Culture and Infancy
VARIATIONS IN THE HUMAN EXPERIENCE

THE CHILD PSYCHOLOGY SERIES

EXPERIMENTAL AND THEORETICAL ANALYSES OF CHILD BEHAVIOR

EDITOR
DAVID S. PALERMO

DEPARTMENT OF PSYCHOLOGY
THE PENNSYLVANIA STATE UNIVERSITY
UNIVERSITY PARK, PENNSYLVANIA

Culture and Infancy
VARIATIONS IN THE HUMAN EXPERIENCE

edited by

P. Herbert Leiderman
Stanford University Medical School
Stanford, California

Steven R. Tulkin
State University of New York
Buffalo, New York

Anne Rosenfeld
Washington, D.C.

ACADEMIC PRESS, INC.   *New York   San Francisco   London   1977*
A Subsidiary of Harcourt Brace Jovanovich, Publishers

Academic Press Rapid Manuscript Reproduction

ACADEMIC PRESS, INC.
111 Fifth Avenue, New York, New York 10003

United Kingdom Edition published by
ACADEMIC PRESS, INC. (LONDON) LTD.
24/28 Oval Road, London NW1

GN
510
.C84

23

Library of Congress Cataloging in Publication Data

Main entry under title:

    Culture and infancy.

        Based on a conference held in June 1973,
    sponsored by Wenner-Gren Foundation for
    Anthropological Research.
        1. Socialization—Congresses.   2. Child
    development—Congresses.   3. Mother and child—
    Congresses.   I. Leiderman, P. Herbert.
    II. Tulkin, Steven R.   III. Rosenfeld, Anne H.
    IV. Wenner-Gren Foundation for Anthropological
    Research, New York. [DNLM: 1. Child development.
    2. Cross—Cultural comparison. WS105 C968]
    GN510.C84   301.15'72   77-1677
    ISBN 0-12-442050-8

Dedication

We would like to dedicate this book to the memory of Dr. William Caudill, who was one of the original organizers of the Wenner-Gren Conference on "cultural and social influences in infancy and early childhood." The field of comparative child development has come a long way since William Caudill started his comparisons of child rearing in Japan and America in the early 1960s, and that progress owes much to his efforts. He has inspired many to view the microcosm of child and family in a dynamic context of time and culture.

Early infancy was of particular interest to Caudill because it represented the first instance of interaction between the naive organism and the culture in which that child would grow. By studying early development, he hoped to discover the origins of cultural programming and to find out how people acquire patterns of social behavior adapted (or maladapted) to their particular culture.

Caudill gave us a detailed understanding of the ways in which Japanese and American cultures are transmitted through the mother–infant interaction. In doing so, he identified many of the unique characteristics of each society as well as their similarities. Beyond this, however, he outlined some of the basic problems that are inherent to any multicultural research, and he suggested a number of ways in which such problems can be overcome. The sum of his work indicates that only a combination of detailed naturalistic observations, controlled studies, and empathic immersion can serve as a proper basis for comparison across cultures. Perhaps this was Caudill's most important legacy.

Had Caudill lived, he would have seen how significant his influence has been. This book, and the ongoing research on cultural differences in infancy that continues to be conducted around the world, attests to the significance of his influence. It is clear that the spirit of Caudill's work will continue wherever multicultural studies of early infancy are carried out with vision, methodological rigor, and proper appreciation for the adaptive capacities of children.

Contents

List of Contributors

MARY D. SALTER AINSWORTH   Department of Psychology, Gilmer Hall, University of Virginia, Charlottesville, Virginia 22901

PEGGY BAN   Educational Testing Service, Princeton, New Jersey 08540

T. BERRY BRAZELTON   23 Hawthorn Street, Cambridge, Massachusetts 02138

H. H. DRAPER   Department of Nutrition, University of Guelph, Guelph, Ontario, Canada

SUSAN GOLDBERG   Department of Psychology, Brandeis University, Waltham, Massachusetts 02154

CHARLES W. GREENBAUM   Department of Psychology, The Hebrew University, Jerusalem, Israel

JEAN-PIERRE HABRICHT   Instituto de Nutricion de Centro America y Panama, Apartado 11-88, Guatemala City, Guatemala, Central America

SANDRA J. JONES   Child Research Branch, Bldg. 15K, National Institute of Mental Health, Bethesda, Maryland, 20014

JEROME KAGAN   Department of Psychology and Social Relations, Harvard University, Cambridge, Massachusetts 02138

ROBERT E. KLEIN   Instituto de Nutricion de Centro America y Panama, Apartado 11-88, Guatemala City, Guatemala, Central America

MELVIN KONNER   Department of Anthropology, Harvard University, Cambridge, Massachusetts 02138

RIVKA LANDAU   Department of Psychology, The Hebrew University, Jerusalem, Israel

ROBERT E. LASKY   Instituto de Nutricion de Centro America y Panama, Apartado 11-88, Guatemala City, Guatemala, Central America

GLORIA F. LEIDERMAN   Peninsula Children's Center, 3860 Middlefield Road, Palo Alto, California 94303

P. HERBERT LEIDERMAN   Department of Psychiatry and Behavioral Sciences, Stanford University School of Medicine, Stanford, California 94305

ROBERT A. LeVINE   School of Education, Harvard University, Cambridge, Massachusetts 02138

MICHAEL LEWIS   Educational Testing Service, Princeton, New Jersey 08540

HOWARD A. MOSS   Child Research Branch, Bldg. 15K, National Institute of Mental Health, Bethesda, Maryland 20014

FRANK A. PEDERSEN   National Institute of Child Health and Human Development, National Institute of Health, Bethesda, Maryland 20014

M. P. M. RICHARDS   University of Cambridge, 5 Salisbury Villas, Station Road, Cambridge, England

ANNE ROSENFELD   Washington, D.C.

JUDITH RUBENSTEIN   National Institute of Child Health and Human Development, National Institute of Health, Bethesda, Maryland 20014

MARTHA JULIA SELLERS   Department of Psychology, Harvard University, Cambridge, Massachusetts 02138

STEVEN R. TULKIN   Department of Psychology, State University of New York at Buffalo, Buffalo, New York 14226

JOHN W. M. WHITING   Department of Social Relations, Harvard University, Cambridge, Massachusetts 02138

PETER H. WOLFF   Children's Hospital, 300 Longwood Avenue, Boston, Massachusetts 02138

CHARLES YARBROUGH   Instituto de Nutricion de Centro America y Panama, Apartado 11-88, Guatemala City, Guatemala, Central America

LEON J. YARROW   National Institute of Child Health and Human Development, National Institute of Health, Bethesda, Maryland 20014

Preface

Multicultural research in child development has a time-honored history, beginning with the work of Margaret Mead. More recently, it has had a renaissance, especially among psychologists and psychologically oriented anthropologists who have attempted to employ more rigorous methods of developmental psychology to examine the variations and consistencies of child development across cultures. Researchers have attempted to broaden the generality of developmental theories to populations other than the usual urban middle-class societies of the Western world. The focus on *infancy* as an area of cross-cultural research is a more recent phenomenon. The importance of social and psychological forces in infancy has been recognized since the theories of Freud, but systematic direct observations were not employed until the last decade. Cross-cultural research on the first year of life is itself in its infancy.

The major research in the field is being done by anthropologists and psychologists, although in fact the field is an intellectual conglomerate, drawing on the theories and methodologies of most behavioral sciences as well as on aspects of pediatrics, developmental biology, nutrition, ethology, and psychiatry. Traditionally, both anthropologists and psychologists have considered early socialization to be within their special domains. Their approaches and their findings, however, have not been well integrated. Psychologists who study child development might describe an infant's social and physical environment in terms of the amount and quality of "stimulation" (toys, mobiles, distinctive vocalization, mother–infant relationships, etc.), or the crowdedness of the home; and early history is often viewed in terms of birth order and parents' background. Anthropologists who study child development generally have quite different perspectives. Their concerns relate to broader aspects of the physical environment (such as climate), to broader aspects of the social environment (such as kinship patterns), or to the traditional cultural attitudes and behavior patterns of the infant's social group. Both anthropologists and psychologists, until recently, have tended to underplay the role of biology (e.g., genetic, physiological–maturational, and medical variables), which interacts with the social factors being studied. Neither of these groups of researchers has, until very recently, attempted to understand the evolutionary significance of the biological or social components that affect socialization processes. Although the approaches of psychology, anthropology, and biological sciences seem quite divergent, each has a great deal to contribute to an understanding of infant socialization. This book, and the conference on which it is based, represents an attempt to nurture such an integration.

In June 1973, an interdisciplinary conference attended by a group of anthropologists, psychiatrists, psychologists, pediatricians, biologists, and child development experts was held, under the sponsorship of the Wenner-Gren Foundation for Anthropological Research to explore the "cultural and social influences in infancy and early childhood." The purpose of the conference was to bring together individuals from different professional backgrounds who had cross-cultural and methodological sophistication in early child development in order to pool our knowledge, to raise issues, and to point out promising paths for future research. This volume, although based on conference papers and discussions, is not a conference report. Rather, it is a summation of what the conferees are thinking and doing in the area of social influences in early childhood, analyzed and presented more systematically than a conference report format permits.

To the extent that the conferees are representative of other workers in the field, the book reflects the current state of art and science, although it does not attempt to review comprehensively all studies of early infant socialization. We have chosen to emphasize research strategy, rather than developmental theory or research results, as a way of fostering an integrated approach to future studies of infant socialization. Although we, like all the conferees, are acutely aware of the need for integration at the theoretical level, and the necessity that research strategy follow systematically from theoretical assumptions, we have found, at the methodological level, a striking unity of approach and perspective that cuts across disciplinary and theoretical boundaries. It is this perspective that we particularly want to share.

The issues raised in this book reflect the concerns and caveats of researchers in a new interdisciplinary field that might properly be called *comparative child development.* As in any effort to communicate across disciplines, some information that is old hat to researchers in one discipline may be new and challenging to those outside it. Because the majority of the contributors to this volume are psychologists, their particular concerns are heavily represented. Yet most of the issues discussed can be considered profitably by anyone tempted to do similar types of comparative studies, whether in developing or developed countries of the world. Many of the problems discussed here are not unique to comparative research, but when seen in the comparative context, can add new dimensions to our understandings.

Among the issues we shall consider are the following:

1. The similarities and differences between cross-cultural studies and comparative studies of child development.
2. The definition and developmental meaning of social class differences across cultures.
3. The uses of within group and across group comparisons.
4. Biological covariance with social factors.
5. Observation and analysis of behavior.
6. The uses of interdisciplinary teams in comparative and cross-cultural studies.
7. Ethical considerations and the role of the researcher; i.e., his "field of force" in the community under study.

For many of the questions, both methodological and substantive, raised in this volume, answers are as yet fragmentary at best. But we believe that the conference, and its distillation in this volume, may give rise to better ways of framing and answering these questions in the future. Because of space limitations, only twenty individuals could attend the conference. They were selected out of a much larger number who might have been included because their work was interesting and relevant to early development, while intimating promising directions for future comparative and multicultural research. As almost all conferees admitted, both before and especially after the conference, sharing research problems and insights across disciplines, like traveling to a foreign culture, is an eye-opener; one finds oneself strikingly sophisticated in some areas and shockingly blind and naive in others. Such a realization can be the beginning of growth in an individual or a field. This volume is dedicated to helping it happen.

Acknowledgments

An edited book is the product of many individuals and help from many institutions. This book would not have been possible without the generous assistance of the Wenner-Gren Foundation, Ms. Lita Osmundsen, and her staff. They not only provided the magnificent location of Burg Wartenstein, Austria, for the conference that gave rise to this volume, but also provided subsequent encouragement and financial support for its publication.

The Center for Advanced Study in the Behavioral Sciences and the Guggenheim Foundation provided the freedom of a fellowship year for one of the editors (P. Herbert Leiderman), during which time portions of this volume were completed. Typing and editorial assistance by Joan Warnbrunn and Miriam Gallaher of the Center staff were most helpful in the early stages of preparation.

Joan DeLoach, of State University of New York (SUNY) at Buffalo, and Tome Tanisawa, of Stanford University, bore major responsibility for typing the manuscript. Their cheerful persistence through many drafts brought the volume to its final stage. Finally, we want to acknowledge the support of our respective universities, Stanford and SUNY-Buffalo, in furnishing the setting and the time to complete the editing of this book despite the many other competing activities.

Part One
Introduction

The human environment is inescapably social. From the
moment of birth, human infants are dependent on others for
biological survival. Psychologically, their cognitive, social,
and emotional development is also predicated on human interaction. Adult independence and self-sufficiency are achieved
gradually through years of contact and interaction with others.
Thus, despite the sometimes heroic efforts of children to
resist the pressures of family and society, the process of
acculturation continues generation after generation. This
process, commonly termed *socialization* by behavioral scientists,
is actually a form of adaptation, since for those who become
acceptably socialized there are physical, economic, and
psychological rewards and benefits; for those who do not, there
can be ostracism, exile, imprisonment, institutionalization,
or even death.

Although this general outline of socialization is commonly
accepted, the specifics of how it works in various cultural
settings are by no means fully understood. The purpose of this
book is to expand the scientific knowledge about the earliest
days and years in a child's life, using information from various
cultures and social groups that illustrates how caretaking
practices interact with biological and maturational givens.
We hope that by presenting these findings we will communicate
the potential advantages of multicultural approaches to the
study of child development.

1

Chapter 1

Overview of Cultural Influences in Infancy

P. Herbert Leiderman
Stanford University School of Medicine

Steven R. Tulkin*
State University of New York at Buffalo

Anne Rosenfeld
State University of New York at Buffalo

Observing and interpreting the interplay of maturational and environmental factors in child development is difficult, even on one's home turf, where subjects are readily obtained, language and cultural barriers are minimal, and relevant social variables likely to be understood by one who shares the same social and cultural milieu as his subjects. In a foreign culture, it is infinitely harder, both practically and theoretically. Yet, for many of the researchers in this volume, there have been compelling scientific reasons for choosing the more difficult course. For anthropologists, whose intellectual commitment is to the study of social organization at the cultural level, the investigation and comparisons of life-styles across cultures is natural and traditional, with research experience in at least one foreign culture a required component of graduate training in most universities. For psychologists and other social scientists unschooled in anthropology, this approach is novel and often difficult, yet potentially very rewarding. In this chapter, we will examine some of the reasons why these scientists have adopted a comparative approach to child development, in at least some of their studies.

*Present address: University of Cape Coast, Cape Coast, GHANA.

3

CROSS-CULTURAL METHODS AND COMPARATIVE CHILD DEVELOPMENT:
A DISTINCTION

Most of the studies reported in this book, while dealing
with comparisons of two or more social groups or cultures, are
not what an anthropologist would call *cross-cultural studies*,
although they may share some common methodology. Rather, they
are what we have chosen to term *comparative child development
studies*. To make the distinction clear, let us review briefly
the background and intent of cross-cultural studies, and show
how they differ from studies of comparative child development.[1]

Cross-Cultural Studies

The cross-cultural approach in anthropology, introduced
by Whiting and Child in 1953, had, as one of its major purposes,
the shift of anthropology from the natural history of the
science to one that was potentially more deductively oriented.
Using the cross-cultural method, a group of cultures can be
associated along a given dimension, and variation across these
cultures can be related to a given cultural practice, value
orientation, or type of behavior. Through this method, whole
cultures--including religious beliefs, economic structures,
family organization, linguistic structures, technological
developments, artistic and cultural styles, etc.--are observed
and compared with one another. Child-rearing attitudes and
practices, as well as patterns of child development, might be
included in cross-cultural investigations, but they are not
their primary focus. In such studies, an attempt is often made
to find underlying structural features of human organization,
so that one can say, for example, that any society with a given
type of religion, or child-rearing practice, will also have a
given type of economic system, or vice versa. The method
enables more inclusive theories to be formulated, and in fact
permits testing of specific hypotheses derived from theoretical
systems within and without the field of anthropology.

In its initial development, much of the focus of the
approach was on social and cultural variables as they related

[1]In this volume, the term *cross-cultural* refers to studies
utilizing the Whiting and Child (1953) format of examining
the interrelationships of various systems on a cultural level.
The term *comparative child development* refers to field and
experimental studies within a limited domain of a culture or
cultures (e.g., child-rearing patterns, problem-solving
abilities, cooperation, etc.). The term *multicultural* refers
to research utilizing or amenable to both of these methods.

to specific behaviors and/or personality, with relatively less emphasis on environmental features, and practically no emphasis on the biological components of the culture. This orientation was, of course, in keeping with the interests of the "culture and personality" (Kluckhahn & Murray, 1948) school of anthropology, then so dominant in the United States, which stressed the psychological domain of personality, especially as influenced by psychoanalytic theory, with some contributions from the learning theories of Hull and others.

It soon became clear that the holistic approach to culture and personality development was imprecise, and, as psychologically trainted anthropologists and psychologists moved into the field, the emphasis of psychology turned from personality development to the development of cognition (see Cole, Gay, Glick, & Sharp, 1971). This new concern with cognitive development, influenced by the social and biological studies on cognition then so widely extant in the field, led to greater concern with more precise measures of social and biological effects on cognitive development. Thus, the requirements for more specific social data, as well as direct assessment of biological factors, became essential. It became clear that treating cultures holistically, using the data from the human area files, was woefully inadequate for the study of cognitive development. It was this lack of an adequate data base that led the Whitings to suggest and introduce their now famous six-culture study (B. Whiting, 1963; J. Whiting & Child, 1966), in which equivalent anthropological and psychological methods could be used by six teams scattered throughout various cultures in the world. Although the number of societies was small, and the methods used by the different teams were not completely comparable, the thrust of the study was to provide a bridge linking cross-cultural approaches with comparable psychological and anthropological approaches for a given culture. The potentiality for adequate cross-cultural approaches was obvious. (Neglected, however, even in this study, was the biological component, only recently introduced as important for understanding infant development and socialization.)

Comparative Studies in Child Development

In contrast to Whiting's cross-cultural approach (presented here in his theoretical remarks in Chapter 3), which obviously requires a monumental team effort, the majority of studies in this volume are more modest in scope. While comparisons may be made across cultural groups, they are focused on only those aspects of the given cultures that appear to be directly relevant to children's developmental experience.

As this volume will often stress, however, regardless of the delimited nature of an investigator's scientific interests, it is both scientifically and ethically essential that he or she understand the broader cultural contexts within which child-rearing is studied. To ignore them is to risk misinterpreting data and losing sight of essential variables influencing behavior, to say nothing of alienating the people being studied.

The questions underlying comparative child development studies are primarily psychological (focusing on the dynamics of individual cognitive, affective, and motor development) rather than anthropological (focusing on the origins and enduring patterns of social structure). Among those theories particularly appropriate to comparative child development studies are those that propose presumably universal laws of development, both biological and psychological, such as Gesell's motor maturational theory, ethological social theories (e.g., attachment theory), Piagetian cognitive theory, psychodynamic social theories, and social learning theories.

Characteristically, the investigator conducting comparative child development studies will use naturally occurring cultural-and/or class-related differences in child-rearing patterns as a way of increasing variation in his or her subject population, or in the social variables affecting that population. Such studies may also be used to test the replicability of findings discovered in one culture and presumed to be universal.

Although not all of the comparative child development studies in this volume demonstrate equal sophistication in the use of the comparative approach across cultures (and differ as well in their sensitivity to relevant biological variables), the investigators represented here, as well as other workers in the field, are gaining new appreciation of the need to adopt not only the methodology of anthropologists, but also their cultural sensitivity, when working outside their own social and cultural milieu. The following discussion of research approaches is addressed, therefore, to future investigators of comparative child development, whatever their disciplines.

HYPOTHESIS SEEKING AND HYPOTHESIS TESTING

Comparative studies of child development have been conducted for a variety of reasons. They can be loosely grouped into two sorts; exploratory and hypothesis testing; or, as Reichenbach (1958) has termed them, studies within the "context of discovery", and those within the "context of justification":

> The scientist who discovers a theory is usually
> guided to his discovery by guesses; he cannot
> name a method by means of which he found the
> theory and can only say that it appeared plausible
> to him, that he had the right hunch, or that he
> saw intuitively which assumption would fit the
> facts. ...The inductive inference is employed
> not for finding a theory, but for justifying it
> in terms of observational data. [Pp. 230-231]

Both types of research are legitimate, compatible, and necessary; however, they follow different logical rules. The first often forms the basis for the second. Studies conducted within the context of discovery, although guided by a rationale, are generally rather freewheeling and exploratory, geared to coming up with a hypothesis or theory, but following no set rules of induction or deduction. Given the relatively young state of the field, it is not surprising that a significant proportion of comparative studies of early development have been of this type [i.e., Ainsworth's (1967) initial study of attachment in Uganda, or Konner's study in the present volume). Studies of the second type, conducted within the context of justification, in which one is testing a hypothesis or exploring the ramifications of a theoretical position, are conducted according to a strict set of logical rules far more easily followed in the laboratory than in the field.

Exploratory Research

As anyone who has conducted child development research in a "foreign" setting can attest, a major rationale for conduct-int such a study is its value as an "eye opener". Doing research outside one's familiar territory has a way of jolting one out of old assumptions, sharpening perceptions, and suggesting new ideas and hypotheses. Not only does one perceive a new culture freshly, but often there is also carry-over to one's own culture, as familiar aspects are viewed anew after one returns from the field. Culture shock, however traumatic, can have profound intellectual benefits. Taking a page from the anthropologists' manual, it might be well to require graduate students outside the field of anthropology to do at

least one comparative study, if only for this reason. The
same may be said for doing comparative research across classes
or subcultural groups in our own society, although the effects
are likely to be less striking.

Exploratory comparative studies have a second value as
preparation for more systematic investigations. An assessment
study can reveal which settings in particular environments have
the best payoffs for studying specific questions later. In
view of the frequent unreliability of older anthropological
and ethnological data, such a study is recommended even when
one intends to enter an unfamiliar culture with hypotheses
already generated.

It is important to point out that exploratory or
hypothesis-generating research involves more than simply
living in a culture and "getting a feel" for its ways of life.
Observers can be rigorous, even in exploration. We need to be
aware of the potential influences of variation attributable to
ecological variables such as settings, and population variables
such as social stratification, as well as more specific sampling
problems such as time of day, season of year, effects of
observers, etc. Finally, we need to be aware of our own
cultural biases and how they can influence our perceptions.

Hypothesis-Testing Research

Not all questions or hypotheses concering child development require or are appropriate for comparative research across
cultures. In fact, as we will discuss later in this volume,
there is often strong justification for studying certain
questions, such as the organizational structure of a behavior,
through the examination of individual differences in one
culture, preferably one's own. Nonetheless, many developmental
questions are particularly appropriate for comparative study.

A primary reason for undertaking comparative study is to
test out the universality of ontogenetic principles, particularly
those that relate to the ontogeny of social or cognitive
behavior. Because the body of knowledge in developmental
psychology is built primarily on studies of children within
the most technologically developed populations, the universality
of many developmental "laws" is still open to question.
Extensive replicative research in populations exhibiting
significant behavioral differences from our own will be
required to dispel such doubts. To some extent, this is already
underway, as current attempts to replicate Piagetian principles
across cultures attest, but far more study is needed.

Questions concerning the effect of early environmental interactions (social and physical) on the course and character of development obviously lend themselves to comparative investigation across cultures and across social classes. For example, many questions regarding the development of attachment, the caretaking conditions that give rise to it, and the consequences in later life of various patterns of early attachment can be clarified enough through a comparative study. In some instances, investigation of attachment behavior outside the usual Western family structure has already challenged accepted theoretical explanations of the dynamics of attachment. By studying early infancy and caretaking in Uganda, Ainsworth found that Freudian theory and acquired drive theory notwithstanding, young Ganda children manifest attachment to individuals not regularly involved in their feeding. Such a finding invites further investigation in other cultures, and reexamination of assumptions and observations in our own culture.

Because of ethical limitations against experimentation and intervention in child-rearing practices, students of infant socialization must depend heavily on the natural experiments provided by cultural variation. Observing behavior in other cultures can expand the range of environmental and experiential variation, and can provide relatively large populations exhibiting behavior too infrequently observed in our own culture for statistical inferences to be made. Because of the natural variation of child-rearing practices throughout the world, it is possible to find natural experiments in which events or social stimuli usually "packaged" together in our society occur in isolation. These instances can provide important tests for theories of development based on observation of American and European populations.

For example, in studying attachment behavior, one must not only distinguish analytically a child's reaction to strange events from his reactions to separation, but must also distinguish the often concurrent events of weaning from these other behaviors. One can find societies in the anthropological literature in which weaning is sufficiently delayed so that weaning effects are negligible among the youngsters studied. For those specifically interested in the effects of various patterns of weaning, it is possible to find in Africa, for example, a range of weaning patterns, from the gradual weaning of the Ganda and Yoruba, to the abrupt practices of the Zulu and Hausa in which a particular day for weaning is chosen in advance and the child is never again allowed to return to the breast. The comparison of gradual and abrupt

weaning could be made in Nigeria alone, using the Yoruba and
Hausa.

Another example of a natural experiment with important
developmental consequences is the Hausa practice of avoiding
interaction with the first-born children from birth. Although
Hausa mothers breastfed their first-born children, they do not
play with them, have eye contact with them, or call them by
name. LeVine (personal communication) has found, in a pilot
study comparing first and later-born children, that, although
the norm of avoidance was not given uniform adherence, there
were systematic differences between the attachment of first
and later-borns to their mothers. Rebelsky and Abele's (1969)
report of child-rearing behaviors among Dutch and American
mothers offers similar possibilities for the study of large
variations in mother-child interaction in Western industrialized
societies in the early months of life.

Social scientists interested in the evolutionary and
historical origins of the family and the adaptive singificance
of child-rearing practices can find, through comparative study
of societies in various stages of development, a fertile ground
for hypothesis testing. Although Konner's study of child-
rearing among the Bushmen (Chapter 13 of this book) as
primarily exploratory, it casts light on one of the earliest
known forms of human society, and reveals that even in this
basic subsistence economy (not unlike the earlier patterns
of hunter-gatherer groups), infant development, particularly
motor development, proceeds extremely well, generally in advance
of American norms. To what extent parental permissiveness and
extensive physical contact, the use of a sling, and participation in a multiage child group early in life contribute to
this developmental pattern remains to be investigated, but
there are many provocative clues for further hypothesis testing.

The important point to remember when reviewing these
studies, however, is that they are not cross-cultural studies:
We do not have data available to tell us about all aspects of
the cultures we are comparing, so we do not know how many other
aspects of acculturation--besides mother-child interaction--
differ. This limits the scientific conclusions that may be
drawn from comparative studies, and definitely suggests that
we must refrain from drawing implications from these studies
about what might be "good" to do in any given culture.

It is also important to remember that comparisons of
child-rearing across cultures can be strengthened significantly
through the study of individual differences within cultures.

One of the major problems in making comparisons across two cultures, or even two social classes, is that, if naturally occurring differences are found, there are an infinite number of reasons to explain those differences. One has to discover whether or not the relationship of variables within each of the instances is consistent. By studying individual differences within each of the groups, one is aware of their range, and can gain a better understanding of the implicit interrelations within the society that seem to be related to these differences. These cautions will be elaborated further in our comments in the concluding chapters.

REFERENCES

Ainsworth, M. D. S. Infancy in Uganda: Infant care and the growth of love. Baltimore, Md.: Johns Hopkins University Press, 1967.

Cole, M., Gay, J., Glick, J. A., & Sharp, D. W. The cultural context of learning and thinking. New York: Basic Books, 1971.

Kluckhohn, C., & Murray, H. (Eds.). Personality in nature, culture and society. New York: Knopf, 1948.

Rebelsky, F. G., & Abeles, G. Infancy in Holland and the United States. Paper presented at meeting of Society for Research in Child Development, Santa Monica, California, 1969.

Reichenbach, H. Rise of scientific philosophy. Berkeley: University of California Press, 1958.

Whiting, B. (Ed.). Six cultures: Studies of child-rearing. New York: Wiley, 1963.

Whiting, J. W. M., & Child, I. L. Child training and personality: A cross cultural study. New Haven: Yale University Press, 1953.

Whiting, J. W. M., & Child, I. L. Field guide for the study of socialization. New York: Wiley, 1966.

Part Two
Theoretical Perspectives

Most multicultural studies of infant socialization have been only minimally tied to theory. This has led some of our colleagues to conclude that multicultural research is not derived from theories about cultures, but only from theories of development. The critical importance of cultural variation has been lost. Therefore, before preceeding with the empirical studies, we would like to present a sampling of theoretical approaches to multicultural research on socialization and early development.

LeVine relates child-rearing practices to adaptation and, therefore, to the survival of the species. He argues that the goals of socialization are closely tied to the stage of development (that is, complexity) of the culture. Whiting suggests an approach to studying these questions, providing examples from the "six cultures" study. Ainsworth ties the previous theoretical papers to a specific area of inquiry (attachment) that has interested psychologists, and demonstrates how the multicultural approach is critical for comprehensive understanding of this phenomenon. Finally, Konner approaches infancy from an evolutionary perspective, attempting a synthesis of anthropological, psychological, and biological viewpoints to broaden our perspective on this most important period in human development.

Chapter 2
Child Rearing as Cultural Adaptation

Robert A. LeVine
University of Chicago

Anthropologists have shown with increasingly convincing evidence over the last forty years that the environments of infancy and early childhood are shaped by cultural values. These values vary widely between human populations and become firmly established in the personal preferences and inner regulations of individuals, who seek to reestablish them in the next generation. Some of the best evidence can be found in the studies by Caudill comparing Japanese and Americans (Caudill & Plath, 1966; Caudill & Weinstein, 1969) and by Whiting, Chasdi, Autonovsky, & Ayres (1966) comparing Zuni, Texans, and Mormons in New Mexico. The values involved are

---

*This paper was written while the author was recipient of a Research Scientist Award (5-K05, MH-18444-02) from the National Institute of Mental Health. The ideas were developed during 1971 and 1972 when he was a fellow of the Center for Advanced Study in the Behavioral Sciences. Field research among the Gusii during 1955 and 1957 was supported by a Ford Foundation fellowship; that among the Hausa during 1969 by grants from the Carnegie Corporation to the Child Development Research Unit, Ahmadu Bello University (Zaria, Nigeria), and from the United States Office of Education to the Early Education Research Center, University of Chicago.

are not specific to situations of infant and child care, but are seen as derived from broad orientations (regarding interpersonal relations, personal achievement, and social solidarity) associated with the social system and its institutional goals. The function attributed to such values in child rearing is that of preparing the individual, through processes not yet well understood, for participation in that system, at some psychic cost to himself.

I believe that this approach to child rearing has proved its worth, particularly in the hands of sophisticated investigators such as Caudill, Whiting, and Spiro (1958), by amassing empirical data to support its assumptions (see LeVine, 1970, pp. 589-593, 603 for a review of those data). At the same time, I believe that factors other than cultural values are involved in shaping the early environment of the child, and that attention to these factors will clarify the context in which values can make their impact. One set of factors is the biological equipment of all human infants that predisposes them toward certain patterns of social responsiveness. Psychobiological investigators have been producing evidence of this for some time (see Freedman, 1974), and we are indebted to Bowlby (1969) for giving it an evolutionary rationale of broad applicability, regardless of whether we accept the specifics of his explanation. Bowlby argues that infant-mother attachment as it develops in humans is the outcome of a phylogenetic process in which attachment was necessary for protection from predators and hence for infant survival. As descendants of the survivors of those environmental conditions, contemporary humans are innately programed for attachment, and child-rearing practices everywhere must be accommodated to this universal tendency. In this respect, then, child-rearing practices reflect the environmental pressures that acted on our hominid ancestors, rather than those that parents experience today, and they can vary culturally only within limits established in the distant evolutionary past without inflicting developmental damage on the child.

The point of this chapter is that cultural evolution within human populations also produces standardized strategies of survival for infants and children, strategies reflecting environmental pressures from a more recent past, encoded in customs rather than genes and transmitted socially rather than biologically. Insofar as the environmental hazards, demands, and opportunities are common to all human populations in their potential effects on infants and children, they act as another set of constraints on cultural variation in child-rearing, but insofar as they differ, or have differed within a past that is culturally present as tradition, then they may form the basis of the cultural variations in child-rearing that have been interesting to anthropologists. In contrast with the innate and panhuman program of attachment that Bowlby (1969) and Ainsworth (1967) have identified, the culturally organized formulae with which this chapter deals are responsive to environmental change within a few generations and tend to reflect major divisions in the conditions of life among the peoples of the world.

My aim in this necessarily speculative analysis is to suggest (1) that culture, no less than biology, contributes to the presumptive basis of parenthood, i.e. to the ways in which parents perceive the task of rearing children; (2) that these ways are "rational" in that they contain information about environmental contingencies previously experienced by the population and assimilated into its cultural tradition; (3) that this information concerns features of the environment that are most salient to the health and welfare of the child, and appropriate responses to them; (4) that a parent who conforms to such customary prescriptions may be unaware of their past or present efficacy, but may view them as religiously or ethically ordained; and (5) that this adaptive component concealed in child-rearing customs must be clarified to understand the constraints within which other cultural values operate and to assess the prospects of change.

ENVIRONMENTAL PRESSURES ON PARENTAL GOALS

In this section I shall present what I regard as the basic goals parents set for themselves as parents, i.e., in their roles as responsible agents for the care of the child, concerned with his present welfare and long-term interests. In other words, this discussion is about what parents want *for* the child, rather than *from* him.

We know parents often want a good deal *from* their children: Among African peoples, for example, parents frequently expect the child to contribute his labor to the domestic productive unit, to give respect to his elders, and--when mature--to support his aging parents. In our society, parents often talk of what they want from their children in terms of affection, enjoyment, and love. Our concern here, however, is what parents want when they take the child's point of view rather than their own, on the assumption that the vast majority of parents must have taken this perspective for the human species to have survived, and that, in any event, most of what parents want *from* their children presumes that the latter's health and welfare have already been taken care of.

Before outlining the goals of parent *qua* parents, I would like to mention the field experiences that led me to this formulation. When I was working among the Gusii of south-western Kenya from 1955 to 1957, I encountered a toddler who had been severely burned in the cooking fire. Discussing this case with other Gusii, I discovered that this was a well-known hazard, covered by the proverb that can be translated "Lameness is up", which means that when children become able to walk they are liable to be maimed. Here was cultural recognition of a condition of risk associated with a stage of motor development. Many years later (in 1969), working among the Hausa in north-western Nigeria, I found that hospitals and dispensaries in the area regularly dealt with an exceptionally large number of infant burn cases during the *harmattan*, that season when the dry wind from the Sahara makes the nights so cold that families tend to keep the evening cooking fire going until morning for warmth. Here again, the risk involved was widely recognized not only by medical personnel but other adults as well, and it occurred to me that the Hausa practice of carrying toddlers on the back and otherwise restricting the mobility of toddlers who can walk might represent an adaptation to the recognition of risk. If true, it would mean that without the practices restricting mobility, many more toddlers would be burnt, which is currently a rare occurrence relative to the number of small children. Since then, I have had anecdotal evidence from other parts of Africa that indicates the Gusii and Hausa are not isolated cases in terms of the existence and recognition of the burn haz rd of cooking fires to small children. Since carrying practice; restricting the mobility of small children who can walk are also widespread in Africa, it may be that perception of the burn hazard, including observation of the serious injuries incurred by burnt children, represents a major environmental pressure to which carrying practices were originally adapted and that continues to maintain them.

This point may seem so obvious as to require no serious attention. But it represents a class of instances in which parental behavior is directed to vital and conspicious short-term goals, while potentially having a less visible impact on the long-term psychological development of the child. In other words, being carried on someone's body a great deal of the time until 18 months of age or older, and having one's exploratory behavior severly limited at the same time may affect the emotional and cognitive development of the child. Whatever those effects are, however, they are not visible to the mother, whereas the risk of being burnt is, and she adapts to that without awareness of possible psychological consequences.

In fact, however, this is not a complete account of the custom. The burn hazard is highly visible and, in some areas, dramatically seasonal, but it is--as the Gusii proverb quoted above suggests--only one of many potential hazards to the infant and small child in a typical African environment. In some regions there is the danger of falling off cliffs or hills, in others those of falling into lakes, rivers, wells, or dye pits, not to mention being run over by cattle or motor vehicles. Given a home environment in which domestic activities are carried on outdoors as much as indoors, with mothers devoting their attention to productive tasks, there is a milieu of physical risk for the infant and small child that goes beyond any specific hazard and to which customs restricting his mobility must have been origianally adapted. Furthermore, once the adaptive solution of carrying on the back is encoded in custom, caretakers can direct their mental and physical activities toward conforming to the custom without concerning themselves with the risks and hazards themselves, thus eliminating the anxieties that could arise in raising children under potentially dangerous conditions.

Another experience affecting my thinking about parental goals has to do with weaning from the breast. In most of rural Africa, children are not weaned from the breast until well into the second year of life and sometimes later, depending on whether the mother becomes pregnant again. In areas where the postweaning diet is very low in protein, child health specialists regard this as a period of great vulnerability to disease and generally support the indigenous custom of prolonged breastfeeding as protecting infants from protein-calorie malnutrition. I have repeatedly discovered (in southern Nigeria and other regions) that, while mothers have no understanding of nutrition in the Western sense, they are guided by cultural belief to adjust the age of weaning to the size of the child. Although a cultural group may recognize eighteen months or two years (or some developmental event) as the ideal age for weaning, a child who is small for his age is definitely weaned later, while one who is larger than average might be weaned earlier. This is in fact medically sound, since heights and weights are used by Western physicians working in malnourished populations as crude but effective indicators of the child's general health status. Here again we have an example of a child-rearing practice, dictated by custom and of significance for the child's psychological development, that seems to represent an adaptation to hazards that threaten the child's survival, rather than a reflection of moral values or repressed motives. These folk practices are based on environmental information, the feedback received by parents about child care--in the latter case, from observations of the child's size compared to that of other children, interpreted as a health indicator; in the first case from observations of child injuries, interpreted as an indicator of environmental perils. In both instances, parents use the feedback to promote the survival of the child.

Such reflections on my field experience led me to the hypothesis that customs of infant and child care evolve as adaptations to environmental features that generations of parents perceive as frequent or especially threatening obstacles to their conscious child-rearing goals. When these customs are functioning adaptively, they provide parents or other caretakers with an established solution to a traditionally recognized problem, eliminating the necessity for parents to consider anew the adaptive function of the custom. One result of this is that parents guided by such customary formulae are frequently unable to explain to an inquiring outsider "why" they are doing what they do. Their behavior is more adaptive than they are aware of or can put into words.

This perspective on child-rearing customs leads to a detailed consideration of parental goals. I propose the following as the universal goals of parents vis-à-vis their children:

1.   The physical survival and health of the child, including (implicitly) the normal development of his reproductive capacity during puberty.

2.   The development of the child's behavioral capacity for economic self-maintenance in maturity.

3.   The development of the child's behavioral capacities for maximizing other cultural values--e.g., morality, prestige, wealth, religious piety, intellectual achievement, personal satisfaction, self-realization-- as formulated and symbolically elaborated in culturally distinctive beliefs, norms, and ideologies.

I submit that if one asks the question "What do parents want for their children?" the answers from all human populations would include and be exhausted by these three categories. These goals are not without structure. There is a natural hierarchy among them, because if Goal 1, the physical health and survival of the child is threatened, it becomes the foremost concern of the parents, since it is prerequisite to Goals 2 and 3. Similarly, if Goal 2 is seriously threatened, it is likely to assume the highest priority in the parental goal structure because it is necessary for Goal 3; i.e., if there is doubt about whether the child will be able to make a living according to group standards of economic role performance, the problem of the child's future subsistence is likely to become of greater parental concern than cultural values seen as unrelated to subsistence. There is also a rough developmental sequence implied in these goals, because in all human populations physical survival and health are of greatest concern during the first years of a child's life, whereas attention to the other two goals can be postponed until his survival seems assured. It may be, as discussed below, that in those populations where infant mortality is so low that the child's survival seem assured in advance, parents are more likely to turn their attention to the development of the child's behavioral capacities at an earlier point in his life.

CULTURAL VARIATION IN PARENTAL GOALS

If parents do in fact organize their thinking about child rearing in this way, then the following hypotheses about cross-cultural variations in child behavior are implied:

1. In populations with high infant mortality rates, parents will have the physical survival and health of the child as their overriding conscious concern, particularly in the early years, and child-rearing customs will reflect this priority.

2. In populations with relatively scarce or precarious resources for subsistence, parents will have as their overriding conscious concern the child's capacity for future economic self-maintenance (broadly defined), particularly after his survival seems assured, and child-rearing customs will reflect this priority.

An important qualification is that the customs that have evolved to deal with these parental concerns tend to relieve or even prevent anxiety on the part of the parents about these issues, so that if the customs are functioning adaptively, parents will not exhibit the amount of affect that can be seen in parents with the same realistic concerns but without the comfort of custom. Thus a parent with a very ill child in a population with a low mortality rate, or one facing unemployment or hunger in the midst of plenty, is likely to experience more anxiety and distress than parents in populations in which death and poverty are frequent, not only because of differential expectations based on social comparison but also because in the latter cases parents are usually provided with cultural solutions that make them feel that their concerns are being taken care of. Hence the paradox that parents in those populations in which infant mortality is highest and subsistence most precarious often manifest relatively little anxiety about these threats to their children. This does not mean, however, that they are not concerned about them but, on the contrary, that the cultural beliefs with which they were raised make them take for granted both the problem and the cultural solution to it, the two tending to be fused in a coherent organization of belief. Any other way of approaching child care seems to them aberrant.

Thus in a population with a high infant mortality rate, a mother will probably find incomprehensible the suggestion that she take certain measures to stimulate her infant's cognitive development so that he will be able to perform well in school. This is not necessarily because she has a short time perspective; in fact, she may have made plans for his betrothal and other aspects of his future. It is more likely to be because she accepts as a given the cultural definition of infancy as a period in which customary caretaking behavior is organized around the goal of survival without consideration of behavioral development as such. Conversely, a mother with a chronically and perhaps fatally ill child in a population with a low mortality rate among infants and children will not necessarily eliminate from her treatment of the infant and concern for his early behavioral development that is institutionalized in her culture. While she recognizes that survival comes first, she is too much a product of that culture to see infancy as a period organized exclusively around survival and physical health. In other words, individual parents do not respond to the threats to their child-rearing goals *de nova*, but in terms of definitions of long-standing common problems, and the solutions to them that are embedded in cultural formulae. It is the individual's use of these cultural formulae and their relations to environmental hazards that are of special concern here.

To provide more concrete illustration of what is implied here, let us consider the first hypothesis stated above: In populations with high infant mortality rates, parents will have the physical survival and health of the child as their overriding conscious concern, particularly in the early years, and child-rearing customs will reflect this priority. In my own African experience and in the accounts of others from tropical places as diverse as Latin America and Indonesia, there is a general picture of infant care that emerges:

1.   The infant is on or near a caretaker's body at all time, day and night.

2.   Crying is quickly attended to and becomes rare relative to Western infants.

3.   Feeding is a very frequent response to crying.

4.   There is, by Western standards, little orgainzed concern about the infant's behavioral development and relatively little treatment of him as an emotionally responsive individual (as in eye contact, smile elicitation, or chatting).

Western observers, scientists and amateurs alike, have tended to conceptualize this pattern as *indulgence* because of the demand feeding, the rapidity of response to crying, the absence of pressure for toilet training, the apparent quiescent contentment of the infants, the inference that the infant's "needs" are being well taken care of. But the term *indulgence* as a folk expression in English also connotes an emotional attitude involving "affection", "warmth", and related attributes on the part of the caretaker, whereas the overt behaviors indicating such an attitude are frequently minimal in the non-Western populations being observed. By using a term like *indulgence* with its strong emotional connotations in our language, we tend to obscure what seems to be the case, namely, that among these non-Western peoples we find "indulgent" behaviors without the emotional attitude that typically accompanies them among our own people. Another way of putting this is that we find a certain pattern of bodily proximity, feeding, responsiveness to crying, and absence of disciplinary training that looks "indulgent" to us, but without the equally "indulgent" maternal behaviors of smiling, eye contact, face-to-face smile elicitation, chatting, cooing, and kissing, that usually supply the psychological context in which we interpret a Western mother's "indulgent" behavior.

How, then, shall we interpret this pattern of infant care? I believe it can be explained as a cultural adaptation to high infant mortality rates among peoples of diverse cultural values. In other words, I do not believe that a satisfactory explanation will be found in terms of a permissive-restrictive

dimension of maternal ideology or any of the other value
dimensions applying to behavior in general rather than in
specific to infancy. My theory is that a high infant
mortality rate are severely limited resources for responding
to disease have shaped a folk pattern of preventive medicine
in infancy that reflects parental concern for the physical
survival and health of the child and is relatively efficacious
in attaining that goal, given the low level of medical
technology.

My argument begins with the point in child care in which
mortality is most frequently experienced. Since comparative
mortality figures are usually given over the first five years
of life, it is often unclear how old most children are at
death, and the medical concern over postweaning malnutrition,
at least, in West Africa, has given many the impression that
the third and fourth years are when most deaths occur. Our
data from the Hausa of northwestern Nigeria and data from
other unpublished studies with which I am acquainted suggest
that the first year of life is by far the period of greatest
mortality. Briefly summarized, our data show the following
results from 86 women over 45 (postchildbearing age), in the
central section of a Hausa market town, who reported 415
live births: 31.8 percent of the infants died before the
age of 5, and of those, 59.8 percent died during the first
year of life and 22.7 percent during the second year of life.
Together, then, 82.5 percent of the deaths in the first five
years occurred before the age of two. Furthermore, since
these postmenopausal women, depending almost exclusively on
their own memories without birth records, are most likely to
have forgotten deaths in the earliest months, it can be
assumed that the actual proportion of eary deaths is even
greater.

It must also be borne in mind that 31.8 percent is a
fairly low under-five mortality rate for a population in the
region. Nearby communities with poorer water supplies and
less access to medical dispensaries show rates ranging up to
60 percent. If this be taken as representive of rural
populations in the tropics, then, it is not unreasonable to
assume that one or two children out of every five born alive
(i.e., at least 20 percent) will not live to their first
birthdays, or that (altogether) one or two out of every four
born alive (at least 25 percent) will not live to their second
birthdays. These death rates, or higher ones, have prevailed
for a long time and must have made an impact on generations
of parents. Where the mortality rate now is lower, the
decline has usually been a recent phenomenon.

Given this extreme threat to survival during the infancy period, the pattern of infant care described above can be seen as an attempt at preventing death. I propose that it represents a constant medical alert, a chronic emergency mobilization to save the child at risk. The infant is kept on or near a caretaker at all times so his condition can be monitored. His cries are immediately attended to so that the caretaker can receive immediate feedback concerning whether they are easily reduced by shaking or feeding; if not, perhaps he is ill. Minimizing his crying from other causes heightens the value of crying as a signal of organic upset, i.e., disease. Frequent feeding, particularly breast-feeding, serves to replace fluids and alleviate the dehydration from diarrhea that is probably the most frequent precipitant of infant death in the tropics. Keeping the infant on someone's body or otherwise restricted prevents the accidental injuries that can lead to death if not properly treated. All in all, though not a highly effective medical system, it is an adaptive response to extreme environmental hazard and probably has more efficacy than is readily apparent.

Western observers have not interpreted the pattern of infant care in this way because they expect individuals mobilized for a medical emergency to appear anxious, whereas tropical parents appear to be calm and even inattentive to their small children. My point, however, is that the customary pattern of infant care consists of rules that in effect, represent an adaptation to a situation of chronic medical risk; the parents and other caretakers who follow the rules do not necessarily experience the state of emergency in their own psychophysiological functioning. It is like the sentry post, which as an aspect of military structure represents an institutional adaptation to the ever-present possibility of unwarranted intrustion; the sentinel who mans the post, however, may be the picture of drowsy boredom as he holds his loaded gun and scans the horizon for intruders. It is possible, especially in a relatively slow-changing society, for an individual to follow the traditional norms of the parental role without experiencing what earlier generations of parents must have experienced as the norms were evolving in response to environmental hazards.

In this pattern of infant care adapted to the risks of disease and death in the earliest years, there is no place for an organized concern about the development of the child's behavioral characteristics and social and emotional relationships; such concerns are postponed until later in his life, when custom provides a basis for confidence in his

continued survival. The lack of parental concern, however,
does not mean that the infant is not developing psychologically,
nor that the pattern of care is not influencing this development
in powerful and perhaps irreversible ways. It only means that
mothers and other caretakers are not monitoring this development,
thinking about it, talking about, or attempting to control it.
Whatever the psychological consequences, they must be of
secondary interest to parents facing the pressures of infant
mortality.

A question that must be faced in this kind of evolutionary
analysis is how the customs evolved, i.e., how did the
parental practices that might have reduced infant mortality
to some degree become established as customary norms attached
to the parental role? The question is particularly problematic
in light of the argument that parents are not necessarily aware
of the adaptive function of the pattern. Thus if innovative
parents did not know that what they did acted to prevent the
deaths of their children, how were they able to convince others
to do it? And how did such a subtle process repeat itself in
so many parts of the world? An answer can only be speculative.
I assume that in a population afflicted with high infant
mortality women who have more surviving children are in a
better position to transmit their ideas of infant care to
the next generation, not only because they have more daughters
and daughters-in-law whom they can influence directly, but also
because the effectiveness of their mothering may lead other
young women to take them as models for imitation and persons
to turn to for advice in matters of infant care. If this
happened generation after generation, it would be possible
for more-adaptive infant care patterns to be selectively
propagated and ultimately institutionalized in a gradual
process of cultural change. Hence the cumulation of "folk
wisdom", eventually to be solidified in custom.

CONCLUSIONS

The relationship of infant mortality to customs of infant
care illustrates a cultural-evolutionary analysis of child
rearing. The customs represent adaptations to environmental
pressures experienced by earlier generations of parents seeking
to realize the universal goals of parenthood. A similar case
could be made concerning the relation of subsistence pressures
to customs of child training related to economic performance.
The point, however, would be roughly the same. Institutionalized patterns of child rearing need to be analyzed as means

by which parents have responded adaptively to their experience of environmental hazards threatening the health or future welfare of their children.

Anthropologists have emphasized the influence on child rearing of broad cultural values concerning morality and social interaction not specific to the situations of infancy and early childhood. These influences cannot be denied, but they should be placed in the context of the culturally organized hierarchy of parental goals suggested in this chapter.

REFERENCES

Ainsworth, M. Infancy in Uganda. Baltimore, Md.: Johns
        Hopkins University Press, 1967.

Bowlby, J. Attachment and Loss. Vol. 1: Attachment. New York,
        Basic Books, 1969.

Caudill, W. & Platt, D. Who sleeps by whom? Parent-child
        involvement in urban Japanese families. Psychiatry
        1966, 29, 344-366.

Caudill, W. & Weinstein, H. Material care and infant behavior
        in Japan and America. Psychiatry, 1969, 32, 12-43.

Freedman, D. G. Human Infancy: An Evolutionary Perspective.
        Lawrence Erlbaum Associates, 1974.

LeVine, R. Cross-cultural study in child psychology. In
        P. Mussen (Ed.) Carmichael's manual of child
        psychology, (3rd ed.). John Wiley & Sons, New York:
        1970.

Spiro, M. E. Children of the Kibbutz. Cambridge, Mass.:
        Harvard University Press, 1958.

Whiting, J. W. M. Chasdi, E. H., Antonovsky, H. R., & Ayres,
        B. C. The learning of values. In E. Z. Vogt and
        E. M. Albert (Eds.), People of Rimrock. Cambridge,
        Mass.: Harvard University Press, 1966.

Chapter 3
A Model for Psychocultural Research

John W. M. Whiting
Harvard University

Over the years, my colleagues and I have developed the so-called Whiting Model for psychocultural research (Figure 3.1). This a heuristic model, and can serve here as a map showing how each of the studies that I will mention relates to all the others.

The arrows in the model represent assumptions about the direction of causation. It should be emphasized that we are dealing with assumptions, not laws or axioms. In some, if not many, instances, the true direction of causation may be the reverse: there may be feedback loops and steps in the assumed

---

*

This chapter is a revised version of the Distinguished Lecturer Address, delivered at the American Anthropological Association meetings, New Orleans, November 29, 1973.
I have always felt more comfortable talking with people about research problems than reading books or thinking by myself.
What I am going to report here about research strategies in psychological anthropology is truly the product of discussions with my colleagues and students while we have struggled together, trying to make sense of our data or working out the details of a research plan. I could not begin to list all of these people, but I must mention one colleague with whom I have worked closely since 1935 and who has contributed immeasurably to the product: Professor Beatrice Blyth Whiting.

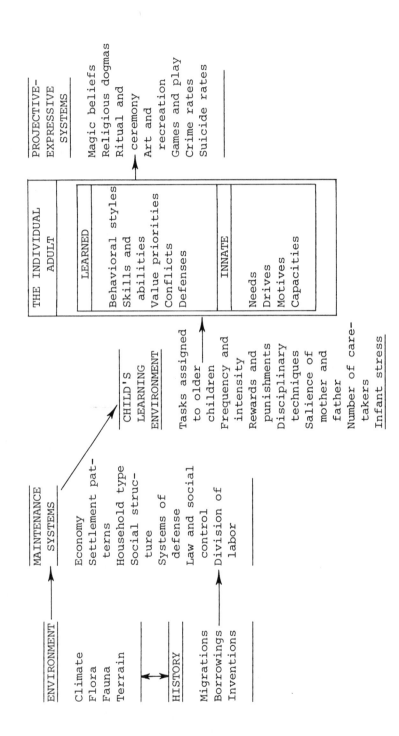

Figure 3-1: A Model for Psychocultural Research

ENVIRONMENT

Climate
Flora
Fauna
Terrain

HISTORY

Migrations
Borrowings
Inventions

MAINTENANCE
SYSTEMS

Economy
Settlement pat-
  terns
Household type
Social struc-
  ture
Systems of
  defense
Law and social
  control
Division of
  labor

CHILD'S
LEARNING
ENVIRONMENT

Tasks assigned
  to older
  children
Frequency and
  intensity
Rewards and
  punishments
Disciplinary
  techniques
Salience of
  mother and
  father
Number of care-
  takers
Infant stress

THE INDIVIDUAL
ADULT

LEARNED

Behavioral styles
Skills and
  abilities
Value priorities
Conflicts
Defenses

INNATE

Needs
Drives
Motives
Capacities

PROJECTIVE-
EXPRESSIVE
SYSTEMS

Magic beliefs
Religious dogmas
Ritual and
  ceremony
Art and
  recreation
Games and play
Crime rates
Suicide rates

sequence may be skipped. The arrows do, however, represent a commonly occurring sequence. The primary reason for making such oversimplified assumptions about causation is that they give rise to a readily testable set of hypotheses. Hypotheses that are difficult or impossible to put in jeopardy are not, in my opinion, very fruitful. Progress in any science is most rapid when an accepted hypothesis is shown to be false, and a new search for truth begins.

It would be impossible to review here even a reasonable sample of the research bearing on the various parts of the model. I will, however, briefly describe a few studies that will, I hope, serve to illustrate the model and elucidate the basic assumptions latent in it.

Most ethnological disciplines make either implicit or explicit assumptions about the needs, drives, and capacities of the individual. Economic anthropology assumes a need for sustenance and shelter. Political anthropology makes certain assumptions about strivings for power and prestige. Cognitive anthropology has an explicit theory about individual strategies of coding and storing information. Symbolic anthropology makes assumptions about the capacity to create and understand metaphor. These assumptions take it for granted that the adult members of all societies have the same psychobiological needs, motives, and capacities. They behave differently only because of the beliefs, values, and techniques of their cultures.

This "natural man" approach has been very effective. There is, indeed, great psychobiological similarity among the peoples of the world. The present model does not deny this, but makes the further assumption that events occurring in infancy or early childhood--what the model collectively terms *the child's learning environment*, and what we often call *socialization*-- make a person something *more* or something *less* than a natural man.

LEARNING ENVIRONMENTS

A full characterization of childhood learning environments would have to include physical, economic, cultural, and interpersonal factors, and would obviously be useless in a model. Before a concept can be incorporated into a model, it must first be reduced to its essential attributes. And, if the model is to be used in different cultures, these presumed attributes must apply in all of them. I will begin by illustrating this process of refinement for the concept of the learning environment that now appears in the Whiting Model.

Using Freud's three-stage conceptualization of psychosexual development (oral to anal to phallic), and our own cultural background, we devised our first list of essential variables for children's learning environments: weaning from the breast, toilet training, and sex training. As Irvin Child and I (Whiting & Child, 1953) reviewed the ethnographic literature, we soon realized that these were not the salient variables in most cultures. Weaning from the breast was relatively unimportant. Toilet training was seldom mentioned as any problem at all. And the socialization of sex turned out to be dealt with by rules governing premarital sexual behavior in late childhood and adolescence, rather than by rules or training during early childhood. Aggression, however, and weaning from the back, or the development of independence, turned out to be problems that had to be coped with in all societies. We therefore added independence training and training for the control of aggression to our list of salient variables. And we dropped the notion of stages in psychosexual development, deciding rather to speak of behavior systems--oral, anal, sexual, dependent, and aggressive.

For each of these variables or behavior systems, we found differences between cultures in (1) the degree of initial indulgence or permissiveness; (2) age at onset of socialization; (3) severity of socialization; and (4) technique of punishment characteristically used by parents and other socializing agents. When the study was completed, it became evident that we had made but a crude beginning. We had learned that parents in most cultures are more concerned with interpersonal relations than with body functions, and had modified our variables accordingly. But further refinements were needed to describe the most important features of the learning environment during infancy and of socialization pressures during childhood.

Irvin Child, Margaret Bacon, and Herbert Barry set out to work on the problem of socialization during later childhood, using both Henry Murray's theory of personality (1949) and the theory of learning advanced by Hull (1943) and Miller and Dollard (1941). They reanalyzed infant indulgence, developing a code to allow cross-cultural evaluation of this variable. More important, they broke independence down into six categories: responsibility, nurturance, self-reliance, achievement, obedience, and general independence. Evaluating the most often used training techniques for each of these categories, they found positive learning to be the most effective.

This reformulation of part of the socialization process in learning-theory terms was useful, but it left out of account both the personal relationship between mother and child and the role of the father in the socialization process. Oedipal rivalry, identification, and superego development had also been bypassed.

The following passage from Freud's New Introductory Lectures (1933) inspired our further work on the superego:

> The role, which the superego undertakes
> later in life, is at first played by an
> external power, by parental authority.
> The influence of the parents dominates
> the child by granting proofs of
> affections and by threats of punishment,
> which, to the child, mean loss of love,
> and which must also be feared on their
> own account. This objective anxiety is
> the forerunner of the later moral anxiety;
> so long as the former is dominant one need
> not speak of superego or conscience. It
> is only later that the secondary situation
> arises, which we are far too ready to regard
> as the normal state of affairs; the external
> restrictions are introjected, so that the
> superego takes the place of the parental
> function, and thenceforward observes, guides
> and threatens the ego in just the same way
> as the parents acted to the child before... .
> The basis of the process is what we call an
> identification, that is to say, that one ego
> becomes like another, ... which results in
> the first ego behaving itself in certain
> respects in the same way as the second; it
> imitates it, and as it were takes it into
> itself. This identification has been not
> inappropriately compared with the oral
> cannibalistic incorporation of another person.

Our initial approach to the problem was through a study of disciplinary techniques as the origins of guilt, or

internalized parental values. Assuming that guilt is most
effectively internalized if punishment consists of withdrawal
of love, Irvin Child and I devised a measure of "love-
oriented" techniques of discipline. Not satisfied with the
reliability of this measure when it was applied solely to
ethnographic reports, we incorporated it into an interview
form that was used to survey disciplinary techniques among
three groups of mothers in the American Southwest--Texans,
Mormons, and Zuni, (Whiting, Antonovsky, Chasdi, & Ayres,
1966)--and then among a large sample of mothers in two Boston
surburbs (Sears, Maccoby, & Levin, 1957).

From these two studies we discovered that interviews were
no more satisfactory than ethnographic reports. Mothers could
not report on their use of love-oriented disciplinary techniques.
We concluded that values are transmitted by frowns, smiles,
touches, and avoidances that are not consciously formulated by
parents as teaching techniques, but that are unconscious
expressions of feelings toward their infants or children.
This body language, however, is a powerful indicator of what
the parents approve or disapprove, and thus provides the
evaluative content of the children's superegos.

A parent's expressive behavior will be effective only if
she or he is salient to the child. Salience depends on two
factors--the degree to which the child is dependent on the
parent and the frequency with which the parent is present and
interacts with the child.

Highly salient parents not only transmit values by
expressive behavior but also serve as models for identification,
an equally important part of the socialization process. In an
attempt to resolve the apparent contradiction between a theory
based only on the strength of love or dependence on the model
and the evidence indicating identifications with the aggressor,
we formulated the status-envy hypothesis (Whiting, 1960).
This hypothesis assumes that identification is a function of
the degree to which the identificant sees the model as
controlling crucial resources such as food and, more important
for infants and young children, comfort, love, and power.

The nonverbal transmission of values and the identification
process are subtle and difficult to measure. Since they both
occur quite automatically and unconsciously, so that interviews
are of little or no use in evaluating them, some other method
must be devised. Observing what goes on between infants and
those who care for them, in natural settings, seems to be a
promising alternative. We have recently tried this in Kenya,

but since we are just beginning to analyze our data, we cannot yet tell how successful it will be. It certainly is very time consuming.

MAINTENANCE SYSTEMS

The important antecedent variables of parent salience and parent-child interaction are also difficult to measure directly. Thus we began to look for indirect ways to assess them. This turned out to be a fruitful approach, not only to these particular variables, but to all sorts of variations in the learning environment. Domestic arrangements obviously vary a great deal from culture to culture (see, for example, Murdock's Ethnographic Atlas, 1962). The independent nuclear family living in a single household is by no means the only or even the common pattern. Various forms of extended and polygynous households are more common among the societies of the world that retain their traditional culture. A polygynous mother who lives in a hut of her own, eats with her children with no other adult present, and shares her bed with her infant rather than her husband might well be far more salient to her children than a mother in a monogamous household in which the father eats with the mother and children, shares in the domestic duties, and sleeps with the mother (Whiting and Whiting, 1975a).

The relative power and control of resources that each parent is perceived to have can also be estimated from proxy or index variables. If strict virilocal residence is the rule, the mother is a newcomer to the community and her relatives live at a distance. By contrast, the father is a member of the community by right of birth, and his relatives are near at hand. This gives him a big advantage over the mother as a desired model for identification, if the households are independent. If the households are extended, however, the distribution of domestic power is quite different. Both parents may be subservient to the natural grandparents, and in domestic matters it is often the parental grandmother who wields the real power.

Extended or independent households based on other residence rules can be examined in the same way, and similar estimates of the distribution of power by sex and generation can be made. Residence rules and household structure thus provide excellent proxy variables to describe variations in the learning environments of children.

Most of the variables we have thus far used to describe

the learning environment have been borrowed from learning
theory or from psychoanalytic theory. Recently, however,
we have turned our attention to attachment theory, which
suggests new variables to investigate. After observing
animals in their natural habitats, Tinbergen, Lorenz, and
other ethologists hypothesized that a young animal becomes
attached to and follows its parents by a process called
imprinting. John Bowlby (1969) borrowed this idea and
developed a theory of attachment to apply to human mothers
and infants. Bowlby insists that attachment differs from
the acquired-drive concept of dependency advanced by learning
theorists. He considers it an instinctive mechanism that
has persisted because of its adaptive value.

In his early formulation of attachment theory, Bowlby
assumed that for "healthy" development an infant should be
securely attached to his biological mother and to her alone.
He has recently modified this extreme view to admit the
validity of subsidiary as well as primary attachments. In
any case, Bowlby hypothesizes that the number of people
taking responsibility for infant care is significant. Since
in many cultures older children, grandparents, aunts, and
uncles share the duties of infant care, there are many
societies where the effect of multiple caretakers can be
studied. Cultures also vary considerably in the degree to
which the father is involved in infant care.

A second hypothesis in attachment theory that is
pertinent here deals with the security of the attachment
between infants and primary caretakers. The degree of
security is commonly measured by noticing what children do
when their mothers leave them, and is presumed to be related
to the degree of physical closeness--i.e., the amount of body
contact--the infants have experienced with their mothers or
primary caretakers since birth. If this presumed relation
is valid, we should be able to estimate security of attachment
by observing whether infants are carried in slings or shawls
when their caretakers are on the move and sit in their laps
when they are resting or, by contrast, are heavily swaddled
or strapped to a cradle board and treated like a package that
can safely be put down. In our own culture, as in some others,
neither of these extremes prevails. In spite of a recent
resurgence of carrying babies around in stomach or hip slings
and in backpacks, many if not most American babies spend hours
each day alone in cribs, playpens, or jump seats. Yet these
babies are also cuddled close at several times during the day,
and are not swaddled or strapped to boards.

Stress theory provides still another variable that belongs in our model learning environment. Seymour Levine (1959), Victor Denenberg (1963), and others have demonstrated in their animal research that stress experienced during infancy has two very important effects on growth and development: (1) it increases the rate of growth, and   (2) it makes the animal bolder in exploring a strange environment when it reaches maturity.   These effects can be observed whether the stress is "physical" (electric shock, violent movement, extreme cold) or "psychological" (repeated separation of a young infant from its mother).

Since it seemed likely that human infants would respond to stress in similar ways, we reviewed the ethnographic literature for evidence of cultural variation in the stress experienced by infants. We found that in some cultures infants are customarily subjected to physically stressful events such as having their earlobes or their nasal septa pierced, or having their heads molded for cosmetic purposes, or being vaccinated or circumcised during infancy, whereas in other cultures infants are carefully protected from such stresses. In addition to these direct measures of physical stress, we found a likely proxy variable for psychological stress--the degree to which infants are separated from their mothers.

These, then, are the variables in the child's learning environment suggested by learning theory, psychoanalysis, attachment theory, and infant-stress theory: the frequency and strength of rewards and punishments during the socialization process, the choice of techniques of disciplines, the timing of various events such as weaning, toilet training, and training for independence; the relative salience of the mother and father as socializing agents; the number of care-takers, and the occurrence of specific stressful events in early infancy.

At this point, I would like to move to the left-hand side in our heuristic model (see Figure 3-1) and specify variables in the maintenance systems of a society that influence its childhood learning environment. The first study to approach this problem was that of Bacon, Barry, and Child (1959), which showed that differences in the subsistence economy of a culture influenced the factors emphasized in training for independence. Cultures with capital investments in cattle and methods of storing agricultural products pressured their children to be responsible, obedient, and nurturant, whereas hunters and gathers who had no such accumulation stores stressed self-

reliance and achievement.[1] More recently, the learning
environments of infants and children in a hunting and gathering
society--that of the !Kung Bushmen--have been described by
Mel Konner (1973) and Pat Draper (1973), with findings
supporting Bacon, Barry, and Child's findings of low pressure
for responsibility in such societies.

Our theory differs from Bacon, Barry, and Child in that
we believe cultural variation in training for responsibility
arises more directly from variation in mothers' workloads
from culture to culture than from variation in capital
accumulation. In cultures where women have a major
responsibility for the primary subsistenance activity,
especially in agricultural societies where the women are the
chief gardeners, the older children are held responsible not
only for domestic chores in general, but for much of the
infant care as well. Complex societies, especially those
that have adopted Western schooling and have a social class
structure with upward mobility related to achievement, are
more likely to stress individual achievement. Thus, the
tasks assigned to older children, whether they be carrying
out domestic chores or learning the three R's, are important
features of a child's learning environment that are dictated
in large part by the maintenance systems of the child's
culture.

Settlement patterns, residence rules, and family and
household structure, which we have shown to be important
proxy variables for crucial parts of childhood learning
environments can be considered part of the maintenance system
of the culture. Social structure is constrained by subsistence
activities, whether the people in question are nomadic hunter-
gatherers, transhumant herdsmen, or settled agriculturalists.

The relationship of history and the environment to a
society's maintenance systems is for the most part beyond the
scope of this paper, but I would like to mention on important

---

[1] A study of children in six cultures (Whiting and Whiting,
1975b) seems to contradict this finding. The more complex
cultures in this sample stressed individual achievement,
whereas the simpler cultures stressed responsibility and
nurturance. However, the two samples are not really
comparable. None of the cultures in the Barry, Bacon, and
Child sample was so complex as the three complex cultures
in the six-culture study; and none of the three simpler
societies in the six-culture study was a hunting and
gathering society.

climatic effect. In cultures located in areas of the world
in which the temperature falls below freezing in the winter,
babies are very likely to be heavily swaddled, carried on
cradle boards or wheeled about in baby carriages and put to
sleep alone in cribs; whereas in warmer climates they are
either naked or lightly clothed, carried in shawls or pouches
in close body contact with the mother, and placed in the
mother's bed at night. Climate also determines to a large
extent whether or not husbands and wives sleep in the same
bed. They usually sleep together in cold climates, apart in
warm climates (Whiting, 1964; 1971).

PROJECTIVE EXPRESSIVE SYSTEMS

Finally we come to the most important question of all.
What difference does all this make? How do children's early
experiences affect the projective-expressive systems of a
culture, as presented at the right-hand side of the heuristic
model (see Figure 3-1)?

The easiest answer, postulating a simple, direct effect--
as the twig is bent, the tree's inclined--has some validity,
but it is not very interesting. If adults brought up in a
given culture enjoy its expressive styles, take seriously the
proper performance of its rituals, and hold firmly to its
magical and religious beliefs simply because they have been
taught them as children, there would be little need for
further research. Once the essential elements of the childhood learning situation were identified for any given culture,
the adult behavior and personality characteristics for that
culture could be predicted. We make a more complex assumption.
All the cultures we have thus far studied make rather heavy
demands on their children, many of which demands have been
described in our discussion of learning environments. Such
demands, we believe, produce enduring conflicts that would be
intolerable and would soon be replaced by neurotic symptoms
unless there were culturally approved modes of defending
against them. We assume, then, that a given culture's
projective-expressive systems arise out of these defensive
struggles--partly consist, in fact, of these necessary and
socially accepted defenses--and differ from those of other
cultures to the degree that its members have distinctive
conflicts to defend against.

Although there have been some attemtps to measure
personality in other cultures directly, by using Rorschach,

TAT (Thematic Apperception Test), and other projective tests, most studies relevant to this right-hand side of the model have used proxy variables for this purpose. Spiro and D'Andrade (1958) and Lambert, Triandis, and Wolf (1959) have shown that the nature of a culture's gods reflects the relations between children and their parents in that culture. Belief in witchcraft can be interpreted as a paranoid defense resulting from severity in the socialization of sex and in training for the control of aggression (Whiting & Child, 1953; Whiting, 1959; LeVine, 1962). Barbara Ayres (1968) has shown the learning environment's influence on music; Barry (1957) its relation to complexity in the pictorial arts; Shirley & Romney its relation to love magic (Shirley & Romney, 1962); Stephens (1961) its influence on menstrual taboos; and Roberts & Barry its relation to a cultural preference for playing games of chance (Roberts & Barry, 1973).

The particular conflict-defense system we focused on was the sexual one. We hypothesized that in cultures where mothers are highly salient in early infancy and fathers become more salient later in childhood, there should be a conflict in sex identity for both boys and girls. If so, then initiation rites at puberty involving circumcision for boys and clitoridectomy for girls might funciton as a means of resolving or defending against this conflict by removing the "feminine" prepuce and the "masculine" clitoris. Cross-cultural tests by Burton and Whiting (1961) and by Judith Brown (1963) supported this interpretation.

The couvade, too, can be interpreted as a defense against a conflict in sex identity. Lee and Ruth Munroe hypothesized that in cultures where mothers are highly salient not only in infancy but later in childhood (because of exclusive mother-infant sleeping arrangements and matrilocal residence rules), the couvade allows men to act out the female role symbolically and ritually, and in a culturally approved manner. A cross-cultural test supported their hypothesis (Munroe, Munroe, & Whiting, 1973).

Our hypothesis about conflict in sexual identity for both sexes, which I call the *cross-sex-identity-hypothesis* for short, was tested in a number of other studies as well. These studies were done on people who had been brought up in the same society but in learning environments that differed in the relative salience of the male and female parents. D'Andrade (1962) worked with children in a Barbadian community in Massachusetts, comparing those brought up with their fathers and those brought up without them. Lynn Kuckenbert Carlsmith

(1964) studied a college and a high school sample, contrasting the half of each group whose fathers had been at home with the half whose fathers had been overseas serving in World War II during the first years of the subjects' lives. The Munroes (1973) followed up their previously mentioned cross-cultural study of the couvade by relating the seriousness with which Black Carib men practiced the ritual to differences in the salience of males in the household during their infancy and early childhood. Harrington (1970) tested the hypothesis on a sample of mentally disturbed teenage boys from upper New York State. Carol Ember (1970) tested it on a sample of Luo children and Sara Nerlove (1969) on a sample of Gusii children. Finally, Robert Daniels (1970) tested the hypothesis on a sample of Kipsigis men. In each of these studies, tests designed to measure individual differences in sex identity were used. In each study, some of the tests supported the general hypothesis and some did not.

Another method of testing the hypothesis consists of determining at the individual level whether or not initiation rites do indeed act as a culturally approved defense. If so, males should be more sure of their manhood and females of their womanhood after the appropriate initiation than before it. There was some confirmation of this in the Daniels study of Kipsigis men, but Herzog (1973) found no support for it among Kikuyu youths tested before and after undergoing circumcision at adolescence. Although not focused on the problem of sex-identity conflict, Granzberg (1973) found a before-and-after-initiation effect on a sample of Hopi youth. I have given a battery of sex-identity tests to samples of Kipsigis, Kikuyu, and Gusii youths before and after initiation, using the Luo, who do not practice circumcision, as a control group. Unfortunately, the data have yet to be analyzed.

At this time, then, the cross-sex-identity hypothesis can neither be rejected nor accepted as proven. There is, however, considerable support for the more general hypothesis that the projective-expressive systems of a culture provide defenses against conflicts engendered in infancy and early childhood.

I have reported the sex-identity problem in some detail because it illustrates a research strategy that is particularly appropriate for psychocultural research. This strategy combines cross-cultural studies in which each culture is a unit with studies in which groups of people brought up in a single culture but with different childhood experiences are the units. These latter studies should be replicated in a variety of different cultures to test the effect of cultural

context, as has been done with the infant-stress hypothesis
(Landauer & Whiting, 1964; Gunders & Whiting, 1968; Whiting,
Landauer, & Jones, 1968). Unfortunately, however, people who
use the cross-cultural method seldom do fieldwork, and few
ethnographers either test their field results cross-culturally
or even use cultural findings when designing their field
studies.

The six-culture study mentioned above represents a somewhat different research strategy: Child rearing was studied
simultaneously in six different cultures, using the same
methods and focusing on the same problems. Data on the history,
environment, maintenance systems, and learning environments
of each culture were collected and reported by the field team
that carried out the research (J. and A. Fischer; K. and R.
Romney; W. and C. Nydegger; T. and H. Maretski; R. and B.
LeVine; L. Minturn). An analysis of standard interviews with
the mothers has also been published (Minturn & Lambert, 1964).

The dependent variable chosen for this study was the
social behavior of children as observed in natural settings.
A monograph reporting the results has been published (Whiting
& Whiting, 1975), but some of the most important findings can
be summarized here. The best predictors of the social
behavior of children between the ages of three and eleven
are, in order of importance, (1) the type of culture in which
the child was reared; (2) the status of the person with whom
the child was interacting; (3) the child's sex; (4) the
child's age; (5) the child's position in the sibling order;
and (6) differences between the child's learning environment
and that of his or her peers.

Of the cultural predictors, the most powerful was the
level of complexity. As reported above, children in simple
cultures are high on nurturance and low on egoism, whereas
children brought up in complex cultures are egoistic and not
very nurturant. A second important cultural variable was
whether or not the ideal household consisted of a monogamous
nuclear family. Children brought up in cultures favoring
nuclear families were high on intimate and sociable interaction and low on aggression, while those brought up in
societies with extended or polygynous households had the
opposite characteristics.

In all six cultures, however, children were more likely
to be nurturant than to make any other response if they were
interacting with infants and similarly to act sociably and to
seek help when interacting with their parents. Also, in all

six cultures girls were more nurturant than boys and boys were more aggressive than girls.

There were difficulties with the six-culture study. The fact that the cultures being studied were so widely scattered over the world led to problems in communication. When one field team discovered a defect in the plan, months sometimes passed before the defect could be remedied and the remedy communicated to all the other teams (Whiting, *et al.*, 1966). Furthermore, it was not feasible to maintain contact with each of the villages over an extended period of time. Partly for these reasons, in our most recent attempt to use the model to guide our research, we have modified our research strategy by choosing a set of communities that are geographically closer together but still markedly different in physical environment, history, maintenance systems, and learning environments. We set up what we call our Child Development Research Unit, and the site we chose was Kenya. Since this project began in 1966, we have gathered the basic demographic and genealogical data on sixteen communities representing eight different cultures and varying degrees of modernization and urbanization.

The Research Unit's attachment to the University of Nairobi represents another major improvement in our previous research strategy. Being attached to the University enabled us to use students as apprentices and research assistants, and to collaborate with members of the faculty. It enabled us to assemble research teams combining the sensitivity of native speakers of the study-site language with the objectivity of outsiders. Kenyan students learned research methods, and we gained a proper repository and disseminating agent for copies of our research reports and for our basic data, ensuring that they will be available to our host country.

I hope the Child Development Research Unit will be the first step in a consortium of research units in many countries, each staffed by indigenous scholars and each with visiting scholars from other units in the consortium. American scholars wishing to join the consortium would have to identify a set of communities in their own countries as well as in the United States, representing different facets of American culture--not limited to the ghettos--set up and maintain research units there, and invite staff members from the units in other countries and cultures to join them as visiting scholars.

In conclusion, I would like to make the general point that those of us who wish to think of ourselves as practitioners of "hard" science have failed to achieve this status in large part because, along with most other social scientists, we have refused to accept the test of replicability. All too readily we report the results of a single study as validated truth, without waiting to see whether anyone else will get the same results with our methods. We are inclined to feel that repeating a study on a different sample or in a different culture is not being creative, and we certainly transmit this feeling to our students. Let us put all our hypotheses in maximum jeopardy.

REFERENCES

Ayres, B.   Effects of infantile stimulation on musical behavior.   In A. Lomax (Ed.), Folk song style and culture (American Association for the Advancement of Science, Publication 88) 1968, Washington, D.C.

Bacon, M., Barry, H. & Child, I.   Relation of child training to subsistence economy.   American Anthropologist, 1959, 61, 51-63.

Barry, H.   Relationship between child training and the pictorial arts.   Journal of Abnormal and Social Psychology, 1957, 54, 380-383.

Bowlby, J.   Attachment and loss.   Vol. 1: Attachment.   New York: Basic Books, 1969.

Brown, J. K.   A cross-culture study of female initiation rites.   American Anthropologist, 1963, 65, 837-853.

Burton, R. V., & Whiting, J. W. M.   The absent father and cross-sex identity.   In W. A. Lessa and E. Z. Vogt (Eds.), Reader in comparative religion.   New York: Harper & Row, 1961.

Carlsmith, L. K.   Effect of early father absence on school aptitude.   Harvard Educational Review, 1964, 34, 3-21.

D'Andrade, R. G.   Father-absence and cross-sex identification.   Unpublished doctoral dissertation, Harvard University, 1962.

Daniels, R. E. By rites a man: A study of the societal and
    individual foundations of tribal identity among the
    Kipsigis of Kenya. Unpublished doctoral dissertation
    University of Chicago, 1970.

Denenberg, V. H. & Whimbey, A. D. Behavior of adult rats is
    modified by the experiences their mothers had as
    infants. Science, 1963, 142, 1192-1193.

Draper, P. Crowding among hunter-gatherers: the !Kung Bushmen.
    Science, 1973, 182, 301-303.

Ember, C. R. Effects of feminine task-assignment on the
    social behavior of boys. Unpublished doctoral
    dissertation, Harvard University, 1970.

Freud, S. New introductory lectures on psycho-analysis.
    New York: Norton, 1933, 89-90.

Granzberg, G. The psychological integration of culture: A
    cross-cultural study of Hopi type initiation rites.
    Journal of Social Psychology, 1973, 90, 3-7.

Gunders, S. M. & Whiting, J. W. M. Mother-infant separation
    and physical growth. Ethnology, 1968, 7, 196-206.

Harrington, C. Errors in sex-role behavior in teenage boys.
    New York: Teachers College Press, 1970.

Herzog, J. D. Initiation and high school in the development
    of Kikuyu youths' self-concept. Ethos, 1973, 1(4),
    478-489.

Hull, C. L. Principles of behavior. New York: Appleton-
    Century, 1943.

Konner, M. J. Aspects of the developmental ethology of a
    foraging people. In N. Blurton Jones (Ed.),
    Ethological studies of child behavior. Cambridge,
    England: Cambridge University Press, 1973.

Lambert, W., Triandis, L., & Wolf, M. Some correlates of
    beliefs in the malevolence and benevolence of
    supernatural beings--A cross-cultural study. Journal
    of Abnormal and Social Psychology, 1959, 58, 162-169.

Landauer, T. K., & Whiting, J. W. M. Infantile stimulation and adult stature of human males. American Anthropologist, 1964, 66, 1007-1027.

LeVine, R. Witchcraft and co-wife proximity in Southwestern Kenya. Ethnology, 1962, 1(61), 291-296.

LeVine, S. J. & Lewis, G. W. The relative importance of experimenter contact in an effect produced by extrastimulation in infancy. Journal of Comparative and Physiological Psychology, 1959, 52, 368-370.

Miller, N. & Dollard, J. Social learning and imitation. New Haven: Yale University Press, 1941.

Minturn, L. & Lambert, W. W. Mothers of six cultures: Antecedents of child rearing. New York: Wiley, 1964.

Munroe, R. L. & Munroe, R. H. Psychological interpretation of male initiation rites: The case of male pregnancy symptoms. Ethos, 1973, 1(4), 490-498.

Munroe, R. L., Munroe, R. H., & Whiting, J. W. M. The couvade: A psychological analysis. Ethos, 1973, 1(1), 30-74.

Murdock, G. P. Ethnographic atlas. Ethnology, 1962, 1(1), 113-134.

Murray, H. Exploration in personality. New York: Oxford University Press, 1949.

Nerlove, S. B. Trait dispositions and situational determinants of behavior among Gusii children of Southwestern Kenya. Unpublished doctoral disseration, Harvard University, 1969.

Roberts, J. M., & Barry, H. Infant socialization and games of chance. Ethnology, 1973, 1(3), 296-308.

Sears, R., Maccoby, E., & Levin, H. Patterns of child rearing. Evanston: Row, Peterson, 1957.

Shirley, R. W., & Romney, A. K. Love magic and socialization anxiety: A cross-cultural study. American Anthropologist, 1962, 64, 1028-1031.

Spiro, M., & D'Andrade, R. A cross-cultural study of some supernatural beliefs. American Anthropologist, 1958, 60, 456-466.

Stephens, W. N. A cross-cultural study of menstrual taboos. Genetic Psychology Monographs, 1961, 64, 385-416.

Whiting, B. B. (Ed.) Six cultures: Studies of child-rearing. New York: Wiley, 1963.

Whiting, J. W. M. Sorcery, sin and the super-ego: A cross-cultural study of some mechanisms of social control. In M. R. Jones (Ed.), Nebraska Symposium on Motivation. Lincoln: University of Nebraska Press, 1959.

Whiting, J. W. M. Resource mediation and learning by identification. In I. Iscoe and H. Stevenson (Eds.), Personality development in children. Austin: University of Texas Press, 1960.

Whiting, J. W. M. The effects of climate on certain cultural practices. In W. H. Goodenough (Ed.), Explorations in anthropology: Essays in honor of George Peter Murdock. New York: McGraw-Hill, 1964.

Whiting, J. W. M. Causes and consequences of the amount of body contact between mother and infant. Paper presented at the annual meeting of the American Anthropological Association, New York, 1971.

Whiting, J. W. M. & Child, I. Child training and personality. New Haven: Yale University Press, 1953.

Whiting, J. W. M. & Whiting, B. B. Aloofness and Intimacy in Husbands and Wives: A Cross-Cultural Study. Ethos, 1975(a), 3(2).

Whiting, J. W. M. & Whiting, B. B. Children of Six Cultures-- A Psycho-Cultural Analysis. Cambridge, Mass.: Harvard University Press, 1975(b).

Whiting, J. W. M., Landauer, T. K., & Jones, T. M. Infantile immunization and adult stature. Child Development, 1968, 39, 59-67.

Whiting, J. W. M., Antonovsky, H., Chasdi, E., & Ayres, B. In E. Vogt and E. Albert (Eds.), Peoples of Rimrock. Cambridge, Mass.: Harvard University Press, 1966.

Whiting, J. W. M., Child, I. L., Lambert, W. W., *et al.*,
    Field Guide for a Study of Socialization.   Six
    Culture Series, Vol. 1.   New York: Wiley, 1966.
    Reprinted by Krieger Publishing Co., Huntington,
    New York.

Chapter 4

Attachment Theory and its Utility in Cross-Cultural Research

Mary D. Salter Ainsworth

The Johns Hopkins University

Attachment theory was first introduced to psychological science by John Bowlby in 1958, and given more definitive and comprehensive formulation by him in 1969. This theory arose from a background of research and was primarily heuristic in intent. It provides an organized set of propositions about early social behavior and development that are nested within a compatible but more comprehensive behavioral theory that might well be characterized as *behavioral biology*. It shares with all contemporary biology a belief in the usefulness of a Darwinian evolutionary perspective. Prior to attachment theory, the two major starting points for research into early social development had been psychoanalytic theory and social learning theory, both of which come in several versions. In my opinion, neither of these important and comprehensive theories gave research into the origins and early development of the child-mother relationship as useful a basis as attachment theory, either for understanding empirical findings already amassed or for launching successful new research.

The almost immediate popularity of the concept of attachment as a basis for research testifies to its filling a need long felt by students of early social development, and yet many who have appealed to its authority have misunderstood it and, I believe, misused it. Attachment theory is part of a new paradigm (Kuhn, 1962) that is not readily assimilated by those who have worked all their scientific lives within the framework of other paradigms. Consequently, contemporary literature on attachment is chaotic, and controversy is active about points that I consider to be phantom issues. I have elsewhere attempted fuller statements of attachment theory (Ainsworth, 1967, 1969, 1972). Here I shall address myself chiefly to those aspects of the theory that seem to have been especially difficult for others to understand and assimilate.

A DEFINITION OF ATTACHMENT

The term *attachment* refers to a relationship between two individuals--a relationship that endures over a relatively long period of their life span. Both following the lead of previous theory and beginning at the beginning of the life span, Bowlby addressed himself primarily to the attachment of an infant to his mother figure. Not all long-lasting relationships are attachments, but the question of just which relationships may be usefully classed as attachments is best deferred until after the characteristics of an attachment relationship have been considered.

Bowlby's attachment theory is acknowledged to stem from an ethological orientation. Attachment may be equated to what the ethologists have termed *bonding*. Infant-mother attachment consists of a bonding of an infant to his mother that endures throughout a more or less extended period of his life span. The attachment of offspring to mother constitutes an important constraint on social organization that is shared by many mammalian species, as well as by many avian species. Because it is a concept relevant to social organization, attachment is a concept useful to anthropologists and to others who are interested in the glue that holds certain important components of social organization together.

John Bowlby was led to borrow the ethological notion of bonding in order to account for the responses of a young child to extended separation from his or her mother. His central question was why a young child protests separation--and continues to protest it--despite the fact that while separated all of the child's survival requirements may be met by a variety of kind and considerate caregivers. It seemed clear to Bowlby that a bond with a specific individual--the mother--persists even though she is absent and even though other people take over her role in caring for the child.

An attachment relationship is obviously not present at birth. A newborn does not protest being removed from his mother and given into the care of a foster mother. The relationship--the attachment--develops over time, and in the human species the time span is substantial, requiring some months. How does it develop? And how do we know when an infant has become attached?

CRITERIA OF ATTACHMENT

The most obvious and most crucial criterion that an infant has formed an attachment to his mother is his prolonged distress if he loses her either permanently or for a period of time long enough to seem to be forever. A separation of no more than several days may cause an infant or young child to despair of ever regaining the figure to whom he or she is bonded. In the study of human beings, however, it is ethically unfeasible to engineer a major separation merely to ascertain whether or not an attachment has been formed.

It is well established that a major separation experience may occasion substantial distress (e.g., Bowlby, 1953; Burlingham & Freud, 1942; Schaffer 1958; Yarrow, 1967). Therefore, it seemed reasonable for Schaffer and Emerson (1964) and others to suppose that the lesser distress activated by minor, everyday separation experiences might serve as a criterion of attachment. In my study of Ganda infants (Ainsworth, 1967), however, I found that some infants who were otherwise clearly attached to their mothers did not protest consistently when their mothers left the room. I concluded that a child may be attached to his mother, perhaps more securely attached than others, and still not consistently protest brief, everyday separations.

At a meeting of the Tavistock Study Group on Mother-Infant Interaction, held in London in 1961, I reported the findings of my Ganda study (1963, 1967), including my finding that some babies who were obviously attached to their mothers did not consistently protest minor separations. I was asked: "How did you know that the child was attached?" This led me to scrutinize the decision-making processes involved in such a judgment, and resulted in the formulation of a catalogue of behaviors that, especially in combination, might serve as a set of criteria of attachment. This catalogue included not only crying when the mother left the room, but also following her, greeting her on her return with smiling, vocalization, excited bounding, reaching, or approach behavior, and a variety of behaviors relevant to physical contact, such as clambering up and clinging. I added the proviso that in the case of each behavior, differential responsiveness to the attachment figure was required before it could be used as a criterion that a baby had become attached. I termed these behaviors *patterns of attachment behavior*, and posited that when a child directs behaviors such as these toward a specific individual, persistently although intermittently over a long period of time, rather than toward other available persons, he or she may be identified as having become attached to that person.[1]

In general, attachment behaviors may be viewed as constituting a class of behaviors that serve to promote proximity or contact with an attachment figure, and to maintain such proximity and contact after it has once been achieved. Nevertheless, some of the same behaviors may be manifested while an infant is still too young to have become attached to a specific figure, even then, they may be viewed as promoting proximity or contact, but indiscriminately, and indifferent as to figure. Some of these behaviors are signaling behaviors, such as crying, smiling, and vocalizing, that promote proximity through attracting a figure to approach or that maintain proximity by inducing the figure to remain close. Others are active behaviors, such as sucking, rooting, and grasping, that serve to maintain contact once it has been achieved.

It is a small step from this to hypothesize that it is through these early proximity-promoting behaviors--and other, later developing ones--that an infant gradually becomes attached. The behaviors first become differentially directed to a specific mother figure, and then become organized together with her as a focus. It is an attractive hypothesis to attribute the differentiation of these behaviors and their increasing focus on one figure rather than another to the positive feedback or reinforcement that an infant receives. Nevertheless, there is much evidence, both clinical and from experimental studies with nonhuman primates (e.g., Harlow, 1963; Harlow & Harlow, 1969), that infants clearly may become attached to mothers who are rejecting, punitive, or actually

---

[1] In addition to the behaviors mentioned above, the list of patterns of attachment behavior included differential crying, differential smiling, and differential vocalization, although I cautioned that these might show only ability to discriminate between figures and not serve as indicators that an attachment had been formed.

brutal, and who thus yield much negative feedback. It seems a more conservative hypothesis that it is the frequency and intensity with which active attachment behaviors are elicited by a specific figure--up to an as yet undetermined asymptote-- that accounts for the formation of an attachment.

It is pertinent in the case of attachment and attachment behaviors to ask the same four questions that Tinbergen (1951) asks about any behavioral system that is a candidate for identification as a species-characteristic system. What activates the behavior, that is, what made the animal do it now? What is its ontogeny? What is its function, that is, its survival value? Why does this kind of animal solve this problem of survival in this particular way?

THE ACTIVATION OF ATTACHMENT BEHAVIOR

What activates attachment behavior? That is, under what circumstances does a young child seek proximity to the attachment figure? Some of these causative conditions are internal or organismic and some are external or environmental. Attachment behavior is more likely to be activated when an infant is hungry, in pain, tired, or ill than when he or she is rested, well fed, and healthy. Attachment behavior is likely to be activated, often at high intensity, when a child is alarmed. Or when the attachment figure moves away, departs, or is absent--and especially if it is inexplicably and seemingly irretrievably lost. Other conditions include the return of an attachment figure after an absence, or after a rebuff either by that figure or by someone else. When the child is at a distance from the attachment figure, but the figure is nevertheless accessible, attachment behavior may be activated intermittently, often at low intensity.

THE ONTOGENY OF ATTACHMENT

What is the ontogeny of attachment? How do attachment behaviors develop, become discriminating, and organize together in a focus on a specific figure? These are the core questions of the research in which I have been engaged for over a decade. Partial answers have been presented in publications to date. The development of crying and its relationship to maternal responsiveness is discussed by Bell and Ainsworth (1972). The development of separation protest, following and greeting behaviors was studied by Stayton,

Ainsworth, and Main (1973), while individual differences in
these behaviors and their organization, together with crying
and with physical contact behaviors, were dealt with by
Stayton and Ainsworth (1973). An interim report on behaviors
relevant to physical contact and their relation to maternal
behavior was made by Ainsworth, Bell, and Stayton (1972).
The issue of differential responsiveness to an attachment
figure in preference to another figure has been dealt with
in regard to locomotor approach behavior by Tracy, Lamb, and
Ainsworth (1976), and in regard to behavior in fact-to-face
situations by Blehar, Lieberman, and Ainsworth (1977). Data
analysis relevant to the development of organization and
focusing has not yet been completed. (This research project
deals only with the first year of life. Research into the
further development of child-mother attachment, in the second
year and beyond, is urgently needed.)

THE FUNCTION OF ATTACHMENT

     What is the function of attachment behavior and, indeed,
of attachment itself? What outcome was so crucial for survival
in the environment of evolutionary adaptedness that proximity-
promoting attachment behaviors were selected and genetically
perpetuated as characteristic of the species? Bowlby's (1969)
hypothesis is that the biological function of attachment and
of attachment behaviors is protection, and perhaps particularly
protection from predators. Although protection from predators
does not seem to be crucial for present-day humans, especially
in the Western world, it is clear that protection from other
dangers is still a very significant outcome of the behaviors
that ensure proximity between a young child and his attachment
figure.

HOW ATTACHMENT BEHAVIOR EVOLVED

     Why does the human species solve the problem of protection
through infant attachment behavior (and reciprocal maternal
behaviors)? The answers to this question must, of necessity,
rest chiefly on inference. The human infant is relatively
helpless at birth, although not as helpless as some other
mammalian infants. However, the period during which human
offspring require protection by an adult is very long indeed.
The hypothesis is generally accepted by students of early men
that they were ground-living primates in a savannah environment

who relied on hunting and gathering for their sustenance.
There is evidence that groups of early men had a home base
from which hunting and foraging expeditions set out, but that
this home base might shift with the season and with changing
food supply. Both during his mother's food gathering
expeditions and when the whole group traveled to a new site,
it was necessary that a young child either be carried by his
mother, or, if he was old enough to walk long distances, that
he follow her reliably. Even in the case of an infant who was
carried on expeditions, it was important that when the mother
did set the child down, when she rested or engaged in other
activities, he could be trusted to maintain a reasonable degree
of proximity to her. Many mammalian young are well endowed
with interest in exploration and play. The human is no
exception, and has in addition a particularly long duration
of the period in which he has keen exploratory interests.
This interest in itself has a very important function in the
human species, in view of the exceptionally long period during
which behavior is relatively labile and when the child is open
to learning the characteristics of the environments to which
he or she is exposed and is acquiring the skills to cope with
them. It is obviously of survival value both that a child
investigate the environment actively and learn thereby, and
that exploratory fervor be tempered by a proximity-maintaining
mechanism that ensures safe exploration.

Although attachment behavior is adapted to the original
environment in which the behavior was evolved, and although
man's present-day environments differ markedly from that
original environment in many instances, it is a fundamental
principle of attachment theory that the genetically-based
species groundplan still disposes infants to behave in ways
appropriate to that original environment. Although in a
present-day Western home and infant may be fairly safe from
harm or danger even when left alone, he is still predisposed
to protest or follow when his mother departs, and he still
seeks to be close to the mother when alarmed. Indeed, it
seems reasonable to hypothesize that the human infant's
behavior is adapted to a mother who is continuously nearby
and who is responsive to his signals. In other words, the
infant's attachment behavior is adapted to reciprocal maternal
behaviors.

LIMITS TO LABILITY OF ATTACHMENT BEHAVIOR

The human species is conspicuous for the lability of its
behaviors and for its great learning potential. Therefore, it

should be no surprise that both infant attachment behaviors and reciprocal maternal behaviors are to some extent labile and modifiable, while still capable of being classed as *instinctive* and *species-characteristic*. They are not infinitely labile, however. Especially in regard to behavioral systems that are crucial for species survival-- and the infant attachment system is one of these--it is reasonable to suppose that there is substantially less lability (that is, less responsiveness to environmental variation) than is the case with other behavioral systems. Present-day Western mothers sometimes believe they can mold their babies to accept almost any caregiving arrangement that suits the mother's convenience, only to be astonished to find that their babies are less flexible than expected. Young children may well respond to an involuntary separation with an intensity appropriate to matters of life and death. Although in the present environment of rearing they might well be perfectly safe although separated, their intensity of response would have been appropriate in the environment of evolutionary adaptedness.

Without in any way minimizing the flexibility of human young, there are limits. If an infant is reared in an environment too disparate from that to which his attachment behaviors are adapted, this behavioral system develops in anomalous form. He may fail to become attached to anyone (e.g., Goldfarb, 1943; Provence & Lipton, 1962) or his attachment relationship may be distorted qualitatively. In our present-day Western environment, an infant without an attachment figure may survive--even though he or she thereby becomes ill-fitted to live a full and useful life in our society--but in man's original environment he probably would not have survived at all. The disposition to become attached is so deep-rooted in our species that it takes very gross departures from normative family rearing to incapacitate it-- either institutional care (which, in my opinion, is very unlikely to be able to meet infants' requirements during the first year especially, no matter how the institution strives to do so) or grossly negligent maternal care at home. So strong is the disposition to become attached, that babies become attached to very "bad" mother figures, as long as they are consistently enough present for an attachment to be formed at all. Furthermore, efforts to suppress attachment behaviors, as in training to eliminate "dependence" and foster the growth of independence, may well backfire, and activate attachment behavior at an even higher level of intensity.

ATTACHMENT VERSUS ATTACHMENT BEHAVIOR

In the course of this discussion, it should have become evident that *attachment* is to be distinguished from *attachment behavior*. Nevertheless, there has been so much confusion in the literature pertinent to this issue that I shall reiterate. Attachment behavior promotes proximity, at first indiscriminately and indifferent as to figure. Attachment is the relationship with a specific figure--the bond. In the normal course of development, attachment behavior, when activated, comes increasingly to be directed toward one or more specific figures and not to anyone who happens to be around-- persistently and over time. Nevertheless, in the very young infant, attachment behavior may be directed toward any available figure, and it will be especially likely to be so activated under conditions of alarm, or when the baby is alone. If the level of activation is sufficiently intense, even an attached child may direct attachment behavior toward an available figure who is not an attachment figure, and who may even be a stranger. Furthermore, if a child has more than one attachment figure, he or she may not protest the departure of one as long as another remains nearby (cf. Kotelchuck, 1972).

For at least the last five decades, psychologists have felt pressed to demonstrate their dedication to science by quantifying their observations. This addiction to quantification sometimes leads to inappropriate conceptualization. It is legitimate to ask whether or not a baby has as yet become attached to anyone. It is conceivable that there may be a relatively brief period after a baby has first become attached when his attachment is weak in the sense of being somewhat unstable and not fully consolidated. During this brief period, one might expect that the infant may at first protest loss of an attachment figure, but accept a new figure relatively quickly. There is no evidence for this, however. Indeed, both Schaffer's (1958) and Yarrow's (1967) work suggests that once a baby is attached he vigorously protests loss and does not act as though caregiver figures are interchangeable. There does not seem to be a gradient.

DEGREE OF INTENSITY OF ACTIVATION OF ATTACHMENT BEHAVIOR

Nevertheless, Schaffer and Emerson (1964) and many others conceive of a strength or intensity dimension to attachment. There is no doubt that attachment behaviors may be activated in varying degrees of intensity in different situations. The term intensity here refers to the intensity of the activation, and not to the strength of the underlying bond. High intensity of activation of attachment behavior may be shown by short latency; by intensity of signaling behavior (such as loud crying, in contrast to soft vocalization); speed of approach; completeness of approach (that is, whether a baby is content with proximity of, say, fifty feet or whether he must be within a few feet of his attachment figure); requiring contact rather than mere proximity to terminate attachment behavior' or, indeed, whether he needs to cling closely, rather than being content with mere touching. Which specific attachment behaviors are manifested may depend on the intensity of activation of the systems. Thus, for example, smiling may occur when the system is activated at low intensity, but not when the activation is intense. Clinging seems reserved for situations of high activation.

Frequency of occurrence of a behavior has often been taken as an indication of its strength. Frequency of activation of attachment behavior, however, depends in part on the situations an infant encounters. A child who is healthy, rested, recently fed, in a familiar environment, with no alarming stimuli present, with mother nearby, and with other interesting objects or people to attend to may emit attachment behavior relatively infrequently and of low intensity. Surely this does not imply that he is more weakly attached than another baby who happens to be hungry, or in an alarming situation, or with mother inaccessible, and who is more likely to emit attachment behavior and at higher intensity. Both frequency and intensity of activation (at least when observed within a relatively short time span) indicate less about the strength of the bond than about the situation in which attachment behavior is activated.

It may be assumed that attachment behavior will be manifested only intermittently and at relatively low intensity in a nonstressful situation. Therefore to obtain any notion of stable individual differences, one must sample behaviors over a substantial time span. In the course of our longitudinal project, each visit to the home lasted for approximately four hours and occurred once every three weeks. Within the four-hour time span of a visit we focused on the situations in which attachment behavior is most likely to be activated--when the mother puts the baby down, when she leaves the room, when she reenters the room, when she gets into a face-to-face confrontation, and the like. Furthermore, it was evident that frequency and nature of attachment behavior varied from one visit to another, sometimes clearly because of illness or some

other obvious condition or circumstance, sometimes not.   In
any event, more stable measures of attachment behavior could
be obtained from several visits than from any one visit,
despite the length of each one.

Within a span of ten or twenty minutes of free play in
the laboratory, there is no reason to suppose that there is
any special instigation to attachment behavior, provided the
mother is present.   Indeed, one might well anticipate that
exploratory behavior elicited by features of the novel
environment might well override attachment behavior.   Under
these circumstances, slight individual differences in the
frequency of various attachment behaviors do not seem likely
to refer to any psychologically meaningful dimension.   This
is why we prefer to use a mildly stressful laboratory
situation in our research.   Since one can assume that the
stresses introduced tend to activate attachment behavior in
all subjects, one has a better basis of comparing individuals
than in a nonstressful situation, in which one can never be
certain whether low-frequency activation indicates the
intensity with which competing behavioral systems are
activated, or whether it indicates weak attachment--or, more
accurately, weak instigation of attachment behaviors.

ATTACHMENT BEHAVIOR IN RELATION TO OTHER BEHAVIORAL SYSTEMS

It is a mistake to study attachment behavior in isolation
and out of context.   Such behavior is but one of a number of
behavioral systems.   In any situation, the extent to which
attachment behavior occurs depends not only on the strength
to which it is activated, but also on the strength of
activation of other competing (or compatible) behavioral
systems.   Attachment behavior is antithetical to exploration.
When exploratory behavior is strongly activated, the infant
tends to leave the vicinity of the attachment figure in order
to move out into the environment in an exploratory fashion.
When attachment behavior is activated, the infant tends to
regain proximity to the attachment figure.   When the mother
is absent attachment behavior tends to be activated, provided
the baby is attached to her, and this necessarily reduces
exploratory behavior.   Therefore, the mother's presence may be
necessary to support exploration, for her absence activates
attachment behavior so strongly as to override the exploratory
system.   This phenomenon I have termed "using the mother as a
secure base from which to explore" (Ainsworth, 1967).

Fearful or wary behavior, on the other hand, tends to

work in the same direction as attachment behavior. An alarming stimulus object not only activates fearful or wary behavior, hence maintaining distance from or moving away from the source of the alarm, but it also tends to activate attachment behavior, hence maintaining proximity to or moving toward the attachment figure. If the attachment figure is accessible and can be relied on to be responsive, then its presence within an optimum range of proximity may tend to reduce or deactivate fear behavior.

Like exploratory behavior, affiliative behavior activated by a conspecific who is not an attachment figure may override attachment behavior, and may result in the baby's moving away from the attachment figure toward the unfamiliar or less familiar one. The same specific behaviors may serve both the affiliative and the attachment systems—although these tend to be low-intensity behaviors, such as smiling, rather than high-intensity behaviors, such as rapid approach and tight clinging. It is as though the precursor attachment behaviors, indiscriminate as to figure at first, may continue to mediate interacton with conspecifics generally, even though they may over time be directed more frequently, and especially more intensely, toward attachment figures.

In some situations—for example, an unfamiliar situation in which attractive toys, and a stranger are present as well as an attachment figure (Bretherton and Ainsworth, 1974)—all four of the behavioral systems discussed above may be activated to a greater or lesser extent—exploratory, fearful and/or wary, attachment, and affiliation. The resultant behavior of the child is likely to reflect the interplay between behavioral systems, with conflict shown in intention movements, and compromises.

QUALITY OF ATTACHMENT VERSUS STRENGTH OF ATTACHMENT

I have repeatedly maintained (Ainsworth, 1967, 1972; Ainsworth & Bell, 1970) that it is impossible in our present state of knowledge to assess strength of attachment. This is in part because the intensity with which attachment behavior is activated is so highly dependent on situational factors and on competing behavioral systems. Yet even when infants are observed repeatedly over a span of time long enough to even out the situational factors that vary from day to day, it is by no means clear that the relatively stable individual differences that emerge are attributable to differences in the strength of the attachment bond. This is because infants differ in the particular attachment behaviors that are most conspicuous (that is, most frequent and/or most intense)[2] in their relations with an attachment figure. Some infants greet the mother enthusiastically after a brief absence and show active and positive behaviors when in physical contact with her; their signaling behaviors tend to be positive in tone, rather than consisting of crying; they tend not to protest when put down, and rarely cry when the mother leaves the room. Other infants are most conspicuous for crying signals in general, and especially when put down or when the mother leaves the room, but rarely show positive behavior when in physical contact with her.

Which pattern of attachment behaviors should be given the greater weight when attempting to assess the strength of the bond? I do not feel prepared to answer this question. On the other hand, I am confident that differences of the sort mentioned above reflect qualitative differences in the attachment relationship. During nearly two decades of research into infant-mother attachment in two societies, in which infant behavior was observed longitudinally in the natural environmnet and in the context of the behavior of the mother and other figures toward the infant, I have not been able to distinguish a satisfactory basis for assessing the strength of attachment once it has been formed, although I believe that I have learned much about assessment of qualitative differences in the attachment relationship.

An evaluative interest in the quality of the infant-mother relationship is certainly not specific to attachment theory. Psychoanalysts, psychiatrists, and clinical psychologists have for many years studied qualitative differences in intimate interpersonal relationships. The chief innovation in our present approach is that qualitative differences in the infant-mother relationship are observed directly in infancy rather than merely being inferred from later behavior and/or

---

[2] The reader may wonder why I use frequency and/or intensity of an attachment behavior as criteria for assessing whether it is differential between figures, while distrusting these as indicators of strength of attachment. Probably the most cogent reason is that when one assesses differentiality each baby acts as his own control. We are not interested in the absolute "strength" of the behavior but in the relative degree to which it is activated by one figure in contrast with another.

fantasy. These qualitative differences in attachment are identified in terms both of attachment behaviors and of behaviors compatible with them. We have been interested in the characteristic organization of attachment behaviors, in their interrelationship both with one another as they are directed toward the specific figure and with behaviors of other kinds. Most specifically, we have been interested in the conflicts between resistant or avoidant behaviors on the one hand and attachment behaviors on the other (Ainsworth, Bell, & Stayton, 1971). We have also been interested in the constellations of attachment behaviors that mediate attachment, and how these vary among individuals (Ainsworth, Bell, & Stayton, 1972; Stayton & Ainsworth, 1973). Finally, we have been interested in the extent to which attachment behaviors are activated or fail to be activated (or are overridden by other behaviors) in different situations, and, if attachment behaviors are activated, the intensity with which they are manifested.

Elsewhere in this volume I have reported our finding a security-insecurity dimension to be the most conspicuous qualitative dimension of infant-mother attachment in both the Ganda and the American samples. Important though this dimension may be, it surely is not the only significant one. Another dimension, for which we have less documentation, is the degree of anger that may be activated simultaneously with attachment behavior. Angry, aggressive, or resistant behavior is antithetical to attachment behavior, and yet obviously it may occur simultaneously with it or in rapid alternation. For example, some babies--both at home and in a strange situation-- may seek physical contact, but at the very point at which they are picked up may push away and want to be put down, only immediately to want up again, and this sequence of reponses is characteristically accompanied by crying, fussing, or tantrum behavior. Let us label this the dimension of *ambivalence*--and it deserves much more intensive empirical study. Another significant dimension appears to be activity-passivity. Some infants (one-year-olds or slightly younger), when the attachment system is activated, typically take the initiative and approach the attachment figure actively; others, presumably motivated just as strongly, are less active, tending to remain sitting and to indicate their desire for proximity through signaling behaviors such as crying or reaching. Very much more research is needed to adequately explore qualitative dimensions of the primary attachment relationship. At present such research seems likely to be more productive than research directed toward measuring strength of attachment.

THE DEGREE OF EXCLUSIVENESS OF ATTACHMENT

Another very significant aspect of infant-mother attachment that needs to be explored much more intensively is degree of exclusiveness of attachment. Both Ainsworth (1963, 1967) and Schaffer and Emerson (1964) have pointed out that a baby may become attached to other familiar figures before, at the same time as, or shortly after becoming attached to the mother figure, and that the baby may be attached to several figures. Bowlby (1958), on the other hand, enunciated a principle of monotropy, implying that it is the mother figure (not necessarily the natural mother, of course) who becomes the principal attachment figure, who is preferred when the chips are down, although there may also be one or more (but only several) secondary or supplementary attachment figures. Kotelchuck (1972) demonstrated that the father could funciton as an attachment figure in an unfamiliar laboratory situation with as much (or nearly as much) effectiveness as the mother. Fleener (1973) demonstrated that two to three hours per day of intensive interaction for three days could build up something resembling an attachment relationship with an initially unfamiliar figure--although there was evidence that the mother remained the preferred figure. Our own strange-situation studies indicate that a baby, when distressed by separation from his mother, may accept close physical contact from a stranger, and even cling tightly to the stranger (although the attachment behavior is likely to be ambivalent).

Much more research is needed to ascertain whether the mother figure is indeed the primary and principal attachment figure, how many other figures a baby may become attached to, the extent to which these other figures may be interchangeable with the principal figure, what functions they do and do not fulfill, and whether new potential attachment figures outside the familiar environment of the home can operate fully as attachment figures or only to a limited extent. Robertson and Robertson (1971) have shown that young children separated from their parents may form close relationships with sensitive foster parents, and that such a relationship can both much reduce separation distress and avert the more serious and pathogenic consequences of separation. Although the foster parent relationship tended to make reunion with the natural mother and father relatively free of the usual kinds of disturbance it was nevertheless clear that the breach of the new tie with the foster parents caused no apparent distress. There are two major points of interest in the research that I propose. To what extent does a secondary or substitute attachment figure function in the same way as the primary attachment figure and thus make up for the absence of that figure wholly or in part? To what extent does separation from a secondary or substitute attachment figure cause distress? In short, to what extent are attachment figures interchangeable? Cross-cultural research is a method par excellence to study these questions, since the caregiving arrangements of different societies differ, and societies other than our own may well provide a more crucial test of whether or not attachment figures are equivalent and interchangeable.

THE VALUE OF CROSS-CULTURAL RESEARCH ON ATTACHMENT

Since Freud (e.g., 19 38) we have believed it entirely likely that the quality of the infant-mother relationship strongly influences the nature of later important inter-personal relationships. We have every reason to believe that different infant-care practices and patterns of maternal behavior have a differential effect in shaping the nature of the infant-mother relationship. If different societies have different practices and different patterns of maternal behavior, cross-cultural comparisons will certainly supplement within-group comparisons in throwing light upon the development of qualitative differences. Cross-cultural studies, perhaps more clearly than intracultural studies, may clarify how infant-mother relationships of different kinds influence later important interpersonal relations--with father, with siblings, with spouse, and so on. On the other hand, studies of the ontogenesis of social behavior as it differs from one society to another should throw much light on the relative outcomes, in terms of the social structure characteristic of one society in contrast to another. The case is very strong for the utility of cross-cultural studies in developmental research, especially research into social development.

Nevertheless, one might well ask in what way the concept of attachment offers a heuristic contribution more important than, or to supplement, other conceptions of infant development. I believe there are two important ways in which it has a special contribution to make. First, it is a concept specific to social development, and as such suggests that there are processes implicit in social development that are unique to it and that cannot be satisfactorily inferred from a general knowledge of processes either of learning or cognitive development. Second, it is a concept implying genetic determinants of early social behavior that for all societies place certain limits beyond which a society cannot push its efforts to mold the child to conform to social demands--at least not without risking gross and maladaptive anomalies of development inimical to the survival of that society. Within these limits, genetically based determinants of infant behavior provide constraints that at least resist efforts to mold--perhaps making some of them entirely impossible.

REFERENCES

Ainsworth, M. D. S. The development of infant-mother inter-action among the Ganda. In B. M. Foss (Ed.), Determinants of infant behavior II. New York: Wiley, 1963.

Ainsworth, M. D. S. Infancy in Uganda: Infant care and the growth of love. Baltimore, Md.: Johns Hopkins University Press, 1967.

Ainsworth, M. D. S. Object relations, dependency, and attachment: A theoretical review of the infant-mother relationship. Child Development, 1969, 40, 969-1025.

Ainsworth, M. D. S. Attachment and dependency: A comparison. In J. L. Gewitz (Ed.), Attachment and dependency. Washington, D.C.: Winston, 1972.

Ainsworth, M. D. S., & Bell, S. M. Attachment, exploration, and separation: illustrated by the behavior of one-year-olds in a strange situation. Child development, 1970, 41, 49-67.

Ainsworth, M. D. S., Bell, S. M., & Stayton, D. J. Individual differences in strange-situation behavior of one-year-olds. In H. R. Schaffer (Ed.), The origins of human social relations. London: Academic Press, 1971.

Ainsworth, M. D. S., Bell, S. M., & Stayton, D. J. Individual differences in the development of some attachment behaviors. Merrill-Palmer Quarterly, 1972, 18, 123-143.

Bell, S. M., & Ainsworth, M. D. S. Infant crying and maternal responsiveness. Child Development, 1972, 43, 1171-1190.

Blehar, M. D., Lieberman, A., & Ainsworth, M. D. S.   Early
    face-to-face interaction and its relation to later
    infant-mother attachment. Child Development, 1977,
    48.

Bowlby, J.   Some pathological processes set in train by early
    mother-child separation. Journal of Mental Science,
    1953, 99, 265-272.

Bowlby, J.   The nature of the child's tie to his mother.
    International Journal of Psychoanalysis, 1958, 39,
    350-373.

Bowlby, J.   Attachment and loss. Vol. 1: Attachment. New
    York: Basic Books, 1969.

Bretherton, I., & Ainsworth, M. D. S.   Reponses of one-year-
    olds to a stranger in a strange situation.   In
    M. Lewis, and L. A. Rosenblum (Eds.), The origins
    of human behavior: Fear.   New York: Wiley, 1974.

Burlingham, D., & Freud, A. Young children in wartime.
    London: Allen & Unwin, 1942.

Fleener, D. E. Experimental production of infant-maternal
    attachment behaviors.   Paper read at the American
    Psychological Association meeting in Montreal,
    August, 1973.

Freud, S. An outline of psychoanalysis.   London: Hogarth,
    1938.

Goldfarb, W.   Effects of early institutional care on
    adolescent personality. Journal of Experimental
    Education, 1943, 12, 106-129.

Harlow, H. F.   The maternal affectional system.   In B. M. Foss
    (Ed.), Determinants of infant behavior II.   New
    York: Wiley, 1963.

Harlow, H. F., & Harlow, M. K.   Effects of various mother-
    infant relationships on rhesus monkey behaviors.
    In B. M. Foss (Ed.), Determinants of infant
    behavior IV. London: Methuen, 1969.

Kotelchuck, M. The nature of a child's tie to his father.
    Unpublished doctoral thesis, Harvard University,
    1972.

Kuhn, T. S. The structure of scientific revolutions. Chicago:
University of Chicago Press, 1962.

Provence, S. & Lipton, R. C. Infants in institutions. New
York: International University Press, 1962.

Robertson, J., & Robertson, J. Young children in brief
separation: A fresh look. Psychoanalytic Study of
the Child, 1971, 26, 264-315.

Schaffer, H. R. Objective observations of personality
development in early infancy. British Journal of
Medical Psychology, 1958, 31, 174-183.

Schaffer, H. R., & Emerson, P. E. The development of social
attachments in infancy. Monographs of the Society
for Research in Child Development, 1964, 29, (3,
Serial No. 94).

Stayton, D. J., & Ainsworth, M. D. S. Individual differences
in infant responses to brief, everyday separations
as related to other infant and maternal behaviors.
Developmental Psychology, 1973, 9, 226-235.

Tinbergen, N. The study of instinct. London: Oxford
University Press, 1951.

Tracy, R. L., Lamb, M. E., & Ainsworth, M. D. S. Infant
approach behavior as related to attachment. Child
Development, 1976, 47, 571-578.

Yarrow, L. J. The development of focused relationships during
infancy. In J. Hellmuth (Ed.), Exceptional infant:
The normal infant, (Vol. 1). Seattle: Special Child
Publications, 1967.

Chapter 5

Evolution of Human Behavior Development

Melvin Konner
Harvard University

> It should, by now, be... obvious
> that there is, indeed, a general
> theory of behavior and that that
> theory is... evolution, to just
> the same extent and in almost
> exactly the same ways in which
> evolution is the general theory
> of morphology. [Roe & Simpson,
> 1958, p. 2]

This theoretical chapter considers what developmentalists may stand to gain by giving attention--that elusive and precious commodity--to the science of evolution; that is to say, substantial attention; something beyond the lip service offered casually in the first few pages of the textbooks. Thanks to various excesses of biological determinism, developmentalists--

---

*
I thank Irven DeVore, Robert Trivers, N. G. Blurton Jones, Marjorie Shostak and Steven Stepak for various forms of assistance. This work was supported by the Foundations Fund for Research in Psychiatry and the Harry Frank Guggenheim Foundation.

who, historically, have concerned themselves with the making
of policy to maximize human potential--have more or less sworn
off biology. Or, to put it more exactly, they have, in general,
signified their intention to operate with the variance remaining
within the limits provided by biology.

Thus many developmentalists find motor development boring,
except insofar as it is deemed responsive to experience. The
question of population differences in behavior is so deeply
politicized that one can scarcely approach it without some
armor of ideology, and the question of sex differences is gaining the same distinction. As for comparative developmental
research--well, a child is neither a rat, a dog, a duckling,
or a monkey. So goes the objection we hear quite regularly.

Having some familiarity with all five of those sorts of
animals, one can scarcely dissent from this opinion. A child
is indeed none of those things, nor, for that matter, is a
duckling a dog, or a rat a monkey. Yet, one insists, there is
much knowledge to be gained about each of those creatures by
looking at all of them.

Backing off from biology was wise step when it happened.
In the early part of this century Haeckel's "biogenetic law"--
to the effect that the course of development recapitulates the
phyletic history of the organism--was overapplied so literally
and indiscriminately that it rapidly outlived its usefulness
(which was, incidentally, as a pillar of the edifice of
evidence for evolution, rather than as a theory of development).
At length it resulted in one of the most famous pieces of
silliness in the history of psychology, its sad monument in a
field that had grown away from it (Freud, [1913] 1938).

At the same time the excesses of "Social Darwinism"--which,
as we now understand, was not Darwinian--caused evolution to
become identified with political and social reaction. In the
United States, Yerkes, Terman, and other psychometricians,
allied with eugenicists in biology and racists in politics,
succeeded in turning down to a trickle, by the early 1930s, a
current of immigration that could have saved the Jews of Europe
(Kamin, 1974). On the other side of the ocean, Lorenz and other
continental ethologists, to their everlasting detriment and shame,
allied themselves, in the name of biology, with the most pern-
icious ideology in human history (Eisenberg, 1972).

So decent people entering anthropology or psychology to
consider various issues in human behavior development were
understandably chary of evolution. The work of Gesell and

Amatruda (1965) and McGraw (1963) on motor development came ultimately to be largely ignored, sex differences to be explained by sex role learning (Kagan, 1964b), and the laws of operant conditioning to be stretched in attempts to account for such phenomena as language acquisition (Skinner, 1957) and the infant's tie to its caretaker (Gewirtz, 1972).

But, with the front door firmly barred, biology was again found in the house, having not only snuck in through the basement and seeped in around the windows, but having also walked calmly in through various other unlocked doors. Piaget's biologizing slipped by, perhaps because he slyly refused to take a stand on the nature-nurture controversy. Still, it became apparent that he was dealing with phenomena whose variance was mostly accounted for by maturation (Flavell, 1963), a fact not surprising when it is considered that he began life as a zoologist. The quantum advance of the 1960s in developmental psycholinguistics laid permanently to rest the notion that first-language acquisition could ever be accounted for by conventional learning theory (Lenneberg, 1964; R. Brown, 1973). Perceptual and cognitive development in infancy (Bower, 1974; Kagan, 1970) acquired an increasingly maturational cast. And, finally, work on the development of fear (Hebb, 1946; Bronson, 1972) and of primary attachment (Bowlby, 1969; Ainsworth, 1967) became "biologized" and set in the context of evolution.

Also, there were some unwanted presences. Scientists and nonscientists alike were addressing the public with poorly formulated notions about the biological basis of aggressiveness (Morris, 1968); territorality (Ardrey, 1966); and intelligence (Herrnstein, 1973), before those notions were subject to adequate scientific scrutiny. None of them has survived even a few years of such scrutiny. But their hold on the public, of course, outlives their real credibility, and that hold itself is a subject worthy of study.

The resistance found among behavioral scientists to behavioral biology is thus understandable and, in certain respects, valuable. But, at last, it is unwise, because if responsible scientists fail to consider the biology of behavior, irresponsible ones will do so, and we will all spend a great deal of time explaining what is wrong with them. The study of behavior, which is a feature of living organisms, is simply a branch of biology, and behavior development research above all should be cognizant of this; because, with the exception of behaviorism, and associationism in perception, every major advance in behavior development research has been biological (Freud, 1920; Piaget, 1971; Gesell & Amatruda, 1965; Carmichael, 1970; Bower, 1974; Bowlby, 1969; R. Brown, 1973).

The major current trends concerning the biological basis of behavior development were all in evidence at the Wenner-Gren Conference (held in June 1973, in Austria). They were represented as follows.

1. Brazelton emphasized the interactive nature of the mother-infant relation, but especially stressed the infant's contribution. Many investigators of infant behavior now recognize as far from trivial the individual differences exhibited at birth, and the ways in which these *shape* parental behavior (Lewis & Rosenblum, 1973).

2. Wolff presented evidence that certain behavioral differences of different populations may arise from genetics rather than culture (cf. Freedman, 1974). He pointed out that resistance to this possibility is a kind of denial of individuality.

3. Kagan reviewed the evidence for the hypothesis that certain features of human behavior and ability are such fundamental features of nervous system function that they will unfold in almost any environment, in a fashion highly resilient with respect to deviation. He pointed out that one would expect natural selection to favor such resilience, cushioning crucial abilities against environmental insult. He repeatedly used the metaphor of metamorphosis, the transformation of caterpillars into butterflies, to emphasize the maturational nature of the emergence of these abilities.

4. Konner emphasized the importance of a phylogenetic, as well as cross-cultural perspective on human development, and presented a description of infancy in the human environment of evolutionary adaptedness. He pointed out that a consideration of the adaptive value of infant behaviors might lead to a consideration of infant abilities otherwise obscured by Western cultural practices, and that a consideration of changes in infant environment since the end of the Pleistocene ere would have heuristic value for intervention studies.

5. DeVore introduced the other members of the conference to certain new features of natural selection theory,

pertaining to behavior between parents and offspring, as well as among siblings, which promise to revolutionize our view of the nature of these behaviors.

Now, these five quite different contributions have in common that each emphasizes a previously neglected *biological* aspect of human behavior development, and each argues to swing the pendulum of behavioral science back in the direction of biology. Here we will consider the specifically *evolutionary* aspects of the potential change. We will touch on all these five biological viewpoints, and others as well, but will concern ourselves centrally with the last two: the theory of natural selection and the facts of phylogenesis. These two currents in the science of evolution have both flourished robustly and grown beyond recognition since half a century ago, the last time they touched significantly the sciences of development.

NATURAL SELECTION

Natural selection has two components that, for purposes of analysis, are usefully separated. The one that comes most quickly to mind is differential viability. Some individuals are more likely than others to die, and are said to be less well *adapted*. It should be noticed, as it often is not, that selection through differential viability operates at each stage of the life cycle from before conception to the end of the breeding period, and not just at maturity. Consequently, an immature individual is constantly balancing two forms of viability--the necessity to survive currently, and the necessity to develop toward viability at maturity. There may be tension between these forms of viability, as in the obvious case in which becoming "tied to a parent's apron strings" may improve current, but reduce ultimate, viability. Much more subtle interactions are possible, and when it is considered that each life-cycle stage may affect all subsequent ones, the balance of selective effects may be very complex.

It will be useful also to introduce the concept of a *selection funnel*. This will be taken to mean a stage of the life cycle in which mortality is very high and in which selection consequently may operate more intensively. A sufficiently intense selection will produce optimal viability at this stage, even though the adaptation necessary may, in the life of the individual, result in suboptimal viability at later stages. Selection funnels may be as common as the reverse case, in which an adaptively neutral feature of the juvenile, such as, perhaps, play, results in improved viability in the adult.

However, differential viability, in spite of its complexity, is only half of the picture of natural selection. In fact, if a population were to have strictly uniform viability--if all the individuals died at the same age--evolution would still proceed apace, by means of sexual selection. Though viability were uniform, reproductive success--the number of offspring left to the subsequent generation--would vary, because sexual attractiveness and sexual effectiveness would vary. If we add to our model population the possibility of death during infancy, we have another source of variability--differential caretaking effectiveness. Thus, in addition to balancing current against future viability the immature individual must balance both against future sexual attractiveness, sexual effectiveness, caretaking effectiveness and other influences on reproductive process. Again, these effects may sometimes oppose each other. An individual may die young but have left so many offspring that selection favors his genotype in spite of his early death. To win at selection roulette means only to maximize surviving, reproducing offspring, a complex sum of all these selective effects.

Some aspects of natural selection theory that have specific implications for infant and parent behavior are now considered along with past applications of each concept, difficulties with it, and testable predictions arising from it. It is hoped in this way to make the heuristic and explanatory value of these concepts apparent.

Selection Funnels

At some stages of the life cycle, mortality is exceptionally high or arises from causes later to disappear or diminish in importance, and selection acting at this stage thus affects all subsequent phases of the organism. In this way the ABO and Rh blood-type distributions of the adult population are determined not primarily by the (very slight) selection pressures operating on them in adulthood, but by maternal-fetal incompatibility during fetal life.

Bowlby's view of attachment rests, in effect, on this concept (1969). Heightened effects of selection by predation at the time of infancy, he argues, have produced in many infant birds and mammals a set of innate proximity-maintaining mechanisms that, by reducing the distance between infant and parent, reduce the rate of predation. Several problems arise from this argument.

First, Bowlby assumes that, because this pattern has been selected for in infancy, interference with it will have deleterious consequences for current or later (adult) phases of the organism. In fact, if a selection funnel is narrow enough, it may produce adaptations in the early phase that result ontogenetically, in later-phase adaptations that are selectively neutral or even deleterious. In other words, it is possible that early attachment to a mother or single permanent mother substitute, so crucial for reduction of the predation rate in infancy, has deleterious consequences for the mental health of the adult, and that the appropriate response to the present reduced predation rate is to *reduce* the strength or exclusiveness of that attachment. It is also possible that, as Bowlby argues, eons of selection have produced later-phase adaptations that result from strong infant attachment but that are advantageous for the organism; or that, as Kagan would argue, early attachment patterns have few or no later-phase consequences. The respective validity of these competing hypotheses can only be assessed by means of longitudinal intervention studies, and not by evolutionary analysis. But the latter points to the problems of importance.

Second, Bowlby's stress on the infant's current survival also leads to neglect of possible adaptive *advantages* for later phases of the organism. Observations of infants in the human environment of evolutionary adaptedness (Konner, 1972; Chapter 12 of this volume) reveals that no infant deaths occur through loss or predation, and that the 20 percent mortality in the first year (Howell, 1975) results from infectious disease. This may be, of course, because the adaptation provided by attachment is essentially perfect. However, observation suggests that proximity to caretakers results in transmission of behaviors essential for subsistence activity and for social and sexual activity. Experiments on rhesus monkeys have shown that interference with the earliest attachments can place the individual at a severe reproductive disadvantage by impairing later sexual and parental behavior (Harlow, 1963). This would constitute as strong a selection force favoring attachment as any pressure arising from current viability. An elaboration of this concept follows.

Teleological Selection

Teleological selection will be taken to refer to early-phase characters of the organism that, although selectively

neutral or deleterious for that phase, are favored for over-
whelming later-phase advantages. The evolution of altriciality,
or prolonged immaturity, is usually accounted for by some vari-
ant of this process. Increasing altriciality, so the argument
goes, in the evolution of man, with its attendant disadvantages--
greater cost to the parent, slower repoductive rate due to
longer generations and reduced litter size--is nevertheless
favored because of overwhelming advantages accruing to the adult,
including larger body and brain size and a larger set of acquired associations and responses.[1]

But, beyond this cliché, which I will scrutinize critically
later, of what use is the concept? In recent years, it has
been applied by investigators studying the details of the
development of skill in infancy (Bruner & Bruner, 1968). Sucking patterns of the newborn, it is argued, in addition to their
obvious effect on current viability, serve as the ontogenetic
foundation of later-phase information processing and mother-
infant interaction schemes that are uniquely human. Thus
evolution, ever conservative, gives a new ontogenetic function
to a phylogenetically old system. Furthermore, it is argued,
the system becomes modified in ways that have nothing to do
with current viability but only to do with effects on later-
phase adaptations. Claims have been made for a uniquely human

---

[1]This has apparently happened in the evolution of the ontogeny
of the human skull. In order to pass a large brain through
the narrow pelvic corridor of an erect biped, it became
necessary to have disarticulated skull plates beyond the time
of birth. Now, no one would suggest that to expose the
infant's brain for a year or more to the jeopardy of sharp
objects and poking fingers is adaptive. Yet is is the inevitable consequence of an ontogenetically prior adaptation that
is so strongly selected for that its advantage outweighs the
later disadvantage. This instance is further complicated by
the fact that the disarticulated sutures have arisen to protect
the large brain that is to become a real advantage only much
later in the life cycle; which, in other words, has been
favored by *teleological selection* (see later discussion).
Finally, the necessity for the adaptation evidently arose in
the first place because of selection for erect posture in the
adult female, a process seemingly far removed from any infant
adaptation. This simple case illustrates what caution is
called for in attempts to analyze the adaptive value of infant
characters.

burst-pause pattern in newborn sucking, unrelated to feeding or breathing, having as its sole purpose the eliciting of the mother's attention so that a rhythmic mother-infant interaction pattern, essential for later-phase viability, will begin to form (Kaye & Brazelton, 1971).

While we can cavil at the extent to which these workers have stressed, again, the old idea of human uniqueness, and while we note that there is no evidence that sucking patterns have any influence on later information processing or mother-infant relations, still, the invocation of evolutionary process is leading to experiments that might not otherwise have been made. We can hope and expect that more attention will be given to the sucking pattern in nonhuman primates, and to the question of late effects of the early pattern.

Selection for Plasticity and Resilience in Development

It has been argued (Kagan, Chapter 11 of this volume), that selection can be expected to have produced a developing nervous system that will be relatively impervious to insult, and whose major behavioral functions will be maintained and emerge normally in spite of wide environmental fluctuations. This corresponds to the notion of canalization in evolutionary biology and embryology (Waddington, 1942), according to which selection is held to have endowed organisms with a small number of developmental tracks, progress along which is regulated by negative feedback. Thus departures from the track (for example, effects of early insults), will be tolerated temporarily, but will result in final correction, so that the end-point reached by the organism will not have been altered. This means, not that normal development is independent of environment, but rather that so wide a range of stimuli can provoke or restore progress along developmental tracks, that the normal outcome is very nearly certain. Broadly speaking, this is a sound view, but it faces three problems.

First, this would seem to be equally true for all organisms, the fact is that organisms vary greatly in the environment dependency of their developing nervous systems. Thus other factors than the necessity to protect vital functions must be operating.

Second, it is difficult to see how natural selection would produce a nervous system with functions developing independent of features of the environment that are continuously present. With respect to such features, selection would lose its cutting edge. Thus, the visual system of kittens does not develop normally without an input of patterned light (Wiesel & Hubel, 1965; Hirsch & Spinnelli, 1970). Why, one may ask, did natural selection not give them a really good visual system, one that would grow reliably with or without patterned light? The reason is probably that, since kittens have never been called on to grow the system in darkness, there was no disadvantage for those that were unable to do so. How generally this principle may be applied remains to be seen, however.

Third, the developing nervous systems of many organisms, including those with the least plastic behavioral functions, may exhibit highly specific forms of environment dependency. For example, salmon become imprinted on the odor of the stream they are raised in, and this accounts for their ability to return after long migrations (Hasler, 1960, 1974). As Richards pointed out at the conference, moths will feed preferentially on the species of leaf they lived on as caterpillars (Thorpe, 1939), a simple effect that survives metamorphosis. A similar process appears to be operating to determine habitat selection in damselflies (Johnson, 1966). The infantile attachment objects of members of many bird species will determine their sexual choice as adults (Hess, 1974). This effect is subsequently modifiable, but at greater cost, and is in any case readily reinstated.[2] Finally, learning paradigms in which rats are trained early in life and the habits allowed to become extinct show that later in life such habits are much more easily reingrained ("reinstated") than established anew in controls, in spite of the fact that experimental and control animals do not differ at all in base-level responding on the task (Campbell & Jaynes, 1966). This interesting phenomenon may have wide applicability and should alert those investigators of early-experience effects who study only base-level adult responding to the hazards of accepting the null hypothesis.

Even for those species whose behavioral repertoire is limited and relatively fixed (and certainly for species that do not fit this description), we must recognize the existence of *facultative* as opposed to *obligatory* adaptations. The former result from selection for a series of adaptations in an organism that inhabits several different niches. Facultative adaptations require a switching mechanism that will enable the animal to "select" (not necessarily consciously or voluntarily) among the several possibilities of the genome, and the switch

---

[2]Much qualification over the years of the original concept of imprinting has made it less mysterious than it seemed at first, but has not really changed its essential outlines.

must be responsive to information in the environment. Early
experience may be a part of the switch in certain animals.
That is, the environment may signal the developing infant
nervous system that certain facultative adaptations will be
required in adulthood, and "tell" it to produce those rather
than others. The well-known (although poorly understood)
mechanism by which rats stressed in infancy became larger and
less fearful as adults (e.g., LeVine & Mullins, 1966; Denenberg,
1964) could conceivably have resulted from such selection.
(One would have to suppose either that being smaller and more
fearful is an advantage in some environments, or that it is
tied to some other parameter that is important. Either of
these suppositions is reasonable.)

Genetic Assimilation

By the mechanism of genetic asssimilation, characteristics,
whether morphological or behavioral, that are at first acquired
during individual life history, come eventually to be genetically determined (Waddington, 1953). While at first blush this
seems to have a Lamarckian cast, it is really not mysterious.
Members of a population who can acquire the character lead the
population into niches where the character is an advantage.
The same individuals are likely to be among the first who exhibit some genetic adaptation for the character, and these
will be selected for in the ordinary way. (Of course, this
must be a situation in which lability for the character is not
at a premium.) A related mechanism, usually called the *Baldwin
effect* (Mayr, 1958), specifies that the initial acquired
character be behavioral, but that the genetic adaptations that
follow may be of a wide variety not limited to genetic changes
underlying the behavior. For example, a bird population
acquires a taste for a new berry, by experiment; adaptations
may follow, affecting the genetic basis of beak shape, color
perception, and digestive enzyme systems. When we consider
that entering a new niche is typically the first step in
specific formation (Mayr, 1963), and that for animals, at least,
a new niche is entered by means of behavior, we may conclude
that something like the Baldwin effect must be very important
in animal evolution. The human or protohuman invention of
the infant-carrying sling may thus have paved the way for the
increase in human altriciality at birth (with its many important consequences, some of which are considered below). The
recently demonstrated fact that chimpanzees can acquire some
rudiments of language (e.g., Rumbaugh, van Glaserfeld, Warner,
Pisani, & Gill, 1974) suggests that genetic assimilation may
have been involved in the evolution of the human capacity for
language. Finally, since juveniles are typically the most
experimental members of a species, exhibiting many apparently

useless behaviors usually called *play*, we may expect that it
is often they who take the lead into a new niche. The first
step in the evolution of language may, indeed, have been taken
by a population of infants and mothers babbling at each other.

Selection for Litter Size and Birth Spacing

   It has been known for many years that animals exhibiting
parental care cannot usually maximize their reproductive
success by maximizing litter or clutch size (number of eggs), or
by minimizing birth spacing (Lack, 1954), because there is a
quickly reached point of diminishing returns, at which investment by parents is thinned so as to jeopardize all the
offspring. Optimal litter or clutch size varies with environmental quality, but in any environment there is a point at
which the total number of surviving offspring will be decreased
by a further increase in clutch size. This phenomenon operates
in humans in relation to birth spacing as well as litter size.
Before the advent of modern medicine, the number of children
surviving from 100 twin pairs was smaller than the number
surviving from 100 singletons, giving humans an optimal litter
size of one (Trivers, 1974). Particularly in developing
countries, but also in the United States (Morley, 1973, p. 304),
neonatal, infant, and early childhood mortality increases with
decreasing birth interval.

   In human hunter-gatherers, as well as in great apes,
natural birth spacing is about four years. Many questions may
be raised regarding the implications of shorter spacing, among
which are direct effects on the young child of reduced length
of intensive care, variations in the intensity of sibling
rivalry, and strain on the mother, with its probable attendant
ill effects on the children. One wonders, also, if the strong
birth-order effects usually found in the study of achievement
motivation are related in any way to length of birth spacing.

Inclusive Fitness Theory and Parental Investment Strategy

   Important recent advances in natural selection theory
have transformed our understanding of parental altruistic
behavior, among other forms of social behavior, and more
generally of parent-offspring relations. These advances have
decisively liberated the study of social behavior from such
concepts as "group selection" and "survival of the species".
(Both these concepts are now widely considered untenable.)
The advances are summarized as follows.[3]

_____

[3]The interested reader is strongly urged to consult the

Inclusive fitness. Invoked initially to explain the remarkable altruism of the social insects, this concept extends the notion of individual fitness to include the individual's blood relatives. A gene for altruism will spread through a population, in spite of the cost to the individual altruist, provided the altruist preferentially helps those most likely to share the gene. These will be his relatives, and the likelihood of a shared gene (and thus of a given degree of altruism) will vary closely with the degree of relatedness (Hamilton, 1964).

Parental investment and sexual selection. In species in which one sex invests more than the other in offspring, this sex will become a limiting resource, and members of the other sex (males, in most birds and mammals) will compete among themselves for access to the first (females). The result will be greater male than female variability in reproductive success (RS; number of reproducing offspring), a variety of special adaptations for fighting in males, and for nurturance in females. Female choice will be seen to guide the course of male evolution by selecting only certain males for fertilization of ova. Sexual dimorphism of varying degrees will result. Species, or populations within species, will be seen to vary systematically along certain parameters. Those high in sexual dimorphism will exhibit high male variability in RS, high promiscuity (or polygamy) in the successful males, low male parental investment, and high male-male competition. Those at the other end of the continuum will exhibit pair bonding with relatively low male promiscuity, low male variability in RS, low male-male competition and high male parental investment (Trivers, 1972). Humans are generally considered to be near but not at this end of the continuum; many species of birds seem to be more strongly pairbonded. But it should be remembered that these adaptations may be facultative. That is, the same species may exhibit different reproductive strategies in different environments.

Parent-offspring conflict. Parent and offspring may be expected to disagree over the degree of parental investment, since the offspring is related to itself more closely than to future siblings, whereas the parent is equally related to all of them. At a certain point in the offspring's growth, the parent will "decide" that the offspring is viable, and will

---

original papers. They have begun to cause a paradigm shift in zoology and ethology and promise to have a similar impact in anthropology and psychology. It appears likely that they will be looked on in the future as a quantum advance in the sciences of behavior.

want to construe its energy in the production of subsequent offspring, while the offspring will be demanding more investment. At a later point, the offspring's "desire" to have siblings, which arises from the same selection pressure that makes parents want offspring, will be sufficient to overcome its own selfishness. The period intervening will be the period of weaning conflict, during which the offspring will be expected to exhibit "tantrums"--signals that deceive the parent into perceiving distress where there is no distress, so as to cajole more investment out of it. Such tantrums are found in a wide variety of species (Trivers, 1974).

Sex ratio theory. Because males are more variable than females in their reproductive success, parents in good environments will be expected to vary the sex ratio of their offspring in favor of males, so as to maximize the number of offspring in the third (F_2) generation. Parents in poor environments will be expected to "want" more females, since inferior males are likely to leave no offspring (Fisher, 1958; Trivers & Willard, 1973).

Theory of competition. The relevant portion of this body of theory holds that competition will be selected to be different among relatives than among nonrelatives. The closer the relationship, the less likely the competitor will be to inflict real harm and the more likely he will be to protest strongly over a small degree of harm inflicted on himself. In other words, the relatedness will make him behave like a parent in the former case and an offspring in the latter (Popp & DeVore, in press).

Relations among juveniles. Except where preparation for adult competition is at a premium, and where population structure makes this possible, juveniles will be expected to aggregate in mixed-age rather than same-age play groups. An individual will be at an advantage choosing an older playmate because of possible investment by that playmate, including transfer of nongenetic information, particularly if the two are related. An individual will be at an advantage choosing a younger playmate because of possible practice of parental behavior. However, where competition among adults is of very great importance, individual juveniles will be expected to try to accustom themselves to it by associating with others as nearly as possible equal in ability (Konner, 19675).

Among investigatable questions raised by this body of theory, the following may be of interest to child psychologists:

1. How do adoptive parents differ from biological parents in parental investment? What causes adoption under various circumstances?

2. What explains variation in human male parental investment?

3. At what age and in what circumstances can children be expected to desire younger siblings, if they have none?

4. Does parental differentation in caretaking of boys and girls vary systematically with environmental quality, as sex ratio theory predicts?

5. Do identical and fraternal twin pairs differ in their competitive behavior?

6. How does varying the age discrepancy between two children affect their interaction?

Many other testable hypotheses readily come to mind. It should be noted that invoking natural selection in these instances does not rule out more conventional explanations. Natural selection is the final cause theory in biology. Its dictates must be met, but they may be met with a wide variety of proximate mechanisms, by means of a wide variety of efficient causes. Unraveling those efficient causes is the business of most of biology, including behavioral science. Yet selection theory may point the way to some of the more interesting ones.

PHYLOGENY OF PARENTAL BEHAVIOR AND OF BEHAVIOR DEVELOPMENT

Apart from the question of how selection may be expected to influence various behaviors during evolution, from considerations arising from Darwinian assumptions, there is the question of what has actually happened in evolution. How are various features of behavior and development distributed taxonomically, and what can we infer from that distribution (and from the fossil evidence) about the history of those behaviors? What are the broad trends and modes of change affecting behavior and development, not at the population level, where specific selective forces are seen to be operating currently, but at the phyletic level, where processes requiring thousands of generations may be in evidence?

Four Misconceptions About Phylogeny and Development

Misconception 1:   "Ontogeny recapitulates phylogeny".
Wrong; but, properly stated, there is a piece of the truth
here.   It is that evolution is opportunistic; it builds on
what it has.   Therefore embryologic and other developmental
events are conserved, while evolution builds on later phases
of the organism.   In other words, ontogeny recapitualtes, not
the adult phases of ancestral forms, but, to some extent, the
early ontogeny of those forms.   Put yet another way, the early
phases of related forms can be expected to resemble one another
more than the adult phases of these forms.   But we must never
look, in human infancy and childhood, for characteristics
resembling those of adults of other animals.   (Carried to a
bizarre extreme, this has at times resulted in the contention
that mental functioning in Western children resembles that of
adults of other human populations.   Evidence for this contention
is, to put it mildly, hard to come by.   But in addition it makes
a travesty of everything we know about the biology and evolution
of human populations.)

Misconception 2:   "The higher the animal, the slower its
development, the less developed it is at birth, and the more
plastic is its behavioral repertoire".   No.   First, there is
no acceptable way of arraying animals in a hierarchy.   Attempts
to do this have been heavily criticized (e.g., Lockard, 1971).
What is interesting about animals is how they differ, not how
they rank.   Second, plasticity is very variable even in closely
related animals, and is by no means always linked to slow
development.   Of two subspecies of deermice (*Peromyscus
maniculatus*), the one that develops faster is more affected by
early experience (Rosen & Hart, 1963).   A review of sensory-
motor development in two prosimian, one Old World monkey and
two New World, monkey species (Ehrlich, 1974) reveals no trends
at all in the rate of emergence of the behavior, and no relation
to the wide differences in learning ability among these animals
in adulthood.   Variation within a species in time of emergence
of the behaviors proves in some instances greater than variation
among widely disparate phyla.

Very broadly speaking, of course, it may be said that
behavioral plasticity increases as we come closer to man
(Lorenz, 1965).   But more specific expectations than this one
should not be held.   Plasticity should not be expected to vary
with rate of development and it should be understood that
plasticity may vary with stage of the life cycle in unexpected
ways, related organisms being more or less plastic at earlier
or later stages of their development.

Above all, no simple notions should be held about state of development at birth. This is not determined by broad phyletic trends, but by necessities specific to individual species, such as the level of predation, the possibility of nest building, the time available for gestation, and the overall length of the life span. State of development at birth need not be correlated with overall rate of development or ultimate behavioral plasticity in any way. Finally, it should not be expected that the rate of development or the state of development at birth in different behavioral and organ systems will be interrelated. Newborn kangaroos and opossums, otherwise the most altricial of all mammals, have highly developed forelimbs and a poorly understood orienting system that carry them from the uterus, across a great expanse of belly, into the pouch, and to the teat, with no assistance from their mothers. Among ungulates, fairly closely related species differ in whether the newborn is able to follow the mother immediately; it is in species (such as wildebeest) that are highly migratory; in a number of others it is cached in a shifting hiding place, and the mother returns periodically until it is able to follow well. Here again, the state of development at birth is determined by the specific demands of the niche, and is unrelated to behavioral plasticity. Hares and rabbits, close relatives, differ as dramatically in their state of development at birth as, virtually, any other pair of mammals (Bourliere, 1955). Humans and other higher primates are precocial in most sensory systems and altricial in most motor systems (except for, in monkeys, clinging). (An extensive discussion of these and other aspects of altriciality and pre-cociality may be found in Ewer, 1968, Ch. 10). Thus it seems that state of development at birth, which, as we will see, determines many other aspects of infant and parent behavior, is in turn the result of specific adaptation, usually by means of the process we have called the *selection funnel* at birth, and follows no grand phylogenetic logic, nor bears any relation to ultimate adult plasticity of the organism.

Here again, the misconception has been carried to bizarre extremes: African motor precocity has been viewed as consistent with an alleged African intellectual inferiority in adulthood, because of some half-baked and silly notions about phylogeny. Of course, there is no good evidence for African intellectual inferiority, and no evidence whatever for any correlation, positive or negative, between infant motor development and later intellectual capacity. But we may point out as well that there is no basis in evolutionary theory for expecting such a relationship.

Misconception 3: "If a behavior is phyletically widespread, it must be a 'fixed action pattern' or 'instinct', and thus genetically based. In this event there is no sense trying to change it". Each step of this syllogism is wrong: First, analogy is not homology. Widely disparate animals may face similar puzzles posed to them by natural selection, and their solutions may look similar, and serve similar functions, without having similar mechanisms. The wings of flies come from thorax; of birds, from forelimbs; of bats, from fingers; and of man from Eastern Air Lines. Bowlby (1969) correctly points out that human infant attachment formation and precocial bird imprinting serve similar adaptive functions. But we need know scarecely more than that, one is completed in several days and the other requires several months, to know that their underlying mechanisms must differ in important ways. The point is that both mechanisms must be investigated separately. All the comparison can do is point to possible features of attachment formation in humans that have received inadequate study.[4]

Secondly, fixed action patterns, which used to be called instincts (Lorenz, 1965) are arrived at by as wide a variety of routes as they are species to exhibit them. For us to accept that a fixed action pattern or a response to a given stimulus (releasing mechanism) is not learned, we must have the evidence of the deprivation experiment, by means of which the relevant information or experience is withheld from the animal during its growth. In this fashion, numerous features of the behavior of virtually any organism studied can be shown to be innate; or at least that, as Lorenz points out (1965, p. 27), to say that they are is "less inexact than the statement that a steam locomotive or the Eifel Tower are built entirely of metal". In human infants, smiling, crying from discomfort, bipedal walking, and language competence are examples of behavioral or cognitive characteristics not dependent on learning for their emergence. However, and here we depart from the classical ethologists, many fixed and perfectly stereotypic action patterns and, more especially, releasing mechanisms, in a wide variety of species, may emerge by routes that depend in important ways on experience. Already mentioned among these are food choice in moths, habitat choice in damselflies, homing in salmon, sexual choice in some pair-bonding birds, and sexual performance in rhesus monkeys. The same evidently, applies to mouse killing by rats (Denenberg, Pache, & Zarrow,

---

[4]Incidentally, the converse notion, that if only humans do it, it must be learned, is also false. Smiling and language competence, both fixed action patterns and strictly speaking, limited to man, are clearly not learned in any usual sense of the word.

(1968) and maternal behavior in rhesus monkeys (Arling & Harlow, 1967). It has even been argued (Lehrman, 1953) that the pecking behavior of chicks immediately after hatching is acquired during gestation, through the training of head movements by the beat of the fetal heart. While this particular instance may be criticized (Lorenz, 1965), the concept is important because it makes a further distinction: behaviors (and releasers) that are innate need not be genetically determined. (Various routes to species-specific fixed action patterns are discussed by Moltz, 1965.) Again, the specific determination of each pattern must be investigated individually.

Now we turn to the belief held by some psychologists that if a behavior, ability, or behavior disorder is genetically determined, it is a waste of time to try to change it (Jensen, 1969). A proper discussion of this point is beyond the scope of this chapter, but because the specter of biology seems to cast such a somber shadow over the making of public policy, it must be mentioned. Wearers of eyeglasses and takers of insulin can testify to the folly of this view. While these are palliative measures and not cures, medical institutions forge bravely ahead from day to day searching for ways of altering conditions in people who have them because of simple gene action. Behavioral scientists can do the same.

Misconception 4: "If animals are so variable, we may as well pay attention to those most closely related to man, since this is where we will learn the most." This view guides the funding of research on monkeys and apes, and the comparative thinking of most behavioral scientists. It is not completely false, but is wrong enough to require comment. Closeness of phyletic relationship is only one of at least four bases for comparing two species, and it sometimes may be misleading. The other three are similarity of reproductive strategy, similarity of ecological adaptation, and similarity of major sensory processes used in communication. The chimpanzee, our closest relative and surely worthy of study, differs from humans living under natural conditions in having a much smaller territorial or home range, doing much less hunting, and exhibiting much less pair bonding (Goodall, 1965). Hunting mammals such as lions exhibit more humanlike patterns of sharing behavior (Schaller, 1972) and teaching behavior (Schenkel, 1966) with respect to offspring than does any higher primate. Foxes, which are pair-bonding hunting mammals, and thus an excellent model for certain aspects of human parent-offspring relations, have scarcely been studied at all.

The rhesus monkey, the model on which we rely almost completely for laboratory manipulation of the growth of social

relations, may not be appropriate at all. The major difficulties
with it are that under natural conditions rhesus live in very
large troops, are highly promiscuous, and are very careful to
keep their infants from other individuals. These are major
differences distinguishing them from human foragers. Indeed,
it has been shown that, in two closely related species of
macaque (bonnet and pigtail), the response of infants to removal
of their mothers when the pair are living in a social context
derives from just such differences in the species' normal guarding
of infants (Rosenblum, 1971). The responses of the infants are
diametric opposites: the bonnet infant is soon adopted by another
female, and soon behaving normally; the pigtail infant enters a
profound depression from which it never fully recovers. In these
and other respects, the pigtail resembles rhesus, our favorite
subject for study; the bonnet, studied only in one or two labor-
atories, resembles humans.[5]

A final example will illustrate the principle of comparison
because of similarity in the sensory processes relied on for
communication. Much has been made in recent years of the fact
that the redoubtable rhesus monkey relies largely on olfactory
signaling for communication in courtship (Michael & Keverne,
1968). While the possibility of similar effects in humans
could receive more attention than it has, it may be of greater
interest to study the ring dove (Lott, Scholz, & Lehrman, 1967),
which we know relies overwhelmingly (as people do) on visual
signaling in courtship. So a close relative, the rhesus, with
its much better sense of smell than ours, is of less value as
a model than a remote relative, the ring dove, which, like
humans, has a poor sense of smell and an excellent sense of
vision, (and, incidentally, is pair bonding, as people are).
Similar considerations may apply regarding the development of
attachment in infancy, although we must note the recent
intriguing demonstration that human infants show preferential
head turning toward their own mothers' breast pads, as opposed
to another mother's, using olfactory discrimination, at the
age of six days (MacFarlane, 1974).

Process in the Phylogeny of Development

This review would be incomplete without mention of some

---

[5]Higher primates differ widely from species to species, and
according to no obvious pattern, in the extent to which females
will permit their offspring to be handled by other animals.
For a review of this interesting, if puzzling, variation, see
Hrdy, 1974.

basic concepts of phylogenesis derived from comparative
embryology. They provide descriptive generalizations regarding events that are known to have happened during the evolution of ontogeny in various phyla (DeBeer, 1951). These
processes are of a much more inductive sort and describe much
more long-term events than the processes discussed earlier
in the chapter. They are descriptive summaries of the history
of various organisms, rather than deductive principles of
change in populations.

At least eight such processes have been named. The names
will not be repeated here, except for the most famous of these,
noeteny, which is usually held to have operated in the evolution of man. As a result of this process, the sexual maturation of the organism is attained earlier in its development, or
the growth rate slowed in relation to it, in such a way as to
make the adult of the descendent resemble the juvenile of the
ancestor. For this reason, it is said, human adults resemble
ape infants and juveniles in various physical characteristics,
more than we do adult apes.

Little purpose will be served by describing the rest of
the terms and concepts (see DeBeer, 1951, for a review). The
main point, which summarizes all of them, is this: the speed
of growth in specific organ systems, the age at termination,
and the length of life all may evolve independetly of one another. New characters may appear at one phase of development,
then shift to another phase or come to occupy more than one
phase. Old characters may disappear by means of the same
processes in similar phase-specific fashion. Such events
affecting ontogeny must, indeed, be among the major processes
by which the form of organisms changes over the history of life.

The concept of *allometry* is usually invoked to describe
the relationship between the size and weight of organ systems
whose rates of growth are not related linearly. It provides
descriptive equations, usually simple exponential equations of
the form $y = bx^k$, where y and x are sizes of the respective organs or body parts and b and k are constants
(Sinclair, 1973). These equations summarize the shape changes
of organisms, whether during evolution or during individual
development.

The significance of allometry in phylogeny is that we may
observe major shape changes during the evolution of a body
part, the significance of which is attributable to other body
size changes, needing to separate adaptive explanation.   In
the evolution of the horse, for example, the face has lengthen-

ed as body size has increased. This is because face length is determined by area of tooth surface necessary for chewing, which, since it depends on the amount eaten, depends on body mass. Body mass increases as the cube of body length, and tooth surface as the square of face length. Therefore, face length must increase faster than (as the 3/2 power of) body length. A recent attempt has been made to apply the same kind of reasoning to the study of human brain evolution (Pilbean & Gould, 1974).

The significance of allometry in individual behavior development lies in the manner in which allometric shape changes affect the behavior of parents and children. It has been noted, for example, that humans, as well as all other mammals and birds, because of allometric shape changes during growth, have young with a characteristic "infant shape", including a head very large, and limbs short, with respect to the torso; a flat face; and eyes very large with respect to the face. These features, in addition to small size and behavioral clumsiness, are pro- posed as releasing mechanisms for parental behavior (Lorenz, 1965), and their universality held to explain the potential for cross-fostering of species, including human affection for young of other species. Allometric shape changes during growth remove the features, and correspondingly reduce the power of the child to release parental behavior.

Among other consequences of allometric shape changes for behavior development, it may be noted that among other problems faced by children learning to walk, their centers of gravity are higher than they will be later, and, among other problems faced by adolescents learning virtually everything, they have to face the embarrassment of having feet and hands that grow faster than the rest of them.

THE EVOLUTION OF HUMAN BEHAVIOR DEVELOPMENT

To be of real use to us, this body of theory must, of course, generate hypotheses, and guide us in our choice of laboratory animal models; but it must be more, as well. It must help us to place the human species in relation to other animals in such a way that we can reconstruct the history of the facts we are most concerned with; the facts of the behavior, and the growth, of parents and children. Only then will evolution illuminate these facts.

An extensive review of the data now available is not

possible here. Even if it were, great gaps would still remain
in the picture. But still we may touch on a few areas of
interest. In each case, probable events leading to the condition found in human hunter-gatherers from their higher
primate ancestors will be suggested. This will be followed
by mention of very recent changes--those that have occurred
in the ten thousand years since the invention of agriculture,
or even more recently, since the industrial revolution.

1. Behavioral status of newborns. Higher primate newborns are generally precocial in sensory systems and altricial
in motor systems, except for clinging ability, which in most
monkeys is present at birth (Ewer, 1968, Ch. 10). Humans are
more altricial motorically at birth than monkeys or apes.
They develop more slowly than apes, which develop more slowly
than monkeys. Monkeys have the shortest, and humans the longest life span. Comparing humans to chimpanzees, it is not
clear that there has been a relative slowing of development.
It seems, instead, that an absolute lengthening of the life
span can account for many of the differences in rate of
development. This lengthening may account for the more
altricial condition of humans at birth, if we assume that
gestation could not be lengthened (see Footnote 1). Surely
the human invention of the sling for carrying infants must
have been an important step in making this more altricial
condition possible; human neonates do not ordinarily cling,
and so must be carried. Also, to evolve a slower rate of
development often requires reduced selection pressure against
offspring (Emlen, 1973; p. 141), which the sling would provide.
This suggests that the exceptionally altricial condition of
human newborns has evolved very recently, probably in the last
million years. This notion is supported by the fact that the
social smile, which makes human infants most attractive to
mothers, does not appear until the second month, and infants
are unattractive at birth, suggesting that selection has not
had time to reduce the age of emergence of social smiling.
(A similar argument was made by Richards [1966] for the golden
hamster. In this species, the length of gestation is shorter
than in other rodents, and mothers are more responsive to pups
at several days of age than they are at birth, suggesting that
the gestation period has shortened recently, and selection has
not had time to make the necessary adjustments in the releasing
characteristics of the pups.)

Very Recent Changes. As the sling is no longer in use, in our
population, Western neonate experiences fewer motor challenges,
less tactile and vestibular stimulation, more temperature main-

tenance challenges, and is kept almost exclusively horizontal in posture instead of largely vertical, in comparison with the condition of neonates in hunter-gatherer societies (see Chapter 12). Judging from the similarity of the hunter-gatherer neonatal condition to that of other higher primates, with respect to these variables, we may infer that we have experienced a sudden change in a pattern that is very old, perhaps tens of millions of years old. The consequences of the change, if any, are unclear, but it is worthy of note that the use of infant sling is now showing a slight tendency to reemerge in certain Western populations.

2.   Nursing behavior of infants and mothers. Age at weaning, frequency of suckling, and rate of sucking have all received substantial attention in the comparative literature. These will be considered in turn.

a.   Weaning. Weaning in higher primates is generally precipitated by the birth of a subsequent off-spring. In many Old World monkeys, this occurs at about a year of age, although in baboons it is usually at two years (DeVore, 1965). In chimpanzees (Goodall, 1967) and in human hunter-gatherers (Konner, 1972; Ch. 12 of this volume) it occurs at about four years. In each case, the age at weaning is equivalent to approximately one-fourth to one-third the age at sexual maturity, so that in spite of the absolute lengthening of the nursing period, its relative length has not changed much during the course of higher primate evolution. (This statement is meant to be extremely general, and is not to be applied to specific variation among monkey species.)

Very Recent Changes. Clearly, a dramatic drop in the age at weaning has occurred in the last few thousand years, beginning with the development of settled agriculture, which seems to lead to a birth interval (and consequently a probable weaning age) of two or three years (Morley, 1973; p. 306), and continuing with the evolution of the advanced industrial state. Research has failed to demonstrate significant sequelae of mode of infant feeding (Caldwell, 1964), but it must be noted that the range of variation under discussion here is scarcely tapped by comparing infants breast-fed for a few months with infants bottled-fed, which is what virtually all of the out-come studies have done. So the consequences of the great drop in age at weaning, for individual development, must be considered an open question.

b. Frequency of sucking. Extensive comparative work
    (Ewer, 1968; Ben Shaul, 1962; Blurton Jones,
    1972b) has suggested that mammals may be useful
    divided into two groups, characterized as *contin-
    ual* or *spaced* feeders in early infancy. Contin-
    ual feeders are those whose infants cling to
    them, such as most primates, bats, and marsupials,
    and those whose infants follow them, such as the
    most precocial ungulates. Spaced feeders are
    those that leave their infants in nests, such as
    tree shrews and rabbits, or in movable caches,
    such as eland and certain other ungulates. Milk
    composition (Ben Shaul, 1962) and sucking rate
    (Wolff, 1968, cited in Blurton Jones, 1972b) are
    correlated with spacing of feeds as follows.
    Continual feeders have more dilute milk, with
    lower fat and protein content, and suck slowly.
    Spaced feeders have more concentrated milk and
    suck quickly. The milk composition and sucking
    rates of higher primates, including people, is
    consistent with a classification of them as
    continual feeders. This is indeed the case for
    most monkeys (Horwich, 1974), chimpanzees
    (Nickolson, n.d.) and human hunter-gatherers
    (Konner, 1972, Ch. 12 of this volume), all of
    which suckle several times an hour.

Very Recent Changes. Humans in Western societies are now
spaced feeders. When this change occurred is unknown, and what
its consequences may be are a matter of speculation. Studies
showing no significant sequelae of the choice between "demand"
and "scheduled" (four-hourly) feeds are of slender interest in
this context, since in Western homes "demand" feeding sorts
itself out to six or seven feeds a day. Not merely the possible
chronic effects of the change from continual to spaced feeding
but also the acute effects on such phenomena as infant feeding
difficulty and "colic", maternal success in milk production,
and prevention of conception, are completely unknown.

c. Rate of sucking. Much discussion (Bruner & Bruner,
    1968; Kaye & Brazelton, 1971; J. Brown, 1973) has
    centered around the differences between human and
    ape newborns in their pattern of nonnutritive
    sucking, and improbable arguments have been mount-
    ed regarding the presumed adaptive value of the
    differences (see pp. 25-27). The essential
    differences seem to be that humans exhibit a
    unique burst-pause pattern and are more easily

distracted from sucking. Two remarks are of
interest here. First, developmental studies are
necessary to show that the human newborn's
unique pattern is not merely a consequence of
greater human altriciality at birth, only to
disappear during the ensuing weeks. Second,
since neither human hunter-gatherers nor apes
typically provide their infants with anything
other than the breast to suck, we must wonder
how a nonnutritive sucking pattern with such
complex presumed adaptive consequences could
ever have been selected for.

　　3.　　Maternal and infant attachment. There have been
recent presentations of evolutionary views of the infant's
attachment to its primary caretaker (Bowlby, 1969) and of the
mother's attachment to the infant (Barnett, Leiderman, Grobstein, & Klaus, 1970; Kennell, Jerauld, Wolfe, Chesler, Kreger,
McAlpine, Steffa, & Klaus, 1974). Bowlby discusses many
similarities in the growth of attachment in infants in various
species, but argues that humans have distinguished themselves
by coming to rely on distal mechanisms of mother-infant
communication for the formation of attachment. He cites the
human newborn's poor clinging ability as evidence for an
evolutionary step away from proximal mechanisms dependent on
physical contact. It will be clear from the foregoing discussion, and from other works (Konner, 1972; Ch. 12 of this volume), that humans, in their environment of evolutionary
adaptedness, exhibit a mother-infant bond in which both continual physical contact and continual prolonged nursing,
figure importantly, just as they do in other higher primates.
The infant sling, not distance from the infant, is what has
obviated the necessity for strong newborn clinging in humans.
Indeed, the gradualness of this transition is evident when it
is considered that none of the great apes is able to cling
well at birth, and that all are supported for a time by the
cradling arm of the mother, who walks three-leggedly for the
first few weeks of the infant's life (Goodall, 1967; Schaller,
1963; Rodman, 1973).

　　In addition to these comments of the bond that clearly
affect both mother and infant, it has been suggested (Leiderman, Leifer, Seashore, Barnett, & Grobstein, 1973; Kennell,
et al., 1974) that events in the first days or even the first
hours of life may affect the mother's subsequent attachment to
the infant. It is true that in all placental mammals there is
extensive mother-infant contact, including handling or licking
stimulation of the infant, during the immediate postparturi-

tional period (Ewer, 1968), and in some mammals such contact appears to be important in the development of maternal attachment (Klopfer & Klopfer, 1968). Human hunter-gatherers exhibit immediate extensive stimulation of the infant and continuous mother-infant contact during the hours and days after birth. Although it seems likely that events of the first few hours could be crucial, and there is evidence that effects of contact during the first few days are not lasting, (Leiderman & Seashore, 1975), the comparative evidence warrants further study of these phenomena.

Very Recent Changes. Especially since the industrial revolution, there have been great changes in the nature of the mother-infant relation, particularly in physical proximity, which has decreased dramatically. Making and breaking of contact with the infant, once accounted for almost exclusively by the infant, is now largely accounted for by the mother. At present, during the first few days of their relationship, mothers and infants may be almost completely isolated from one another, although there are small signs of increasing contact in some populations. The consequences of these changes, for the mother or the infant, if any, are unknown.

4.   Other early social relations.

a.   Male parental investment. Male parental investment has increased greatly during the evolution of humans from their primate ancestors, but this has not taken the form of an increase in the amount of interaction between males and their offspring. Rather, it has taken the form of economic investment, which in nonhuman primates is nil (because they eat very little meat). Still, this does represent a greater investment by human males, as would be predicted from the fact that humans are more or less pair bonding (see p. 15). It is worth noting, however, that males among marmosets, the other pair-bonding primates, exhibit extensive interaction with infants, carrying them 70 percent of the time (there are usually twins) and giving them to their mothers only to nurse. (For a review of male parental behavior in primates, see Mitchell & Brandt, 1971.)

Very Recent Changes. In all known human cultures, males exhibit an extremely minor direct role in relation to small children and especially to infants, and human hunter-gatherers

may be included in this generalization. While the latter may
show more father-infant contact than is shown in our own
culture (West & Konner, 1976), it may be said that father-
infant relations have changed relatively little, if at all,
since the hunting-gathering period. However it appears that
they may do so in some Western populations, in the very near
future. It will be of interest to observe the relative
success of this effort to increase father-infant contact.

      b.   Relations with infants and juveniles. In all
higher primates, including human hunter-gatherers, the very close mother-infant bond is
mitigated, for the mother, by the presence of
other adults and, for the infant, by the presence
of a multiage juvenile play group, and easy object
for the infant's transition to a wider social
world (Konner, 1975; see Leiderman, Ch. 16 this
volume). Same-age peer relations are nonexistent
in human hunter-gatherers and in apes, because of
demographic considerations, and tend to be more
possible in monkeys, although even here exclusively
same-age peer groups are rare. Thus there appears
to have been a gradual increase in the multiage
nature of the juvenile play group during the
evolution of man.

    Very Recent Changes. Same-age peer groups, even in earliest
childhood, have largely replaced the multiage play group. Consequences of this change for efficiency of child care, of the
social integration of the infant, and of the intergenerational
transfer of information, especially information about infant and
child care, have yet to be explored.

    5.   Observational learning, teaching, and play. In all
animals, some accumulation of information about the environment
and some acquisition, or at least, sharpening of skills, must be
effected during development. The three means provided by selection for these purposes may be considered separately.

      a.   Observational learning. Improvement of rate of
learning by observation of conspecifics has been
shown for a number of mammals (e.g., Chesler,
1969). In herbivorous mammals, especially those
whose infants follow them or are carried around
by them, transmission of information about food
sources and food extraction is effected by this
means. This is clearly one of the adaptive
functions served by the mother-infant bond in

nonhuman higher primates and in human hunter-
gatherers, in addition to the predation-reducing
function. (It appears [Chesler, 1969] that the
mother is a more effective object for observational learning enhancement in kittens than is a
strange conspecific, as might be expected.)
Even quite complex skills such as termite fishing
in chimpanzees (Goodall, 1967), can be acquired,
or have their acquisition facilitated, in this
manner. Infants among human hunter-gatherers
acquire the rudiments of digging for roots, crack-
ing nuts, and pounding with a mortar and pestle
by the end of the second year of life, by observing their mothers engaging in these skills, and
imitating them (Konner, 1972).

b.   Teaching. As distinct from observational learning,
teaching requires actual efforts by adults or older
juveniles to aid in the process of acquisition.
Not merely being available for observation, but
deliberate modeling when the action is really
purposeless, or active encouragement, or simplify-
ing the task to provide graded steps, are required.
Such behavior is rarely observed in nonhuman
primates, and efforts to stretch certain features
of their parental behavior to make it seem more
like teaching (e.g., Whiten, 1975) impress one
more strongly with how little teaching they really
do. Carnivores, on the other hand, including lions
(Schenkel, 1966), tigers (Schaller, 1968), and
otters (Ewer, 1968, Ch. 10) commonly engage in
substantial teaching behavior that functions to
transmit hunting and prey-catching skills. Feline
mothers bring back half-dead prey that their young
then kill and eat; lead cubs and kittens on
expeditions whose main purpose seems to be
acquainting the young with stalking; and partially
kill prey on the hunt, leaving the young to finish
if off and intervening when the prey shows signs
of escaping. Human hunter-gatherers have available,
of course, a unique means of information transfer:
language. Most teaching about hunting occurs in
the form of storytelling and answering questions,
means unavailable to hunting cats. So it is not
surprising that the teaching actions described
above for cats occur very infrequently in human
hunters, and that linguistic information transfer,
observational learning, and play are the main

means of acquiring hunting skills. It must be
noted that fathers sometimes make play bow and
arrow sets for their sons, but the boys often
make these themselves. It must also be noted
that boys learn much about tracks, game movements, and local landscape while following their
mothers during gathering trips. Girls acquire
much of the information they need about food
gathering during the same expeditions, also, with
apparently little active teaching.

c.   Play.   Much print has been expended regarding the
functions of play (e.g., Lorenz, 1965; Loizos,
1966; Ewer, 1968), and the evidence suggests that
it serves the functions of exercise, acquisition
of information about the environment and about
conspecifics, and sharpening, or, more rearely,
acquisition of subsistence and social skills.
In some mammals, it is clear that the deprivation
of opportunities for play in early life have
serious deleterious consequences on social and
reproductive skills. It may be noted (Ewer,
1968; Ch. 11) that, broadly speaking, the most
intelligent mammals (primates, cetacea, and
carnivora) are the most playful; the two qualities
probably increase synergistically. Also, if an
animal is very short-lived, the young do not
appear to play very much, probably because there
is too little time for them to gain much from
playing (Ewer, 1968, Ch. 11).

Finally, the composition of play groups has
received comparative attention (Konner, 1975),
as summarized earlier. Because of the multiage
nature of hunter-gatherer and other higher
primate play groups, information acquisition
and practice of skills are effected in a context
in which teaching, observational learning, and
play are combined and, in effect, become one
process.

Very Recent Changes.   Since the hunter-gatherer era, the
percentage of information transfer accounted for by teaching
has greatly increased, and that accounted for by observational
learning and play correspondingly decreased. Also, the context
of information transfer has become overwhelmingly that of
adult to child or adult to same-age peer group of children,
rather than from older to younger child. Usually this change

is attributed to the greater amount, greater complexity, and less "organic" nature of the information to be transferred. Undoubtedly this explanation has some merit. But it will be of interest to follow the emergent trends toward mixed age grouping, individual pacing, and "open" (playful?) classrooms in schools, and to attempt to assess the efficiency of these other very ancient means of information transfer.

6. <u>Stages and patterns of growth</u>. The evolution of the human condition at birth has been considered above. Two other stages of human growth, that of adolescence and that of the "five-to-seven shift" (White, 1974), deserve comparative attention. Both these stages are clearly biological in nature, resembling metamorphosis. Adolescence occurs in other higher primates, including a growth spurt as well as sexual maturation. While the age of adolescence is much later in humans than apes, and later in apes than monkeys, the ages, as suggested above, are roughly proportional to the life span, so that the question of relative postponement of adolescence during human evolution is an open one. But the principal student of the five-to-seven shift (White, personal communication, 1976) has recently come to the view that the old Bolk thesis about human neoteny may have some merit. According to this thesis, most of the events of adolescence have, in the course of evolution, become postponed, thus producing the so-called latency period, during which some aspects of growth are slowed. If this is so, the five-to-seven shift may be the remnants of the onset of adolescence. Clearly, only attention to preadolescent growth spurts, if any, in nonhuman primates can resolve this question.

It may be of interest also to note that the five-to-seven shift begins soon after the time when, in hunting-gathering populations, a child's next sibling is born. It is tempting to speculate that selection has provided for a quantum step in the direction of physical and behavioral adulthood not long after the child's dependence on its mother has to be sharply curtailed.

<u>Very Recent Changes</u>. The reduction of birth spacing has been discussed above. It is interesting to note that schooling, a very recent phenomenon indeed, appears to take cognizance, in its age of onset, of the child's biological readiness (as provided by the five-to-seven shift), even though much learning that goes on in school is clearly possible earlier.

Finally, no discussion of this sort would be complete without mention of recent secular trends in growth at adolescence. It is well established that in many of the world's populations, though especially in European and American ones, there has been a dramatic increase in adult stature, decrease in the age at menarche, and decrease in the age at termination of growth in stature. The age at menarche has dropped about four years and the age of termination of growth more than five years, during the last century (Tanner, 1970).[6] This is not the place to discuss the causes of these trends, but it may be noted that they constitute a biological change in the course of growth that has enormous potential ramifications. The central challenge they present to psychologists is to determine whether emotional and intellectual growth patterns are changing at a similar rate. If they are not, then clearly earlier onset of sexual maturity presents threats to mental health and social welfare that must be guarded against. If they are, then clearly our view of adolescent rights and privileges, and our notion of what an adult is, must be substantially revised.

SUMMARY AND CONCLUSION

Evolutionary concepts and facts relevant to the understanding of the development of behavior have been presented. First, elements of natural selection theory as it applies to parent and child behavior were outlined. Second, major misconceptions about the phylogeny of behavior and development were discussed. Third, broad processes of the phylogeny of development were mentioned. Finally, an attempt was made to array the comparative evidence in such a way as to infer the evolutionary history of some aspects of infant behavior, parent behavior, and developmental process. These histories were then set against the very recent changes in these characters, changes probably too recent for selection to have adequately responded to them.

Much nonsense has been written about the evolution of behavior and development, and much glib talk has put many sensible people off of it as a useful area of study. It is hoped that this review may function to tighten up some of the loose thinking, and persuade some skeptics that there is indeed value in it. Not only must it guide our choice of subjects for laboratory and field comparative study; not only can it point to phenomena needing study in human children; but it may, by

---

[6]These trends seem to be ending in populations with very high socioeconomic status, where they may also have started earlier. Thus the trends are not expected to continue indefinitely.

providing historical depth, affect our concept of our nature, and so, as well, of our future.

REFERENCES

Ainsworth, M. D. S.   Infancy in Uganda: Infant care and the growth of attachment.   Baltimore, Md.: The Johns Hopkins University Press, 1967.

Ardrey, R.   The territorial imperative.   New York: Atheneum, 1966.

Arling, G. L., & Harlow, H. F.   Effects of social deprivation on maternal behavior of rhesus monkeys.   Journal of Comparative and Physiological Psychology, 1967, 64, 371-377.

Barnett, C. R., Leiderman, P. H., Grobstein, R. & Klaus, M.   Neonatal separation: The maternal side of interactional deprivation.   Pediatric, 1970, 45, 197-205.

Ben Shaul, D. M.   The composition of the milk of wild animals.   International Zoological Year Book, 1962, 4, 333-342.

Blurton Jones, N. G. (Ed.)   Ethological studies of child behaviour.   Cambridge, England: Cambridge University Press, 1972, (a).

Blurton Jones, N. G.   Comparative aspects of mother-child contact.   In N. G. Blurton Jones (Ed.), Ethological studies of child behaviour.   Cambridge, England: Cambridge University Press, 1972, (b).

Bourliere, F.   Natural history of mammals.   London: Harrap, 1955.

Bower, T. G. R.   Development in infancy.   San Francisco: W. H. Freeman, 1974.

Bowlby, J.   Attachment and loss. Vol. 1: Attachment.   London: Hogarth, 1969.

Bronson, G. W.   Infants' reactions to unfamiliar persons and novel objects.   Monographs of the Society for Research in Child Development, 1972, 37 (3).

Brown, R. A first language. Cambridge, Mass.: Harvard
    University Press, 1973.

Brown, J. V. Nonnutritive sucking in great ape and human new-
    borns: Some phylogenetic and ontogenetic character-
    istics. In J. F. Bosma (Ed.), Fourth Symposium on
    Oral Sensation and Perception: Development in the
    Fetus and Infant. Washington, D.C.: U.S. Government
    Printing Office, 1973.

Bruner, J., & Bruner, B. Process of cognitive growth: Infancy.
    Worcester, Mass.: Clark University Press, 1968.

Caldwell, B. The effects of infant care. In M. L. Hoffman &
    L. W. Hoffman (Eds.), Review of Child Development
    Research, Vol. 1. New York: Russell Sage Foundation,
    1964, 9-87.

Campbell, B. A., & Jaynes, J. Reinstatement. Psychological
    Review, 1966, 73, 487-480.

Carmichael, L. The onset and early development of behavior.
    In P. H. Mussen (Ed.), Carmichael's Manual of Child
    Psychology, Vol. 1, 3rd Ed. New York: Wiley, 1970.

Chesler, P. Maternal influence in learning by observation in
    kittens. Science, 1969, 166, 901-903.

DeBeer, G. R. Embryos and ancestors. Oxford: Oxford University
    Press, 1951.

Denenberg, V. H. Critical periods, stimulus inputs, and
    emotional reactivity: A theory of infantile stimulation
    Psychological Review, 1964, 71, 335-351.

Denenberg, V. H., Pachke, R., & Zarrow, M. X. Killing of mice
    by rats prevented by early interaction between the
    two species. Psychonomic Science, 1968, 11, (39).

DeVore, I. (Ed.) Primate behavior. New York: Holt, Rinehart
    and Winston, 1965.

Ehrlich, A. Infant development in two prosimian species:
    greater galago and slow laris. Developmental
    Psychobiology, 1974, 7, (5), 439-454.

Eisenberg, L. The human nature of human nature. Science,
    1972, 176, (4031), 123-128.

Emlen, J. M. Ecology: An evolutionary approach. Reading,
    Mass.: Addison-Wesley, 1973.

Ewer, R. F. Ethology of mammals. London : Elek, 1968.

Fisher, R. A. The genetical theory of natural selection.
    New York: Dover, 1958.

Flavell, J. H. The developmental psychology of Jean Piaget.
    Princeton, N.J.: Van Nostrand, 1963.

Freedman, D. F. The biological basis of human infancy.
    Washington, D.C.: Erlbaum, 1974.

Freud, S. A general introduction of psychoanalysis. New York:
    Washington Square Press, 1920.

Freud, S. Totem and taboo. In A.A. Brill (Ed.), The basic
    writings of Sigmund Freud. New York: Random House,
    1938. Originally published 1913.

Gesell, A., & Amatruda, C. S. Developmental diagnosis,
    normal and abnormal child development. New York:
    Harper & Row, 1965.

Gewirtz, J. L. (Ed.) Attachment and dependency. Washington,
    D.C.: Winston, 1972.

Goodall, J. Chimpanzees of the Gombe Stream Reserve. In I.
    DeVore (Ed.), Primate behavior: Field studies of
    monkeys and apes. New York: Holt, Rinehart and
    Winston, 1965.

Goodall, J. Mother-offspring relationships in chimpanzees.
    In D. Morris (Ed.), Primate ethology. Chicago:
    Aldine Press, 1967.

Hamilton, W. D. The genetical evolution of social behavior.
    Journal of Theoretical Biology, 1964, 7, 1-52.

Harlow, H. F. The maternal affectional system. In B. M.
    Foss (Ed.), Determinants of infant behavior, Vol. 2.
    London: Methuen, 1963.

Hasler, A. D. Guideposts of migrating fishes. Science, 1960,
    131, 785-792.

Hasler, A. D. Olfactory imprinting in migrating salmon.

Paper presented at the Society for Neuroscience, Fourth Annual Meeting, St. Louis, Missouri, October 20-24, 1974.

Hebb, D. O.   On the nature of fear. Psychological Review. 1946, 53, 259-276.   Also: In P. H. Mussen, J. J. Conger, & J. Kagan (Eds.), Readings in child development and personality. (New York: Harper & Row, 1965.)

Hess, E.   Imprinting.   Chicago: University of Chicago Press, 1974.

Herrnstein, R. J.   I.Q. in the meritocracy.   Boston: Little Brown, 1973.

Hirsch, H., & Spinnelli, D.   Visual experience modifies distribution of horizontally and vertically oriented receptive fields of cats.   Science, 1970, 168, 869-871.

Horwich, R. H.   Regressive periods in primate behavioral development with reference to other mammals. Primates 15, (2-3: 141-149), 1974.

Howell, N.   The population of the Dobe Area !Kung.   In R. Lee & I. DeVore (Eds.), Kalahari Hunter Gatherers. Cambridge, Mass.: Harvard University Press, 1975.

Hrdy, S.   The care and exploitation of nonhuman primate infants by conspecifics other than the mother.   In Rosenblatt, Hinde, & Shaw (Eds.), Advances in the study of behavior. New York: Academic Press, 1974.

Jensen, A.   How much can we boost I.Q. and scholastic achievement?   Harvard Educational Review, 1969, 39, 1-123.

Johnson, C.   Environmental modification of habitat selection in adult damselflies.   Ecology, 1966, 47, 674-676.

Kagan, J.   Acquisition and significance of sex typing and sex role identity.   In M. L. Hoffman & L. W. Hoffman (Eds.), Review of Child Development Research, Vol. 1. New York: Russell Sage Foundation, 1964, (a).

Kagan, J.   Attention and psychological change in the young child. Science, 1970, (b), 170, 826-832.

Kamin, L. J.   The science and politics of I.Q.   New York: Wiley,

1974.

Kaye, K., & Brazelton, T. B. Mother-infant interaction in
      the organization of sucking. Paper presented at
      Annual Meeting of Society for Research in Child
      Development, 1971.

Kennell, J., Jerauld, R., Wolfe, H., Chesler, D., Kreger, N.,
      McAlpine, W., Steffa, M. & Klaus, M. Maternal
      behavior one year after early and extended post
      partum contact. Developmental Medicine and Child
      Neurology, 1974, 16 (2), 172-179.

Klopfer, D. H., & Klopfer, M. Maternal "imprinting" in goats:
      Fostering of alien young. Zeitschrift fur Tier-
      psychologie, 1968, 25, 862-866.

Konner, M. Aspects of the developmental ethology of a
      foraging people. In N. G. Blurton Jones (Ed.),
      Ethological Studies of Child Behavior. Cambridge,
      England: Cambridge University Press, 1972.

Konner, M. Relations among infants and juveniles in comparative
      perspecitve. In M. Lewis & L. Rosenblum (Eds.),
      The Origins of Behavior. Vol. 3: Friendship and Peer
      Relations. New York: Wiley, 1975.

Lack, D. The natural regulation of animal numbers. London:
      Oxford University Press, 1954.

Lehrman, D. A critique of Konrad Lorenz' theory of instinctive
      behavior. Quarterly Review of Biology, 1953, 28,
      337-363.

Leiderman, P. H., & Seashore, M. J. Mother-infant neonatal
      separation: Some delayed consequences in parent-
      infant relationships. Ciba Foundation Symposium
      33 (New Series), Amsterdam: Elsevier, 1975.

Leiderman, P. H., Leifer, A. D., Seashore, M. J., Barnett, C. R.,
      & Grobstein, R. Mother-infant interaction: Effects
      of early deprivation, prior experience and sex of
      infant. In J. I. Nurnberger (Ed.) Biological and
      environmental determinants of early development.
      Association for Research in Nervous and Mental
      Disease, 51, 154-173. Baltimore: Williams & Wilkins,
      1973.

Lenneberg, E. H. A biological perspective of language. In
        E. H. Lenneberg (Ed.), New directions in the study
        of language. Cambridge, Mass.: M.I.T. Press, 1964.

Levine, S., & Mullins, R. F. Jr. Hormonal influences on brain
        organization in infant rats. Science, 1966, 152,
        1585-1592.

Lewis, M., & Rosenblum, L. The effects of the infant on its
        caregiver. New York: Wiley, 1973.

Lockard, R. Reflections on the fall of comparative psychology:
        Is there a message for us all? American Psychologist,
        1971, 26 (2), 168-179.

Loizos, C. Play in mammals. In P. Jewell & C. Loizos (Eds.),
        Play, territoriality and exploration in mammals.
        New York: Academic Press, 1966.

Lorenz, K. Z. Evolution and modification of behavior. Chicago:
        University of Chicago Press, 1965.

Lott, D., Scholz, D. S., & Lehrman, D. S. Exteroceptive
        stimulation of the reproductive system of the female
        ring dove (Streptopelia risoria) by the mate and the
        colony milieu. Animal Behavior, 1967, 15, 433-437.

MacFarlane, A. Olfaction in the development of social
        preferences in the human neonate. Paper presented
        at the CIBA Foundation Symposium on the Parent-
        Infant Relationship, London, November 1974.

Mayr, E. Behavior and systematics. In A. Roe & G. G. Simpson,
        (Eds.), Behavior and Evolution. New Haven, Conn.:
        Yale University Press, 1958.

Mayr, E. Animal species and evolution. Cambridge, Mass.:
        Harvard University Press, 1963.

McGraw, M. The neuromuscular maturation of the human infant.
        New York: Hafner, 1963.

Michael, R. P., & Keverne, E. Pheromones in the communication
        of sexual status in primates. Nature, 1968, 218,
        746-749.

Mitchell, G. & Brandt, E. Paternal behavior of primates. In
        Poirier (Ed.), Primate socialization. New York:
        Random House, 1971.

Moltz, H. Fixed action patterns. Psychological Review, 1965, 72, (1), 27-47.

Moltz, H., & Robbins, D. Maternal behavior of primiparous and multiparous rats. Journal of Comparative Physiological Psychology, 1965, 60, 417-421.

Morley, D. Pediatric priorities in the developing world. London: Butterworths, 1973.

Morris, D. The naked ape. New York: McGraw-Hill, 1968.

Nicolson, N. A comparison of early behavioral development in some captive and wild chimpanzees. Manuscript of the Stanford Outdoor Primate Facility, Stanford University, 1974.

Piaget, J. Biology and knowledge. Chicago: University of Chicago Press, 1971.

Pilbeam, D. & Gould, S. Size and scaling in human evolution. Science, 1974, 186, (4167), 892-901.

Popp, J., & DeVore, I. Aggressive competition and social dominance theory. In D. Hamburg & J. Goodall (Eds.), The Behavior of the Great Apes. New York: Holt, Rinehart, and Winston, (in press).

Richards, M. P. M. Activity measured by running wheels and observation during the oestrous cycle, pregnancy and pseudopregnancy in the golden hamster. Animal Behaviour, 1966, 14, 303-309.

Rodman, P. Population composition and adaptive organization among Organ-utans of the Kutai Reserve. In R. Michael & J. Crook (Eds.), Comparative Ecology and Behavior of Primates. New York: Academic Press, 1973.

Roe, A., & Simpson, G. G. Behavior and evolution. New Haven, Conn.: Yale University Press, 1958.

Rosen, J., & Hart, F. Effects of early social isolation upon adult timidity and dominance in peromyscus. Psychological Reports, 1963, 13, 47-50.

Rosenblum, L. Kinship interaction patterns in pigtail and bonnet macaques. Proceedings Third International Congress on Primates, Zurich, 1970, Vol. 3, 79-84,

Rumbaugh, D., von Glaserfeld, E., Warner, H., Pisani, P., &
    Gill, T.   Lana (chimpanzee) learning language: A
    progress report. Brain and Language, 1974, 1,
    205-212.

Schaller, G. The mountain gorilla: Ecology and behavior.
    Chicago: University of Chicago Press, 1963.

Schaller, G. The deer and the tiger. Chicago: University of
    Chicago Press, 1969.

Schaller, G. The Serengeti lion. Chicago: University of
    Chicago Press, 1972.

Schenkel, R. Play, exploration and territoriality in the wild
    lion. In Jewell and Loizos (Eds.), Play, exploration
    and territory in mammals. (Symposium of the Zoo-
    logical Society of London, No. 18). London: Zoo-
    logical Society of London, 1966.

Scott, J. The effects of early experience on social behavior
    and organization. In Etkin (Ed.), Social behavior
    and organization among vertebrates. Chicago:
    University of Chicago Press, 1964.

Sinclair, D. Human growth after birth. London: Oxford
    University Press, 1973.

Skinner, B. F. Verbal behavior. New York: Appleton-Century-
    Crofts, 1957.

Tanner, J. M. Physical growth. In P. Mussen (Ed.), Carmichael's
    manual of child psychology (Vol. 1, 3rd ed.). New
    York: Wiley, 1970.

Thorpe, W. H. Further studies on pre-imaginal olfactory
    conditioning in insects. Proceedings of the Royal
    Society of London, 1939, B 127, 424-433.

Trivers, R. L. Parental investment and sexual selection. In
    B. Campbell, (Ed.), Sexual selection and the descent
    of man 1871-1971. Chicago: Aldine, 1972.

Trivers, R. L. Parent-offspring conflict. American Zoologist,
    1974, 14, 249-264.

Trivers, R. L. & Willard, D. E. Natural selection of parental
    ability to vary the sex ratio of offspring. Science,

1973, <u>179</u>, 90-92.

Tulkin, S. R., & Leiderman, P. H.   Mother and infant in Japan
        and America: A synthesis of several recent papers
        of William Caudill. <u>Cultural and Social Influences</u>
        <u>in Infancy and Early Childhood</u>, (Burg Wartenstein
        Symposium No. 57). Wenner-Gren Foundation for
        Anthropological Research, 1973.

Waddington, C. H.   Canalisation of development and the
        inheritance of acquired characters. <u>Nature</u>, 1942,
        <u>150</u>, 563.

Waddington, C. H.   Genetic assimilation of an acquired
        character. <u>Evolution</u>, 1953, <u>7</u>, 118.

West, M. M. and Konner, M.   The role of the father: An
        anthropological perspective. In M. Lamb (Ed.), <u>The</u>
        <u>role of the father in child development.</u>   New York:
        Wiley, 1957.

White, S.   Review of mental health: From infancy to adolescence
        and social change in the mental health of children.
        <u>Contemporary Psychology</u>, 1974, <u>19</u>, 499-500.

Whiten, A.   Observations of teaching behavior in a gorilla.
        Manuscript of the Department of Psychology, Oxford
        University, Oxford, England, 1975.

Wiesel, T. & Hubel, D. J.   Extent of recovery from the effects
        of visual deprivation in kittens. <u>Journal of</u>
        <u>Neurophysiology</u>, 1965, <u>28</u>, 1060-1072.

Wolff, P. H.   Sucking patterns of infant mammals.   In <u>Brain,</u>
        <u>Behavior and Evolution</u> (Vol. 1), 1968.

Part Three
Empirical Studies

It should be obvious from previous discussions that comparative child development research requires a special integration of biological, psychological, and anthropological approaches. Most researchers are trained in only one of these disciplinary areas, and the work in the following pages reflects this. If none of the studies in this volume exemplifies fully the approach we now believe to be essential, there are many that can serve as good models for various aspects of future, better-designed studies. In these pages, we will discuss how the papers exemplify both the progress and problems of current research.

LIMITATIONS

As we look at the empirical studies included in this section, despite their relatively sophisticated design and the generally high level of appreciation of the problems of conducting psychological studies in "foreign" cultures, they share (with some exceptions) common limitations as well, at least as viewed with the wisdom of hindsight. In the geographical distribution of the studies, industrialized, Western nations such as the United States and England are heavily represented. While there are studies in Israel,

Japan, and Mexico, the majority of studies were conducted in Africa. The investigators, all white, English-speaking, and, all but two, Americans, have sometimes used indigenous talent as interviewers or observers, but not as coauthors.

With the exception of the anthropologist investigators, most of the investigators have been relatively unfamiliar with the foreign culture they have studied, have spent little time there, may not have known the language, and have based their findings on a fairly short observation period, with little or no follow-up. Sample selection and size has been, in some cases, haphazard, with the choice of specific site and subjects determined by nonscientific factors. In many studies, controls of social class or socioeconomic factors have not been fully explored. Similarly, in almost all studies except those specifically focused on medical and biological variables, these factors have not been sufficiently considered. Very few of the investigators have attempted to describe or measure fully the infant's physical environment surround, and the social environment has usually been limited to the infant's contacts with caretaker (usually mother). Fathers, siblings, extended family members, visitors, animals, etc., are typically ignored.

Except for Ainsworth's study, the papers are largely atheoretical. The choice of problems and methods for study are usually based on the researcher's own theoretical assumptions concerning child development but rarely are these assumptions explicitly stated and tested. There is a dearth of attitudinal data that might provide a clue to the motivation or meaning of caretaking behavior as it relates to larger cultural values and attitudes.

The absence in most studies of highly trained, coequal colleagues from the cultures or social groups under study has undoubtedly led to an overly Western, middle-class emphasis in techniques, assumptions, and interpretations, although this is difficult in most instances to document. Surely, our particular concern with cognitive development is evident; affective, social, and moral development and their inter-relation are given secondary focus.

The intracultural studies, with the exception of Richards', have tended to be rather narrow in focus as well, ignoring many key biological, medical, and physical environmental variables. While in many studies social class and socioeconomic differences are explored, the use of traditional SES (socioeconomic status) measures still leaves many questions concerning their salience for child development and the familial environment.

STRENGTHS

Despite their limitations, these studies represent significant progress in the study of child development, and each provides deeper insight into aspects of development previously unexplored, or studied with less precision or perspective.

Among the studies of infancy across cultures, Ainsworth's study of the Ganda is exemplary in the translation of a broad-ranging theoretical approach into precise hypotheses meticulously studied across cultures.

Brazelton exhibts extreme sensitivity to the biological and medical variables impinging on child development, and recognizes the great importance of early observation, assessment of maternal health and background, and appreciation of individual variability among infants.

Draper's paper demonstrates profound appreciation of the complexities of assessing human nutritional status, and provides a check to ready generalizations concerning the influence of pre- and post-natal nutritional influences on cognitive or other aspects of development.

Goldberg's Zambia study provides fresh insight into questions of "precocious" development, and gives further credence to the role of vestibular stimulation and "permissive parenting" in encouraging early development.

Greenbaum and Landau's observations of verbal behavior in Israeli infants from diverse social and cultural background are unique in that they assess families who are economically very disadvantaged but provide active verbal stimulation to infants. The data reveal a potentially universal developmental principle relating to the way social background variables affect the timing of emergent skills.

Kagan demonstrates how cross-cultural comparisons can establish the presence of invariant sequences in social and cognitive development, thereby enabling the developmental psychologist to focus on the possible biological and psychological processes involved in these invariants. As an illustration of the value of this approach, he reports his work on the ontogenesis of object permanence in the second half of the infant's first year of life, illustrating how experimental work in several cultures contributes to our understanding of an important shift of cognitive development in the infant's earliest years.

Konner's study of the Kalihari San illuminates many of the same developmental stimuli as Goldberg's, but conducted in a setting considered to be the earliest extant from human society, provides provocative clues for the adaptive meaning of child-rearing patterns in human evolution.

Lewis and Ban, investigating urban and rural Yugoslav child-rearing, have delved more than most into the meaning of comparisons across and within cultures. Their examination of both similarities and differences, and their attempt to find a common base for comparison among diverse studies of similar aspects of development, shows us both how far we can go with available data, and how far we still need to go in devising studies that are designed a priori to obtain comparable data across a variety of settings.

Wolff's paper brings us back to the biological roots of cultural and individual differences, and reminds us that, despite current philosophical and ethical preferences to view children and adults from diverse cultural and racial groups as actually or potentially similar and equal, there are nonetheless culturally and genetically determined differences in basic physiologic functioning that must be recognized.

The next group of studies emphasizes variations within a single culture, generally using social class as one important variable among others to differentiate groups within a single society.

Klein's study takes an important first step in assessing the effects of nutritional variation on both mother-infant interaction and cognitive development. Combining the behavioral assessments used in this study with the nutritional assessments suggested by Draper provides an excellent model for studying nutrition and early development.

The Leidermans' exploration into the developmental meaning of socioeconomic differences in a non-Western culture, and their attempt to discover culturally and developmentally meaningful measures of economic position, provides a model for those conducting studies in many cultures, including our own.

Moss and Jones, looking at the relation between child-rearing attitudes and behavior in our own culture have discovered class-related discrepancies that should stimulate greater appreciation of the importance of maternal personality and expectations. Their numerous attempts to understand the class differences they found provide a model for attempts to decipher the complexities of the social class variable.

Richard's study, also within his own culture, in many respects comes closest in design to the type of comprehensive investigation we advocate for future child development studies. Longitudinal, encompassing parental attitudes and behavior, medical and social background, as well as infant variables ranging from biological characteristics at birth through motor, social, and affective development, this study provides a wealth of data, albeit on a relatively narrow base of subjects. A variety of observational and measurement techniques are used, at many intervals, although this study, like the others in this volume is somewhat weak in measures of the physical environment. The heavy stress on medical and biological variables, and the recognition of individual variability among infants is a welcome foil to many overly psychological studies of development.

Tulkin's observations in his own culture provide us with a way to look at the meaning of social class as it affects many aspects of child development. In addition to psychological variables, medical and environmental variables have been given some, although perhaps not enough, attention. Tulkin's study raises the important point that the meaning of the same behavior may be different in different groups and settings. When attitudinal data (obtained but not presented here) are combined with the careful behavioral observations reported here, we will better understand how parental social position and behavior interrelate and shape the child's world.

Yarrow, Pederson, and Rubenstein, investigating the development of black infants in their own culture, have addressed themselves to differentiating the complexity of the infant's proximal environment, analyzing the impact of social stimuli (their modality, contingency, affective expression, and variety), as well as aspects of the inanimate environment of a host of infant variables (social-affective, cognitive, and motor). While limited in scope, this study provides a valuable model for fine analysis of the ways that specific aspects of the infant's physical and social environment differentially affect aspects of the developing child, and goes far beyond many similar explorations of the effects of environmental "stimulation" or "deprivation" on child development.

A.
Infancy Across Cultures

Chapter 6

Infant Development and Mother–Infant Interaction Among Ganda and American Families*

Mary D. Salter Ainsworth
The Johns Hopkins University

During a period of nine months in 1954-1955, I undertook a study of infant care practices, mother-infant interaction, and infant development in a sample of semiacculturated Ganda village mother-infant pairs. For three years before going to Uganda, I had been associated with John Bowlby and his research team, who were investigating the effect on personality development of separation for the mother in early childhood. This research experience convinced me that interruption of a

---

*

The study of Ganda infants and mothers was supported by the East African Institute of Social Research, Kampala, Uganda, at that time directed by Dr. Audrey I. Richards. I am grateful for her help and for that of my assistant Mrs. Kate Kibuka. The Baltimore study has been supported by Grants 62-244 of the Foundations' Fund for Research in Psychiatry, R01 HD 01712 of the United States Public Health Service, by the Grant Foundation, and by the Office of Child Development; this support is gratefully acknowledged. I also deeply appreciate the cooperations of many associates and assistants who have helped in the analysis of the data; they are too numerous to be listed here, but have been acknowledged in the publications cited in this chapter.

young child's attachment relationship could have gravely
adverse effects on his subsequent development, and it made
me very eager to investigate the development of that early
relationship. I wondered what went on between an infant and
his mother during the first year of life that has such impact
on his subsequent development. In the 1950s, there had been
no published report of systematic observation on the development of the infant-mother relationship, although there had
been plenty of theorizing.

I went to Uganda as a wife accompanying her husband.
Otherwise I would probably not have undertaken a cross-cultural
study, much as I now value this approach. When I arrived in
Uganda, still working on material relevant to Bowlby's
Tavistock research project, European pediatricians, who were
knowledgable about Bowlby's work from his 1952 monograph for
the World Health Organization, urged me to undertake a study
of the effects of separation among Ganda infants. They
pointed out that it was customary among the Ganda to separate
infants from their mothers at the time of weaning. Some
suggested that this early separation might account for the
fact that adult Ganda were "affectionless"--at least in their
European view.

Although I did not assume there was an undue preponderance
of "affectionless character" among the Ganda, I was enthusiastic
about the opportunity to study separation that did not involve
institutionalization and that, because it was supported by
ancient custom, did not necessarily imply familial disruption,
rejection of the infant, or illness. Yarrow (1963, 1967) has
since demonstrated that "pure" separation, involving a shift
of mother figures, without illness, institutional experience,
or other untoward events, arouses substantial distress and
disturbance in infants old enough to have formed a "focused
relationship" with the initial mother figure.

In the 1950s, however, it was still doubted by many that
separation per se could have adverse effects; these were
attributed to concomitant circumstances. I therefore envisaged
an experiment of opportunity. I would observe infants before
weaning, learning what kind of relationship they had established
with their mothers as a baseline against which later developments could be viewed. I assumed that some of these infants
would be separated, according to custom, but that others would
not, since old customs were breaking down in Ganda society
through the influence of European acculturation. I would
follow both separated and nonseparated groups, and be in a
position to assess whether "pure" separation had adverse

effects or not. Some months were then spent in gaining some competence in the language (Luganda) and familiarity with the customs of the people, eliciting the cooperation of the appropriate chiefs, and explaining my proposed project to village assemblies.

Soon after I began my study of unweaned babies, it became evident to me that the separation that took place at weaning, if it took place at all, was a token separation for but a day or so; that the real separation, if any, occurred at about the time another baby was born; and that it was unlikely that families would arrange to send their babies away even then, as long as my project provided them with the various benefits I had arranged to sustain their cooperation. Although the "experiment of opportunity" therefore had to be abandoned, I had nevertheless my first opportunity to study the development of the infant-mother relationship in the first year of life. What had been intended as a baseline became the focus of the study, and I added to my original nucleus of infant subjects a number of younger infants who were not close to the time of weaning.

Thus, although not so intended at the outset, this project came to focus on the development of infant-mother attachment (Ainsworth, 1963, 1967).[1]   Its most significant yield included an identification of a number of patterns of attachment behavior, identification of several phases of development distinguished from one another in terms of the attachment behavior conspicuous in each, and the recognition of individual differences in the way babies had organized their several attachment behaviors. It appeared that no single criterion of attachment would suffice.

This cluster of findings from the Ganda study provided the chief aims of a much more intensive and systematic study of the development of infant-mother attachment in a sample of white, middle-class, American mother-infant pairs. Each of the previously identified patterns of attachment behavior was to be studied in detail, and, in conjunction with the investigation of the organization of attachment behavior, it was proposed to ascertain what features of maternal behavior influenced individual differences in the quality of the attachment relationship. If infants of two societies,

---

[1]
Throughout this chapter, it will be understood that Ainsworth (1967) is the basic reference for the Ganda study.

differing as widely as Ganda villagers and white, middle-class Americans, resembled each other closely in their attachment behaviors and the ways in which these developed and became organized, the implication would be that these are likely to be species-characteristic behaviors, and that both the normative course of development and environmental factors influencing deviations from it may be viewed as comprehending a common set of developmental principles.

I have been given opportunity elsewhere in this volume to summarize my theoretical orientation, so I shall not give an account of it here, except to state how it related to my Ganda project. Shortly before I left the Tavistock research team to go to Uganda, John Bowlby had become interested in the potentialities of ethology as inspiring a fresh theoretical orientation that might provide a much more satisfactory explanation of a child's responses to separation than could the then popular psychoanalytic or other "secondary-drive" theories. I resisted this nudge to revise my way of viewing the early mother-child relationship--until I began actually to observe infants and mothers in interaction during the first year of life. At that time, previously valued theory seemed totally inadequate, and the new view, sparked by ethological research and principles, seemed increasingly salient. Since then, John Bowlby and I have been jointly concerned with developing new theory that better fits the facts of early social development, and the findings of the two studies I refer to in this paper have helped to provide significant empirical support for such theory.

Even though my Ganda study led directly (although with some time lag) to my study of American infant-mother pairs, a comparison between the two studies does not approximate an ideal cross-cultural study, because their procedures differed greatly. Therefore, it will be necessary for me to cast my comparisons in general terms, rather than in the form of precisely measured differences between the two samples.

METHODS

Subjects

The Ganda sample consisted of 28 babies, 15 boys and 13 girls. Nine were first-born, 7 of them girls. Some of the participating families were contacted directly, some through chiefs, and some were volunteers from among the neighbors of participants. The families differed widely in degree of acculturation and in educational and socioeconomic level. Seven of the infants lived in polygynous households, 8 in nuclear families, and 13 in a modified extended family arrangement. Although none of the households were truly "extended", most included more adults than does the typical Western household. None of the babies lived alone with their mothers, but the presence of fathers varied greatly from one family to another.

The American sample consisted of 26 infants, 16 boys and 10 girls. Six of the infants, all boys, were first-born. The families were contacted through pediatricians in private practice, usually before the birth of the baby. All families were intact. One of the mothers had full-time employment throughout most of the infant's first year, and five others had full- or part-time employment for short periods. One family had a maternal grandmother present for most of the baby's first year and two had daily housekeepers to assist in the baby's care.

Home Visits

All infants in both samples were observed chiefly in their own home environment. At the time observations began, the Ganda babies ranged in age from two days to 80 weeks, with a median age of 24 weeks. At the time observation ended they ranged in age from 15 weeks to two years, with a median age of 46 weeks. As subjects were added to the sample from time to time, the span of the observations differed, ranging from 7 to 38 weeks, with a median span of 27 weeks. In short, a combination of longitudinal and cross-sectional methods was used to study Ganda development.

The visits to the Ganda homes were planned to occur every two weeks and to last for two hours. There were many irregularities, however. Some visits were missed, and frequent brief visits were interspersed between regular vistis-- chiefly rapport maintaining, but with some observational yield. At the insistence of the mothers, the visits took place always in the afternoons. Ganda women, responsible for raising food for their families, typically spent their morning hours working in their gardens. In the afternoon, they were usually at leisure and ready to entertain visitors. My interpreter (a well-educated Ganda woman, with a natural talent for fieldwork) and I were entertained in the livingroom, together with whomever else visited. We did not have the opportunity to follow the mother throughout her daily routine nor to inspect all parts of the living quarters. Our visits were devoted almost equally to interview and to direct observation.

The American sample--all of whom lived in the Baltimore area--were visited throughout the first year. After one or more preliminary visits, the participating families were visited once every 3 weeks, from 3 to 54 weeks. The visits lasted approximately four hours, and occurred at varied times of the day. The mothers proceeded with their usual routines, and the observers could see at first hand all aspects of the baby's life except what took place overnight. Direct observation was given first place, with interview of the mothers very secondary and taking place chiefly when the baby was napping.

At approximately 51 weeks, all but one of the Baltimore sample were introduced to a standardized strange situation in the laboratory. Here it was possible to observe the balance between attachment behavior and exploration in an unfamiliar environment, and also the infant's responses to brief separations and to a stranger under controlled conditions. The situation closest to this that occurred with the Ganda infants was visiting the well-baby clinic--transportation to which was offered to participating families as an inducement to cooperation. Not all the infants were taken there, and those who did went at different ages; furthermore, the observer was often too busy with the logistics of trans- portation to be able to observe their reactions to this unfamiliar situation.

Data Analysis Procedures

Data analysis procedures were much more numerous and elaborate in the Baltimore project than in the Ganda study. In the Baltimore project, the basic procedure was detailed coding of behavior of both mother and infant in several "critical" situations--situations most likely to elicit infant attachment behavior. Infant crying was also coded. This coding was supplemented by a variety of tabulations, and by ratings of maternal behavior as it appeared in inter- action with the infant. Classificatory procedures were also used, but for the most part these were superseded by quantitative procedures or at least supported by multivariate analysis.

In the Ganda project methods of data analysis were necessarily much cruder. No systematic coding could be done, but rather I had to be content with mere tabulations--nose

counts--of babies who did and did not display a specified
behavior, or of age of onset of observed behaviors. Several
relatively simple rating scales were devised, but these dealt
with variables that were crudely defined in comparison with
those rated in the Baltimore project. One classifactory
system was devised, and rated variables were checked against
it by means of a simple median test.

COMPARISON OF FINDINGS

     First and most important, I was very much more impressed
by the similarities between the two samples than by their
differences. Furthermore, I was impressed with the wide range
of individual differences within each sample, and with the
ways in which individual differences in maternal behavior were
linked to differences in infant behavior, the same kind of
relationships holding in both samples. There were, however,
cultural differences in infant-care practices, to which some
differences in infant behavior seemed attributable. This
paper will deal with a few of these, and will also give
attention to the ways in which this comparison of two societies
throws light on general developmental principles.

Feeding Practices and Behaviors

     Perhaps the most conspicuous differences between the Ganda
and the Baltimore samples concerned feeding. Twenty-seven of
the 28 Ganda babies were primarily breast-fed. Thirteen were
offered the breast not only when hungry, but often also for
mere comfort, and usually in response to minimal signals.
Eight were fed according to a schedule, usually a very
flexible one. The remaining seven were fed when the mother
judged them to be hungry but rarely if ever for mere comfort.
At night, however, nearly all Ganda babies were fed when they
awakened, and hence "on demand". A conspicuous feature of
the feeding of the majority of Ganda babies from about the
middle of the first year onward was the degree of initiative
they took in seeking the breast when they wished it. They
would approach the mother, fumbling in the folds of her dress,
and sometimes find and manage the breast without assistance.
This active initiative was most characteristic of demand-fed
babies--especially those who had been given the breast for
comfort.

     Of the American sample only 4 were breast-fed, and 22
bottle-fed (Ainsworth & Bell, 1974). In many cases how the

mother characterized her feeding practices bore no relation to what she did. In only 11 cases could the mother be described as heeding her baby's signals in regard to when she fed him. One of these practiced thoroughgoing and consistent demand feeding, sometimes for mere comfort, very much like her Ganda counterparts. Six used flexible schedules, often with "snacks" between scheduled feedings. Four tried hard to gratify their babies, but overinterpreted infant signals and substantially overfed them. The other 15 mothers heeded infant signals little or not at all, either attempting to force rigid or too widely spaced schedules, or impatiently terminating feeding too soon, or coaxing or forcing the baby to take enormous quantities so that he would sleep long and be little trouble, or, in some instances, being entirely arbitrary in the timing of feedings. Among the American mothers, degree of responsiveness to infant signals in the feeding situation in the first three months was a representative indication of the degree of excellence of other concurrent mothering practices (as indicated by high correlations with a number of detailed measures), and also highly predictive of the mother's sensitivity to infant signals throughout the rest of the first year. Although comparable measures are lacking for the Ganda mothers, my impression is that more of them than of the Baltimore mothers were sensitive to infant signals and communications, and fewer of them insensitive, rejecting, inaccessible, or interfering.

As might be expected, babies in the American sample, so few of whom were breast-fed, did not show the active initiative in instituting feeding that was characteristic of a majority of Ganda infants. Only one did so, and this was the baby who was breast-fed consistently on demand and for comfort. None of the other breast-fed infants did so, perhaps because they were weaned too soon to the bottle, and it is usually difficult for a bottle-fed baby to take initiative in securing his own bottle.

Weaning is gradual among the Ganda. First the daytime feedings are gradually dropped out, but the infant is still given the breast on demand during the night. About two weeks later, if the infant has accepted the new daytime regimen, the nighttime feedings are abruptly terminated. Present-day Ganda infants are weaned at about 12 months of age (Welbourn, 1958), although, in the memory of my Ganda informants about old customs, weaning traditionally took place between two and three years of age. In my Ganda sample (except for the baby who was bottle-fed from the beginning), only eight were weaned during the span of my observations. Three of these were

schedule-fed babies, and none on final weaning was disturbed
for longer than a day or two. Of the five demand-fed babies,
the one weaned latest--at 22 months of age--responded well to
final weaning, becoming much more self-reliant and grown up,
although still with a secure, healthy attachment relationship
with his mother. The other four demand-fed babies, who were
finally weaned at 32, 49, 50, and 57 weeks respectively, were
markedly disturbed. They showed extremely heightened and
insecure attachment behavior, crying easily, constantly hanging
onto mother's skirts, trying to get at her breast, and becoming
very distressed if she left for even a minute. None had
recovered from this phase of anxious attachment by the time
the study ended from 5 to 11 weeks later.

Weaning took place substantially earlier among the four
American breast-fed babies--at 18, 20, 28, and 35 weeks
respectively--with the bottle being substituted for the breast.
(Both Ganda and Baltimore babies had a substantial proportion
of their nourishment from "solid" foods before weaning.) None
of these four Baltimore babies were disturbed by weaning, not
even the one fed on demand for comfort. This baby "weaned
herself" at 35 weeks, showing a decided preference for finger
food and for her older brother's bottle, which was left handy
for him if he wished it and which was also easily accessible
to her.

Although the numbers of infants are too few to support
statistical comparisons, emphasis has been given to response
to weaning because it illustrates very well the way in which
cross-cultural comparisons contribute to the resolution of
theoretical issues. The issue here is the role of feeding in
the infant-mother attachment relationship.

Bowlby (1969) and I (e.g., Ainsworth, 1972) have defined
an attachment behavior is one that promotes proximity or
contact. Attachment behaviors (including those that are
present during the first few weeks, which are indifferent as
to figure, and those that emerge later) gradually become
directed toward specific persons, the mother figure and
perhaps a few others. Indeed, I believe that it is through
these behaviors that an infant becomes attached. However,
our hypothesis is that, in accordance with environmental
influences, different babies mediate their attachment through
different organizations of attachment behaviors. Sucking and
rooting are clearly to be characterized as attachment
behaviors because through them even a neonate is active in
gaining and maintaining contact with his mother figure,
particularly a breast-feeding mother. For an attachment to

be formed, however, not all attachment behaviors need be involved. Thus, for example, Harlow's work (e.g., 1958) showed that infant rhesus monkeys became attached to a terry-cloth surrogate mother figure despite the fact that she yielded no milk and provided no appropriate "aliment" for the "sucking schema", to use Piaget's (1936, 1952) terminology. Nevertheless, there is a long tradition, partly popular and partly psychoanalytic, that infants become attached to the figure that feeds them *because* she feeds them. Many psycho-analysts have referred to weaning as the first major trauma that a young child experiences. Furthermore, an ethological and evolutionary conception suggests that in mammalian species it would be of survival advantage for an infant to gain and to maintain contact with his lactating mother. How is the paradox presented by these conflicting pieces of evidence and opinion to be resolved?

My hypothesis, resting largely on the comparison of Ganda infants who were breast-fed on demand and for comfort with the rest of the Ganda sample on one hand and with the American sample on the other, is as follows. Under circumstances in which an infant through his own active attachment behavior, including sucking and rooting and also reaching, grasping, and approaching, can gain contact with an actual or potential attachment figure who is also his food source, his feeding behaviors become an integral part of the organization of his attachment relationship. The circumstances under which this integration is possible are: (1) when the baby is fed contingent on his own behavior, including both his signaling behavior and his more active contact-seeking behavior, as in thoroughgoing demand feeding; (2) when the baby is breast-fed, so that the food-providing source and the attachment figure are one and the same; and (3) when weaning is deferred until after an attachment has already been established. Under these circumstances, feeding behavior is so enmeshed in the organization of the attachment relationship that weaning may threaten the whole relationship. Indeed, the four younger, demand-fed, Ganda infants responded to weaning in the same way that young children respond to their mothers after a major separation experience. Attachment behaviors are greatly heightened, and the set goal that monitors proximity has been newly set for closer proximity, so that the child is now distressed whenever his mother is absent or indeed when he is not in actual contact with her, and seems constantly anxious lest he lose her altogether. If, however, weaning is deferred until the child is two or three years old (unless it is carried out suddenly and traumatically, as Albino & Thompson [1956] described for the Zulu) it may coincide well enough with a child's increasing capabilities for and interest in self-reliant behavior that it does not shake the child's confidence in his mother's accessibility or threaten his attachment relationship. This seemed to be the case for the Ganda boy finally weaned at 22 months, although even he was very anxious during the gradual weaning process.

If a baby is bottle-fed, or if feeding is not contingent on his own behavior--as in the case of infants who are either schedule-fed or more arbitrarily fed--then feeding behavior splinters off, as it were, from the other package of attachment behaviors and does not become integrated into the attachment relationship. Under these circumstances, weaning does not threaten the attachment relationship. Sucking behavior may become linked with a nonnutritive source such as a pacifier or a thumb, or feeding behavior may become linked with a bottle or with food that a baby can manage for himself. In either case, both sucking and other feeding behavior become detached from the main cluster of attachment behaviors, and thus so indifferent to the attachment relationship that frustrations, however disturbing in themselves, do not threaten the integrity of the attachment relationship. This is my hypothesis, and the confirmation thereof probably rests on further cross-cultural studies, with samples including larger numbers of breast-fed babies, fed on demand, and not weaned until 12 months or later (i.e., after the attachment has become well-established), compared with samples of bottle-fed, schedule-fed, and/or early-weaned infants.

Availability of the Mother

The Ganda, even traditionally, lacked extended households. In all the families we visited, it was the mother who was primarily responsible for the infant's care. On the other hand, only eight babies lived in households in which parents were the only adults, and none lived alone with their mothers without at least another child in the household. The typical Ganda village mother must work in her garden for a certain portion of the day, a period usually occupying only the morning hours. If she has someone with whom to leave the baby while she works, she leaves him behind. Five mothers had no "baby-sitter" and so took the baby along to the garden. Four of these babies were laid on a mat in the shade, and only one was slung on his mother's back while she worked.

A 7-point scale was devised for rating the amount of care given by the mother to the baby. The modal rating of 4--"The mother is chiefly responsible for the care of the baby but leaves him for relatively short periods while she works in the garden; to some extent she shares mothering duties with others"--was obtained by 10 mothers. This scale distinguished at the 5 percent level of significance, according to a median test, among three groups of infants--secure-attached, insecure-attached, and not-yet-attached.

Both the secure- and insecure-attached groups showed a variety of attachment behaviors that, in sum, were considered to indicate that an attachment had been formed to the mother as a specific figure. These two groups were distinguished from each other on the basis of crying frequency, with the secure group crying substantially less. (These classifications were made on the basis of preweaning behavior, and hence do not take into account the postweaning period in which even some infants who had previously been securely attached became quite anxious.) The not-yet-attached group included four infants, aged respectively 8 1/2, 8 1/2, 11, and 12 months. (One 4-month-old was not included in the comparison.) Despite having passed the age at which other Ganda infants showed clear signs of attachment, these did not even show attachment behavior differentially directed toward their mother.

No mother of the not-yet-attached group received ratings higher than 2 with respect to amount of care. These babies were left regularly by their mothers for long periods of time and were given relatively little care by her even when she was available to give it. Although the secure-attached group tended to receive more care from the mother than the insecure-attached group, there was considerable overlap between them, which suggests that other variables besides sheer amount of mother's care influence the degree of security of the infant-mother relationship.

One of the several variables that were examined was total amount of care. It might be hypothesized that care from other figures would compensate for relative lack of care by the mother. A 7-point scale was devised for rating total amount of care given by all adults and children who shared mothering duties, including the mother. The top rating of 7 was given in 10 cases in which the baby was given much "mothering" and was alone only when asleep. There was one baby whose total amount of care seemed to compensate for her mother's long absences; this securely-attached baby received a rating of 3 for mother's care, but 7 for total care. Total amount of care did not, however, discriminate significantly among the groups, despite the fact that the not-yet-attached infants all received ratings of 2 in total care. Although they received some mothering beyond minimum routine requirements, they were left alone for much of the time, even when they were awake. Two of these mothers had been impressed with the convenience of European methods and left their babies in a crib in a bedroom nearly all the time, and one mother of twins kept them for most of the time outside in a baby carriage. In short, although most Ganda infants had one or more care-givers in addition to the mother, the total amount of care received from all of them seemed less important than the amount of care received from the mother in determining secure attachment formation.

I do not mean to imply that the supplementary care given by other caregivers in the mother's absence is unimportant. Nor am I suggesting that a baby becomes attached only to his mother if he becomes attached at all. Indeed, these Ganda babies became attached to one or a few other figures at about the same time they became attached to their mothers. Although most of these other figures were caregivers, in some cases they were fathers or older children who merely interacted with the baby and were not responsible for his routine care.

In our Baltimore sample, only one household included an adult other than the parents--the maternal grandmother--and she was present only for part of the baby's first year. Two had 5-day-a-week housekeepers who helped care for the baby. Only one mother had a full-time job for most of the baby's first year, and a second began full-time work when the baby was 11 months old. Three others had part-time work for brief periods of the baby's first year, and a fourth was so occupied helping her husband in his work that she had the equivalent of an outside job. Thus most of the sample were cared for exclusively by the mother at least during the day. In comparison with the Ganda women, nearly all of whom worked in their gardens at least throughout the mornings, relatively few of the American mothers had work outside the home.

On the other hand, the American babies were left alone even when awake to a much greater extent than were the Ganda infants, except for the not-yet-attached Ganda infants, who were ignored perhaps even more than the most ignored American babies. All the American infants became clearly attached to their mothers, even those whose mothers were least available to them. The two who had care from housekeepers seemed to become attached to them, although in each case the mother was demonstrably the preferred attachment figure. An attempt was made to assess the availability of the mother and of all caregivers together by means of two 9-point rating scales, but the much more detailed observational data obtained for the

American sample made it clear that there were wide individual differences in the mothers' psychological accessibility to the infant when she was at home that had to be taken into account, in addition to the proportion of time that she was physically present. Indeed, attention turned to dimensions of maternal behavior altogether more subtle than those that had been used in the analysis of the Ganda data, of which perhaps the most important were several measures of maternal sensitivity and responsivenesss to infant signals.

Maternal Sensitivity to Infant Signals

In the case of the Ganda, it was possible only indirectly to assess maternal sensitivity to infant signals. This was done by a 7-point rating scale devised to measure the mother's excellence as an informant. The top rating of 7 was obtained by eight mothers who were identified as excellent informants, who volunteered information and gave much spontaneous detail about their babies. My inference was that they were sensitively perceptive of the signal value of the infant's behavior, whereas mothers who were poor informants were not so much uncooperative with me as imperceptive of the nuances of infant behavior. This scale distinguished at the 5 percent level of significance among secure-attached, insecure-attached, and not-yet-attached groups.

In the analysis of the American data, there were two kinds of maternal measures directly pertinent to sensitivity and responsiveness to infant signals. The first were derived from coding maternal responsiveness to infant crying signals; the second were rating scales dealing with various aspects of sensitivity to infant signals generally.

Infant Crying and Maternal Responsiveness.   Each episode of infant crying observed during a visit was coded. For each quarter of the first year, two measures of infant crying were derived from this coding: (1) the mean frequency of crying episodes per waking hour, and   (2) the mean duration of crying in minutes per waking hour. Two measures of maternal unresponsiveness to infant crying were also derived from this coding: (1) the mean number of episodes per hour altogether ignored by the mother, and   (2) the mean duration of maternal unresponsiveness to crying in minutes per hour.

Silvia Bell and I (Bell & Ainsworth, 1972) addressed ourselves to the question of the existence of a cause-and-effect relationship between degree of maternal responsiveness to crying and amount of infant crying. We found no stability

in infant crying until the second half of the first year.
Babies who cried much at the beginning were not necessarily
those who cried conspicuously much at the end of the first
year. There was, however, a significant degree of stability
in maternal unresponsiveness to crying throughout the infant's
first year, so that mothers who were unresponsive to crying
at the beginning tended to continue to be so. Within the
first quarter-year the amount of infant crying and degree of
maternal responsiveness were quite uncorrelated. But within
each of the second, third, and fourth quarters, mothers who
were relatively unresponsive had infants who cried relatively
much. Significant correlations were found between maternal
unresponsiveness in one quarter and infant crying in the
subsequent quarter; indeed, for the duration measure, maternal
unresponsiveness in any one quarter was significantly correlated
with amount of infant crying in all subsequent quarters, except
that the correlation fell somewhat below a 5 percent level of
significance between maternal behavior in the first quarter
and infant crying in the fourth. On the other hand, until the
second half of the first year there was no consistent tendency
for amount of infant crying in one quarter to be correlated
with maternal unresponsiveness in subsequent quarters.

From the comparison of maternal and infant behaviors in
regard to stability and the cross-quarter correlations, Bell
and Ainsworth concluded: (1) the effect of maternal behavior
on infant behavior is greater than the effect of infant
behavior on maternal behavior (at least in regard to crying);
(2) maternal responsiveness to crying tends to reduce the
tendency of a baby to cry in later months; and (3) babies who
cry relatively much by the second half of the first year have
had a history of maternal unresponsiveness to crying in
earlier months. It takes about three months for this effect
to become established; tiny babies do not respond immediately
to maternal ignoring and delay by crying even more. By the
second half of the first year, however, an infant's persistence
in crying seems to affect his mother's behavior, suggesting
the establishment of a vicious spiral--mothers who are
unresponsive to the crying of a tiny infant have babies who
cry more later on, which in turn further discourages the mother
from responding and results in a further relative increase in
infant crying. For mothers who are responsive, of course, a
"virtuous spiral" is established.

General Sensitivity to Infant Signals. Silvia Bell and I
(Bell & Ainsworth, 1972) also presented evidence that infant
crying in the fourth quarter of the first year was no longer
exclusively an expressive signal, but at least sometimes a mode

of communication directed specifically to the mother.   In
addition, babies who possessed relatively varied, subtle, and
clear modes of noncrying communication tended to cry relatively
little, and to have mothers who were relatively responsive to
crying signals. Since we had also found that mothers who are
responsive to crying signals tend to be responsive to all kinds
of infant signals, we concluded that it is this general
sensitivity to signals that tends to foster the development
of infant communication.

It was not possible, however, to code infant noncrying
signals in the same way that crying had been coded, if only
because the entire behavioral repertoire of the infant has
signal value to a sensitively perceptive mother. Instead,
the assessment of general sensitivity or insensitivity to
infant signals was tackled by means of a 9-point rating scale,
with detailed behavioral definition of five anchor-points 1,
3, 5, 7, and 9. This scale defined sensitivity to signals in
terms of four processes. The highly sensitive mother   (1)
received the baby's signals,   (2) interpreted them accurately
and without distortion,   (3) responded to them promptly, and
(4) responded to them appropriately. The highly insensitive
mother tended to be unresponsive to signals either because she
was too preoccupied or defended to perceive them, or because
she chose not to respond.

Significant correlations between other measures derived
from detailed behavioral coding of maternal behavior gave
evidence of the validity of the sensitivity-insensitivity
ratings. Thus mothers who were sensitive to signals tended
neither to ignore crying episodes (-.41) not to be slow to
respond to crying (-.58) nor to be ineffective in their
intervention to infant cries (-.42); they tended to
acknowledge the baby in "enter-room" episodes (.60), to pick
up the baby relatively frequently merely to show him affection
(.62), but not to pick him up interferingly (-.51) or
frequently but briefly (-.50); and they tended infrequently
to intervene physically to control the baby's activity (-.44).
Maternal sensitivity-insensitivity to infant signals was also
significantly correlated with a number of measures derived
from detailed codings of infant behavior. Positively related
were: positive response to being held (.71), positive
greeting to the mother entering the room (.50), positive
response to being put down (.43), and incidence of following
the mother when she leaves the room (.40). Negatively related
were: duration of crying (-.63), negative response to being
held (-.53), and crying when mother leaves the room (-.40).

In short, maternal sensitivity-insensitivity to infant signals appears to be related to a variety of maternal behaviors and infant-care practices, including sensitivity to infant signals relevant to the feeding as described earlier. It is also related significantly to a variety of infant behaviors that suggest a security-insecurity dimension in the infant's relationship with his mother.

Security-Insecurity in the Infant-Mother Attachment Relationship. In the American sample, assessment of the quality of the infant-mother attachment relationship was approached in two ways. One type of assessment was based on infant behavior in a controlled, laboratory "strange situation" at the end of the first year (Ainsworth, Bell & Stayton, 1971). Space is insufficient here for a description of this technique. Suffice it to say that an infant's strange-situation behavior was found to be closely related to his behavior in the home environment. The other approach was a multiple factor analysis of measures derived from detailed codings of fourth-quarter infant behavior (Stayton & Ainsworth, 1973). Here we shall report the loading of the various measures on only the first factor, which was identified as reflecting an insecurity-security dimension of the attachment relationship.

The behavior with the highest loading on the insecurity-security factor was crying when the mother leaves the room (.875). Other behavioral variables with high positive loadings were frequency of crying episodes (.733), duration of crying (.719), and crying when the mother enters the room (.661). Also positively loaded, but less conspicuously so, was a negative response to being put down after having been held (.379). Behavioral variables with negative loadings on this factor, and thus related to the secure rather than to the insecure end of the dimension, were positive greetings to the mother when she entered a room (-.593), positive response to being held (-.344), and positive response to being put down (-.534).

Since infant behaviors toward the insecure pole were significantly and positively related to measures of maternal unresponsiveness to crying and negatively related to ratings of maternal sensitivity to infant signals, Donelda Stayton and I suggested that the extent to which a baby's attachment relationship with his mother is of secure or insecure and anxious quality depends largely on the extent to which the mother in earlier months has been sensitive and responsive to the baby's signals.

Thus a detailed analysis of the data from the Baltimore sample offers substantial support to the hypothesis stemming from the Ganda data, namely that behind the relationship between quality of attachment and amount of mother's care lay other maternal variables, including perceptive responsiveness to the infant, and that frequency and intensity of crying when mother left the room was related to a security-insecurity dimension of the attachment relationship rather than to its strength. Furthermore, these findings are congruent with the implications of the findings stemming from an analysis of infant-mother interaction in feeding, reported earlier.

Physical Contact

A direct comparison between the Ganda and American samples in regard to physical contact was impossible because of differences in the conditions of observation. It will be recalled that home visits to the Ganda were made during leisure hours in the afternoon, whereas visits to the Baltimore babies were made at varying times of the day, during which the mother pursued her usual routines. Nevertheless, I am under the clear impression that Ganda infants, especially in the early months, experience much more physical contact than do American middle-class infants.

Inquiries were made of Ganda mothers about how much they held their babies. Of 27 informants, 17 replied "much", 4 "some", and 6 "little". Four of those who replied "little" had babies who were not yet attached. The other two, whose babies were judged to be securely attached, were observed to hold the baby and interact with him much, to belie their reports that the baby was held little. On the other hand, two mothers who reported that they held the baby "much" were observed to hold him little during visits, and from other interview information could be inferred to hold him relatively little. One had an insecure-attached baby and the other one not yet attached. I was inclined to trust observation more than interview, despite the fact that our visits yielded inadequate sampling of the infant's day. According to observations, secure-attached babies tended to be held much, not-yet-attached babies little, while amount of maternal holding varied in the insecure-attached group.

Excluding the four not-yet-attached babies who were usually confined to cribs or baby carriages, the babies in the Ganda sample who were as yet unable to sit alone were invariably held by someone, not necessarily the mother, throughout the two-hour visits except for portions thereof when they were asleep. If a baby fell asleep while being held, however, he was not necessarily put down. Babies who were able to sit spent at least part of the visit sitting near the mother, rather than on someone's lap. Those who were capable of locomotion spent most of the visit on the floor, and were able on their own initiative to explore, to play with any other infants who were present, or to approach and perhaps seek contact with anyone. Almost invariably the figure with whom a mobile infant spontaneously sought contact was the mother. It was easy for a Ganda infant to clamber up on his mother's lap, as she sat on the floor. It was extremely rare for a mother, or any other adult, to reject the contact-making advances of an infant under these circumstances.

The play-by-play records of behavior of the babies in the Baltimore sample made it possible to calculate how much time a baby spent in contact with each figure present during the visit. During the first-quarter visits the average mother held her baby for 21 minutes per waking hour, but this diminished to 5.8 minutes in the fourth quarter. The decrease was almost entirely accounted for by a reduction in holding for feeding. Whereas nearly all Ganda infants were free to move about on the floor when not being held, this was not the case for most of the American sample, who were frequently confined to cribs, infant seats, jump chairs, highchairs, or playpens when they were neither asleep nor being held.

Because physical contact was so ubiquitous among Ganda infants not yet capable of locomotion (except for the four kept in crib or baby carriage), no effort was made to relate amount or quality of physical contact with infant behavioral variables. For the American infants, however, an analysis was undertaken--complete as yet for only first- and fourth-quarter behavior--of the relationships between maternal and infant behaviors relevant to physical contact (Ainsworth, Bell, & Stayton, 1972). Intercorrelations among maternal behaviors themselves suggest two major clusterings. First, the mother who holds her baby for a relatively long time each time she picks him up, especially when she picks him up for nonroutine purposes, tends not to pick him up frequently. A relatively large proportion of her holding time is characterized by tender and careful holding. Infant behaviors associated with this pattern, both within quarter and when first-quarter maternal behavior is correlated with fourth-quarter infant behavior, are to respond positively to being held and yet, even in the first quarter, to respond positively to being put down. In the fourth quarter, babies who responded cheerfully to being put down moved off, in about half the "put-down" episodes, into independent exploratory activity. A second clustering implies that mothers who pick up their babies relatively frequently tend to hold them for relatively short periods, especially for nonroutine purposes. These mothers tended to pick their babies up in an abrupt and interfering manner and to hold them ineptly or even inadequately. Infant behaviors associated with this pattern are negative response to being held, negative response to being put down, and, in the fourth quarter, active initiation of being put down.

It thus appears that relatively much physical contact, holding of tender and careful quality, and pick-ups solely to give affection do not tend to addict a baby to physical contact or to "spoil" him. On the contrary, a baby who has experienced "good" contact tends by the end of the first year to be able to move away from his mother to explore his world, whereas a baby who has had more conflicted experiences of contact tends to be ambivalent about it--often negative while in conflict, perhaps squirming to be put down, but then often immediately protesting or seeking to be picked up again. These findings are generally congruent with my impressions of Ganda mother-infant interaction.

Sensorimotor Development

In the Baltimore project, the Griffiths' infant intelligence scale was administered at intervals. Although test equipment had been ordered for use in the Ganda study, it did not arrive in time, and I therefore had to rely on observation of relatively crude milestones of development-- such as achievement of sitting, crawling, and walking. After my fieldwork had been completed, some of the Ganda sample were tested by Dr. Marcelle Geber, who used the Gesell Infant Schedules.

Locomotor milestones were achieved by nearly all of the Ganda sample substantially in advance of the Griffiths' norms, and my impression was that language development was also accelerated. Fourteen infants of the sample were tested by Geber--all whose mothers could be induced to cooperate. Eleven received developmental scores above 100. Of the other three, one two-year-old was very negativistic to the testing, although he had seemed accelerated during my period of observations, and two showed acute stranger anxiety. These latter two tested above 100 a year later. In all, Geber (1960) tested 252 Ganda infants, and found them accelerated during the first year especially. For example, of those tested between 6 and 9 months of age, 95 percent received developmental scores

above 100. Although locomotor development was most
accelerated, thus confirming my impression, Geber found all
aspects of development represented in the Gesell schedules
to be precocious.

I attributed this acceleration in sensorimotor development to three main features of Ganda infant-care practices,
and, in general, Geber and Dean (1957) offered a similar
explanation. I suggested that the fact that Ganda infants
were held so much during the first few months of life required
much postural adjustment, which in turn strenthened neck and
trunk musculature, thus facilitating locomotor development.
To this I now would add the likelihood that the vestibular
stimulation implicit in being brought to and maintained in an
upright position facilitated a state of alert inactivity
conducive to visual exploration of the environment (Korner
& Thoman, 1970). Second, the extensive floor freedom
experienced by the typical Ganda infant as soon as he acquires
locomotion is likely to encourage exploratory activities of
all kinds. Third, the fact that the baby is nearly always
with people, and often in the midst of a socially interactive
group, provides him with substantially more interpersonal
interaction than the average American infant experiences, and
this also is likely to facilitate sensorimotor as well as
social development.

The infants in my middle-class American sample tended also
to be accelerated in their sensorimotor development, as
reflected by the fact that all but two regularly obtained
quotients exceeding 100 in the course of their several testings.
The results of the Ganda and Baltimore testings are not
strictly comparable, however. Different instruments were used.
Only half the babies of the Ganda sample were tested, and then
only once, at least while they were infants. Furthermore, the
American infants were tested by the observer, who became a
somewhat familiar person over the course of a year, while the
Ganda infants were tested by a complete stranger. There is no
doubt, however, that Ganda locomotor development was much more
accelerated than that of the Baltimore infants, whereas
perhaps the other lines of sensorimotor development were
roughly similar in their degree of acceleration.

In the American sample, Silvia Bell and I attempted to
identify those features of infant care that were most highly
correlated with DQ (Developmental Quotient) in the fourth
quarter of the first year (Ainsworth & Bell, 1974). Of seven
measures so far found to correlate with DQ, two had
correlation coefficients as high as .56--maternal sensitivity

to infant signals and the amount of floor freedom permitted
the baby by his mother--although the two were entirely
uncorrelated with each other. The multiple correlation
coefficient of these two variables with DQ was, however, .63.
Adding other measures of maternal behavior to the multiple
correlation further raised it to .70. These findings provide
some confirmation to the hypotheses suggested by the Ganda
study of ways in which infant-care practices and mother-infant
interaction may facilitate sensorimotor development. In
addition, that the level of DQ is enhanced by maternal
sensitivity to signals suggests that an infant's development
is facilitated by having his behavior responded to contingently.

Separation Protest and Fear of Strangers

There is no substantial difference between the Ganda and
Baltimore samples in regard to either a catalogue of attachment
behaviors or the order in which they emerge. Nevertheless,
differences appeared in two behaviors linked to attachment--
separation protest and fear of strangers--and these differences
seem attributable to differences in experience for infants of
the two cultures.

Age of onset of separation protest was essentially the
same. Ganda babies typically began to cry when the mother
left the room at about 20 to 24 weeks of age, while the
American babies showed the onset of this behavior at a median
age of 22 weeks (Stayton, Ainsworth, & Main, 1973). It was in
frequency of separation protest that the two samples appeared
to differ. The Baltimore infants cried, on the average, in
only about one quarter of "mother-left-room" episodes in the
last half of the first year, whereas it is my impression that
the average Ganda infant cried more consistently than that.
Both Ganda and Baltimore infants were more likely to cry when
left alone than when left in company, and, once mobile, they
were more likely to follow than to cry if they were on the
floor and free to follow when the mother left.

As reported earlier, frequency of crying when mother left
the room is associated, in the Baltimore sample, with the
insecure end of an insecurity-security continuum, although all
infants displayed this behavior at one time or another, of
course. Among the Ganda also, more consistent separation
protest seemed characteristic of the insecure-attached rather
than of the secure-attached group. Indeed, the fact that
some of the secure-attached group rarely protested minor,
everyday, separation situations convinced me that separation
protest was an unsatisfactory single criterion of attachment

and prompted me to examine other attachment behaviors that
might serve as alternative criteria. Furthermore, my
interpretation that the weaning disturbance manifested by
comfort-fed infants was essentially anxiety about maternal
accessibility and responsiveness after the breast was withheld was largely supported by the great intensification of
separation protest occurring in the postweaning period.

Nevertheless, intense separation protest was indeed more
frequent, even before weaning, in the Ganda than in the
American sample, despite the fact that the proportion of
securely-attached babies seemed perhaps larger in the Ganda
sample. In my judgment, this is attributable to two major
factors. First, the American babies had more experience with
frequent maternal goings and comings than had Ganda infants.[2]
During our visits, American mothers left the room 3.4 times
per hour, on the average, whereas Ganda mothers were unlikely
to leave as often as once per hour. The typical mother in
the American sample left her baby for fairly long periods in
one place, often enough confined, and came in and out
frequently in the course of her household activities. In
contrast, the Ganda mother, when she left her baby to work
in her garden, left him for a period of three or four hours
or more. When she was at home, she tended either to stay put
or to take the baby with her. Thus the securely-attached
American infant presumably developed expectations that when
his mother left him, say, to go to the kitchen or even upstairs,
she would return soon, and perhaps the baby learned also that
she would be readily summoned if he needed her. Secure in
such expectations, her many brief departures in the familiar
environment of the home came to activate protest infrequently.
In contrast, even the securely-attached Ganda infant built up
expectations that his mother's departure signified a longer
absence during which his mother was inaccessible to his
signals, so that even when left in the familiar home environment with familiar caregivers her departure tended to activate
protest, unless the baby were able to follow his mother when
she left. In short, it seems that separation protest is much

---

[2]
In the American sample, frequency of mother's leaving the
room was found not to be significantly correlated with
frequency of infant separation protest. Nevertheless, the
difference between the Ganda and American samples is so
substantial in regard to both frequency of leaving and
duration of daily absence that this conclusion seems a
plausible one to me.

influenced by an infant's confidence in his mother's
accessibility, and the expectations that constitute that
confidence are influenced by real-life experiences.

Since alarm is known to activate attachment behavior
as well as fear behavior, another possible influence making
separation protest more conspicuous in the Ganda sample is
that the infants were more alarmed by the presence of the
visitors as strangers than were the Baltimore infants. For
the Ganda sample, then, the mother's becoming inaccessible
by departing probably compounded the fear already activated
by the stranger to intensify separation protest (Bowlby,
1973). During the last quarter of the first year, Ganda
infants who had earlier seemed merely reserved with my
interpreter and me began to show a more marked constraint
or overt avoidance, despite the fact that by then we were
not total strangers. Infants whom we *began* to visit at the
same age, however, and to whom we were indeed strangers,
tended to manifest intense anxiety by clinging tightly and
persistently to their mothers, looking or turning away if
our eyes met even momentarily, and screaming desperately if
the mother attempted to give him to either of us to hold.
After such experiences with Ganda babies, it was a surprise
to me that the babies of the American sample rarely showed
more than temporary wariness of the visitor, and almost never
the intense fear reaction displayed by some of the Ganda
babies. Even when encountering a total stranger in a
strange situation, few of the 106 Baltimore one-year-olds
that we have observed showed clear-cut fear (Bretherton &
Ainsworth, 1974).

To me, the most reasonable explanation is that the two
samples differed in the extent of their general experience
with strangers and that infants living in Ganda villages fear
strangers because they have little experience with any people
except their own families, immediate neighbors, and visiting
relatives. Konner (1972) reported that Zhuñ/twa infants not
only were intensely afraid of strangers and extremely slow to
accept them, even over a period of weeks, but seemed equally
fearful of white- and of black-skinned strangers. Certainly
these Bushmen rarely encounter people other than those of
their own tightly knit group. The babies in the American
sample, on the other hand, were early taken, and relatively
frequently, to supermarkets and other places where they
encountered unfamiliar people in great variety, under
circumstances of proximity and often interaction and even
contact.

Let us return, however, to the link between separation protest and fear of strangers that was suggested earlier. It is my hypothesis that a baby is more likely to be afraid of strangers not only if he has had less experience than others with this class of people, or if his previous experience with strangers (or a stranger) has been painful, but also if he has more anxiety than others about his mother's accessibility and responsiveness--that is, if his attachment relationship is insecure. There is some support for this hypothesis from my American data, particularly regarding responses to a stranger in a strange situation. The Ganda sample, however, provides the most convincing cases. The four babies who were weaned at about a year of age after having been breast-fed on demand and were thrown into anxiety about their mother's accessibility and responsiveness suddenly showed a remarkable increase of intensity in their fear of strangers. These few cases were so striking that they led me to a strong hypothesis that there is a link between separation anxiety and fear of strangers, despite the fact that I do not agree with Spitz (1965), who postulated that fear of strangers is generally reducible to fear of loss of the mother and that the onset of stranger anxiety is *the* indication that attachment ("true object relations") has been formed.

SUMMARY AND DISCUSSION

In any given population, rearing variables that possibly influence infant development are frequently interlocked to such an extent that analytic efforts cannot tease them apart. Since the variables that tend to appear together in one society may appear in different constellations in another, cultural comparisons provide an opportunity to assess the independent influence on development of different infant- and child-rearing practices. If, in addition to a comparison of central tendencies, the analysis of variables in each of two societies includes an analysis of individual differences within each, the comparisons are likely to be especially productive.

Although an ideal study would use identical methods with both or all societies being compared, this ideal is perhaps both unrealistic and in some instances mistaken, if, for example, techniques and methods developed in observing one society provide a distorting filter for viewing and assessing practices in another. Both the Ganda and the Baltimore studies were undertaken at a time when the scientific study of social development in infancy had scarcely begun, and refined techniques of observation and assessment were lacking. The Ganda study was essentially descriptive, and the few efforts to classify and quantify data in order to discover the relationships between mother and infant variables were necessarily crude. Nevertheless, the findings and hypotheses emerging from the Ganda study were very helpful when dealing with the infinitely more intensive and hence more complex data of the American sample.

Before summarizing these findings and hypotheses, I should like to comment upon the methodology that was common to the studies of both societies.   In both I used naturalistic observation in the child's home environment, and I strongly urge this procedure for comparative cultural studies. No matter what other supplementary procedures are employed to assess infant development, the essence of comparison is to examine any differences that are apparent in infant development as they may be related to cultural differences in methods of infant care, maternal behavior, and the like. It is my belief that the best way of assessing these "background" variables is to observe them directly, rather than relying entirely on interview procedures.

When beginning the Ganda study, I certainly had given thought to the various maternal and infant behaviors that I wished to study. Nevertheless, there had been so little pertinent previous research that I did not wish to limit my observation by setting up a checklist of behaviors that would be observed on a time-sampling basis. I was afraid I would thereby miss behavioral phenomena that had not occurred to me in advance. Furthermore, I felt that the rigid kind of "spectator" observing that the checklist and time-sample method would impose might undermine the bases of cooperation that I had managed to establish with the Ganda families--which at first was tenuous at best. By the time I began my American study, I had accumulated such a complex list of infant and maternal behaviors to observe that a continuous, coherent narrative account seemed clearly superior to what could be derived from a checklist. Any checklist comprehensive enough to include all that I hoped to observe would be totally impractical. Furthermore, I had learned so much from the Ganda study beyond my initial hypotheses, expectations, and points of interest that I did not wish to limit myself to a number--even perhaps an extensive number--of a priori foci of observation.

The disadvantages of the naturalistic narrative account are substantial. Data analysis is extremely time consuming, both because one must first identify the behavioral variables one wishes to highlight and because it is extremely laborious to process the data in order to yield quantitative data. The advantages of the checklist, time-sample methodology are that quantitative processing of the data is relatively fast, and, furthermore, in comparative studies, there is a common, objective basis of comparison. Caudill and Weinstein (1969) used this method to very good effect, although it must be pointed out that Caudill had intimate knowledge of both the Japanese and the American cultures that he was comparing and used this skillfully in interpreting the findings of the quantitative comparison. I maintain, nevertheless, that the checklist method of observing confines one to preconceived variables, and leaves little possibility of discovering new and important behavioral variables or relationships between these and the variables one had set out to observe. Similar limitations pertain to standardized tests and to controlled laboratory situations, valuable though these may be as supplements to naturalistic observation and narrative recording.

Let us remind ourselves at this point that the scientific value of cultural comparisons of infant and child development is that different societies may have different constellations of rearing conditions that provide something akin to the "experiment of opportunity". Without undue or unethical meddling, one hopes to be able to assess the effects of different environmental influences on development as they naturally occur in different societal contexts. Let us not blind ourselves to the unusual features of the unfamiliar society by limiting ourselves to variables or to procedures based on the familiar society--our own.

Nevertheless, I wish that, after having completed the analysis of our American sample, the methods therein devised could be applied in a second study of Ganda infant-mother pairs--just as the observation and analysis of the American sample had been originally influenced by the Ganda study. Since this is impractical, however, I must be content with the returns of an incomplete comparison, and with the fact that some of the yield of this comparison is in the form of hypotheses and pointers for future research rather than definitive conclusions.

First, in regard to feeding and weaning practices, the within-Ganda analysis, as well as the Ganda-American comparison, has led to an important hypothesis about the role of feeding behavior in the formation of the infant-mother attachment relationship. Furthermore, both analyses have thrown new

light on "demand" feeding, cast doubt on earlier studies that
concluded that variations in feeding practices had no effect
on development, and strongly suggest the desirability of
further and more intensive research into the effects of
demand- versus scheduled-feeding.

A within-sample Ganda analysis pointed toward the
significance of a security-insecurity dimension of the infant-
mother attachment relationship and its link to both maternal
availability and maternal sensitivity to infant behavior. A
within-sample American analysis confirmed the security-
insecurity dimension and also led to a refinement of our
understanding of maternal availability. The American study
emphasized responsiveness to crying signals specifically and
sensitivity to infant signals generally, whereas, in the
Ganda sample, main emphasis was given to the relatively crude
variable of amount of time that the mother was physically
accessible. Undoubtedly, both accessibility and responsiveness
are important facets of availability. To assess their
relative influence on infant development is of considerable
importance for an understanding of the effects of a mother
working and/or placing her child in day care. Our current
Ganda-American comparisons are relevant to this problem, but
point to the desirability of further research specifically
directed toward assessing the interaction between these two
interrelated dimensions of maternal care.

In regard to the influence of physical contact on infant
development, comparative data from Ganda and American samples
were not exploited to the full. The modal pattern of much
physical contact in early infancy was so striking in the
Ganda sample that individual differences were not explored.
Within the American sample data analysis is still incomplete,
but enough has emerged to suggest that a relatively large
amount of physical contact of good quality in early infancy
facilitates rather than hinders later development toward
independent exploration and self-reliance--a finding entirely
compatible with the Ganda data and quite contrary to the fear
of many mothers that such treatment "spoils" children.

In both frequency of separation protest and intensity of
fear response to strangers, there were differences between
the typical American and typical Ganda infant. Comparisons
of infant-care practices pointed toward differences possibly
affecting these behaviors, while at the same time being
indifferent to the quality of infant-mother attachment.
Nevertheless, within each sample there remained the likelihood
that both are also linked to the degree of anxiety in the
attachment relationship.

Despite the fact that our assessments of sensorimotor development were confined to the measure offered by standardized tests of global development, the Ganda–American comparisons and the within-sample American analysis pointed to some specific features of infant-rearing conditions that may facilitate cognitive development. Orthogonal variables that seem facilitatory are contingent response by the mother figure to infant signals and freedom to explore. The Ganda study suggests that general opportunity for interpersonal interaction may be a facilitatory variable and that the amount of early physical contact, especially that involving upright holding, may especially facilitate locomotor development. More investigation of these variables and their relationship to various aspects of cognitive development is obviously indicated.

REFERENCES

Ainsworth, M. D. The development of infant-mother interaction among the Ganda. In B. M. Foss (Ed.), Determinants of infant behavior II. New York: Wiley, 1963.

Ainsworth, M. D. S. Infancy in Uganda: Infant care and the growth of love. Baltimore, Md.: Johns Hopkins University Press, 1967.

Ainsworth, M. D. S. Attachment and dependency: A comparison. In J. L. Gewirtz (Ed.), Attachment and dependency. Washington, D.C.: Winston, 1972.

Ainsworth, M. D. S., & Bell, S. M. Some contemporary patterns of mother-infant interaction in the feeding situation. In A. Ambrose (Ed.), Stimulation in early infancy. London: Academic Press, 1969.

Ainsworth, M. D. S., & Bell, S. M. Mother-infant interaction and the development of competence. In K. J. Connolly and J. S. Bruner (Eds.), The growth of competence. New York: Academic Press, 1974.

Ainsworth, M. D. S., Bell, S. M., & Stayton, D. J. Individual differences in strange-situation behavior of one-year-olds. In H. R. Schaffer (Ed.), The origins of human social relations. London: Academic Press, 1971.

Albino, R. C., & Thompson, V. J. The effects of sudden
    weaning of Zulu children. British Journal of
    Medical Psychology, 1956, 29, 177-210.

Bowlby, J. Maternal care and mental health (2nd ed. Monograph
    Series, No. 2). Geneva: World Health Organization,
    1952.

Bowlby, J. Attachment and loss. Vol. 1: Attachment. New
    York: Basic Books, 1969.

Bowlby, J. Attachment and loss. Vol. 2: Separation: Anxiety
    and anger. New York: Basic Books, 1973.

Bretherton, I., & Ainsworth, M. D. S. Responses of one-year-
    olds to a stranger in a strange situation. In M.
    Lewis and L. A. Rosenblaum (Eds.), Origins of human
    behavior. Vol. 2: Fear. New York: Wiley, 1974.

Caudill, W., & Weinstein, H. Maternal care and infant
    behavior in Japan and America. Psychiatry, 1969,
    32, 12-43.

Geber, M. Problems posés par le dévelopment du jeune enfant
    africain en function du son milieu sociale. Le
    Travail Humain, 1960, 23, 97-111.

Geber, M., & Dean, R. F. A. Gesell tests on African children.
    Pediatrics, 1957, 6, 1055-1065.

Harlow, H. F. The nature of love. American Psychologist,
    1958, 13, 673-685.

Konner, M. Aspects of the developmental ethology of a
    foraging people. In N. Blurton Jones (Ed.),
    Ethological studies of child behavior. Cambridge,
    England: Cambridge University Press, 1972.

Korner, A., & Thoman, E. B. Visual alertness in neonates as
    evoked by maternal care. Journal of Experimental
    Child Pshychology, 1970, 10, 7-78.

Piaget, J. The origins of intelligence in children (2nd ed.).
    New York: International Universities Press, 1952.
    Originally published 1936.

Spitz, R. A. The first year of life. New York: International
    Universities Press, 1956.

Stayton, D. J., & Ainsworth, M. D. S.   Individual differences in infant responses to brief, everyday separations as related to other infant and maternal behaviors. Developmental Psychology, 1973, 8, 226–235.

Stayton, D. J., Ainsworth, M. D. S., & Main, M. B.   The development of separation behavior in the first year of life: Protest, following and greeting. Developmental Psychology, 1973, 8, 213–225.

Welbourn, H. F.   Bottle feeding: A problem of modern civilization.   Journal of Tropical Pediatrics, 1958, 3, 157–166.

Chapter 7

Implications of Infant Development Among the Mayan Indians of Mexico

T. Berry Brazelton

The advantages of comparing child-rearing behavior across cultural groups are many: (1) other cultures present the opportunity to look at different modes of interactional behavior, often with a more objective eye than in one's own culture; (2) the variability that other groups present can offer a spectrum of possibilities by which one's own cultural practices can be measured; (3) in a stable culture, the practices have been sifted for generations, and may represent conscious and unconscious efforts of the group to preserve certain characteristics in their children that are necessary to the group's survival; (4) the opportunity to document such experiments of nature and to observe them in their natural settings seems preferable to the disadvantages of setting up experimental manipulations that may create unnatural distortions within the culture and that may perturb interaction patterning in parents. Particularly in a culture that is as unsettled as is our current one for child-rearing in the United States, there is a real danger of influencing young parents in unpredictable directions by suggestion and by their interpretation of the goals of the observer.

I first came to multicultural research in infancy via the study of normal development in a psychoanalytic setting at the Putnam Children's Center in Boston. In an intensive study of each parent before delivery, we were attempting to predict

the effects their personalities would have in shaping the
baby. After a very few new babies, we realized that the
individuality of each baby shaped his environment as powerfully
as his parents shaped him. In other words, the nature-nurture
effect was that of a constantly developing interaction. In
order to assess the relative contribution of the baby to this
interaction, I began to try to assess differences in neonates
at birth and before the environment began to affect them. In
an effort to free myself from my own cultural prejudices, which
contributed to unconscious judgments about "good" or "bad",
"weak" or "strong" behavior on the part of the neonate and his
parents, I turned to multicultural studies. It seemed like a
desirable strategy to select cultures whose customs and child-
rearing practices were stable and whose adults were clear in
their expectations for their offspring.

     At first glance, the issues seem simpler in another
culture; but the complexity in a familiar cultural setting is
not accessible to a naive observer. As understanding of the
new culture increases, the complexity is uncovered, and one
rapidly begins to agree with Levi-Strauss (1966) that
primitive cultures are not simpler except in the eyes of the
beholder. For example, the "observer effect" on them must be
seen as important, since it involves the evil-eye beliefs
that are at the root of their powerful defenses against being
understood and absorbed by others. Also, environmental
variations in nutrition and infection, whose powerful influence
on development are rapidly becoming understood, become major
variables if one is to interpret differences in the children
of other cultures.

     The most basic issue in understanding early development
is that of the relative importance of nature versus nurture.
We are just beginning to understand the dependence that each
has on the other. The formulation *behavioral phenotype =
genotype × environment* may be an acceptable way of recognizing
the interplay of these factors. No longer must we look at
infants as malleable or helpless. Nor is it fair to look at
parents and the environment they provide as if it were entirely
their responsibility. In pediatric practice, I have been
impressed by the power of individual differences in human
infants at birth to shape their mother's reactions to them
(Brazelton, 1963). Although the mother may come to the delivery
with a wide potential for mothering her new infant, the kind of
infant she produces powerfully determines how she reacts to the
baby. This earliest interaction seems to "set" her attitudes
toward her child in ways that are suggestive of the imprinting
of maternal attachment described by Bowlby (1969). So powerful

are the infant's characteristics in setting her attachment behavior that I would like to venture that the behavior of her infant may become the basis for the characteristics that dominate a whole culture. The strength of the culture may be preserved in the kind of infants that it produces.

In an effort to document behavioral differences in neonates, and to see their interactions with child-rearing practices that have been selected over generations in an isolated culture, we are here reporting on our observations of infant development among the Mayan Indians of Southern Mexico (Brazelton, Robey, & Collier, 1969). Neurological-behavioral examinations and unstructured observations of neonates at birth and in the first week of life revealed striking inborn differences between these infants and a control group from our own culture. Developmental testing of Indian infants under one year of age showed minimal differences when compared to United States norms in the sequence and timing of developmental steps. However, the effects of their distinctive child-rearing practices on these infants was demonstrated in subtler ways, i.e., in the development of personality characteristics and imitative learning of expected roles that enabled the child to fit into his environment and to perpetuate the culture of these isolated, "primitive" people.

ZINACANTAN--THE SETTING FOR THE STUDY

The Zinacantecos of highland Chiapas, in Southeastern Mexico, are a culturally distinct tribe of Indians who live in scattered mountain-villages in relative isolation. For twenty years, they have been the subject of intensive anthropological study by the Harvard Chiapas Project, led by Evon Vogt of the Harvard Anthropology Department. Project members, including George Collier, have gathered extensive background information on the society and have developed a fine rapport with its leaders, which enabled us to observe deliveries, examine newborns, and test small infants, despite the pervasive suspicion with which outsiders are viewed (Collier, 1962).

Description of the Zinacantecos

Unlike many aboriginal hunting and gathering groups in the United States whose cultures were destroyed by the encroachment of civilization, the Zinacantecos have remained

successful agriculturalists who have been able to defend themselves from assimilation by dominant Mexican civilization
despite 400 years of close contact with it. Indeed, their
cultural integrity and Indian identity are strong, and non-
conformity leads individuals to unhappy roles outside the
society (Colby & Van Den Bergh, 1961).

The total population of about 8,500 is surrounded by other
Indian tribes with whom, however, there is almost no intermarriage. The typical living unit is headed by an older male
and is made up of his children, and his married sons and their
offspring who live in his house or in adjacent dwellings. Men
of such a unit cooperate in farming and share with each other
the expenses of rituals, sickness, and all the life crises,
while the women of the group prepare its food and clothing.
Ordinarily, then, the immediate family group is much larger
than our own, and the infant in a single household has many to
mother him.

A typical house has one room about twenty feet square, with
a dirt floor, windowless walls of mud or split boards, and a
high, peaked, thatched roof with a smoke hole. Family members
sleep on planks or mats around the periphery of this room,
where cooking is done over the quiet, perpetually burning fire
in the center.

Theirs is not an idle life; men and grown boys are usually
at work in the fields, while older girls and women are busy
with household tasks and care of the young. A child is
expected to assume adult tasks and responsibilities by the
sixth or seventh year, and is given increasingly difficult
chores from infancy (Blanco & Chodorow, 1964).

Zinacanteco artistic expressions are subtle and muted;
their joy in speech, drinking, and complex ritual is a more
important creative outlet than are their handicrafts, which,
although extensive, tend to be prescribed, functional, and
uniform. Unaware of the magnificent achievements of their
Mayan ancestors, they are concerned only with survival and the
present. They make sparse reference to past history in their
folklore and worry little about future unforeseeable events.
Individual self-expression is not a goal, and conformity is
highly valued and respected.

As in many primitive cultures, illness is widespread;
sanitation is nonexistent, and the incidence of gastrointestinal
disorders and parasitism is extremely high. Pneumonia,
tuberculosis, and infectious diseases of childhood are endemic.

Although precise figures do not exist, we estimate that 30 percent of the children die before the age of four, half of these in infancy (Vogt, 1966). Modern medicine is available at free clinics in a nearby Spanish town; nevertheless, the Zinacantecos rely on local shamans or curers to treat most illness, which they believe has its origin in loss of the soul occurring through supernatural causes.

Although Zinacanteco nutrition seemed quite adequate, on the surface, as eggs and meat frequently supplemented the staple bean-and-corn tortilla diet, it became obvious that subclinical malnutrition was fairly widespread. Babies were small, and growth into adulthood seemed stunted, compared to United States averages. The effects of malabsorption of limited protein and chronic, frequent gastrointestinal infection could not be discounted. However, severe malnutrition that might permanently damage the infants' central nervous systems did not seem to be present.

Zinacanteco cultural practices involving infant and child care are remarkably uniform. As in other primitive cultures with extended families, knowledge is passed on by the immediate presence of experienced older family members at the time of birth and thereafter. No special rites or practices are carried out while a woman is pregnant, and no pharmacologic agents are given before or during delivery. The midwife, always present during childbirth, does not employ any particular obstetrical techniques, but supports and encourages the mother in labor (Anscheutz, 1966). Immediately after the birth, elaborate rituals are performed, with the newborn lying naked near the fire. Prayers and incantations by the midwife exhort the gods to bestow on the child all the manly or womanly attributes necessary for success in the Zinacanteco world. The infant is then clothed. A long, heavy skirt extending beyond the feet, which is worn throughout the first year by both sexes, is held in place by a wide belt or cinch wrapped firmly around the abdomen. Then the newborn is wrapped in additional layers of blankets to protect him from "losing parts of his soul". This swaddling acts as a constant suppressant to motor activity (Lipton, Steinschneider, & Richmond, 1965; Bloch, 1966), as well as defending him from outside evil. Infants' faces are covered except during feedings, especially during the first three months, to ward off illness and the effects of the "evil eye".

During the first month after delivery the mother is confined, with the infant held wrapped in her arms or laid supine beside her as she rests. Thereafter, the child is carried in a rebozo on the mother's or another woman's back when not feeding. Siblings often care for infants, carrying them on their backs in imitation of the mother, although rarely playing with them (Blanco & Chodorow, 1964). Indeed, during the first year, they are never propped up to enable them to look around; nor are they talked to or stimulated by eye contact with family members, or put on the floor to explore on their own.

Striking in this culture is the frequent nursing of the infant, facilitated by the dress of adult women--a handwoven blouse, slit deeply under the arms to provide easy access to the breast. Breast-feeding is performed in response to any activity on the part of the infant, rather than to any more direct expression of hunger. A baby is never allowed to cry from hunger.

In general, social and visual stimulation are minimal throughout the first year, while kinesthetic and tactile forms of interaction are maximal.

PROCEDURE

The author, John S. Robey, M.D., both pediatricians and George A. Collier, Ph.D. in Anthropology, carried out the major portion of the study during the summers of 1966-1969. In all the summers, the pediatricians participated for one month each, while the anthropologist and an Indian guide located subjects and interpreted language and cultural practices. The study consisted of three parts, the first focusing on characteristics of the newborn at birth and in the first week of life, using the Brazelton Neonatal Scale (Brazelton, 1973); the second on mother-child interaction in the first nine months, using the Rheingold (1960) evaluation of four-hour samples in the villages; and the third on developmental milestones during the first year, using the Bayley (1961) and Knobloch (Knobloch, Pasamanick, & Sherard, 1966) scales at each month.

We observed deliveries and were allowed to examine a total of five neonates in this first week of life. Although the sample is small, they are the *only* neonates ever observed and documented in this group. Since these observations, seven other babies have been evaluated and they too replicate the behavior we documented in these five tables. The twelve observations of the newborns falls into three categories.

The first category was an unstructured observation period of thirty minutes during which the infant was with his mother. At this time, we recorded spontaneous activity and the neonate's responses to stimuli that occurred naturally (environmental sounds, light changes, handling by the caretakers, and the baby's own internal stimuli). Of particular interest to us was the infant's motor activity and states of consciousness (see Appendix A), e.g., how the infant moved from state to state, the buildup of tension before he nursed, and his mode of falling asleep afterward.[1]

We recorded the quality of his responses--his ability to attend to or modulate his response to a stimulus in these unstructured periods. Nursing and mothering practices were described in detail as we observed them.

A pediatric examination was made on each visit, with special attention given to the infant's maturity, state of nutrition, and hydration. Since our equipment was necessarily limited to a stethescope and tapemeasure, because of the parents' fear of intrusion on the integrity of the infant's soul, a large part of this assessment depended on observation and palpation. No blood sampling was possible without endangering our chances of continuing our study among the Indians.

A neurological-behavioral evaluation was recorded on each infant twice in the first week (Brazelton scales). This assessment was based on that outlined by Andre-Thomas, Chesni, and Saint-Anne Dargassies (1960), Prechtl and Beintema (1964), and on behavioral tests of Graham, Matarazzo, and Caldwell

---

[1]"State of consciousness" or "state" is one of the most important variables in any observation period. Reactions to stimuli must be interpreted within the context of the presenting state of consciousness. These reactions vary markedly from state to state in each infant. State depends on physiological variables such as hunger, nutrition, degree of hydration, time within the wake-sleep cycle of the infant, etc. The patterns of states as well as the movement from one state to another appear to be important characteristics of infants in the neonatal period. This kind of evaluation may be the best predictor of the infant's receptivity and ability to respond to stimuli in a cognitive sense. Our criteria for determining states are based on our experience and on that of others.

(1956). Presentation of stimuli and the elicitation of reflexes were flexible, and we attempted to produce optimal responses. Our categories included:

1. Motor activity. Both spontaneous and elicited responses were recorded; they included quantity, tempo, freedom, and fluidity of movement, tremulousness, startle activity, preferred movement, and positions at rest. A general assessment of the infant's buildup of activity, tempo, use of states, general tone, irritability, vigor, maturity, and organization of reflex activity was made. Passive movements were scored according to Andre-Thomas, Chesni, & Saint-Anne Dargassies (1960).

2. Sensory responses. Stimuli were presented at appropriate times and reactions recorded: tactile reaction to stroking around the mouth, on the belly and estremities, etc.; kinesthetic reaction to handling, rocking, and cuddling, and changing the subject's position; auditory reaction to voice, rattle, and bell; visual reaction to observer's or mother's face, fixation, and pursuit of red ball (Brazelton, Robey, & Scholl, 1966); sucking mother's breast or observer's finger; temperature changes, observed when infant was undressed or uncovered for a period; and reaction to restraint or swaddling, as was achieved by the tight cinch around the abdomen and the swaddling effect of the rebozo.

At the end of the thirty-minute period of observation of spontaneous responsive activity, we scored each of the twelve infants on a 5-point scale. A general assessment of the infant's state, behavior, motor activity and tempo, tonus, maturity, irritability, and consolability, vigor, adaptation to repeated sensory stimuli, and general behavioral organization also was recorded at the end of this period of observation.

In addition to these neonatal observations four-hour observation periods of mother-child interaction were made, using infants of different ages from one to nine months. We attempted to use Rheingold's (1960) method for sampling interaction at prescribed intervals but found that we had to modify it to suit our purposes. In this culture, interaction between mother and child was infrequent and each event was extremely significant. Timed sampling missed many of these events. Therefore, all events occurring in this dyad were recorded in detail and timed accurately; we focused on whether mother or infant initiated the interplay, its purpose, and its outcome. Rheingold's categories for mothering activities and infant behavior were followed according to her criteria. The number and quality of each were recorded.

In this aspect of the study, we used the Knobloch-Pasamanick (1966) adaptation of the Gesell scales the first summer and the Bayley (1961) scales the second summer. Motor development and social interaction were also scored. Testing of infants over nine months of age proved impossible because of the marked degree of stranger anxiety that appeared before twelve months and interfered with observations. Each infant was tested once, and a second time one month later.

RESULTS

To summarize the results of these examinations.

Delivery Examination

Of the five Zinacanteco newborns examined in the first week, two were examined at birth. In each case, the delivery was easy. The young mother was given no medication during labor. Toward the end of the second stage, she knelt before her own mother while her husband pulled on a cinch around her waist, putting downward pressure on her fundus. The midwife instructed her with each labor pain, received the infant on delivery and tied the cord. In one case, she manually extracted the placenta when it did not come easily. Then the young baby was kept undressed for a thirty-minute period in front of the fire, with no protection against the cold other than a blanket at his back, while chants were sung and rituals performed on his behalf. This provided us with a rare opportunity to observe and record his behavior immediately after delivery.

Both infants were typical of the other newborn Zinacantecos we examined later in the neonatal week. They were small, weighing about 5 lb., average length was 18 in., head circumference was 12½ in. Apgar scores for both were 9-9-9 at 1, 5, and 15 minutes. In appearance and behavior, they were mature, with no apparent anemia or dysmaturity. Although they were the size of premature infants in our country, they had none of the jerky movements or snapback of the limbs characteristic of a premature infant. Their limb movements were free and smooth, and they lay quietly on the blanket, looking around the room with alert faces for the entire hour after delivery. In addition to quiet motor activity, they demonstrated a striking sensory alertness. Repeatedly in the first week, all five infants would alert, become quiet, and slowly turn toward a voice. When lighting was adequate in the dark huts, they alterted to the red ball visual stimulus and followed it back and forth as it was moved; on one occasion, a baby followed for sixty seconds without interruption. Vertical excursions of 30° from neutral were easy to elicit. We noted frequent head movement to augment such pursuit, and only rarely would startles or jerky motor activity interrupt this attentive state.

In order to evaluate the distinctive characteristics of these Zinacanteco infants, we compared their performance with that of three Caucasian infants to whom we administered, on each day of their first week of life, the same neurological-behavioral protocol used for their Zinacanteco counterparts. These controls had experienced normal spontaneous delivery from unmedicated and unanesthetized mothers after forty weeks of normal gestation without any complications of pregnancy. Their Apgar scores were 8-9-9 or over, and pediatrically and neurologically, they were normal in the first week after birth.

Table 7-1 shows tested performance differences for the two groups of infants. Each infant was rated on a scale from 1 to 5 (low to high) on test items listed by general category of response. The figures given for each item are the averages of the ratings for the infants of each group.

Although the small size of our samples does not allow statistical treatment of the data, certain differences speak for themselves. We shall summarize the most important ones.

Spontaneous movement. While the output, tempo, and freedom and excursion of limb movements were initially low for both groups of infants, they increased gradually from day-to-day for the United States controls, but not for the Zinacantecos. Both the freauency and duration of hand-to-mouth activity were initially lower in the Zinacantecos than in the controls, and, by the fifty to seventh day, were much reduced in the Zinacantecos, while increasing in the controls. Spontaneous startles and tremulousness were much lower at all times in the Zinacantecos, while their fluidity and freedom of movement were rated consistently high. In general, the Zinacantecos were distinguished by high freedom and fluidity, but low output of spontaneous movement.

TABLE 7-1. Observations of Zinacanteco infants (ZI) and U.S. Controls.

Number of infants examined

	At Birth		On Day 1		On Day 2		On Day 3		On Day 4		On Day 5		On Day 7		
	ZI	US	ZI	US	ZI	US	ZI	US	ZI	US	ZI	US	ZI	ZI	US
	2	3	3	3	2	3	2	3	1	3	1	3	2[a]	2[b]	3

Average ratings of performance, scaled from 1-5 (low to high)

Spontaneous Movement

	At Birth		On Day 1		On Day 2		On Day 3		On Day 4		On Day 5		On Day 7		
	ZI	US	ZI	US	ZI	US	ZI	US	ZI	US	ZI	US	ZI	ZI	US
Output	2	2	2.5	1	2	2	2	2	2	3	1	4	1	3	4
Tempo	2	2	2	1	2	2	2	2	2	4	2	4	2	2	4
Limb excursion	2	3	2	2	2	2	3	3	2	4	2	4	1	2	4
Hand-to-mouth															
Frequency	2	4	3	3	2	3	3	4	2	4	1	4	1	2	4
Duration	1.5	3	3	3	1.5	3	2	4	2	4	1	4.5	1	2	4.5
Spontaneous															
startles	1	4	2	4	2	4	1	3	2	3	1	3	1	1	2.5
Tremulousness	1	4	1	4	1.5	4	1	3	1	3	1	3	1	1	3
Fluidity of movement	4	2	4	2	3	2	3.5	2	4	3	3	3		4	3
Freedom of movement	3	4	3.5	2	3.5	3	3.5	3	3	4	2	4	2	3	4.5

161

Elicited Responses

	ZI	US	ZI	US	ZI	US	ZI	US	ZI	US	ZI	US	ZI	US	ZI	US
TNR	2	2	2.5	3	1.5	3	2	3	2	3	2	3	2	3	2	4
Pull-to-sit	2	2	2.5	3	1.5	3	2	3	2	3	2	3	2	3	2	4
Head lag	2	2	2.5	2	2	2	2	2.5	3	3	3	3	2	2	3	4
Head control	3	3	3	2	2	2	3	3	2	3	2	3	4	3	4	4
Prone placement																
Crawl	2	3	3	2	2	2.5	3	3	2	3.5	2	3.5	1	2	2	4
Head raising and turning	2	3	3	2	2	3	3	4	2	3.5	2	4	1	2	1	5
Moro																
Extension to flexion	3	3.3	3.5	3	2	3	3	4	2	4	2	5	1	3	3	4
Ankle clonus	1	3	2	4	1	3.5	1	4	2	4	2	3	1	1	1	3
Pinprick (intensity and speed)																
Grasp (hands)	4	4	4	3	2	3	3	4	2	3	2	2	1	3	2	2
Placing	3	4	3.5	3	3	3	3	3	4	4	3	4	2	3	3	3
Stepping	3	4	3.5	2	3	3	3	2	3	3	3	3	1	3	3	4
Rooting	3.5	3	4	2	3	3	3.5	4	4	4	2	2	4	4	4	4
Sucking	4.5	3	5	2	4	2	4	4	5	3.3	4	2	5	4	4	4
Passive Movement																
Range	4	3	4	2	4	3	4	3	4	2.5	4	3	2	4	3	3
Resistance	1	3	2	2	1	2	1	3	2	4	1	4	4	2	4	4
Recoil	1	3	1	3	1	2	1	4	1	4	1	3	1	2	3	3
Muscular consistency	2.5	3	2.5	2	2	2.5	2	4	2	3	2	3	2	3	3	4

162

	ZI	US	ZI	US	ZI	US	ZI	US	ZI	US	ZI	US	ZI	US
Sensory Responses														
Eyes Blink	3	3	2	3	3	3	3	3	3	4	3	3	3	3
Adaptation	4	3	3	4	4	4	3	3	4	3	3	4	3	4
Visual pursuit	4	3	4	2	3	2	3	1	3.5	3	3	3	4	4
Amp. persistence	4	3	3	2	3	2	3	2	3.5	2	2	2	5	5
Vestibular (head and eyes)	3	3	3	3	3	3	3	3	3	3	3	3	2	3
Auditory	4	3	4	3	3	2	3	2	4	3	3	3	3	4
Adaptation	4	3	3	2	3.5	2	3	2	3	2	2	3	3	3
General Assessment														
Modulation of states	4	3	4	2	4	2	4	1	4	2	4	3	3	4
Organization (spread of resonses, habituation, quality of performance)	4	3	4	2	3	2	4	2	4	3	3	4	3	4
Adaptation to repeated stimuli	4	3	4	3	4	3	3	4	4	3	4	4	3	4
Consolability	5	3	4	2.5	3	2.5	3	3	4	3	4	5	4	4
Maturity	4	3	4	2	3	2.5	3	3	4	4	4	4	3	3
Rapidity of buildup	2	3	3	4	2	5	2	5	3	4	1	4	1	3
Tempo at height	2	4	3	4	2	4	2	3	3	4	1	3	2	3

	ZI	US	ZI	US	ZI	US	ZI	US	ZI	US	ZI	US	ZI	US
Irritability	1	3	2	4	2	4	2	4	1	3	1	3	1	3
Vigor	2.5	3	2.5	3	2	3	2	4	3	4	2	4	2	5
General tonus	2	4	3	2	3	2	2	3	3	3	2	4	3	4

[a] In cinch.

[b] Out of cinch.

Reprinted from: Brazelton, T.B., Robey, J.S. & Collier, G.A., Infant development in the Zinacantico Indians of Southern Mexico. Pediatrics, 1969, 44, 274–283.

Elicited responses. Zinacanteco infants were similar to the controls, during the first two or three days, in tonic neck responses, in head lag and head control on being pulled to sit, in their crawling and head control when placed in a prone position, and in the completeness of Moros. After two or three days, however, the controls scored increasingly higher in these responses. With ankle clonus and in the intensity of spread of pinprick response, the Zinacantecos were consistently lower throughout the first week. In placing, stepping, and grasp, they differed little from the controls. In sucking and rooting, their performance was consistently excellent. The effects of the cinch around the belly apparently restrained many of these responses by the seventh day. In general. the Zinacanteco infants maintained throughout the first week the muted level of these responses seen at birth, while their United States counterparts increased in the intensity of their responses.

Passive movement. In range of passive movement, the Zinacantecos scored slightly, but consistently, higher than the controls; but in resistance, recoil, and muscular consistency, their responses were noticeably more muted.

General assessment. In modulation of states, the Zinacanteco infants scored consistently higher than their United States counterparts. Their moderately high organization of responses, adaptation to repeated stimuli, consolability, and maturity exceeded those of the controls in the first days; however, the controls equaled or surpassed the Zinacantecos in their degree of these responses by the end of the first week. In rapidity of buildup, tempo at height, irritability, and vigor, the Zinacantecos scored consistently lower than the controls throughout the first week, while both groups had roughly the same level of general tonus. In general. the Zinacanteco infants' scores did not change appreciably during the first week, while the controls increased in their level of organization, adaptation, consolability, and maturity.

In summary, Zinacanteco infants motor activity from birth was freer, more fluid, nontremulous, and only moderate in vigor, without the "over-shooting" or overreaction that tends to interfere with prolonged or repeated responses to sensory stimuli as seen in North American infants. Spontaneous startles were rare; responses to the elicited Moro were somewhat subdued in the Zinacantecos; the general disorganization of states and lack of coordination that we are accustomed to see on Days 1 and 2 in North American infants (Brazelton & Robey, 1965) was not evident in these neonates. State behavior was also dissimilar to that of United States babies, the Zinacantecos maintaining quiet, alert states for long periods, with slow, smooth transitions from one state to another. We recorded none of the deep sleep, intense crying, or intense sucking states observed in the American controls. The apparent control of state and motor behavior in Indian infants seems to be of a higher order, permitting repeated and prolonged responses to auditory, visual, and kinesthetic stimuli in the first week of life.

OBSERVATION PERIODS

Twelve Zinacanteco infants ranging in age from one to nine months were the subjects of our four-hour observations of mother-child interaction. Parents, although bewildered by the purpose of our four-hour visits to their homes, quickly resumed their normal activities, while other family members and occasional visitors chatted with them and with our guide.

Rheingold's categories of mothering and infant activities were the basis for our observations. Rather than following her time sampling procedures, however, we recorded the frequency and duration of interaction continuously throughout each observation.

For each subject of the four-hour observations, the number and duration of each mothering and infant activity is listed in Table 7-2. Although we have established no controls for these observations, certain differences from mother-child patterns in our own culture are striking and obvious from a comparison with Rheingold's data (although ours are not sampled figures, but represent all events). The major differences were emphasized in our minds because of our twenty-five years of experience as pediatricians in middle-class United States.

For example, Zinacanteco mothers rarely attempted to elicit social responses from their infants by looking at their faces or talking to them. Even during feedings, when the mother would preen the baby, her glances were perfunctory and without expectation of response.

The infants were rarely placed on the floor or bed, except when kept supine and swaddled beside the mother during the month of her post partum confinement. Older infants were held in mother's lap, arms, or on her back in the restraining rebozo.

TABLE 7-2. Ratings from four-hour observations of mother-child interaction.

Mothering Activities	1(1)	2(1)	3(1)	4(3)	5(3)	6(4)	7(6)	8(7)	9(8)	10(8)	11(9)	12(9)
Total number of caretakers	1	1	1	1	4	2	1	1	1	1	2	5
Number of glances at infant's face	3	4	3	2	3	3	1	1	1	1	4	0
Number of times talking to infant	10	0	0	4	1	5	0	1	4	3	2	0
Number of diaperings	4	4	1	2	1	1	1	1	3	1	4	0
Total minutes hold child in rebozo	0	0	0	50	94	0	180	30	0	0	58	111
Total minutes holding in arms or lap	25	40	110	185	143	142	60	210	176	240	182	227
Total minutes leaves child on bed	215	200	130	5	3	98	0	0	64	0	0	0
Number of breast feedings	3	6	3	7	9	4	2	5	3	6	7	9
Total length of feeding, min.	24	38	14	37	63	30	15	35	15.5	48	30	35
Number of times siblings were breastfed	3	3	–	–	–	–	–	–	–	9	2	10
Age of siblings, years	1.5	3	–	–	–	–	–	–	–	3	2	3
Total minutes of sibling feeding	10	15	–	–	–	–	–	–	–	20	5	29

Infant Activities	1(1)	2(1)	3(1)	4(3)	5(3)	6(4)	7(6)	8(7)	9(8)	10(8)	11(9)	12(9)
Total minutes of sleep	205	55	100	33	30	93	180	30	60	15	58	111
Total minutes awake	35	185	140	207	210	147	60	210	180	225	182	129
Total number of vocalizations	0	0	0	1	3	0	0	1	3	2	5	5
Number of times cries briefly	7	5	8	3	2	0	1	3	1	1	3	3
Number of times mouths hands	0	0	1	3	3	3	3	5	3	3	5	5
Number of times plays with toys	0	0	0	1	1	0	0	0	7	3	2	1

Reprinted from: Brazelton, T.B., Robey, J.S., & Collier, G.A., Infant development in the Zinacantico Indians of Southern Mexico. Pediatrics, 1969, 44, 274–283.

168

Breast-feedings were notably frequent, as high as nine times in a four-hour period. (In four families, siblings were breast-fed as often as ten times a day.) The primary purpose of feeding appeared to be to quiet the child's restlessness when he would not be lulled in the rebozo on the mother's back by her rhythmic grinding of the corn.

The most striking feature of infant activity was the paucity of vocalizations. Indeed, during three observations, *no* vocalizations were heard. Cries were brief and were quickly terminated by the mothers' quieting activities.

These infants rarely mouthed their hands and never sucked their fingers. The youngest infants spent most of their time covered and asleep with the confined mother. Older infants were never offered pacifiers and only rarely toys, and never placed on the floor to crawl or stand at the furniture. They remained mostly in their mother's arms or lap, or on her back in a rebozo. In the rebozo, they might reach for her braid or beads, or for passing objects as she moved, and sit up or bounce, as though in a rocking chair. Although they were quieter and less demanding than middle-class United States infants, their activity and motor development was normal in spite of the limitations of the rebozo.

TESTS OF DEVELOPMENT

We tested 93 healthy, normal infants, ranging in age from birth to nine months, for gross and fine motor performance (Figure 7-1), and for mental age as judged by social behavior, language development and adaptive behavior in response to test objects (Figure 7-2). Each infant was tested once and, where possible, retested by a second observer one month later. We used the Knobloch-Pasamanick adaptation of the Gesell scales in 1966 and the Bayley scales in 1967.

Test items were administered with the infant in his mother's lap in the hut or, occasionally. outside on a mat. The examiner sat nearby and presented blocks, toys, and other test items on a small square board platform held on his knees. Curious onlookers inevitably gathered around us in this setting and added their comments as we tested. This excitement produced enough anxiety of strangers in infants older than nine months to prevent their being tested. Both the Knobloch-Pasamanick and the Bayley scales required the use of test objects with which the Zinacanteco infants were totally unfamiliar, such

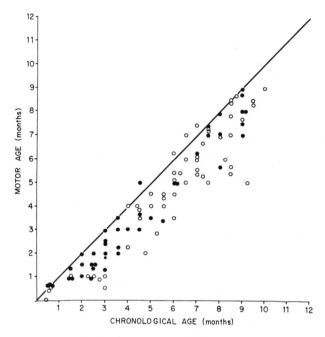

Figure 7-1.   Estimates of motor age plotted against
chronological age: Knobloch-Pasamanick
scale (●); Bayley scale (○). The diagonal
line indicates the statistical norm of
United States infants.

as cubes, rattles, balls, spoons, and cups; the children had
to be taught how to use these objects before their performance
could be scored. Novelty was met with impassive faces in tested
children and parents alike. Repeatedly, infants watched us
carefully as we demonstrated the use of test objects, imitated
each movement we had made to score a success on the test, and
then dropped the object without any of the exploration or
experimental play we would have seen in United States babies.

Because Zinacanteco mothers never place their infants in
a prone position, doing so, as required for certain items of
motor development testing, uniformly elicited distress, masking
the motor performance being tested. Finally, several items
rating the quality of vocalization could not be scored because
of the paucity of social babbling and imitation of language in
the Zinacanteco infants.

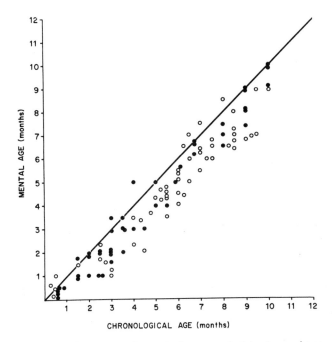

Figure 7-2. Estimates of mental age plotted against
chronological age: Knobloch-Pasamanick
scale (●); Bayley scale (○). The diagonal
line indicates the statistical norm of
United States infants.

Despite these problems, the ratings from the Knobloch-
Pasamanick and the Bayley scales gave comparable results,
although the administration of the latter and its scoring
were somewhat easier and more precise. Both scales permitted
performance on items to be grouped, thus yielding an estimate
of mental age and motor age for each child that could be
compared with his chronological age. Although data were
collected from three different Zinacanteco hamlets, all three
were culturally similar and since there was no statistical
difference in performance between them the results were pooled.
The results are summarized in Figures 7-1 and 7-2, and in
Table 7-3.

In Table 7-3, differences in performance of the Zinacantecos
from United States norms are summarized. For each Zinacanteco
infant, the estimated mental and motor ages in months were

TABLE 7-3. Differences from United States norms of mental and motor ages observed in Zinacanteco infants.

Scale Used	Difference in mental age from U.S. norms		Difference in motor age from U.S. norms		Number of Subjects
	Mean	Standard Deviation	Mean	Standard Deviation	
Knobloch-Pasamanick Scale (administered by Robey and Brazelton)	0.61	0.60	0.88	0.61	40
Bayley Scale (administered by Robey)	1.24	0.76	1.51	0.91	36
Bayley Scale (administered by Brazelton)	0.74	0.59	0.78	0.75	17

Reprinted from: Brazelton. T.B., Robey, J.S., & Collier, G.A., Infant development in the Zinacanteco Indians of Southern Mexico. Pediatrics, 1969, 44, 274-283.

subtracted from his chronological age in months, yielding differences whose averages across subjects would be zero if the subjects did not differ from United States norms; they would be significantly greater than zero if they lagged behind these norms. The Table gives the mean and standard deviation, in months, of these differences from United States norms of mental and motor age among the Zinacanteco children. The results were derived from the Knobloch-Pasamanick scale the first summer, and from Robey's administration of the Bayley scale and Brazelton's administration of the Bayley scale in the second summer.

From Table 7-3, it can be seen that the differences from United States norms are positive. Despite variation in size of sample and test administrators, the Zinacanteco infants lagged behind by about one month, with no increasing decrement with increasing age (Figures 7-1 and 7-2).

The difference from United States norms in motor age is consistently higher than that of mental age.[2] Further, there was a Pearson product moment correlation (r) between the differences from United States norms in motor age and mental age. It was 0.66 for the Knobloch-Pasamanick ratings and 0.42 for the Bayley ratings (both significant at the 0.01 level), indicating a tendency for high lag in motor age to accompany high lag in mental age.

Finally, the lack of agreement in Table 7-3 regarding the differences from United States norms of Zinacanteco performance warrants some comment. We attribute the considerable spread of the distribution of these differences to the peculiar circumstances and difficulties inherent in the testing situation, especially those of reacting to the novelty of the test setting and procedures, which modified the infant's test response. The differences between Robey's and Brazelton's

---

[2]This difference is highly significant for the Knobloch-Pasamanick data $(\rho = 0.01)$, approaches significance for Robey's data $(\rho = 0.10)$, and not significant, and not significant though suggestive for Brazelton's Bayley data, as indicated by t-tests performed on the values of mental and motor age differences across subject. Two extremely large values of motor age difference in Robey's data, 4.2 and 4.3, were Winsorized back to the next largest value, 3.2, in the computations so that they would not unduly influence the results. If left unaltered, they would only have decreased the ρ value.

administration of the Bayley scale, however, reflected a
definite observer effect. Brazelton tended to vary the scale
to elicit the *best* performance available in each infant.
Robey followed Bayley's manual recommendations more literally.
We felt that the differences in our results indicated that.
with an approach that was more sensitive to their needs than
to the requirements of the test, these people could score
significantly higher on our scales. This must be kept in mind
as one scores a group who are not in any way acquainted with
our structured evaluations of their performance.

In summary, in the first year of their motor and mental
development, Zinacanteco infants seemed to lag consistently
one month behind United States norms. Nevertheless, this lag
did not increase with age, reflecting the Zinacantecos'
apparent passage through essentially the same sequence of
development at approximately the same rate as is characteristic
of North American infants.

DISCUSSION

Descriptions of the salient characteristics of Zinacantecan
and U.S. parents and infants are given in Appendix B and will
not be summarized here. The complexities of assessing an
infant's behavior and its interaction with an environment may
well be demonstrated by this "pilot" study in another culture.
I felt, and feel, that it is vital for us to assess and attempt
to account for as many of the variables as possible. There is
no real way of assessing the effect of a foreign observer on
the mother-infant dyad. We were automatically endowed with
"the evil eye" until I assured mothers that I was a "curer"
and could counteract it if I had it. However, the effects
of stranger anxiety in the baby were powerfully reinforced
by his parent's constant anxiety about our presence. We were
unable to relate to babies after nine months of age because
this effect was so powerful. But the impact of strong
differences in the behavior and expectations that were
demonstrated early in mother-infant interaction were powerful
variables and their effect on the baby's development seemed
apparent.

Using neonatal observations as a first step has many
advantages. If we really believe that the formula for
development is genotype × environment = phenotype, we can
only begin to make educated guesses about the genotype, as
well as the infant's first environment (the uterus), from

neonatal assessments. At birth, we are already assessing an
evolved phenotype.

The genotype of these Mayans was felt to be pure. Natural
selection has been enhanced over the last 400 years by
environmental forces such as survival in a high altitude,
infection, being isolated in a peace-loving community, intermarriage among closely related people--coupled with the values
that determine selection of mates for their survival value.
(These are mainly such attributes as an Asian look, quiet
strengths and industriousness, submerged aggression, and
willingness to conform to group expectancies and to accept
clear-cut sexual identies without overt ambivalence.)

The influence of high altitude with relative hypoxia and
polycythemia, along with the powerful effects of intrauterine
protein malnutrition and infection and of the constant, regular
activity of the pregnant female, may be reflected in the neonates by their superb state control and their slow, liquid
movements. They were not depleted, undernourished or under-
hydrated--but they were small. Scrimshaw, Taylor, and Gordon
(1968) claim that subclinical protein malnutrition coupled
with intrauterine infection produces small babies who are then
prone to high rates of infant mortality. Perhaps slow, liquid
movements are a behavioral equivalent of undernutrition in
utero in a particular genetic strain of infants. Their
fluidity, lack of interfering motor activity, and well-regulated
state and autonomic control thus lends a reinforcing background
for what appears to be auditory and visual precocity in the
immediate neonatal period. Whether it is real precocity or a
condition resulting from lack of competition from motor activity,
coupled with a quiet environment after delivery, awaits other
studies. The effect of such a difference in this behavior for
the neonate and for his parent must be a powerful shaper for his
nurturing environment.

Neonates in our culture are more motoric, and the reflex
motor responses that are interspersed in spontaneous and
elicited behavior interfere with prolonged periods of alertness
in the U.S. babies. Zinacanteco babies' state behavior is then
not only less labile, but also the peaks of sleep and awake
states are leveled off--deep sleep and wide-awake crying
differing in quantity and quality between the two groups. This
modulated, smoothed-out behavior is reflected in more stabilized
autonomic control also. A neonate in our culture who was left
uncovered for thirty minutes would be either shivering, or
crying to keep up his body heat, or would be in a cardiovascular
collapse from heat loss. Not only do there appear to be genetic

differences between these two groups--Freedman and Freedman (1969) have replicated these same neonatal differences in U.S. born Oriental babies--but the effects of different intrauterine environments are already interacting with these genetic differences to produce these very different neonates. Subclinical malnutrition, if it is present in these Indians, as Scrimshaw postulates, is produced by parasitism and infection in the mother, rather than being caused by inadequate intake of protein and calories. Cord bloods taken from a sample of Guatemalan Indian neonates (Scrimshaw, Taylor, & Gordon, 1968) show a factor of ten times increase in gamma globulins, which reflects infection that has crossed the placenta. (Information on gamma globulins is lacking in our sample of Zinacanteco neonates.) The intrauterine effects of relative hypoxia, of a cold climate, of a culture eliciting slow moving, constant industry, and rocking behavior on the part of the mother, of little ambient noise or raising of the voice, of no overt aggression--all suggest that intrauterine conditioning may be of a very different order. Perhaps these influcence the Zinacanteco baby toward a kind of autonomic and motoric stability that is reflected in his neonatal behavior.

The immediate paranatal experience--no drugs, no interference with the natural course of labor and delivery, emotional support for the mother, emphasis on subdued, rather passive participation of the mother in the delivery--is reenacted in a similar experience for the newborn. He is left undressed for a period--a stressful period from an autonomic aspect. No attention seems to be given by the mother to the neonate's alert sensory responses at this time. But the infant manages the necessary temperature control in a strikingly different way from U.S. neonates, and is then placed in a swaddled, face-covered position alongside his mother. The mother then sets up a mode of immediate contingent responsiveness to the infant's needs--*before* he can build up to express a need, feel the importance of it, make a demand, and then find it gratified. There is *no* experience in early infancy that could contribute the framework for self-motivated demand, frustration, and then gratification--a cycle that must be important in setting up a model for self-initiated and reinforced independence in our U.S. culture.

The child-rearing emphasis is on subdued motor activity and on averting a demand-response pattern. When the infants' motor activity was elicited in our test situation, the lactating mothers' breasts leaked milk. In the U.S. culture, such a "let-down" response follows a baby's cry. These Zinacanteco mothering responses seem to reinforce quiet passivity and low

motor activity in the earliest neonatal interactions. None of
the efforts to "jazz up" babies to respond with smiling,
vocalizing, *or* motor behavior that mothers use in an interaction in our culture are *ever* utilized in Zinacantan. Quiet,
nondemanding babies are the desideratum. They are kept near
the mother or a surrogate from the immediate extended family.
A fussy baby is treated as if he were sick. Curing ceremonies,
sedative herbs, isolation of mother and baby in "healing" smoke-
filled huts are instituted to "cure" him. Only when the baby
gives up its crying are the mother-infant pair allowed to resume
a normal life. Although the concern of the mother is great as
her baby cries, she handles her responses with less overt
anxiety than do mothers in our culture. In the U.S., regular
crying episodes that are likely to occur at the end of the day
are almost universal in nuclear middle-class families
(Brazelton, 1963), and they often seem reinforced by the
anxious practices that parents institute to try to suppress
them.

Differences in the stimulation provided by mother-infant
interactions in the U.S. and Zinacantecan cultures are dramatic.
Zinacantecan infants are not reinforced contingently for
vocalizing, smiling and motor development; yet, they continue
to develop, as reflected in the results of the Bayley scales.
Although performing slightly below the level of U.S. infants,
the Zinacanteco infants do walk on time, and can also be coaxed
to smile, vocalize, and speak on time. The quality of these
responses may differ; but the "milestones" we are testing do
not vary significantly. We must, then, begin to see that we
are producing only qualitative differences by emphasizing
contingent reinforcement in our culture. For example, we must
see that adequate tactile. kinesthetic, auditory, vibratory,
and other sensory stimulation, even though it is not contingently
reinforcing, can provide an adequate framework for normal,
albeit slightly more stereotyped development of all kinds.

These findings suggest that the imitative mode for learning
may adequately replace a more experimental "accretion" model.
Imitation may serve well for the quantitatively adaptive learning
we see in this Zinacanteco group, and imitation as a learning
mode may be activated by stimuli that seem noncontingent and are
not directed through the usual visual and verbal channels. In
this group, other modes of interaction seem sufficient to provide
the matrix for this kind of learning. But this model may not be
sufficient for more complex models necessary to our technological
society (see Brazelton, Tronick, Adamson, Als, & Weise, 1975).

The most striking differences between our culture's child-

rearing practices and those of the Zinacantecos seem to be in
the area of creating in middle-class children in the U.S. an
air of anxious expectancy for individualized performance. The
child in the U.S. is expected to be independent and self-
motivated, i.e., under a real head of steam to express himself
or herself, and to sort out the ingredients for each new
developmental step from the rather overwhelming mass of stimuli
that are offered from the environment to spur the individual on.
The multiplicity of choices that this offers must create a
difficult decision at each step. The fact that the individual
can choose what is needed to help, or that he or she can maintain
enough inner drive to master one's own next step, is testimony
in part to the powerful forces of maturation and of his or her
coping mechanisms. Seeing the Zinacanteco baby develop in the
face of quiet, firm suppression of active exploratory behavior
certainly adds another dimension to the powerful influence of
maturation of the central nervous system along with other modes
for furthering development.

    In our culture, mastery of the many choices that are
presented is coupled with early emphasis on being independent.
All of our earliest practices press the baby to find his own
sources of comfort, to find his own ways of waiting for and of
demanding a feeding, and to establish independent sleep
patterns and rhythms of sleep that are optimal for receiving
stimulation when it will be available. As a result, the baby's
activity is highly charged with an independent exploration of
the environment, with much sorting of what works and what does
not. This must reinforce the need for self-reliance and also
lead to the kind of self-questioning that we see in adults in
our culture. Much of this is good, but the anxiety that
accompanies it is also reflected in the ambivalence that
characterizes most of our middle-class parents. So it seems
to me that our culture sets the stage in infancy, especially
for boys, for early independence, a searching for individuality,
an intense drive to successful mastery, self-questioning, and
a kind of devaluation of help from those around who might offer
help. We seem to demand from our children a kind of precocity
and self-reliance that does not lead to trust in relationships.
Almost universal is a devaluation of those who are not intensely
motivated toward success. Unreasonable fear of inadequacy and
a fear of dependency or inactivity must follow. One of the most
serious problems for and with young parents in our culture is
that they cannot trust their own reactions toward a dependent
new baby, and their relationship is fraught with tension and
ambivalence about the burden the baby places on their own
fragile and inadequate resources.

The Zinacantecos thus offer a "simpler" model of child-rearing, handed on and reinforced without apparent self-questioning from generation to generation. The result of their handling of babies seems to be to set up a mode of imitative learning that is adapted to the culture's emphasis on equality and interdependence. The patterning for the anlage of these characteristics is made in the earliest weeks and months after birth. Obviously, the inferences from infancy to adult behavior are oversimplified, but this comparative cultural look does present one who might wish to intervene in our culture's child-rearing practices with a question as to whether we have not demanded too much of our infants--and may be setting the stage for chaos in later life.

APPENDIX A

ASSESSMENT OF INFANT STATES

AWAKE STATES

1.   Eyes generally open; semidozing, activity level low, with interspersed mild startles from time to time; reactive to sensory stimuli, but delay in response often seen; state change after stimulation frequently noted.

2.   Eyes open; considerable motor activity with thrusting movements of extremities; intermittent crying, few spontaneous startles; reactive to external stimulation, with increase in startles or motor activity, but discrete reactions difficult to distinguish because of general high activity level.

3.   Alert, bright look--seems to focus attention on source of stimulation such as a sucking object, visual or auditory stimulus; impinging stimuli may break through, but with some delay.

4.   Characterized by intense crying or sucking activity that is difficult to break through with stimulation.

SLEEP STATES

1.   Light sleep with eyes closed; low activity level, with random movements and mild spontaneous startles; responsive to internal and external stimuli, with startle equivalents, often with a resulting change

of state.

2.   Deeper sleep, with little spontaneous activity
      except startles or startle equivalents (Wolff,
      1966); at quite regular intervals, external
      stimuli produce startles with some delay;
      suppression of startles rapid; state changes
      less likely.

3.   Deep sleep with no spontaneous activity other than
      a few mild startles at regular intervals; external
      stimuli do not seem to penetrate and no behavioral
      response may be noted for long periods; this state
      is most readily induced by a prior period of
      disturbing stimulation (Brazelton & Robey, 1965).

APPENDIX B

APPARENT DIFFERENCES

ZINACANTECO   U.S.

Genetic

   Asian, mongoloid in   Mixed genetic pool
   appearance
   Intermarriage for 600
   years

Intrauterine Influences

   High altitude, relative   Active, noisy environment
   hypoxia polycythemia   surrounding mothers
   Quiet environment around   Diet adequate
   mother   No history of drugs or
   Constant rhythmic move-   infection
   ment of mother   No bleeding or difficulties
   Protein ingested by mother during pregnancy
   in pregnancy but possibly
   increased parasitism and
   infection interfering
   with utilization

ZINACANTECO	U.S.

Delivery

No drugs or other
ingestants
Home delivery with
support from all the
family

If "natural childbirth",
still some minimal
premedication
Hospital delivery and
anxieties surrounding
it

At Birth

1. Infants--Tiny but well
   developed, not immature
   or dysmature.
   Extremes of sleep and
   crying states rarely
   seen and shortlasting
   Move slowly from one
   state to another
   Prolonged alert states
   with high degree of
   visual and auditory
   responses maintained,
   aided by low degree
   of motor interference
   Motor activity smooth,
   mature, well-modulated,
   freedom of movement
   Autonomic control
   impressive--little
   need for self-consoling
   Little hand-to-mouth
   activity

1. Infants--Variable size and
   stages of maturity
   Active and labile state
   changes, extremes seen
   frequently
   Shorter alert periods,
   difficult to maintain
   due to interfering of
   motor or reflex responses
   Motor activity more
   intrusive, jerky. over-
   reactive
   Poorer autonomic control
   and demanding attention
   from environment
   Need to console self
   actively
   High hand-to-mouth activity

2. Parents--Anticipate high
   mortality and depend on
   religious practices
   versus evil eye, as well
   as cultural practices in
   which they place faith--
   such as isolate mother
   and baby together, feed
   before upset or active,
   wrap and cover face to
   keep soul together and
   to protect from evil eye

2. Parents--Expect live, viable
   child due to medical
   intervention, hence rely
   on iatrogenic customs--
   such as leave alone
   (versus infection), feed
   every four hours (hospital
   routine) does not hurt to
   cry (hospital practice)--
   overstimulation of noisy,
   brightly lit wards

ZINACANTECO	U.S.
3. Immediate Attachment Behavior--Wrapping, cinching in to keep soul together Covering face, swaddling and wrapping, keeping close by--no eye contact, frequent breast-feedings	3. Immediate Attachment Behavior--Combination of intensity and distance Look at--eye contact, touch Actively stimulate to visual, auditory. and motor responsiveness Turn over responsibility to other caretakers in beginning Unconsciously influenced by iatrogenic rules

Immediately After Delivery

Baby left unswaddled and uncovered in front of fire for thirty minutes--partially exposed in this period Quiet, dark huts--minimal handling	Much handling, spanked, airway cleaned out--given injection and eyedrops Loud, noisy, overlighted delivery room

Initial Period After Birth

Swaddled next to mother	Sent to nursery for bath and swaddling

Feeding Behavior

Fed before infant hungry--in response to activity rather than after infant's realization of hunger, so that he could feel rewarded by being fed Takes peak off the build-up-gratification cycle Dependency on frequent gratification from care-taker. Breast used as pacifier in every way. Five times as many feedings as U.S., but total duration same Little anxiety on surface about whether she is	Fed every four hours or slight variation. Tend allow hunger to build up, baby cries and realizes hunger, then fed Response is in part a measure of reaction to baby's active demand (leads to cycle of independence?) Early solid feeding and feed self--all pushing infant toward independence and individuality in feeding area. Anxiety about giving baby enough, and also about choice of feedings. Choices and

ZINACANTECO	U.S.
doing right about it. E.g., if has not enough milk, pragmatically gives infant to another woman, who does No early feeding, solids are split into infant's mouth in second half of 1st year, and feeds self with family by end of year. Not weaned by mother--weans self at five years. Perfunctory stimulation at feeding time--no real play together	critics around her re-inforce mother's feedlings of inadequacy. Weaned early--by 6 to 9 months. Interaction at feeding time goes on all along

Mouthing of Hands

ZINACANTECO	U.S.
Infant almost never sucks fingers No 'loveys' or crutches	Finger sucking common--ambivalence in many. Mothers mobilized by it Independence reinforced by 'loveys' such as thumbs or fingers for sucking, blankets to carry, etc.

Crying

ZINACANTECO	U.S.
Never "allowed" to cry Crying very uncommon and short-lived No real buildup to crying state Fussing at low level Fussing that can not be suppressed treated as an illness, baby and mother isolated in smoke-filled hut for curing ceremonies, given herbs. Everyone supports and feeds mother of crying child Breast-fed frequently, but no other unusual efforts to suppress baby	Crying expected up to a point and often treated as a sign of spirit More than unusual crying treated by: 1. Left to cry it out 2. Pacifier 3. More stimulation--visual, handling, anxious frequent feedings, or 4. Treated as sign of disturbance and sedatives given the baby Ambivalence at a peak in parents

ZINACANTECO	U.S.

Sleep Practices

Amount of sleep--very
little different but
deep sleep seemed shorter
in duration during night,
and more inactive sleep
in day while in serape
on mother's back

Little effort to press in
to diurnal cycle of long
sleep at night

Breast-feeding frequent at
night and in response to
movement of baby

Sleep between parents
wrapped up between them
until next baby, then
with siblings after two
years

Children go to bed when
tired or when parents
go to bed

Baby pressed to sleep at
night from first. When
this doesn't work, either:
1. Left to cry it out or
2. Treated with anxious,
   ambivalent intervention

Given a substitute 'lovey'
early

Expected to have motoric,
rhythmic behavior to
comfort self every four
hours through night

If wakens at night, parents
caught between inclination
to go to child and letting
him deal with it himself.
If not a "set" bedtime,
parents feel caught and
guilty about having him
up. Child disintegrates
at end of day to be
provocative, excited, and
out of control

Play Practices

Little opportunity for
visual, tactile
exploration by infant in
first four months.
Tactile, kinesthetic,
auditory, oral stimulation
high, but received
passively

Short periods available
for visual exploration
around each breast-
feeding, but no overt
response given from the
mother. However, short
opportunities for visual
information may be
heightened by association
with feeding

High premium on visual,
auditory stimulation and
face-to-face interaction.
Carried very little

Infants jazzed up in infant
seat or on bed to excited
responses. All of this
associated with "distance"
behavior from parents.
Much time to be on own for
exploration and learning.
This heightens independent
exploration of environment
and of self

Learning by "accretion"--
after exploration,
serendipity, and
assimilation

ZINACANTECO	U.S.
Suppression of smiling, vocal, motor exploratory behavior. When it can be suppressed no longer (e.g., when baby is on mother's back), she secretly enjoys and supports it but does not heighten or tease it on No real frustration or excitement about new steps in learning seen in either mother or baby-- more a passive expectation in parents. Learning by imitation--large hunks of behavior imitated by baby after maturation readies the ground for its acquisition. Little active reinforcement from environment	Self-motivation high and fuels acquisitive kind of trial and error learning Frustration before and excitement after each new step points to the kind of self-motivation and sense of independent achievement. Pressure from environment to learn new steps by practicing, teasing, stimulating the behavior

REFERENCES

Andre-Thomas, C. Y., Chesni, Y., & Saint-Anne Dargassies, S. Neurological examination of the infant. London: National Spastics Society Monograph, 1960.

Anscheutz, M. A study of midwives in Zinacantan. Unpublished doctoral dissertaion, Harvard University, 1966.

Bayley, N. Bayley scales of mental and motor development: Collaborative perinatal research project. Bethesda, Md.: National Institute of Neurological Diseases and Blindness, 1961.

Blanco, M. G., & Chodorow, N. J. Children's work and obedience in Zinacantan. Unpublished report, Anthropology Department, Cambridge, Mass.: Harvard University, 1964.

Bloch, A.   The Kurdistani cradle story.   Clinical Pediatrics,
        1966, 5, 641-643.

Bowlby, J.   Attachment and loss.   Vol. 1: Attachment.   New
        York: Basic Books, 1969.

Brazelton, T. B.   The early mother-infant adjustment.
        Pediatrics, 1963, 32, 931-935.

Brazelton. T. B.   Neonatal behavioral-neurological evaluation.
        London: National Spastics Society Monographs No. 5.
        1973.

Brazelton. T. B., & Robey, J. S.   Observations of neonatal
        behavior: The effect of perinatal variables, in
        particular that of maternal medication.   Journal
        American Academy of Child Psychiatry.   1965, 4,
        613-619.

Brazelton. T. B., Robey, J. S., & Collier, G. A.   Infant
        development in the Zinacanteco Indians of Southern
        Mexico.   Pediatrics,   1969, 44, 274-283.

Brazelton, T. B., Robey, J. S., & Scholl, M. L.   Visual
        behavior in the neonate.   Pediatrics, 1966, 37,
        284-289.

Brazelton, T. B., Tronick, E., Adamson, L., Als, H., & Weise,
        S.   Early mother-infant reciprocity.   CIBA Foundation
        Symposium, 1975, 33, 137.

Colby, B. N., & Van Den Bergh, P.   Ethnic relations in South-
        eastern Mexico.   American Anthropoligist, 1961, 63,
        4-12.

Collier, G. A.   The life cycle in Zinacantan.   Unpublished
        doctoral dissertation, Harvard University, 1962.

Freedman, D. G., & Freedman, N.   Behavioral differences between
        Chinese-American and American newborns.   Nature,
        1969, 224, 227.

Graham, R. K., Matarazzo, R. C., & Caldwell, B. M.   Behavioral
        differences between normal and traumatized newborns.
        Duke University Psychological Monographs, 1956, 70,
        427-435.

Knobloch, H., Pasamanick, B., & Sherard, E. S. Jr.   A
    developmental screening inventory for infants.
    Pediatrics, Supplement, 1966, 38, 1095-1099.

Levi-Strauss, C. The savage mind.   Chicago: University of
    Chicago Press, 1966.

Lipton. E. L., Steinschneider, A., & Richmond, J. B.   Swaddling,
    a child care practice: Historical, cultural and
    experimental observations. Pediatrics, Supplement,
    1965, 35, 521-528.

Prechtl, H., & Beintema, O. The neurological examination of
    the full-term newborn infant. London: Heinemann,
    1964, National Spastics Monograph, 12.

Rheingold, H. L. The measurement of maternal care. Child
    Development, 1960, 31, 565-570.

Scrimshaw, N. S., Taylor, C. E., & Gordon, J. E.   Interactions
    of nutrition and infection (WHO Monograph Series
    No. 56). World Health Organization, 1968, Washington,
    D.C.

Vogt, E. Los Zinacantecos Mexico, D. F. Institute Nacional
    Indigenista, 1966.

Wolff, P. H. The causes, controls, and organization of
    behavior. New York: International Universities
    Press, 1966.

Chapter 8

Biological, Cultural, and Social Determinants of Nutritional Status

H. H. Draper

University of Illinois at Urbana-Champaign

This paper will attempt to deal with the general
principles of nutritional assessment and to characterize
the network of biological, cultural, and social variables
that influence nutritional status. Illustrations will be
drawn from the literature and from personal observations on
two diverse cultures: rural Mississippi blacks and northern
Alaskan Eskimos.

METHODS OF NUTRITIONAL ASSESSMENT

Methods employed to appraise the nutritional status of
populations range in complexity from simple anthropometric
measurements of height, weight, or head circumference to

*

The studies on Alaskan Eskimos cited in this paper were
supported by a research grant (GB-28361) from the U.S.
National Science Foundation. The author greatefully
acknowledges the assistance of Delia C. Protacio in
performing the riboflavin analyses, Roma Raines Bell and
James G. Bergan in conducting the lactose and sucrose
tolerance tests, and Kenrad E. Nelson in supplying clinical
data on the Mississippi subjects.

comprehensive medical examinations coupled with biochemical analyses of blood and urine and a quantitative dietary survey. In practice, the selection of methods is often determined by pragmatic considerations of resources, personnel, or logistics. Basic anthropometry is readily performed and yields gross correlates, but a meaningful interpretation of anthropometric data requires (in addition to relevant standard) information relative to the consumption of specific nutrients, the general state of health of the population and factors affecting the composition of the diet. Comprehensive cross-sectional surveys yield information on the prevalence and severity of specific nutritional problems and, if carefully performed, can give a reliable indication of the immediate cause of these problems in terms of indigenous patterns of food consumption. Even sophisticated cross-sectional surveys, however, may fail to provide a full understanding of the reasons for the nutritional status quo. Such an understanding requires a comprehension of the dietary traditions of individual cultures. This can be achieved only through longitudinal multidisciplinary studies. Failure to appreciate the nonnutritional values attached to foods by diverse cultures has been a prime obstacle to intervention programs in malnourished populations.

A manual of techniques of nutritional assessment has been published by the U.S. Interdepartmental Committee on Nutrition for National Development (1957). These methods have been used, with appropriate modifications, in some thirty-odd surveys carried out in countries around the world. A revised version has been prepared by the U.S. Public Health Service and published in the National Nutrition Survey Guidelines and Procedures (1970). Clinical, biochemical, and dietary procedures and standards are pescribed for different age groups, including pregnant and lactating women, infants, and small children. A brief evaluation of the rationale underlying these methods, and of their limitations, is included here.

Clinical Examination

Nutritional health can be evaluated only within the context of general health. A clinical examination conducted by a physician experienced in the diagnosis of nutritional diseases is therefore an important component of any program of nutritional assessment. In societies lacking modern sanitation facilities, the origins of nutritional disorders frequently are found in infectious diseases and parasitic infestations rather than in simple dietary inadequacies.

Infectious diseases affect nutritional status in a number

of different ways. Chronic or intermittent diarrhea, a common affliction in infancy and early childhood in primitive societies, impedes the digestion of food in the intestine as well as the absorption of nutrients released during digestion. Some nutrients, including milk sugar (lactose) and sucrose, are digested by enzymes located on the surface of cells of the intestinal mucosa that are sloughed off during protracted periods of enteritis and dysentery. The undigested sugars draw extracellular water into the intestine by osmosis, causing gas formation, cramps, and noninfectious diarrhea. These symptoms may extend into the postinfection period until a normal mucosal cell population has been reestablished. Persistent diarrhea also leads to depletion of electrolytes and escalating nutritional problems caused by weakness and appetite depression. Fever causes an accelerated catabolism of nutrients in the tissues and an increased loss of vitamins and minerals in the urine.

Any physiological disturbance, whether of infectious, metabolic, or emotional origin, that depresses appetite will have secondary effects on nutritional status. In affluent societies, the diet contains excess concentrations of some nutrients that are sufficient to satisfy minimal requirements even during periods of moderately reduced food intake. In the United States, for example, the food chain contains twice the quantity of protein required to satisfy the per capita protein requirement. A reduction of 50 percent in food intake during a disease episode, therefore, may be of little consequence as far as protein nutrition is concerned. For a child subsisting on a low-protein diet, however, such an episode may have serious nutritional consequences. In some societies, the diet is a precarious source of essential nutrients even when consumed in normal amounts by the healthy child. When consumed in reduced amounts during a protracted illness, it leads to multiple nutritional deficiencies. In the absence of a modern medical facility where the effects of anorexia associated with prolonged illness can be countered by administration of vitamin supplements, electrolyte solutions, and protein hydrolysates or amino acids, the nutritional sequelae of chronic illness can be very serious. The importance of eliminating the causes of inappetance as a prime strategy in dealing with undernutrition is therefore evident. The critical nutrients under most circumstances are protein and some of the water-soluble vitamins (principally thiamine, riboflavin, and niacin).

Biochemical Analyses

Diagnosis of mild or moderate deficiencies of vitamins

TABLE 8-1. A Comparison of the Riboflavin Status of Holmes County, Mississippi, Blacks and Wainwright, Alaska, Eskimos (1971).

Age Years	Standards[a]			Alaskan Eskimos			Mississippi Blacks		
	Deficient	Low	Acceptable	Deficient	Low	Acceptable	Deficient	Low	Acceptable
1-3	< 150	150-499	$\geq$ 500	0	0	2	28	19	14
4-6	< 100	100-299	$\geq$ 300	0	0	11	22	31	19
7-9	< 85	85-269	$\geq$ 270	0	1	19	17	29	28
10-15	< 70	70-199	$\geq$ 200	1	2	39	32	65	90
> 15	< 27	27-79	$\geq$ 80	0	0	65	25	112	383
Totals				1	3	136	124	256	534
% Distribution				0.6	2.1	97.3	13.6	28.0	58.4

[a]The abbreviation μg stands for urinary riboflavin per g creatinine (O'Neal, Johnson and Schaefer, 1970).

and minerals is generally based on the levels of these nutrients in the blood or urine. In some cases, the activity of specific vitamin-dependent enzymes can be determined, such as the thiamine-dependent enzyme transketolase in red blood cells. For most nutrients, standards have been developed for blood or urine concentrations that are equated with "acceptable", "low", or "deficient" status. (O'Neal, Johnson and Schaefer, 1970.) In Table 8-1 this classification is applied to urinary riboflavin values recorded for Mississippi blacks and Alaskan Eskimos. There is a natural association between most B-complex vitamins and protein that is reflected in the favorable riboflavin status of northern Alaskan Eskimos. The unsatisfactory riboflavin nutriture of some Mississippi black children is associated with a starchy, low-protein diet and a limited consumption of milk. The biochemical phase of nutrition survey generally provides the most reliable indication of nutritional status with respect to specific nutrients. Unfortunately, there is no satisfactory biochemical indicator of moderate protein deficiency. Serum protein levels are often misleading. In studies on Alaskan Eskimo and Mississippi black children, for example, serum protein levels were frequently higher in the latter although protein intake was known to be lower. (Draper, unpublished results.) An electrophoretic separation of serum proteins (Table 8-2) revealed that serums from blacks contained a large γ-globulin fraction, indicative of infections and infestations during early childhood. Serum albumin is a more reliable index of protein nutriture than total serum protein, but consistent depressions are seen only under conditions of severe deprivation.

TABLE 8-2. Distribution of Serum Proteins in Twenty-Five Mississippi Black Subjects with Elevated Serum Protein Values.[a]

	Normal Range (%)	N		
		<Normal	Normal	>Normal
Albumin	55-77	25	0	0
α_1-Globulin	2-5	0	24	1
α_2-Globulin	7-11	0	9	16
β-Globulin	8-12	1	10	14
γ-Globulin	10-20	0	4	21

[a]Children and adults of both sexes. Normal serum protein level 6.5-8.2 grams per 100 ml (1).

Diet Survey

Diet assessment is conceptually the least complicated component of a comprehensive nutrition survey. Operationally, it is generally the most difficult and least satisfactory. Two general approaches are customary. One is a personal or family dietary recall extending over the previous twenty-four hours, sometimes coupled with a questionnaire on the frequency with which various foods or groups of foods are customarily consumed. The other is a dietary record of the kinds and amounts of foods consumed over a period of days (usually three to seven), compiled in the home by a trained recorder with the aid of food models or a diet scale. Either method is fraught with significant quantitative errors, even in the hands of skilled interviewers. Nutrient intake is calculated from standard tables of food composition. Most of the available data are for single foods prepared by standard methods, whereas many native foods are mixtures prepared according to local customs. Also, the dietary of industrialized societies contains an increasing proportion of "fabricated foods" of variable composition. Diet assessment in semicommunal cultures is particularly difficult. Eskimo children, for example, may frequent several houses in the course of a day and derive a substantial portion of the daily diet from these visits.

Despite these difficulties, a diet survey often provides important information relative to the nutritional milieu. A dietary explanation of biochemical findings may be found from even qualitative diet records. For instance, low urinary riboflavin concentrations in Mississippi children were found to be associated with a lack of milk in the diet of certain families. Assessment of children's diets in industrialized societies has been made more difficult by a trend away from the traditional three-meals-a-day pattern of food consumption and toward a pattern of frequent snacks consisting predominantly of manufactured foods. As an aid to nutritional evaluation, some countries now require food manufacturers to state the nutrient content of their products on the container.

CULTURAL AND SOCIAL CONSIDERATIONS

Nutrition as a biological science appears to have achieved one of its major historic goals: the ability to formulate diets from pure compounds that will sustain experimental animals (and, by inference, human beings) in a state of nutritional health throughout a normal life span.

This accomplishment implies that all of the nutrients essential for human health are now identified. Eventually, certain additional trace elements probably will be added to the list, but these do no appear to be of much practical importance. Conceptually, therefore, the diet of any discrete population should be susceptible to analysis in terms of its capacity to provide adequate amounts of these essential nutrients, and it should be possible to devise modifications that will compensate for deficiencies of specific items.

Experience gained from intervention programs in both industrialized and nonindustrialized societies, however, has shown that this is a simplistic approach to the solution of malnutrition. Apart from considerations of economics, agriculture, and disease, the diet of any society is influenced by cultural values placed on individual foodstuffs that may be unrelated to their nutritional value. In affluent societies, which have removed most of the material obstacles to adequate nutrition, such values constitute the main barrier to diet improvement. Food choices based on such values are not necessarily deleterious but any beneficial nutritional fallout is coincidental rather than the product of a conscious decision.

Numerous illustrations could be cited of the impact of cultural traditions on nutritional status. Vitamin A deficiency (probably the most serious vitamin deficiency disease of children in the world today) is most prevalent in countries, such as Indonesia and Thailand, that are suited to the growing of leafy vegetables that are good sources of vitamin A activity. Yet the per capita consumption of vegetables in Indonesia, according to Food and Agriculture Organization statistics for 1960-1965, is less than one-quarter of that in the United States. The nutritional value of green vegetables as a supplement to white rice, the basic food staple, is not generally accepted. In the face of this cultural constraint, the current strategy for prevention of blindness caused by vitamin A deficiency in children is to administer massive doses of the vitamin by injection. This is clearly a stop-gap measure. A long-term solution will require an educational program aimed at modifying the current dietary pattern to take greater advantage of the supply of indigenous foods.

The necessity of considering cultural attitudes toward foods in attempts to alter nutritional status is further illustrated by the experience of Cassel (1955) with remedial

programs among the Zulus. Green vegetables could be introduced into the diet because there was no cultural prejudice
against them. Eggs, on the other hand, were rejected, because
they were used in certain religious rituals and because their
consumption was regarded as indicative of greed (i.e., an
unwillingness to exercise restraint until the egg could be
transformed into a chicken). Traditional beliefs militated
against the drinking of cow's milk by women, but this
constraint could be circumvented by the use of powdered milk,
because milk in this form was not associated with the tribal
cattle.

A preference in some societies for polished rice over
brown rice leads to beriberi, a classic example of "status
malnutrition" brought about through cross-cultural influences.
Unmilled rice contains enough vitamins (including thiamin) and
good-quality protein to serve unsuccessfully as a staple food
for a population with access to modest amounts of other plant
or animal foods.

The record of survival of many isolated societies is
evidence of the basic adequacy of their historic diets. Most
nutritional crises among these societies were the result of a
breakdown in the food supply or of a deterioration in the
quality of the diet brought about through contact with other
cultures. The present-day nutritional plight of the Zulus is
a case in point (Cassel, 1955). Their traditional cereal
staple was millet, which they supplemented with milk and meat
obtained in the course of their roving pastoral existence.
Their history is that of an aggressive, hardy society. As a
result of contact with white settlers, millet was supplanted
by maize, because of its greater yield, and herding was confined
to reservations that soon became eroded through overgrazing.
These changes reduced the Zulus to a state of nutritional
impoverishment.

The survival of Eskimos residing in the northernmost
regions of Alaska and Canada involved a successful adaptation
to a remarkably narrow diet base, (Draper, in press). Land
and sea mammals (with available amounts of fish) constituted
the dietary staples. At that latitude, native plant foods
were of negligible nutritional importance. This diet
supported a slow population growth over many centuries until
contact with white whalers generated epidemics of disease
that caused a sharp decline in numbers.

Evaluation of the historic Eskimo diet in terms of modern
knowledge of nutritional requirements indicates that, despite

its usually restricted character, it was capable of furnishing
adequate amounts of all essential nutrients. Vitamin C, a
substance generally associated with plant foods, was obtained
from raw or lightly cooked animal foods. There is little
historic evidence of deficiency diseases among the Eskimos.
Most of their nutritional crises, like those of other isolated
cultures, derived from episodes of famine, in this instance
caused by the misfortunes of hunting. Contact with outsiders
reduced the risk of famine, but led to new problems arising
from adulteration of the native diet with foods of generally
lower quality. Introduction of processed foods into the
Eskimo diet has been followed by increases in the incidence
of atherosclerosis, diabetes, and obesity, i.e., the hallmarks
of malnutrition in industrialized societies.

Although food habits are generally considered to be among
the oldest and most ingrained traditions, it is impressive how
rapidly the diet patterns of previously isolated populations
change following interaction with industrialized societies.
Diet records taken in 1972 in the Eskimo village of Wainwright,
Alaska, revealed a pervasive influence of processed foods,
particularly on the diet of the young (Draper, 1976). Breast
milk had been supplanted by canned milk. Chicken was frequently
identified as the favorite meat dish despite the historic
dependence of this population on indigenous animals for food.
Carbonated beverages, confectionary foods, and baked goods had
become major items in the diet of children with generally
devastating effects on dental health. The cost of these food
items (inflated by long-distance air transport) was partially
offset by a subsidized federal food stamp program. Many Eskimo
families qualified for this program on the basis of their low
cash income. For the most part, these changes in diet came
about in the span of one generation. Hunting now is engaged in
as much for sport and excitement as for food. With the added
advantages of modern firearms, power boats, and mechanized land
vehicles, the present-day population is better equipped to
sustain itself as a hunting society than were its predecessors.
However, its cultural values are no longer those of a hunting
society, and the village now looks to Western industrialized
society for many of its nutritional needs.

NUTRITION IN EARLY CHILDHOOD: SOME CROSS-CULTURAL EXPERIENCES

In this section, some illustrations are given of multifaceted nutritional problems of children belonging to two
diverse cultures: rural Mississippi blacks and northern

Alaskan Eskimos.

Nutritional Anemia

Iron-deficiency anemia, one of the most prevalent nutritional problems of children, is often the result of an interplay of biological, socioeconomic and behavioral factors. Rural Mississippi black children share with most others the risk of anemia that derives from the low iron content of milk and the fact that there are few iron-rich solid foods. In recent decades, their iron intake, like that of most inhabitants of industrialized countries, has been reduced by the abandonment of iron in favor of aluminum cooking pots. Examination of four- and five-year-old children revealed that 31 percent were harboring *Ascaris*, an infestation known to interfere with the absorption of iron from the intestines. A loss of iron also could be inferred from frequent episodes of infectious diarrhea that were associated with inadequate sanitation facilities and a moist, warm climate. Additionally, a longitudinal study revealed that geophagia was practiced by about 40 percent of pregnant women and by 15 percent of preadolescent children (Vermeet & Frate, 1975). One of the nutritional sequelae of geophagia is that the absorption of iron and other divalent cations is reduced by chelate formation with colloidal clays in the lumen of the intestine. Considering the complexities of this situation, it is paradoxical that the anemia of iron deficiency is sometimes referred to as *simple nutritional anemia*.

Obesity

Overweight has been observed to be more prevalent among the lower than the upper classes in industrialized societies (Stunkard, 1968). One of the explanations offered for this apparent paradox is that adiposity has not been stigmatized by people in lower socioeconomic groups, many of whom still regard it as a sign of general well-being. Obesity was found to be particularly pervasive among rural Mississippi blacks (Nelson, K.E., & Draper, H.H., unpublished results). The average body weight of women of child-bearing age was significantly above the mean for black women in the United States generally, which in turn is higher than the mean for white women (Nelson, K.E., personal communication, April 8, 1971).

The correlates of obesity (atherosclerosis, diabetes, hypertension) were much in evidence. "Definite" hypertension ($\geq$ 160/95) was recorded in 39.7 percent of adult females between the ages of 18 and 79 years (Nelson, K.E., personal communication, April 8, 1971); "severe" hypertension ($\geq$ 200/120) was observed in 8.5 percent of adults of both sexes. Hypertension is probably a factor in a high rate of perinatal mortality. These observations are consistent with the known susceptibility of American blacks to high blood pressure.

In contrast to U.S. blacks, the incidence of hypertension, diabetes, and atherosclerosis in Eskimos has been found to be remarkably low. Acculturation has been accompanied by some increase in the occurrence of these diseases, but a comparison of the prevalence of hypertension in the two populations made in 1971 reveals a marked difference in all age groups except the elderly (Table 8-3). The low incidence of hypercholesterolemia and atherosclerosis among Eskimos, who have relied for generations on a high-fat diet almost exclusively of animal origin, provides an interesting paradox for epidemiologists, who generally consider that such a diet is conducive to cardiovascular disease. Hence, Eskimos have been prime subjects for cross- cultural research into the relaitonship between diet and the occurrence of atherosclerosis and diabetes.

Modern pediatric medicine has discouraged the philosophy that "fat babies are happy babies" and has substituted the admonition that "fat babies make fat adults". Obesity in infants is associated with hyperplasia of the adipose tissues (i.e., an increased number of fat cells), whereas adult obesity is due primarily to hypertrophy (an enlargement of existing cells). There is evidence that individuals who develop a large number of adipocytes as children have a greater propensity for fat accumulation as adults. While this concept may be valid, it is clearly not the sole explanation of adult obesity and it does nothing to explain childhood obesity.

Attempts to rationalize the prevalence of obesity among blacks in terms of differences in metabolism, diet composition or anthropometry have not been enlightening. No differences have been found in basal metabolic rate. The high carbohydrate content of the diet is an unlikely explanation, since the cereal diet of many Asian societies is equally high in this component. By this token, the high-fat native diet of Eskimos should produce an exaggeration of the problem, whereas historic evidence indicates that this was not the case. Obesity is a particular concern in blacks because of its association with hypertensive, atherosclerotic cardiovascular, and cerebral disease (Finnerty, 1971).

TABLE 8-3. A Comparison of the Prevalence of High Blood
Pressure (HBP) Among Northern Alaskan Eskimos
and Rural Mississippi Blacks (1971).[a]

Age Range	Reference Blood Pressure	Alaskan Eskimos		Mississippi Blacks	
years	systolic/diastolic	Total N	% HBP	Total N	% HBP[b]
0-9	$\geq$ 130/90	83	0	119	6
10-19	$\geq$ 140/90	93	1	262	18
20-29	$\geq$ 140/90	27	4	40	20
30-39	$\geq$ 150/90	43	2	55	53
40-49	$\geq$ 160/90	26	0	71	65
50-59	$\geq$ 160/90	25	8	108	59
60- +	$\geq$ 160/95	38	42	151	63

[a] Males and females in comparable proportions from each
population sample.

[b] Includes 8.5 percent of the adult sample with severe
hypertension ($\geq$ 200/120).

Clinical examination of Mississippi blacks revealed a
further possible ingredient in the etiology of obesity in this
population. Although they reside outside the well-recognized
"goiter belt" that surrounds the Great Lakes in the United
States, 16 percent of the women of reproductive age were found
to have palpable goiters (Nelson, K. E., personal communication,
April 8, 1971). A diet survey revealed a high consumption of
home-grown "greens" (spinach, kohlrabi, cabbage, and turnip
leaves), which are known to contain natural goitrogens. To
what extent hypothyroidism induced by these compounds may be
a factor in the unusual incidence of obesity in this
population is unknown.

Lactose Intolerance

From a cross-cultural standpoint, the genetic code appears to be consistent with respect to which biochemical constituents of the body must be obtained from the environment (i.e., the biochemicals that cannot be synthesized in the cells). As far as is known, all racial and ethnic groups require the same essential nutrients. Biochemical individuality in quantitative nutritional needs has been well documented, but such variations (with the exception of the vitamin D requirement, which is affected by skin pigmentation) do not appear to follow a racial pattern.

Despite this general rule, there are striking differences in the capacity of different racial and ethnic groups to digest certain sugars. Most ethnic groups other than those of northern European descent experience a decline in the synthesis of lactase (an intestinal enzyme required for the digestion of milk sugar) in early childhood and are able to tolerate only small quantities of milk as adults. Although this phenomenon has been generally described in a racial-ethnic context, adult retention of the ability to synthesize lactase appears to be an acquired trait that is related to a cultural tradition of herding (Kretchmer, 1970). The practice of dairying favored survival of mutants having this lactase-synthesizing ability, regardless of their racial origins. While Negroes are generally regarded as lactose intolerant, African tribes such as the Fulani and Tussi, which have a history of dairying, continue to synthesize lactase as adults. Studies on progeny derived from outmarriages between these tribes and members of nonherding societies indicate that lactose tolerance is an incompletely dominant genetic trait (Kretchmer, 1970). Variability in the capacity of different populations to digest a lactose load is illustrated in Figure 8-1.

Fifty-gram lactose load tests conducted on Alaskan Eskimos revealed the expected pattern of intolerance (intestinal cramps, flatulence, and diarrhea) (Bell, Draper, & Bergan, 1973). However, administration of a series of graduated doses revealed that nineteen out of twenty adult subjects were asymptomatic after a 10-gram load (equivalent to the amount of lactose in a cup of milk--see Table 8-4). This study indicated that most Eskimos can tolerate up to 3 cups of milk per day, or its equivalent in other dairy foods, if such foods are consumed in at least three portions at intervals of several hours. Intolerance for lactose per se is not a serious nutritional consideration; its nutritional significance stems from the fact that it may deprive nutritionally vulnerable subjects,

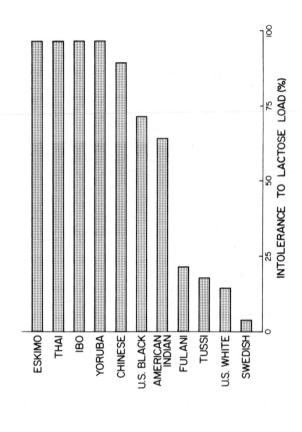

FIGURE 8-1. Variations in the Response of Different Populations to an Oral Lactose Load. Adapted from Kretchmer (1972).

TABLE 8-4. Symptomatic Response of Twenty Adult Alaskan
Eskimos to Graduated Lactose Loads.

	Lactose Load (grams)		
	10	20	30
No. first experiencing symptoms	1	8	4
No. with symptoms at this intake or less	1	9	13
% with symptoms at this intake or less	5	45	65

such as the growing child and the pregnant and lactating woman,
of other important nutrients present in dairy products.

Calcium Deficiency

   Milk consumption by Eskimos traditionally ended at weaning
age. The protein and vitamin needs of the growing child were
met by the predominantly meat diet. But meat is very low in
calcium, and while variable quantities of this element were
obtained from the bones of fish, it appears that Eskimo
children (like many children in cereal-eating societies)
subsisted on about half the dietary calcium recommended for
children in industrialized countries. Yet calcium deficiency
in Eskimo children and adults has never been identified as a
significant nutritional problem.

   The explanation of this apparent anomaly has been provided
by recent biochemical research on a sophisticated mechanism
of metabolic adaptation to low dietary intakes of calcium.
This vitamin D-dependent mechanism provides for an increase
in the efficiency of absorption and retention of calcium when
the intake is low, and it apparently accounts for the ability
of diverse populations to adapt to a wide range of calcium
intakes.

Vitamin D Deficiency

   There are major differences among races with respect to
the capacity to synthesize vitamin D in the skin. These
differences are significant in the prevention of rickets in
children and of osteomalacia ("adult rickets") in pregnant

and nursing women. Vitamin D is formed in the skin by
photochemical processes induced by the ultraviolet rays
present in sunlight. Since adequate exposure to sunlight
obviates the need for vitamin D in the diet, it has been
proposed that this vitamin be reclassified as a hormone.

However, not all cultures may be capable of fulfilling
their vitamin D needs through exposure to sunlight. Many
Eskimo children receive no direct sunlight for several weeks
during midwinter. Furthermore, their skin is almost
completely covered with heavy clothing during much of the year.
It is doubtful, therefore, that Eskimos could have survived
without access to vitamin D in fish, seal, and whale oils.

The efficiency of vitamin D synthesis is reduced by skin
pigments that absorb part of the energy of ultraviolet rays.
In fair-skinned northern Europeans, vitamin D synthesis
proceeds very efficiently, whereas in black- and brown-skinned
races synthesis is inhibited. Indeed, a need to regulate the
synthesis of vitamin D has been offered as a possible
explanation of the origin of skin color (Loomis, 1970).
According to this hypothesis, light skin was advantageous in
northern latitudes, because of a paucity of sunlight, whereas
dark skin was advantageous in equatorial areas, where a
surfeit of sunlight posed a danger of vitamin D toxicity. In
light-skinned subjects living in tropical areas, this danger
is counteracted by tanning. An interesting corollary of this
theory is that the children of recent Pakistani immigrants
into the United Kingdom have been found to exhibit a high
incidence of rickets.

Sucrose Intolerance

A rare form of intolerance to disaccharides has been
recently characterized in Alaskan and Greenland Eskimos. The
symptoms are similar to those seen in lactose intolerance, but
in this instance they are due to a genetic block in the
synthesis of sucrase, an intestinal enzyme required for the
digestion of cane and beet sugar. The anomaly follows a
familial pattern that is unrelated to the pattern of lactose
intolerance (Bell, Draper, & Bergan, 1973). Primary sucrase
deficiency appears to be a nutritional problem to which
Eskimos are uniquely susceptible, and although the incidence
is relatively small, for those affected it presents major
difficulties of adaptation to processed foods now being
inserted into the general diet. Sucrase deficiency is a
nutritional problem created by acculturation. The virtual
absence of sucrose from the native diet of northern Alaskan

Eskimos over many centuries obviated the need for sucrase, and hence there was no selection pressure in its favor. It is only in recent times that its absence has been a biological disadvantage.

Sucrase deficiency can be diagnosed either by observing the gross symptoms that ensue following sucrose ingestion, or by monitoring blood glucose concentration after a standard oral sucrose load as done in the standard lactose tolerance test. Figure 8-2 illustrates the failure of the blood glucose titer to rise following administration of sucrose to five intolerant subjects and the normal increment that followed ingestion of sucrose by a tolerant subject (Bell, Draper, & Bergan, 1973). The "flat" glucose curves denote an inability to split sucrose into its component sugars, glucose and fructose.

PERSONAL CONSPECTUS

The foregoing discussion points up the need for a multi-disciplinary approach to the study of nutritional problems. Social scientists are capable of providing a dimension to such studies that is beyond the scope of biomedicine. However, there is an a priori requirement to characterize the *status praesens* by rigorous application of the nutritional, biochemical, and clinical sciences. This requirement seldom has been satisfied in nutritional studies carried out by social scientists. Conversely, few surveys conducted by biologists have adequately considered the influence of cultural food habits on nutritional status.

There is a tendency among students in the social sciences (and others) to draw simplistic conclusions about the role of nutrition in the evolution of primitive societies. These conclusions are generally based on popular or pseudo-scientific assertions about the importance of specific foodstuffs in mental or physical development. In terms of current dietary recommendations for the general U.S. public, the native diet of northern Alaskan Eskimos, for example, may be regarded as disastrous, since it is essentially devoid of three of the four main food groups said to be necessary for a balanced diet (fruits and vegetables, cereals, and dairy foods). Yet for centuries this diet sustained an active, vigorous society under extremely harsh environmental conditions. There is nothing unusual about the metabolism of Eskimos that enabled them to survive on this diet, as demonstrated by the Arctic

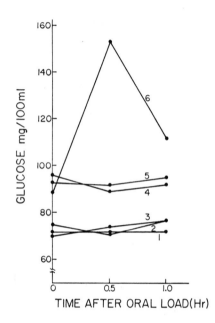

Figure 8-2.   Blood glucose response of five sucrose-intolerant adult Eskimos (Subjects 1 to 5) and one tolerant individual (Subject 6) given a 50-g oral sucrose load (Bell, Draper, & Bergan, 1973).

explorer V. Stefansson, who maintained himself in good health
on the same diet under medical surveillance for two years.
His experience was an illustration of the fact that there are
no essential foods; there are only essential nutrients.
Analyzed in terms of its capacity to provide essential
nutrients, the native Eskimo diet (as traditionally prepared
and consumed) is capable of sustaining nutritional health in
any human population. However, it requires more than a casual
acquaintance with the essential nutrient requirements of man,
the metabolism of these nutrients, the composition of native
foods and the dietary traditions of Eskimos to make this
assessment.

In the wake of recent evidence of significant malnutrition
in the United States, there has been a call for the training of
more scientists along interdisciplinary lines. Such scientists,
it is argued, would be better able to deal with the broad
spectrum of cultural, socioeconomic, and biological factors
involved in malnutrition. Attempts to devise graduate
curricula appropriate to this objective, however, have
encountered serious difficulties. Social science departments
have tended to embrace the concept of a graduate well trained,
for example, in social anthropology, with "a couple of courses
in nutrition". Graduate departments of nutrition, on the
other hand, commonly admit students with no previous courses
in nutrition, providing they have sound undergraduate
preparation in analytical, organic and physical chemistry,
biochemistry, physiology, and microbiology, i.e., subjects
in which social science students generally have little, if
any, preparation. Generally speaking, neither department is
willing to compromise its basic curriculum for the sake of a
program of interdisciplinary training. Consequently, the
student entering such a program is confronted with the
necessity of completing what amounts to two complete curricula
before beginning his dissertation research. Few students are
willing and able to undertake a training program of this
magnitude, or to keep abreast of developments in multiple
disciplines after graduation.

A more productive approach to the study of nutritional
problems can be made by multidisciplinary teams of
investigators trained in depth in their respective disciplines.
Scientific communication among the members of such teams
generally presents no serious difficulties and the quality of
research is likely to be superior to that achieved by graduates
of interdisciplinary training programs. Under the International
Biological Program, teams of investigators consisting of social
anthropologists, psychologists, physiologists, nutritionists,

physical anthropologists, geneticists, and physicians engaged
in successful collaborative research on human adaptability in
the Arctic. For most of those involved, this experience
verified the feasibility of multidisciplinary research and
illustrated the additional benefits that can be derived from
an integrated approach to research on human populations.

REFERENCES

Bell, R. R., Draper, H. H., Bergan, J. G. Sucrose, lactose
and glucose, tolerance in nothern Alaskan Eskimos.
American Journal of Clinical Nutrition, 1973, 26,
1185.

Cassell, J. A comprehensive health program among South
African Zulus. In B. J. Paul (Ed.), Health, culture,
and community. New York: Russell Sage Foundation,
1955.

Draper, H. H. A review of recent nutritional research in the
Arctic. In Proceedings of the Third International
Symposium on Circumpolar Health. Toronto:
University of Toronto Press, 1976, R. S. Shephard
and S. Itoh (Eds.).

Draper, H. H. The aboriginal Eskimo diet in modern perspective.
American Anthropoligist (in press).

Draper, H. H. The nutritional status of Alaskan Eskimos. In
O. L. Kline and C. G. King (Eds.), Nutritional
Adaptation to the Environment. Human Adaptability
Coordinating Office International Biological Program,
University Park, Pennsylvania, 1976, 3.

Finnerty, F. A. Hypertension is different in blacks. Journal
of the American Medical Association, 1971, 216, 1635.

Kretchmer, N. Lactose and lactase. Scientific American, 1972,
227, 70.

Loomis, W. F. Rickets. Scientific American, 1970, 223, 76.

O'Neal, R. M., Johnson, O. C., & Schaefer, A. E. Guidelines
for classification and interpretation of group blood
and urine data as part of the National Nutrition
Survey. 1970, Pediatric Research, 4, 103.

Rantakallio, L., & Väänänen, M. The effects of social and economic background on the hospitalization of children during the first five years of life. In Proceedings of the Third International Symposium on Circumpolar Health. Toronto: University of Toronto Press, 1976.

Stunkard, A. J. Environment and obesity: Recent advances in our understanding of regulation of food intake in man. Federation Proceedings, 1968, 27, 1367.

U.S. Interdepartmental Committee on Nutrition for National Development. Manual for Nutrition Surveys. Washington, D.C.: U.S. Government Printing Office, 1957.

Vermeer, D. E., & Frate, D. A. Geophagy in a Mississippi County. Annals of the Association of American Geographers, 1975, 65, 414.

Chapter 9

Infant Development and Mother–Infant Interaction in Urban Zambia

Susan Goldberg

Brandeis University

From the outset, my work in Zambia was intended to serve several purposes. The immediate aim of the research was to explore the relationship between patterns of mother-infant interaction and later infant development. At the same time, I hoped to find out whether the techniques of observation and assessment with which I was familiar would be applicable to research in a different cultural context. I thought of my work in 1968-1970 as a pilot exploration. It was only after I had been working in Zambia for several months that an additional purpose became evident to me. I had to choose a text for a course in development at the University of Zambia and I soon realized that all the existing texts were about white, middleclass children, usually in the United States. I would like to think that the studies reported in this volume and others like them will make it possible for students outside the United States and Western Europe to use texts that include studies of children relevant to their own environments. That is, a Zambian University student should be able to read some material about child development in Zambia or at least a Central African country.

When I arrived In Zambia, I had recently coauthored a paper that suggested a way in which mother-infant interaction might be related to infant cognitive development (Lewis & Goldberg, 1969). We argued in that paper that early contin-

gency experience enables infants to develop the expectancy
that their behavior has results and is effective. This
expectancy subsequently motivates exploration, learning, and
practice of new skills, thus facilitating development.
Furthermore, the most important source of early contingency
experience is the mother. Prompt maternal responses related
in a consistent way to the infant's behavior should enhance
development. Several reports of precocious infant development
in previously studied African samples had emphasized the
contribution of traditional patterns of infant care to this
precocity (Falade, 1960; Geber, 1958; Ramarasona, 1959). The
relationship between mother and infant described in these
papers suggested a high incidence of physical proximity and
contact, prompt maternal responses, and a high degree of
maternal indulgence. These conditions should enhance the
probability of the infants' receiving more frequent contingency
experiences than typical European and American infants, who
spend long periods alone in their beds in separate rooms. I
observed and was told that Zambian infants were rarely left
alone. They were carried by their mothers in a cloth sling a
good part of the day, slept with their mothers at night, and
were breast-fed on demand. Assuming that Zambian infants'
contingency experiences were probably quite different in
amount and kind from those of American infants we have studied
(Lewis & Goldberg, 1969), I wondered whether individual
differences in mother-infant interaction would still have the
predicted relationship to later development. Would Zambian
infants whose mothers were more attentive and responsive be
those who showed more rapid development?

The remainder of this chapter describes the general plan
of the study and the characteristics and living conditions of
the sample, and reports data on mother-infant relationships
and sensorimotor development. After discussing the relationship between measures of early mother-infant interaction and
infant development, I attempt to evaluate the impact of the
work in Zambia from a broader yet personal perspective,
indicating how it has influenced my thinking about infant
development and research in general.

DESIGN AND SUBJECTS

The original plan of the study was to follow a group of
approximately 40 infants from the age of four months through
the remainder of their first year with periodic visits to
their homes for observation and testing. All testing and

interviewing was carried out between December 1968 and March 1970 by two female Zambian research assistants.[1] Table 9-1 indicates the data collected, the number of infants involved, and the age of the infants at each visit.

TABLE 9-1.   Data Collection Schedule

x Age and Range	Environment and Care	Motor Development	Sensorimotor Development
2 months	demographic data		
4.2 months (3.8-4.4)	coded observation of motor-infant interaction (N = 39)	Bayley Motor Scale (N = 39)	
6.5 months (5.8-7.3)			Prehension Scale (N = 33)[a] Object Permanence Scale (N = 32)[a] Space Scale (N = 33)[a]
9.8 months (8.8-10.4)			Prehension Scale (N = 5 infants who had not completed scale 6 months only)[a] Object Permanence Scale (N = 25)[a] Space Scale (N = 23)[a]
12.2 months (11.7-13.4)	Home Stimulation Inventory (N = 25)[b]	Bayley Motor Scale (N = 16)	Object Permanance Scale (N = 23)[a] Space Scale (N = 21)[a]

NOTE: N = the number of infants for whom data are complete.
[a]From the Albert Einstein Scales of Sensorimotor Development (Escalona & Corman, 1966). [b]Caldwell (1969).

[1]The work of Phideas Nguluwe and Margaret Kateya in enlisting families in the study, interviewing mothers, and observing and testing infants was invaluable. Leslie Beck assisted with observation and data analysis. This research was carried out while the author was a member of the Human Development Research Unit, University of Zambia.

We began with 21 girls and 18 boys born to families
residing in Matero, a high-density suburb of Lusaka, Zambia's
capital city. (Ten additional infants whose data are not
included in any analysis were visited as pilot subjects.)
Families were located from an earlier house census of Matero.
Within a selected geographical area, the research assistants
visited every family likely to have an infant (every family
that reported no children under two in the census). Those
with infants were included if the infant was the appropriate
age, was breast-fed, appeared to be healthy, and there was no
report of difficulty with pregnancy, delivery, or infant
health. Twenty of these infants had been born at home with
a female relative assisting. The remainder had been born in
Lusaka Central Hospital. No attempt was made to control size
of family, tribal background, or parental education and
occupation. The families ranged in size from 3 to 17 persons
($\bar{x}$ = 7.2). There were 19 nuclear families and 20 extended
families. Tribal background varied, and 16 different tribes
were represented. The length of time the parents lived in
Lusaka varied (2 to 17 years, $\bar{x}$ = 8.3) but none of the
parents had been born in Lusaka. These were recently
urbanized families who were in the process of adapting rural
traditions to urban life. Fathers' occupation and schooling
varied. The sample included fathers who were laborers, truck
drivers, clerks, policemen, and small businessmen. All but
three fathers had completed primary school and five had gone
to secondary school. Most mothers had one to three years of
schooling, although one had completed secondary school.

Such heterogeneity would never be acceptable in an
experimental sample in most studies. In all my previous work,
I had selected subjects so as to restrict or control variables
such as socioeconomic status and ethnicity. But I did not
think of this study as an experimental one. I thought of it
as primarily observational. In such a study, a reasonable
strategy is to sample a geographic area in such a way as to
obtain a representative sample. That is, one tries to mimic
the variability of such factors as socioeconomic status,
ethnicity, and length of residence in the total population
for the area. In fact, I did not adopt this strategy either.
My primary concern was with the relationship between maternal
behavior and infant development and I wanted, first of all,
to ensure the cooperation of families and, secondly, to ensure
that there would be variability of maternal behavior. If I
were to selectively control population variables, there was
always the danger of finding out that the sample was then
homogeneous with respect to maternal behavior. If I were to
systematically vary population variables, I might find that

I had varied conditions of no relevance for maternal behavior.
On some dimensions, such as social class, I had no basis for
selecting levels, since I could not conceptualize social class
in Western terms for this population. The most important
aspect of the work, I thought then (and still think), was to
get into homes and look. The niceties of experimental method
seemed to be an obstacle to doing this. While experimental
methods were, I thought, inappropriate at the outset, I hoped
that the outcome of the observational work would point to
some questions that could be answered experimentally, in
Zambia or elsewhere.

FINDINGS

Living Conditions

     The following description of living conditions is based
on data collected at the first visit as well as on subsequent
observations in the homes.

     Matero borders on Lusaka's heavy industrial area. The
houses of stucco with corrugated metal roofs are close together along unpaved streets. Houses vary somewhat in size
but the families we visited lived in two or three rooms. None
had inside plumbing or electricity (although twenty-three had
battery operated radios). Those who were fortunate had a
nearby water tap and outhouse shared with several other
families. Those less fortunate used water taps and pit
latrines at a distance. Three families had wood burning
stoves in the house, but most cooked outside on a wood or
charcoal fire. Typically, charcoal would be used after pay-
days, when money was available. Thereafter, as charcoal and
money were exhausted, the mother would gather wood. Most
family activities, including meal preparation, washing of
clothing and eating utensils, eating, and socializing took
place outside on the veranda or on mats in the yard. Grass
around the houses was rare, but some families planted flowers
or decorative plants and some vegetables. Most of the women
grew corn in nearby fields during the rains (November to
March). Corn is the staple crop and the traditional diet is
based on cornmeal porridge (*nsima*), eaten with meat, vegetables,
groundnuts (peanuts), or fish, particularly a small, high-
protein fish called *kapenta*. This is a nourishing diet, but
in the city, lack of money and knowhow, and the availability
of beer and soft drinks, make malnutrition a major problem
and probably a basic cause of high infant mortality. The most

frequent immediate causes of infant deaths are gastroenteritis,
respiratory infections, and the complicating effects of measles.
Medical care is widely available in free government clinics,
but lack of transportation and little understanding of how to
use such facilities (i.e., when to go, what to tell, what to
ask) combine to make services inadequate.

Family Life

The following description is based on data elicted via
the Home Stimulation Inventory (Caldwell, 1969), administered
at a separate visit after the twelve-month assessment. The
inventory consists of a series of statements that are checked
as being typical of the family (yes) or not typical (no). It
includes some items judged solely on the basis of information
given by the mother (e.g., the mother has not punished the
child physically more than once in the previous year) and
some items rated on the basis of observation during the visit
(e.g., mother praises child at least once during the visit).
It has eight parts, each of which reflects the Western middle-
class conception of a "good" home environment:

Part I.   Measures frequency and stability of contact with
          adults (e.g., child spends part of the visit on
          mother's lap). We added two items to this
          section, to record the amount of time the child
          was carried on the mother's back in a sling, and
          the infant's sleeping arrangements.

Part II. Concerned with vocal and developmental stimu-
          lation (e.g., mother encourages new behavior).

Part III. Reflects frequency and kind of mother-child
          play (e.g., mother structures play periods,
          mother sometimes sings to the child).

Part IV. Reflects the emotional tone of the home (e.g.,
          mother praises child during the visit).

Part V.   Concerned with restrictions on the child's
          freedom of movement (e.g., child's clothing
          allows freedom of movement).

Part VI. Reflects the range of the child's experiences
          (e.g., how frequently the infant goes along to
          market, church, or on social visits).

Part VII. Reflects the physical condition of the home (e.g., play area is safe and free of dangerous things).

Part VIII. Omitted because it concerns play materials not available to any of the infants in our sample.

Table 9-2 summarizes the data from the Home Stimulation Inventory. The score on each subscale is the number of yes responses for each family, and the total is the sum of these subscores. High scores reflect Western conceptions of the "ideal" home environment.

TABLE 9-2. Scores on Home Stimulation Inventory.

Part	Information	Mean	Range	Maximum Possible Score
I	Adult contact	7.0	7-9	10
II	Intentional stimulation	3.8	1-7	9
III	Play contact	5.1	2-10	10
IV	Emotional climate	4.1	1-6	10
V	Restrictions	3.3	2-4	6
VI	Breadth of experience	5.1	3-7	8
VII	Physical environment	5.5	2-9	10
Total		33.0	24-40	63

The most striking characteristic to me is the high frequency and stability of adult contacts for these infants. No infant's family scored below the midpoint of the scale. Similarly, on Part IV, no family scored above 6 of a possible 10 in expression of emotional climate. We will discuss this in more detail later. Typically, breadth of experience also was rated high as the infant was involved in all aspects of family life. Aside from maintenance activities, the major family activities were social in nature. Families did not report regular recreational activities but 23 reported frequent regular visits with family and friends, and 23 mothers said they exchanged regular visits with other women with children. Eighteen infants went regularly to church and 15 to markets and shops. In general, there seemed to be little concern for adapting family life to the needs of the infant. Although children are highly valued, Zambian families are not "child centered". Children are expected to adjust to family life. The family continues its regular activities and it is taken for granted that the infant will be there. Little consideration is given to whether the activity is suitable for the infant, to the convenience of taking an infant along, or the chance that the infant may interfere with adult activities. Indeed, family maintenance occupies a major portion of the mother's time, particularly in the mornings, and the available time for fussing over the infant is limited. Infants are therefore exposed to a wide variety of people, places, and experiences early in life. Families are large by Western standards. Although school-aged siblings are often in school, the schedule of three daily shifts in local schools ensures that they are home a good part of the day. High unemployment rates in Lusaka also increase the probability that adult men are home during the day. Thus the mother and child are embedded in a densely populated social context.

This picture of family life is consistent with that described by Munro (1968) for a better-educated and more affluent group of Zambians in Lusaka. Rent in Munro's sample was K24-32, compared with K3.50-8.50 (in 1968-1970, K1 = 1.40 dollars) in our sample. Half of Munro's fathers had been to secondary school as compared with the five in our sample. However, frequent contact with adults, great variety of experience, and emphasis on social interactions were characteristic of both samples and thus appear to be a pattern typical of urban Zambia rather than a function of social class.

In addition to using relevant items on the Home Stimulation Inventory, we coded interaction behavior during

a ten-minute observation at the four-month visit, and questioned
the mothers about feeding and weaning at the twelve-month visit.

Interview Data

All of the infants were breast-fed initially and the
majority (22 of 25) were still breast-fed at one year. Of
those who had been weaned before a year, one was weaned at
9 months when her mother had to be hospitalized, one at 4
months on the "advice" of a doctor (by a mother judged in all
respects to be lowest in responsiveness to the infant), and
one had been weaned at 11 months because her mother judged
her ready. It appears that under normal circumstances most
infants are nursed throughout the first year. Of the still-
nursing mothers, we inquired when they planned to wean the
infant. The answers were difficult to interpret. Some
replied that they had plenty of time for that, that they did
not worry about it or specified an age that the child had
already passed. At most, we could only conclude that weaning
was not a pressing concern for these mothers of one-year-olds.

In general there was little scheduling of feeding or
other caretaking activities. Only five mothers reported that
they tried to keep the infant on a schedule of any kind.

It is customary for nursing infants to sleep with their
mothers, and 19 infants were still sleeping with their mothers
at one year. One slept with a sister, one with a grandmother,
and 4 slept in beds of their own.

Especially when very young, these infants are constantly
with their mothers, with a grandmother or other substitute
caretaker, carried in a cloth sling on the back. When the
infant is too young to sit, the sling serves as a cot, playpen,
buggy, and feeder. As the infant gets older, more time is spent
sitting on a mat or on the floor and by a year the sling is
more often primarily a mode of transport. All of our mothers
said they would still carry their one-year-olds if going somewhere and taking the child. Sixteen mothers said that they
still carried the child regularly and of these, eight were
willing to carry the child for long periods of time.

There seemed to be little conscious stimulation of infant
development. For example, only six mothers said they encouraged
the baby to do new things. No mother bought toys for the
purpose of stimulating development, but this is not surprising,
since only four infants had toys of any kind. These were dolls,
balls, toy dishes, and cars. Most mothers said that their

babies played with materials found around their homes such as old tins, crockery, sand and water, sticks and stones, pieces of cloth, bottle-tops, and boxes. However, we rarely saw infants playing with anything, and few mothers (seven) said they structured the infant's play or demonstrated use of play-things. Few (six) were observed to give the child an activity or engage in verbal games during the interview. Thus, it is likely that opportunities to engage in manipulative play with objects in the home occurred incidentally rather than through a mother's structuring of the environment.

At the same time, there were few restrictions and little interference with the infant. All but one mother said they allowed the child "messy" play and no mother was observed to interfere with a child during the visit. Only five children were judged to be dressed in restrictive clothing and no mother made use of any baby equipment or barriers to restrain the infant's movements. If the children did not nap on their mother's backs, they slept on a mat or bed from which they could get out on their own when awake. The major restriction seemed to be the use of the cloth sling. I have argued else-where (Goldberg, 1972) that even after an infant is able to reach and retrieve objects and is capable of some form of locomotion, long periods of being carried in the sling continue to provide high levels of stimulus change. However, these are brought about through the action of the mother rather than through the developing locomotor and manipulatory skills of the infant. Thus, a large portion of the infant's experience in the sling at older ages is passive rather than active. Time spent in the sling is therefore a restriction of exploratory activity, a limit on "floor freedom" for older infants. (In a later section, the relationship between our test scores and carrying practices is considered in more detail.)

There seemed to be little show of either positive or negative emotion toward the infant. No mother was observed to shout at her infant, nor did any mother scold or complain about the child more than once during the visit. However, 17 reported using punishment of a physical nature more than once in the previous week. Three mothers were observed to show affection by hugging, kissing, or caressing the infant during the visit. Most (18 of 25) showed pleasure when the visitor praised the child and 16 praised the child themselves. Favorable comparisons with another child were made spontaneously by eight mothers. These are, of course, ways in which a Western mother reveals feelings about a child and it may well be that Zambian mothers express these same feelings through other behaviors to which the inventory was not sensitive.

Observation Data

At the four-month visit we included a short (ten-minute) observation of mother and infant before any testing was introduced. An observation period of this length does not give a detailed picture of the ongoing mother-infant inter- action, but, rather, a sample of interaction under potentially stressful conditions. We kept the observation short because we viewed it as a trial situation for our coding system. Because of the difficulties in working outdoors, we were unable to coordinate the two observers' time periods for reliability checks. A single observer therefore watched and coded all mother-infant pairs. We hoped that even with these limitations the most salient characteristics of the mother-infant relation- ship would emerge.

Most observations took place outdoors, and the mother was told we would watch the baby for a while before doing any test- ing. We did not tell the mothers they too were being observed, nor did they seem to be conscious of our doing so. For example, one mother left us alone with her infant and went inside to prepare for a trip to market. Another, the mother of twins, fed the infant we were not observing for most of the observation. During the observation period, the observer recorded in each ten-second period the occurrence of mother and infant behaviors. For the mother, these included looking at, smiling at, vocalizing to, feeding, holding, and playing with the infant. For the infant, we recorded active movements, crying, smiling, vocaliza- tion, eating, and quiet play.

The first analysis of the data involved tabulation of the number of ten-second periods in which each maternal and infant behavior occurred. The mean range of frequencies are entered for each behavior under the column headings in Table 9-3. These frequencies are presented for the girls and boys combined as there were no significant sex differences either in infant behavior or in maternal behavior toward the two sexes. The most frequent behaviors for the mothers were holding, looking, and touching their infants, while the predominant activities for infants were active movements, quiet play, and vocalization. Vocalizing, feeding, and play were infrequent maternal activities. It is not surprising that there was little feeding in the short observation period. However, the low rate of maternal vocaliza- tion is surprising in view of the fact that infants vocalized in about one-third of the ten-second periods. Several other studies report that adult vocalization is the predominant response to infant vocalizations (Gewirtz & Gerwitz, 1969; Lewis & Ban, this volume; Lewis & Wilson, 1972). The frequencies

TABLE 9-3.   Frequency and Range of Infant and Maternal
Behaviors.

Infant Behavior	x̄ Frequency	Range	Maternal Behavior	x̄ Frequency	Range
Active behavior	52.0	21-60	Hold	41.5	0-60
Play	20.7	0-57	Look	35.2	4-60
Vocalize	19.8	1-49	Touch	21.9	0-59
Smile	8.1	0-37	Smile	13.2	0-32
Eat	5.2	0-54	Play	6.8	0-44
Cry	2.2	0-6	Vocalize	3.7	0-21

NOTE: Data represent the number of ten-second periods in which
a behavior occurred. The possible range is 0-60.

for maternal behaviors shown in Table 9-3 reflect a high degree
of physical contact and show proximal stimulation (holding and
touching) as predominant modes of interaction over distal
stimulation (looking and vocalizing). This is consistent with
the initial impression that a high level of physical contact
between mother and infant was typical of mother-infant pairs
in Zambia.

A second tabulation of the data was undertaken in order to
examine some of the interactive relationships. Since we did not
attempt to record the order in which behaviors occurred in any
ten-second period, this analysis was limited to occurrences
within the same ten-second period without regard for whether
mother or infant initiated interactions. For each possible
combination of mother and infant behavior, we tabulated the
number of ten-second periods in which both occurred. Thus we
asked, for example, of all the periods in which the infant
vocalized, what was the number in which he or she was also
held, the number in which he or she was also looked at, etc.
The sum of these joint frequencies was then divided by the
number of times that particular infant behavior occurred to
give an index of the amount of maternal behavior occurring
simultaneously with that infant behavior. Similarly, we

computed for each maternal behavior the ratio of total joint
occurrences with infant behaviors divided by the frequency of
maternal behavior, as a measure of infant activity occurring
simultaneously with that maternal behavior. These measures
of simultaneously occurring activity may also be considered
to reflect, in the first case, maternal responsiveness to
infants; and in the second, infant responsiveness to mothers.
Table 9-4 presents the mean ratios of simultaneous activity
for mothers in relation to specific infant behaviors.
Table 9-5 presents the mean ratios of simultaneously occurring
activity for infants in relation to specific maternal behaviors.
In each case, separate means are reported for boys, girls, and
sexes combined. The number of subjects differs in each cell
because all possible behaviors did not occur in each observation.

TABLE 9-4. Mean Scores: Maternal Activity Simultaneous
with Infant Behaviors.

| | Infant Behaviors | | | | | |
	Move	Play	Vocalize	Smile	Eat	Cry
With Boys	2.04	1.80	1.88	2.30	2.81	2.32
N	17	15	17	13	5	11
With Girls	2.12	2.09	2.25	2.30	3.04	2.77
N	22	21	22	19	5	7
Combined	2.08	1.96	2.08	2.30	2.91	2.65
N	39	36	39	32	10	19

Note first that (Table 9-4) mothers are most active (have
high ratios of simultaneous activity) during feeding and crying
and are least active (have lowest ratios of simultaneous
activity) when the infant is engaged in quiet play. The
pattern of maternal activity with girls and boys is very
similar. The rank order correlation between mean scores for
girls and boys is .94 ($p < .01$, 1-tailed). The only reversal
that occurs is that for girls, mothers are more active in
relation to vocalization than movement, while the reverse is
true for boys. In each case, this difference is marginally
significant ($p < .07$ by sign test for boys and for girls).
Table 9-4 also shows that, for every behavior except smiling,
mothers were more active with girls than with boys. The

differences between the mean scores for boys and girls are significant only for eating and crying, both of which include only a small number of subjects. However, the consistent direction of differences is striking. Thus, although we found no differences in frequency of maternal behaviors with girls and boys, there do appear to be subtle sex differences in the patterning of interactions.

TABLE 9-5. Mean Scores: Infant Activity Simultaneous with Maternal Behaviors

	Maternal Behaviors						
	Hold	Look	Touch	Smile	Play	Feed	Vocalize
Of Boys	1.74	1.90	1.88	1.85	2.61	1.71	1.90
N	14	17	13	17	8	5	12
Of Girls	1.75	1.85	2.13	2.14	1.84	2.06	1.93
N	18	22	17	22	12	5	17
Combined	1.74	1.87	2.02	2.01	2.14	1.90	1.92
N	32	39	30	39	20	10	29

When we examine the pattern of activity ratios for infants in relation to specific maternal behaviors, the rank order correlation between boys' and girls' scores is -.09. Thus, although mothers show a highly consistent pattern of activity in relation to infant behavior regardless of sex of infant, infants' activity patterns in relation to maternal behavior differ according to the sex of the infant. That is, the sex differences in behavior are greater for infants than for mothers. Although there are differences in mean activity ratios between girls and boys in relation to specific maternal behaviors, none of these differences are statistically significant.

For the group as a whole, infants show least activity in relation to maternal holding and looking, which are the most frequent behaviors of mothers. Comparison between mean activity ratios for specific maternal behaviors (by sign test) revealed that holding was associated with less simultaneous

activity for girls than were touching ($p < .03$), smiling
($p < .02$), or vocalization ($p < .07$). Boys were more active
in relation to smiles than to holding ($p < .01$). The only
significant difference for the combined group was between
activity simultaneous with holding and with smiling ($p < .01$).
This suggests that being held, which is a high-frequency event,
has less salience for Zambian four-month-olds than relatively
infrequent behaviors such as smiling and vocalization.

Thus, the observation data indicate that Zambian four-
month-olds experience a high degree of physical contact and
proximal stimulation, while distal interactions such as vocal
communications are less common. Although the frequency of
maternal and infant behaviors is not a function of sex of
infant, there are subtle sex differences in the patterning of
mother-infant interaction when we examine simultaneously
occurring behavior. Finally, the analysis of simultaneous
activity suggests that infants are more active in relation
to infrequent maternal behaviors such as smiling and vocalizing
than to frequent behaviors such as holding and looking.

Sensorimotor Development.

At 6, 9, and 12 months, we administered the Albert
Einstein Scales of Sensorimotor Development (Escalona & Corman,
1966). These scales are based on Piaget's observations and
theories about early cognitive development (Piaget, 1952, 1954).
We used three subscales that test prehension (P), eye-hand-
mouth coordination; spatial concepts (S), ability to follow and
predict movements of objects in space, and spatial relations;
and object permanence (OP), the notion that objects exist
independently of sensory contact with them. Each scale consists
of a series of items that have been chosen to represent the
stages and substages described by Piaget and have been shown
empirically to constitute an ordinal scale (Corman & Escalona,
1969). The value of these scales is that unlike standardized
infant tests, they not only have a theoretical unity but focus
on the qualitative characteristics of behavior at each stage
rather than on number of items passed or failed. A brief
description of Stages III to VI, the span of stages observed
in this study, with typical items from the scales, follows.

> Stage III. The infant first becomes interested in the
> effects of actions, and repeats behaviors that
> produce interesting results such as hitting a
> dangling toy and watching it (P), or follow-
> ing a vertically dropped object visually (S
> or OP).

Stage IV.   The infant begins to coordinate the
behaviors of Stage III to obtain simple
goals such as removing a cloth covering the
experimenter's face (OP), or relocating
visually an object that moved too fast to
be followed (S).

Stage V.   Active trial and error appears and the infant
can vary approaches to the same goal. For
example, the contents of a container can be
moved by reaching into it or by turning it
over (S).

Stage VI.   The infant is capable of predicting outcomes
of simple behavior sequences. For example,
when given a set of nested boxes, differential
behavior is shown in opening them depending
on whether or not the child has seen a toy
put into the innermost box (OP).

The scales were administered and scored according to the
manual. Although specific materials are suggested, the actual
manipulations can be carried out with whatever materials appeal
to the child. These scales appear to be adaptable to trans-
cultural use. Our testing materials included a variety of
small manufactured toys, cloths, pillows, and cups (as hiding
places), and materials available at the child's home, such as
eating utensils, sticks, and stones, or pieces of food. All
infants were tested by the same Zambian female, with a second
Zambian female and the author observing and scoring. In no
case did the two observers disagree on the most advanced major
stage achieved by a child. The overall agreement was 85 to 100
percent, with disagreements occurring primarily in judging
numbers of successes where a specific number of successes was
required to pass an item.

An infant's score was the stage (indicated by roman number)
and substage (indicated by arabic numeral) associated with the
most advanced items passed. For computational purposes, these
scores were transformed to ordinal scores according to developmental sequence. In the following discussion, we will use
stage scores, since they refer to qualitative characteristics
of congnitive functioning, as indicated earlier.

Prehension

Corman and Escalona (1969) describe the Prehension (P)

Scale as being suitable for infants from three weeks to 7 months of age.   At 6 months, our sample represented the upper age range and a large proportion of the infants were performing at Stage III, the most advanced level possible.   Only 5 of 33 subjects were scored as performing at Stage II levels.   By 9 months all subjects had completed Stage III; therefore, we did not repeat this scale at 12 months.   Since there was so little range in scores, we did not use these data in any further analysis.   The range of ages at which the subjects in the Corman and Escalona (1969) validation sample completed Stage III on the P scale was 6.7 to 12.6 months, suggesting that our sample was more advanced in eye-hand coordination at 6 months than infants in the validation sample.

Spatial and Object Permanence Scales

Tables 9-6 and 9-7 summarize the data on the OP and S scales, with the age ranges reported by Corman and Escalona (1969) for each major stage.   At every age, Zambian infants were more advanced on Space Scale performance than on Object Permanence (6 months, $p < .02$; 9 months, $p < .04$;   12 months, $p < .001$ by sign test).   In general, the stage levels achieved by our sample are within what we would expect on the basis of the Corman and Escalona data.

TABLE 9-6.   Percent of Subjects in Each Stage: OP Scale.

	Age in Months		
	($N = 33$) 6	($N = 24$) 9	($N = 23$) 12
Stage III (4.0-9.6)[a]	33	0	0
Stage IV (5.6-10.3)	63 1/3	91	43
Stage V (6.8-11.4)	3 1/3	9	52
Stabe VI (8.3-19.7)	0	0	5
Group Mean	IV - 1	IV - 3	V - 1

[a]Age ranges for entering each stage from Corman & Escalona (1969).

TABLE 9-7.   Percent of Subjects in Each Stage: S Scale

	Age in Months		
	(N = 33) 6	(N = 25) 9	(N = 21) 12
Stage III (4.9-8.9)[a]	24	0	0
Stage IV (5.1-9.5)	76	96	4
Stage V (8.2-11.2)	0	4	92
Stage VI (10.1-14.3)	0	0	4
Group Mean	IV - 2	IV - 4	V - 7

[a] Age ranges for entering each stage from Corman & Escalona (1969).

We experienced extreme difficulty in administering these scales. With few exceptions, these infants did not appear to be highly motivated to follow and search for objects. Golden and Birns (1968) reported similar difficulties in testing U.S. children from poor, broken homes on the OP scale and described some of the unorthodox methods used to elicit optimal performance from these infants. We adopted many of these techniques at the outset: the use of food as lures, use of the mother or a sibling as experimenter, and repeated visits. In fact, we often made third and fourth visits to a single child, in comparison with Golden and Birns' two visits. Difficulty in testing was particularly acute at 9 months, when it was complicated by what appeared to be the infant's acute stranger anxiety. At this age, we often visited several times before doing any testing at all. At 12 months, the situation had improved but we still found some infants difficult to test. Often, repeated removal of objects upset the child and terminated the session.

The rank order correlations between ages for the OP and

S scales are shown in Table 9-8. They are generally positive
but low, indicating that infants did not necessarily retain
their ordinal position with respect to the group from age to
age. This is what we would expect to find if sensorimotor
development proceeds in fixed sequence, but not at a fixed
rate. The infant must master each stage as a prerequisite
for attaining the next, but the rate at which stages are
reached may depend on a variety of factors that change over
time, such as physical health and maturation, family situations,
and specific experiences available to the infant.

TABLE 9-8.   Age to Age Correlations: OP and S Scales.

	6 Months	9 Months	12 Months
6 months	--	.32	.45[a]
9 months	.44[a]	--	.33
12 months	.23	.15	--

NOTE: -OP above the diagonal (--), S below.

a
$p < .05$.

Home Stimulation, Maternal Behavior, and Sensorimotor Development

The rank order correlations between scores on the Home
Stimulation Inventory and performance on the S and OP scales
at each age-level are shown in Table 9-9. The majority of the
correlations are essentially zero and the one significant
correlation does not fit any particular pattern. This is
consistent with previous work with Piagetian scales showing no
difference in sensorimotor development attributable to home
environment as indicated by social class (Corman & Escalona,
1969; Golden & Birns, 1968). Wachs, Uzgiris, and Hunt (1971)
found social class differences in sensorimotor performances,
but these appeared primarily in the case of eliciting responses
and number of trials needed to achieve the required number of
successes. We did not make any formal record of ease of
testing each infant, but clearly this is valuable information,

TABLE 9-9. Rank Order Correlations: Home Stimulation Inventory Versus Sensorimotor Scales.

Age	OP			S		
	6m	9m	12m	6m	9m	12m
N	23	18	17	23	20	16
Part I	.10	-.02	-.31	.18	.07	.16
Part II	.00	-.37	.02	-.09	-.29	.23
Part III	.33	-.02	-.05	.05	-.04	.08
Part IV	.19	-.26	.08	.15	.18	.16
Part V	.16	-.10	.00	-.06	.07	.13
Part VI	-.47[a]	.08	.03	.03	.31	-.32
Part VII	.08	.18	-.16	.01	.22	.12
Total	.07	-.29	-.28	.04	.09	.17

[a] $p < .05$

particularly in a sample such as ours, where we did encounter
difficulties in testing many infants.

Of particular interest in the Home Stimulation Inventory
data is the finding that intentional stimulation of development
by the mother was unrelated to sensorimotor performance. The
small numbers of infants whose mothers reported that they
stimulated their infants, or were actually observed to stimulate development, were indistinguishable from the rest of
the sample.

Further independence of home environment and sensorimotor
performance is demonstrated in our finding that neither family
size or structure (nuclear versus extended), nor home verus
hospital birth (all of which probably reflect degree of
Westernization) had any significant relationship with sensorimotor performance.

Table 9-10 presents the rank order correlations between
measures of maternal behavior at 4 months and performance on
the S and OP Scales at 6, 9, and 12 months. Contrary to our
expectations, the correlations are predominantly negative.
All reported probabilities are therefore two-tailed. There
is little evidence of a clear relationship between maternal
behavior at 4 months and later performance on the Space Scale.
However, for the Object Permanence Scale, the correlations become increasingly negative with age and, in fact, most of the
significant correlations are between 12-month OP scores and
earlier maternal simultaneous activity. The more active a
mother was with her child at 4 months, the less advanced was
OP performance at 12 months. Other studies have shown OP
scores to be positively related to measures of mother-infant
interaction (Bell, 1970; Decarie, 1965; Serafica & Uzgiris,
1971; Yarrow, this volume). In these studies, mother-infant
interaction was assessed concurrently with (within a short
period) or subsequent to testing of Object Permanence. Thus,
it is not clear whether Object Permanence was dependent on
the mother-infant relationship, or vice versa, or, more likely,
both. In the present study, we were interested in predicting
later infant performance from earlier maternal behavior and
hypothesized that more attentive and responsive mothers would
have infants who later exhibited more mature sensorimotor
performance. It is also important to note that simple
frequency counts of maternal behavior were, for the most part,
not related to sensorimotor scores. It was only in measures
of simultaneous activity, which take account of the infant's
behavior, that the relationship between OP scores and maternal
behavior is evident. However, we need to ask why it is that

TABLE 9-10. Rank Order Correlations: Maternal Behavior at Four Months Versus Sensorimotor Scales.

Maternal Behaviors (4m)	OP			S		
	6mo.	9mo.	12mo.	6mo.	9mo.	12mo.
Proximal Stimulation	.05	-.14	-.29	.18	.01	.17
Distal Stimulation	.00	-.19	-.33	.13	-.02	-.11
Total Stimulation	.05	-.26	-.50[a]	.27	-.03	.13
Activity Simultaneous with Vocalization	-.24	-.18	-.50[a]	.27	-.15	-.09
Activity Simultaneous with Movement	-.10	-.28	-.42[a]	.05	-.04	-.03
Activity Simultaneous with Play	.07	-.30	-.60[b]	-.01	-.17	-.16
Activity Simultaneous with Smile	-.48[a]	-.34	-.56[b]	-.40	-.01	.45

[a] $p < .05$

[b] $p < .01$

more attentive and responsive mothers have infants who show
less mature performance and why the effect of this early
responsiveness is increasingly negative as the child matures.

Maternal behavior toward infants is generally found to be
strongly related to the age of the infants (Lewis & Ban, 1971;
Lusk & Lewis, 1972; Moss, 1965, 1967). The most sensitive
mother is one whose behavior is adjusted to the current skills
and behaviors of her infant. Thus, the mother who is responsive
to her 4-month-old will, if she continues to be responsive,
behave quite differently toward the same child at 12 months.
Indeed, the mother who perpetuates the pattern of mothering
that was appropriate at 4 months is probably not responding to
the capabilities of her infant as he gets older. When we
observed mothers with their 4-month-olds, we saw them in a
situation where they maintained physical proximity to the child,
a typical situation in everyday life, since most infants were
carried on their mothers' backs for long periods. We observed
that mothers were more likely to use proximal modes of
stimulation with their 4-month-olds and although looking was
relatively frequent, smiling and vocalizing were not.
Typically, it is reported that proximal stimulation decreases
with age of infant while distal stimulation increases (e.g.,
Lewis & Ban, 1971; Lusk & Lewis, 1972; Moss, 1965, 1967).
Furthermore, Yarrow (this volume) found a low relationship
between proximal and distal stimulation of 5 1/2-month-old
infants by their mothers, and concluded that mothers had
preferred patterns of stimulation. I would suggest that the
proximal modes of stimulation are preferred by Zambian mothers
and continue to be preferred as long as the infant is carried
in the sling. I argued, earlier in this chapter, that the
experiences provided by this carrying method are particularly
appropriate to the stimulation of young infants. Later, when
the infant is capable of locomotion and manipulation, the
sling provides passive experiences and limits opportunities
for active exploration. Perhaps those mothers who continue
to carry their infants for long periods of time as they
mature do, in fact, perpetuate earlier patterns of interaction
both with the mother and with the inanimate world.

Carrying Practices and Infant Development

With this possibility in mind, we reviewed the Home
Stimulation Inventory data on maternal carrying of infants.
We were able to group infants according to the amount of time
the mother said she spent carrying at 12 months. We do not
know how long each infant was carried at earlier periods but
it is probably safe to infer that infants who were carried a
long time at 12 months were carried at least that long when

younger, and similarly infants who were not carried at one year or were carried minimally were likely to have been carried less at earlier periods as well. We then examined scores on the Space and Object Permanence Scales as well as Bayley Motor Scale performance for these groups of infants.

On the Bayley Motor Scale, there were no differences in the performances of 4-month-olds as a function of time being carried. At 12 months, those infants who were not carried at all showed the most advanced motor behavior (Kruskal-Wallis analysis of variance by ranks, $H = 6.1$, $p < .02$, 2 df).[2] The comparisons for the Space Scale Scores showed that there was a tendency for those infants who were carried least to show more advanced behavior at all ages, but this difference was not significant at any age. On the Object Permanence Scale, there was a significant difference in performance at 6 and 12 months, according to the amount of time the infant was carried (6 months, $H = 23.3$, $p < .001$, 3 df; 12 months, $H = 10.4$, $p < .02$, 3 df). At 6 months, the infants who were carried most showed the most advanced behavior, while at 12 months the infants who were carried least obtained the most advanced scores.

These findings appear to support the notion that sling experience facilitates early development and restricts later development. However, it can also be argued that the amount of time the infant is carried may reflect developmental maturity rather than determine it. That is, the child who seems to be less mature is treated like a younger infant and carried, while the more mature child is treated appropriately and left alone more frequently. In order to explain the finding that 6-month OP scores were more advanced for infants carried more frequently, we would have to argue that for some reason the more mature infants are carried more (perhaps because it is more dangerous to leave them on the ground). At present, it seems more parsimonious to say that the sling provides experiences appropriate to early development but serves as a limitation on exploratory opportunities for the older infant. A number of

---

[2] For most comparisons, the subjects were divided into four groups in which long, short, irregular, or no carrying were characteristic. Because the number of infants tested on the Bayley Motor Scales at twelve months was smaller than any other sample, the infants were divided into three groups with long, short, or irregular, and no carrying.

authors have emphasized the beneficial effects of the sling
on infant development (Ainsworth, 1967; Geber, 1958; Konner,
1972). Although no one so far has commented on its limitations
in later infancy, there is abundant evidence to indicate that
infants with more opportunities to explore, more "floor
freedom", show better test performance (Beckwith, 1971; Collard,
1971; White, 1972; Williams & Scott, 1953).

It is also important to consider the possibility that
amount of time spent in the sling is primarily an index to
other characteristics of home and family conditions that
influence development. Infants who were carried little or not
at all were more likely to have been born in the hospital than
at home, to sleep alone rather than with the mother or a
relative, and to be in better health--all characteristics that
may reflect Westernization. We have already indicated that
hospital versus home birth and family size and structure were
not related to sensorimotor performance. This is true for
motor performance as well. The number of infants sleeping
alone (four) was too few for statistical analysis, but there
is no striking evidence that these four infants were more
advanced in development than the rest of the group.
Unfortunately, we do not have adequate records for these
infants. The mothers' reports indicated that six infants
were seriously ill during the study. Four of these infants
were in the group that was carried most. Adequate health
records would be a vital addition to any follow-up study of
this population. Thus, on the basis of the evidence currently
available, it appears that the strongest relationship is, in
fact, between mother's carrying practices and performance on
the motor and sensorimotor tests. There was no clear
relationship between 12-month carrying practices and 4-month
observation data. Those infants who were carried most were
least advanced in motor and sensorimotor development, while
those who were carried least showed the most advanced
performance.

LeVine (1973) has suggested that extensive carrying of
infants is most likely to occur in societies with high infant
mortality rate. When infant deaths are frequent, it is argued,
infant survival becomes a high-priority parental goal. The
physical proximity between infant and caretaker provided by
extensive carrying ensures continual attention to the infant
and rapid responses to infants' needs, and is thus adaptive
for infant survival. I believe that traditional carrying
practices may also have as an incidental effect the production
of children who are conforming and obedient, behavior patterns
that are valued in traditional societies. The restriction of
exploration and the high degree of passive experience that

seems likely to occur for older infants under prolonged
carrying may also reduce motivation for individual mastery
and independence that are not valued in traditional societies.
(See Freedman, 1975; Appleton, Clifton, & Goldberg, 1975.)
Those infants in our sample who were carried least seemed to
come from more Westernized families who were perhaps more
certain about infant survival and may have been more tolerant
of independent behavior in their children.

SUMMARY

The data can be briefly summarized as follows:

1.   Infants and mothers customarily interacted in an
       environment that was densely populated with other
       family members and where the major family activities
       beyond maintenance were social in nature.

2.   Infants spent long periods of time in physical
       contact with their mothers. Typically, they were
       carried most of the day and slept with the mother
       at night. The observation data indicated that
       holding, touching, and looking were the most frequent
       maternal behaviors, while vocalizing to the infant
       was notably rare.

3.   Although there were no sex differences in infant or
       maternal behaviors when only frequency of
       activities was considered, sex differences did
       appear when patterns of simultaneous activity were
       analyzed.

4.   Sensorimotor development was within the ranges
       indicated for the validation sample on the Albert
       Einstein Scales. Difficulties encountered in
       administering these tests made interpretation of
       infant performance ambiguous.

5.   There was no relationship between measures of home
       stimulation and sensorimotor performance. Typically,
       mothers were not concerned with stimulation of new
       behaviors and development. Infants of mothers who
       reported or were observed to stimulate development
       did not differ from the rest of the sample in
       sensorimotor performance.

6. Measures of maternal behavior from the 4-month observation, particularly those based on simultaneous behavior in relation to the infant, were negatively related to infant performance on the OP scale.

7. An attempt to explain this negative relationship led us to analyze test performance in relation to amount of time infants were carried at one year.

PERSPECTIVE AND HINDSIGHT

There are clearly many limitations in these data. If they had been collected elsewhere, I would hesitate to talk about them. If I were to plan such a study again, I would do it differently. But what have I learned from all of this anyway? The important insights for me were not in the data per se. They were in the perspective I gained about my own assumptions and attitudes, about the nature of research, and about what is important to study.

I began with the question of whether the methods I had imported from the United States would be appropriate for research in another cultural context. I learned that in many respects they were not. Were I to study maternal behavior in Zambia again, I would begin at a more descriptive level and I would define maternal behavior differently. I had, in fact, unwittingly defined maternal behavior as "that which is done by the mother". In most Western countries, the mother is the exclusive caretaker in an environment that contains few other people. Studies in the U.S. that attempt to investigate the effects of "multiple mothering" have traditionally assumed that this is a form of deprivation (e.g., Caldwell, Herscher, Lipton, Richmond, Stern, Eddy, Drachmau, & Rothman, 1963).

In Zambia, polymatric families are the rule rather than the exception, and are certainly not considered to be deprivation conditions. The mother is usually the primary caretaker, but the infant's interactions with siblings and adults are more frequent than they are in American homes. The same amount and kind of activity is distributed differently over a variety of people, and surely this must be an important aspect of maternal behavior. The same amount and kind of maternal attention might have different effects according to the number of people who dispense it (see Leiderman & Leiderman, this volume). Furthermore, the effect of others in the family can also be seen in the behavior of the mother alone. In our

sample we found that mothers in small families gave more total
stimulation to their infants. We also found that looking,
talking, playing, and smiling were more frequent modes of
interaction for mothers in extended families than for those
in nuclear families. These findings suggest that as the size
of the family increases, to the extent that the mother's
responsibilities increase, she is less available to the infant.
However, the availability of other caretakers, as in the
extended family situation, may allow the mother to share child-
care responsibilities and free her to engage more often in
noncaretaking activities with the infant such as talking and
play. Household composition has been found to influence
infant care in both cross-cultural (Whiting, 1961) and intracultural studies (Munroe & Munroe, 1971). I am suggesting
that these effects are found both in the infant's interactions
with others and in the interaction with the mother.

In the course of this study, it also became clear to me
that infant tests are not culture-free. It is easy to suppose
that, because they do not involve language and because infants
have had minimal exposure to cultural influences relative to
older children or adults, cultural biases play little role in
infant tests. This is not the case. Performance on infant
tests depends on the subject's experiences. For example, even
when very young, infants have experienced a particular kind
of handling. The experience of being held upright to test
head and neck control must be different for a Zambian baby,
who is normally upright, than for a European baby who is
normally supine. Secondly, familiarity with materials can
affect an infant's manipulatory responses. Collard (1971)
found that infants who were more familiar with a toy showed
more variety and less repetition in manipulative play.
Thirdly, the expectations of mothers with respect to testing
situations are undoubtedly communicated to their infants. In
the U.S., mothers have some familiarity with infant testing,
whereas Zambian mothers do not. The experience of a European
visiting Matero was clearly an unusual one for these mothers.
Children were open in dragging their mothers to look at the
"Mzungu" and trying to touch my hair, but mothers must also
have found my visiting novel and peculiar. Finally, I have
suggested (Goldberg, 1972) that some of the difficulties we
had in administering the sensorimotor tests may reflect
socialization pressures on Zambian infants. Failure to perform,
especially in searching for hidden objects, may reflect an
unwillingness to persist when an adult (by withdrawing a toy)
has imposed restrictions.

In view of these observations, it is of interest that a

recent study that also used the Albert Einstein Scales (Dasen, 1973) with an African sample reported that infants had difficulty with manipulation of objects and were *more oriented toward the social environment than the physical environment*. We have emphasized the importance of social activities in the family life of our sample. It may be that the instruments of Western psychology in fact test responses to that aspect of the environment that is least salient for Zambian infants.

Two years was much too short a time to accomplish what I had hoped to do in Zambia. I felt keenly the absence of inter-disciplinary teamwork during the study. I needed the advice of medical colleagues, of sociologists, and of anthropologists. I began more or less in a vaccum, in trying to understand everything. Most of all, I wanted independent verification of my impressions and judgments. Much later I discovered, in my reading of such books as Women in the Field (Golde, 1970), Stranger and Friend (Powdermaker, 1966), and Never in Anger (Briggs, 1972), that many of the problems that I found over-whelming were not unique. They were problems commonly experienced but rarely discussed among workers in the field. In search of colleague substitutes, I began a long and continuing odyssey through the literature of anthropology and animal behavior. At the end of two years, I had just begun to make the contacts with other schools of the University and with appropriate ministries that I had needed to make in 1968. But I was also just beginning to see what the questions were. I felt as if I had to leave too soon.

The value of long-term commitments to work in another culture cannot be emphasized enough. There are an embarrassing number of studies in the literature that suffer from lack of it (Warren, 1972). What is lost when an investigator spends a few months administering a test to a rarely tested sample and calls it a study is the most valuable part of comparative work in another culture: the opportunity to absorb the cultural context, the chance to be shaken by it, and the experience of struggling to understand it.

It is rare that we have opportunities to expose ourselves to experiences of this kind as adults. What I have described will be recognized by good Piagetians as an experience with disequilibrium. I am suggesting that cross-cultural experiences produce a fundamental kind of disequilibrium in which the work of equilibration requires questioning of one's self and one's basic assumptions. It is in this process that new ideas and research themes are generated. I believe that, painful as such experiences are, they are necessary if we are to move beyond the stage of "formal operations" in understanding human behavior.

REFERENCES

Ainsworth, M. D. S. Infancy in Uganda. Baltimore, Md.: Johns Hopkins University Press, 1967.

Appleton, T., Clifton, R., & Goldberg, S. The development of behavioral competence in infancy. In F. D. Horowitz (Ed.), Review of child development research, (Vol. 4). Chicago: University of Chicago Press, 1975.

Beckwith, L. Relationships between attributes of mothers and their infant's IQ scores. Child Development, 1971, 42, 1083-1097.

Bell, S. M. The development of the concept of objects as related to infant-mother attachment. Child Development, 1970, 41, 291-311.

Briggs, J. L. Never in anger: Portrait of an Eskimo family. Cambridge, Mass.: Harvard University Press, 1972.

Caldwell, B. Inventory of home stimulation. Unpublished manual, Children's Center, Syracuse University, Syracuse, New York, 1969.

Caldwell, B., Hersher, L., Lipton, E. L., Richmond, J. C., Stern, G., Eddy, E., Drachman, R., & Rothman, A. Mother-infant interaction in monomatric and polymatric families. American Journal of Orthopsychiatry, 1963, 33, 563-664.

Collard, R. R. Exploratory and play behaviors of infants reared in an institution and in lower- and middle-class homes. Child Development, 1971, 42, 1003-1015.

Corman, H. H., & Escalona, S. K. Stages of sensorimotor development: A replication study. Merrill-Palmer Quarterly, 1969, 15, 351-362.

Dasen, P. R. Preliminary study on cognitive development among Ivorian children (Baolé and Ebrié): Sensorimotor intelligence and concrete operations. Early Child Development and Care, 1973, 2, 345-354.

Descarie, T. G. Intelligence and affectivity in early childhood. New York: International Universities Press, 1965.

Escalona, S. K., Corman, H. H. Albert Einstein scales of sensorimotor development. New York: Albert Einstein College of Medicine, Department of Psychiatry, 1966.

Falade, S. Le developpement psychomoteur de jeune Africain du Senegal au cours de sa premiere annee. Concours Medical, 1960, 82, 1005-1013.

Freedman, D. G. Human infancy: An evolutionary perspective. New York: Halstead Press, 1975.

Geber, M. The psychomotor development of African children in thier first year and the influence of mother behavior. Journal of Social Psychology, 1958, 47, 185-195.

Gewirtz, H. B., & Gewirtz, J. L. Caretaking settings, background events and behavior differences in four Israeli child-rearing environments: Some preliminary trends. In B. M. Moss (Ed.), Determinants of infant behavior (Vol. IV). London: Methuen, 1969.

Goldberg, S. Infant care and growth in urban Zambia. Human Development, 1972, 15, 77-89.

Golde, P. Women in the field. Chicago: Aldine, 1970.

Golden, M., & Birns, B. Social class and cognitive development in infancy. Merrill-Palmer Quarterly, 1968, 14, 137-149.

Konner, M. J. Aspects of the developmental ethology of a foraging people. In N. Blurton Jones (Ed.), Ethological studies of child behavior. Cambridge, England: Cambridge University Press, 1972.

LeVine, R. Comments at Wartenstein Symposium No. 57, Cultural and social influences in infancy and early childhood, June 1973.

Lewis, M., & Ban, P. Stability of attachment behaviors: A transformational analysis. Paper presented at meeting of the Society for Research in Child Development, Minneapolis, 1971.

Lewis, M., & Goldberg, S. Perceptual-cognitive development in infancy: A generalized expectancy model as a function of mother-infant interaction. Merrill-Palmer

Quarterly, 1969, 15, 81-100.

Lewis, M., & Wilson, C. D.   Infant development in lower-class American families.   Human Development, 1972, 15, 112-127.

Lusk, D., & Lewis, M.   Mother-infant interaction and infant development among the Wolof of Senegal.   Human Development, 1972, 15, 58-69.

Moss, H. A.   Methodological issues in studying mother-infant interactions.   American Journal of Orthopsychiatry, 1965, 35, 482-486.

Moss, H. A.   Sex, age and state as determinants of mother-infant interaction.   Merrill-Palmer Quarterly, 1967, 13, 19-36.

Munro, D.   A survey of pre-school children's environments in a Lusaka suburb (Human Development Research Unit Report No. 9).   Lusaka: University of Zambia, 1968.

Munro, R. H., & Munroe, R. L.   Household density and infant care in an East African society.   Journal of Social Psychology, 1971, 83, 3-13.

Piaget, J.   The origins of intelligence in children.   New York: International Universities Press, 1952.

Piaget, J.   The construction of reality in the child.   New York: Basic Books, 1954.

Powdermaker, H.   Stranger and friend.   New York: Norton, 1966.

Ramarasona, Z.   Psychomotor development in early childhood in the Tananarive region.   Working paper, Meeting on the Basic Psychology of African and Madagascan Populations.   Conference on Southern Africa, Publ. No. 51, Tananarive, Madagascar, 1959.

Serafica, F. C., & Uzgiris, I. C.   Infant-mother relationship and object concept.   Paper presented at meeting of the American Psychological Association, Washington, 1971.

Wachs, T., Uzgiris, I. C., & Hunt, J. M.   Cognitive development in infants of different age levels and from different environmental backgrounds.   Merrill-Palmer

Quarterly, 1971, 17, 283-318.

Warren, N. African infant precocity. Psychological Bulletin, 1972, 78, 353-367.

White, B. L. Fundamental early environmental influences on the development of competence. In M. E. Meyer (Ed.) Third Symposium on Learning: Cognitive Learning. Bellingham, Wash.: Western Washington State College Press, 1972.

Whiting, J. W. M. Socialization process and personality. In F. L. K. Hsu (Ed.), Psychological Anthropology. Homewood, Ill.: Dorsey Press, 1961.

Williams, J. R., & Scott, R. Growth and development of Negro infants. Child Development, 1953, 24, 103-121.

Chapter 10

Mothers' Speech and the Early Development of Vocal Behavior: Findings from a Cross-Cultural Observation Study in Israel

Charles W. Greenbaum
and
Rivka Landau
Hebrew University of Jerusalem

The influence of early verbal stimulation on the later cognitive development of the child has been discussed by a number of writers, particularly those interested in language development (Friedlander, 1970; Lenneberg, 1969; McNeill, 1966; Holzman, 1974; Ryan, 1974; Bruner, 1975). The nature of this influence remains unclear, however, largely because the relation between adult speech and infant vocalization is itself not well understood. The present study examines the vocal behavior of infants at various ages in the first year of life and its relation to selected aspects of adult speech by comparing a number of child-rearing environments. It is one of a series of studies dealing with adult-infant inter- action in several environmental settings in Israel. Such cross-cultural comparisons may enable us to determine the components of vocal behavior that are subject to environmental influence, and those that represent developmental stages of mastery by the child, relatively independent of environmental influence.

There are few studies on the relationship between early vocal behavior and the verbal behavior of adults. The findings reported by Cameron, Livson, and Bayley (1967) suggest that infant vocalization predicts later intelligence, at least for females. Brodbeck and Irwin (1946) and Irwin (1948) also studied the development of vocal sounds in the infant and have traced the increase in complexity and diversity of such sounds with age of the infant. A later study (Irwin, 1960) reported that reading to infants has a beneficial effect on their vocal development. A number of experimental studies (Ramey & Ourth, 1971; Rheingold, Gewirtz, & Ross, 1959; Weisberg, 1963) have also found that it is possible to condition vocalization of infants by using systematic stimulation and reinforcement procedures. In none of the latter studies, however, has the *quality* of the vocalization been analyzed.

There have been some studies of adult stimulation and infant speech in the infant's natural environment. Beckwith (1971) reported correlations between mothers' verbalization at an early age (8.7 months) with infants babbling at a later age (10.0 months). Tulkin (see Tulkin, 1970; Tulkin & Kagan, 1972) found that middle-class mothers provide more and different stimulation for their ten-month-old infants than do lower-class mothers. (See Holzman, 1974; Landau, 1976.)

Since these studies were performed in a variety of contexts and with children of different ages, it is difficult to compare them. It may be ventured that verbal stimulation (or rein-forcement) for vocal responses of young children is effective in influencing infant vocalization that occurs immediately after exposure to such stimulation. There is some hint in Irwin's (1960) and Beckwith's (1971) studies that stimulation at an earlier age may have effects on later verbalization. However, the specific influence of stimulation on infant speech over an extended period in the course of a day has not been established.

OVERVIEW OF DESIGN

The study from which the present report is taken has attempted to explore in detail the relationship between behaviors of infants and other people in their environment in the course of a typical day. The design of the study was cross-sectional and developmental (studying children at the ages of 2, 4, 7, and 11 months of age) and cross-cultural (sampling at each of the above ages in five environments: middle-class, lower-class, institution, kibbutz, and Bedouin Arab). The age groups were selected to provide critically different stages in the child's development, and the environments to provide variation in the type and amount of stimulation provided to the child.

A number of hypotheses are possible in a study of this kind, considering the large number of responses being studied. Formulation of any hypothesis concerning the relation between environment and infant response must be considered a two-stage process. The first stage consists of assessing the behavior of individuals in the infant's environment, indicating the makeup of the special psychological environment for the child. In this stage, the behavior of the child is described as well. The second stage consists of determining the functional relations between the behaviors of the child and the behaviors of others. For example, a study of infant vocalization requires that the rate of infant vocalization be determined, as well as the rate of behaviors of others in the environment that are likely to affect vocalization. Others' responses may serve as stimuli (before vocalization) and/or reinforcers (during or after vocalization).

An hypothesis concerning relationships between others' responses and those of the infant may be tested only after base rates have been determined. The present report is thus part of the first stage of an overall analysis of the relation between the infant and its environment. Such an assessment has been suggested by a number of theoretical approaches (Baker & Wright, 1955; Brunswik, 1956; Gewirtz, 1969; Lewin, 1951). All of these emphasize in different ways the necessity for detailed analyses of the social environment in order to understand individual behavior.

ENVIRONMENTS

The basic purpose of the larger research on which this study is based was to contribute to the understanding of the effects of the environment on development and learning in infancy. This chapter reports specifically on the speech of the mother (or caretaker in the institution environment) and the vocalization of the infant. The cultural comparative design was employed in order to study the possible influences of particular dimensions of the environment on the early learning of the infant, as well as to study the behavior of the child in the different environments. The terms *culture* and *environment* are not identical, but they are related to each other. We suggest that the culture provides the direction for socially significant behaviors in which people engage. These adult behaviors then provide a meaningful part of the environment for the growing child.

The environments studied thus serve as independent factors in a natural experiment. We attempted to select environments that differed from each other in crucial dimensions of stimulation they provide the child. At the same time, we wished to preserve some comparability among these environments. The basic dimensions we studied were the richness of the environment in amount, rate, and variety of stimulation provided the child, and the presence of a permanent caretaking figure. There are indications of the importance of these factors in an enormous number of previous studies. However, their precise impact, and their interaction with the behavior of the child, has never been adequately understood.

With regard to the relative richness or poverty of the environment, we addressed ourselves first to the possible differences between social classes. Differences in amount and type of verbal interaction between parents and children in middle- and lower-class environments have been pointed out by many writers (e.g., Bernstein, 1961; Hess & Shipman, 1965; Tulkin & Kagan, 1972) indicating that the verbalization of middle-class mothers may be more frequent and more varied than that of lower-class mothers, even at early ages. In the present study we were interested in seeing if similar social class differences could be found in Israel, and how other environments would compare with middle- and lower-class U.S. samples.

In studying the effects of richness of stimulation, it was important to observe an environment in which environmental conditions were simple, but in which a "culture of poverty" did not necessarily exist. This was done in order to distinguish the effects of the cultural environment from those of poverty per se. The cultural environment, apart from poverty, would also be differentiated from lower- and middle-class urban Jewish environment. The culture chosen was the Bedouin Arab, whose Israeli members live for the most part in tents in the Southern (Negev) desert plain in Israel. In addition to considerations of comparison, the Bedouin culture is interesting in its own right, and its child-rearing practices have never been system-atically studied.

The second dimension, relative presence of mother, was studied by comparing the above environments with others in which the mother was not present a good deal of the time. The mother is present most of the time in the middle-class, lower-class, and Bedouin environments. In the kibbutz, on the other hand, the mother is present less. While she remains very active in the caretaking process, she leaves a good part of the caretaking to another person, the Metapelet, or child caretaker. In the institution, the mother is almost never present. This environment includes children who are not living in their homes. The deprivation of mother's presence is thus extreme.

The five environments, then, differ both in degree of richness of stimulation and degree of mother-care provided. With regard to richness of stimulation, the middle class and kibbutzim are presumably the best established. The institutions are not to be considered "poor" economically; all medical, nutritional, and other needs are well provided for. On the other hand, we may hypothesize that the institutions are the poorest in stimulation provided the child. The Bedouin and lower-class environments should come between these extremes.

With regard to presence of mother, the three home environments provide for the largest amount of such presence, followed by the kibbutz, where mother-presence is still high, and the institution, where the mother is usually not present at all. Each environment can be seen as a case study in itself, with its own unique possibilities for influencing the child.

DESCRIPTION OF THE ENVIRONMENTAL SETTINGS

Middle- and Lower-Class Environments

The families of the middle- and lower-class infants in our sample are urban apartment dwellers. Criteria for social class were judged on the basis of occupation and education. Information concerning these variables was taken from official birth record forms filed with the Ministry of Health at the time of birth, and/or interviews with the parents. All middle-class parents were in white-collar positions--government officials, lecturers in universities, or members of the free professions. All parents had at least a high school education and most had some university education. The lower-class parents were engaged in unskilled or semiskilled positions or were engaged in private business. None had more than nine years of education. In order to control for country of origin, we included only Jewish parents whose family origins were in Western (English-speaking, South American, or North European) countries. All families had both a mother and a father living at home, and no mother was working at the time her child was in the study.

The differences between middle- and lower-class samples
in our study may be fewer than in studies performed in other
countries, since all parents in the present study were
apartment dwellers, were fairly young, and had no more than
two children. Thus, some of the differences in habitat between
middle and lower class found in other studies, such as over-
crowding, were not found here. All apartments in our sample
contained at least two and a half rooms in additon to a kitchen,
and many had three or four rooms. Most also had a veranda in
which the child could be placed if the weather was good. All
children slept in cribs--and all had some toys in their rooms.
The nature and variety of the toys was noted and will be dealt
with in subsequent reports.

The Kibbutz

Descriptions of the kibbutz, including the environments
in which the children live, are available in a number of sources
(Spiro, 1956; 1958; Talmon-Garber, 1972). All kibbutz parents
in our sample were born and raised on the kibbutz, and all had
attended high school.

The kibbutz infants lived in a children's house under the
care of a special caretaker. The children's houses generally
contain a large amount of play equipment and toys. Usually no
more than four such infants of somewhat varying ages live in
one room of the house. The children's house is usually placed
in a grassy, shaded area in which children can be put outside
for naps. The location of the children's house is such that it
can be reached by a few minutes' walk on the part of the parents
either from work or from their apartments. The mother usually
feeds the baby in the children's house at the younger ages (two
and four months). The feeding of all the children generally
takes place at about the same time, and they are taken out of
the children's house late in the afternoon for two to three
hours. During this time, the child is in or near the parent's
apartment. Usually the father is present and the time is spent
playing with the child, napping, or relaxing.

Landau (1976) presents an analysis of the degree to which
mothers contribute to stimulation of the infant in each of the
environments studied here. She reports that the kibbutz mother
provides a large share of such stimulation, though her
contribution is less than that of mothers in the other four
home environments.

The Bedouin

The Bedouin Arabs of the Negev desert live in tents or

huts, usually in proximity to the members of the extended
family or clan. Larger groupings, or tribes, live in the
same general area. An excellent description and analysis of
Bedouin kinship systems is found in Marx (1967). The requirement
to sample only second-born children was not held to among the
Bedouin or in the institutions due to the smaller population
from which the children were drawn and the consequent difficulty
in obtaining such a sample.

The Bedouin tent is usually divided into two areas. One
contains a fire and serves as a kitchen and work area for women.
A larger area, usually containing carpets, is set off by a
hanging partition and provides a reception room for guests
during the day, and sleeping quarters at night.

Infants spend most of their time with their mothers, being
carried about either by hand or in a sling device. They sleep
in a hammock inside the tent, or on the floor on a pile of
blankets. Some children are swaddled in rags, which are changed
from time to time, while a few wear diapers. There are few toys
in evidence, but the children play with anything that comes to
hand, including pieces of rope, wood, carpet, or furniture.
At times domestic animals--such as goats, chickens, or dogs--
walk through the tent.

Families among the Bedouin were larger than those among
the Jewish populations studied. The older children often help
with household chores and with care of the young. In addition,
members of the extended family including mothers or aunts of
the parents, are often present to help.

Institutions

The two institutions in which children in this study were
living are physically well kept; the children receive constant
medical attention, and they are well clothed and fed. Children
live six or seven to a room. A head nurse is in charge of three
or four such rooms. However, there is a lack of a constant caretaker in the lives of the infants. The head nurse cannot form
close relationships with the infants, since she is responsible
for a relatively large number of children. Much of the day-to-
day care is in the hands of student nurses who come and go in
the course of the day, and leave permanently for other duties
after a few months. The children are left on their own for long
periods of time. Most interaction occurs during caretaking
periods.

The infants in the institutions were placed because of

problems at home, some financial, and some personal. Many are
candidates for adoption--while some will return to their
original families.

METHOD

Subjects

     All infants in the study were males. Five children were
studied at each age level in all environments (except for the
Bedouin) for a total of 20 in each environment. Four children
were studied at each age level among the Bedouin, for a total
of 16. In all, the data for 96 infants are reported.

     The ages selected for study in this research were chosen
so as to provide the possibility of observing different stages
in a child's development of social responses (see Gewirtz, 1965).
At two months, the infant's response is relatively undifferenti-
ated. At four months, its response, as indicated by smiling
to both social and nonsocial objects, is stronger. Seven months
represents a time when social responses become more discriminating
among people. At eleven months, the social and nonsocial response
systems are more varied, and may, at least in part, be under the
voluntary control of the child.

Procedure

     All children were observed in their natural habitats for
the equivalent of one typical waking weekday, to be called a
behavior day. The observation was spread over two days in all
environments except the Bedouin: It began on the afternoon of
one day (beginning about lunchtime) and continued until the
infant went to sleep. The second day's observation began the
next morning and concluded at approximately the same hour that
the observation had begun on the previous day. A single
observer was used in these environments. The child was the
focus of the observation. If he was moved from one place to
another, the observer followed.

     In the Bedouin environment, there were two differences in
the observation procedure, owing to conditions that made
extended observation difficult. There two observers were used,
and both morning and afternoon observations were carried out on
the same day. The observers worked one at a time, relieving
one another at hourly intervals.

The observers, six female students of psychology, all had Bachelor's degrees or were senior undergraduates. They were trained in the observation procedure for about six months prior to starting work.

Observation system. The observation system used in the present study was influenced by one developed by Gewirtz and Gewirtz (1965, 1968). It requires the sequential notation of various vocal, motor, emotional, and play behaviors of the child, and the affectional, verbal, helping, caretaking, restraining, and play behaviors of the people with whom the child comes into contact. A comprehensive presentation of the system is given in Greenbaum (1968) and other details may be found in Greenbaum and Landau (1972).

The system provided for the notation of over 100 responses of the infants and over 100 responses of any persons who came into contact with them. It discriminates between those responses made to the child by other individuals while in the child's immediate vicinity, and those made while the individual was some distance away, in the background. Notation was made of responses of the child that elicited responses in the other, and those of other individuals who elicited responses in the child. Only the child's responses and the responses of people who came into contact with him were noted.

Notation was made by pencil into a specially designed spiral notebook. Behaviors were noted sequentially by a special code. A page in the notebook was turned each half-minute, providing a thirty-second time location for each response. The observer remained in the background throughout and initiated no contact with the infant under observation.

The behavior categories to be examined in the present report include two major verbal categories used by the adult: sentences and questions. (In the institution environment, the behavior of the caretakers who had responsibility for the child was recorded.) The present study does not distinguish between verbalizations directed at the child and those directed at others in the child's environment, and thus gives the total amount of stimulation to which the child was exposed. Three central categories of vocalization by the infant are dealt with: vowels, discrete consonants, and vowel-consonant combinations. The use of words by the older infants in our sample is also reported and a brief summary of infant imitation of adult vocalization is presented. These responses account for a major portion of the child's total vocal output in the course of a day.

Reliability. The responses to be reported showed inter-
judge agreement percentages (number of agreements divided by
number of agreements plus number of disagreements) averaging
73 when omission of responses is not considered an error. The
percentage is 55 when omission is considered an error. The
results reflect agreement percentage aggregated over eleven
special observations performed by two observers at a time,
both before and during performance of the research. The lower
level of reliability when omission is considered can be traced
partly to errors of omission of maternal behaviors, probably
due to the fact that the child, not the mother, was the focus
of the observation. Agreement among observers is adequate
for a complex system such as the one described here, and shows
that when a response was perceived by an observer it was
generally perceived accurately. Gewirtz and Gewirtz (1965;
1968), who obtained comparable results with a similar observation
system, point out that omissions indicate underestimation of
behavior and not inaccuracy in observer discrimination.

Dependent measures of behavior. The principal measure
used in this report is the rate of responding per half minute
of time for each response, for an entire behavior day. These
rates are reported separately for the mother and for the infant.
Rates were calculated by dividing the total number of times a
response was emitted during the observation by the number of
half-minute observations units included in the behavior day for
each infant. With regard to the mother, this measure reflects
the amount of stimulation to which she exposed the child in
the course of a behavior day.

RESULTS

The data presented in Figures 10-1 to 10-5 show mean rates
for each response for mother and child. The data in each graph
were subjected to a 4 × 5 (age × environment) analysis of
variance, using the Miami MANOVA program (Clyde, Cramer, &
Sherin, 1966). In addition, trend tests were performed, to
determine whether linear, quadratic, or cubic trends could
be discerned among the age differences.

Verbalization of Mothers and Institutional Caretakers

Figure 10-1 presents the mean exposure to sentences spoken
by the mother. There is a striking *decrease* with age in the
amount of exposure to sentences in all environments,
$F(3, 76) = 3.59$, $p < .017$. The overall decreasing linear
trend is significant, $p < .01$. In addition, the difference

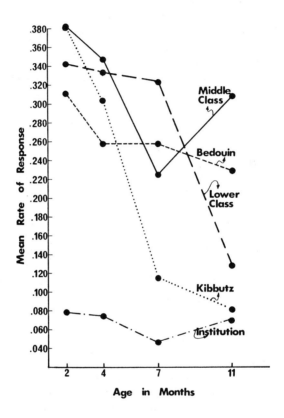

Figure 10-1.   Mean rate of sentence utterances by mothers
in presence of infants for each age and
environment.   (For institutions, caretakers'
data are presented.)

among environments is significant, $F(4, 76) = 6.83$, $p < .001$, due largely to the low stimulation received by the institutionalized infants.

The rate of questions asked by the mother is also related to both age and environment (Figure 10-2). The effect for environment $F(4, 76) = 15.00$, $p < .001$ shows the two urban environments, middle- and lower-class, to be clearly higher than the others in amount of mother's asking of questions. There is a difference among ages, $F(3, 76) = 2.90$, $p < .04$, expressing itself again in a decrease in exposure to a verbal response of the mother (not discernible for the Bedouin) in the later ages, as opposed to the earlier ones. The significant interaction effect $F(12, 76) = 2.03$, $p < .03$ confirms that the differences between environments are not uniform across age groups, the Bedouin and institutionalized infants having a distinctly different profile.

The low incidence of Bedouin mothers, question asking is not typical for most responses. The Bedouin infants are generally exposed to similar amounts of verbal stimulation, according to most measures, as the other home environments. It should be noted that the amount of stimulation to which the institutionalized child is exposed is quite low, even when *all* caretakers' behavior is considered. Thus the institutionalized infant is exposed to less stimulation from all his caretakers than a child in most environments receives from his mother alone.

Similar results with some variations are obtained when other aspects of the mother's verbal behavior are considered-- e.g., isolated words, baby talk, and calling the child by name. These data are not presented here for reasons of brevity. Thus, the child does *not* become increasingly exposed to verbal stimulation from the mother as he develops through the first year of life; if anything, in most environments he is exposed to less such stimulation as he grows older. This may be partially due to the fact that there is somewhat less interaction with the child in terms of caretaking (changing, feeding, etc.) at the later ages. Future studies in this series will explore the relationship between presence of an adult and amount of stimulation to which the child is exposed.

Vocalization of Infants

The data for infants' vowel expression are presented in Figure 10-3, which presents mean rate of vowel expression. It indicates significant effects of environment,

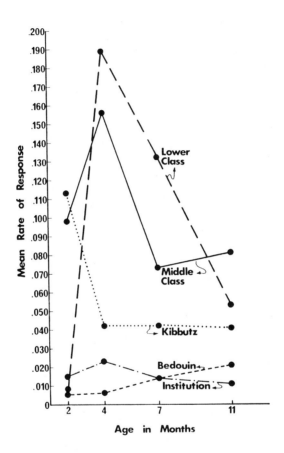

FIGURE 10-2. Mean rate of questions asked by mothers in presence of infants for each age and environment. (For institutions, caretakers' data are presented.)

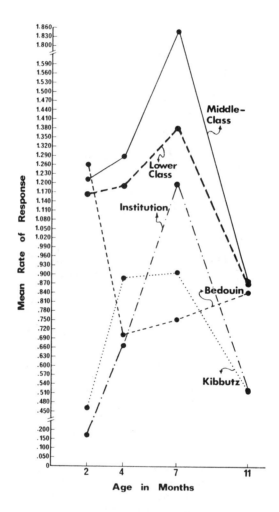

FIGURE 10-3.   Mean rate of vowels emitted by child for
each age and environment.

$F(4, 76) = 5.43$, $p < .001$, and age, $F(3, 76) = 3.85$, $p < .01$. It is clear that the children in the two urban home environments express more vowels than children in the other environments in the three upper age levels. Independently of this effect, there is a general and significant ($p < .05$) curvilinear trend, indicating that the vowel response initially increases with age and then decreases. This is true for all environments except for the Bedouin, who seem to show a reverse trend. Vowel responding, then, can clearly be affected by the environment, an effect that appears together with a trend that is not linear with age. Similar conclusions may be drawn from a study of vowels repeated within the same breath, not shown here. While there is a significant effect of age, reflecting some increase between two and eleven months, there does not appear to be a clear linear trend for any of the environments.

Figures 10-4 and 10-5 present the data for expression of vocalizations involving consonants. Inspection of both figures indicates that the picture here is different from the one given by the data on vowels. Figure 10-4, showing the mean rate of expression of single, isolated consonants, reveals a clear effect for age, $F(3, 76) = 17.33$, $p < .01$, with the sharpest increase in all environments occurring between seven and eleven months of age. This is indicated in the significant linear ($p < .001$) and quadratic ($p < .05$) trends that the data yield.

Figure 10-5 shows the mean rate of emission of vowel-consonant combination, such as *ab*, *eek*, etc. Age is the only significant influence on this response $F(3, 76) = 9.45$, $p < .01$, and only the linear trend is significant ($p < .001$). In a sense, this response represents the "purest" effect of age: a clear linear effect, with no other trends or effects discernible. This is a relatively complex response. The beginnings of a difference between environments, with some assumed to be somewhat richer in stimulation (kibbutzim, middle class, and Bedouin) than others (lower class, institutions), can be discerned at eleven months. This may indicate that vowel-consonant combinations are now mature enough to be affected by the environment, and that the effects will become stronger at later ages.

Words. Distinguishable words appear only at eleven months of age in our sample, and then with low frequency. Differences among environments are not significant, but it is worthwhile noting the extremes. Kibbutz children, who experienced the sharpest dropoff in the amount of speech to which they were exposed, spoke more words per time unit than any other group. Institutionalized children spoke no words at all.

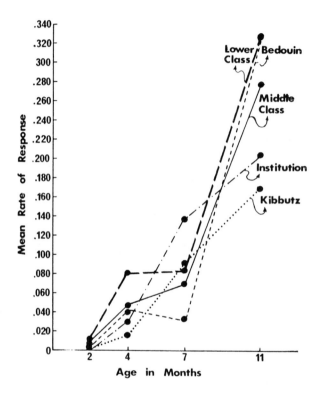

FIGURE 10-4. Mean rate of discrete consonants emitted
by child for each age and environment.

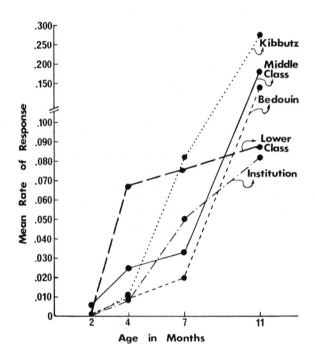

FIGURE 10-5.   Mean rate of vowel-consonant combinations
emitted by child for each age and environment.

This result may indicate some crucial variables involved in the passage from vocalization to language. A threshold level of stimulation is probably necessary for early vocalization and babbling. This level is clearly reached by the institutionalized children, who are not markedly different from others in measures of preverbal babbling presented earlier. The low level of stimulation may be insufficient for the early development of speech, however. To test this hypothesis, it is necessary to determine what qualitative factors in the mother's interaction with the child affect the development of speech.

Imitation. Imitation was defined as infants' behavior that clearly has common properties with those of immediately preceding adult (or other) behavior. Very little direct imitation of vocal behavior of adults by infants was observed; the amount of vocal behavior occurring without imitation was greater by many times than that occurred in the context of imitation. Clearly, then, a very large proportion of vocal behavior occurs in the absence of direct, immediate imitation, though imitation could still play a key role in the development of such behavior. The amount of imitation the child engages in is not related in any simple manner of degree of vocalization. More detailed data on imitation and other aspects of the child's vocal development will be presented in subsequent reports.

DISCUSSION

Role of Adult Stimulation in Early Development of Vocalization

Some parallels between the results reported here and those presented in our previous reports (Greenbaum & Landau, 1972) should be noted. The first is the lack of relationships between specific responses of the child and relevant responses of the mother, as indicated by inspection of the age trends of responses for each participant. Indeed, the amount of mother's talk to which the child is exposed clearly decreases with age, a result consistent with that of Cohen and Beckwith (1976). The explanation for infant learning of vocalization is thus not a simple one. Two obvious factors that should affect such learning--amount of verbal stimulation to which the child is exposed, and amount of imitation--do not relate to the development of infant vocalization in a simple manner. In our previous report, similar results were found in respect to decreasing laughing of mothers to infants, with increasing laughing of infants as age increases.

Analyses on this level do not necessarily mean that imitation of adult behavior is unimportant. Only overt, immediate imitation was studied. We do not know how much, if any, of infant vocalization occurring at each time point may actually have been imitations of parental vocalization. In addition, comparisons of gross rates of response by infant and child give only an imprecise estimate of "relation" or mutual influence. Discovery of precise contingency relationships between mother and child will require different methods of analysis, to be utilized in future treatment of the data. These will examine types of adult stimulation, especially those directed specifically at the child, which were not treated separately in this report.

There is at least one implication in the reported data concerning the effect of adult stimulation on the development of infant response: in the environments studied here, sheer quantity of stimulation does not necessary result in increased infant response in a home environment. In fact, development of consonants increases linearly with age in spite of the fact that verbal stimulation from the mother decreases. The mother in the kibbutz environment, who was the least stimulating of the mothers at later ages in terms of sheer quantity, seems to produce verbally well-developed children. Examination of the behavior of the child caretaker in the kibbutz (metapelet) does not change this picture.

Discrepancies between Experimental and Observational Data on Vocalization

How are these findings to be integrated with the experimental evidence (Ramey & Ourth, 1971; Rheingold, Gewirtz & Ross, 1959; Weisberg, 1963) that vocalization of the infant is subject to the influence of stimulation and reinforcement on the part of the adult? One possible answer is that the infant in the short term (the few minutes necessary for experimentation) will respond readily to the influence of stimulation or reinforcement once rapport with the child has been achieved. Infant vocalization is an ongoing process, however, and such experiments say little about the large amounts of vocal behavior the child engages in during the course of a day. The level and variety of adult stimulation that affect the infant's vocalization in natural settings over the long term are not well understood from experimental work alone.

A second consideration is the nature of the child's response. The results presented here indicate that the

influence of environment is primarily on well-developed
responses such as vowels and quickly repeated consonants.
Environment did not have a discernible effect on sounds that
were still in a formative stage of development. The
experimental reports mentioned do not distinguish among
different characteristics of infant sounds. It can probably
be assumed, however, on the basis of our results, that the
effect of the mother on the infant's vocalization in the first
year of life is felt most strongly on vowels and well-learned
consonants. Definite conclusions concerning such an
hypothesis must wait until the influence of other adults
besides those reported here have been studied. At least one
report (Rebelsky & Hanks, 1971) has indicated that fathers
spend little time vocalizing to their infants.

Environmental Influence on Behavior Is Highly Selective

The considerations outlined above should be evaluated in
the context of the general problem of the influence of the
environment on behavior. As in our previous report (Greenbaum
& Landau, 1972), environment was found to have a clear effect
on certain responses and not on others.

What is the key to the seemingly highly selective
influence of environment on behavior? We suggest the following
hypothesis. Response systems that are in an early stage of
development seem to be relatively unaffected by environment,
while response systems over which the child has attained some
degree of mastery may be affected by the environment to a
significant degree. The clear implication is that the
environment will not significantly affect a response until it
has reached a certain level of attainment. This level may be
indicated by its maximum rate of occurrence in the course of
a normal day, at an age when there are no differences among
environments. We may call this the *age of maximum rate* for a
particular response. After this age of maximum rate with no
difference among environments, differences among the
environments appear.

The responses that develop early, such as the vowel
response, have clearly passed the age of maximum rate by the
time of two months of age. Therefore, the influence of the
environment is already apparent at the age of two months.
Other responses such as the complex vocalization indicated by
discrete consonants and by vowel-consonant combinations do
not yet reflect the influence of the environment.

Valuable information is available in previous studies that

have analyzed test data in order to find trait profiles
common to a number of populations (Guttman, 1967). However,
the use of a rate measure taken over several hours of
observation in a natural setting shows promise of being a
central indicator in understanding the behavior of the infant,
yielding information not available through testing techniques.

Some Implications for the Development of Language

     The foregoing considerations may shed light on some ideas
put forward by Lenneberg (1967; 1969) concerning the development of language. Lenneberg reports (see Lenneberg, Rebelsky,
& Nichols, 1965) that children of deaf parents do not differ
from children of hearing parents in early vocal development,
in spite of clear differences in the amount and type of
stimulation that each group receives. On the basis of this
and other data, Lenneberg states that "language capacity
follows its own natural history. The child can avail himself
of this capacity if the environment provides a minimum of
stimulation and opportunity" (1969, p. 637).

     The evidence for this statement in our data is mixed.
Support for Lenneberg's position is found in the result that
institutionalized infants did not differ greatly from infants
in the more stimulating kibbutz or home environments in either
vowel or consonant development. On the other hand, there are
some differences among environments in vowel and repeated
consonant development, though these do not seem to be correlated
with differences in sheer amount of maternal stimulation.
Perhaps more importantly, no institutionalized child speaks
words by the age of eleven months, while there are infants in
each of the other environments who do. It is reasonable to
assume that this may be due to the lower level of verbal
stimulation received by the institutionalized infants. This
result is clearly at variance with Lenneberg's (1967; 1969)
proposals that onset of language development is unaffected by
environment. There is a strong possibility that a deprived
environment in the first year of life may adversely affect
certain key responses in a child's vocal development in the
long-range sense.

The Uses of Systematic Comparative Culture Observation

     The data presented here comprise only a beginning of a
number of analyses we plan to carry out. They should suffice,
however, to point to the uses of systematic cultural
comparisons by means of observation in natural settings. Such
studies should help to focus on specific effects of the

environment on particular response systems of the growing infant.

Research done in this fashion can study effects over a long time span (several hours or longer) than is generally utilized in experimental studies. Most critically, it may be that only systematic, observational, and naturalistic comparison among cultures containing wide differences in type and amount of stimulation to which they expose the child can provide us with the meaning of developmental indicators. Such comparisons will tell us when the developmental phase has run its course and when the influence of the environment begins to make itself felt.

In this context, a number of features of the approach used in our present study should be pointed out. One is that the study is multicultural--studying five different child-rearing environments. The use of this number of environments permits comparisons that highlight similarities and differences not possible when a smaller number of environments are studied. Thus, many comparisons show no differences between middle- and low-class environments--unlike a number of previous studies. Indeed, in the use of questions middle- and lower-class mothers are more like each other than they are to those of other environments. In addition, middle-class infants of seven months of age are clearly higher in emission of vowels than infants in all other environments. This indicates a high degree of such behavior in comparison, not only to lower-class infants (who are, again, actually closest to them), but to other environments as well.

On the other hand, *lack* of difference among five environments, when behavior changes with age, is powerful evidence of development relatively free of environmental influence. This is the case for the development of consonants and consonant-vowel combinations, and may be true of other behaviors as well.

The findings demonstrate the potential that is inherent in the use of systematic multicultural comparisons. Further analyses will attempt to discover other aspects of the nature of environmental influence on the child, and of the child's influence on other people in his environment.

REFERENCES

Barker, R. G., & Wright, H. F. The Midwest and its children.
New York: Harper & Row, 1955.

Beckwith, L. Relationships between infants' vocalizations
and their mothers' behaviors. Child Development.
1971, 17, 211-226.

Bernstein, B. Social class and linguistic development: A
theory of social learning. In A.M. Halsey, J. Floud,
& C. A. Anderson (Eds.), Education, economy and
society. New York: Free Press, 1961.

Brodbeck, A., & Irwin, O. C. The speech behavior of infants
without families. Child Development, 1946, 17,
145-156.

Bruner, J. S. The ontogenesis of speech acts. Journal of
Child Language, 1975, 2, 1-19.

Brunswik, E. Perception and the representative design of
psychological experiments. Berkeley, Calif.:
University of California Press, 1956.

Cameron, J., Livson, N., & Bayley, N. Infant vocalizations
and their relationship to mature intelligence.
Science, 1967, 157, 331-333.

Clyde, D. J., Cramer, E. C., & Sherin, R. J. Multivariate
statistical programs. Coral Gables, Fla.: University
of Florida, 1966.

Cohen, S. E., & Beckwith, L. Maternal language in infancy.
Developmental Psychology, 1976, 12, 371-372.

Friedlander, B. Z. Receptive language development in infancy:
Issues and problems. Merrill-Palmer Quarterly,
1970, 16, 7-51.

Gewirtz, H. B., & Gewirtz, J. L. Caretaking settings, background events, and behavior differences in four
Israeli child-rearing environments: Some preliminary
trends. In B. M. Foss (Ed.), Determinants of
infant behavior (Vol. 4). London: Methuen, 1968.

Gewirtz, J. L. The course of infant smiling in four child-
rearing environments in Israel. In B. M. Foss (Ed.),

Determinants of infant behavior (Vol. 3). London: Methuen, 1965.

Gewirtz, J. L. Mechanisms of social learning: Some roles of stimulation and behavior in early human development. In D. Goslin (Ed.), Handbook of socialization theory and research. Chicago: Rand-McNally, 1969.

Gewirtz, J. L., & Gewirtz, H. B. Stimulus conditions, infant behaviors, and social learning in four Israeli child-rearing environments: A preliminary report illustrating differences in environment and behavior between the "only" and the "youngest" child. In B. M. Foss (Ed.), Determinants of infant behavior (Vol. 3). London: Methuen, 1965.

Greenbaum, C. W. Assessment of the reinforcing environment in preschool children. Unpublished progress report submitted to Bureau of Research, U. S. Office of Education, 1968.

Greenbaum, C. W., & Landau, R. Some social responses of infants and mothers in three Israeli child-rearing environments. In F. Monks, W. Hartup, & J. de Wit (Eds.), Determinants of behavioral development. New York: Academic Press, 1972.

Guttman, R. Cross-population constancy in trait profiles and the study of the inheritance of human behavior variables. In J. N. Spuhler (Ed.), Genetic diversity and human behavior (Publication No. 45). New York: Viking Fund Publications in Anthropology, 1967.

Hess, R. D., & Shipman, V. Early experience and the socialization of cognitive modes in children. Child Development, 1965, 36, 869-886.

Holzman, M. The verbal environment provided by mothers for their young children. Merrill-Palmer Quarterly of Behavior and Development, 1974, 20, 31-42.

Irwin, O. C. Infant speech: Development of vowel sounds. Journal of Speech and Hearing Disorders, 1948, 13, 31-34.

Irwin, O. C. Infant speech: Effect of systematic reading of stories. Journal of Speech and Hearing Research, 1960, 13, 190-197.

Landau, R. The extent that the mother represents the social stimulation to which the infant is exposed: Findings from a cross-cultural study. Developmental Psychology, 1976, 12, 399-405.

Lenneberg, E. H. On explaining language. Science, 1969, 164, 635-643.

Lenneberg, E. H. Biological foundations of language. New York: Wiley, 1967.

Lenneberg, E. H., Rebelsky, F., & Nichols, I. A. The vocalization of infants born to deaf and hearing parents. Human Development, 1965, 8, 23-37.

Lewin, K. Behavior and development as a function of the total situation. In D. Cartwright (Ed.), Field theory in social science: Selected theoretical papers by Kurt Lewin. New York: Harper & Row, 1951.

Marx, E. Bedouin of the Negev. Manchester, England: Mancherster University Press, 1967.

McNeill, D. Developmental psycholinguistics. In E. Smith and G. Miller (Eds.), The genesis of language. Cambridge, Mass.: M. I. T. Press, 1966.

Ramey, C. T., & Ourth, L. L. Delayed reinforcement and vocalization rates of infants. Child Development, 1971, 42, 291-297.

Rebelsky, F., & Hanks, C. Fathers' verbal interaction with infants in the first three months of life. Child Development, 1971, 42, 63-68.

Rheingold, H., Gewirtz, J. L., & Ross, W. Social conditions of vocalizations in the infant. Journal of Comparative and Physiological Psychology, 1959, 52, 68-73.

Ryan, J. Early language development: Towards a communicational analysis. In M. P. M. Richards (Ed.), The integration of a child into a social world. Cambridge, England: Cambridge University Press, 1974.

Spiro, M. Kibbutz: Venture in utopia. New York: Schocken, 1956.

Spiro, M. Children of the kibbutz. Cambridge, Mass.: Harvard University Press, 1958.

Talmon-Garber, Y. Family and community in the kibbutz. Cambridge, Mass.: Harvard University Press, 1972.

Tulkin, S. R. Mother-infant interaction in the first year of life: An inquiry into the influences of social class. Unpublished doctoral dissertation, Department of Social Relations, Harvard University, 1970.

Tulkin, S. R. & Kagan, J. Mother-child interaction: Social class differences in the first year of life. Child Development, 1972, 43, 31-42.

Weisberg, P. Social and non-social conditioning of infant vocalizations. Child Development, 1963, 34, 377-388.

Chapter 11

The Uses of Crosscultural Research in Early Development

Jerome Kagan

Harvard University

Although systematic observations of children in settings
other than the United States and Europe have become more
frequent during the last decade, the selection of a community
is often based more on logistic convenience than on the special
characteristics of the setting. The purpose of this chapter is
to discuss some of the uses of cross-cultural investigation of
the opening years of life from the perspective of the developmental psychologist, illustrating some of them with recent data
on cognitive functioning in the infant.

TO PROBE A FUNCTIONAL RELATION MORE COMPLETELY

The essence of a scientific discipline is a coherent set
of functional interrelations among well-defined variables.
These relations form the elements that a theory attempts to
coalesce into a logically consistent structure. Often the
relation between pairs of variables is not linear. The form
of the function changes with different values of the independent

[1]The research reported in this paper was supported, in part, by
grants from the Grant Foundation and the Foundation for Child
Development.

variable. Because certain magnitude ranges of the predictor
variable may not occur in the setting in which the investigator
lives, it is useful to travel to a culture where those magnitudes
can be found. Darwin discovered in the Galapagos conditions he
could not have observed in England: two neighboring islands
with identical climates containing morphologically different
members of the same species. These observations contributed
to his eventual rejection of the climatological interpretation
of speciation.

There are many functional relations in development, the
specification of which requires sampling in more than one
locale. The relation of malnutrition to physical growth, of
peer interaction to social behavior, of schooling to cognitive
ability, and of variety of experience to cognitive development
are just a few. For example, among middle-class American
families there is no reason to suspect a relation between amount
of caloric intake during pregnancy and either mortality of the
infant or intellectual capability in the young child. But
among populations existing on marginal diets, a condition that
exists in rural subsistence farming villages in less well-
developed countries, there is a relation between caloric intake during pregnancy and both the likelihood of infant
mortality and the child's verbal ability at four years of age
(Klein, 1975).

TO DEMONSTRATE UNIVERSALITY IN A GROWTH SEQUENCE OR IN PSYCHOLOGICAL FUNCTIONING

A second purpose of cross-cultural research is to
determine if a particular phenomenon, either a growth sequence
or a particular functional relation, is universal. Over twenty
years ago, Brown and Lenneberg (1954) assumed that a culture's
specific language terms for color would influence the salience
of those colors in memory, and they published a report on
American adults in support of that idea. Recently, Heider
(1972a, 1972b) reported that particular focal colors are better
remembered in some cultures despite absence of a lexical name
for them. The suggestion that evaluation, potency, and passivity seem to be universal connotative dimensions is a classic
instance of the use of cross-cultural research to discover
universals in human semantic systems (Osgood, May, & Miron,
1975). Later in this paper, we shall suggest that there seems
to be an invariant sequence involving the amplification of
memory during the first year of life.

TO REFUTE A HYPOTHESIS

Perhaps the most powerful use of cross-cultural study is to gather data that refute a functional relation that has become popular. As Popper (1962) has noted, this is a common use of empirical observations in mature disciplines. Although developmental psychology does not have many well-formed hypotheses, the validity of a few can be examined through cross-cultural study. John Bowlby (1969) and Mary Ainsworth (1967) have argued in the past that separation anxiety was a sensitive index of the level and intensity of the infant's attachment to his mother, where attachment was assumed to covary with the quality and duration of the mother-infant interaction. Because extensive variations in the quality of the mother-child interaction in the United States are hard to find, it is useful to test that idea in settings where the infant has either minimal daily contact with a single care-taker or almost continual contact. These data have been gathered, and the growth function for separation distress is similar for children exposed to a wide variety of daily contact with their mothers. We have gathered data on the developmental course of separation protest over the first two and a half years of life in American children as well as in children growing up in settings outside the United States. The non-American samples included lower-class Ladino families living in the city of Antigua, Guatemala; Indian families residing in isolated agri-cultural villages on Lake Atitlan in northwest Guatemala; Israeli kibbutsim, where infants spend most of the day in an infant house; !Kung San families living in the Kalahari Desert. In all four of these groups, the occurrence of crying following maternal departure when the infant was left with a stranger was minimal prior to 9 months, increased to a peak value between 12 and 15 months, and then declined (Kagan, 1976).

Additionally, we have studied separation distress in a longitudinal sample of American children (Caucasian and Chinese) attending a day-care center five days a week from three and a half through twenty-nine months of age. Each child of the same sex, social class, and ethnic group who was being raised at home. The child's reactions to his mother's departure (leaving him alone in a strange room) were observed regularly from three and a half to twenty-nine months of age. The growth function for protest was identical for both day-care and home-reared children and, as in the other settings, protest did not occur reliably until nine months of age and peaked during the second year (Kagan, 1976). Because the growth function for separation protest was similar for all groups, despite the enormous variation in duration and quality of mother-infant contact, it seems that the original hypothesis should be questioned.

Consider as a second example the suggestion, based on psychoanalytic theory, that suppression of anger and aggression should lead to psychological symptoms and, perhaps, somaticization. Among the Utku Eskimo of Hudson Bay, with whom Jean Briggs spent twenty months, displays of anger in a child after age two are followed by a "silent treatment". Although the child is initially upset, after a few years there are no tantrums and little interpersonal aggression (Briggs, 1970). But the psychological symptoms that are presumed to result from suppressed anger are absent.

Consider, as a final example, the hypothesis originally proposed by Geber (1956), that motor development matures more rapidly in African than in European infants because of innate racial differences. Super (1976) has recently reported that motor development in Kipsigis infants growing up in the village of Kokwet is only advanced, relative to Americans, for sitting, standing, and walking--responses that Kipsigis mothers deliberately teach their babies. The Kipsigis infants are not advanced over Americans in crawling or rolling over, and these are responses that Kipsigis mothers do not encourage. Super's data provide a challenge to the hypothesis that the motor development of African children is innately different from those of Caucasians.

UNDERSTANDING THE CULTURE

These three uses of cross-cultural work aim at nomothetic statements about human functioning. But there are many who believe that study of individuals in other societies is of value even though transfer of principles to another community might not be possible. The purpose is to understand the psychological functioning of another group and to learn of the coherences that exist for that community. This attitude is common in both biology--where study of the ecology of mountain goats is done for its own sake--as well as in developmental psychology where one probes a phenomenon that is confined to a particular era in the life span. Study of the form and growth function of the Babinski reflex probably produces no information that helps us understand the functioning of the six-year-old. But that is not sufficient reason to ignore this event. It is a lawful phenomenon and therefore invites understanding. To know that the Indians of Santiago Atitlan regard hard work, cleverness, and wealth as the essential qualities of the ego ideal of adult men aids our understanding of the functioning of that community.

MODERN PROBLEMS IN EARLY DEVELOPMENT

There are many contemporary issues in developmental psychology that can be informed by cross-cultural investigation. A key proposition in Piagetian theory states that there are invariant sequences in cognitive development. Affirmation or refutation of that proposition demands cross-cultural study. The remainder of this paper deals with some of these issues in the context of one segment of development; the period from about six to twenty months of life. The data to be summarized imply that there is an invariant growth sequence during the last half of the first year that seems to involve, in part, the amplification of short-term memory and the coordination of memory and behavior.

THE ENHANCEMENT OF RETRIEVAL AND COMPARATIVE PROCESSES

The corpus of data generated by many investigators over the last ten years seems to require the positing of a new set of developmental processes that emerge by eight months of age that seem responsible for a variety of phenotypically different phenomena. Although temporal covariation among manifestly different phenomena does not necessarily imply a common mechanism, the scientist's affection for parsimony invites an attempt to invent a unitary process or, at least, a small number of processes.

The Growth Of Attentiveness To Discrepant Events.

Toward the end of the first year the infant frequently displays more prolonged attention to a variety of discrepant events than he did when he was six or seven months old. If an interesting event is shown to infants from four through thirty months of age, in either a cross-sectional or longitudinal design, there is often, but not always, a U-shaped relation between age and fixation time, with a trough around seven to nine months. For example, if masks or drawings of a human face are shown to children four through thirty-six months, attention is prolonged at four months, markedly lower at seven to eight months, but increases through the second and third years (Kagan, 1972). This developmental function for attention to facial masks holds not only for American children, but for rural Mexican (Finley, Kagan, & Layne, 1972) and Guatemalan children as well (Sellers, Klein, Kagan, & Minton, 1972). Moreover, the U-shaped function holds for nonsocial visual events and, even more important, for attentiveness to speech.

We recently studied the growth function for attentiveness to speech in American children and isolated Indian children living in northwest Guatemala. The child heard a four-second meaningful phrase for ten or twelve trials followed by five transformation trials of either nonsense or nongrammatical speech, followed by three more presentations of the original standard. The variable of interest was search behavior during the presentation of the auditory information. Search was defined as the maintenance of a quiet, alert posture together with saccadic movements of the eyes during the presentation of the stimulus event. Intercoder reliability for search was over + .90. The growth function for search behavior was curvilinear in both samples with a trough at seven to eight months of age.

Both the American and Indian infants passed through a brief period at seven to eight months when attentiveness to speech was at a nadir, after which attention increased. If we interpret the trough in attention at seven months as indicating easy assimilation of the event, why is it that a few months later the same event seems to be more difficult to assimilate? Of the many possible interpretations, we favor the idea that the new competence involves the ability to retrieve the schema of the original standard, to compare it with the discrepant event in the perceptual field, and to attempt to resolve the discrepancy between the two. The three- to six-month-old is attentive to the event because he is trying to assimilate it to an existing schema. Because that process proceeds more quickly at seven to eight months, attentiveness is reduced. The one-year-old, however, is able to hold the representation of the past experience in short-term memory for a much longer period, but more important, attempts to generate the relation between past and present. The increased search behavior after eight months reflects that cognitive process.

Inhibition To A Discrepant Event.

Prior to seven months the infant frequently reaches at once for a novel object presented following repeated presentations of a familiarized standard, while eleven-month-olds show a short but obvious delay before reaching for the novel object (Parry, 1973; Schaffer, Greenwood, & Parry, 1972).

The capacity for generalized motor inhibition to an unexpected event is not new, for newborns will inhibit both limb movement and sucking in response to a sudden onset of visual or auditory stimulation and three-month-olds will inhibit an operantly trained kicking response if presented with a mobile different from the one on which they have been trained (Fagan, Rovee, & Kaplan, 1976). These instances of motor inhibition in the young infant seem to be reflexive, automatic reactions to a discrepant event, rather than the volitional inhibition of a goal-directed reaching response that characterizes the older infant.

Apprehension To Discrepant Events

    Another major change that occurs at this time is a dramatic increase in the likelihood of facial wariness, inhibition of play, and crying in response to an event whose major character- istic is that it is a discrepant transformation of an earlier or immediately past experience. Scarr and Salapatek (1970) exposed infants two to twenty-three months of age to six different discrepant or novel events--stranger approaching the child, a visual cliff, a jack-in-the-box, a mechanical dog that moved, facial masks, and a loud noise. Infants younger than seven months rarely showed any behavioral signs of wariness to- ward any of these events. The peak display of wariness usually occurred between eleven and eighteen months for most of these episodes. Additionally, inhibition, facial wariness or overt distress in response to unfamiliar people or maternal departure is infrequent prior to seven months, grows dramatically between that time and the middle of the second year, and then declines. As indicated earlier, the growth function for separation distress is similar among children being raised in different settings and tends to peak during the second year. It is important to note that the growth function for separation distress in blind child- ren is not much different from that noted for those with sight. Fraiberg has gathered detailed longitudinal observations on ten blind infants who were seen bimonthly in their homes (Fraiberg, 1975; Adelson & Fraiberg, 1974). The distress to separation emerges between ten and nineteen months, with a median age of about eleven months, close to the median age for sighted infants. This is remarkable, considering the fact that the child cannot see if the parent is present. The incentive event for the dis- play of distress is the unexpected absence of the mother's voice or the sounds that accompany her bodily movements.

Enhancement Of Memory, Activation Of Structures, And The Coordination Of Action With Retrieved Structures.

We believe that the temporal concordance of increased
attentiveness and inhibition, wariness, and distress in response
to discrepant events are caused by the emergence of several
related cognitive competences. These include the ability (1)
to retrieve a schema related to the child's present experience
following minimal exposure to a new event and minimal incentive
cues in the immediate field, and (2) to retain that schema in
memory while the child compares the retrieved structure with
the present, in an attempt to resolve the discrepancy or inconsistency. Support for these hypotheses come from two similar
studies of this age period. The first, conducted by Nathan Fox,
was a short-term longitudinal investigation of eight, healthy,
middle-class Caucasian American children who were observed
monthly in both home and laboratory from six to thirteen months
of age. The procedures administered are described as follows.

1. **Vacillation.** In this procedure, the child is allowed
   to play with an attractive toy for thirty seconds.
   After the period of familiarization, the toy was
   removed, the examiner distracted the infant, and
   thirty seconds later the examiner presented simultaneously the familiar toy and a new toy. The major
   dependent variable was occurrence and duration of
   vacillation; the length of time the infant looked
   back and forth between the new and familiar toy.

2. **Object permanence.** The children were administered a
   series of tasks requiring them to find an object they
   had watched the examiner hide, in the standard object
   permanence paradigm.

3. **Object permanence: "A not B", with delays.** Each child
   was administered the "A not B" variation of the standard object permanence problem, with either a three- or
   seven-second delay between the time the object was
   hidden at location B and the time when the child was
   permitted to reach for it.

There was remarkable concordance among the eight children
in the age at which the infants met the criterion for each of
these tasks (see Table I). All children displayed vacillation
by six to seven months. One month later, all children had
passed the simple object permanence task, followed a month
later by successful performance on the "A not B" problem with

a three-second delay. By ten months, all eight solved the
"A not B" problem with a seven-second delay.

TABLE 11-1. Age (In Months) At Which Each of Eight
American Infants Mastered The Four Procedures

Procedure	Infant							
	A	B	C	D	E	F	G	H
Vacillation	6	7	7	7	6	6	6	7
Simple object permanence	7	8	8	8	7	8	7	7
"A not B" 3-second delay	8	8	8	9	9	9	8	8
"A not B" 7-second delay	8	9	9	10	9	10	9	9

Additionally, Robert Klein, Elena Hurtado and I have
performed a cross-sectional study of Indian children from the
villages of San Pedro and San Marcos on Lake Atitlan. The
eighty-seven infants, between five and twenty one months of
age, were administered three of the procedures used in the
American study (vacillation, simple object permanence, and
"A not B" with a three-second delay) and, additionally, inhibition to novelty. All procedures were administered in the
child's home. In the inhibition to novelty problem, the infant was shown the same identical toy for six repeated trials,
each lasting about eight seconds. On the seventh trial, the
infant was shown a single novel toy. Latency to reach for the
toy was coded on each trial, and the behavior of interest was
the tendency to inhibit reaching for the novel toy on the
critical seventh trial. The procedure was repeated three times,
with threee different pairs of toys. The criterion for inhibition was an increase of at least one second in the latency to
reach for the new toy compared with the last presentation of
the familiarized toy.

The performances of the Indian children on these four procedures also fell into an invariant sequence. In both villages,
vacillation occurred before inhibition to novelty, and both
occurred before successful solution of the two object permanence
problems. Table 11-2 presents the earliest age at which any
child met the criteria for "success" on the tasks and the age
at which half the children met the criteria for these procedures.

TABLE 11-2. Sequence of Developmental Milestones In San
Pedro and San Marcos Children

Response	Youngest Age At Which Any Child First Met Criterion		Age At Which 50 Percent Of Group Met Criterion	
	San Pedro	San Marcos	San Pedro	San Marcos
Vacillation on 2 of 5 trials	5 mos.	7 mos.	5-6 mos.	8 mos.
Inhibition to novelty on 2 of 3 trials	6	8	8	9
Simple object permanence	7	9	7-8	10-11
Object permanence A not B (3-sec. delay)	7	11	10	11

Although the Cambridge children tended to be a little more
advanced than the more isolated Indian infants in the appearance
of these milestones, perhaps because of greater environmental
variety and better health, the sequence of victories was
remarkably similar in both cultures. The results of the studies
imply that enhancement of short-term memory may be one of the
central competences that emerges during the last half of the
first year. Schaffer (1974) has also suggested that the new
cognitive competence that emerges at this time is the ability
to activate from memory schemata for absent objects, and to use
them to evaluate a situation.

The new capacity to retrieve structures for events not in
the immediate field can help to explain some of the phenomena
described earlier. For example, let us apply this idea to the
inverted U-shaped function for attention to visual or auditory
events. The increase in attention after seven months can be
explained if we assume that the older infant is able to
retrieve a representation of a repeated experience, hold it
in memory, and try to relate it to the discrepant event in the
perceptual field. If the event is a mask, the child retrieves

his representation of a regular face and tries to generate the relation between his knowledge of the normal face and the mask in front of him. As long as a trace of the past event remains articulated and the infant continues to attempt to relate it to present experience in the service of understanding, he remains attentive. The appearance of motor inhibition in the inhibition to novelty situation implies that the child may be generating structures representative of the earlier event.

We also believe that the growth function for separation distress requires, as a necessary, although not sufficient, condition, the enhanced ability to retrieve schemata of prior events and to hold them on the stage of awareness for a longer period of time. Following departure of the mother, the ten-month-old child generates from memory the schema of her former presence in the room and holds that schema in memory while comparing it with the present. If the child cannot resolve the inconsistency inherent in the comparison, he becomes uncertain and may cry. But that hypothetical sequence is not completely satisfactory, for several reasons. First, the one-year-old occasionally cries as the caretaker walks toward the exit-- before she has left the room. Second, the child does not cry or become upset in similar situations when he compares past and present and cannot resolve the discrepancy contained therein. For example, the one-year-old becomes puzzled, but usually does not cry, when he fails to find a toy under a cover after having watched an adult place an object there several seconds earlier. Moreover, the one-year-old compares past with present all through the day in a myriad of contexts, but distress is not a common event during most of the child's waking hours.

It appears, therefore, that additional processes must be postulated if we are to explain the robust separation findings. A likely possibility is that the enhanced ability to retrieve and hold a schema of the past is correlated with the ability to generate anticipations of the future. We assume that the eight-to nine-month old has a new capacity, best described as the disposition to attempt to predict future events and to generate responses to deal with discrepant situations. The child tries to cope instrumentally with the unfamiliar experience; he did not try to do that earlier. If the child cannot generate a prediction or instrumental response, he is vulnerable to un-certainty and distress. Distress is more likely to appear to separation than to other surprises in the child's daily life, because his schemata for the mother and her presence are highly salient. Distress does not occur to most discrepant experiences in the laboratory or the child's daily encounters, because the events are relatively unfamiliar.

We are left with one final puzzle. Why does the presence of a familiar person or setting reduce dramatically the occurrence of uncertainty and crying to maternal departure? And why does the presence of the mother, especially if she is close by, reduce the likelihood of fear to many discrepant events? Although there are many possibilities (e.g., there is a continuum of uncertainty and within that continuum each child has a threshold, or the infant classifies contexts into familiar or unfamiliar), a possibility we favor is that the presence of a familiar person or setting provides the child with opportunities for responses to make when uncertainty is generated. Recognition of the opportunity to issue an action buffers uncertainty. Distress does not occur when the mother leaves the child with the father, because his presence provides the child with a potential target for a set of behaviors. This interpretation is profoundly cognitive, for the infant does not have to move toward the father or the familiar figure; he only has to know that the parent is present.

In sum, the protest following separation during the latter part of the first year requires the postulation of the following hypothetical sequence.

1. The ability to retrieve from memory schemata of past salient events with minimal incentive cues and to hold those representations on the stage of short-term memory so that comparison of past and present is possible. The essential competence is the enhanced ability to hold a retrieved schema in awareness for a longer period of time.

2. The attempt to predict possible future events and to generate instrumental reactions to deal with discrepant experience.

3. The inability to resolve the inconsistency between past and present, to predict future possibilities, or to generate a coping reaction.

4. If there is no opportunity to issue a behavior to the preceding state of uncertainty, distress mounts and crying is likely to occur.

We are not suggesting that the child under seven months does not retrieve past experience. Existing research indicates that the three-month-old, and even the newborn, will dis-habituate to an event that is a transformation on a habituated standard. The very young infant can retrieve a schema for a

past event. However, establishment of the schema may be slower
and the retrieval competence vulnerable to long delays. The
major differences between the ten-month-old and the three-month-
old are, in our opinion, that the older child can establish a
schema more quickly, can retrieve it with minimal stimulus in-
centives in the immediate field and after a longer temporal
delay between the two events; and that the older infant can
hold representations of past and present in short-term memory
for a longer period of time. Because of these competences, the
older child shows both more prolonged attention to discrepant
events and is more vulnerable to uncertainty, because he is
permitted a longer period of time to work at resolving the
discrepancy between schema and current experience. The disposition to generate cognitive structures or actions that
attempt to relate past and present or deal with the discrepant
present are as important as the increased ability to hold past
experience in short-term memory.

We believe that these new functions are the direct consequence of maturational changes in the central nervous system;
assuming, of course, that the child is growing up in an environment that contains some variety. It may not be a coincidence
that the proportion of quiet sleep, which is relatively constant
from three to nine months, shows a major increase at nine to
ten months, the age when these processes emerge (Emde & Walker,
1976). Because many physiologists believe that the neural
control of sleep shifts from brainstem to forebrain mechanisms
during the first year (McGinty, 1971), it is reasonable to
suggest that the diverse behavioral changes that suddenly and
rather uniformly appear toward the end of the first year in
children from different cultures are released by structural or
biochemical events that are essential elements in ontogenesis.

REFERENCES

Adelson, E., & Fraiberg, S. Gross motor development in infants
        blind from birth. Child Development, 1974, 45, 114-
        126.

Ainsworth, M. D. S. Infancy in Uganda. Baltimore, Md.: Johns
        Hopkins University Press, 1967.

Bowlby, J. Attachment and loss. Vol. I: Attachment. New York:
        Basic Books, 1969.

Briggs, J. Never in anger. Cambridge, Mass.: Harvard University Press, 1970.

Brown, R. W., & Lenneberg, E. H. A study in language and cognition. Journal of Abnormal and Social Psychology, 1954, 49, 454-462.

Emde, R. N., & Walker, S. Longitudinal study of infants' sleep: results of fourteen subjects studied at monthly intervals. Psycho-physiology, 1976, 13, 456-461.

Fagen, J. W., Rovee, C. K., & Kaplan, M. G. Psychophysical scaling of stimulus similarity in three-month-old infants. Journal of Experimental Child Psychology, 1976, 22, 272-281.

Finley, G. E., Kagan, J., & Layne, O. Development of young children's attention to normal and distorted stimuli. Developmental Psychology, 1972, 6, 288-292.

Fraiberg, S. The development of human attachments in infants blind from birth. Merrill-Palmer Quarterly, 1975, 21, 315-334.

Geber, M. Developpement psycho-moteur de l'enfant Africain. Courrier, 1956, 6, 17.

Heider, E. R. Universals in color naming and memory. Journal of Experimental Psychology, 1972a, 93, 10-20.

Heider, E. R., & Olivier, D. C. The structure of the color space in naming and memory for two languages. Cognitive Psychology, 1972b, 3, 337-354.

Kagan, J. Do infants think? Scientific American, 1972, 226, 74-83.

Kagan, J. Emergent themes in human development. American Scientist, 1976, 64, 186-196.

Klein, R. E. Malnutrition and human behavior. Paper presented at Conference on Malnutrition and Behavior, Cornell University, Ithaca, New York, 1975.

McGinty, D. J. Encephalization and the neural control of sleep. In M. B. Sterman, D. J. McGinty, & A. M. Adinolfi (Eds.). Brain development and behavior. New York: Academic Press, 1971.

Osgood, C. E., May, W. H., & Miron, M. S. Cross-cultural
    universals of affective meaning. Urbana: University
    of Illinois Press, 1975.

Parry, M. H. Infant wariness and stimulus discrepancy. Journal
    of Experimental Child Psychology, 1973, 16, 377-387.

Popper, K. R. Conjectures and refutations. New York: Basic
    Books, 1962.

Scarr, S., & Salapatek, P. Patterns of fear development during
    infancy. Merrill-Palmer Quarterly, 1970, 16, 53-90.

Schaffer, H. R. Cognitive components of the infant's response
    to strangeness. In M. Lewis & L. Rosenblum (Eds.),
    The origins of fear. New York: Wiley, 1974.

Schaffer, H. R., Greenwood, A., & Parry, M. H. The onset of
    wariness. Child Development, 1972, 43, 165-175.

Sellers, M. J., Klein, R. E., Kagan, J., & Minton, C.
    Developmental determinants of attention: A cross-
    cultural replication. Developmental Psychology,
    1972, 6, 185.

Super, C. M. Environmental effects on motor development: The
    case of African infant precocity. Developmental
    Medicine and Child Neurology, 1976, 18, 561-567.

Chapter 12
Infancy Among the Kalahari Desert San

Melvin Konner

Harvard University

In 1963 Irven DeVore and Richard Lee made their first field visit to the !Kung[1] San of northwestern Botswana. The !Kung hunt and gather for a living. In spite of many differences, people the world over who hunt and gather for a living share certain features of social and cultural life in common. Among these are small band size; seminomadic mobility; fluid group structure with little strict adherence to rules of residence, land tenure, inheritance, and marriage; resolution

---

[1]These are the same people often referred to as "Bushmen". Because this term is used in Southern Africa as a racial slur, it has been dropped from scholarly use, and the word San substituted. The !Kung are one of six San language groups.

---

*I am grateful to Irven DeVore, Jerome Kagan, N. G. Blurton Jones, and Steven R. Tulkin for various forms of assistance, support, and friendship from the inception of this work to the present, and to Marjorie Shostak for her help and companionship throughout. Financial support has come from the National Science Foundation (GS-2603), the National Institutes of Health (5-R01-MH-13611), the Milton Fund, and the Foundations' Fund for Research in Psychiatry.

of conflict by group fission; and extreme flexibility of adaptive (subsistence) strategies. Moreover, these features may be seen to result from the common demands of a common subsistence pattern. Since this was the very subsistence pattern that characterized human adaptation during 99 percent of the history of the genus *Homo*, it was deemed essential to pursue the study of modern hunting and gathering peoples as an adjunct to the study of human evolution.

The !Kung San in contact with the Harvard project were a population of about one thousand individuals living in the northwest corner of the Kalahari Desert, within a few miles either side of the border between Botswana and Namibia (Southwest Africa), from about fifty to about one hundred and fifty miles south of the Caprivi Strip. They live in a number of semipermanent or temporary village camps, each consisting of from 15 to 40 people. Within a village camp, residents are related to one another through a wide variety of blood and marital ties. More than a single village camp often locate in the vicinity of a given waterhole, giving rise to a total effective population of daily social contact of from 35 to 120. When a group in a village camp moves, as they do for both brief, subsistence-related trips and for more stable relocation, most of its members usually stay together. This makes it meaningful to speak of the *band* as the basic population unit, provided that it is not conceived of as permanent, highly structured, or territorial.

The environment is classed as semiarid, annual rainfall varying from 7 to 23 inches, the soil mostly sand covered with thorny bushes and trees. The seasons are a wet season of about two or three months; a long, hot, dry season, including two or three months of daily temperatures over 100; and a two-month winter, including six weeks of near-freezing night temperatures.

Subsistence of the contact population is variable, but most subsist primarily, and some exclusively, by gathering and hunting wild vegetable and animal foods. Vegetable foods, collected by women, provide from 50 to 80 percent of the diet by weight. Both the caloric and nutritional value of the diet have been assessed and appear to be adequate, more so than a great many other African diets, which tend to be low in protein and narrow in nutritional range. Subsistence maintenance is achieved with an average of three days' work a week, so that leisure time is abundant. (These general remarks about the !Kung may be substantiated and extended by reference to the forthcoming volume Kalahari Hunter-Gatherers, edited by Lee and DeVore (Harvard University Press).

BACKGROUND OF THE INFANCY STUDY

At the time this study was conceived, infancy had become
a major focus of interest for psychologists (Kessen, Haith,
& Salapatek, 1970), ethologists (Hinde & Spencer-Booth, 1968),
and students of the evolution of behavior (Bowlby, 1969).
Draper's excellent work on !Kung childhood (1972) was beginning to produce some interesting results pertaining to infancy,
but was to focus ultimately on the effects of subsistence
ecology on later childhood. So it seemed wise to plan a
specific study of infancy as part of the long-range Harvard
project. Like other aspects of the expedition, this study
suggested itself with a certain amount of urgency. Hunter-
gatherer life did not seem destined for a lengthy future, and
with it would pass an important chapter in our knowledge of
human infancy, especially of the evolution of human infancy.
That is, its importance lay not mainly in its uniqueness as
an ethnological variety, but in its position as representative
of a group of societies resembling, in their basic subsistence
ecology, the original human sociocultural form.

The study of infancy was carried out over twenty months
between 1969 and 1971 in the !Kangwa, Dobe, and /Du/da areas
of northwestern Botswana. It was made technically possible
only by the context of the larger expedition, since an infant
study cannot be carried out without a secure rapport with the
community, or without exact ages for the infants. The ages of
subjects were available thanks to the basic demographic work
of Howell, Lee, and Draper; and the rapport, thanks to all the
previous expedition participants, was excellent.

Previous reports of our investigations of infancy among
the !Kung include a theoretical examination of the implications
of our observations for understanding the evolution of attachment, especially Bowlby's theory of attachment (DeVore &
Konner, 1974; Konner, 1972), and a study of sex differences in
the behavior of two- to five-year-olds (Blurton Jones & Konner,
1973). The present chapter attempts a more quantitative
presentation of some of the observational data, as well as a
presentation of some test data, and extends the earlier
theoretical perspective in terms of the new data.

There are several reasons for taking an interest in !Kung
infancy, in terms of behavioral science strategy. One is that,
like any cross-cultural research, it broadens the variability
available for study. It has the effect of giving us more
variance with which to address any theoretical issue, and,
occasionally, may disabuse us of false notions, explicit or
tacit, of the universality of some Western infant behaviors

or caretaking procedures. Unlike most cross-cultural research,
however, it also adds a temporal or evolutionary and
(potentially) causal dimension to the extent that we can guess,
by extrapolation from modern hunter-gatherers, what adaptations
in infant care and development must be characterized *ancestral*
populations of hunter-gatherers. We reason from what we know
of hunter-gatherer sociobiology and subsistence ecology and
how the latter appear to affect infancy. Finally, it gives us
leads, to be checked in an appropriately broad cross-cultural
context, on possible universal features of human infant care,
infant behavior, and development. This, in turn, gives us a
basis for cross-species comparisons.

In concluding the introductory material, three points
should be emphasized. First, the !Kung mother-infant bond is
close, of long duration, and characterized by general indulgence
of infant demands while remaining low in restriction of infant
operations on the world. Second, this relationship exists in
a very dense social context; the mother-infant pair is typically
in constant contact with other adults (relatives and friends).
This overall social context is in marked contrast to the
isolation of American mothers, and probably goes a long way
toward making the very indulgent !Kung pattern of child care
emotionally possible for mothers. Third, the infant graduates
from his strong attachment to his mother to an attachment to a
multiage child group. This transition begins at the end of the
first year and is largely complete several months after the
birth of the next sibling, usually at age three or four. It is
important to note that this child group is not a peer group
(see Draper, 1972). Indeed, given the demographic limitations
of foraging subsistence, the likelihood that there would
ordinarily be enough children of the same age at the same place
at the same time to form a peer group is very low. Multiage
groups have the following implications: (1) older children in
the group will discharge many caretaking functions of the mother
and father, thus largely obviating the need for parental vigil-
ance after age three or four; (2) the infant's transition from
interaction with parents to interaction with children is
facilitated by the fact that much of the behavioral equipment
he already has for social relations, exercised in relation to
adults is also appropriate in relation to older children,
whereas it would not work as well with peers; (3) cultural
transmission in general can be carried out more on a child-to-
child basis, as opposed to adult-to-child only; and (4) the
acquisition of caretaking behaviors themselves is greatly
facilitated by older children's experience with infants in
these groups.

TYPICAL INFANT POSITIONS AND THE INFANT SLING

From the earliest days of life and throughout the first
year, three positions characterize infant posture: (1) awake--
held sitting or standing in the lap of the mother or other
caretaker, or on the ground immediately in front of the caretaker (since there are no chairs, adults are typically sitting
on the ground); (2) in the infant sling at the mother's side,
either awake or asleep; or (3) lying asleep on a skin or cloth
on the ground beside the mother. At later ages, sitting on the
ground beside the mother is added to these three. Infants are
rarely permitted to lie down while awake. Mothers consider that
this is bad for infants and that it retards motor development.
(This is the opposite of the folk belief in the Northwestern
United States where vertical posture is considered bad, at least
for very young infants. Hence, presumably, the American parental
practice of laying babies down in a horizontal position all the
time.)

The sling merits specific description because it differs
in important ways from carrying devices in many other nontechnological societies, and from all the carrying devices now
acquiring some commercial success in the Northeastern United
States. It is maximally nonrestrictive, leaving the arms and
legs freely moving; it allows constant skin-to-skin contact
between mother and infant; and it keeps the infant on the
mother's side (hip) rather than on her back or front. The
side position has the following noteworthy features: (1) the
infant sees what the mother sees, thus sharing her view of the
social world and the world of objects, especially a close view
of work in the mother's hands, and eye-level contact with
children, who take considerable interest in babies; (2) the
infant has constant access to the mother's breasts, which are
uncovered, and, after the development of visually directed
reaching, feeds whenever he or she likes; and (3) infants
have constant access to cosmetic and decorative objects hanging
around their mother's neck, and often occupy themselves by
playing with them. These objects appear to function for the
infant as do mobiles and other objects hung in American cribs.
This is important because the latter have been shown to
significantly accelerate sensorimotor development during the
first six months (White & Held, 1967).

NURSING AND WEANING

Newborn infants are not fed the colostrum and are put to

the breast when milk appears. If this is only a day or so
later, the infant will not be fed until then. If it is longer,
the infant will be fed by another lactating woman. (This last
statement is based on mothers' reports rather than observation.)

Infants are fed whenever they cry and frequently when they
do not cry. As mentioned above, when the infant is able to
reach for the breast, he feeds himself at his leisure. This
results in short (a few seconds to fifteen minutes), frequent
(several times an hour during the day) feeds. At night, infants
sleep immediately beside their mothers, face to face, and are
fed several times, at least whenever they cry. Such feeds may
occur without the mother awaking.

The modal age of weaning is during the fourth year, as may
be seen from Figure 12-1. The figure shows cross-sectional
data on the number of infants and children at each age who were
nursing at the time when they were first contacted. Weaning is
gradual and generally takes place some time during the mother's
next pregnancy, being completed before the birth of the sibling.
If there is no next sibling, nursing will usually continue until
after age five and may continue, with much reduced frequency,
until age eight. Supplementing of nursing with a wide range
of foods sometimes premasticated begins around the age of six
months.

The process of weaning is mild, but the child's reaction
is sometimes severe, and the child may behave in a depressed
manner for weeks or even months. However, some children effect
this transition with no such difficulty.

PHYSICAL CONTACT WITH MOTHER AND OTHER CARETAKERS

The extent of physical contact between the infant and
mother during the first two years is shown in Figure 12-2.
The graph shows *passive* physical contact only, excluding active
touching of the mother by the infant.

The sample in this graph consists of thirty-one infants,
ranging in age from 1 to 94 weeks, each observed at from 1 to
4 age points, for a total of 54 age points. Each age point
consists of three spot observations per infant. The spot
observation was made immediately on entering the village camp
and before the mother or infant noted the observer's presence.
The proportions of observations per age point per child for
which there was passive physical contact was averaged over

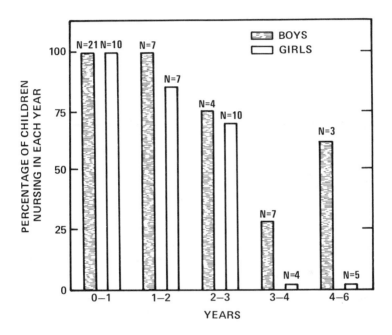

Figure 12-1.   Nursing behavior--cross-sectional data.

arbitrary age groupings to give data points on the graph.   Each
dot represents from two to eight infants.

The data indicate a gradual decline in passive physical
contact from a high of about 70 percent in the first months to
about 30 percent in the middle of the second year.   There is
also a nonsignificant divergence of the sexes after about 20
weeks, with the females having more passive physical contact
than the males.

Other data (Blurton Jones & Konner, 1973), from observations of two- to five-year-old !Kung children in the same area,
show that girls are more likely than boys to be passively

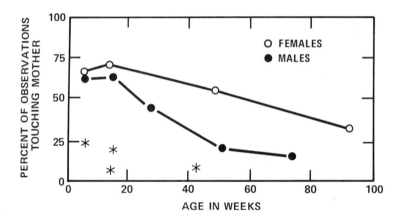

Figure 12-2.   Passive touching, spot observations.

touching or within two feet of the mother, suggesting that the
sex difference in infancy persists (Mann-Whitney U, $p < .05$).
Draper's (1972) study of the behavior of !Kung children of all
ages found that girls were more likely to be in the presence
of adults in the immediate village camp vicinity, and less
likely to be in contexts where there were only children present.

The asterisks on Figure 12-2 represent an effort to
present some comparison data from published reports on English
and American infants. The first point on the graph represents
on 8-day-old infant studied by Richards and Bernal (1972)
in Cambridge, England. They published a 24-hour diary kept
for this infant by its mother as typical of their much larger

sample. The percentage includes all time spent out of the cot, either being fed or being bathed, as a proportion of total waking time. The next group of infants is drawn from Rheingold's (1960) study comparing home-reared (H) and institution-reared (I) U.S. infants at three and a half months of age. These data are from observations, rather than diaries (one observation every 15 seconds for several hours). Again, the percentages include all the time the infant was held, plus basinette time, on the theory that infant bathing may be a parental effort to establish contact in a culture where "purposeless" physical contact is largely unacceptable. The ten-month data are from Tulkin's (Tulkin, 1970; Tulkin & Kagan, 1972) study of social class differences in infant girls in Boston. The data, from time-sequence observations, showed no class differences in physical contact, so the 60 subjects were pooled to form the proportion.

Both the !Kung and the admittedly makeshift "Western" data show declining physical contact with age, the total amount of physical contact being very much greater for the !Kung infants. Note especially that the order of magnitude of the difference in the Rheingold study between the home-reared (H) and institution-reared (I) infants is small compared with the difference between normally reared American and !Kung infants.

Other studies of American infants, including studies comparing American infants to Japanese and Dutch infants, confirm the low percentage of physical contact time and suggest that this phenomenon may be generalizable to advanced industrial societies. Moss (1967), studying first-born American infants, found that "Total holds" constituted between 15 and 27 percent of observation time for three-week-old to three-month-old infants. Rebelsky and Abeles (1973) found that "Hold" constituted the following percentages of 36 spot observations over three hours: American two-week-olds (N = 10), 17.2 percent; American twelve-week-olds (N = 10), 12.2 percent; Dutch two-week-olds (N = 11), 15.3 percent; Dutch twelve-week-olds, (N = 11), 17.5 percent. Totaling Caudill and Weinstein's (1969) categories "In arms", "Diapers", and "Dresses", gives figures of 29 percent and 21.1 percent for Japanese and American three-month-olds, respectively (N = 30 in each culture). Tulkin's (1970 and this volume) data, gives "Total physical contact" as 11.2 percent for sixty ten-month-old Boston girls, with no difference between professional and working class. Only Lewis and Ban's data (this volume) depart somewhat from the overall picture of low physical contact in industrialized societies, showing that 32 American twelve-week-olds were held for 42.7 percent of a two-hour observation and 18 Yugoslavian twelve-week-olds for 32.6 percent.

However, even the highest of these figures amounts to only about one half of the !Kung infant percentages at comparable ages. Turning to less-acculturated samples produces a picture closer to that of the !Kung. Klein and colleagues (personnal communication, 1974), using an observation format closely resembling that of the Tulkin study and the San study, observed infants in a rural area of Guatemala and found percentages of physical contact ranging from 19 to 36 percent. Brazelton (this volume), observing twelve Mayan infants in Zinacantan, a peasant community in Mexico, found that they were held an average of 60.4 percent of a four-hour observation. In contrast to the San data, however, this percentage increases through the first year.

In summary, if the orphanage infants observed by Rheingold (1960) are "deprived" of physical contact as compared with infants living at home, then normally reared American infants would appear to be similarly "deprived" as compared with !Kung infants.

Whether it makes sense to talk of "deprivation" at all will depend on studies of the *consequences* of different degrees of early physical contact. Several facts, however, point to the importance of this type of experience in evolution:

1.   American child-training practice (middle-class, as of 1940) is found to be low in the indulgence of dependency (which would include physical contact in infancy), as compared with a worldwide ethnographic range (Whiting & Child, 1953).

2.   In a recent cross-cultural study of mother-infant physical contact, Whiting (1971) found that amount of physical contact was correlated with mean annual temperature. Since man evolved in a context of tropical hunting and gathering, the likelihood is high that the !Kung pattern of high mother-infant physical contact would have characterized human populations during the Pleistocene.

3.   Laboratory studies of macaques (M. mulatta: Hinde & Spencer-Booth, 1968; M. nemestrina: Jensen, Bobbitt, & Gordon, 1968) show an age curve of mother-infant physical contact starting at close to 100 per-cent, declining to 50 percent during the first fifteen weeks, and thereafter declining much more gradually until the end of the first year. Apart from the greater amount of contact for the first few weeks,

the curve is similar to the !Kung curve. While these
are laboratory curves, Hinde and Spencer-Booth show
that the presence or absence of social context does
not alter the pattern drastically. DeVore (1963)
and Jay (1963) describe mother-infant relations in
free-ranging baboons and langurs, and their data also
indicate high physical contact. The research in
general indicates that high mother-infant physical
contact is a basic higher primate pattern. The
!Kung infant data together with the Whiting (1971)
study and the comparisons noted from other observations
suggest that man did not evolve away from this pattern,
at least not to the extent of the major departure
exhibited by Western infant care, until the tropical
hunting and gathering mode of subsistence was left
behind.

CONTACT WITH OTHER PERSONS

Data were also collected in the spot observations on the
amount of passive physical contact with anyone, including the
mother. Boys showed greater increases in contact, compared to
Figure 12-2, than girls. Thus the boys seem to be making up
some of their "reduced" maternal contact by having contact
with individuals other than the mother in second year. As yet,
the data have not been analyzed to determine who these people
are.

Figure 12-3 presents an analysis of the participation by
older children in the course of an infant observation. (These
are not spot observations, but 15-minute, time-sequence
observations, six per age-point per infant, in which the
observer's presence was known to those being observed.)
Female children interact more with infants of both sexes than
do males. There also appears to be a same-sex preference
operating, so that girls play more with girl infants and boys
play more with boy infants.

Data from observations of two- to five-year-olds in
London and among the San conducted by Blurton Jones and
Konner (1973) showed that English children in this age group
are more likely to be face-to-face with the mother than are
!Kung children (Mann-Whitney U; girls, $p < .02$; boys, $p < .002$)
and less likely to be face-to-face with other children (girls,
$p < .02$; boys, $p < .10$). This finding suggests that despite
early intensive contact between !Kung mothers and infants,

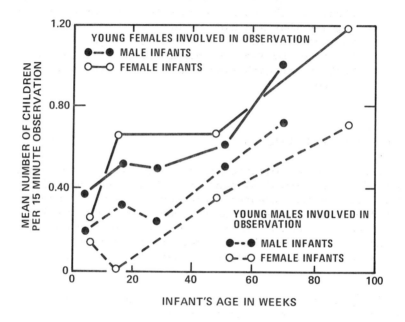

Figure 12-3.   Sex of juveniles involved with male and
female infants.

these infants do not become excessively attached. The maximum
number of feet from the mother during the hour of observation
was greater for the !Kung than for English children (girls,
$p < .10$; boys, $p < .02$), and there was no difference between
the cultures in the amount of time touching or within two
feet of the mother. If anything, there is a suggestion that
English children in this age group are more involved with
their mothers than are !Kung children, and independently
recorded facial expression data (Blurton Jones, personal
communication) support this suggestion.

NONPHYSICAL INTERACTIONS IN INFANCY

It is sometimes argued that while mothers in nontechnological societies have many physical interactions with their infants, wean them late, and nurse them frequently, such mother-infant pairs are low in vocal and visual interaction (e.g., Kagan & Klein, this volume). Conversely, mother-infant pairs in Western samples are seen as making up what they lack in physical interactions involving proximal receptors through more extensive interactions involving distal receptors. This notion finds support in the data on mother-infant interaction in Guatemala (Klein, this volume), where physical interaction is relatively high and vocal interaction relatively low. Thus it seemed important to examine the validity of this notion in the San, where physical contact is especially high, weaning especially late, and nursing especially frequent. To this end, frequencies of various mother and infant behaviors involving communication through distal receptors were calculated for all San infants between the ages of 32 and 53 weeks (mean age 45.0 weeks) for comparison with Tulkin's (1970, and this volume) sample of sixty ten-month-old girls in Boston.

The results of this comparison are displayed in Table 12-1. Frequencies are all converted to the percentage of all 5-second periods in which the behavior occurred. The data for middle- and working-class Boston girls are presented separately, and the data for infants in Guatemala (Klein, this volume) are presented for ages eight and twelve months as well as mean percentage. The observation methods used in Guatemala and for the !Kung were both adopted from Tulkin's. Unfortunately, the !Kung infants in this age group were seven boys and two girls, and this should be considered when comparing them to Tulkin's sample, which is all girls, and to the Guatemala sample, which is equally representative of both sexes. The method, as applied to the !Kung involved observing each infant in its mother's presence for 15 minutes at a time, six times for each age point, with all behavioral items coded every 5 seconds. Total observation time for this particular body of data was 90 minutes for each of seven infants and 180 for each of two mothers.

As Table 12-1 shows, the hypothesis that interactions using proximal and distal mechanisms of communication are reciprocally interrelated is not applicable to the !Kung. !Kung infant vocalization and caretaker vocalization are at the frequency level shown by the Boston working class, although lower than that of the middle-class sample. Similarly, for the measure "Percentage of reciprocal vocalization"--the percentage of all infant vocalizations followed in the same or immediately subsequent 5-second period by a caretaker vocalization--the !Kung frequency is again

TABLE 12-1. Percentages of Five-Second Time Blocks In Which Behaviors Occurred.

BEHAVIOR	!Kung (7M, 2F)		Boston Middle-Class (Tulkin) (30F)		Boston Working-Class (Tulkin) (30F)		Guatemala (Klein) (10M, 10F)	
	MEAN	S.D.	MEAN	S.D.	MEAN	S.D.	MEAN	S.D.
Infant Vocalization	22.77	8.14	25.90	4.88	23.13	5.58	17.78	7.13
Percent Reciprocal Vocalization	15.08	5.35	21.62	10.37	16.12	8.84	--	--
Caretaker Vocalization	10.32	1.52	15.56	7.46	10.31	6.01	3.78	1.94
Percent Response To Spontaneous Freta	78.07	17.93	[61.86]	--	[47.80]	--	--	--
Face to Face With Mother	2.91	2.61	3.85	3.95	1.85	1.86	--	--
Face to Face With Anyone[a]	4.55	1.11	[4.08]	--	[2.31]	--	--	--
Infant Smiles	3.89	2.62	2.47	1.12	1.92	1.41	--	--

[a] Percentages reported in brackets for Tulkin's sample were extrapolated from other measures. See text for explanation.

TABLE 12-1: Continued

LEVELS OF SIGNIFICANCE,   2-Tailed t-Test

Infant Vocalization

       Middle versus Guatemala: t = 4.68, $p <$ .01

       Working versus Guatemala: t = 2.91, $p <$ .01

           No other significant differences

Percentage Reciprocal Vocalization

       Middle versus Working: t = 2.17, $p <$ .05

           No other significant differences

Caretaker Vocalization

       Middle versus Working: t = 2.95, $p <$ .01

       Middle versus !Kung: t = 2.04, $p <$ .05

       !Kung versus Guatemala: t = 8.64, $p <$ .01

           Other comparisons with Guatemala
           highly significant

           No other significant differences

Face to Face With Mother

       Middle versus Working: $p \approx$ .02

           No other significant differences

Infant Smiles

       !Kung versus Working: t = 2.86, $p <$ .01

       !Kung versus Middle: t = 2.28, $p <$ .05

           No other significant differences

---

at about the level of the Boston working-class girls.[2]

Considering the percentage of 5-second intervals in which
the infant and mother were in the face-to-face position, the
!Kung figure falls between that of the two Boston classes.
Data on "Face to face with anyone" were available only for the
!Kung, but were extrapolated for the Boston samples (bracketed
figures) as follows. Data were available for the Boston
samples for the vocalizations and physical contact of both
mother and other caretakers. For each class and each variable,
the percentage of total frequency contributed by caretakers
other than the mother was calculated, and for each class the
two percentages were averaged to provide an indicator of the
percentage of total interactions the infant had with caretakers
other than the mother. (These percentages were 24.6 percent
for the working class and 5.9 percent for the middle class.)
These figures were then used to extrapolate "Face to face with
anyone" from "Face to face with mother" for these samples.
The resulting figures for both classes are lower than for the
!Kung.

"Percentage of response to spontaneous fret", or percentage
of all episodes of spontaneous fretting that were followed by
any positive maternal response in the same or subsequent 5-
second interval is also shown. ("Spontaneous" fretting is
defined as any fretting not caused by the caretaker, e.g., in
cleaning or adjusting the infant.)

Finally, for smiling, a principal signaling mechanism of
the infant, the !Kung figure is higher than that of the Boston
middle class and more than double that of the working class.

To summarize: while !Kung infants have very much more
physical contact with their mothers than do English and
American children, they have a good deal of contact with others
as well, and they have comparable amounts of interaction with
their mothers through distal mechanisms such as looking, smiling, and vocalizing. The responsiveness of the mothers to
the infants' signals, as measured by percentage of reciprocal

---

[2]Numerous studies (e.g., Goldberg & Lewis, 1969) have shown
that girls at this age have more verbal interactions with
their mothers than do boys, the differential representation
of the sexes in the !Kung and Boston samples biases the
comparison against the conclusion that !Kung frequencies
are equally high, thus strengthening the present argument.
Note that both infant vocalization and caretaker vocalization
are considerably lower in Guatemala than for either !Kung or
Boston samples.

vocalization, is comparable to that of American working class mothers (of girls) and, as measured by percentage of response to spontaneous frets, greater than that of either American working-class or middle-class mothers.

NEUROMOTOR MATURATION AND NEUROMOTOR LEARNING

As part of an effort to assess as many different aspects of !Kung infant development as feasible, neuromotor development tests were administered. A neurological assessment schedule for infants up to 10 days of age (Prechtl & Beintema, 1964) was administered to ten infants. For older infants, a neuromotor development schedule based on the work of McGraw (1963) was used (see Richards & Bernal, n.d.). This test has the advantage of more elaborate and detailed descriptions of motor behaviors and stages than is found in other infant tests, which should improve one's confidence in comparisons of samples assessed by different investigators.

Figures 12-4 to 12-7 report comparisons between the sample of !Kung infants and the original McGraw (1963) sample on the age of attainment of four aspects of neuromotor development. Other phases showed similar patterns; the data is available from the author.

The !Kung sample consists of 21 infants tested at various ages, though some infants were tested at more than one age. The McGraw sample is a larger longitudinal one tested weekly, and thus monitored much more closely than the !Kung sample, some of whom were tested only once. This would mean that the entry of one of McGraw's infants into a phase would have been noted within one week of its occurrence, whereas a !Kung infant's entry into a phase might be noted only a month or more later. This would tend to bias the data against the hypothesis that !Kung infants are precocious.

The points on the !Kung line represent percentages of infants whose ages fall within 100-day blocks. The points on the McGraw line represent percentages of infants actually tested at the specific age indicated. In spite of this bias, in two of the four measures the !Kung infants are performing in phase earlier than the American infants.

Figure 12-4 shows the attainment of the phase of sitting characterized by the ability to maintain an erect sitting posture without support from the arms. Figure 12-5 shows the

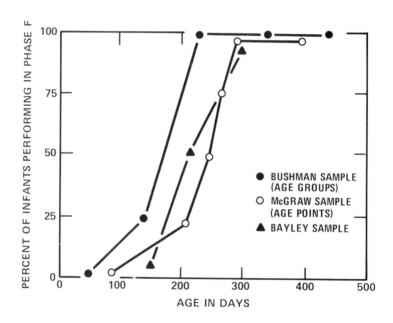

Figure 12-4.   Sitting, resistive aspect (Phase F:
                Independent sitting)

attainment of the phase of rising, characterized by the ability,
in the testing situation, to rise from the supine position on
the ground, without assistance and without holding on to anything, to the erect standing position. Figures 12-6 and 12-7
show the phases of walking with both hands held, and initial
walking without assistance (three steps without hands held)
but without heel-toe progression or synchronous arm movements,
respectively. These latter two graphs show descending as well
as ascending segments because they do not represent the highest
stage of a given locomotor development sequence, and so show
infants passing out of the phase as well as into it.

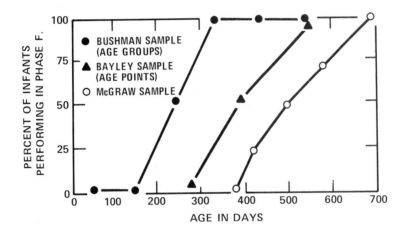

Figure 12-5.   Assumption erect posture (Phase F:
              Independent rising [or higher])

Figures 12-4 and 12-5 indicate a motor advancement of
!Kung infants compared with American infants; Figure 12-6
shows no difference; and Figure 12-7 shows a slight reversal
of this trend.   The Baylay (1969) age norm for independent
walking indicates that the McGraw sample may be walking a
bit earlier than the American norm, assuming that McGraw and
Bayley were looking at the same behavior.   On the whole,
considering that the procedures biased the data in favor of
the McGraw longitudinal sample, it seems reasonable to conclude that !Kung infants are advanced in motor development in
some areas as compared with their American counterparts.[3]

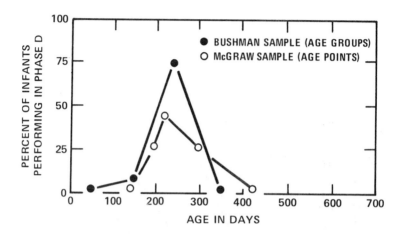

Figure 12-6.   Erect locomotion (Phase D: Deliberate
stepping, hands held)

<hr>

[3]Recent work by Dana Robinson and Nancy Chang in the Department
of Anthropology at Harvard has confirmed the precocity of
!Kung infants in these areas by following Konner's procedure
using the McGraw Scale on a new sample of American infants of
mixed socioeconomic backgrounds.

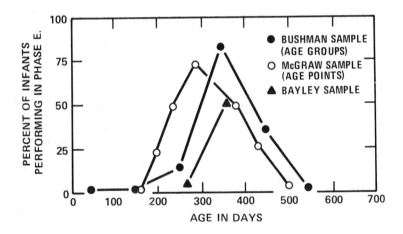

Figure 12-7.   Erect locomotion (Phase E: Independent
walking)

The question of why this is so is a complicated one.   The
precocity of African infants in motor performance as they
develop (though not at birth) is a well-accepted phenomenon
(LeVine, 1970), and Warren's (1972) cogent critique of the
research, while it points to the need for more careful work
in this area, does not convincingly dispel one's belief in
the phenomenon.

A first explanation that comes to mind is that the genetic basis of the developmental rates may exhibit some sort of racial polymorphism. One would expect, if this were so, to find differences at birth. While one well-known study has found such differences (Geber & Dean, 1967), its methodology has been severely criticized (Warren, 1972). Warren's restudy of the same Uganda population failed to find evidence of precocity at birth, and Geber's own study of African newborns in Zambia also failed to find evidence of precocity (Brazelton, personal communication). Infants of the !Kung, who are considered racially distinct from these other African populations, also do not give evidence of perinatal precocity (Konner, 1972).

While the absence of differences at birth makes the existence of genetic differences less likely, it is possible for postnatally emerging differences in developmental rate to be genetically based. Before reaching this conclusion, however, one would want to rule out the possibility of environmental influence. It was the opinion of Ainsworth (1967) that the precocity of her (and Geber's) Uganda infants in the first two years resulted from the exercise and stimulation of unrestricted freedom of movement and from being held all the time.

While the question of how much these neuromotor developmental rates are subject to environmental influence and learning has been a controversial one, Zelazo, Zelazo, and Kolb (1972) have demonstrated that exercise of the placing and walking reflexes of the newborn for only 12 minutes a day during the first eight weeks not only greatly increases the response rate for these reflexes, but also accelerates the attainment of walking alone by six to eight weeks as compared with control groups. Passive exercise of the legs also had an accelerating effect, but one significantly smaller than that of active exercise.

Considering the exceptional amount of experience in the vertical position, held sitting and held standing, that !Kung infants have during the earliest weeks and indeed throughout infancy, the Zelazo finding strongly suggests the explanation that this experience has an accelerating effect on neuromotor maturation. While the age of independent walking itself is not accelerated, neither is the walking reflex at birth (usually) specifically exercised. Perhaps, as Zelazo et al. have suggested, the marked acceleration of the age of first independent walking depends on exercise of the centrally organized mechanism of walking, rather than just muscle exercise.

Another factor that demands attention is the !Kung parental attitude toward motor development. This attitude was examined in child behavior seminars held with several groups of !Kung men and women. While their belief about most aspects of development involves a sort of cognitive-alimentation-adaptation view ("The child plays and teaches himself") with some basis in maturation for the behavior, they do not believe in the maturation of motor milestones. They insist that a child not taught to sit, crawl, stand, and walk will never perform these behaviors (even as late as age three) because the bones of his back will be "soft" and "not tightened together". They therefore follow a training routine for each of these behaviors. Infants too young to sit are propped in front of their mothers in the sand with a wall of sand around their buttocks to support them. When they fall, they are propped up again. Incipient walkers are lured with bits of food to push the limits of their ability.

In general, it seems reasonable to accept the explanation of environmental influence for the partial precocity of !Kung infants. In view of recent evidence for the lability of these developmental systems, it would be wise to investigate this possibility in all cases of population differences in motor development rates. The burden of proof seems to have shifted to those who believe these differences are genetically based. They will have to either show conclusively that there are population differences in motor capacity at birth, and that these are not the result of differences in prenatal care, maternal nutrition, or perinatal insult; or show that there are population differences in postnatal development rates where there are no differences in aspects of parental care and experience that are likely to affect these rates.

COGNITIVE DEVELOPMENT IN EARLY INFANCY

In an effort to assess some dimensions of cognitive development, the Einstein Scales of Sensorimotor Development (Corman & Escalona, 1970; Escalona & Corman, 1969), based on the infant studies and sensorimotor development theory of Piaget (1954, 1962) were administered. Only the results from the Prehension Scale, for infants up to six months old, have been analyzed so far. These results are presented in Figure 12-8.

The scale is ordered into stages, each consisting of several items all believed to reflect the same level of cognitive maturity. The scalability of the items, that is

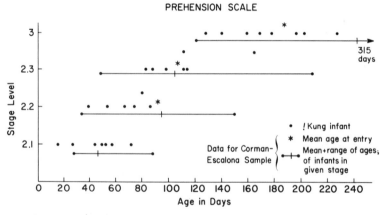

Figure 12-8.   Prehension Scale of the Einstein Scales
of sensorimotor development

the consistency of clustering within the stages, has been
demonstrated for a sample of American infants (Corman &

Escalona, 1970). It was our impression that the clustering was very similar for !Kung infants, but our sample (eighteen infants in all, from five to eight per stage) was not sufficiently large or sufficiently longitudinal for a statistical demonstration of clustering. Strictly speaking, this is a flaw in the comparison.

Figure 12-8 shows the four stage levels of prehension discontinuously along the y-axis, and age on the x-axis. Each !Kung infant performing at a stage level is represented by a dot, while the mean and range of the Corman and Escalona data is shown by the horizontal line.

Important items in the various stages are shown in Table 12-2. According to the instructions in the manual (Escalona & Corman, 1969), infants are scored as performing in stage if they make two or more separate reponses appropriate to the stage, or if they make one response on two or more separate trials. There were two observers, and both had to agree that a response had been make before it could be scored. The ages of the !Kung infants in a stage on the graph were compared with the midpoints, for individual American infants using the Mann-Whitney U test (two-tailed). The !Kung infants are younger than the American midpoint ages for Stage 3 ($p = .002$) and Stage 2.3 ($p < .002$) and younger than the American age *at entry* for stage 2.2 ($p < .02$).

Thus the general trend is for !Kung infants to be ahead of American infants in the Corman-Escalona sample on these indicators of very early cognitive or sensorimotor development. Clearly these items are not free from the influence of motor maturation. No available test of infant intelligence is (although Tulkin's [1971] study has made important progress in this direction). Still, behaviors such as the Stage 3 items "Shakes rattle with regard to sound" and "Transfers object from hand to hand with visual regard" have as their crucial features the mutual articulation of two separate sensorimotor systems (or *schemata*), reflecting, presumably, the maturation of some central organizing mechanism. It seems reasonable to suggest that !Kung infants are advanced with respect to a cognitive development factor (in the first six months) that is separate and distinct from their advanced neuromotor maturation.

In attempting to explain this difference, one thinks first of environmental enrichment, since many studies (e.g., Fowler, 1972; Robinson & Robinson, 1971) have now shown that social and environmental enrichment significantly enhances the cognitive development of infants. Figures 12-2 and 12-3 and

TABLE 12-2.   Prehension Scale Items Administered
              (Brief Summary)

---

1. Infant touches, rubs, scratches, or grasps objects or
    surfaces. Stage 2.1.

2. Infant touches, grasps, releases, regrasps, releases,
    and regrasps in continuous sequence. Stage 2.1.

3. Infant brings any portion of his hand to his mouth.
    Stage 2.1.

4. Infant touches hands together in any way. Stage 2.1.

5. Object placed in infant's hand, out of visual field:
        Response 1: After 3 seconds or more, object is
                     brought to the mouth, without visual
                     regard. Stage 2.1.
        Respones 2: As above, but with no delay. Stage
                     2.2.
        Response 3: Visual regard, 3 seconds or more, be-
                     fore bringing to mouth. Stage 3.

6. Object presented visually, infant's hand out of visual
        field:
        Response 1: Sucking movements or mouthing of hand
                     (3 times) while looking at object.
                     Response must begin only after present-
                     ation. Stage 2.2.
        Response 2: Energetic arm waving or groping follow-
                     ing presentation. Stage 2.3.
        Response 3: Reaching following light touch of
                     infant's hand with object. Stage 2.3.
        Response 4: Hand to mouth followed by reaching and
                     touching object. Stage 2.3.
        Response 5: Coordinated reach and grasp. Stage 2.4.

7. Object presented visually, infant's hand in visual field:
        Response 1: Infant looks alternately at object and
                     at hand. At least four shifts in focus.
                     Stage 2.3.
        Response 2: Infant reaches for and contacts object.
                     Stage 2.3.

8. Hand regard.
        Response 1: Transient but repeated hand regard.
                     Stage 2.1.

TABLE 12-2:   Continued

Response 2:   Longer, continuous regard, at least four
seconds. Stage 2.2.

9.   Infant's hand grasped and restrained by examiner, out of
infant's visual field (twice with each hand):
Response 1:   Infant tries to free hand, without
visual regard. Stage 2.2.
Response 2:   Infant turns to look at hand and/or
face of examiner. Stage 2.3.

10.   An object is place in infant's mouth. Infant brings one
or both hands to object as if holding at his mouth.
Stage 2.2.

11.   Infant transfers object from one hand to the other with
visual regard. Stage 3.

12.   Sustained shaking of rattle while facial expression and
movement indicate attentiveness to sound. Three
separate occasions. Stage 3.

Table 12-1 indicate that !Kung infants are receiving considerable social stimulation in the first months, both from the
mother and from other individuals. White and Held (1967) have
shown that one aspect of sensorimotor development, the growth
of visually directed reaching, can be significantly accelerated
by the presence of hanging objects in the infant's crib.
Observations suggest that cosmetic and decorative objects
hanging around the !Kung mother's neck within reach of the
infant in her lap or in the sling serve much the same function
as the White and Held crib mobiles.

One final factor deserves mention in relation to this
cognitive advancement: the fact that !Kung infants have much
more experience in the vertical position than do their
American counterparts. Vertical and horizontal positions have
very different effects on levels of altertness, particularly
in early infancy.

A number of investigators of infant cognition (Bower,
Broughton, & Moore, 1970; Bruner, 1968) have found that
positioning young infants (who cannot as yet sit) in a vertical

or semivertical posture in an infant seat improves their performance on cognitive tasks. Vertical posture is also linked
to a phenomenon known as the *orthostatic pressor reflex*. This
is a response in infants of the adrenal medulla, in which the
vertical posture results in greater production of adrenal
medullary hormones, as indicated by the rate of urinary
excretion of catecholamines (Harper, 1972). Since blood
pressure rises, inhibiting ACTH secretion in this situation,
the upright posture could, conceivably, tend to inhibit the
stress response. This, in turn, might conceivably have a
facilitating effect on attention, and, consequently, on
cognitive learning.

Vertical posture is well known as a soothing device for
crying infants (Oken & Heath, 1963), including newborns
(Korner & Grobstein, 1966). Korner and Grobstein demonstrated
that eye opening and visual scanning occurred more frequently
($p < .01$) in newborns held upright against the shoulder than
in controls. The combined stimuli of this experimental treatment are more similar to experiences of !Kung infants than
American and other Western infants. Korner and Thoman (1970)
and Korner (1972) extended these experiments, finding that of
six interventions with crying newborn infants, vestibular
stimulation had a far more powerful effect in evoking visual
alertness than did contact (Korner, 1972), and that raising
the infant, in an infant seat, to the vertical position, without contact, was effective, although it was not as effective
as the same intervention with contact. In sleeping newborns
the only two interventions which elicited any visual activity
were interventions entailing vestibular stimulation and the
upright position (Korner, 1972). Referring to Humphrey (1965)
and Langworthy (1933), Korner reasons that the vestibular system
is a likely principal mediator of early stimulation effects
because it is one of the earliest myelinated (beginning at 4
months gestational age) and is fully mature at birth.
In another study, unrelated to infant posture, White and
Castle (1964) showed that twenty minutes of additional physical
handling per day increased the amount of visual exploration in
infants observed after 30 days of such handling (beginning at
one week of age). While this treatment did not significantly
affect sensorimotor test performance, the authors hypothesized
that increased visual attentiveness together with increased
movement in an enriched environment would constitute the optimal
circumstances for visual-motor development. These are
essentially the conditions experienced by !Kung infants. Korner
would probably argue that the key independent variable in the
handling was vestibular stimulation rather than contact. The
important point would seem to be that all the candidates for

"key variable" in these studies--vestibular stimulation, upright posture, and physical contact--have some effect on
attentiveness, at least in crying infants. All are almost
continuously present in the !Kung infant's stimulus envelope,
whether in the sling or in the lap of the mother or other
caretakers. Thus the natural environment of !Kung infants
resembles, in several respects, a well-designed infant stimulation program.

But the data on accelerated neuromotor and cognitive performance must be viewed with caution. Early acceleration of
development in African infants has sometimes been found to
disappear or even reverse itself after infancy (LeVine, 1970).
The best explanation for this is the change to a protein-poor
diet at weaning, which does not happen for !Kung infants, but
still one cannot assume that these early advances are lasting,
or that sensorimotor intelligence is related to later intelligence. It has even been argued (Warren, 1971) that accelerated development may be harmful, since man is an altricial
animal needing his long immaturity for learning. This argument,
which by a logical extension would constitute a defense of
retardation, must be taken with a grain of salt. But much more
needs to be known about the long-term effects of specific early
advances.

The data do show, however, that intensive mother-infant
contact and extreme indulgence of infant dependency are not
incompatible with adequate neuromotor and cognitive development. They may even encourage it, as Ainsworth (1967) has
argued. The data also confirm the lability of developmental
systems in relation to early stimulation and learning.
Finally, they emphasize two independent variables, vertical
posture and vestibular stimulation, which are receiving increasing attention from developmental scientists, and which
may prove to have marked effects on infant development.

COMPARATIVE DATA: DENSITY OF SOCIAL CONTEXT AND THE COURSE OF
MOTHER-INFANT INTERACTIONS

The notion that density of social context may regulate the
degree of maternal indulgence of infant dependent demands (and/
or the extent of infant dependent demands) is supported by
laboratory studies of three primate species (Hinde & Spencer-
Booth, 1967; Kaplan, 1972; Kaplan & Schusterman, 1972; Wolfheim,
Jensen, & Bobbitt, 1970). Hinde and Spencer-Booth observed
mother-infant pairs of rhesus monkeys (*Macaca rhesus*) longit-

udinally, with and without the long-term presence of other
animals. In isolated pairs, they found that mothers avoided
and left infants more, although infants approached and followed more, than in group-living pairs. Isolated pairs were more
frequently physically separated than group-living pairs. The
amount of time spent more than two feet from the mother,
expressed as a proportion of total time off the mother, was
higher for isolates during the first 10 weeks of life, and
higher for the group-living subjects from 11 weeks on. This
finding may suggest that, when infants are still motorically
immature and have little control over distance from mother,
isolate mothers will maximize it. When locomotor facility
emerges (8 to 17 weeks), isolate infants can minimize the
distance, subverting their mothers' attempts to escape them.
Finally, isolate mothers tended to carry infants on their backs
rather than in the ventral position during transport, after the
infants climbed on them from behind, instead of from in front,
as was more common in group-living infants.

In Kaplan's (1972) similar study of squirrel monkeys
(*Saimiri sciureus*), mothers in isolated pairs avoided and
punished their infants more and retrieved them less than mothers
in group-living pairs, and isolate-pair infants made more
attempts to play with mothers and stayed closer to them, although (at least at some ages) group-living infants nursed more.
Grooming and looking at infants, likely indicators of maternal
concern, was done more by group-living mothers. Thus the
pattern for isolate pairs of greater infant dependent demands
with lower maternal indulgence of them, resembles that found
for rhesus monkeys. One anomalous finding was that group-
living mothers make more attempts to shake off their infants.
This could conceivably arise from their greater frequency of
nursing, at least at some ages.

Wolfheim, Jensen, and Bobbitt (1970) also found a similar
pattern in pigtailed monkeys (*Macaca nemestrina*). Mothers in
group-living pairs (infants age 14 to 15 weeks) were more
retentive, spent more time in ventral contact with their infants, and nursed more than mothers in isolate pairs. Data
from later ages were not presented. The authors interpreted
this finding in terms of protectiveness of infants, who may
come to harm from other group members. Hinde and Spencer-
Booth offered a similar interpretation. In view of Lancaster's
(1971) data on maternal retentiveness in free-ranging vervet
monkeys, this explanation seems plausible. However, Kaplan's
suggestion that isolate mothers are under so much steady
pressure from the infant and only the infant that they are
not inclinded to indulge them ("familiarity breeds contempt")

seems equally plausible. Hinde and Spencer-Booth (1971) summarized the effects as follows:

> The infant's relations with its mother are affected
> by the other females present, for infants living
> alone with their mothers were off them more, and
> went to a distance from them more, than did infants
> with group companions present. Since the infants
> living alone with their mothers were rejected more
> and played a larger role in maintaining proximity
> with their mothers, the difference was primarily
> due to the mothers. [p. 113]

This is the view most pertinent to the human data.

A comparison between !Kung and American or English early
childhood would seem to be analogous in some respects to these
laboratory comparisons. Roughly speaking, the situation of
the !Kung mother-infant pair in the band context resembles that
of the group-living monkey pairs, while the Western middle-class
mother and infant, alone together much of the time, resemble
the isolated monkey pairs. Exhibiting high physical contact
and frequent nursing in the first two years, !Kung mother-infant relations seem to produce, nonetheless, two- to five-year-
olds who, in familiar group contexts, interact less with their
mothers and more with other children as compared with English
two- to five-year-olds, and also tend to go a greater maximum
distance from their mothers. This cultural difference in developmental course parallels the greater initial indulgence of
the group-living mothers and the developmental course of
proximity to the mother in rhesus monkeys.

Two other parallels are of interest. A subsequent
experiment with the same squirrel monkeys (Kaplan & Schusterman,
1972), placed the infants in a choice situation, so that they
could either be near their mothers, a strange adult female, a
strange infant, or an empty cage. Results indicated that the
group-reared infants showed a greater perference for their own
mothers than did the isolate-pair infants. The authors interpreted this as indicating "preference" and the "closeness" of
the relationship. To view it another way, the "choice" situation in the experiment may be frightening to the infants, given
the authors' description of their behavior. (That is, it may
in effect be a fear of strangers test.) It may simply be more
frightening to the more indulged group-reared infants, just as
fearfulness in !Kung infants is greater than that in American
infants (Konner, 1972).

Finally, Hinde and Spencer-Booth (1967) found that locomotor milestones and certain aspects of sensorimotor development
(corresponding to several behaviors in Items 5 and 6 of Table
12-2) appeared earlier in rhesus infants from group-living as
opposed to isolate pairs, just as !Kung sensorimotor development is advanced relative to American.

To summarize, the theory proposed to account for the
developmental course of attachment found in these data is as
follows. The dense social context, by providing ample alternative stimulation for both mothers and infant, improves the
likelihood that mothers will accept the dependent demands of
infants. Paradoxically, this results in decreased proximity
seeking and other dependent demands at later ages, except in
intensely fear-provoking situations. This proposed relationship between early indulgence of dependency and later reduced
dependency runs so contrary to classical notions of reinforcement and even common sense that no amount of evidence seems
sufficient to make it acceptable. Yet a major recent review
of the attachment literature (Maccoby & Masters, 1970) found
this relationship to be confirmed by almost all the studies of
human children that raised this question.

Some theoretical adjustment to accommodate these data
seems in order. An ordinary reinforcement model would predict
that indulgence of dependency, that is, reward of dependent
behaviors with satisfaction of the infant's needs would increase the incidence of the behaviors. Actually, the reverse
is the case.

In Ainsworth, Bell, and Stayton's (1972) longitudinal
study of infant attachment, infant crying and maternal response
to crying were unrelated in the first three months, but lack of
maternal response in the first quarter of the first year was
related to increased infant crying duration and frequency in
the second quarter. The same relationship was obtained between
Quarters Two and Three and Quarters Three and Four. This is
the opposite of the effect predicted by the "spoiling" theory
(e.g., Spock, 1968).

If we assume, as Bowlby (1969) has tried to show, that
attachment behaviors are part of the normal biological functioning of the infant--instinctual, if you will--and thus difficult to extinguish without drastically disrupting the basic
homeostasis of the organism, the data begin to make more sense.
Attachment behaviors are not randomly occurring operants.
Some, at least, such as crying and contact seeking, are
behavioral manifestations of organismic distress. They cannot

be extinguished by ignoring them, any more than shivering in response to cold can be extinguished by ignoring it. Ignoring them simply increases the distress, and so increases the manifestations of the distress.

Ainsworth, Bell, and Stayton (1972) suggest that mothers who respond promptly are reinforcing manifestations of distress that occur at progressively lower arousal levels. In other words, infants who come to feel confidence in their mothers' basic responsiveness will come to signal their needs less dramatically, while infants with less responsive mothers will habitually proceed directly to higher arousal level manifestations. This is not only because they have learned that higher levels are necessary (an operant strengthening), but also because their mothers' unresponsiveness gives them added cause for distress (a positive feedback effect).

"Spoiling" theorists might argue that what Ainsworth and her colleagues are comparing are not responsive and unresponsive mothers, but responsive and inconsistent mothers. That is, the unresponsive mothers are ultimately responding, but erratically, thus applying the most effective reinforcement schedule (intermittent reinforcement) to the strengthening of the high arousal level distress manifestations. The biologically based view would argue that this "inconsistency" is almost inevitable, stemming from the fact that mothers are not well suited to ignoring their offsprings' distress. Some background variables, such as isolation of the mother-infant pair, make them better able to do this. It may be that such conditions, in the long perspective of human evolution, are in some sense abnormal.

Recommendations, such as those of Spock, encouraging maternal unresponsiveness enhance the impact of these background variables on a mother-infant relationship that has evolved away from maternal indulgence of early dependency since the hunter-gatherer era. Whether proposed as practical solutions to parental annoyance and exhaustion or as "ultimate goods" for the child, these recommendations must be viewed with skepticism by developmental scientists in view of the current available evidence. Ainsworth, Bell, and Stayton's "cry-babies", who had had less responsive mothers, reached the point where they fussed even when greeting their mother. That is, the unresponsive mothers were faced with infants who began to fret at their mothers' mere appearance. This is not what mothers are hoping for when they follow Spock's "unspoiling" advice.

It is ultimately possible to stop crying by ignoring it.
This is what happens in infants completely separated for long
periods from their mothers, after the development of attachment.
The effect is described as protest, followed by depression,
followed by a kind of affectless adaptation. There is evidence
that such separations are not conducive to optimal mental
health (Ainsworth, 1962; Bowlby, 1962). There is also evidence
emerging on the long-term effects of short separations. In
rhesus monkeys (Hinde & Spencer-Booth, 1971), infants who were
separated from their mothers for one or two 6-day periods between twenty and thirty weeks proved, at 12 months of age, to
be significantly more reluctant to enter and stay in a strange
environment than were controls; and, at 30 months, the subjects
who had been separated were less active, and engaged less in
social play and more in nonsocial manipulative play. Thus even
short separations at certain ages can have significant long-
term effects. As for less drastic varieties of unresponsiveness,
such as letting a child cry himself to sleep, or the relative
physical separation characteristic of Western mother-infant
pairs, long-term effects are still unknown.

MOTHER-INFANT CONTACT FROM AN EVOLUTIONARY PERSPECTIVE

Extending the above analysis more widely on a phylogenetic
range, Blurton Jones (1972) analyzed comparative data from a
number of mammals on patterns of infant care, and concluded that
mammals in continuous proximity to their young differed from
those that cache or nest their young in certain predictable
ways (see also Ben Shaul, 1962). Most important are that the
"cachers" feed their young at widely spaced intervals, have
high protein and fat content in their milk, and have high
sucking rates, whereas "carriers" (including followers) feed
more or less continuously, have milk with low protein and fat
content, and have low sucking rates. Humans, along with all
other higher primates studied, have the milk composition and
sucking characteristics of continuous proximity, or "carrier"
species.

Considering these comparative data in relation to the
hunter-gatherer data on mother-infant contact, it makes sense
to suggest that such contact was close in man during most of
human evolution. (!Kung infants are fed more or less continuously.) However, Harlow's (1958) now classic research on
deprivation in infant rhesus monkeys clearly demonstrated that
"contact comfort" alone is more important than feeding alone
in the development of attachment. This suggests that mother-

infant physical contact has an importance of its own completely distinct from its relation to the spacing of feeds.

This entire complex of adaptations--milk composition, sucking rate, the need for "contact comfort"--evolved in response to strong selection pressure favoring close mother-infant contact. This pattern is characteristic not only of foraging man, but of higher primates in general, and so must have considerable antiquity. As Bowlby (1969) cogently argues, the danger of infant loss through predation is a part of this selection pressure, especially in an altricial species. Close contact, however, has other selective advantages. It results in an attachment that prevents the newly mobile toddler from getting lost, and produces long-term proximity to adult models of subsistence-related behaviors. It may also reduce the likelihood of contracting illnesses, which constitute the major threat to life in infancy. One adaptive risk of strong attachment, the later failure to separate, is probably much reduced in the dense social context characteristic of human foragers, where the mother has the constant company of adults and the infant has the constant attraction of a multiage child group.

From such comparisons, we are beginning to understand the dominant mode of infant care and early social relations that is natural to humans and closely related animals. This knowledge will point the way for research on the consequences of departures from this pattern.

SUMMARY AND CONCLUSION

A number of conclusions can be drawn from the study of !Kung infant care, behavior, and development.

1.   Infants are in physical contact with their mothers or other individuals for a very large portion of the time in keeping with the pattern common to hunter-gatherers and higher primates in general.

2.   Infants are not restricted and have ample social and environmental stimulation, along with opportunity for self-stimulation.

3.   Infants are held vertical during most of their waking time and receive extensive vestibular stimulation.

4.   The transition away from close mother-infant contact

is facilitated by the presence of a multiage child
group which becomes a major focus of the child's
social behavior after a sibling is born.

5. Infants are advanced in some aspects of neuromotor
   development compared with American infants. This is
   probably attributable to their extensive experience
   in vertical postures and to conscious training
   efforts undertaken by their parents.

6. Infants in the first six months are advanced, compared
   with American infants, in certain measures of cognitive (sensorimotor) development. This is probably
   attributable to the unusually high density of social
   and cognitive stimulation, both generally and in
   specific relation to behaviors tested, in their
   developmental milieu. Their cognitive development
   may also be influenced by vertical posture, in so
   far as the latter appears to facilitate alertness
   and sensorimotor exercise.

!Kung infant life is far from ideal. Infant mortality is
very high. In spite of mitigating factors, many infants
respond to weaning and the birth of a displacing sibling with
a long period of depression, and they may remember this dis-
appointment throughout thier lives. However, the general rules
are indulgence, stimulation, and nonrestriction. The first of
these has been quantitatively shown to be greater than that in
advanced societies and the second roughly equal in terms of
distal mechanisms and greater in terms of proximal ones. Although the data on restrictiveness in infants have not been
analyzed, !Kung two- to five-year-olds show less proximity to
their mothers, fewer interactions with their mothers, and more
interactions with other children than is the case for London
children in the same age group. Also, one's impression of
infant restriction is that it is lower among the !Kung.

Further analysis of the !Kung data will include quantitative analysis of restrictiveness as well as a wide range of
mother-infant interaction variables at all ages. However,
sufficient evidence is available to support the hypothesis
that infant indulgence and stimulation have decreased since
the hunting-gathering era. The importance of research to
determine the consequences of this change of human behavior,
development, and mental health, an area now shrouded in
ignorance, need hardly be emphasized.

REFERENCES

Ainsworth, M. D. S. Deprivation of maternal care. Geneva:
    World Health Organization, 1962.

Ainsworth, M. D. S. Infancy in Uganda. Baltimore, Md.: The
    Johns Hopkins University, 1967.

Ainsworth, M. D. S., Bell, S. M., & Stayton, D. J. Individual
    differences in the development of some attachment
    behaviors. Merrill-Palmer Quarterly, 1972, 18, 123-
    144.

Bayley, N. Manual for the Bayley scales of infant development.
    New York: Psychological Corporation, 1969.

Ben Shaul, D. M. The composition of the milk of wild animals.
    International Zoological Year Book, 1962, 4, 300-332.

Blurton Jones, N. G. Comparative aspects of mother-child
    contact. In N. G. Blurton Jones (Ed.), Ethological
    studies of child behavior. Cambridge, England:
    Cambridge University Press, 1972.

Blurton Jones, N. G., & Konner, M. J. Sex differences in the
    behavior of Bushman and London two- to five-year-olds.
    In J. Crook & R. Michael (Eds.), Comparative ecology
    and behavior of primates. New York: Academic Press,
    1973.

Bower, T., Broughton, J., & Moore, M. Infant responses to
    approaching objects: An indicator of response to
    distal variables. Perception and Psychophysics,
    1970, 9, 193-196.

Bowlby, J. Maternal care and mental health. Geneva: World
    Health Organization, 1962.

Bowlby, J. Attachment and loss. Vol 1: Attachment. London:
    Hogarth, 1969.

Bruner, J. Processes of cognitive growth in infancy. Heinz
    Werner Lectures, Vol 3. Worcester, Mass.: Clark
    University Press, 1968.

324   MELVIN KONNER

Caudill, W., & Weinstein, H. Maternal care and infant behavior
    in Japan and America. Psychiatry, 1969, 32, 12-43.

Corman, H., & Escalona, S. Stages of sensorimotor development:
    A replication study. Merrill-Palmer Quarterly, 1970,
    15, 351-361.

DeVore, I. Mother-infant relations in baboons. In H. Rhein-
    gold (Ed.), Maternal behavior in mammals. New York:
    Wiley, 1963.

DeVore, I., & Konner, M. J. Infancy in hunter-gatherer life:
    An ethological perspective. In N. White (Ed.),
    Ethology and psychiatry. Toronto: University of
    Toronto Press, 1974.

Draper, P. !Kung Bushman childhood. Unpublished doctoral
    dissertation, Harvard University, 1972.

Escalona, S., & Corman, H. The Einstein scales of sensorimotor
    development. Unpublished manuscript, Department of
    Psychiatry, Albert Einstein School of Medicine, 1969.

Fowler, W. A developmental learning approach to infant care
    in a group setting. Merrill-Palmer Quarterly, 1972,
    18, 145-175.

Geber, M., & Dean, R. F. A. Precocious development of newborn
    African infants. In Y. Brackbill & G. G. Thompson
    (Eds.), Behavior in infancy and early childhood.
    New York: The Free Press, 1967.

Goldberg, S., & Lewis, M. Play behavior in the year-old infant:
    Early sex differences. Child Development, 1969,
    40, 21-31.

Harlow, H. F. The nature of love. American Psychologist, 1958,
    13, 673-685.

Harper, L. Early maternal handling and preschool behavior of
    human children. Developmental Psychobiology, 1972,
    5, 1-5.

Hinde, R., & Spencer-Booth, Y. The effect of social companions
    on mother-infant relations in rhesus monkeys. In D.
    Morris (Ed.), Primate ethology. Chicago: Aldine,
    1967.

Hinde, R., & Spencer-Booth, Y. The study of mother-infant interaction in captive group-living rhesus monkeys. Proceedings of the Royal Society, 1968, 169, 177-201.

Hinde, R., & Spencer-Booth, Y. Effects of brief separations from the mother on rhesus monkeys. Science, 1971, 173, 111-118.

Jay, P. Mother-infant relations in langurs. In R. Rheingold (Ed.), Maternal behavior in mammals. New York: Wiley, 1963.

Jensen, G. D., Bobbitt, R. A., & Gordon, B. N. Sex differences in the development of independence of infant monkeys. Behaviour, 1968, 30, 1-14.

Kaplan, J. Differences in the mother-infant relations of squirrel monkeys housed in social and restricted environments. Developmental Psychology, 1972, 5, 43-52.

Kaplan, J., & Schusterman, R. Social preferences of mother and infant squirrel monkeys following different rearing experiences. Developmental Psychology, 1972, 5, 53-60.

Kessen, W., Haith, M. M., & Salapatek, P. H. Human infancy: A bibliography and guide. In P. Mussen (Ed.), Manual of child psychology. New York: Wiley, 1970.

Konner, M. J. Aspects of the developmental ethology of a foraging people. In N. G. Blurton Jones (Ed.), Ethological studies of child behavior. Cambridge, England: Cambridge University Press, 1972.

Korner, A. State as variable, as obstacle, and as mediator of stimulation in infant research. Merrill-Palmer Quarterly, 1972, 18, 77-94.

Korner, A., & Grobstein, R. Visual alertness as related to soothing in neonates: Implications for maternal stimulation and early deprivation. Child Development, 1966, 37, 867-876.

Korner, A., & Thoman, E. Visual alertness in neonates as evoked by maternal care. Journal of Experimental Child Psychology, 1970, 10, 67-78.

Lancaster, J. Play-mothering: The relations between juvenile females and young infants among free-ranging vervet monkeys (Cercopithecus aethiops). Folia primatologica, 1971, 15, 161-182.

Lee, R., & DeVore, I. Kalahari hunter-gatherers. Cambridge, Mass.: Harvard University Press, in press.

LeVine, R. Cross-cultural study in child psychology. In P. Mussen (Ed.), Manual of child psychology. New York: 1970.

Maccoby, E., & Masters, J. Attachment and dependency. In P. Mussen (Ed.), Manual of child psychology. New York: Wiley, 1970.

McGraw, M. The neuromuscular maturation of the human infant (2nd ed.). New York: Hafner, 1963.

Moss, H. Sex, age and state as determinants of mother-infant interaction. Merrill-Palmer Quarterly, 1967, 13, 19-36.

Oken, D., & Heath, H. A. The law of initial values: Some further considerations. Psychosomatic Medicine, 1963, 25, 3-12.

Piaget, J. The construction of reality in the child. New York: Basic Books, 1954.

Piaget, J. The origins of intelligence in children. New York: Norton, 1962.

Prechtl, H. F. H., & Beintema, D. The neurological assessment of the full-term newborn infant. London: Heinemann, 1964.

Rebelsky, F., & Abeles, G. Infancy in Holland and the United States. Unpublished manuscript, Boston University, 1973.

Rheingold, H. The measurement of maternal care. Child Development, 1960, 31, 565-575.

Richards, M., & Bernal, J. An observational study of mother-infant interaction. In N. G. Blurton Jones (Ed.), Ethological studies of child behavior. New York: Cambridge University Press, 1972.

Richards, M., & Bernal, J. Neuromotor development scale.
Unpublished manuscript, Cambridge University, Unit
for Research on Medical Applications of Psychology.

Robinson, H. B., & Robinson, N. M. Longitudinal development
of very young children in a comprehensive day care
program: The first two years. Child Development,
1971, 42, 1673-84.

Spock, B. Baby and child care (Rev. ed.). New York: Pocket
Books, 1976.

Tulkin, S. R. Mother-infant interaction in the first year of
life: an inquiry into the influences of social class.
Unpublished doctoral dissertation, Harvard University,
1970.

Tulkin, S. R. Infants' reactions to mother's voice and
stranger's voice: Social class differences in the
first year of life. Paper presented at the Meeting
of the Society for Research in Child Development,
Minneapolis, Minnesota, April 1971.

Tulkin, S. R., & Kagan, J. Mother-child interaction in the
first year of life. Child Development, 1972, 43,
31-42.

Warren, N. African infancy and early childhood: Unpublished
manuscript, University of Sussex, 1971.

Warren, N. African infant precocity. Psychological Bulletin,
1972, 78, 353-367.

White, B. L., & Castle, P. W. Visual exploratory behavior
following postnatal handling of human infants.
Perceptual and Motor Skills, 1964, 18, 497-502.

White, B., & Held, R. Plasticity of sensorimotor development.
In J. Hellmut (Ed.), Exceptional infant. Vol 1:
The normal infant. Seattle: Special Child Publications,
1967.

Whiting, J. Causes and consequences of the amount of body
contact between mother and infant. Paper presented
at the Meeting of the American Anthropological
Association, New York, November 1971.

Whiting, J., & Child, I. Child training and personality. New
    Haven: Yale University Press, 1953.

Wolfheim, J. H., Jensen, G. D., & Bobbitt, R. A. Effects of
    group environment on the mother-infant relationship
    in pigtailed monkeys (Macaca nemestrina). Primates,
    1970, 11, 119-124.

Zelazo, P. R., Zelazo, N. A., & Kolb, S. "Walking" in the
    newborn. Science, 1972, 176, 314-315.

Chapter 13

Variance and Invariance in the Mother-Infant Interaction: A Cross-Cultural Study

Michael Lewis and Peggy Ban

Educational Testing Service

Most current emphasis in the literature of individual difference is on the study of difference, although it is not unreasonable to look at similarity as well as difference. In fact, arguments could easily be offered that would stress that individual similarities far outweigh differences, and that, in the study of psychological processes, it might be more profitable to study how people are similar rather than different. Thus, rather than show that three-year-olds are different from five-year-olds, it might have more heuristic value for psychological theory to show how a three-year-old can be (or perhaps cannot be) made to act like a five-year-old. This would apply, of course, for individual differences as well. In fact, the "psychology of difference" should take its place with Looft's (1971) conceptualization of the "psychology of more".

Interestingly, it is logically not possible to state that people are the same, since for n number of demonstrations one is always able to argue that an $n + a$ demonstration of

*

The data gathered for this report and the data analysis were supported by the Spencer Foundation. Appreciation is given to Susan Lee-Painter for data analysis and to Dr. Carolyn Edwards for her helpful comments.

differences would be found. However, it is locically easy to
argue for differences; any one demonstration allows us to
state difference. Notwithstanding, this logical consideration
must give way to a more psychologically meaningful one. Thus,
not all differences should be considered psychologically
meaningful.

We strongly feel it is time to explore similarity as well
as difference. In order to determine whether it was reasonable
to discuss both the variance and invariance in the mother-
infant interaction, it was necessary to obtain cross-cultural
data. We had already gathered data from an African culture,
Senegal, (Lusk & Lewis, 1972), and it was thought that another
culture representing European values, both rural and urban,
would be helpful for exploring this problem. Yugoslavia was
chosen mainly because one of us (Peggy Ban) was shortly going
to visit that area.

We shall present first a description of the culture from
which the data were gathered. The report is that of a trained
observer (Peggy Ban) who is married to a Yugoslavian and is
able to speak Serbo-Croatian. This is a narrative obtained
after eight weeks of living in these two, the rural and the
urban, communities.

DEMOGRAPHIC DESCRIPTION OF YUGOSLAVIA

Yugoslavia is a country made up of a number of diverse
regions that, historically, evolved quite independently of
one another. It was not until 1918, after the collapse of
the Hapsburg Empire that had incorporated a part of it, that
the territory of Yugoslavia was defined by national borders.
The region studied is known as Croatia, one of six republics
of Yugoslavia. The city sample was drawn from Zagreb, capital
of Croatia, and the rural sample from Zapresic and Bistra
two villages lying approximately 10 miles to the north of the
city.

Until 1918 Croatia was a part of the Austro-Hungarian
Empire. Loosely speaking, the people of Croatia shared with
the Empire a common culture, involving education style
(German), architecture (central European), religion (Roman
Catholic), and government. In the following sections, we shall
more specifically characterize the city and village samples
of the present study.

City

Many of the city sample were children of university-
educated parents. Since only 10 percent of the Yugoslav
population ever attend a university, these people represent
a fairly specialized, professional segment of society, and
are in some sense equivalent to the highest social class, as
described by Hollingshead (1957). The religious affiliation
of these people is "distantly" Roman Catholic, since very few
city people attend the church and use the affiliation only to
celebrate the baptism of their children and, less frequently,
to sanction marriage, which is now a state function. People
with Communist Party affiliation have, of course, relinquished
all religious ties. In the present sample, it is not known
who are party members.

Nearly all of the city sample live in small apartments,
located near the center of the town. Often, the parents of
either the mother or father share the apartment as well,
resulting in fairly crowed living quarters by American standards. For instance, it is not unusual for four adults and a
baby to share a three- or four-room apartment. The reasons for
the density are the shortage of available urban housing and the
need for a grandparent to be available to watch the baby when
the mother returns to work, which occurs in nearly all cases.
Mothers are permitted six months to one year paid maternity
leave and once this is expended, most mothers return to full-
time work (7 a.m. to 3 p.m. in most cases). Since pay is low
in Yugoslavia, it is considered necessary for mothers to work,
but, in contrast to current attitudes in the United States,
most Yugoslav mothers remark that they would prefer full-time
motherhood. It is quite possible that the prospect of returning
to full-time employment within a year in some way tempers the
young Yugoslav mothers' attitudes toward their babies.

All of the city apartments were clean and well-furnished.
Usually the baby sleeps in a crib in the parents' bedroom.
Babies under six months are given few toys.

Few appliances were available in the home. Generally,
television sets, small refrigerators, and gas stoves were
present. Much less frequently were washing machines and
dishwashers observed. Often the grandmother assumed many of
the household chores, including cooking meals, which suggests
that even with the unavailability of many appliances, the
mother was generally free to attend to the child.

Yugoslav fathers, returning from work around 3 p.m. in
the afternoon, have a relatively greater amount of time in

which to observe or interact with their young babies. Most
fathers, when present, voluntarily interacted with the babies.

The typical Yugoslav week-day involves early arising,
around 6 a.m., so that the father can leave for work around
7 a.m. Household chores and daily food shopping are done in
the morning. Cooking the main meal begins around 1 p.m.
When the father returns at 3 p.m. the family eats the main
meal, then, customarily, rests for an hour afterward. Evening
is spent in relaxing at home, incidental shopping (stores are
open from 6 to 8 p.m.), going to local cafes, or entertaining
family or friends. A light snack is usually eaten around
9 p.m.

Village

Both Zapresic and Bistra, the sites of the rural sample,
can be characterized as villages. Zapresic, however, is undergoing extensive sociological change, which is important to
understanding fully the nature of the families residing there.

As recently as one generation ago, all the residents of
both villages were dependent on farming for subsistence. The
peasant-style homes and most of the fields remain today;
however, a dramatic transition is in evidence. Young men now
seek and obtain industrial employment as laborers, and many
travel daily into the highly industrialized outskirts of
Zagreb. This new type of employment brings in more currency
than would be available to the family through farming alone.
In some cases, this is evidenced by the reconstruction and
new building of homes with larger and more convenient styles
(including indoor plumbing). New homes have two stories, with
brick and stucco facings and red tile roofs. A few families
have acquired television sets.

Home interiors, family structure, and most importantly,
social interactions, appear to be as yet unaffected or minimally
affected by the changes. The social density, like that in the
cities, is quite high, and as many as six to eight adults were
observed living "under one roof"--all belonging to the family.

Home furnishings in the villages remain generally very
simple, with only necessities present. In many cases, the
bedroom and kitchen are the only two centers of activity. The
kitchens, with chairs and a table, apparently substitute for
living rooms, and most rural observations took place there.

With the high social density, the mothers have ample

opportunity for interaction with other adults, as well as with the baby. Most young village mothers are not employed. Apart from attending the baby, they occasionally work in the fields or the garden (this, of course, is seasonal, but quite demanding of time in spring and summer), or attend to the few farm animals that are nearly always present, and to the household chores, which are more demanding in such homes. For instance, most did not have hot running water and at least two did not have indoor water at all.

Because of the small family income, the women often must sew and knit the clothing, spend more time cooking (although prepared bread is available daily to nearly all women), and generally devote more time to household chores than their city counterparts.

A routine village day would require a very early arising, generally between 5 and 6 a.m. Husbands go off to work early, and women and occasionally older men are left at home. (By older men we mean nonemployed grandfathers, generally.) The women do the chores during the entire morning. With a young baby, a great deal of time is devoted to the wash, which must be done by hand and traditionally is boiled on the stove, since there is great fear of exposing the baby to bacteria. Cooking the main meal, as in the city, begins between noon and one o'clock. Husbands return home from work between 3 and 4 p.m., since often they must travel some distance. Immediately, the main meal is eaten, the after-meal rest is taken, and then remaining chores are attended to. The evening is spent most often at home, where the family sit together and talk. Most village people are in bed before 10 p.m.

Ecological Differences in Cultures

As we read this description, we cannot help being struck by the differences that exist between the people of these communities and those of our own--those that make up the samples usually studied in this country. A few differences are most obvious, ones that many of us might assume to have importance for child-rearing practices. The family structure is the most obvious. From the description we learn that there are large numbers of adults living together under one roof. The adult-child ratio is much higher than that which we encounter. Moreover, in our poor communities, those we call *lower-class*, we tend to find fewer adults per nuclear family, whereas in poor Yugoslav families there are even more.

Physical space differences, as a function of the small

homes and large numbers of people, also appear to be striking.
In American middle-class homes, rooms are carefully
differentiated by function (e.g., kitchens for eating in and
bedrooms for sleeping in), and most often infants and children
have their own rooms. This is certainly not so in Yugoslav
homes.

Differences between the cultures in the number of toys
are great. Our culture calls for many varied objects with
which to enlighten the child; the Yugoslav culture deemphasizes
or ignores this source of stimulation to the point that Yugoslav
infants have few, if any, playthings. The consequences this
might have for child-rearing may be vast.

Also striking, in terms of what we observe within our own
homes, is the absence of modern conveniences, the lack of hot
water, and the lack of appliances for cleaning, preparing food,
and caring for the environment. How many families studied by
American psychologists wash their infants' diapers by hand?
This practice should result in the mother's being less centered
around her child, her time and energy devoted to "housework".

These few examples make it clear to us that there are
vast and potentially quite important differences between the
city and village Yugoslavian households we have just described,
and the American households we have so often studied. Given
all these differences, what about the interaction between a
mother and her very young infant? It is possible that mothers,
regardless of their cultural backgrounds or social class,
behave in similar ways, and that infants too share similarities?

A point we would like to make is that social class and
cultural differences as they apply to child care are related
to ideologies, that is, general belief systems, rooted in both
the cognitive and the affective systems. These belief systems[1]
(rather than specific behaviors) and their consequences may be
more related to child development outcomes than we recognize.
Belief systems lead to a wide variety of maternal behaviors,
which in turn have consequences in the development of the child;

---

[1] Unfortunately, belief systems are difficult to measure.
Attitude questionnaires have had a singular lack of success.
Exactly how to tap into these beliefs is not yet clear.
Perhaps neither the study of attitudes (as obtained from the
subject) nor single behaviors (as obtained from observation)
is sufficient, but rather some multivariate procedure
utilizing multiple measures in a variety of situations is
required.

however, because we cannot sample all of the maternal
behaviors, there may be less connection between the behaviors
we do sample and outcome than between belief system and outcome.
This may be so since belief systems may be a more adequate way
to cluster maternal behaviors than the study of specific
behaviors themselves. As behaviorists, or at least persons
committed to aspects of behaviorism, we may err in only looking
at very limited behavior-outcome relationships rather than
considering the broader values-outcome relationship.

     Consider these examples. In one family, a father must
work long hours and has little time to spend with his child.
However, the child is told that the father is working (i.e.,
not with the child) in order to provide money for the family.
In a second family, the father also spends little time with
his child, but this is not due to the amount of time he needs
to spend working. Behaviorally both fathers spend the same
amount of time with their children; however, the consequences
for the child may be quite different. Likewise, consider an
American mother who keeps her child alone in a dark, cold
room, as compared to a Dutch mother who does the same. The
outcomes in the two instances will be different because the
same behavior is serviced by different beliefs. Since in the
American family being left alone is not the norm, while in the
Dutch family it is, the meaning of the maternal act may be
quite different; hostility or rejection in one case, normal
affection in the other.

     In the general case, what we are arguing for is the study
of *behavior-in-context*. By *context*, we mean not only the
ecological context (where the behavior takes place), but also
the cultural meaning of a particular behavior. Unless we
carefully study the context in which the behavior occurs we
may make serious errors in interpretation. How many of us,
interested in such issues as cultural or social class
differences, have sufficient commerce with the groups under
study to understand properly how the behaviors we observe are
embedded in the culture or subculture?[2] To infer meaning from

---

[2]One way to study meaning is by studying behavior in context.
To do this, it is important to utilize members of the meaning
group being studied. This presents a special problem, since
it is necessary to obtain a community member who understands
both the experimenter's culture (including the scientific
procedure or parts of it) and his own. This may not always
be possible, since each may act to distort the other. Imagine
a cultural value of a group that has as its premise the
assumption that members do not tell each other unpleasant

behavior without context (in a broad sense) is folly. Without
such data or in the absence of understanding the ideology, the
observation of behavior may be worthless. There are a variety
of means for understanding the behavior. One method is to
gather information about the broad views and beliefs,
independent of the observational procedures, that is, by
living within the community, using community members as guides,
and studying the belief systems themselves.[3]

Another way to approach this problem is to study behavior
in its situational-interactive context. By *situational context*,
we mean the circumstances under which the behavior occurs. We
have speculated that both physical location and situational
context play a crucial role in the infant's evolving meaning
systems (structures) and should be studied in order to understand the maternal as well as infant behaviors. In studies of
infant vocalization behavior, Lewis and Freedle (1973), Lewis
and Freedle (1975) were able to demonstrate the effectiveness
of studying situational context.

The interactive context ideally is combined with the
situational. Most studies of infant behavior (including
cross-cultural or cross-social class) concern themselves with
the question of how much behavior of a selected type is
exhibited by either the infant or its caregiver. For example,
how much vocalization does the infant or mother produce in x
minutes of observation? To study behavior this way has the
advantage of ease of data collection and high reliability.
It is assumed to be interactive in the sense that the behavior
occurred when the infant and its caregiver were together.
However, such data, if interactive at all, tap a very low
level of interaction (Lewis & Painter, 1973). More importantly,
this method does not generate the behavior-context type of
analysis that may be important. Thus, a more truly interactive

---

things. How does the intermediate observer from both the
culture and the examining culture get around this psychological
situation? To press for unpleasant information, or even to
realize that the culture has this "unreal" view, is to be no
longer a member of the culture and therefore of limited use
in getting at the contextual basis of the behavior. It is
not an easily solved problem and one too often superficially
examined.

---

[3]We have not directly spoken to the issue of where beliefs come
from. We have suggested that they are both cognitively and
affectively based and are a consequence of the organism's
interaction with his world. The origin of beliefs is a most
important subject, one that requires study in itself.

study must be undertaken as well. By using interactive measures, we may learn more about the meaning of the behavior than by the use of frequency data alone.

In the present study, we collected data on two social class groups (if we wish to consider the Yugoslavian city and village samples as different social classes) in a culture that is by many characteristics quite different from our own. It is most important to inquire first what caregiving functions this culture demonstrates and secondly how they might be similar to our own. Our research concerns variance and invariance in the mother-infant interaction and, ultimately, its relationship to belief systems.

To explore this problem, the first issue was how to study these infants and their mothers. We had been working on a variety of techniques for measuring the dyadic interaction between the child and its caregiver (see Lewis, 1972; Lewis & Lee-Painter, 1973; Lewis & Wilson, 1972). It must be recognized that our problem was to obtain as dynamic a picture of the infant-caregiver relationship as possible, and not merely a frequency count of behavior. This dynamic description is necessary if we are to look at behavior in context rather than as just the occurrence of behavior.

The 18 Yugoslavian subjects were all twelve weeks old (+ one week); 9 were from the city, 9 from the villages. Table 13-1 presents pertinent demographic data on these infants and their parents. In order to compare the Yugoslavian with American data, we have used the data from a larger longitudinal study of American mother-infant interaction; some of these data have already been reported (Lewis, 1972). The American sample consisted of twelve-week-old infants. Their sex and socioeconomic status (SES), determined by the Hollingshead Two-Factor Index of Social Position (1957), are presented in Table 13-1.

Ways of measuring the mother-infant interaction have been of considerable interest to us, and to this end we established both a procedure and a methodology for obtaining and scoring these data. We used a dynamic set of measures that explore not only the frequency of occurrence of behavior but also "who does what to whom and when". This procedure allows us to observe behavior in its situational-interactive context. We can observe not only how much looking or vocalizing the mother directs to her infant but also, and more importantly, how much the mother does this when the infant does something. In this way, the context of the mother's vocalization is

TABLE 13-1. Demographic Data

Yugoslavian Sample

Subject	Age	Years of Education	Occupation		Subject	Age	Years of Education	Occupation
Village Male					Village Female			
501	22	8	truck driver		502	28	8	factory worker
503	39	8	factory worker		504	22	8	factory worker
505	35	8	factory worker		506	36	8	truck driver
507	30	11	painter		508	31	6	construction worker
509	37	11	carpenter		X̄	31.1	8.5	
City Male					City Female			
511	36	17	electrical engineer		510	27	12	building foreman
513	22	15	student/model		512	32	18	orchestra conductor
515	32	17	architect		514	24	11	mechanic
517	30	16	chemical engineer		X̄	28.9	14.9	
519	30	16	university student					
521	27	12	building foreman					

Summary of Yugoslavian Sample

	Males	Females	Total	X̄ Education Father
Village	5	4	9	8.5
City	6	3	9	14.9

American Sample

SES	Males	Females	Total	X̄ Education Father
I	2	3	5	19.4
II	4	4	8	15.6
III	4	5	9	13.5a
IV	3	0	3	12.0
V	4	3	7	11.3b

a one infant has no father
b three infants have no father

established.

To obtain data on the mother-infant interaction, it was necessary to observe each dyad over a relatively long period in a naturalistic setting. Each infant was seen in its own home at three months of age (+ one week). Contact with the American mothers was made in a variety of ways: through the mother's initiative, through birth announcements in the news-paper, and through church groups in lower socioeconomic areas. For the Yugoslavian sample, contact was made through well-baby clinics where records were kept on every child. Those who were three months old were contacted and seen. For the villages, this included almost all the infants who were three months old. The city sample was more selective, the selection basis being similar to what we find in this country--that is, the sample was composed of those willing to paritipate.

We have reported the reliabilities of observations of this type before (Lewis, 1972). The observer of our Yugoslavian sample, the reliabilities were moderate (ranging from rho's of .55 to .95 for overall frequency of behavior). While there is no reason to assume that observer differences account for any differences in the data, this cannot be discarded since no Yugoslavian reliabilities could be obtained.

As with the American sample, the Yugoslavian mothers were instructed that the observer was interested in studying the infant's behavior. The observer remained out of the infant's sight. We stressed that it was the infant who was to be observed. Moreover, the mother was to try to forget the presence of the observer and not engage her in conversation. When conversation was attempted, the observer reminded the mother that she was to ignore her. Prior to observation, the observer spent time with the mother with the aim of putting her at ease.

Although every attempt was made to make the observation session as natural as possible, the presence of the observer is bound to have an effect. This problem has been discussed before (Lewis & Goldberg, 1969); in spite of the problems, however, this is the only procedure available for collecting this type of data.

The observation data were collected using a checklist sheet. Each sheet represents 60 seconds, divided into six 10-second columns. Infant behaviors are listed in the upper portion of the sheet, while caregiver behaviors are in the lower portion. When a behavior not listed on the sheet occurs

the observer writes it in. For the most part, the infant
behavior categories are self-explanatory and include vocalize,
feed, smile, extra movement, fret/cry, quiet play, and noise/
nonvocalization. The "extra movement" category consists of
all gross physical movements, such as limb movement or body
rolling. "Quiet play" consists of the child watching a toy
move or playing with his fingers, and noise/nonvocalization
is similar to extra movement, except that noise accompanies
the behavior (by kicking feet against the crib). It is clear
that these behaviors are not totally exclusive, reflecting a
further difficulty in studies of this sort. Although the
behaviors have some overlap, observers are, in general, able
to differentiate between them. Maternal behaviors listed
include touch, hold, vocalize, look at, smile/laugh, play,
feed, change clothes, rock, vocalize to others, read, or
watch television. Mother's touch and hold categories
distinguish between a discrete touch versus physical support.
If during a "hold" the mother also discretely touches the
child, both categories would be scored. Finally, the
categories of read/watch television and vocalize to others
indicate that the mother is involved in activities *not*
directed toward the child.

For each 10-second interval the observer checked off the
occurrence of both infant and mother behaviors, also recording
when possible which behaviors preceded which.

If the infant closed its eyes for longer than 30
consecutive seconds, observation stopped. For both samples
in order to obtain two full hours of eyes-open data, a
minimum of two hours of observation and on some occasions as
much as three or four hours were necessary. In fact, for
one-third of the sample, two visits to the home were required.
Only one hour of observation was obtained for the Yugoslavian
sample. For the purpose of comparison, the Yugoslavian data
were adjusted upward to represent two hours. This was felt
appropriate, since observation of time differences in the
American sample failed to indicate that time influenced
behavior in any systematic pattern.

METHODS OF DATA ANALYSIS

Various levels of interactive analysis are possible with
these types of data. In several papers (Lewis, 1972; Lewis
& Lee-Painter, 1973; Lusk & Lewis, 1972), some of the more
obvious were discussed. In the present paper we shall consider

three methods of data analysis.

The simplest is the *frequency distribution*; that is, how much of each behavior the infant exhibited in the two hours of observation. The same data analysis is possible for the mother's behavior. While these data tap very little of the nature of mother-infant interaction, they are included to facilitate comparison with other studies, as well as to use as a basis for comparing the interaction data.

The simultaneous behavior within 10-second involves the number of 10-second units for which both child and mother behaviors occur. Since it is often difficult to determine exactly which of the pair initiates a behavior sequence and the time duration of the sequence, a more conservative approach is to restrict the analysis to a 10-second time unit, recognizing that it is an arbitrarily selected unit. This measure may have use as an overall interaction measure.

Under directional interactive analyses, two categories of interactive behavior are possible for each specific behavior. For example, consider the infant's vocalization. One question to be asked is whether the vocalization was a response to a maternal behavior or an initiator of a maternal behavior, these being scored as two separate categories. This is accomplished by scoring "1" for initiating and "2" for responding. Each maternal behavior also has two possible direction components. While we have illustrated directionality for vocalization data, it can be applied to all behavioral categories.

There are, of course, many more measures of interaction for which individual measures may be obtained. For example, one might also look at length of interaction or density of response.

OBSERVATIONAL DATA

Frequency of Occurrence

Following first the traditional presentation of data, we report the mean frequency of behavior. The data in Table 13-2 represents the mean number of 10 seconds in which the particular behavior occurred. The data are presented by culture, social class, and sex.

TABLE 13-2. Behavior Frequencies: Mean Number of 10-Second Periods.

Infant Behaviors	Total		Male		Female		Yugoslavia		United States				
	Yugo.	U.S.	Yugo.	U.S.	U.S.	Yugo.	City	Village	I	II	III	IV	V
Vocalize	154.4	170.8	159.4	172.1	169.2	146.5	147.3	161.6	102.4	121.0	220.3	175.7	235.4
Movement	156.2	96.5	164.9	87.4	106.7	142.6	151.1	161.3	75.3	72.2	72.0	48.7	189.4
Fret/Cry	90.4	77.3	104.9	72.8	82.3	67.7	100.2	80.7	99.0	114.8	60.9	62.7	47.4
Play	418.6	108.0	423.5	99.3	117.9	410.9	359.1	477.3	99.0	142.8	120.3	77.3	93.9
Smile	25.8	37.3	25.5	36.6	35.8	26.3	33.5	18.0	23.9	29.4	39.0	24.3	53.7
Maternal Behaviors													
Touch	113.0	126.7	116.9	128.7	124.5	108.9	128.7	97.3	92.2	135.4	123.8	137.7	163.6
Hold	234.7	307.3	198.0	356.9	251.0	292.3	265.3	204.0	231.9	264.8	352.5	356.7	361.6
Vocalize	270.2	257.2	247.5	227.1	291.3	306.0	312.9	227.6	227.9	215.0	313.9	293.7	244.7
Look	374.6	174.3	344.2	145.1	207.4	422.3	407.3	341.8	169.7	111.6	173.3	166.7	229.4
Smile	99.8	33.0	97.1	37.0	28.4	104.0	105.8	93.8	17.6	25.2	35.9	31.7	55.6
Play	79.8	86.8	71.6	84.3	89.5	92.6	109.6	50.0	44.9	84.6	118.1	78.0	110.0
Rock	31.6	10.1	28.7	14.5	5.0	36.0	23.3	39.8	12.0	20.8	5.0	8.0	8.0
Voc/Other	104.4	96.7	109.1	109.5	82.3	97.1	80.9	128.0	113.3	61.0	84.8	182.7	77.7
Read/TV	1.9	48.5	3.1	57.1	38.9	0.0	3.8	0.0	25.4	5.2	62.0	8.3	111.00

Infant Behavior.   In the overall comparison between the U.S. and Yugoslavian infants, there is relatively little behavioral difference. Yugoslavian infants show significantly more movement than American children (Mann-Whitney U test, $\rho < .01$);[4] however, the difference is significant only for boys ($\rho < .02$). Yugoslavian children also show very much more quiet play than American children ($\rho < .001$).

If we look at the ordering of behavior, we find that across groups there is a high consistency of infant activities. Infants, regardless of background, show the most frequent behaviors to be vocalization and quiet play while the least are smiling and fret/cry. In fact, the correlation beween the U.S. and Yugoslavian samples is rho = .83, while between the two Yugoslavian groups (city versus village) it is rho = .91. It would appear then that for infants' behaviors there is relatively little cultural or social class difference to be observed in terms of their frequency data.

Maternal Behavior.   The maternal data found in Table 13-2 reveal some interesting differences. For example, American mothers tend to hold their infants more than Yugoslavian mothers do ($\rho < .10$), especially for male infants ($\rho < .01$); however, Yugoslavian mothers rock their infants more than American mothers ($\rho < .05$). Finally, Yugoslavian mothers look and smile at their infants more than American mothers ($\rho < .001$). Unlike in the American sample, in the Yugoslavian sample there was almost no reading or television watching (mostly because there were few books and television sets). Thus, behavior directed away from the infant is not comparable across cultures, except for vocalizing to others, where there were no Yugoslav-American differences. There were no significant Yugoslavian city-village differences in maternal behavior.

While Yugoslavian mothers do seem to make more distal contact in terms of looking at their children than do American mothers, there are no vocalization differences in terms of frequency of occurrence. The proximal contact is almost equal if one allows for a sytle difference between hold and rock. While these differences may reflect some underlying processes, it is important to note that Yugoslavian and American mothers behave in much the same manner. For both groups the three most frequent behaviors are hold, vocalize,

---

[4]All tests are nonparametric and are Mann-Whitney U tests unless otherwise stated. All ρ values are two-tailed.

and look. In fact, there is a rho of .85 (ρ < .001) between
the nine maternal activities for the two samples, indicating
that in general the mothers behave in the same way (in terms
of frequency), regardless of culture. The correlation between
the Yugoslavian city and village is rho = .88 (ρ < .001).

TABLE 13-3. Percentage of 10-Second Periods in which an
Infant Behaved and There Was a Simultaneous
Maternal Behavior.

	Yugoslavia N	United States N
Total	.68 (18)	.70 (32)
Male	.64 (11)	.72 (17)
Female	.74 (07)	.68 (15)
U.S. SES Level I		.69 (09)
II		.59 (05)
III		.88 (08)
IV		.78 (03)
V		.69 (07)
Yugo. City	.74 (09)	
Yugo. Village	.62 (09)	

Before examining the interactive data, we shall briefly
present the interactive percentages, these being the mean
number of 10 seconds in which an infant and maternal behavior
occur simultaneously. This is a parameter of responsivity
which we have used. Table 13-3 presents the data which
indicate that mothers in this observational setting are in
general highly responsive. Moreover, there are no significant
differences to be observed between any of the groups.

Interaction Data

Interaction data allow us to look at behavior in its

situational-interactive context. By seeing what elicits the
behavior in either member of the dyad and what behaviors
reinforce it, the observer has a better chance to understand
the behavior's meaning and the beliefs underlying it.
Certainly the interaction data contain considerably more
information than does behavior frequency. It has been our
observation that two behaviors are particularly revealing in
terms of cultural or ideological meaning. These two, infant-
maternal vocalization and infant fret/cry-maternal response,
have both been shown to be especially effective in differentiating the beliefs underlying social class differences in
American families (Lewis & Wilson, 1972).

Infant-Maternal Vocalization. Table 13-4 presents four
divisions that compose the dyadic relationship centering around
vocalization. The top left section involves an infant
initiating a vocalization and the mean number of 10-second
periods in which there were a variety of maternal responses.
The top right of the Table shows the mean number of 10-second
periods an infant responds with a vocalization to a variety
of maternal behaviors. The lower left of the Table contains
data on maternal initiation of a vocalization and the variety
of infant responses, while the lower right shows the maternal
vocalization as a response to a variety of infant-initiated
behaviors. We shall consider first the infant vocalization
data, both as a response to and elicitor of maternal behavior.

The Yugoslavian data, like the American, shows that the
vocalization-vocalization relationship is the strongest; that
is, an infant vocalization is most likely to elicit a maternal
vocalization, just as a maternal vocalization is most likely to
elicit an infant vocalization. In fact, the Yugoslavian and
American data are remarkably similar. The correlations
between the Yugoslavian and American samples are rho = .86
(p < .001) and rho = .76 (p < .001) for infant vocalization
elicits maternal behavior, and maternal behavior elicits infant
vocalization, respectively. A difference exists in the absolute
rate of response: American mothers are more likely to "vocalize
in response" to their infants' vocalizations than are Yugoslavian
mothers (Z = 2.26, p < .01). Interestingly, while the American
mothers tend to vocalize somewhat more in response to infant
vocalization, Yugoslavian mothers initiate more vocalization
to their infants than do American mothers.

Maternal vocalization as either an initiator of or a
response to other infant behaviors shows the same pattern of
high agreement between the American and Yugoslavian samples:
maternal vocalization is more likely to be responded to by

TABLE 13-4. Vocalization Interaction Matrix.

Maternal Behaviors	Infant initiates vocalize, mother responds						Mother initiates. infant responds with vocalization					
	Male		Female		Total		Male		Female		Total	
	Yugo.	U.S.	Yugo.	U.S.	Yugo.	U.S.	Yugo.	U.S.	Yugo.	U.S.	Yugo.	U.S.
Touch	0.54	1.50	2.00	0.55	1.12	1.08	8.00	4.07	4.28	6.55	6.56	5.16
Hold	0.00	1.29	0.28	0.18	0.12	0.80	1.10	3.64	2.58	8.09	1.66	5.60
Vocalize	14.72	32.07	22.86	37.00	17.88	34.24	25.28	18.43	27.72	29.27	26.22	23.20
Voc/Other	0.36	1.29	0.00	0.64	0.22	1.00	1.46	0.00	0.28	0.27	1.00	0.12
Look	1.82	2.86	3.72	1.73	2.56	2.36	11.46	4.79	6.86	8.45	9.66	6.40
Smile	2.00	2.86	7.14	2.64	4.00	2.76	11.46	4.64	8.00	7.45	10.12	5.88
Play	0.00	0.57	0.28	0.36	0.12	0.48	5.46	5.71	2.00	10.64	4.12	7.88
Change					0.00	0.12					0.88	0.72
Feed					0.22	0.32					0.22	0.80
Rock					0.22	0.12					0.34	0.04
Read					0.00	0.12					0.00	0.20

Infant Behaviors	Mother initiates vocalize, infant responds						Infant initiates vocalize, mother responds with vocalization					
	Male		Female		Total		Male		Female		Total	
	Yugo.	U.S.	Yugo.	U.S.	Yugo.	U.S.	Yugo.	U.S.	Yugo.	U.S.	Yugo.	U.S.
Vocalize	25.28	18.43	27.72	29.27	26.22	23.20	14.72	32.07	22.86	37.00	17.88	34.24
Movement	0.72	2.57	1.72	2.18	1.12	2.40	7.08	11.50	12.86	10.09	9.34	10.88
Fret/Cry	0.72	1.93	0.86	2.45	0.78	2.16	17.46	16.86	14.00	21.00	16.12	18.68
Play	0.36	1.71	0.00	1.00	0.22	1.40	0.72	3.00	0.58	1.45	0.66	2.32
Smile	14.90	9.79	14.58	13.09	14.78	11.24	1.28	2.86	2.00	1.82	1.56	2.40

346

an infant vocalization than by a smile. There were no
significant mean differences. Moreover, Yugoslavian babies
are more likely to smile as a *response* to a maternal behavior
than as an *initiator*. This is consistent with the American
data.

Thus, when one looks at the vocalization data in the
context of its interaction there are relatively few differences
between the samples. It might also be noted that there were no
significant differences within the Yugoslavian sample itself;
the village and city samples show the same pattern as the overall data. The data, then, indicate that there are large
invariances between a mother and her infant in regard to their
vocalization behavior. That is, certain types of responses
within this dyadic relationship remain constant across these
divergent groups.

Infant Fret/Cry--Mother's Response. A particular interesting context in which to observe behavior of the dyad is the
fret/cry behavior of the infant and the corresponding response
of the mother. Unlike vocalization, this relationship is
asymmetrical, in that we find no data (or reason) for studying
the responses of the infant to the mother's cry. The study of
this particular aspect of the interaction is usually revealing
for it is here that belief systems is more likely to make
itself felt. For example, in the study by Lewis and Wilson
(1972) we observed differences between the social classes in
the mothers' response to their infants' fret/cry behavior.
Most striking was the fact that middle-class mothers tended
to touch their infants as a response to their cries, whereas
lower-class mothers tended to look at and vocalize to their
infants. Investigation of these differences by looking at
other aspects of the data suggested that they had little to
do with caring or not caring for their infants (i.e., mothers
responded with the same *density* of response--only the style
of response differed). Indeed, it is often assumed that the
lower-class mother is less concerned than the middle-class
mother with her child. The data on their response to distress
would at first glance suggest this in that distal behaviors
(such as look and vocalize) are often assumed to be less
comforting than the proximal (touch, hold, and rock). However,
closer analysis indicates that these behaviors may be in the
service of beliefs and strategies both similar to and
different from those of the middle class mothers. Mothers
of both classes report their desire that their children be
able to adapt to a hostile, hard, and difficult social world.
The middle-class mother's strategy for her child's adaptation
may be to protect him from the hostile world for as long as

possible, while the lower-class mother's strategy may be to get her child "used to" the hostile world as soon as possible.

Let us look now at the infant fret/cry interaction data presented in Table 13-5. Several findings again reflect the types of invariances we have seen before. First, as we would expect, infant fret/cry is most usually an initiator of a mother's response rather than a response to a mother's behavior. Thus, while vocalization is equally used by both members as a response and an initiator, fret/cry is used as an infant initiator of maternal responses. The maternal responses also suggest invariances across the cultures; thus, across the Yugoslavian and American samples mothers tend to behave similarly (rho = .79, $p < .001$), with the three most frequent responses to a fret/cry being vocalization, touch, and look. Likewise, infant fret/cry as a response shows a similar pattern across the Yugoslavian and American samples (rho = .91, $p < .001$).

If we look at the mean data, we find no difference, although we note that Yugoslavian mothers are slightly more responsive, in general, than American mothers (mean number of 10-second responses across all 11 behaviors is 26.56 for Yugoslavian and 24.44 for American samples). Interestingly, while Yugoslavian mothers tend to be more responsive, American mothers vocalize and play more with their children in response to their fret/cry behavior.

Observation of the city and village samples within Yugoslavia indicates some differences. The mothers of the city group vocalize more in response to their infants' fret/cry than the village mothers (mean of 10.56 versus 5.56, $p < .05$), while the village mothers tend to respond more proximally to their infants by touching and holding in response. Thus, the Yugoslavian city mothers are similar in this regard to the lower-class American mothers and the rural Yugoslavian mothers are similar to the middle-class American mothers. This is counter to what was expected. We can offer no explanation except to conclude it is a chance finding.[5]

---

[5] Observation of the demographic data of Table 13-1 leads one to conclude that the city-village differences within the Yugoslavian culture might be the same as social class differences, defined by the Hollingshead scale (1957), in the American culture. If one were to consider the education and occupation level of the fathers, then the city-village distinction would be SES I versus SES V. In some sense, one could claim that social class differences, as distinct from

TABLE 13-5. Fret/Cry Interaction Matrix.

	Infant initiates fret, mother responds						Mother initiates, infant responds with fret					
	Male		Female		Total		Male		Female		Total	
	Yugo.	U.S.	Yugo.	U.S.	Yugo.	U.S.	Yugo.	U.S.	Yugo.	U.S.	Yugo.	U.S.
Touch	2.90	1.50	1.72	2.27	2.44	1.84	0.36	0.29	1.14	0.64	0.66	0.44
Hold	1.46	1.00	1.72	1.27	1.56	1.12	0.18	0.14	0.28	0.36	0.22	0.24
Vocalize	17.46	16.86	14.00	21.00	16.12	18.68	0.72	1.93	0.86	2.45	0.78	2.16
Voc/Other	1.10	0.14	0.28	0.00	0.78	0.08	0.00	0.00	0.00	0.00	0.00	0.00
Look	3.64	1.71	1.42	0.91	2.78	1.36	0.72	0.74	0.00	0.27	0.44	0.20
Smile	2.00	0.14	1.14	0.27	1.66	0.20	0.36	0.00	0.00	0.00	0.22	0.00
Play	0.54	0.43	0.00	1.18	0.34	0.76	0.18	0.00	0.00	0.00	0.12	0.00
Change					0.00	0.08					0.34	0.04
Feed					0.22	0.28					0.00	0.00
Rock					0.66	0.04					0.00	0.00
Read					0.00	0.00					0.00	0.00

If we look at infant fret/cry as a response to a maternal behavior, we find relatively little difference between samples or between categories of maternal behavior. This, of course, is due to the fact that fret/cry so rarely occurs as an infant response. In both samples, when it does occur, it occurs most often as a response to a maternal vocalization, another invariance.

---

culture, could be compared. The frequency data of Table 13-2 present no support for this assumption. That is, the Yugoslavian city families are not behaving like the American SES I nor are the village families like the American SES V. In fact, if anything, the Yugoslavian city families are more similar to the SES V, while the Yugoslavian village families are more similar to the American SES I groups. This may not be surprising, when we consider that the Yugoslavian city families and SES V American families are most likely to have mothers who work. This, of course, raises the issue as to what is meant by social class. Inquiry into this question supplies few answers, and these are usually restricted to such obvious differences as education and income levels. Like cultural differences, such obvious differences as education and income must be carrier variables for the more important psychological variables of beliefs and values. The distinctions we make as a function of social class must eventually give way to those dealing with what we have called belief systems, for, unless we make this shift, we may be dealing with a relatively insignificant system of classification. Such a shift should not alarm us, since our use of social class to demonstrate differences has never been grounded on a sound theoretical basis. In fact, social class data reflect our desire to find individual differences rather than to discover process. Our attention should be drawn to process rather than difference. The use of divergent groups should facilitate our knowledge of process, since it may increase the variability of both maternal and infant behavior; however, to stop at differences is false science. The problems of social class as a construct are never more obvious than in cross-cultural studies. That we continue to use it may underline concerns that do not truly belong in the realm of a science of psychology.

GENERAL INVARIANCES ACROSS CULTURES

What emerges from this detailed description of the Yugoslavian city and village and the American samples? It becomes apparent that there are more similarities than differences, more invariances than variances. Even the variances seem to be substitutions rather than absolutes. Thus, for example, while Yugoslavian mothers show more proximal behaviors in response to infant stress, American mothers show more distal behaviors. Even so, there is remarkably little difference between the behavior of our two samples of American and Yugoslavian dyads. This is in spite of the fact that the demographic description would lead one to conclude that large differences exist between the worlds of the Yugoslavian and American infants. This is rather remarkable, when one considers the seemingly all-pervasive difference between the cultures (and subcultures). How could this be?

One possibility is that while there are large differences between the cultures there are also similarities in child-rearing practices. From an anthropological point of view both cultures show similarities. For example, in both the infant sleeps in its own crib; spends much time not being held; most probably is breast-fed for less than six months; stays inside the house a good deal of the time since it is a cold climate part of the year; and finally, adults rather than children are involved in the infant's care. Thus, it is possible that these two cultures are more alike than we thought. In order to look at cultures which differ on these, as well as other dimensions, we compared data from several other studies: Rebelsky and Abeles' (1969) study in Holland; Lusk and Lewis' (1972) study of the Wolof of Senegal; and Goldberg's study in the United States and Zambia (1970).

Unfortunately, only a limited amount of similar data was collected across studies and this all involved frequency of occurrence data. For each of the five cultures, American, Dutch, Zambian, Senegalese, and Yugoslavian, we could obtain data on frequency of maternal touch, hold, vocalize, smile, look at, and play with infant. Because of limited information, only the rank order of these behaviors is available for each culture.

Table 13-6 presents the data. The coefficient of concordance ($w = .575$, $p < .01$) indicates that there is invariance among the five widely divergent cultures. Even at this gross level, there is high intercultural consistency in maternal behavior. In general, at this age maternal play

is a relatively infrequent occurrence, as is maternal smiling.
Maternal vocalization and holding is a relatively frequent
occurrence except in Zambia where vocalization is low.

TABLE 13-6. Rank Order of Frequency of Selected Maternal
Behavior by Cultures.

Rank	Zambian $N = 38$	Dutch $N = 11$	Senegalese $N = 10$	American $N = 32$	Yugoslavian $N = 18$
1	Hold	Look	Vocalize	Hold	Look
2	Look	Hold	Touch	Vocalize	Vocalize
3	Touch	Vocalize	Hold	Look	Hold
4	Smile	Touch	Smile	Touch	Touch
5	Play	Smile	Look	Play	Smile
6	Vocalize	Play	Play	Smile	Play

Spearman Rank Order Correlations between Cultures

U.S.	→ Holland	.77
	→ Yugoslavia	.71
	→ Zambia	.35
	→ Senegal	.49
Holland	→ Yugoslavia	.94
	→ Zambia	.54
	→ Senegal	.26
Yugoslavia	→ Zambia	.30
	→ Senegal	.35
Zambia	→ Senegal	-.14

Interestingly, when individual correlations are computed (see Table 13-6), the highest correlations are between the Dutch-Yugoslavian mothers followed by the American-Dutch, and American-Yugoslavian. The two African cultures show little relationship to one another (they are from widely different parts of the African continent), and their correlations with the three Western groups are moderately low. Thus, even in the midst of invariance there are variances, which if we knew more about the specific cultures we could explain.

The detailed interaction data would seem to support the belief that young infants and their mothers (substitute care-givers in some cases) interact in some predictable and invariant manner. For example, in all cultures sampled, both mother and infant use vocalization behavior as a response to and elicitor of the other's behavior. Infant smile is almost always a response to a maternal behavior, and fret/cry is almost always an elicitor of rather than a response to maternal behavior. Across all cultures, maternal smile and play occur infrequently, while hold and look are relatively frequent. These are just some examples of the invariances. Closer inspection with data more sensitive to mother-infant inter-action would, no doubt, reveal much more. This is not surprising, since the needs of the human infant and the abilities of the human mother should be universal. That there is relatively great *similarity* in the infant-mother relation-ship in the face of such cultural *divergence* suggests several possible conclusions.

First, one might conclude that because there are relatively few measurable differences in different cultures' modes of behavior toward their infants, what happens in infancy may not be relevant for subsequent adaption to the cultural values. While we do not necessarily believe this to be the case, increasing evidence suggests that little individual stability in intellectual functioning, at least as measured by conventional psychometric instruments, exists in the opening years (Lewis, 1973; Lewis & McGurk, 1972) and that there is relatively little consistency between birth and two years in terms of temperament variables (Bell, Weller & Waldrop, 1971).

An alternative hypothesis is that we have not observed the proper variables. In the first and simplest case, the behaviors most of us have been studying may have been a poor guess as to the variables really affecting subsequent infant development. In the second case, these may have been improper variables, because we have looked at behavior rather than belief systems. Thus, even if the behaviors observed show no differences, the beliefs and values underlying them might still produce differential outcomes. Implied here is that total cultural context is more important than isolated behaviors, and that the absence of either books or the time to read to the child (behaviors we measure and think important) tells us little about the cognitive and motivational thirsts for knowledge. These latter may be instilled without immediately obvious behavioral manifestations, thus resulting in the mismatch between behavior and outcome and the match between belief systems and outcome. Further, it may be necessary to explore the quality of the behaviors rather than their occurrence as a frequency or as a response. The quality of the behaviors may be different in different settings, e.g., what type of "holding" is going on? It may be the case that holding in the arms is quite different depending on its embeddedness in other simultaneous behaviors. Holding and vocalization may be a "different" type of holding than holding and reading a book.

Finally, these results suggest that we may do well to turn our attention to the invariances in infants' social-emotional as well as cognitive worlds. One research strategy would be to determine in what respects people (in this case children) are alike and how the human condition, like the world we live in, imposes certain types of invariances, the meanings of which manifest themselves differentially, depending on the context in which they occur.

REFERENCES

Bell, R. Q., Weller, G. M., & Waldrop, M. F. Newborn and preschooler: Organization of behavior and relations between periods. Monographs of the Society for Research in Child Development, 1971, 36 (1-2), Serial No. 142.

Goldberg, S. Infant care in Zambia: Measuring maternal behaviour (Human Development Research Unit Report 13). University of Zambia, 1970.

Hollingshead, A. B. Two-factor index of social position. New Haven, Conn.: Author, 1957.

Lewis, M. State as an infant-environment interaction: An analysis of mother-infant interaction as a function of sex. Merrill-Palmer Quarterly, 1972, 18, 95-121.

Lewis, M.   Infant intelligence tests: Their use and misuse. Human Development, 1973, 16, 108-118.

Lewis, M., & Freedle, R.   Mother-infant dyad: The cradle of meaning.   In P. Pliner, L. Krames, & T. Alloway (Eds.), Communication and affect: Language and thought.   New York: Academic Press, 1973.

Lewis, M., & Freedle, R.   The mother and infant communication system: The effects of poverty.   Paper presented at a symposium, Ecology and Social Class: Socialization, Cognitive and Language Development, at the Biennial Conference of the International Society for the Study of Behavioral Development, Surrey, England, July 1975.

Lewis, M., & Goldberg, S.   Perceptual-cognitive development in infancy: A generalized expectancy model as a function of the mother-infant interaction.   Merrill-Palmer Quarterly, 1969, 15, 81-100.

Lewis, M., & Lee-Painter, S.   An interactional approach to the mother-infant dyad.   In M. Lewis & L. Rosenblaum (Eds.), The effect of the infant on its caregiver: The origins of behavior, Vol. 1.   New York: Wiley, 1973.

Lewis, M., & McGurk, H.   The evaluation of infant intelligence: Infant intelligence scores--true or false?   Science, 1972, 178, 1174-1177.

Lewis, M., & Wilson, C. D.   Infant development in lower-class American families.   Human Development, 1972, 15, 112-127.

Looft, W. R.   The psychology of more.   American Psychologist, 1971, 26, 561-565.

Lusk, D., & Lewis, M.   Mother-infant interaction and infant development among the Wolof of Senegal.   Human Development, 1972, 15, 58-69.

Rebelsky, F., & Abeles, G.   Infancy in Holland and the United States.   Paper presented at the meeting of the Society for Research in Child Development, Santa Monica, California, March 1969.

Chapter 14
Biological Variations and Cultural Diversity: An Exploratory Study

Peter H. Wolff

Children's Hospital
Boston, Massachusetts

Extensive field observations and controlled comparisons of development in different cultures have led anthropology to the conclusion that behavioral differences across mating populations are overwhelmingly determined by environmental factors--by climate and food sources, historical accident, socioeconomic forces, child-rearing practices, and the like (Morgan, 1877; Kroeber, 1939; Murdock, 1959; Erikson, 1950; Mead, 1940; Whiting, 1964; Kluckhohn, 1962). The contribution of biological (genetic) factors to cultural differences has either not been considered or else has been dismissed as being of trivial consequence. The infant's capacity to adapt to nearly all stable cultures and acquire any natural language, the dearth of empirical evidence for a genetic determination of behavioral differences across groups, and a natural reluctance to assume that human populations are destined by heredity to develop along fixed lines, have conspired to

---

*

Work for this presentation was completed while the author was supported by a Career Scientist Award MHK-3461 from the National Institute of Mental Health, and the Children's Hospital Medical Center Mental Retardation and Human Development Research Program (HD 03-0773).

preserve the view that cultural diversity is determined exclusively by environmental factors, and that intrinsic group differences in behavior are not a fruitful domain of anthropological inquiry.

Having discarded the notion of immutable racial "types" for a rational formulation of population gradients, physical anthropology was free to explore the Mendelian patterns of inheritance for discrete physiological and morphological variables (see, for example, Mayr, 1970; Makela, Eriksan, & Lehtovaara, 1959; Mourant, 1954; Race & Sanger, 1968; Kretschmer, Hurwitz, Ransome-Kuti, & Dungy, 1971). Such trait comparisons have generally been devoid of political connotations, and do not lend themselves to odious value judgements. The member of one mating group is not likely to be offended by the observation that a particular haptoglobin fraction is represented less frequently among his peers than in other groups; nor are such differences likely to be misused for political and economic exploitation. Yet biological variations across mating groups having more direct implications for behavior and psychological development are generally viewed with skepticism and suspicion, or condemned as socially undesirable, and therefore understandably avoided. The claim that cultural differences can be explained exhaustively by environmental factors therefore remains, in effect, untested.

Major advances in behavior genetics have traditionally come from controlled breeding experiments on subhuman species. While the findings of such studies are important in their own right, their relevance for the analysis of intrinsic differences across human cultures has been slight. In place of controlled breeding experiments, human behavior genetics has acquired most of its information from family pedigrees and cotwin comparisons, which have revealed an array of isolated traits under greater or lesser genetic control (for reviews, see Fuller & Thompson, 1960; Garn, 1965; Alland, 1967). The comparison of identical twins reared apart and reared together has extended the domain of behavior genetics to include personality characteristics and mental diseases once assumed to be exclusively under environmental control (see, for example, Shields, 1962; Gottesman, 1963). Yet family pedigrees and twin comparisons have contributed little to our understanding of biological variations in behavior across mating groups. Selective breeding by sexual selection and geographic isolation should in principle serve as imperfect human analogues to artificial breeding experiments, and permit a partial analysis of genetic factors contributing to human psychological development. For reasons not inherent to the problem itself, such comparisons have rarely been made, so that

only a few variables of biological origin contributing to
group behavioral differences have been isolated, and we do
not know how many others may exist.

If behavioral diversity across human groups were as
powerfully determined by environmental factors as the available
evidence suggests, one might well question the wisdom of
pursuing empirical observations that are likely to harbor a
potential for social abuse (Chomsky, 1973). Yet an ethical
case could also be made for the pursuit of studies identifying
mating group differences, and against the dangerous premise
that individuals or groups of individuals must be the same in
order to be equal. Rather than continuing to avoid the issue
of behavioral differences across relatively isolated populations,
we may have to come to terms with the probability that they
exist, exposing false claims of difference on scientific grounds
rather than by egalitarian rhetoric, distinguishing biological
identity from the principle of social equality, and working
toward a social structure in which all human groups are equal
regardless of, or perhaps even because of, their intrinsic
differences (Von Humboldt, [1793] 1903; Dobzhansky, 1962, 1972).
If social equality depended on genetic identity, only monozygotic
twins would be equal; and even they are very often different at
birth (Inouye, 1961). If equality among culturally diverse
groups depended on their biological identity, then cooperation
among nations for their mutual survival would come into question
each time a biological difference with behavioral implications
were discovered (see, for example, Guttman, 1963; Spuhler &
Lindzey, 1967; Freedman, 1971). One might therefore draw the
alternative conclusion that we should proceed with a systematic
description of human subgroup differences, in order to guarantee
their equality, and in the home that enough differences will be
identified so that one day no single trait or set of traits can
any longer serve as a basis for erroneous typological classification, ideological excess, or political persecutions; so that
children can grow up with a genuine acceptance of biological
variations without drawing the traditional conclusion that some
groups are better than others or that equality depends on
identity.

A comparison of vasomotor responses to alcohol in Caucasoid
and Mongoloid populations will certainly not bring us much
closer to such a Utopian social structure. Yet it was necessary
to begin somewhere; I selected a trait for study that could be
analyzed objectively and quantitatively, a trait which
differentiated clearly between two major mating populations,
even if its relevance for behavioral development was not
immediately apparent.

Travelers to the Far East have frequently observed that Mongoloid Asians flush bright red after drinking small quantities of alcohol (Kalow, 1962). Having made the same observations during an extended stay in Japan, and having seen the same phenomenon repeatedly during briefer visits to Taiwan, Korea, and Viet Nam, I was intrigued by the possibility that these surface differences might reflect a physiological variation across mating groups that would have broader implications for behavioral development. Anecdotal reports by Asian colleagues indicated that the alcohol flushing response is a complex event, and that its indirect effects on behavior may extend beyond alcohol flushing. Women with a flushing trait, for example, were reluctant to volunteer, because the alcohol flush was a source of embarrassment to them; among those who volunteered and blushed heavily, several stayed away from work for hours until the flush had subsided. Many individuals reported that they usually avoided drinking in public, so that they would not be seen with a bright red face.

Japanese and Chinese culture distinguishes individuals who turn red from those who turn "blue" after drinking. Folklore associates turning red with a happy disposition, whereas turning "blue" is said to reflect a morose aggressiveness and a strong stomach for alcohol. I did not examine the association between temperament and vasomotor response to alcohol, but tested a few Mongoloid subjects who were known to "turn blue" to alcohol.

Some subjects complained of an "allergy" to alcohol; among these, a few reacted to drinking beer or whiskey with flat red blotches of the face, arms, and abdomen that persisted long after the facial flush had receded. The allergic response was more pronounced to certain kinds of commercial alcoholic beverages (beer and unfortified wine) than to dilute ethanol, and may have been a direct response to distillation or fermentation products other than ethanol (Harger & Hulpieu, 1956).

Among Mongoloid subjects who turned bright red soon after starting to drink, there were several who reported that they could drink large amounts of alcohol without becoming ill. I had opportunity to observe some of these individuals while they were drinking in a social context and to confirm their claims for a considerable alcohol tolerance. Such a tolerance in sensitive individuals suggests that flushing is probably not a mild form of the "acetaldehyde syndrome" (Goodman & Gilman, 1970).

THE STUDY

The findings of this report are based on a comparison of
flushing responses in American-born Caucasoid adults and
infants, and adults and infants of the Mongoloid major mating
population (Garn, 1965). The experimental group included:
(1) Japanese adults and newborn infants born, raised, and
tested in Japan; Taiwan Chinese adults and infants born,
raised, and tested in Taiwan, and adults raised on the Chinese
mainland; Korean adults born, raised, and tested in Korea;
(2) American-born and -reared adults of Chinese or Japanese
parents who were raised primarily on Western diets; (3)
adult "Amerasians" or Caucasoid-Mongoloid parents who were
raised in the United States on American diets; and (4) American
Indian adults of the Eastern Cree nation. On a questionnaire,
most Asian Mongoloids reported that they drank rarely or not at
all in social circumstances, but a small subgroup reported
drinking regularly and in relatively large amounts. The
American Indian group included individuals who were accustomed
to drinking large amounts of alcohol (beer or wine) as well as
individuals who rarely if ever drank.

The control group consisted of American-born Caucasoids
whose parents were second- to fifth-generation immigrants from
Western and Eastern European countries (Scandinavia, Germany,
England, Scotland, Ireland, Italy, Yugoslavia, and Poland).
Caucasoids in the habit of drinking moderate or large amounts
of alcohol were excluded from the sample; there were no
statistical differences in mean alcohol consumption between
Caucasoid and Mongoloid groups.

In the early phase of the study, adult subjects were
given ethanol in the form of commercial alcohol beverages;
infants received small quantities of fortified wine in 5
percent glucose and water, adjusted for body weight. To
control for the effect of fermentation or distillation products
other than ethanol, later groups were given an equivalent
amount of alcohol as 95 percent ethanol in orange juice.
Caucasoids were always given 35 to 50 percent more alcohol per
body weight than comparable Mongoloid groups, to control for
minor variations in the dose-response curves.

The flushing response was recorded from a transillumination
densitometer (ear oxymeter) and measured as changes in optical
density of the earlobe. The incidence and relative intensity
of flushing were also noted by visual inspection. The densitometer was modified by a Wratten filter with a peak light transmission at 805 mu (the isosbestic point for reduced hemoglobin

and oxyhemoglobin), so that deviations from baseline
reflected changes in total blood volume, regardless of blood
oxygen saturation (see Figure 14-1). Objectively measured
increases in optical density always preceded visible flushing;
and some individuals responded only to the change in optical
density and had not visible flush.

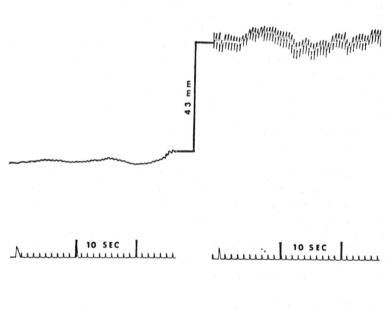

a   b

Figure 14.1.   Increase of optical denisty and pulse
pressure in earlobe after alcohol ingestion, in a Chinese
adult male: (a)   baseline recording; optical density begins
to increase 80 seconds after completion of drinking;   (b)
after 8 minutes, relative optical density has increased by
43 mm.   Changes in pulse pressure are indicated by an
increase in phasic excursions of the channel registering
optical density.

Pulse pressure changes were recorded from the same densitometer and measured as changes in the relative width of periodic excursions made by the recording pen (see Figure 14-1). The pulse pressure oscillations measured from the earlobe were phase-correlated with heart rate measured by EKG, as well as with pulse rate measured by finger plethysomograph. Skin temperature changes were measured on the forehead, cheek, and inner surfaces of the lower arm by thermistor. Once the baseline recording of physiological parameters had stabilized, individuals were asked to drink the measured amount of alcohol as quickly as possible within limits of comfort; recording was continued for 45 minutes after the subjects had completed drinking the test dose. Throughout the trial, adults were asked to report changes in bodily sensations that might be associated with drinking.

Of infants and adults of Mongoloid groups living in Japan, Taiwan, or Korea, 70 to 80 percent showed an increase in optical density of the earlobe and flushed visibly to inspection within 3 to 7 minutes after ingesting small amounts of alcohol (0.14 to 0.30 ml/kg body weight); another 15 percent of Mongoloids showed no measurable vasomotor response of the facial vessels, whereas five Mongoloids showed a vasomotor *constriction* of the facial vessels. American-born half-Caucasoid/half-Mongoloids and one-quarter-Mongoloid/three-quarter-Caucasoid hybrids flushed with the same frequency and intensity as pure Mongoloids and showed a similar increase of facial temperature and measured pulse pressure.

Of Caucasoid infants and adults, 85 percent showed no detectable vasomotor changes after drinking significantly larger amounts of alcohol than Mongoloids (0.36 to 0.46 ml/kg body weight). Less than 10 percent of Caucasoids responded with a measurable increase of optical density in the earlobe, and a slight change in pulse pressure; and only three of these showed a definite facial flush. Two individuals responded to alcohol with a measurable vasomotor constriction. Mating group differences in vasomotor response to alcohol was statistically significant for each comparison between the Caucasoid and one of the several Mongoloid populations (see Tables 41-1 and 14-2).

An increase of optical density in the earlobe was correlated with an increase in pulse pressure ($r_s = 0.76$) $p < .01$; See also Figure 14-1); and racial differences in pulse pressure changes to alcohol were significant ($X^2 = 11.4$, $p < .001$). The increase of optical density

TABLE 14-1. Flushing responses and increases of optical density and pulse pressure in the earlobe, after ingestion of alcohol.

Group	Sample Size (No.)	Visible Flushing (No.)	Optical Density Increase < 5 mm (No.)	Optical Density Mean Increase for Total (mm)	Pulse Pressure Measureable Increase (No.)	Pulse Pressure Mean Increase for Total (%)
Caucasoid						
Adults	34	1	2	1.1	1(?)	5(?)
Infants	20	1	1	1.7	0	
Japanese						
Adults	38	32[a]	34[a]	36.8+	33[a]	257
Infants	25	17[a]	17[a]	16.8+	9	
Taiwanese						
Adults	24	19[a]	20[a]	37.7+	19[a]	246
Infants	10	9[a]	9[a]	14.6+	4	
Korean						
Adults	20	14[a]	10[ab]	17.4+[b]	9[ab]	161

NOTE: In each case, the Caucasoid population is compared to a corresponding Mongoloid group.

[a] Ethnic group differences are significant at *p* < .001, chi-square test; +*p* < .001, *t*-test;

[b] The records of six Korean subjects could not be analyzed reliably because of line-voltage disturbances.

TABLE 14-2. Vasomotor responses to alcohol in various Mongoloid populations.

	Sample Size (No.)	Visible Flushing (No.)	Optical Density		Pulse Pressure		Mean Temperature Increase for cheek (%)
			Increase < 5 mm (No.)	Mean Increase for Total (mm)	Measureable Increase (No.)	Mean Increase for Total (%)	
Caucasoids	50	2	3	4	1	3	0.1
Americans of pure Mongoloid ancestry	15	12[a]	13[a]	64[c]	13[d]	280[c]	1.6[c]
Americans of half-Caucasoid/half-Mongoloid ancestry	20	18[a]	18[a]	59[c]	18[a]	304[c]	2.2[c]
Americans of 1/4 Mongoloid 3/4 Caucasoid ancestry	4	3	3	43	3	160	1.8
American Indian	30	15[a]	22[a]	20.1[c]	23	98.0[c]	+1.21[c]
a. Making no or little use of alcohol	17	9	15[b]	25.0[c]	13	152[c]	+1.6
b. Making frequent use of alcohol	13	6	7[b]	9.2[c]	7	25[c]	+0.7

NOTE: In each case, the Mongoloid or mixed group is compared to the Caucasoid group. Group differences between "pure" and "half-Mongoloids" are not statistically significant. Since facial flushing could not be observed directly in Indians with a dark skin, the number of individuals with a visible flush is lower than the number of individuals showing an increase of optical density or pulse pressure.

[a] Group differences are significant at $p < .001$.   [b] $p < .05$, by chi-square test.

[c] $p < .001$ by t-test.

in the earlobe was associated with an expectable increase of skin temperature on the forehead and cheek ($r_s = 0.74$, $p < .001$), but not with temperature changes on the lower forearm.

Many Mongoloid adults reported a variety of dysphoric symptoms, including pounding in the head, sleepiness, numbness, headache, muscle weakness, and motor instability, that were rarely reported by the Caucasoids, who had consumed larger doses of alcohol (see Table 14-3).

TABLE 14-3. Subjective symptoms after alcohol consumption in Caucasoid and Mongoloid adults.

Symptom	Group			
	Caucasoid ($N = 34$)		Mongoloid ($N = 78$)	
	%	No.	%	No.
Hot in stomach	5.8	2	52.5[a]	41
Palpitations	0	-	25.7[a]	20
Tachycardia	2.9	1	43.5[a]	34
Muscle weakness	2.9	1	25.7[b]	20
Dizzy	8.6	3	37.2[b]	24
Sleepy	5.8	2	33.4[b]	26
Falls asleep	0	-	18.0[b]	4

[a] $p < .001$

[b] $p < .01$

American Indians reacted to the test dose of alcohol like Asian Mongoloids and unlike American Caucasoids. Prior drinking experience attenuated, but did not suppress, the flushing response in the Indian group. Indians with a history of habitual drinking flushed less than Indians who never drank, but still responded significantly more often and more intensely than Caucasoid nondrinkers. It was impossible to infer the causal relation between prior drinking experience and intensity of flushing from these observations. Relatively insensitive individuals might, for example, be less reluctant to drink and therefore report a more extensive drinking history; habitual drinkers, on the other hand, might have developed a pharmacodynamic tolerance to ethanol (Isbell, Fraser, Wikler, Belleville, & Eisenman, 1955; Mendelson, Stein, & Mello, 1965). Some Asian Mongoloid adults without the alcohol flush reported that they liked to drink and that drinking had never caused them any discomfort; some individuals with an intense alcohol flush who had drunk moderately or heavily for a number of years had noticed no change in the intensity of their response, whereas others had observed a gradual attenuation of the flushing reaction after the occasional or frequent use of alcohol over a number of years.

Five Asian individuals who responded to the usual test dose of alcohol with a measureable vasomotor constriction (turning "blue") were also asked to drink larger amounts of ethanol. Three of them continued to respond with a vasomotor constriction after drinking two or three times the usual test does; and all three reported that one or both of their parents "turned blue" to alcohol. The other two turned bright red after drinking twice the test dose that had produced a vasomotor constriction, and showed a vasodilatation in the earlobe and a rise of temperature in the face. Although the paradoxical response of "turning blue" to alcohol was observed in only a small sample, its occurrence strengthens the suspicion that the automatic nervous system contributes to the facial vascular response to alcohol. It suggests that group differences in response cannot be attributed exclusively to variations in levels of circulating alcohol, differences in rates of alcohol metabolism, or variations in levels of the circulating products of ethanol metabolism.

My studies on alcohol flushing (see Wolff, 1972, 1973), anecdotal observations by others (Kalow, 1962), and a recent replication by Ewing, Rouse, & Pellizzani, (1974) indicate that Caucasoids and Mongoloids differ in their vasomotor sensitivity to alcohol, and that the group differences are independent of geographic boundary or previous exposure to alcohol. The persistence of the flushing response among first- and second-generation Mongoloid-Caucasoid hybrids further suggests that the flushing response is associated with a genetic variation, although the mechanism of transmission remains for the present unknown.

One parsimonious biological explanation for the phenomenon would attribute the group variations to a quantitative difference in one or more enzyme for alcohol metabolism. Fenna, Mix, Schaeter, & Gilbert (1971) have reported that American Indians and Eskimos metabolize alcohol more slowly than do Caucasoids. Ewing, Rouse, & Pellizzani (1974) were unable to replicate this observation, and offered the alternative hypothesis that Mongoloids and Caucasoids differ in rates of acetaldehyde metabolism, even though they were not able to demonstrate statistically significant mean differences in blood acetaldehyde levels in Caucasoids and Mongoloids after drinking. To date, no one has observed differences in rates of alcohol absorption from the gastrointestinal tract between American Indians and Caucasoids (Fenna *et al.*, 1971). Delayed rates of alcohol metabolism would also not account for the group differences in vasomotor flushing response, since these became apparent within 3 to 5 minutes after the start of drinking, and within 40 to 70 seconds after the start of intravenous alcohol infusion (Wolff, 1973). If the facial flushing to alcohol of Mongoloids were a function of acetaldehyde retention (for example, because of an "acetaldehydase deficiency"), one would expect sensitive individuals to respond with dynamic respiratory difficulties, nausea, copious vomiting, sweating, etc., whenever they drank alcohol in significant quantities. Although many Asian Mongoloids experienced some unpleasant side-effects from drinking the test does, none complained of such dramatic symptoms. Moreover, some who flushed intensely were nevertheless able to drink large amounts of alcohol without becoming ill.

Alternatively, one might attribute the observed differences to group variations in autonomic nervous system sensitivity to alcohol. Garn (1965) has suggested that the domain most likely to reveal racial differences in behavior would somehow be related to the autonomic nervous system. His inference is based on reports of racial variations in vasomotor reactivity to heat and cold (Mechan, 1955; Wyndham & Morrison, 1958; Hammel, Elsner, LeMessurier, Anderson, & Milan, 1959; Elsner, Nelms, & Irving, 1960); variations in response to autonomic drugs such as atropine and physostigmine (Chen & Poth, 1932; Scott, 1945); and variations in the galvanic skin response (Malmo, 1965; Lazarus, Tomita, Opton, & Kodama, 1966; Kugelmass & Lieblish, 1968).

Central nervous system depression of sympathetic vasomotor centers has generally been proposed as the mechanism responsible for vasodilatation of the facial skin vessels after alcohol ingestion (Goodman & Gilman, 1970; Whelan, 1967). Vasomotor control of the skin vessels, however, varies greatly over different areas of the body surface, and at least three distinct mechanisms of vasomotor control have been described (Hertzman, 1950). Most skin vessels of the limbs and trunk are supplied by sympathetic adrenergic vasoconstrictor fibers, whereas parasympathetic cholinergic fibers play either no or only a negligible role (Hertzman, 1950; White, Smithwick, & Simeone, 1952; Whelan, 1967). The facial skin is supplied primarily by adrenergic vasoconstrictor fibers from the cervical sympathetic ganglia; it may also be provided with cholinergic fibers but their origin and function remain obscure (White, Smithwick, & Simeone, 1952; Wertheimer, Redisch, Hirschhorn, & Steele, 1955; Mitchell, 1956; Hamilton, 1956). Sympatholytic agents and ganglionic blockers that raise the skin temperature of the toes, fingers, and trunk have little or no effect on the face. Exposure to cold and heat produces marked temperature changes in the fingers and toes, but has no effect on the forehead or cheek. Adrenolytic and ganglionic blocking agents that raise the skin temperature of the arms and legs (e.g., methyl amonium chloride, hexymethyl dibenzolate) do not affect the temperature of the facial skin. Agents that lower the temperature of the facial region do not influence the peripheral skin, whereas locally acting drugs like histamine and nicotinic acid raise the facial temperature but do not affect the skin temperature over the rest of the body surface (Wertheimer *et al.* 1955).

In view of an apparent specialization in vasomotor control over the facial skin, and the restriction of the alcohol flush to the same area, I speculated that the mating group differences in alcohol flushing might be associated with specific variations in the vasomoter control of the "blush" skin, and began to explore the effect of autonomic drugs on the alcohol flush. To date, only the effects of atropine sulfate on the alcohol flushing response have been tested systematically.

Sixteen Mongoloid adults with a demonstrated flush and 8 Caucasoids, 3 of whom flushed, were given 1 mg of atropine sulfate by mouth one hour before the alcohol test and two hours after the last meal. All subjects had a dry mouth just before starting to drink the alcohol. Nineteen of 24 subjects (13 of 16 Monoloids, 5 of 8 Caucasoids, including 2 who flushed to alcohol) showed a significant increase in facial flushing after atropine sulfate premedication (X^2 = 8.6, $p < .01$). The potentiating effect of atropine was inversely related to the intensity of alcohol flushing without atropine medication (r_s = .85, $p < .01$). The three Mongoloid subjects with the most intense alcohol flush (without atropine)

had a *diminished* response to the combination of atropine and
alcohol, whereas the three individuals with a vasoconstrictor
response to alcohol alone had a visible flush and a measureable
increase of optical density. Test-retest comparisons of the
flushing response to alcohol alone had shown that the intensity
of flushing was a stable characteristic of the individual, and
that a "regression to the mean" would not account for the
observed effect of atropine premedication.

Atropine also modified the alcohol effect in pulse pressure
although the results are difficult to interpret, since atropine
depressed baseline values of pulse pressure before alcohol
ingestion (p = .005), and reduced the absolute increase in
pulse pressure after alcohol ingestion   (p < .05); thus the
ratio in changes of pulse pressure relative to baseline was
increased (X^2 = 7.56, p < .01). Changes in facial skin
temperature in response to alcohol ingestion were not affected
by atropine, but atropine modified the temperature response of
the peripheral skin. Without atropine premedication, alcohol
raised the temperature by 0.21° F; with atropine premedication
however, alcohol caused a decrease in temperature of 1.27° F.
The modifying effect of atropine on the peripheral skin (forearm) with alcohol ingestion was statistically significant, both
in Mongoloid and Caucasoid individuals (t = 3.41, t = 2.87,
p < .01). A number of subjects in both groups complained of
feeling cold within 15 minutes after drinking when they had
been premedicated with atropine, but not after alcohol alone.

I can offer no satisfactory explanation of these results
until other autonomic drugs have been tested thoroughly. If
current information about the central depressing effects of
alcohol on vasomotor centers is valid, atropine sulfate should
not alter the response to alcohol. If the alcohol flush were
a mild acetaldehyde response, there should also be no effect
from atropine. If the cholinergic vasodilator fibers to the
facial region are functional, atropine should partially
inhibit the flushing response. The possibility that atropine
would potentiate the alcohol flush was not considered, since
there is, to my knowledge, no evidence that the facial skin
is innervated by cholinergic vasoconstrictor fibers.

The traditional classification of the autonomic nervous
system by its two sympathetic and parasympathetic functions
is probably an oversimplified model of actual circumstances
that does not adequately account for a number of contradictory
findings. Yet the autonomic nervous system appears to
contribute directly or indirectly to the alcohol flushing
response, without, however, excluding a parallel contribution

of metabolic factors to racial differences in the alcohol
flushing response.

A qualitatively different form of vasodilatation that is
clearly mediated by central neural pathways is the blushing
response to emotional stimulii. Since this uniquely human
affect expression is among the most difficult to hide from
others, it is surprising that almost no new information has
been added to the phenomenology of blushing since the time
of Darwin's classic description in 1873. While emotional
blushing and alcohol flushing are similar in appearance when
they are fully expressed, their patterns of onset and waning
differ sufficiently to suggest that they are by no means
homologous. Alcohol flushing is first seen in the soft
tissues around the eyes, where it adds the characteristic
appearance of red circles; from there the flush spreads
slowly to the cheeks, the ears, the forehead and the neck
over a period of 5 to 15 minutes. The alcohol flush lasts
for at least an hour and the red circles may persist for
several hours after the rest of the face has returned to
normal. Emotional blushing usually begins in the neck or
cheek regions, and then spreads and vanishes very rapidly.
Darwin's original description and clinical observations
indicate that the topography of emotional blushing differs
significantly from the pattern of alcohol flushing, and that
it may be mediated by different peripheral neural pathways.

Many more Mongoloid than Caucasoid subjects blushed when
I asked for "innocuous" biographical information, but it is
difficult to assess the meaning of such differences, since
the questions and the context in which they were asked may
have had qualitatively different connotations for the two
groups. The concordance between blushing and alcohol flushing
was striking enough, however, so that each subject was asked
to estimate his or her general tendency to blush in
embarrassing or shameful situations. "Pure" Asian Mongoloids
reported a predisposition to blushing more often than
Caucasoids, but the differences were not statistically
significant $(X^2 = 2.29;\ p > .10)$; American-born Mongoloid-
Caucasoid hybrids reported blushing more frequently than
Caucasoid Americans $(X^2 = 8.3;\ p < .01)$, and American
Indians did not differ from Caucasoids. When the groups were
divided by sex, males in each Mongoloid group (Asian-born
Chinese, Japanese, or Koreans; American-born Chinese and
Japanese; Caucasoid-Mongoloid hybrids; or American Indians)
reported a predisposition to blushing in embarrassing
situations more frequently than males in the Caucasoid group;

and for each comparison of male groups, the differences were statistically significant (from $p < .01$, to $p < .001$), whereas there were no racial differences in the tendency to blush among females. Caucasoid females blushed more often than males $(X^2 = 4.4,\ p < .05)$, and no such sex differences were noted in the Mongoloid or hybrid subgroups.

Since a subject's assessment of his or her tendency to blush may not reflect the actual predisposition accurately, I felt it would be desirable to test the blushing trait more rigorously. Objective methods for provoking a blush that have cross-cultural validity are difficult to formulate. Yet it is common-sense knowledge, I believe, that individuals who tend to blush under natural circumstances will also do so with reasonable predictability when attention is called to this trait. As an experimental stimulus to provoke facial blushing, I therefore asked subjects pointed questions about their blushing while they were being tested before the ingestion of alcohol.

Seventeen of 19 subjects who had reported a tendency to blush also responded to the provocative question with an increase in optical density of the earlobe and they blushed visibly. Nine of the 11 individuals who had reported that they never or rarely blushed also had no measureable vasomotor response to the provocative question. The high concordance between subjective reports and objective measures of blushing $(X^2 = 10.93,\ p > .001)$ suggests that people are able to accurately report their predisposition to blush.

In pure Mongoloids as well as hybrid groups, there was an association of alcohol flushing with measured emotional blushing $(X^2 = 8.75,\ p < .01;\ X^2 = 9.4,\ p < .01,$ respectively), as well as with reported blushing $(X^2 = 12.8,$ $p < .001)$. The number of Caucasoids who flushed to alcohol was too small to determine the association of their alcohol flushing with emotional blushing.

The close association between the two forms of vasomotor dilatation in the face might therefore be adduced as partial evidence of autonomic control over alcohol flushing. The association between the two phenomena, however, was demonstrated statistically and does not take the exceptions into account. Two Caucasoid individuals with pathological blushing ("erythrophobia"), examined in the same manner, showed marked fluctuations of optical density in the earlobe to psychic stress as well as marked lability of other autonomic responses, but did not flush to alcohol. Some subjects who flushed intensely to alcohol did not blush to psychic stress, whereas others blushed dramatically to psychological provocation but failed to flush to alcohol. These observations do not permit any firm conclusion about specific mechanisms but they are compatible with the assumption of an intrinsic difference in vasomotor lability across relatively isolated mating populations that codetermines variations in facial flushing to both psychological and pharmacological provocation. Since most societies that have been identified as "shame cultures" (Benedict, 1934; Piers & Singer, 1953) belong to the Mongoloid major mating population, one might further speculate that a lowered threshold for autonomic activation of the facial skin vessels will on one hand influence the drinking patterns of a culture, and on the other contribute to the biobehavioral expression a society will choose as the preferred mode for exercising social sanctions. An implicit awareness of a biological variation might in this way be incorporated into a culture's value systems and social controls.

One obvious and facile extrapolation from the observations reported here would assume a direct cause-and-effect relation between vasomotor sensitivity and the prevalence of alcoholism. Subjects who flushed to alcohol reported dysphoric bodily symptoms after drinking. It has been reported that Mogoloids may need less alcohol than Caucasoids to achieve the same level of intoxication. Japanese road traffic laws in fact specify a blood alcohol concentration of 0.5 mg percent as *prima facie* evidence of driving under the influence, whereas the level specified by U.S. traffic laws is three times as high (Iribe, 1968; National Safety Council, 1954). Even if traffic laws were a valid reflection of group differences in alcohol tolerance rather than of variations in concern for public safety, and even if it could be demonstrated that Mongoloids do not "hold their liquor" as well as Caucasoids, such differences contribute very little to our understanding of a biological predisposition to alcoholism. Yet this unwarranted conclusion has been drawn from the limited evidence on group differences in vasomotor flushing to alcohol.

If group differences in vasomotor flushing are at all pertinent to the biology of alcoholism, the effect will almost certainly prove to be indirect, and demonstrable only in relation to prevailing social conditions. In Japan, for example, pathological drinking was rare before the Second World War, even though drinking to excess on designated occasions was not only tolerated but encouraged by local tradition (Sargent, 1967). With the rapid economic reconstruction of Japan along American lines, and the radical social changes that followed after the occupation in 1945 (Caudill, 1962; Ishino, 1962; Vogel, 1963), alcoholism has become a psychiatric problem of major proportions. By 1964, Japan had one of the highest rates of alcoholism in the world, and 15 percent of all psychiatric hospital admissions were for alcoholism (Sargent, 1967).

Among the Chinese and Taiwanese populations of Taiwan, at most ten cases of chronic alcoholism were reported during the 17 years up to 1963, whereas the "true" aborigines of Taiwan, who are a disenfranchised minority of Southern Mongoloid extraction (Chai, 1967), are said to have a significant problem of alcoholism (Chafetz, 1964). In Thailand, alcoholism has increased from a low baseline at an alarming rate (Chafetz, 1964), since large numbers of foreign troops were stationed in that country and imported an excess of foreign capital and alien values. The incidence of pathological drinking among American Indians before the arrival of the white man is not well documented; but there is no question that American Indians today suffer one of the highest rates of alcoholism in the world (Dozier, 1966); Eskimos probably did not taste alcohol before they were "civilized", but today the rate of alcoholism is reaching epidemic proportions (Fenna *et al.*, 1971).

Such observations expose the absurdity of any claims for a direct causal relation between a genetic variation in vasomotor sensitivity to alcohol and predisposition to alcoholism. Taiwanese, Chinese, Koreans, Vietnamese, Japanese, and American Indians (and, for inference, probably also Taiwan aborigines, Thai, and Eskimos) all show the same vasomotor sensitivity to alcohol. Yet the prevalence of alcoholism differs greatly in the several cultures, and within a culture it has changed radically with historical circumstances over relatively short periods. An inherent sensitivity to alcohol may, however, interact with the social structure to modify patterns of drinking. In each culture populated primarily by members of the Mongoloid mating group that has shifted rapidly from a low to a high rate of alcoholism, the change occurred at a time when the traditional social structure was undermined by the incursion of alien values. Social disintegration may be a sufficient cause for alcoholism in any society, but an intrinsic vasomotor sensitivity to alcohol may accelerate the process. Within the strictures of a stable culture, the combination of highly visible flushing response and dysphoric symptoms may inhibit uncontrolled drinking as long as the society respects traditional sanctions. When that society is overwhelmed by alien values, the same biological sensitivity that previously protected against alcohol excess may contribute to a rapid increase of uncontrolled drinking and an eventual rise in the rate of clinical alcoholism. If this speculation has any merit, it should alert us to the danger that other Asian groups may be particularly susceptible to clinical alcoholism as they are inundated by Western "values" and as their society disintegrates.

Even if autonomic responsivity proves to be a critical variable for explaining group differences in alcohol sensitivity, the extent information does not justify a typological classification of Caucasoid and Mongoloid groups along a dimension of autonomic stability/lability. Freedman (1971), for example, has observed that Mongoloid infants are less perturbable and more consolable than Caucasoid infants-- in other words, that they are less labile, whereas the observations reported here might suggest that Mongoloids are more labile. Assertions concerning the biological basis of behavioral variations across mating groups must be particularly meticulous when defining the limits of relevance of their behavioral domain; otherwise, a relatively neutral and well-documented observation leads to false extrapolations and eventually to invidious group comparisons.

At the same time, the testable question remains whether mating group differences in facial flushing reflect more extensive differences in autonomic reactivity, and whether those differences influence the ways in which the various cultures direct the development of their children in keeping with an implicit awareness of biological variations.

The autonomic response of newborn infants has been studied in some detail (Lipton, Steinschneider, & Richmond, 1965; Lewis, Kagan, Campbell, & Kalafat, 1966; Steinschneider & Lipton, 1965), but, to my knowledge, there are no systematic cross-cultural comparisons of autonomic function in newborn infants. Freedman's (1971) observations come close, but they were organized in terms of temperamental categories rather than physiological variables and did not measure autonomic nervous system function. Such studies would be of particular interest, since racial differences in autonomic responsivity may provide one important means of exploring the interaction of biology and society in determining cultural differences across relatively isolated mating populations.

The observations I have reported are fragmentary and do not warrant firm conclusions about racial differences in

autonomic nervous system reactivity. Yet, comprehensive
assessment of factors that determine cultural differences must
at least consider the contribution of biological variations.
To identify the rationalize intrinsic differences among
individuals, between sexes, and across mating populations is
all the more important today, when the moral and legal
prerogatives of individuality, and of deviation from an
accepted norm, are threatened by a "scientific psychology"
that hopes to control behavior through psychological and
pharamacological techniques in the hope of shaping us all into
one synthetic homogenate where all will be equal because no
one is anything.

REFERENCES

Alland, H. Evolution and human behavior. New York: Natural
    History Press, 1967.

Benedict, R. Patterns of culture. New York: Houghton-Mifflin,
    1934.

Caudill, W., & Scarr, H. A. Japanese value orientation and
    culture change. Ethnology, 1962, 1, 53-91.

Chafetz, M. E. Consumption of alcohol in the Far and Middle
    East. New England Journal of Medicine,1964, 271,
    297-301.

Chai, C. K. Taiwan aborigines. Cambridge, Mass.: Harvard
    University Press, 1967.

Chen, K. K., & Poth, E. J. Racial differences as illustrated
    by the mydriatic action of cocaine, euphthalmine
    and ephedime. Journal of Pharmacology and Experi-
    mental Therapeutics, 1932, 36, 429-445.

Chomsky, N. For reasons of state. New York: Vintage, 1973.

Darwin, C. The expression of emotion in animals and man.
    London: Murray, 1873.

Dobzhansky, T. Mankind evolving. New Haven, Conn.: Yale
    University Press, 1962.

Dobzhansky, T. Genetics and the races of man. In B. Campbell
    (Ed.), Sexual selection and the descent of man.

Chicago: Aldine, 1972.

Dozier, E. P. Problem drinking among American Indians.
Quarterly Journal of Studies in Alcoholism, 1966,
27, 72-87.

Elsner, R. W., Nelms, J. D., & Irving, L. Circulation of heat
to the hands of Arctic Indians. Journal of Applied
Physiology.

Erikson, E. H. Childhood and society. New York: Norton, 1950.

Ewing, J. A., Rouse, B. A., & Pellizzani, E. D. Alcohol
sensitivity and ethnic background. American Journal
of Psychiatry, 1974, 131, 206-210.

Fenna, D., Mix, L., Schaefer, O., & Gilbert, J. A. L. Ethanol
metabolism in various racial groups. Canadian
Medical Association Journal, 1971, 105, 472-475.

Freedman, D. G. Genetic influences on development of behavior.
In G. B. A. Stoelinga & J. J. Van der Werff ten
Bosch (Eds.), Normal and abnormal development of
behavior. Leiden: Leiden University Press, 1971.

Fuller, J. L., & Thompson, W. R. Behavior genetics. New York:
Wiley, 1960.

Garn, S. M. Human races (2nd ed.) Springfield, III.: Thomas,
1965.

Goodman, L. S., & Gilman, A. The pharmacologic basis of
therapeutics (4th ed.) New York: MacMillan, 1970.

Gottesman, I. I. Heritability of personality: A demonstration.
In G. A. Kimble (Ed.), Psychological monographs:
General and applied (American Philosophical Society)
1963, 77, 1-21.

Guttman, R. A test for a biological basis for correlated
abilities. In E. Goldschmidt (Ed.), The genetics
of migrant and isolated populations. Baltimore, Md.:
Williams and Wilkins, 1963.

Hamilton, W. J. (Ed.) Human anatomy. New York: St. Martin's
Press, 1956.

Hammel, H. T., Elsner, R. W., LeMessurier, D. M., Andersen,

H. T., & Milan, F. A.   Thermal and metabolic responses of the Australian aborigine exposed to moderate cold in summer.   Journal of Applied Physiology, 1959, 14, 605-615.

Harger, R. N. & Hulpieu, H. R.   The pharmacology of alcohol. In G. N. Thompson (Ed.), Alcoholism.   Springfield, III.:   Thomas, 1956.

Hertzman, A. B.   Vasomotor regulation of the cutaneous circulation.   Physiological Reviews, 1950, 39, 280-306.

Inouye, E.   Similarity and dissimilarity of schizophrenia in twins.   Proceedings of the Third World Congress of Psychiatry (Vol. 1).   Toronto: University of Toronto Press, 1961.

Iribe, K.   The standards of intoxication based on the measurement of alcohol in the saliva.   In Japanese-American Conference on Alcohol Medical Studies.   Tokyo: Japan, Ministry of Education, 1968.

Isbell, H., Fraser, H. F., Wikler, A., Belleville, R. E., & Eisenman, A. J.   An experimental study of the etiology of "rum fits" and delirium tremens. Quarterly Journal of Studies in Alcoholism, 1955, 16, 1-33.

Ishino, I.   Social and technological change in rural Japan. In R. J. Smith and R. K. Beardsley (Eds.), Japanese culture: Its development and characteristics. Chicago: Aldine, 1962.

Karlow, W.   Pharmacogenetics.   Philadelphia: Saunders, 1962.

Kluckhohn, C.   Culture and behavior.   New York: Glencoe Free Press, 1962.

Kretchmer, N., Hurwitz, R., Ransome-Kuti, O., & Dungy, C. Intestinal absorption of lactose in Nigerian ethnic groups.   Lancet, 1971 (August 21), 392-395.

Kroeber, A. L.   Cultural and natural areas of native North America.   Berkeley: University of California Press, 1939.

Kugelmass, S., & Lieblich, I.   Relations between ethnic origin and BSR reactivity in psychophysiological detection. Journal of Applied Physiology, 1968, 52, 158-162.

Lazarus, R. S., Tomita, M., Opton, E., & Kodama, M. A. Cross-cultural study of stress-reaction patterns in Japan. Journal of Personality and Social Psychology, 1966.

Lewis, M., Kagan, J., Campbell, H., & Kalafat, J. The cardiac response as correlate of attention in infants. Child Development, 1966, 37, 63-72.

Lipton, E. L., Steinschneider, A., & Richmond, J. B. The autonomic nervous system in early life. New England Journal of Medicine, 1965, 273, 147-152, 201-208.

Makela, O., Erikson, A. W., & Lehtovaara, B. On the inheritance of the haptoglobin serum groups. Acta Genetica et Statistica Medical, 1959, 9, 149-166.

Malmo, R. B. Finger-sweat prints in the differentation of low and high incentive. Psychophysiology, 1965, 1, 231-240.

Mayr, E. Population, species and evolution. Cambridge, Mass.: Harvard University Press, 1970.

Mead, M. Social change and cultural surrogates. Journal of Educational Sociology, 1940, 14, 92-110.

Mechan, J. P. Individual and racial variations in vascular response to a cold stimulus. Military Medicine, 1955, 116, 330-334.

Mendelson, J. H., Stein, S., Mello, N. K., Effects of experimentally induced intoxication on metabolism of ethanol-1-c^{14} in alcoholic subjects. Metabolism, 1965, 14, 1255-1266.

Mitchell, G. A. G. Cardiovascular innervation. London: Livingston, 1956.

Morgan, L. H. Ancient society. New York: Holt, 1877.

Mourant, A. E. The distribution of human blood groups. Oxford: Blackwell, 1954.

Murdock, G. P. Africa. New York: McGraw-Hill, 1959.

National Safety Council, Committee on Tests for Intoxication. 1953 Uses of Chemical Tests for Intoxication. Chicago: National Safety Council, 1954.

Piers, G., & Singer, M. B. Shame and guilt. Springfield, III.: Thomas, 1953.

Race, R. R. & Sanger, R. Blood groups in man. Oxford: Balckwell, 1968.

Sargent, M. J. Changes in Japanese drinking patterns. Quarterly Journal of Studies in Alcoholism, 1967, 28, 709-722.

Scott, J. G. Eyes of West African Negroes. British Ophthalmology, 1945, 29, 12-19.

Shields, J. Monozygotic twins. London: Oxford University Press, 1962.

Spuhler, J., & Lindzey, G. Racial differences in behavior. In J. Hirsch (Ed.), Behavior genetic analysis. New York: McGraw-Hill, 1967.

Steinschneider, A., & Lipton, E. L. Individual differences in autonomic responsivity: Problems of measurement. Psychosomatic Medicine, 1965, 27, 446-456.

Vogel, E. F. Japan's new middle class: The salary man and his family in a Tokyo suburb. Berkeley: University of California Press, 1963.

Von Humboldt, W. Plan einer Vergleichenden Anthropologie (Unpublished fragment, 1793). (Vol. 1). Berlin: Behr, 1903.

Wertheimer, L., Redisch, W., Hirschhorn, K., & Steele, J. M. Patterns of surface temperature response to various agents. Circulation, 1955, 11, 110-114.

Whelan, R. F. Control of peripheral circulation in man. Springfield, III.: Thomas, 1967.

White, J. C., Smithwick, R. H., & Simeone, F. A. The autonomic nervous system. New York: MacMillan, 1952.

Whiting, J. Effects of climate on certain cultural practice. In W. Goodenough (Ed.), Explorations in cultural anthropology: Essays in honor of G. P. Murdock. New York: McGraw-Hill, 1964.

Wolff, P. H.   Ethnic difference in alcohol sensitivity. Science, 1972, 175, 449-450.

Wolff, P. H.   Vasomotor sensitivity to alcohol in diverse Mongoloid populations. American Journal of Human Genetics, 1973, 25, 193-199.

Wyndham, C. H., & Morrison, J. F.   Adjustment to cold of Bushmen in the Kalahari Desert. Journal of Applied Physiology, 1958, 13, 219-225.

B.
Infancy Within Cultures

Chapter 15

Relationship of Infant/Caretaker Interaction, Social Class and Nutritional Status to Developmental Test Performance among Guatemalan Infants

**Robert E. Klein, Robert E. Lasky,
Charles Yarbrough, and Jean-Pierre Habicht**

Institute of Nutrition of Central America and Panama

and

Martha Julia Sellers

Harvard University

The data discussed in this paper were gathered in the context of a longitudinal study of the effects of malnutrition on mental development. Our interest in child-rearing practices and their possible relationship to cognitive development is stimulated by the fact that in apparently homogeneous subsistence farming communities of about 1,000 inhabitants, we find simple measures of family wealth and parents' reported child-rearing practices to be powerful predictors of preschool age psychological test performance (Klein, Freeman, Kagan, Yarbrough, & Habicht, 1972). In addition, child-rearing practices may affect both nutritional status and cognitive development, and for this reason they are important in any attempt to estimate the relationship between cognitive development and malnutrition. For these reasons, we undertook an exploratory study of child-rearing practices and of the relationship between child rearing, family social structural status, infant nutritional status, and mental and motor development during the first two years of life.

---

*This research was supported by Contract No. PH43-65-640 from the National Institute of Child Health and Human Development, National Institutes of Health, Bethesda, Maryland.

METHOD

This study was conducted in four isolated subsistence farming communities in eastern Guatemala. The communities range in size from 800 to 1,200 inhabitants and the average family income is about $200 per year. There are approximately 150 births per year in the four communities combined, and for the last four years, health, nutritional, socioeconomic, and psychological data have been regularly collected on all children under seven years of age in the four communities.

Subjects

Sixty-four infants were randomly selected for study from an ongoing longitudinal study in Guatemala. Data on Nutritional status, family socioeconomic status and psychological test performance were available for almost all the children in the sample.

Caretaker/infant interaction patterns were measured for the 64 children at either 8, 12, or 16 months of age, using a schedule adapted from Tulkin (1970). Each child was observed in his house for five, 30-minute periods on alternate days. The observers used a checklist procedure, wherein each of the variables being coded was checked if it occurred during a five-second period. Each variable could be noted only once in any five-second interval. Two observers collected all of the caretaker/infant interaction data. Percentages of agreement between observers were calculated for two-minute segments for each variable, by dividing the number of agreements by the number of agreements and disagreements. The percentages ranged from .67 to 1.00 with the median percentage above .80 for each variable.

The infant/caretaker variables examined in this report were defined as follows:

1. Total physical contact is the sum of Items 1a and 1b.

    a. Subject-initiated physical contact: all episodes of physical contact initiated by the infant, both with and without an affective component (i.e., touching and carrying the infant as well as kisses, tickles, embraces, etc.).

    b. Other-iniated physical contact: the same as Item 1a but initiated by a caretaker.

2. Location of the mother: the amount of time the mother spends at a distance greater than one meter from the child.

3. Play alone: the amount of time the infant spends playing alone without intervention by a caretaker.

4. Total positive vocalization by infant is the sum of Items 4a and 4b.

    a. Positive vocalization while alone: vocalizations or verbal expressions, including babbling as well as discrete words or phrases not produced in a social context or in exchange with a caretaker.

    b. Positive social vocalization: all positive vocal activity as defined in Item 4a but directed toward or in interchange with a caretaker.

5. Total caretaker vocalization is the sum of Items 5a and 5b.

    a. Verbalizations directed toward the infant.

    b. Verbal activity on the part of the caretakers directed to the child in order to control his activity.

6. Total verbal interaction: defined as variable 4 plus variable 5.

7. Total social interaction is the sum of Items 7a and 7b.

    a. Subject-initiated social interaction: this includes social interaction or play initiated by the infant with one or more of the caretakers, and involves the active participation of both the infant and the caretaker.

    b. Other-initiated social interaction: the same as Items 7a except that the social interaction was initiated by one or more of the caretakers.

Nutritional and Socioeconomic Status

Estimates of nutritional status for the infants are based

on two indices of anthropometric growth: height and head circumference. These measurements were taken at 9, 12, and 15 months and thus do not correspond exactly with the ages at which the caretaker/infant interaction observations were made. All measurements were done by a single anthropometrist whose reliability was over .95 for head circumference and height.

The quality of the family's house, which is a strong predictor of preschool psychological test performance, was used as the index of family socioeconomic status. This housing index is based on a 6-point scale that summarizes construction materials, size, and cleanliness of the dwelling.

Mental and Motor Assessment

All psychological testing was conducted in adobe buildings constructed to simulate the interior of the children's homes.

Mental and motor development of the subjects was evaluated by a Composite Infant Scale, made up of items selected from the Bayley, Cattell, Merrill-Palmer, and Gesell infant scales. This test was applied at 6, 15, and 24 months and generated a mental score and a motor score. Four psychometrists collected the infant mental and motor score data. Intertester reliabilities ranged between .82 and .87.

RESULTS

The results are discussed in terms of the four classes of variables being considered. The caretaker/infant interaction data are summarized first, and then the relations between caretaker/infant interaction, nutritional status, and socio-cultural factors are reviewed. Finally, caretaker/infant interaction, sociocultural status and nutritional status are discussed in the context of their relations with the indices of mental and motor development.

Caretaker/Infant Interaction

The data for the five caretaker/infant interaction sessions were first analyzed to see if behavior patterns changed across sessions. No systematic differences were found for any of the variables across the five sessions and for this reason the data were averaged and are presented in terms of a "typical" half hour in an infant's day. Table 15-1 presents means, standard deviations, minimums and maximums, and per-

TABLE 15-1. Means, Standard Deviations, Minimums and Maximums, and Percentages for Average Half-Hour Behaviors.

| | 8 Months | | | | | | | | | |
| | Males (N = 12) | | | | | Females (N = 10) | | | | |
INFANT - CARETAKER VARIABLES	X̄	SD	MIN	MAX	%	X̄	SD	MIN	MAX	%
Physical Contact (Total)	70.25	50.00	11	176	19.5	100.90	79.85	21	302	28.0
Subject-initiated	31.25	19.87	6	66	8.7	48.60	49.52	3	180	13.5
Other-initiated	39.00	46.53	1	133	10.8	52.30	38.32	11	123	14.5
Location of Mother (> 1 meter)	81.17	40.04	28	149	22.5	54.50	55.49	5	200	15.1
Play Alone	278.92	42.86	209	231	77.5	294.30	23.23	254	318	81.8
Vocalizations Infant (Total)	63.50	18.89	30	91	17.6	62.90	30.49	24	109	17.5
(+) Vocalization Alone	59.00	15.56	29	76	16.4	59.60	30.37	20	106	16.6
(+) Vocalization Social	4.50	6.42	0	24	1.2	3.30	1.49	1	6	0.9
Vocalizations Caretaker (Total)	9.17	6.02	1	22	2.6	10.00	5.89	4	21	2.8
(+) Vocalization	6.00	4.10	1	13	1.7	6.70	4.76	2	15	1.9
Verbal Control	3.17	2.48	1	10	0.9	3.30	2.21	0	6	0.9
Verbal Interactions (Total)	72.50	22.05	37	109	20.1	72.90	30.36	28	119	20.3
Social Interaction (Total)	20.16	10.26	4	42	5.6	20.00	8.26	10	40	5.5
Subject-initiated	10.33	8.03	0	30	2.9	7.70	4.52	0	17	2.1
Other-initiated	9.83	4.57	4	18	2.7	12.30	7.13	6	28	3.4

12 Months

Physical Contact (Total)	124.50	78.44	21	250	34.5	128.75	59.86	51	226	35.7
Subject-initiated	33.60	22.43	9	73	9.3	47.58	24.54	8	89	13.2
Other-initiated	90.90	71.83	3	221	25.2	81.17	53.03	3	168	22.5
Location of Mother (> 1 meter)	104.90	78.51	6	226	29.1	101.83	63.40	1	185	28.3
Play Alone	278.80	17.74	254	311	77.4	290.08	20.66	247	318	80.6
Vocalizations Infant (Total)	69.80	35.19	31	144	19.4	59.75	18.08	30	93	16.6
(+) Vocalization Alone	63.90	30.56	29	134	17.8	54.17	20.05	24	88	15.0
(+) Vocalization Social	5.90	5.36	0	18	1.6	5.58	3.55	0	12	1.6
Vocalizations Caretaker (Total)	17.10	8.72	11	38	4.8	17.59	7.30	8	36	4.9
(+) Vocalization	9.70	6.34	3	25	2.7	9.42	4.27	3	17	2.6
Verbal Control	7.40	3.37	0	12	2.1	8.17	3.83	4	19	2.3
Verbal Interactions (Total)	86.89	37.82	44	168	24.1	77.50	22.29	41	121	21.5
Social Interaction (Total)	26.90	7.70	17	43	7.5	27.33	6.04	19	39	7.6
Subject-initiated	12.70	7.44	4	29	3.5	14.08	5.88	7	24	3.9
Other-initiated	14.20	4.32	7	23	3.9	13.25	5.31	7	22	3.7

16 Months

Physical Contact (Total)	91.00	57.33	38	214	25.3	70.60	24.16	35	108	19.6
Subject-initiated	39.60	15.19	22	62	11.0	46.10	23.45	22	99	12.8
Other-initiated	51.40	45.24	6	153	14.3	24.50	21.72	2	63	6.8
Location of Mother (> 1 Meter)	108.20	89.53	16	325	30.1	74.50	42.89	24	170	20.7
Play Alone	255.50	24.74	211	297	71.0	278.60	20.31	247	310	77.4

Vocalizations Infant (Total)	61.50	21.23	44	104	17.1	52.40	21.47	24	96	14.5
(+) Vocalization Alone	50.90	20.94	31	98	14.1	46.20	19.29	22	88	12.8
(+) Vocalization Social	10.60	7.63	3	24	2.9	6.20	3.58	2	12	1.7
Vocalizations Caretaker (Total)	37.10	21.17	10	75	10.3	31.80	9.14	22	46	8.8
(+) Vocalization	21.00	13.18	3	49	5.8	16.90	6.51	8	27	4.7
Verbal Control	16.10	8.13	6	27	4.5	14.90	5.22	5	23	4.1
Verbal Interactions (Total)	100.44	31.44	59	163	27.9	84.00	27.42	47	142	23.3
Socail Interaction (Total)	26.90	12.01	12	51	7.5	23.10	10.57	9	48	6.4
Social-initiated	15.80	8.47	6	31	4.4	17.70	9.24	7	38	4.9
Other-initiated	11.10	5.51	6	24	3.1	5.40	3.27	1	11	1.5

NOTE: All numbers (except percentages) refer to the number of 5-second intervals in which the behavior occurred. The possible range is 0–360. Since more than one type of behavior can occur in a 5-second block, the variables are not mutually exclusive.

centages for the average half-hour behaviors in each of the categories scored.

Each of the variables in Table 15-1 was subjected to an age (3) × sex (2) analysis of variance. Only three behavioral differences were associated with the sex of the child across the age range studied. Girls initiated more physical contact with their caretakers than did boys ($F = 3.29$, $df = 1,63$, $p < .10$) and played alone more than boys ($F = 6.10$, $df = 1,63$, $p < .025$). In addition caretakers initiated more social play with girls than with boys at eight months; however, this pattern reversed at sixteen months ($F = 3.37$, $df = 2,63$, $p < .05$).

The absolute levels of behavior recorded for the variables, presented in Table 15-1, are generally quite low. For example, at all ages, mothers spend 70 percent or more of their time at a distance greater than one meter from their children. Eight and twelve-month-old children play alone 80 and 79 percent of the time, respectively. The figure drops significantly at sixteen months ($F = 3.38$, $df = 2,63$, $p < .05$), but still is approximately 75 percent.

In addition to the fact that mothers spent a large part of their time at some distance from the infants and that the children spent long periods of time playing alone, the level of caretaker vocalization was also low. Positive verbal behavior directed toward the child, including verbal control and prohibitions, ranged from about 3 percent of the half-hour period at eight months of age to nearly 10 percent by sixteen months.

In contrast, the total amount of physical contact was found to be quite high. Both subject-initiated physical contact and contact initiated by others (mother or other caretaker) ranged between 18 and 35 percent. Significantly more physical contact initiated by caretakers was recorded at twelve months of age than at either of the other two age levels ($F = 4.73$, $df = 2,63$, $p < .025$).

Although there were fairly high levels of physical contact between the subjects and their caretakers, relatively little of this contact involved active social play. Social play initiated by either the subject or the caretaker ranged from about 6 to 8 percent of the average half-hour between eight and sixteen months of age.

Nutritional Status

The infants in this study were selected at random from villages where chronic mild-to-moderate malnutrition is endemic. The growth curves of infants in villages such as these are generally similar to those found in developed countries until around 4 to 6 months of age. However, beginning at around 4 to 6 months, growth in height, weight, and head circumference falls off rapidly, and the majority of these children never achieve their full physical growth potential.

Infants are exclusively breast fed during the first few months and supplementary feeding is frequently inadequate and often started too late to avoid malnutrition. Infants are typically weaned between fifteen and twenty-four months of age, frequently due to the impending arrival of another child. The growth decrements among children in these villages have been shown to be directly associated with malnutrition, since experimental programs in supplementary feeding of infants and preschool children produce substantial improvements in physical growth (Division of Human Development/INCAP, 1975).

Our interest in nutritional status in the context of this study is twofold: First, we are interested in assessing the relationship between mild- to -moderate protein-calorie mal- nutrition and mental and motor development. In addition, we are interested in the possible implications of lowered nutritional status, and perhaps concomitantly reduced infant responsivity, for caretaker/infant interaction patterns.

Table 15-2 presents the means and standard deviations for hight and head circumference for the subjects in this study as well as norms for rural Guatemalan children and for children in the United States (McCammon, 1970).

Here it can be seen that the present sample is representative of the larger Guatemalan sample with the exception of the twelve- month-old boys, who are approximately 1 SD below the Guatemalan norms for both height and head circumference. Both the present sample and the Guatemalan sample lag far behind the North American standards for both height and head circumference.

Family Socioeconomic Status

Socioeconomic status (SES), defined here as the quality of the house, is based on a 6-point scale that summarizes the quality of house construction, size, and general cleanliness. This housing index has been shown to be related to nutritional

TABLE 15-2. Height and Head Circumference of the Sample and Norms for Rural Guatemala and U.S.A. (Denver).

Height (Cm)

Age in Months	Sample				Guatemala				U.S.A.			
	Male		Female		Male		Female		Male		Female	
	$\bar{X}$	SD	$\bar{X}$	SD	$\bar{X}$	SD	$\bar{X}$	SD	$\bar{X}$	SD	$\bar{X}$	SD
9	66.8	2.9	66.2	2.0	66.7	2.7	65.0	2.5	71.9	2.7	69.9	2.1
12	66.1	2.1	67.0	3.0	69.3	2.9	67.8	2.8	75.5	2.8	74.1	2.3
15	73.0	3.9	71.4	2.7	71.9	3.2	70.1	3.1	78.9	2.8[a]	77.4	2.5[a]

Head Circumference (Cm)

Age in Months	Sample				Guatemala				U.S.A.			
	Male		Female		Male		Female		Male		Female	
	$\bar{X}$	SD	$\bar{X}$	SD	$\bar{X}$	SD	$\bar{X}$	SD	$\bar{X}$	SD	$\bar{X}$	SD
9	42.6	1.5	43.1	0.9	43.3	1.5	42.5	1.4	45.3	1.1	44.1	1.2
12	43.1	1.4	44.2	1.6	44.5	1.5	43.3	1.4	46.6	1.2	45.4	1.3
15	44.6	1.1	43.7	0.9	45.2	1.4	43.8	1.4	47.4	1.2[a]	46.2	1.3[a]

[a]Estimated.

status as well as to psychological test performance between 3 and 7 years of age in the villages from which the infant sample was selected (Klein *et al.*, 1972). Family socioeconomic status was included in the study in order to examine its relationship to nutritional status during infancy, caretaker/infant interaction patterns, and infant mental and motor development.

Table 15-3 presents the intercorrelations among the nutritional, SES, and mother/child interaction variables. For these and for subsequent analyses, the sexes are combined to obtain the largest possible number of subjects for the correlations.

The strongest relations between infant/caretaker interaction variables and indices of nutrition status were in verbal behavior. Total positive infant vocalizations correlated with height at eight and sixteen months ($r = .58$, $df = 20$, $\rho < .01$; $r = .51$, $df = 15$, $\rho < .05$) as did the index of total verbal interaction ($r = .59$, $df = 20$, $\rho < .01$; $r = .49$, $df = 15$, $\rho < .10$). Other than these relatively strong relations, there were only a few other significant correlations between indices of nutritional status and infant/caretaker interaction variables: height at twelve months and vocalizations by caretaker ($r = .40$, $df = 18$, $\rho < .10$) and head circumference and play alone at eight months ($r = .50$, $df = 20$, $\rho < .05$).

There were several indications of more positive infant/caretaker relations for better homes. The socioeconomic status index correlated negatively with play alone at eight months of age ($r = .54$, $df = 20$, $\rho < .01$), indicating that infants from better houses spent less time playing alone than did infants from poorer houses. In addition, total vocalization by the caretaker was positively correlated with quality of the house at eight months of age ($r = .43$, $df = 22$, $\rho < .05$) as was positive vocalization by the caretaker at eight and twelve months of age ($r = .49$, $df = 22$, $\rho < .05$; $r = .38$, $df = 19$, $\rho < .10$).

Nutritional status and family socioeconomic status are not closely related at eight and twelve months of age; however, at sixteen months both height and head circumference are positively correlated with the housing index ($r = .45$, $df = 17$, $\rho < .10$).

TABLE 15-3. Intercorrelations Between Nutritional, SES, and Mother/Child Interaction.

INFANT/CARE-TAKER VARIABLES	HEIGHT			HEAD CIRCUMFERENCE			HOUSE			SEX		
	N = 22	N = 20	N = 17	N = 22	N = 20	N = 16	N = 22	N = 21	N = 19	N = 22	N = 21	N = 19
	8 mos	12 mos	16 mos	8 mos	12 mos	16 mos	8 mos	12 mos	16 mos	8 mos	12 mos	16 mos
Physical Contact (Total)	-.25	-.14	-.19	-.35	-.31	.07	.02	-.18	-.01	.18	.04	-.12
Subject-initiated	.04	.08	-.25	.10	-.11	-.26	-.28	-.32	-.21	.14	.22	.07
Other-initiated	-.21	-.15	-.03	-.41	-.23	.10	.12	.01	.26	.25	-.01	-.28
Location of Mother	.21	.07	-.16	-.20	-.15	-.03	-.06	-.38[a]	.07	-.43[b]	-.13	-.19
Play Alone	.28	.15	-.15	.50[b]	.22	-.27	-.54[c]	-.02	-.37	.08	.39[a]	.42[a]
(+) Vocalizations Infant (Total)	.58[c]	-.08	.51[b]	-.02	-.30	.27	-.14	-.18	.12	-.03	-.09	-.27
(+) Vocalization Alone	.60[c]	-.09	.45[a]	-.06	-.25	.16	-.20	-.14	.10	-.04	-.05	-.15
(+) Vocalization Social	.42[b]	.03	.16	.24	.04	.09	.09	-.05	.30	.08	-.06	-.33
Vocalizations Care-taker (Total)	.11	.40[a]	.31	-.21	.17	.14	.43[b]	.32	.11	.10	.05	-.03
(+) Vocalization	-.03	.38[a]	.39	-.33	.00	.12	.49[b]	.38[a]	.14	.08	.01	-.13
Verbal Control	.20	.33	.00	.34	.23	-.05	.01	.08	-.06	.14	.14	-.00
Verbal Interaction (Total)	.59[c]	.07	.49[a]	-.03	-.14	.16	-.04	-.18	.10	.00	-.14	-.25
Social Interaction (Total)	.00	-.31	.08	-.23	.04	.29	.15	.24	.00	.03	.03	-.22
Subject-initiated	.04	-.26[b]	.05	-.07	.23	.23	.09	.25	.01	-.24	.03	-.06
Other-initiated	-.09	-.49[b]	.25	-.29	-.32	.36	.11	.08	.03	.15	-.04	-.61[c]

Nutritional Status

	Nutritional Status	Height	Head Circumference	House	Sex
Nutritional Status	1.00	.27	.64[c]	-.30	.00
Height	.27	1.00	.73[b]	-.31	.00
Head Circumference	.64[c]	.73[c]	1.00	.45[a]	.00
House	-.30	-.31	.45[a]	1.00	-.07
Sex	.00	.00	.00	-.07	1.00

[a] < .10
[b] < .05
[c] < .01

397

Relationship Among all Variables and Mental and Motor Development

Mental and motor development scores were available for most of the infants. These assessments were done at 6, 15, and 24 months of age, and thus the points of measurement differ from those at which infant/caretaker interaction was assessed (8, 12, and 16 months). Table 15-4 presents the correlations for infant/caretaker interaction variables, family socioeconomic status, indices of nutritional status, and mental and motor performance scores. The correlations have been computed for ages closest to those at which infant/caretaker interaction was measured. The number of subjects for these correlations varies slightly from those presented earlier because mental and motor performance data were missing from some subjects as some ages.

Mental performance at six months of age was correlated with height measured at nine months of age ($r = .42$, $df = 19$, $\rho < .10$) as was motor performance ($r = .61$, $df = 19$, $\rho < .01$). In addition, total verbal interaction measured at eight months correlated with six-month motor performance ($r = .42$, $df = 19$, $\rho < .10$). Thus, children taller at nine months of age performed better at six months on mental and motor subscales than did shorter children.

However, nutritional status at twelve months of age was not related to either mental or motor performance at fifteen months. Nutritional status and infant/caretaker interaction measured at fifteen and sixteen months were not correlated with mental test scores; however, children who had higher levels of physical interaction with their caretakers performed slightly better on the motor subscale ($r = .43$, $df = 14$, $\rho < .10$).

Finally, correlating fifteen month nutritional status and sixteen month infant/caretaker interaction measures with mental and motor score performance at twenty=four months of age, we find that head circumference is related to mental performance ($r = .47$, $df = 13$, $\rho < .10$). Performance on the motor subscale is strongly correlated with head circumference ($r = .64$, $df = 13$, $\rho < .01$), and less strongly with sex ($r = .48$, $df = 13$, $\rho < .10$), and negatively with verbal environment ($r = -.48$, $df = 13$, $\rho < .10$).

DISCUSSION

The purpose of this study was to explore the relations

among four classes of variables: infant/caretaker interaction, nutritional status, family socioeconomic status, and mental and motor performance. In general we found that most of the activities involving caretakers and infants seemed to be directed primarily toward caretaking rather than verbal and social stimulation per se. Similarly, infant/caretaker interaction was not closely related either to nutritional status or to family socioeconomic status. The positive correlation between nutritional status and family socioeconomic status found in investigations of similar populations between ages three and seven years was not apparent at either 8 or 12 months of age, but was present by 16 months. Presumably, what we are seeing here is the emergence of a closer and closer relationship between family socioeconomic status and nutritional status with age.

Mental and motor performance also seems to be increasingly related to nutritional status across the age range studied. The exception to this was the absence of correlations for 15-month test performance. This may be due in part to the relatively poor level of nutritional status for the 12-month-old boys. Head circumference measured at 15 months of age predicted both mental and motor performance at 24 months.

There have been relatively few investigations of the effects of mild to moderate protein-calorie malnutrition, on infant mental and motor development. (See Klein, Yarbrough, Lasky, & Habicht, 1974; Klein, Irwin, Engle, & Yarbrough, 1976; Lasky, Lechtig, Delgado, Klein, Engle, Yarbrough, & Martorell, 1975.) However, the findings of Chavez, Martinez, Muñoz, Arroyo, and Bourges (1972) are generally consistent with the results reported here. Chavez reports that only after 12 months of age does he find relationships between nutrition, social variables, and developmental test performance. We do not know, of course, whether these relations emerge because of changes in the measures that are used or from the processes being evaluated.

Several studies have been conducted in which severely malnourished children were evaluated before, during, and after nutritional rehabilitation (Cravioto & Robles, 1965; Chase & Martin, 1970; Pollitt & Granoff, 1967; Yatkin & McLaren, 1970). All these investigators report marked reduction in both mental and motor test score performance among severely malnourished children. In general, test scores are found to improve with nutritional rehabilitation. It is not clear whether there are long-term effects of severe malnutrition during infancy on subsequent psychological test performance. Thus, the question of

TABLE 15-4. Correlations Between Mental and Motor Scale Performance, Family SES, Nutritional Status, Infant/Caretaker Interactions, and Sex of the Child.

Age at which Measures Were Taken (Months)		Mental	Motor
		(6 Months)	
	(N = 21)		
--	Sex	.17	.07
--	House	-.27	-.29
9	Height	.42[a]	.61[c]
9	Head Circulference	.19	.37
8	Verbal Environment	.35	.42[a]
8	Social Interaction	.02	.15
8	Physical Interaction	.04	.00
		(15 Months)	
	(N = 20)		
--	Sex	.02	.37[a]
--	House	-.06	-.02
12	Height	.17	.03
12	Head Circumference	.21	.01
12	Verbal Environment	.14	.04
12	Social Interaction	.00	-.15
12	Physical Interaction	-.25	.25
	(N = 16)		
--	Sex	-.18	.20
--	House	-.03	.23
15	Height	.19	.21
15	Head Circumference	-.20	.14

400

		(24 Months)	
16	Verbal Interaction	.19	-.23
16	Social Interaction	-.26	.15[a]
16	Physical Interaction	.05	.43[a]
	(N = 15)		
--	Sex	.04	.48[a]
--	House	.36	.18
15	Height	.38[a]	.31[c]
15	Head Circumference	.47[a]	.64[a]
16	Verbal Environment	.01	-.48[a]
16	Social Interaction	-.34	.00
16	Physical Interaction	-.37	.06

a < .10.
b < .05.
c < .01.

whether or not there are long-term implications for retarded psychomotor development associated with malnutrition during infancy remains to be answered.

REFERENCES

Chase, H. P., & Martin, H. P. Undernutrition and child development. New England Journal of Medicine, 1970 282, 933-939.

Chavez, A., Martinez, C., Muñoz, M., Arroyo, P., & Bourges, A. Ecological factors in the nutrition and development of children from poor rural areas. In Proceedings of the Western Hemisphere Nutrition Congress Vol. 3, 1971, P. L. White & N. Selvey, (Eds.), Mount Kisco, New York: Futura Publishing Co. Inc., 1972, 265-269.

Cravioto, J., & Robles, B. Evolution of adaptive and motor behavior during rehabilitation from Kwashiorkor. American Journal of Orthopsychiatry, 1965, 35, 449-464.

Division of Human Development/INCAP. Nutricion, crecimiento, y desarrollo. Boletin de la Oficina Sanitaria Panamericana, 1975, 78, 38-51.

Klein, R. E., Irwin, M. H., Engle, P. L., & Yarbrough, C. Malnutrition and mental development in rural Guatemala: An applied cross-cultural research study. In N. Warren (Ed.), Advances in cross-cultural psychology. New York: Academic Press, 1976.

Klein, R. E., Yarbrough, C., Lasky, R. E., & Habicht, J. P. Correlations of mild to moderate protein-calorie malnutrition among rural Guatemalan infants and pre-school children. In Symposia of the Swedish Nutrition Foundation XII. J. Cravioto, L. Hambreus & B. Vahlquist, (Eds.), Uppsala: Almquist & Wiksell, 1974, 168.

Klein, R. E., Freeman, H. E., Kagan, J., Yarbrough, C., & Habicht, J. P. Is big smart? Journal of Health and Social Behavior, 1972, 13, 219-225.

Lasky, R. E., Lechtig, A., Delgado, H., Klein, R. E., Engle, P., Yarbrough, C., & Martorell, R. Birth weight and psychomotor performance in rural Guatemala. American Journal of Diseases of Children, 1975, 129, 566-570.

McCammon, R. W. Human growth and development. Springfield, Ill.: Thomas, 1970.

Pollitt, E., & Granoff, D. Mental and motor development of Peruvian children treated for severe malnutrition. Revista Interamericana de Psicologia, 1967, 1, 93-101.

Tulkin, S. R. Mother-infant interaction in the first year of life: An inquiry into the influences of social class. Unpublished doctoral dissertation, Harvard University, 1970.

Yatkin, U. S., & McLaren, D. S. The behavioural development of infants recovering from severe malnutrition. Journal of Mental Deficiency Research, 1970, 14, (Part I), 25-32.

Chapter 16
Economic Change and Infant Care in an East African Agricultural Community

P. Herbert Leiderman and Gloria F. Leiderman

Stanford University School of Medicine

[1]The field work reported in this paper was supported by a Carnegie Foundation grant to Professor John W. M. Whiting, Harvard University. The data analyses were aided by a grant from the Grant Foundation to Professor P. H. Leiderman, Stanford University. Portions of this paper were completed when the first author held a Guggenheim fellowship and was in residence as a fellow at the Center for Advanced Studies in the Behavioral Sciences, 1973-1974.

The authors wish to thank Dr. Helena C. Kraemer, Stanford University, for statistical consultation, Mrs. Ellen K. Curtis for her research assistance, Tome Tanisawa for manuscript typing, and our Kenyan research assistants, Beatrice Babu and Arthur Mgritta, who facilitated data collection. We are especially grateful to the participating families and children whose forebearance, patience, and cooperation made this study possible.

Comparative developmental research provides the opportunity to examine assumptions about child-rearing in our society that might otherwise go unrecognized. One such assumption is the presumed benefit to be derived from an exclusive mother-infant caretaking system on the child's subsequent social and cognitive development. In our own society, where the nuclear family is the norm, the mother generally has the major or exclusive responsibility for an infant's care during the earliest years. Despite variations from this norm, this system of caretaking has been assumed to be ideal. Observers have noted this relationship in more traditional societies, supporting this assumption. In this chapter, we shall examine the validity of the assumption of an exclusive mother-infant caretaking system in more traditional societies, and report on some of the consequences of caretaking systems for infant development as they might affect the purported ideal exclusive mother-infant relationship.

In addition to examining assumptions, comparative psychological research provides the opportunity to use social and psychological constructs derived from research in one society in another society where they may have potential research utility. An example of such a concept is social stratification, whether based on education, income, life-style, or some other descriptive status. In our society, social class, as an index of stratification, has been helpful in understanding some of the social forces influencing the development of a child (Hess, 1970). Although social class is frequently confounded by other variables, and its influence poorly understood, it can serve to point up developmental issues. Social class or other categories of social stratification have rarely been used in comparative psychological or cross-cultural research. Western behavioral scientists who work in non-Western societies frequently treat these societies as if they were relatively homogeneous. While homogeneity may characterize traditional societies, it is quite likely to be the exception rather than the rule in transitional societies extant throughout countries in the developing world. Therefore, a second purpose of this paper will be to look at some aspects of social stratification in a society in transition, to ascertain whether the concept has some utility in understanding child-rearing practices and infant development in a non-Western society.

DESCRIPTION OF THE COMMUNITY

The agricultural community we studied is located in the temperate highlands of central Kenya approximately twenty-five miles northwest of Nairobi. Residents of the community are members of the Gikuyu[2] tribe, a group noted by many observers to be eager to adopt Western political, social, and economic values. People in the village have had more than fifty years of contact with British settlers. They were obviously influenced by European standards, as indicated by five viable Christian churches representing Catholic, Protestant, and Orthodox faiths. Although subsistence agriculture is still dominant in the community, the practice of raising crops to sell for cash has become more frequent. Some men in the community combine farm work with jobs in Nairobi. The population of the village with its surrounding farm area is approximately 5,000 individuals.

The community covers an area of approximately ten square miles. The village center, located four miles from the nearest paved road leading to Nairobi, consists of a market and meeting place, surrounded by a series of small shops in well-constructed stone buildings. Several small restaurants, selling tea, beer, and food, serve as social centers for the men.

Three sections within the community were identified on the basis of distance from village center, type of family structure, and size of family plots of land. The section nearest to the village center consists of small houses constructed of rough-sawn lumber with tin roofs arranged close together on small plots of land usually one quarter acre in size. Some of the families in this central section have plots of land adjacent to their houses, while many others have small plots a distance away. The major crops grown are maize and beans. A few chickens are kept, and very rarely, a cow.

A second section of the community consists of traditional Gikuyu compounds, typically occupied by polygynous families. Here the houses are of traditional circular construction with thatched roofs. They are generally arranged in groups of four or five, on plots of land at least two acres, and, in some cases, more than four acres in size. Families residing in this section have sufficient land to keep cows and chickens. They have more land then do those in the village center on which to grow staple crops.

A third section of the community is made up of families

---

[2]Gikuyu is the traditional form employed by J. Kenynatta in designating this tribe. The European form is Kikuyu. The traditional name will be used here.

living in modern rectangular houses, on plots of land greater
than two acres. Frequently, adjoining plots belong to members
of the same lineage. Most of the individuals in this section,
therefore, have extended family relationships, with the
husband's brothers' families and grandparental generations
living in houses on the same plot, or houses on contiguous
plots of land.

The predominant household arrangement was monogamous, there
being only nine polygynous families (see Table 16-1) in the
sample studied. This may not be representative of the total
community. Although there are considerable economic and status
differences within the community, these differences are not
related to place of residence, to educational level of the
father, nor to the degree of acceptance of "modern" attitudes.

TABLE 16-1. Description of Sample ($N = 67$).

Family Structure	Percent
Monogamous	
Nuclear	32
Patrilocal	29
Matrilocal	07
Polygynous	12
Divorced, Separated, Widowed	12
Unmarried	08
Number of Children	
Infant only	18
2	16
3	10
4	12
5	12
6	10
7	06
8 or more	16

Water could be bought at one of two pumps in the village center or taken from a nearby river. Families with greater economic resources are able to obtain tin rain barrels to collect water from their roofs; some have taps in their home compounds. Fuel for cooking and warmth is usually obtained by the women in the household who walk distances of one to five miles to cut wattle trees, then carry the loads of wood to their homes. Families with sufficient cash resources can purchase fuel from "charcoal burners" who deliver to the village center.

Cash crops consist mainly of pyrethrum, which is grown cooperatively within the community. Some families with cows are able to sell surplus milk to a milk cooperative. A few families keep sufficient chickens to sell eggs commercially, although none of the families in the sample did so on a large scale.

Health care is obtained at a community health center manned by a medical assistant, located five miles away, and reached by walking. A mobile health team comes to the village irregularly. We provided medical attention one-half day per week to the infant and his immediate family in a village clinic specially developed by us for the research project.

The Community in Transition

Shortly after our arrival in the village, it became obvious that our assumption of consistent close contact of a mother with her infant during the infant's first year was erroneous. We observed considerable variation in infant care patterns. Frequently more than one caretaker was involved in addition to the mother, generally an older female sibling of the infant, possibly a male sibling or an adolescent woman hired for the purpose, or, very occasionally, a grandmother. Further, it became obvious that our original assumption regarding social and economic homogeneity within the community was not warranted. We decided, therefore, to take advantage of the heterogeneity of the community (see Table 16-2) and of the varied caretaking practices to study the influences of economic stratification and infant caretaking patterns on infant development.

In order to understand the rapidly changing circumstances within this community, it might be helpful to provide a brief history and description of the Gikuyu people (Cagnolo, 1933; Fisher, 1956; Kenyatta, 1953; Lambert, 1956). The Gikuyu have lived in the highland area of central Kenya for at least the past 300 years. The traditional Gikuyu family was

TABLE 16-2.   Social Stratification and Modernizing
Influences ($N = 67$).

Occupation of Father	Percent	
Job with salary (trained)	42	
Job with salary (non-trained)	09	
Business	09	
Part-time work	02	
Subsistence farmer, < 2 acres	14	
Subsistence farmer, 2-4 acres	06	
Subsistence farmer, > 4 acres	04	
Unemployed	14	

Education	Mother Percent	Father Percent
None	41	18
Standard 1-4	25	25
Standard 4-6	10	02
Standard 7-8	13	42
Teacher Training or Form I-II	07	13
Technical Training	04	00

Educational Materials in Household	Percent
None	24
One	12
Two	07
Three or more	57

Land Owned	Percent
None	14
< 1.9 acres	43
2-3.9 acres	29
4-9.9 acres	07
> 10 acres	07

Languages Spoken	Mother Percent	Father Percent
Kikuyu only	37	14
Kikuyu & Swahili	29	27
Kikuyu & English	02	00
Kikuyu, Swahili & English	32	59

Nairobi Travel	Mother Percent	Father Percent
Daily	03	55
Weekly	11	11
Monthly	38	14
Yearly	35	09
Never	13	11

polygynous, men having several wives, each of whom lived in her own house with her children on the husband's or his family's compound. Although the Gikuyu have been described as having pastoral antecedents, they have been predominantly agricultural over the past 200 years. Since the turn of the century, the Gikuyu have been in contact with the British military and with colonial settlers, with varying effects on the men and women. Traditionally, men had responsibility for cattle herding, for protecting the family against human or animal predators, and for opening up land for the women to cultivate. With the arrival of Christian missionaries, some men received formal education. Pacification between tribal groups also enabled men to turn from their role of protection to participation in the contemporary economy through jobs in government, teaching, and the trades. Jobs, however, are still few in number; and despite varying amounts of formal education, many men are both unemployed and lacking either traditional or modern function within the society.

For the women, contact with British settlers and with missionary schools has been less direct, although many have become members of Christian churches. Women receive less education than the men (see Table 16-2), and continue to perform the traditional agricultural activities necessary for feeding the family and caring for home and children.

The major changes occurring within the family for the women have involved two components: (1) the number and spacing of children, and (2) the amount of help that she has available to accomplish her multifarious activities. Gikuyu married women traditionally were responsible for child-care, agricultural work, fetching of fuel and water, and occasionally petty trade involving exchange of surplus food crops. A married woman was usually assisted in many or all of these activities by her older children, generally female, or, when not available, male children. If neither of these was available, then her younger female sibling might come to assist her, at least until her own children became old enough to help. Given the press of modern Gikuyu men and women toward educating their female and male children, young girls from ages seven through twelve are not currently available to assist their mothers. The mother must then utilize children younger than age seven who are not yet in school, or, if more fortunate, the mothers hire young women who are older than age twelve to assist with the chores.

The change in the number of children in any given family is likely due to the increased health care and improved sanitation within the community. Since both pride and traditional practices require many progeny, the shift from polygynous to monogamous families, accompanied by higher infant survival, has increased the number of children.

DESCRIPTION OF THE SAMPLE

Our sample consisted of 67 infants and their mothers. Originally, 90 families were selected out of an estimated population of 100 families to whom infants were born during the period from 1 July to 31 December 1969. Eighteen of these infants were used as controls and will not be reported on here. Five infants and their families were lost to the study because of either having moved from the area or because of absence from two or more tests or interviews.

Information about the families was obtained by two female University of Nairobi undergraduate students, fluent in both Gikuyu and English, through interviews with mothers and by observations in the homes. Ethnographic data were collected on both the mother and father, as was demographic information including age, education, current employment, household density, and economic resources available to the family. In addition, home observations were made on the availability of modern amenities such as calendars, books, and playthings, to obtain information that might yield additional economic stratification indices.

The age, birth order of the parents, and the number of years married are presented in Table 16-3. The Table shows that the group is a relatively diverse one in terms of age, birth order of parents, and the number of years married although all are members of the Gikuyu tribe. Most of the men and about half of the women had lived in the community since it was moved from a former site one mile away at the end of

TABLE 16-3. Description of Sample (N = 67)

Age	Mother Percent	Father Percent
15-19	01	
20-24	25	17
25-29	21	
30-34	24	38
35-39	13	
> 40	16	
Birth Order of Parents		
1	11	22
2	18	24
3	27	17
4	18	16
5-6	20	17
7-8	06	04

Years Married	Percent
Unmarried	08
1-4	22
5-9	25
10-14	17
15-19	10
20-24	10
> 25	08

the "Mau Mau rebellion" in 1958.

NARRATIVE DESCRIPTION OF DAILY ACTIVITY OF MOTHER, CARETAKER, AND INFANT

In order that the reader may better understand the mother's role, we shall describe a typical day for mother, caretaker, and infant in the village before presenting the results. The activity of the vast majority of women in the sample centers about the household, the agricultural fields, the market, and, on weekends, the church. Typically, a woman arises before dawn, kindles the fire, and starts cooking moring tea and the midday meal. The mother nurses her infant while she goes about her household tasks. When the mother journeys to fetch

water or wood, she is often accompanied by an older daughter,
aged anywhere from five years to early adolescence, who helps
the mother cut wood and carry water. If the infant accompanies
the mother, he is strapped to her back by means of two towels,
with his head uncovered if the weather is suitable, or covered
if not. On the return journey, the infant might be carried
against the mother's chest, or strapped on the daughter's back,
since the mother is carrying a very heavy load on her back.

On those days when the mother goes to her fields to
cultivate her crops or perform other seasonal tasks, young
girls or occassionally boys assist her. In general, the mother
will take her infant regularly to the fields until he is three
or four months of age. She may have the caretaker with her to
watch the infant while she works, stopping work to nurse him.
In the early afternoons, she frequently returns home from the
fields to manage the affairs of the other children and to
proceed with household tasks.

At the end of the day, mother and children gather for an
early evening meal. In the evening, the husband might spend
time with the mother and children, or he might prefer to
socialize with his male friends in the village center. Most
families retire fairly early, frequently shortly after dusk.
The infant sleeps with his mother, and the other young children
sleep in special places within the hut or very near the mother.

Two days a week, the mother visits the central market
within the village or goes to a more distant market. The
market, of course, provides the opportunity for socializing
with other women, and is used for this purpose as well as for
commercial transactions. Frequently the younger infant
accompanies the mother. If the infant is brought along, an
older sibling might accompany the mother to help carry him.
Otherwise he will be left at home with a caretaker, particularly
if the mother chooses to trade at a distant market.

If the mother holds an outside position, the routine is
different. Such a woman might be a nursery school teacher
or work in a shop in the village center. She leaves the infant
at home with a caretaker, returning at midday to take care of
him. Even though they are away from home during much of the
day, these mothers spend considerable time with their children
and husbands when they are at home.

The role of the infant caretaker and mother's helper is
an important one. The caretaker might have completed two years
of "nursery school", finishing by the age of eight years. If
fortunate, she also might have had from three to five years of

primary school. The caretaker is usually old enought to know
the responsibilities of the household, yet young enough to
want to be included in the children's games and activities.

In her typical day, she gets up with the mother and helps
about the house. She frequently accompanies the mother to
collect fuel and water, usually taking responsibility for the
infant on these journeys. She goes with the mother to the
fields where she either assists in cultivating and planting,
or cares for the child while the mother performs her chores.
If the young girl is left at home to care for the infant, she
is solely responsible for his care. She provides food if he
is old enough to take supplemental food, or, if he is still
nursing, she carries him to the mother in the fields. Depending on the interest and sense of responsibility of the young
caretaker, she might watch the infant extremely carefully, or
do so in a more desultory manner, giving in to the temptation
of playing with her friends and siblings while overseeing his
activities. Most of the caretakers take their responsibilities
very seriously, however, and many are genuinely interested in
and involved with the young infants in play as well as in caretaking tasks.

From the typical infant's vantage point, his first year
might be considered as the halcyon period of his life. He
spends the first four months in almost constant contact with
his mother. He is fed on demand, accompanies her on journeys,
and sleeps with her. By four months of age, he has seen or
heard most of the activities in the household and has been
physically stimulated by being in touch with and by being
carried by his mother and his many siblings. He probably has
little directed social interaction with his mother, at least
in the form of verbal communication, but has had a considerable
amount with his siblings and with other children. His father
has likely looked at him but has neither held him nor played
with him, although this pattern appears to be changing as
fathers in the more modern group take more direct interest in
their young infants.

By five or six months, the infant may be with his caretaker almost half of any day, although for much of that time
the caretaker might be carrying him while involved with play-
mates or household chores. His mother continues to nurse him
on demand when present; but she will not always be immediately
available, so he is fed other foods or must wait to be nursed.
By six or seven months of age he is allowed greater freedom
and may be put on the ground to play. His mother is still a
central figure in his life, but during the latter part of the
infant's first year, his caretaker and other siblings play an

increasingly important part in his social life.

INFANT CARETAKING

In order to determine who actually does the caretaking for
the Gikuyu infant during the first year, we adapted a method
developed by Munroe and Munroe (1971). Unscheduled periodic
visits for five minutes were made to the household by a research
assistant who observed and recorded whether the infant was
sleeping, cared for, played with, moving about and, particularly,
whether involved in social interactions with the mother or other
individuals. Caretaking was categorized further as to whether
the infant was merely being held, carried, or simply close to
the mother or to other caretakers. If in a given five-minute
period the behaviors were rapidly changing, then the initial
observation was recorded. The mothers or infant caretakers were
not apprised of the visit in advance. Three village residents
educated at the high school level were trained in these
observation techniques and were examined periodically for
reliability.

Mother, caretaker, and infant were seen in the course of
daytime activities between 8:00 a.m. and 6:00 p.m. Each household was visited at least eight times and at most twenty-three
times over a period of nine months, with an average of fifteen
observations per household. Maternal and caretaker scores
were calculated and expressed as a percentage of that particular
behavior in relation to the total number of observations made
for either the mother or caretaker in that household. In three
households the mother was always observed caring for the infant,
and in two households, the mother was never observed caring for
the infant. Agreement between observers using this technique
was greater than 80 percent for a series of ten observations
done simultaneously.

The data in Figure 16-1 indicate that the mother is the
primary caretaker of the infant until he reaches five months
of age. From that time on, the mother is the principal caretaker for less than 50 percent of the observations of the group,
other caretakers gradually taking over more responsibility.
For the remainder of the infant's first year, a young female
caretaker under age twenty is observed with the infant for
approximately 40 percent of the observations, and a young male
or an older female for the remaining 10 percent of the
observations.

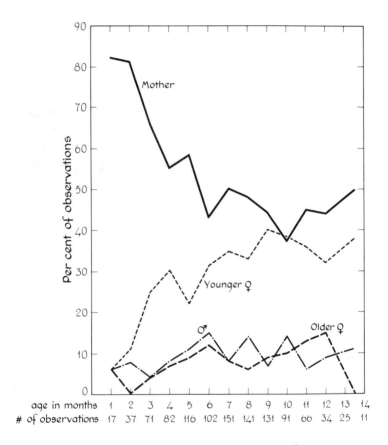

FIGURE 16-1.   Identification of caretaker.

The question of what the mother or caretaker actually does
in relationship to the infant is clearly more important than
her mere presence. Because of the relatively few observations
of older women and males, we shall report the behaviors related
only to the mothers and the young female caretakers. The data
are shown in Figure 16-2, summarized for the entire year.
Developmental changes in the infant are not taken into account,
and, therefore, these data can be considered only as trends for
the group. More detailed observations during specific phases

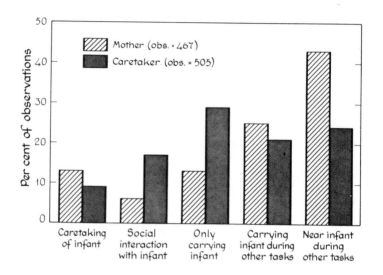

FIGURE 16-2.   Summary of maternal and caretaker behavior during infant's first year.

of development are indicated.

The major differences between caretakers and mothers are found in social interaction with the infant, carrying the infant, and being near the infant. Mothers spend a greater proportion of their daytime activities being near infants than do caretakers. Caretakers are in social interaction with and/ or carrying infants for a greater proportion of the observations. Caretakers and mothers spend about the same proportion of observations in physical caretaking activities and in carrying infants while doing other tasks. These findings indicate that while mothers may be involved in supervision of their infants (i.e., by being near), they rely on the caretaker for many direct infant care functions. The caretaker, and not the mother, is the major purveyor of physical stimulation, in the form of carrying, and of psychosocial stimulation in the form of directed social interaction, especially during the second half of the infant's first year of life. The implications of these findings will be discussed in relationship to the cognitive performance of the infants later in this paper.

Despite reported observations (Jelliffe & Bennett, 1972) that the African mother is with her infant almost constantly during the first year, this is clearly not the case for mothers of this community, at least during daytime hours. Ethnographic reports by Fisher (1956) confirm these observations. The mother is not free to be with her infant constantly in an agricultural community, and must rely on others for infant caretaking. If anything, she is, by Western standards, a working mother with part- or full-time help. Whether or not she chooses this mode of caretaking when other options are available will be dealt with in the next section.

FAMILIAL ECONOMIC LEVEL

Having found that considerable variability exists in infant care arrangements, we next attempted to determine whether the mothers who were sole caretakers did this through economic necessity or through preference. We reasoned that mothers with greater economic resources would be less obligated to provide for the necessities of family survival through their own labor and, therefore, would have more time to devote to their infants. On the other hand, mothers with greater economic resources--that is, cash income derived from their own work or from their husband's employment--might choose to hire someone to assist with infant care; thus, these mothers might spend less time with their infants. Further confusing possible predictions are the conflicting models derived from European and American life. Some mothers might value spending more time with their infants and arrange their lives accordingly if it is economically feasible. Contrasting with this orientation is one derived chiefly from the "British colonial" viewpoint, which provided a model of help for the mother in the form of nurses, or governesses, in the early child-rearing period. Therefore, on the basis of our knowledge of the economic resources available to the mother and British colonial or American middle-class child-care attitudes alone, it would be difficult to predict a priori the child-care patterns adopted by the mother.

We determined the economic level of the family by selecting demographic items from interview questionnaires and observations of the household that were thought to best characterize the economic circumstances of families within the village. They were (1) the amount of land available to the family, (2) the presence of cash income, (3) the number and type of cows owned by the family, (4) the number of

chickens kept by the family, and   (5) the source of water
supply. This choice of items was based on knowledge of the
criteria used by the individuals within the community to
determine differences in familial economic level. Each of
the demographic items was scaled to obtain an index of
familial economic level. The correlation between individual
scores and the total family economic index is shown in
Table 16-4. The composite scores seem to best represent the
variations we observed within the community.

TABLE 16-4. Familial Economic Level.

Total Score Verus Subscores

(Spearman Rho)

Cash Income	$+.55^a$ (58)
Amount of Land	$+.55^a$ (58)
Number of Cows	$+.58^a$ (59)
Number of Chickens	$+.40^a$ (65)
Source of Water	$+.55^a$ (65)

[a] $p < .001$

All of the families in the sample were divided into three
economic level groups of approximately equal numbers based on
these composite scores. A typical family of the lowest economic
level might be characterized as having little or no land to
farm, no cash income, no cows, and few chickens, and would
obtain water from the river or from a distant village pump.
A family in the middle economic range might own two to four
acres of land, have no cash income, no cows, few chickens, and
obtain water either from the village pump or from a neighbor
who could afford a water tap. A family in the upper economic
group would typically possess a farm of at least two acres
(generally more than four), have a cash income, one to four
ordinary cows or one specially bred milk cow, several chickens,
and obtain water from the village pump or from a source within
the home compound--from either a storage tank or an outdoor
tap.

ECONOMIC LEVEL AND CARETAKING ACTIVITIES

Our next step was to examine the relationship between familial economic level and the maternal and caretaker activities involving the infant. The correlation between the percentage of observations over the entire year at which mothers were present and taking care of their infants and the familial economic level was -.51, $p < .01$. This finding indicates that mothers of the higher economic level group spend a smaller proportion of their daytime hours directly involved with infant care. The more affluent Gikuyu women utilize the traditional system for infant caretaking, and those women from the lower economic level families who cannot arrange to have help are required to care directly of their infants. When maternal presence is related to the educational attainment and to modern attitudes of the mother (assessed by the method of Inkeles & Smith, 1975), a negative, although not significant, relationship was found. Where women have the economic resources and social opportunity, they choose to have help with infant care.

If we look at caretaking behavior in more detail, we find some interesting differences between mothers and caretakers according to economic level. The "spot" observations made it possible to determine the mother's or caretaker's activity in relationship to the infant. This activity was divided into four categories: (1) social, defined as direct interaction by mother or caretakers with the infant; (2) caretaking, direct activity of a utilitarian nature such as feeding and bathing; (3) proximity, mother or caretaker presence within ten feet of the infant but not otherwise involved with the infant; and (4) carrying the infant, providing physical but not social stimulation. The patterns of interaction for mother and for caretaker were calculated separately for each of the three economic level groups. Table 16-5 shows that the three economic groups differ in the proportion of time that mothers are present. The pattern of caretaking is similar for the lower and middle economic level groups. Mothers spend more time than caretakers in physical caretaking and being near (proximity) the infant; caretakers spend a greater proportion of their time in social activities and in carrying. The higher economic level group differs from this pattern in that the caretakers spend a lower proportion of time carrying the infant, and a greater proportion of time in close proximity to the infant and taking care of him, as compared to the mother. There is some suggestion that mothers in the higher economic group may spend more of their daytime activities in social interaction with the infant than do the mothers in

TABLE 16-5. Pattern Of Maternal and Caretaker Activity by Economic Level (Total Observations = 972, Expressed in Percent).

| | Familial Economic Level | | | | | |
| | Low (N = 24) | | Mid (N = 24) | | High (N = 19) | |
	Mother	Caretaker	Mother	Caretaker	Mother	Caretaker
Presence	70 percent	30 percent	49 percent	51 percent	35 percent	65 percent
Activity						
Social	6	14	5	20	9	16
Caretaking	14	7	14	8	18	13
Proximity	38	22	38	19	41	35
Carrying	42	57	43	53	31	36

both the lower and middle economic level families.

Thus, we find differences in caretaking behavior based on the economic stratification of the families in this sample. Where mothers have greater economic resources, they seem to have more time for social interactive activities with their infants, probably because they need to devote less time to utilitarian activities. Higher education of women in the higher economic level families cannot explain the results, since the education levels of mothers in both the higher and middle economic groups is about the same, averaging two years of primary school, somewhat higher than the lower economic group mothers who average one year of primary school.

It is also interesting to observe that the caretakers in the middle and higher economic group families spend more time in social interaction with the infants than do those in the lowest group. It is possible that the mothers in the two higher economic group families instruct their caretakers to engage in these activities. We might turn this explanation around, however, and speculate that the infants in these families have a greater social potential by being better nourished; they may, therefore, solicit more social behaviors from their caretakers than do the infants in the lowest economic group. Similar findings on maternal-infant interaction and economic stratification have been obtained from families in the United States (Tulkin & Kagan, 1972; Hess, 1970).

To this point, we have demonstrated that the Gikuyu infant does not have mother as the exclusive caretaker during his first year of life. Further, we have demonstrated that there exists considerable economic stratification even within a relatively homogeneous agricultural society and that this stratification has consequences for both the type and amount of infant caretaking performed by the mother and by the mother surrogate, i.e., the caretaker. The question that now remains is whether these differential activities have any influence on the infant's cognitive development.

INFANT EVALUATION

Infant cognitive performance was determined by means of the Bayley Test of Infant Development (Bayley, 1969) given in standardized form by a British-educated Kenyan nurse, a member of the Gikuyu tribe. She was trained to administer the test through a series of pilot tests of infants not involved in the study. She reached a reliability of 85 percent agreement on test items passed with the investigators for the final two of ten infants. Infant testing began January 1970, and continued through September 1970. Twenty-three of the infants were born between July 1 and September 30, 1969 and were tested at regular intervals between 6 and 14 months. Forty-four were born between October 1 and December 31, 1969 and were tested periodically between 1 and 9 months of age. All the infants were tested at least three times. The interval between tests for those most frequently tested was approximately 2 months. Additional testing was done on a subsample at 1-month intervals, providing a larger number of tests for other purposes. Sixty-five of the infants were tested at least four times and the other two infants only three times. Testing was done either in the morning or in the afternoon, but only at times when the infants were judged to be awake and alert.

Our method of elucidating the relationship between infant test performance and familial economic level took advantage of the fact that each infant was tested several times in the first year. We were thereby able to determine a rate of development as well as a simple level of performance. To determine the rate of development, a straight line was fitted to the log of the number of items passed on each test against the age of the child for the mental (perceptual-sensory) and motoric (psychomotor) portions of the test. This statistical approach yielded a slope, representing the rate of psychological development, and an intercept, representing the average level for the child. These fitted curves were a reasonable approximation to the actual scores obtained, in that they reduced the variance of the sample means by over 70 percent for all but two infants. Performance at age six months was the point selected for determination of the intercept, since all infants in both groups had scores at the six-month age point. All scores for individual infants were related to the total Gikuyu sample means (see Leiderman, Babu, Kagia, Kraemer, & Leiderman, 1973) and not to United States norms.

FAMILIAL ECONOMIC LEVEL AND INFANT TEST PERFORMANCE

The relationship between infant test performance and familial economic level was determined by correlating the slope and intercept for the mental and motor tests with the index of familial economic level. For the total sample of 67 infants and their families, a correlation of +.39 between

mental score intercept and economic level, and a correlation
of -.32 for the slope and economic level were obtained. Both
are significant at p < .01. Figures 16-3 and 16-4 graphically
illustrate the infant mental and motor test performance by
family economic level. The positive relationship between
economic level and infant mental performance is found when
the level of performance rather than the rate of development
is utilized. Indeed, the rate of development is inversely
related to economic level, suggesting that environmental
influences occurring after birth tend to bring the scores of
the infants from different economic levels closer together
over time.

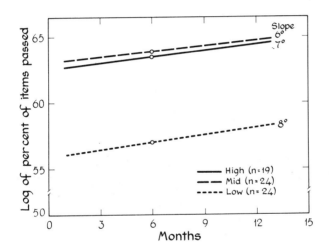

FIGURE 16-3. Familial economic status and infant test
performance (mental test).

Our interpretation of these data is that the difference
in performance level between these infants is either present
at birth, or it begins very early postnatally. One possible
explanation is that either genetic and/or prenatal factors,
such as maternal nutrition, are crucial in determining these
scores, since the social influences have had little time to
manifest themselves. Countering this biologically based
argument is the finding that a postnatal social variable,
maternal work load, is negatively related to mental test

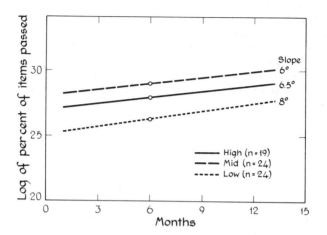

FIGURE 16-4.   Familial economic status and infant test
performance (motor test).

performance, $r = -.45$, $p < .01$. Details of this aspect of
the study will be reported elsewhere. This finding and the
attendant explanations must, however, be corroborated by
additional data collection and analysis not possible within
the bounds of this particular research.

Maternal and Caretaker Behavior and Infant Test Performance

        Considering the number of variables that may influence
an infant's cognitive development, and the wide variation of
maternal and caretaker behavior observed, it is difficult to
quantify the relationships between caretaker behavior and
infant test performance without taking into account complex
social environmental variables. We previously reported
(Leiderman & Leiderman, 1974a, 1974b) that infant performance
on standardized cognitive tests was positively related to
caretaker's presence, especially for the mental portion of
the test, and suggestively positive for the motor portion.
This finding seemed to hold for infants in the lowest economic
level families and was less strong for infants from families
in the middle and higher economic levels.

An approach to understanding the effects of the caretaker's behavior on cognitive performance is to assess particular
qualities of the caretakers. One clear attribute of the caretaker is her age. We predicted that those infants who had older
and, consequently, more mature caretakers would receive more
adequate caretaking than those infants raised by younger caretakers. Table 16-6 shows the average caretaker in each of the
three economic groups. The middle economic group had the
youngest caretakers, the highest economic level group had the
oldest caretakers. These findings are consistent with our field
observations that the lowest economic level families tended to
have insufficient finances to afford school fees (required for
all schools in Kenya) and, therefore, had older female siblings
not in school who were available to help with the care of the
infants. The highest economic group infants similarly had older
caretakers, because mothers of this group were able to hire nonfamilial caretakers for this purpose. In contrast, the middle
economic level families tended to send their girls to school,
but had insufficient extra cash resources to hire older caretakers. They were forced to rely on younger caretakers. It
should be noted, however, that there is wide variation in the
caretakers' ages within each group, so the infants of any one
economic group were exposed to caretakers of varying ages.
Despite the seeming curvilinearity of the relationship, the
overall linear correlation between familial economic level
and the age of the caretaker is +.35, $p < .01$.

TABLE 16-6.   Relationship of Age to Caretaker to Familial
Economic Level.

	Low Ec. Level	Mid Ec. Level	High Ec. Level	Correlation
Age in years	13.9	10.6	20.2	+.36, $p < .01$
$N =$	(12)	(16)	(16)	

We next categorized the data into three groups based on
the age of the caretaker: under eight years of age, eight to
twelve years of age, and over twelve years of age. The data
in Table 16-7 show that the age of the caretaker is positively
related (+.36, $p < .01$) to infant mental test scores

TABLE 16-7. Relationship of Age of Caretaker to Test Performance.

Bayley Test Score	Age of Caretaker			Correlation
	8 Years	8-12 Years	12 Years	
	N	*N*	*N*	
Mental 1-6 months	101.1 (17)	96.7 (12)	103.1 (14)	+.08, N.S.
Mental 7-12 months	98.1 (18)	97.7 (12)	107.7 (14)	+.35[a] ($p < .01$)
Motor 1-6 months	99.7 (17)	100.0 (12)	102.7 (14)	.18, N.S.
Motor 7-12 months	101.4 (18)	98.8 (12)	102.7 (14)	.03, N.S.

[a]Partial correlation coefficient controlling for economic level = +.25 ($p < .05$).

NOTE: N.S. means not significant.

summarized over the age period of 7 to 12 months. The relationships for the mental test for the age period 1 to 6 months, and
for the motor test for age periods 1 to 6 months and 7 to 12
months, were not significant. (The summarized mental scores for
the 7 to 12 months age period were determined in the same manner
as the scores for the entire 1 to 12 month period reported in
Leiderman and Leiderman (1974a). These summarized scores for
the half-year period obviously are based on fewer test scores
than for the summarized one-year scores.)

Since we have previously demonstrated that the economic
level of the family is related to mental performance, we
partialed out this variable, thereby reducing the correlation
to +.25, $p < .05$. Even though we statistically eliminated
the effects of economic level, there is still a significant
positive correlation between caretaker age and mental test
performance for the second six months of the infant's life.
This finding suggests that age (presumably indicating greater
social maturity in infant caretaking) of the caretaker does
have an influence on the child's performance in the last half
of the first year, independent of the economic level of the
family. Thus, we can conclude with some degree of certainty
that the presence of an older female caretaker assisting the
mother has the effect of increasing the infant's test
performance. It should be recalled that this is the same age
period when the caretaker takes over more responsibility for
the infant, further supporting the argument that the caretaker's
actions play some part in the infant's cognitive development.

MATERNAL AND CARETAKER BEHAVIOR AND SOCIAL DEVELOPMENT

We have emphasized in this paper some of the demographic
factors that may influence cognitive performance during the
infant's first year. The emphasis on cognitive and motoric
performance should not be construed to mean that we believe
these components to be the most important aspects of an
infant's functioning in the earliest years.' Rather, cognitive
measures have been emphasized because they are more readily
quantifiable and because they can be related to social-affective
developmental processes. We believe social development to be
an equally important, if not a more important, developmental
process in the infant's first year. In looking at some
familial social variables, such as caretaking arrangements,
we have reported elsewhere (Leiderman & Leiderman, 1974a)
that the infant's affective reactions to a stranger approaching
and mother's leaving are related to the infant caretaking

arrangement (i.e., *monomatric*, a single maternal figure, and *polymatric*, more than one maternal figure). Infants in a polymatric system tended to react more negatively to a stranger's approach, and more negatively to mother's departure than did infants raised in a monomatric caretaking arrangement. Therefore, not only is cognitive performance influenced by social and demographic factors, but social-affective behavior of the infant is also influenced by some of the same factors. Whether the social-affective developmental processes in the infant's first year are related to later social-affective development, or whether the infant's early cognitive development predicts later school performance, cannot yet be started. Given the variety of environmental variation expected to impinge on the child during the preschool years, it would seem unlikely that they would be highly predictive. More important for this research and other comparative psychological research, would be our findings that economic and social environments available to the infant have measurable affects on psychological development. Undoubtedly, these environmental influences become increasingly powerful with the increasing age of the infant, but they are operative even during the first year. Thus, it is no longer possible to assume either a homogeneity of caretaking arrangements or a constancy of social forces within a relatively homogeneous society even over the short time span of the infant's first year.

DISCUSSION

We began this chapter by raising two issues. The first concerned the assumption of exclusive maternal caretaking of infants in agricultural non-Western societies where the mother has the major household and agricultural tasks. The second issue, related in part to the first, dealt with accessibility to economic resources by the family, thereby affecting the maternal work load and infant caretaking activity. Both issues have been relatively neglected in studies of non-Western communities, although both have been considered as having important implications for child-rearing practices in our own society.

Contrary to popular accounts, we found that the East African mother is not an exclusive infant caretaker. This finding is comprehensible, when one takes into account the numerous demands on her time in her role as agricultural worker and household manager, as well as infant caretaker. Therefore, one important finding in this study is the identification of the mother's helper, the child-caretaker, and of the central role she plays in the infant's care, especially from the time the infant reaches five months of age, and continuing throughout the remainder of the infant's first year. The lack of research emphasis on the auxiliary caretaker role in infant care in developing countries is remarkable indeed, when one considers that anthropological observations of this phenomenon in Bali between 1936 and 1939 were reported by Mead (Mead & MacGregor, 1951). LeVine (1970) reported similar observations for sub-Saharan Africa. On the basis of these observations and our findings, it should be obvious that no discussion of infant care patterns in more traditional agricultural societies can be complete unless auxiliary caretakers for the infant are taken into consideration. The high value placed on the exclusive maternal caretaking system by Western behavioral scientists is apparently a by-product of a cultural bias based on economic factors and the nuclear family form in our society.

An important observation derived from this work on the auxiliary caretaker is recognition of the change in the infant caretaker occurring through the modernization of and/or economic change in the community. In the past, usually a younger relative of the infant's mother or an older sibling of the infant. Although we found many infant caretakers with these characteristics, we found some families without a secondary caretaker and some families with caretakers below the age of eight years. The key change in the community accounting for fewer auxiliary caretakers, or for caretakers younger in age, is the greater educational opportunity provided girls as well as boys. Families who send their children to school lose the services of an important infant-caretaker of the requisite age for at least part of the day. Some families with sufficient economic resources can pay both the required school fees and hire a nonfamilial caretaker. Less affluent families who do send their daughters to school quite likely have the disadvantage of a less mature infant caretaker. Since we have shown that more mature caretakers are associated with higher infant performance on standardized tests even when the important variable of family economic level is controlled for, the decrease in age of infant care-takers has important implications for a developing society. The question of whether differential infant cognitive performance at this early age bears any relationship to the child's later cognitive and social development remains open. We have shown, however, how the potential benefit of a local primary school to a community may have negative consequences for other aspects of the community, for example, its infant and child-care system.

A second result concerning the caretaker is the greater importance of the caretaker as a source of social interaction for the infant as compared to the mother. Regardless of familial economic level, the caretaker appears to spend more daytime activity in talking to and playing with the infant than does the mother. Because the mother's daytime role is so demanding, with every pressure toward utilitarian aspects of infant care, the amount of time she has for purely social activities with her infant is relatively small, leaving much of this interaction to her older children. She still remains the person preferred by the infant, especially in times of stress, but social interactive relationships for the infant and young child are oriented toward peers. Although there are considerable variations in this play relationship between infant and peers across families within the community, the infant with a secondary caretaker has a greater likelihood of being socially stimulated by these peers than by a hard-working mother who is his sole caregiver.

These findings are of particular relevance for develop- mental models that have long been based on the centrality of parental, primarily maternal, socialization of the infant in the earliest years (see Bowlby, 1969). The emphasis in these models is on the dyadic relationship and omits other possibly significant relationships. These rudimentary dyadic models of socialization, when combined with developmental research on later years of childhood, almost imply an "assembly-line" pattern of socialization. The mother is thought to be the major socializing agent until the infant is age two, the father is added when the infant is aged three through six, a few peers or siblings are brought in for the child from ages six through twelve, and peers are considered as the exclusive socializing agents from ages thirteen to eighteen. Such a model neglects the potential socialization by older peers in the infant's and child's earliest years, and, of course, the parental and other adult socialization operative in the adolescent years.

The limitations of this descriptive model are obvious for societies both in the developed and developing worlds. Our findings emphasize the centrality of the infant's older peer as a socializing agent even in the early postnatal period. The secondary caretaker, serving in a socializing role, has the characteristics of both a child and an adult, and thus may have an advantage over the parent in passing on aspects of the culture to the infant and young child. This transmission through the older peer occurs at a younger age in developing societies than it does in Western societies, and may have the effect of easing the infant's transition into the larger community. The facilitating hand of a helpful older peer to aid the infant's movement into the larger world is one marked difference between the Gikuyu infant and the American middle-class infant, where this transition to a larger society occurs at ages later than amongst the Gikuyu.

We have emphasized the social interactive role of the secondary caretaker because of possible enhancement of the child's language development and later social and cognitive development. Bayley (1970) has reported on the positive relationships between early verbal abilities and later intellectual function. Clarke-Stewart (1973) in her study of United States' infants found somewhat greater specificity of interactive consequences than did Bayley. Verbal stimulation was positively related to infant's language competence, and maternal responsiveness to infant's expression of emotion. Therefore, the type and amount of social interaction provided by caretaker and/or mother can have important consequences for the infant's later psychological development.

The second main issue raised in this chapter concerns the effects of familial economic level of infant care practice, and subsequent effects on physical, psychological, and social development of the child. Although there were several bases for judging stratification in the community, such as education, church membership, clan and lineal membership, and status of grandfather, we chose the familial economic level, because it differentiated maternal and paternal behavior within the community, was easily measured, and provided a direct link to the postulated effects on the child. For example, at the biological end of the developmental spectrum, familial economic level could be thought to influence infant development through the mother's nutritional status during pregnancy. It has been reported by Lechtig, Delgado, Lasky, Klein, Engle, Yarbrough, and Habicht (1975), and Lechtig, Delgado, Lasky, Yarbrough, Klein, Habicht, and Behar, (1975) that decreased protein intake in the prenatal period can have negative consequences for the infant's later cognitive development. Although we were not able to ascertain prenatal nutrition in this study, we were able to measure height and weight of the infants periodically, and to perform physical examinations at least twice during the year on each infant. There was no evidence of clinical malnutrition on clinical examination of the infants. (It should be noted that all infants in our study were breast-fed throughout the first year of life, with largely carbohydrate supplementation added from about six months on for some of the infants.) We found that the weight of the infant, but not the height, was related to the index of familial economic level (r = +.40, p < .01). Details of the relationship between physical growth and psychological development will be reported elsewhere.

On the social side of the developmental spectrum was our observation that maternal caretaking practice was related to familial economic level. While we cannot delineate the circumstances to account for this relationship, we believe that one explanation is the extent of the maternal work load, including the mother's command over external resources to aid her in her household and infant-caretaking functions. If the mother's work load is heavy because of both the size of her farm and the size of her family, and she is also without cash income from her husband's job or from the sale of her extra crops, she may well have little opportunity for anything other than the most utilitarian aspects of child care. If, however, her farm is small, the nuber of children few, and she has a cash income, then she has a smaller work load and/or the ability to hire individuals to help her. This latter circumstance potentially could provide her with more leisure time to spend in play or in social interaction with her infant. An additional factor, not systematically studied, may be the interaction between source of income and mother's work load.

The confounding of the relationship between adequate nutrition and maternal work load as they affect infant care is exemplified by the lore in the community that the average family needs about two acres to have sufficient food for the year. A typical mother farms this amount of land and easily takes care of her family. With more than two acres, the mother may feed her family more adequately, but it involves more work and less time for infant caretaking. With less than two acres, her work load is lighter, but there is also less food. The work load of the mother thus becomes a crucial variable. Through this analysis, we believe we have demonstrated that family economic level, albeit a crude index of stratification, can provide clues for more definitive analyses of social forces within the family and within the community affecting the biological and psychological development of the child.

CONCLUSIONS

Beyond the actual findings reported in this chapter, this research emphasizes the necessity of being prepared to observe existing patterns of behavior when doing comparative psychological research, rather than relying on preformed views. Our original research plan had been to utilize the expected prolonged mother-infant contact in an East African agricultural society to examine the development of maternal-infant relationships during the infant's first year. We had assumed a homogeneity of infant care practice in a relatively homogeneous social system. We rapidly ascertained that differences in familial economic resources made a critical difference in a mother's daily activities, and, in turn, in her child-care practice. In some families, the mother was the sole caretaker; in others, she had significant amounts of help. Thus, we were forced to take into account the crucial role of the surrogate caretaker in helping the infant's mother with her everyday activities. Although we had not anticipated these variations, we found them inherently interesting, with enough potentially significant implications for child developmental research to make them the focus of our endeavors.

Our finding of a shift from a polymatric form of infant caretaking to a monomatric form, whether due to changing attitudes of women, educational opportunities for young girls, or economic necessity, raises many questions for developing societies as well as for our own. What are the merits or demerits of these systems? Under what cultural conditions are they best operative? In the West, we have had almost two generations of experience with the monomatric form, and have only been gathering evidence on these questions within the past decade. The polymatric form has probably existed within agricultural societies for several centuries. Given the lack of evidence for the advantages or disadvantages of these systems, it would be unfortunate if societies in the developing world moved to the monomatric form and, conversely, if societies in the developed world moved to the polymatric form without taking into account the benefits and costs of each system.

We have attempted to demonstrate how concepts and observations from one society can have important implications for another society; and not unidirectional, from the industrial Western world to the agricultural communities of the Third World. However, it should be obvious that conclusions about child care practice in one society cannot simply be applied to another without taking into consideration the functional relationship of the infant caretaking system to the familial social system, the economic resources within the community, and the value orientation regarding children extant in the culture.

Finally, from the point of view of public policy and more
fundamental developmental research, the study of early child
development in different societies offers the opportunity to
understand the relative contributions of social, psychological,
and biological influences on infant growth and development.
At the same time, these comparative psychological studies can
indicate how these influences are modified and shaped by
cultural forces, to enable the child to adapt to new challenges
of rapid change in our own society, and as well in societies in
less-developed parts of the world.

REFERENCES

Bayley, N. Bayley scales of infant development. New York:
    Psychological Corporation, 1969.

Bayley, N. Development of mental abilities. In P. Mussen (Ed.),
    Carmichael's manual of child psychology (3rd ed., Vol.
    1). New York: Wiley, 1970.

Bowlby, J. Attachment and loss. Vol. 1: Attachment. London:
    Hogarth Press, 1969.

Cagnolo, C. The Akikuyu--Their customs, traditions and folk-
    lore. Nyeri Catholic Mission, Nyeri, Kenya, 1933.

Clarke-Stewart, K. A. Interactions between mothers and their
    young children: Characteristics and consequences
    (Monograph No. 38, Society for Research and Child
    Development). 1973, University of Chicago Press,
    Chicago.

Fisher, J. The anatomy of Kikuyu domesticity and husbandry
    (Monograph, Department of Technical Cooperation,
    Overseas Development Administration). London:
    Eland House, 1956.

Hess, R. D. Social class and ethnic influences on socialization.
    In P. Mussen (Ed.), Carmichael's manual of child
    psychology (Vol. 2). New York: Wiley, 1970.

Inkeles, A., & Smith, D. H. Becoming modern. Cambridge, Mass.:
    Harvard University Press, 1975.

Jelliffe, D. B., & Bennett, F. J. Aspects of child rearing in
    Africa. Journal of Tropickal Pediatric and

Environmental Child Health, 1972, 18, 25-43.

Kenyatta, J. Facing Mount Kenya, The tribal life of the Kikuyu. London: Secker and Warburg, 1953.

Lambert, H. E. Kikuyu social and political institutions. London: Oxford University, 1956.

Lechtig, A., Delgado, H., Lasky, R. E., Klein, R. E., Engle, P. L., Yarbrough, C., & Habicht, J. Maternal nutrition and fetal growth in developing societies: Socio-economic factors. American Journal Diseases of Children, 1975, 129, 434-437.

Lechtig, A., Delgado, H., Lasky, R. E., Yarbrough, C., Klein, R. E., Habicht, J., & Behar, M. Maternal nutrition and fetal growth in developing countries. American Journal Diseases of Children, 1975, 129, 553-556.

Leiderman, P. H., & Leiderman, G. F. Affective and cognitive consequences of polymatric infant care in the East African highlands. In A. D. Pick (Ed.), Minnesota symposia on child psychology (Vol. 8). Minneapolis: University of Minnesota Press, 1974 (a).

Leiderman, P. H., & Leiderman, G. F. Familial influences of infant development in an East African agricultural community. In E. J. Anthony & C. Koupernik (Eds.), The child in his family--children at a psychiatric risk (Vol. 3). New York: Wiley, 1974 (b).

Leiderman, P. H., & Seashore, M. J. Mother-infant neonatal separation: Some delayed consequences. In Parent-infant relationships (CIBA Foundation Symposium 33). Amsterdam: Elsevier, 1975.

Leiderman, P. H., Babu, B., Kagia, J., Kraemer, H. C., & Leiderman, G. F. African infant precocity and some social influences during the first year. Nature, 1973, 242, 247-249.

LeVine, R. Quoted in Psyche and Environment. Psychoanalytic Quarterly, 1970, 38, 191-216.

Mead, M., & MacGregor, F. C. Growth and culture. New York: Putnam, 1951.

Munroe, R. N., & Munroe, R. L. Household care and infant care in an East African society. Journal of Social Psychology, 1971, 83, 3-13.

Tulkin, S. R., & Kagan, J. Mother-child interaction in the first year of life. Child Development, 1972, 43, 31-41.

Chapter 17

Relations Between Maternal Attitudes and Maternal Behavior As a Function of Social Class

Howard A. Moss and Sandra J. Jones
National Institute of Mental Health

A popular and effective strategy for identifying the determinants of child behavior is through the study of contrasting groups. Once clear group differences emerge, it becomes possible to search for their antecedents. Thus, in constructing a theory of psychological development, the study of contrasting groups facilitates identifying and conceptualizing those events that were instrumental in contributing to personality formation. This research strategy provides the social scientist with a naturalistic analogue of the experimental method associated with the laboratory.

Livson (1973) has suggested that it would be profitable to analyze data separately for a variety of homogeneous subgroups, and to use the presence or absence of "generality of results across groups" as a basis for stimulating theoretical speculations. Studies of sex and social class differences, as well as cross-cultural comparisons, have made effective use of the technique of contrasting groups for the purpose of testing or deriving developmental hypotheses. Research by Kagan and Moss (1962) on sex differences, Kohn (1963) on social class, and Caudill and Weinstein (1969) on cross-cultural comparisons are examples of studies where information based on contrasting groups was used to derive theoretical concepts associated with parental treatment and child behavior. Most of these studies have made use of markedly divergent groups, since this, of course, maximizes the differences that can be observed and facilitates tracking or reconstructing the antecedent factors that produced these group differences. In contrast, the research to be reported on in this chapter compares groups that are relatively close in terms of the general culture from which they were drawn--different sectors of a middle-class population of the kind frequently used in developmental studies.

As part of a longitudinal study on family development[1] carried out by the Child Research Branch of the National Institute of Mental Health, a sample of mother-infant pairs was studied by means of interviews, questionnaires, home observations, and experimental procedures. The present report deals with those aspects of the data concerning the relations between ratings of maternal attitudes as judged from inter- views conducted during the last trimester of first pregnancy, and selected mother-infant behaviors assessed when the infants were three months of age. A major objective of our research was to evaluate the relative contribution of different determinants of maternal behavior. The attitudes of the mother concerning the values and satisfactions associated with caring for infants is one of the factors that should contribute to maternal behavior. Since distinctive characteristics of the infant might interact with and influence the expression of these attitudes as well as affect maternal behaviors, there would seem to be a definite methodological advantage in assessing maternal attitudes prior to the birth of the infant. The last trimester of the pregnancy was selected for this interview, since it was felt that by this time women would be more likely to have mobilized their feelings and attitudes about prospective parenthood and be more sensitized and articulate in expressing these views, while remaining relatively independent of strong influences that might be

---

[1]This longitudinal program, in addition to the mother-infant study, includes the study of early marriage directed by Dr. Robert Ryder, the analysis of newborn behavior carried out by Dr. Thomas Douthitt and Dr. Raymond Yang, and a preschool assessment supervised by Dr. Charles Halverson. Each project studied the same sample, at different develop- mental stages, so that a longitudinal assessment could be generated by interrelating the data among each of these independent cross-sectional studies. Dr. Richard Bell . directed the overall longitudinal program.

produced later on through exposure to their infant.

We felt there was still another advantage in interviewing women at the latter stage of pregnancy. Women who are about to have their first infant are under considerable psychological pressure to reorganize their view of themselves and their imminent role in society. For these women, the prospect of motherhood is often strange and discontinuous from their previous life experiences. At the same time, these subjects often manifest a greater acceptance of themselves as persons and reflect an ingenuousness that somehow appears to be related to their consciousness of bearing a child. It may be for this combination of reasons that women during the third trimester of pregnancy seem particularly eager to communicate with psychologically trained professionals and are able to do so in a remarkably nondefensive and candid manner. In two of our studies, we found that pregnancy interviews were more productive and freer than follow-up interviews with the same mothers when their infants were about three and one-half months of age, even though we were considerably more acquainted with these subjects by the time of the second interview. Therefore, we feel that the timing of our pregnancy interview was particularly effective in terms of producing rich and reliable information.

Research efforts have yielded inconsistent findings regarding the relationship of maternal attitudes and behaviors. Moss and Robson (1968), Tulkin and Cohler (1973), Caldwell and Hersher (1964), and Clarke-Stewart (1973) all have shown some support for maternal attitudes being related to behavior; whereas Becker and Krug (1965), in their review of research using the Parent Attitude Research Instrument, present a negative picture. Evaluation of these various findings suggests that there is a much greater chance of identifying an association between attitudes and behavior when the content of the respective attitudes and behaviors are cognate, when they are functionally related to one another, or when they deal with developmental issues that are salient at the time of assessment. Although attitudes assessed from both interviews and questionnaires have predicted to behavior, there is some evidence that interview-derived information provides stronger relations to behavior than do the questionnaires that are currently available. In some unpublished data, Moss and Robson found that maternal attitudes assessed during pregnancy through interviews and the Schaeffer Pregnancy Research Inventory were significantly interrelated, but that only the interview measures were related to maternal behaviors when the child was three months old. Another consideration in evaluating the predictive power of maternal attitudes is that these attitudes, much as one would expect, show more consistent relations to maternal than to child behavior. More information is needed concerning the effect of maternal behavior on child behavior before we can hope to establish the relation between maternal attitudes and child behavior.

There is also evidence that maternal attitudes are more predictive of both maternal and child behavior of middle- and upper-middle than for lower-class samples (Becker & Krug, 1965; Tulkin & Cohler, 1973). Although the basis for this social class difference has not been established, these findings support our decision to dichotomize our cases on a dimension associated with social class.

In previous studies (Moss, 1967; Moss & Robson, 1968) involving smaller samples, we examined the relation between maternal attitudes assessed before the birth of the infant and later maternal behavior. These studies provided guidelines for the selection of variables that were included in the present study. Generally, it was found that maternal attitudes were positively associated with functionally similar later maternal behaviors. The data to be reported here serve, in part, as an attempt to replicate these earlier findings.

SAMPLE

The sample consisted of 121 primiparous mothers and their infants. They were all native-born, white, and were living in the greater Washington, D.C., metropolitan area at the time of the study. This sample was dichotomized in terms of the husband's educational level (EL), resulting in 60 families in the lower EL group, and 61 families in the upper. There were 35 male and 25 female infants in the lower group and 29 male and 32 female infants in the upper. The mean number of years of schooling for the lower EL group was 12.92 for the wives (range, 12 to 16 years) and 13.02 for the husbands (range, 10.5 to 15). The mean years of schooling for the upper EL group was 14.77 for the wives (range, 12 to 18) and 16.94 for the husbands (range, 16 to 20). The religious composition of the two groups was quite similar (approximately 50 percent Protestant, 35 percent Catholic, and 15 percent Jewish). In this sample, there were four mixed marriages between Christians and Jews, all of which occurred in the upper EL group. The geographical origin of wives from both groups was quite comparable.

The overall sample proved to be highly heterogeneous as to demographic variables such as income level, occupation, religious background, and geographical origin. Although all of the subjects were drawn from the Washington, D.C., area, many had moved there from other parts of the country either as children with their parents or on their own as young adults to seek employment, to attend college, to get married, etc. About 50 percent of the wives grew up in the D.C. area. Approximately 12 percent were reared in rural settings, another 12 percent had moved several times while growing up, and the remainder came from towns and cities of various sizes throughout the United States. Even for those subjects who grew up in or around D.C. there was variability in background, since the many kinds of neighborhoods that exist in a metropolitan area were represented in our sample. Therefore, although we made some effort to control the makeup of our sample by restricting our cases to native-born whites, we ended up with what appears to be a heterogeneous cross-section of families. This heterogeneity in demographic characteristics also extended to variations in attitudes, beliefs, and life space experiences among members of our sample. Thus we feel limited in being able to draw normative conclusions from our results. Instead, our analyses are directed more toward establishing dimensions on mother-infant behavior and in identifying the connections between the functioning of the mother and the child. Some of the limitations associated with this heterogeneous sample are partially overcome by having dichotomized our cases on the basis of education and having reported results separately for these two sub-groups. Therefore some tentative generalizations may be made about these two respective groups.

The fact that our subjects were studied so intensively by different investigators adds a richness to our data and presents a unique opportunity to link behaviors across distinct developmental stages. However, we feel that large-scale, comprehensive data collection programs such as ours often pay a price for the magnitude of their operation. Some of the risks associated with ambitious research efforts are that they may become administratively unwieldy, may result in an impersonal and superficial association with subjects, and may make careful monitoring of data collection impossible, so that what one gains in statistical power from larger samples may be lost because of increased error variance.

The following illustrates the kind of problem we experienced in conducting our longitudinal research. The marriage assessment, from which our mother-infant cases were obtained, started out by surveying a large sample of subjects

(2,000 cases). Only a small proportion of these cases could be followed up at subsequent stages by our staff because of the amount of time our procedures required. Furthermore, administratively we were unable to monitor accurately whether some of the cases were not followed up because the couple had moved and could not be reached, or because some subjects were less willing to accept the pressures and imposition of participating in our data collection procedures. Thus we are faced with an unknown degree of self-selection of those who participated in this research. In addition, since our study of mother-infant behavior was part of a longitudinal assessment, we were geared to studying specific subjects on an age-related schedule that necessitated spurts of high-velocity data collection. These pressures to collect a great deal of data over short periods of time impeded our acquiring the type of in-depth familiarity with our subjects that we regard as important, at a conceptual level, for integrating complex psychological phenomena and for generating original hypotheses concerning the organization of behavior.

The educational classification we used for dichotomizing our sample is merely a convenient index for identifying the reference group or social class to which our subjects were likely to belong. We are interested in social class because it is more functional than education per se in forming and transmitting the differing attitudes and values concerning infant care. As suggested by Kohn (1963) and Caudill and Weinstein (1969), occupational experiences both directly and indirectly shape interpersonal attitudes and values, and thus contribute to the nature of the interactions parents share with their children. Since occupational experience may be important both as an indicator of social class membership and as an agent for shaping parent-child interactions, we have included information concerning the occupational makeup of our two EL groups.

Table 17-1 shows the most frequently occurring occupational categories for the husbands in our sample, and Table 17-2 lists the most frequent categories for the wives.[2] In each of these tables, the occupation information is presented separately for the lower and upper EL groups.

As would be expected, there were distinct differences in the occupational makeup of the two EL groups for the husbands.

[2]This was based on most recent occupation, since at the time of the study many of the wives had stopped working because of pregnancy.

TABLE 17-1. Most Frequent Occupation for Husbands.

Lower EL Subjects		Upper EL Subjects	
Occupation	Frequency	Occupation	Frequency
Salesman	7	Student (preparing for advanced degree)	11
Store manager	6	Engineer	8
Computer operator	3	Scientist	6
Policeman	3	Accountant	5
Draftsman	3	Lawyer	4
Programmer	3	Programmer	3
Construction worker	3	Teacher	3
Telephone installer	3	Mathematician	2
Insurance agent	3	Public relations	2
Truck driver	2		
Self-employed	2		

About 40 percent of the lower EL husbands were associated with the business world, either directly as salesmen, or through the management of business enterprises. Another 15 to 20 percent of this group functioned as skilled workers, while an equal percentage of the lower EL men had semiskilled jobs. On the other hand, almost 60 percent of the upper EL husbands were employed as scientists or professional men, with an additional 20 percent studying for advanced degrees that in all likelihood would prepare them for the scientific/professional work force. There was minimal overlap in the occupational categories of the lower and upper EL men.

The differentiation between occupations of the lower and

TABLE 17-2.   Most Frequent Occupations for Wives.

Lower EL Subjects		Upper EL Subjects	
Occupation	Frequency	Occupation	Frequency
Secretary	22	Secretary	14
Clerk	8	Teacher	11
Saleswoman	4	Clerk	5
Teacher	3	Programmer	4
Hair dresser	2	Analyst	3
Bank teller	2	Student	3
Dental technician	2	Nurse	3
Nurse	2	Manager	2
Manager	2	Dental technician	2
X-ray technician-receptionist	2	Bookkeeper	2
Administrative consultant	2	Housewife	2
Writer-artist (commercial)	2	Social worker	2

upper EL wives was much less than for their husbands.
Approximately 50 percent of the lower and 30 percent of the
upper EL wives held secretarial-type positions. About 10
percent of both groups had ancillary or technical jobs in
the medical profession. The greatest distinction between
these two groups for the wives was that close to 25 percent
of the upper EL women held the type of professional positions
that require an academic degree (teachers and social workers),
whereas only about 5 percent of the lower EL women fitted
this category.

METHOD

Pregnancy Interview

The mothers were interviewed in our laboratory during the third trimester of their first pregnancy. A standard interview schedule was followed that dealt with the expectant mother's feelings of well-being, concerns and attitudes about the pregnancy, expectations about maternal functioning, investment in being a mother, interest and pleasure in caring for infants, identification and affectional patterns with her own parents, and affectional and sexual behavior in the marriage. Our primary interests were to determine, before the birth of the child, the amount and type of contact the mother would seek with her infant, and the degrees to which her maternal behavior would be influenced by the infant's state or her own predisposition to be responsive.

The pregnancy interviews were used for rating (on a 9-point scale) a series of global variables relevant to the various dimensions and issues under study. One staff member conducted the 121 pregnancy interviews and then listened to tape-recordings of these interviews in order to make the necessary ratings. A second staff member rated 24 of these cases for the purpose of establishing interrater reliabilities. Four of these pregnancy interview variables were selected to be included in the present analysis. The choice of these four interview variables, as well as of the eight home observation variables, was based on findings from previous studies (Moss, 1967; Moss & Robson, 1968) and from theoretical expectations that these two sets of variables should be related to each other. Abridged definitions and the reliabilities for the interview variables are as follows:

1. Degree of depression during pregnancy (interrater reliability, .83). This variable rates both the frequency and intensity with which the subject has experienced overt depression during her pregnancy. She may demonstrate a depressed mood, psychomotor retardation, and describe more or less constant feelings of sadness, discouragement, or crying spells.

2. Degree that infant is seen in a positive sense (interrater reliability, .71). This variable assesses the extent to which the subject views an infant as gratifying, pleasant, and nonburdensome. She stresses the warmer, more personal, and

rewarding aspects of the infant.

3.   Degree of interest in affectionate contact with the
     infant (interrater reliability, .88). This variable
     assesses the amount of interest the expectant mother
     exhibits at the prospect of holding, cuddling, and
     rocking her infant. Evidence for such interest
     might be seen in her looking forward to such contact
     with pleasure, wanting to breast-feed to be closer,
     enjoying physical contact with other infants she
     has cared for, and being upset at the idea of having
     a "noncuddly" baby.

4.   Degree of interest in social interaction with the
     infant (interrater reliability, .90). This variable
     assesses the degree to which the mother describes
     herself as getting pleasure from looking, smiling,
     talking, and playing with infants. Particular
     emphasis is given to her interest in evoking these
     behaviors in her infant and engaging in reciprocal
     social interactions.

Home Observations

     Two 6-hour naturalistic observations were conducted in
the home when the infant was three months of age. The
observations started at 9:00 a.m. and occurred on two non-
consecutive days, but within a week of each other. The
observations for the 121 cases were divided among three female
observers. Prior to the first home observation, the observer
assigned to that case made a brief introductory visit to the
home in order to structure the observational procedures for
the mother, establish rapport with her, and to assist her in
working out any discomfort she might experience in having an
observer present in the home.

     A modified time-sampling procedure was used for coding
the observational data. The time-sampled variables included
both maternal and infant behaviors. The infant variables
dealt largely with the state of the infant (asleep, awake,
crying, etc.). The maternal variables pertained to caretaking
activities (feeding, burping, diapering, etc.), contact
(holding or attending the infant), stimulation of the infant
(visual, tactile, auditory, and motion), and social-affectionate
behaviors (smiles, speech, and kisses). For each minute of the
observation the observer placed a check in a column for each
behavior that occurred in that particular minute. Thus, a

score of 360 was the maximum that could be achieved for any
one variable for each 6-hour observation. In addition to the
time-sampled codings, a more refined measure was obtained
concerning the infant's cry and the maternal response to the
cry. This consisted of starting two stopwatches when the
infant began to cry, one to record the duration of the cry
and the other to record the latency of any maternal behavior
associated with approaching and soothing the crying infant.
The scores for the two 6-hour observations were summed to give
one score for each measure.

Correlation coefficients were computed between the scores
for the time-sampled variables obtained from the two
observations. Since the scores for the two observations were
summed for each variable, the obtained correlations were
corrected using the Spearman-Brown formula. The corrected
reliability coefficients ranged from .74 to .89 with a mean
of .81 for the seven time-sampled variables used in the present
analysis. A reliability of .54 was obtained for the Maternal
Responsiveness score, which was a timed measure. At regular
intervals throughout the data collection, the observers went
in pairs to homes not included in the regular sample to obtain
reliability data on the observational variables. Twelve cases
were studied for each combination of the three observers.
After the reliability data were recorded, the observers
reviewed their respective records in order to determine and
correct for any indiosyncratic biases or drift that may have
developed over the three-year data collection period of the
study. The definitions and observer reliabilities for the
eight home-observational variables included in the present
analysis are given in the following list. Each of the
reliabilities reported is the average for the three combinations
of observers.

1. Mother holds infant (average interrater reliability,
    .99). Mother holds the infant in any manner so that
    the primary support for the infant is provided by
    the mother's body or extremities.

2. Mother caretakes (average interrater reliability,
    .99). Mother changes diaper or bathes infant.
    Score from the time mother initiates activity until
    infant is once again completely dressed.

3. Mother initiates socializing with infant (average
    interrater reliability, .80). The mother plays with
    infant or talks and smiles and attempts to evoke a

response from infant.

4. Mother smiles (average interrater reliability, .90).
    Any smile by mother directed at the infant that
    occurs within his field of vision.

5. Mother talks to infant (average interrater reliability,
    .98). Any vocalization of the mother that is directed
    to the infant (include talking, singing, and whistling).

6. Vis-a-vis (average interrater reliability, .97).
    Eye-to-eye contact between the mother and infant
    occurring at a distance of not more than four feet.
    A mutual pause and fixation must occur for this
    variable to be scored.

7. Mother kisses infant (average interrater reliability,
    .62). Mother kisses infant anywhere on body.

8. Maternal responsiveness (no reliability data). This
    measure is the average latency, in seconds, of the
    maternal response to infant protest (either fusses
    or crying).

The mean scores for the two EL groups were compared for
each of the home observation and pregnancy interview variables
that were included in the present analysis. Table 17-3 shows
the mean, standard deviations, and the *t*-values based on
comparisons between the upper and lower EL groups for the
pregnancy and home observation variables.

The upper and lower EL groups were not significantly
different on any of the home observation variables. However,
the upper EL group received significantly higher pregnancy
interview ratings than the lower EL group for the variables
Interest in affectionate contact with infant ($t = 2.33.$,
$p < .05$), and *Interest in social interaction with infant*
($t = 2.31$, $p < .05$). The lower EL group received significantly
higher scores for the interview variable that related *Depression
during pregnancy* ($t = 2.52$, $p < .05$).

The main analyses consisted of correlating each of the
four pregnancy ratings with maternal variables coded from home
observations when infants were three months old. These
correlations were computed separately for the two EL groups
in order to determine whether different patterns of correlations
or different levels of predictability of interview material

TABLE 17-3. Means, Standard Deviations, and t-values for Comparisons between Upper and Lower EL Groups.

| | Lower EL Group | | Upper EL Group | | |
	Mean	S. D.	Mean	S. D	t-values
Interview Variables					
Depression	5.36	1.95	4.38	2.24	2.52[a]
Infant seen in pos. sense	6.37	1.84	6.00	2.27	.97
Interest in affect. contact	5.67	1.78	6.43	1.81	2.33[a]
Interest in social interaction	5.82	1.67	6.53	1.73	2.31[a]
Home Observation Variables					
Holds infant	157.62	68.82	156.44	55.02	.10
Caretakers	49.63	20.03	45.11	18.89	1.27
Initiates socail	65.62	30.44	66.82	39.79	-.18
Smiles at infant	66.45	33.70	73.46	38.70	-1.05
Talks to infant	202.23	71.88	195.72	68.15	.51
Vis-a-vis	117.43	44.09	109.51	43.24	.99
Kisses infant	24.97	23.42	20.56	20.20	1.10
Maternal responsiveness	91.47	63.59	90.28	64.77	.10

[a] $p < .05$, two-tailed test.

451

were associated with the respective social class membership,
as represented by our dichotomized sample. In addition to the
use of the four selected interview variables, the complete
list of thirty-five interview variables was factor analyzed,
and factor scores derived from this analysis were correlated
with the selected set of home observation variables for the
two EL groups. The comparisons of correlations between the
two EL groups are exploratory in nature, since no specific
hypotheses were generated for predicting different results
for these two groups. However, it was assumed that for both
groups the pregnancy ratings would be associated with the home
observation variables.

RESULTS

    Tables 17-4 and 17-5 show the intercorrelations among the
pregnancy interview variables and three-month home observation
variables, respectively. The findings in each of these Tables
are presented separately for the lower and upper EL groups.
These data are presented in order to assist in the interpretation of the correlations between the pregnancy and the
home observation variables.

    There is indication in Table 17-4 of low to moderate
overlap among some of the interview variables, so that the
results reported in the following sections, which show the
correlations for each of the interview variables with the home
observation variables, were not completely independent from
one another. In particular, the variables *Infant seen in a
positive sense*, *Interest in affectionate contact*, and *Interest
in social interaction* tend to cluster together, especially for
the upper EL group. Nonetheless, the shared variance between
any pair of correlated variables in this Table tends to range
only between 0 to 28 percent, suggesting that these variables
were rated with sufficient independence to warrant separate
presentation of results. Although it is not the intent of
this paper to present a technical analysis of the organizational
structure of the home observation variables, it can be readily
observed in Table 17-5 that there are substantial intercorrelations among many of these variables, and that in
particular the social behaviors form a strong nucleus. This
holds up for both the lower and upper EL groups. The high
intercorrelations among many of these observation variables
help account for the fact that these variables often show
similar patterns in their relation to the pregnancy interview
variables.

TABLE 17-4. Intercorrelations among Pregnancy Interview Variables for Lower and Upper EL Groups Separately.[a]

	Depression	Infant seen in positive sense	Interest in affectionate contact	Interest in social interaction
Depression		-.18	-.13	-.42[c]
Infant seen in positive sense	-.16		.53[c]	.41[c]
Interest in affectionate contact	.07	.43[c]		.35[b]
Interest in social interaction	.02	.16	.33[b]	

[a] The correlations for the lower EL group are presented on the lower left, and for the upper EL group on the upper right.

[b] $p < .01$ significance level.

[c] $p < .001$ significance level.

TABLE 17-5. Intercorrelations among the Maternal Home Observation Variables for Lower and Upper EL Groups Separately.[a]

	Holds Infants	Care-takers	Initiates Socializing	Smiles at infant	Talks to infant	Vis-a-vis	Kisses infant	Maternal responsiveness
Holds infant	--	.17	.38^c	.20	.50^d	.35^c	.30^b	.14
Caretakes	.27^b	--	.53^d	.48^d	.49^d	.57^d	.21	.17
Initiates socializing	.30^b	.35^c	--	.84	.72^d	.81^d	.54^d	.16
Smiles at infant	.28^b	.36^c	.72^d	--	.56^d	.77^d	.64^d	.09
Talks to infant	.53^d	.51^d	.64^d	.65^d	--	.72^d	.38^c	.26^b
Vis-a-vis	.35^c	.42^d	.57^d	.66^d	.72^d	--	.41^d	.21
Kisses infant	.19	.27^b	.50^d	.28^b	.40^c	.33^c	--	.18
Maternal responsiveness	.20	.09	.09	.12	.19	.04	.16	--

[a]The correlations for the lower EL group are represented on the lower left, and for the upper EL group on the upper right.

[b] p < .05 significance level.

[c] p < .01 significance level.

[d] p < .001 significance level.

454

Within each of the EL groups separate correlations are presented for the mothers with male infants (35 lower and 29 upper EL) and mothers with female infants (25 lower and 32 upper EL). This was done since studies of mother-infant inter-action frequently show sex differences, and these differences are often helpful in explicating theoretically important aspects of the relationship.

Table 17-6 shows the correlations of each of the pregnancy interview variables with the selected set of home observation variables. In general, these findings are quite consistent and striking in showing significant correlations between pregnancy ratings and maternal behavior for the upper, but not for the lower, EL mothers. All of the significant correlations that were observed for the upper EL group occurred in the predicted direction, and in most cases the correlations for the male and female subgroups showed the same pattern.

Specifically, the highlights of the findings are as follows: Upper EL mothers who showed evidence of being depressed during the pregnancy interview were less likely to initiate social behavior, smile, talk, and engage in "vis-a-vis" interaction with their infants when they were three months of age.

The pregnancy ratings on *Degree infant is seen in a positive sense* are highly related, for the upper EL mothers, to the whole cluster of home observation variables reported in Table 17-6. Thus, this pregnancy rating for these mothers was associated with their social, nurturant, and affectionate behavior toward their infants. Again, these correlations were comparable for both male and female infants. What seems particularly striking in Table 17-6 is the contrast of extensive significant findings for the upper EL group, but a complete dearth of findings for the lower EL group.

The pregnancy rating on *Degree of interest in affectionate contact with infants* was significantly associated with maternal behaviors only for the female infants of upper EL mothers. For these subjects, interest in affectionate contact was related to social, affectionate, and nurturant overtures from the mother. Nonsignificant, but parallel trends occurred for the upper EL males, and the only statistically significant pooled correlation was between *Interest in affectionate contact* and *Kisses infant*. The fact that this emerged as the strongest relation conforms to expectations, since these two variables reflect a specific and similar motive that can be directly expressed in verbal or physical behavior.

TABLE 17-6. Correlations Between Pregnancy Ratings and 3-Month Maternal Behaviors

	Holds infant	Care-takes	Initiates Social	Smiles at infant	Talks to infant	Vis-a-vis infant	Kisses infant	Maternal responsiveness
Degree of Depression								
Upper EL (total)	-.16	-.19	-.31[a]	-.36[b]	-.36[b]	-.29[a]	-.21	-.06
Upper EL males	-.01	-.22	-.35	-.37[a]	-.37[a]	-.40[a]	-.22	-.03
Upper EL females	-.27	-.14	-.27	-.33	-.34[a]	-.19	-.22	-.09
Lower EL (total)	.18	-.24	.04	.17	.01	.05	.11	.10
Lower EL males	.19	-.18	.02	.11	-.05	-.01	.05	.11
Lower EL females	.17	-.33	.06	.25	.12	.12	.22	.10
Infant Seen in Positive Sense								
Upper EL (total)	.25[a]	.13	.34[b]	.33[b]	.29[a]	.37[b]	.45[c]	.40[b]
Upper EL males	.32	-.01	.38[a]	.28	.40[a]	.49[b]	.43[a]	.47[b]
Upper EL females	.21	.34[a]	.35[a]	.43[a]	.24	.31	.48[b]	.45[b]
Lower EL (total)	.10	-.20	-.03	-.05	-.03	.05	.03	.03
Lower EL males	.06	-.19	-.07	-.04	-.10	.06	.03	-.01
Lower EL females	.16	-.20	.02	-.07	.08	.03	-.12	.11
Interest in Affectionate Contact								
Upper EL (total)	.09	.07	.22	.23	.15	.16	.42[c]	.23
Upper EL males	-.18	.26	.19	.27	.18	.30	.30	.25[b]
Upper EL females	.28	.06	.34[a]	.34[a]	.26	.13	.54[b]	.48[b]
Lower EL (total)	.18	.03	-.07	.08	.02	.09	-.06	-.11
Lower EL males	.26	.12	-.29	.01	.01	.13	-.16	-.18
Lower EL females	.05	-.16	.28	.20	.04	.03	.17	.02
Interest in Social Interaction								
Upper EL (total)	.15	.34[b]	.35[b]	.28[a]	.37[b]	.38[b]	.29[a]	.39[b]
Upper EL males	.11	.52[b]	.40[a]	.25	.49[b]	.53[b]	.18	.25
Upper EL females	.19	.17	.32	.31	.26	.25	.39[a]	.41[a]
Lower EL (total)	.08	-.03	-.12	-.08	-.05	-.02	-.16	.04
Lower EL males	.11	.04	-.16	-.03	.08	.13	-.20	-.03
Lower EL females	.10	-.17	-.03	-.11	-.30	-.21	-.06	.10

[a] $p < .05$
[b] $p < .01$
[c] $p < .001$

Finally, the pregnancy ratings on *Interest in social interaction with the infant* were highly related to most of the three-month maternal behaviors, but, again, only for the upper EL group. Although the upper EL male and female subgroups exhibited similar trends, there was also some suggestion of different correlational patterns. The category *Interest in social interaction* was significantly correlated with mostly the home observation variables dealing with social maternal behaviors for the upper EL males. For the upper EL females, the pregnancy rating was significantly associated only with those maternal behaviors reflecting affection and nurturance. This sex difference is somewhat surprising, since, if anything, it was expected that a maternal interest in social interaction would have been most strongly related to cognate social behaviors for the female infants. However, the differences in correlations between the upper EL male and female groups were not statistically significant, and in some instances these differences were quite negligible, so that they could easily represent random variations.

The four pregnancy interview variables used in the present analyses were drawn from a total set of 35 pregnancy variables. These variables were developed and rated with the objective that they might each, to a degree, be unique in predicting some aspect of maternal functioning. Nonetheless, it seems highly reasonable to anticipate moderate overlap among these 35 variables, both on conceptual grounds and in terms of rater halo effect. The pregnancy interview variables were factor analyzed in order to examine the dimensions that underlie the 35 variables. A principal components factor analysis yielded four rotated (varimax) pregnancy interview factors. Interview variables that had loadings of .40 or higher on a factor were used in deriving factor scores on that factor for each of the subjects. Thus each prospective mother had 4, rather than 35, scores based on the pregnancy interview ratings. The intercorrelations among these four factor scores[3] ranged from .40 to -.34 with a mean of .00. Appendix A groups the interview variables according to those factors for which they had factor loadings of .40 or more. The obtained factor loadings are shown next to the respective interview variable.

Summary descriptions of these four factors are as follows:

---

[3]Although the original rotated factors were orthogonal, correlations of greater than zero among the factor scores resulted because only loadings of greater than .40 were selected in deriving the factor scores.

Factor 1. Positive orientation toward infants and toward the maternal role.

Factor 2. Fearfulness and sense of inadequacy.

Factor 3. Predisposition toward providing and seeking social and physical stimulation.

Factor 4. Establishes close and affectionate ties with family members.

These four pregnancy interview factor scores were correlated with the eight home observation variables that were included in the previously discussed analyses. These results are presented separately for the lower and upper EL subjects in Table 17-7, and the results for the factor scores are consistent with those results shown in Table 17-6. That is, the pregnancy interview factors were related to maternal behavior for the upper, but not for the lower, EL subjects. Factor 1, which depicts a positive orientation toward infants and toward the maternal role, was related to social, affectionate, and nurturant maternal behaviors for the upper EL wives toward both their sons and their daughters. Again, for the upper EL subjects, Factor 3, which deals with the positive mother's predisposition toward providing and seeking stimulation, was related to most of the three-month maternal behaviors for male infants; while Factor 4, which encompasses close and affectionate ties toward family members, was related to the maternal behaviors for the female infants. On the other hand, Factor 2 showed little relation to the home observation variables for any of the subgroups that were studied. In sum, the pregnancy interview factors, which were based on all of the interview ratings, showed trends similar to the findings obtained for the individual interview variables. The advantages of the factor scores are that they efficiently summarize the information obtained from the pregnancy interviews, and they provide results that indicate that the findings observed for the selected interview variables did not inadvertently involve capitalizing on chance relations. On the other hand, the individual interview variables remain useful in that they explicate specific conceptual links to various maternal behaviors, a level of analysis that is important in terms of our current status in theory construction about mother-infant interaction.

The findings that the upper EL male and female subgroups each exhibited similar patterns of correlations between the pregnancy ratings and the home observation variables serves as

TABLE 17-7. Correlations Between Pregnancy Interview Factors and 3-Month Maternal Behaviors

Interview factors	Holds infant	Care-takes	Initiates Social	Smiles at infant	Talks to infant	Vis-a-vis	Kisses infant	Maternal responsiveness
Upper EL total sample								
1	.24	.13	.24	.30[a]	.20	.30[a]	.43[c]	.32[a]
2	-.03	-.12	-.04	-.11	.01	-.05	-.18	-.30[a]
3	.03	.40[b]	.30[a]	.31[a]	.19	.33[a]	.30[a]	.38[b]
4	.16	.06	.19	.17	.02	.08	.30[a]	.03
Upper EL males								
1	.27	.28	.25	.29	.28	.45[a]	.40[a]	.41[a]
2	.10	.05	-.05	-.09	.05	-.05	.01	-.19
3	-.03	.62[c]	.46[b]	.40[a]	.32	.60[c]	.25	.44[a]
4	-.29	.07	-.06	.14	-.22	-.06	.02	.04
Upper EL females								
1	.22	.06	.28	.37[a]	.19	.21	.46[b]	.37[a]
2	-.12	-.24	-.02	-.11	-.01	-.05	-.30	-.48[b]
3	.07	.27	.21[b]	.26	.09	.16	.34[a]	.43[a]
4	.51[b]	.16	.46[b]	.30	.34[a]	.26	.51[b]	.22
Lower EL total sample								
1	.12	-.06	-.03	.04	.01	.01	.01	.01
2	.09	-.07	.06	.08	.02	.06	.01	-.10
3	.00	-.11	.00	.02	.02	-.05	-.12	.10
4	.19	.14	-.06	.16	.07	-.04	.12	.13
Lower EL males								
1	.14	.02	-.10	.10	.01	.05	.02	.05
2	.12	-.05	.03	-.02	.04	.01	-.04	-.14
3	.07	-.16	-.07	-.01	.12	.03	-.22	.02
4	.26	.16	-.15	.13	.03	-.01	-.01	.00
Lower EL females								
1	.08	-.16	.04	-.05	.00	-.08	-.02	.16
2	.02	-.11	.10	.23	-.04	.15	.10	.02
3	-.08	-.03	.12	.09	-.14	-.11	.08	.20[a]
4	.06	.11	.05	.19	.13	-.11	.34	.44[a]

[a] $p < .05$

[b] $p < .01$

[c] $p < .001$

a replication of the reported findings. In addition, for a
previous sample studied by our laboratory (Moss & Robson, 1968),
we also obtained correlations between pregnancy ratings and
home observation variables similar to those coded in this
study. One difference was that this earlier study involved two
6-hour observations at one month of age as well as one 6-hour
observation at three months. Although the earlier findings are
not as striking, they generally correspond with the findings
reported in Table 17-6 for the upper EL subgroups. In particular
the results involving the one-month observations provide farily
solid evidence for replication. One reason for the one-month
scores providing more consistent evidence for replication may
be that they were based on *two* 6-hour observations (as in the
present study) and thus consisted of more stable and reliable
scores than was the case for the three-month observations.

DISCUSSION

     The fact that maternal attitudes during pregnancy were
positively associated with later maternal behaviors is easily
reconcilable in terms of most theoretical positions concerning
mother-child relations. What is enigmatic is the fact that
significant correlations between maternal attitudes and
behaviors occurred only for the upper and not for the lower
EL group. On theoretical grounds, it seems plausible to
expect the same pattern of results to emerge for both groups.
It therefore becomes necessary to search for some elements in
the subculture, or style of functioning, of the lower EL
subjects that would interfere with a direct translation of
maternal attitudes into maternal behavior.

     Before attempting to explain our results it should be
pointed out that other investigators have obtained findings
similar to ours showing that maternal attitudes relate to
behavior mainly for middle-class subjects. Tulkin and Cohler
(1973, p. 104) collected home observation data on a sample of
middle-class and working-class mother-infant pairs, and
correlated the maternal behaviors with the maternal attitude
scores they obtained on these subjects. Their correlations
strikingly paralleled those reported above. Maternal attitudes
were extensively related to behavior for the middle-class, but
were negligibly related for the working-class mothers. Their
explanation for this social class effect is that "mothers in
these two social strata perceive their role in their children's
development differently... . The working-class mothers felt
they could have little influence over the development of their

infant". In addition to these findings, Becker and Krug (1965, p. 529) conclude in their review article that "covariation of Parent Attitude Research Inventory (PARI) scores with measures of child behavior have shown promising implications primarily with homogeneous middle-class families". Thus, the consistent results from these different reports suggest that we are probably dealing with a reliable phenomenon.

As an explanation for the lack of findings in the lower EL mothers, it seems possible to assume that their pregnancy interviews may have been less informative, and their interview ratings less reliable, than those obtained for the upper EL mothers. Education is associated with verbal ability, and for this reason the lower EL women may have lacked the skill to communicate their attitudes effectively during the course of the pregnancy interview. Also, the upper EL mothers may have come from a comparable background, and probably had similar reference groups to that of the interviewer. These circumstances may have facilitated the rapport and openess of the upper EL subjects with the interviewer. Along the same lines, because of greater similarity with the upper EL mothers, the interviewer may have been more "tuned in" to their statements and thus rated them more reliably than the rating of the lower EL mothers. In order to test this assumption, the average interrater reliabilities for the total list of thirty-five interview variables were compared for the lower and upper EL mothers. The average reliability was .73 for the lower and .81 for the upper EL mothers. Although the difference in mean correlations between the two groups is in the suggested direction, this difference is hardly sufficient to account for the lack of results for the lower EL mothers.

Another possible explanation of why the pregnancy ratings did not predict maternal behavior for the lower EL women is that their behavior may have been more susceptible to external forces than was the case with the upper EL women, so that their own predispositions were subordinated. This would be consistent with the interpretation suggested by Tulkin and Cohler (1973) for the social class differences they observed. Examples of this susceptibility to external forces would be instances where stimuli originating from the infant controlled the situation, or where attitudes of the father indirectly shaped the mother-infant interaction. Our data present opportunities to partially test these assumptions.

The home observation data include infant and maternal behaviors that are functionally related to each other. That is, certain infant behaviors appear to have the potential or

"stimulus pull" for evoking particular maternal behavior.
High correlations between these reactive (contingent) variables
could suggest that the mother is especially responsive and
tractable to the related mode of stimuli exhibited by the
infant. Correlations are presented in Table 17-8 to determine
whether lower EL mothers are more responsive (show higher
correlations) than upper EL mothers for a set of these
functionally related mother-infant behaviors. The coupled
variables presented are *Infant protests* with both *Mother holds*
and *Caretakes; Infant vocalizes* with both *Mother talks* and
Imitates infant vocalizations; and *Infant smiles* with *Mother
smiles*. These correlations are presented separately for male
and female infants for the two EL groups.

The only significant correlations that occurred that
suggest that the lower EL mothers may have been selectively
more under the control of their infants were between *Infant
protests* and *Mother holds* and *Caretakes*, but these correlations
were significant only for the lower EL males. The other coupled
variables tended to be correlated at the same level of
significance for both the EL groups. An interesting sex
difference in this Table is that *Infant vocalizes* was
significantly correlated with *Mother talks* for both of the
female but neither of the male groups. This finding is in
keeping with the tendency for social behavior and social
learning to more frequently characterize interaction with
female than with male infants (Moss, 1974). Even if higher
correlations had occurred for the lower EL mothers for these
reactive variables, we would have had to have been exceedingly
cautious in interpreting such results since these correlations
would not enable us to conclusively establish whether it was
the mothers who were being responsive to the infants or vice
versa.

Data from our project also were examined to determine
whether there was any evidence to suggest that the lower EL
husbands indirectly influenced the three-month maternal
behavior of their wives. There is some precedent for this
assumption, since Hoffman (1963) found that in working-class
families certain attitudes of the husbands were more highly
correlated with the wives' behavior toward their children than
were the wives' own attitudes. We administered a questionnaire
concerning traditional familiy attitudes to all our subjects
prior to the birth of their infants. The purpose of this
questionnaire was to attempt to develop an indirect measure for
predicting parental behavior. Both the husbands' and wives'
scores on this questionnaire were correlated with the 42 home
observation variables we studied (32 maternal and 10 infant
variables). In order to determine whether the husbands from

TABLE 17-8. Correlations between Reactive (Contingent) Home Observation Variables.

	Lower EL Group		Upper EL Group	
	Males (N=35)	Females (N=25)	Males (N=29)	Females (N=32)
	Infant Protests			
Mother holds	$.41^b$	.02	.12	-.06
Mother caretakes	$.49^c$	-.19	.18	.05
	Infant Vocalizes			
Mother talks	.25	$.56^b$	.20	$.39^b$
Mother imitates vocalization	$.40^b$	$.47^b$	$.35^a$	$.38^a$
	Infant Smiles			
Mother smiles	$.67^c$	$.47^b$	$.53^c$	$.76^c$

[a] $p < .05$ significance level.

[b] $p < .01$ significance level.

[c] $p < .001$ significance level.

the lower EL group were exerting a greater influence than their wives on the home observation scores, the number of significant correlations were counted and compared for the husbands and wives from both groups. Since correlations were computed separately for male and female infants, there were a total of 84 correlations for each group. We found that 21 of the correlations of the lower EL husbands, compared to 13 of their wives' correlations, were significant at the 10 percent level or better. On the other hand, for the upper EL subjects 8 of the husbands' and 13 of the wives' correlations between the questionnaire scores and the home observation variables achieved this level of significance. Thus, there is indirect evidence that the attitudes of the lower EL husbands somehow may have had a greater influence than the attitudes of the lower EL wives on the three-month mother-infant interaction scores. The opposite seemed to be true for the upper EL subjects.

We have presented some evidence to try to understand why the pregnancy interview material was not predictive of the home observation scores for the lower EL group. Although no single aspect of this evidence is by itself particularly convincing, the results of these analyses suggest some factors that, for the lower EL subjects, may have been operating that interfered with obtaining direct correlations between pregnancy ratings and maternal behavior. (See Tuddenham, Brooks, & Milkovich, 1974; Zegiob & Forehand, 1975.)

These findings suggest that, even in seemingly homogeneous samples, there may be subgroups that differ as to family values, social structure, and style of functioning. Comparisons among these subgroups can provide results that are as striking and as informative as those observed among phenotypically more divergent groups. The consequence of pooling groups that are dissimilar in family background factors is that findings characteristic of the respective groups in the total sample might become diluted or masked, because of different patterns of results for the various subgroups. Also, results obtained from separate studies dealing with the same subject matter, but where the samples were drawn from somewhat different sectors of a middle-class population, would be less likely to support or replicate one another.

REFERENCES

Becker, W. C., & Krug, R. S. The parent attitude research instrument--A research review. Child Development, 1965, 36, 327-365.

Caldwell, B. M., & Hersher, L. Mother-infant interaction during the first year of life. Merrill-Palmer Quarterly, 1964, 10, 119-128.

Caudill, W., & Weinstein, H. Maternal care and infant behavior in Japan and America. Psychiatry, 1969, 32, 12-43.

Clarke-Stewart, K. A. Interactions between mothers and their young children: Characteristics and consequences. Monographs of the Society for Research in Child Development, 1973, 153, 1-109.

Hoffman, M. L. Personality, family structure, and social class as antecedents of parental power assertion.

Child Development, 1963, 34, 869-884.

Kagan, J., & Moss, H. A.   Birth to maturity.   New York: Wiley,
    1962.

Kohn, M. L.   Social class and parent-child relationships: An
    interpretation.   American Journal of Sociology,
    1963, 68, 471-480.

Livson, N.   Developmental dimensions of personality: A life-
    span formulation.   In P. B. Baltes & K. W. Schaie
    (Eds.), Life-span Developmental Psychology Personality
    and Socialization.   New York: Academic Press, 1973.

Moss, H. A.   Sex, age, and state as determinants of mother-
    infant interaction.   Merrill-Palmer Quarterly, 1967,
    13, 19-36.

Moss, H. A.   Early sex differences and mother-infant interaction.
    In R. C. Friedman, R. M. Richart, & R. L. VandeWiele
    (Eds.), Sex Differences in Behavior.   New York: Wiley,
    1974.

Moss, H. A., & Robson, K. S.   Maternal influences in early
    social visual behavior.   Child Development, 1968,
    39, 401-408.

Tuddenham, R. D., Brooks, J., & Milkovich, L.   Mothers' reports
    of behavior of ten-year-olds: Relationships with sex,
    ethnicity and mother's education.   Developmental
    Psychology, 1974, 10, 959-995.

Tulkin, S. R., & Cohler, B. J.   Childrearing attitudes and
    mother-child interaction in the first year of life.
    Merrill-Palmer Quarterly, 1973, 19, 95-106.

Zegiob, L. E., & Forehand, R.   Maternal interactive behavior
    as a function of race, socioeconomic status, and sex
    of the child.   Child Development, 1975, 46, 564-568.

APPENDIX A

PREGNANCY INTERVIEW VARIABLES	FACTOR LOADINGS

FACTOR 1

Nurturance toward infant	.87
Degree infant is seen in positive sense	.85
Positive attitude toward maternal role	.85
Investment in maternal role	.76
Rate of relationship to infant	.65
Contingent maternal behavior	.61
Degree pregnancy is satisfying experience	.56
Nurturance to husband	.52
Degree of interest in affectionate contact with infant	.46
Maternal coping	.46
Preference for infant versus older child	.45
Expected autonomy-control toward infant	.42
Experience caring for infants	.40
Degree of aversion to fussy, irritable infant	-.49

FACTOR 2

Generalized apprehension	.86
Proneness to disorganization under stress	.84
Apprehension over health and well-being of infant	.61
Dependence	.54
Degree of depression during pregnancy	.47
Contingent maternal behavior	-.41
Confidence in maternal skills	-.74
Confidence in overall adequacy	-.78

FACTOR 3

Mother as source of stimulation (orientation)	.74
Degree of interest in social interaction with infant	.73
Mother as source of stimulation (voice)	.69
Degree of preference for active, responsive, high-drive child	.57
Maternal coping	.55
Overall interest in sexual relations	.47

FACTOR 4

Physical affection received from father	.79
Physical affection received from mother	.74
Identification with father	.49
Rate of relationship to husband	.48
General affectionate demonstrativeness	.47
Identification with mother	.42
Degree of interest in affectionate contact with infant	.41

Chapter 18

An Ecological Study of Infant Development in an Urban Setting in Britain

M. P. M. Richards

Cambridge University
Cambridge, England

The aim of the research project to be reported in this
chapter may be stated very simply: we hoped to provide a
description of the development of a sample of children in
their first few years in a city in England. We set out to
build a developmental ecology that would describe the children's
interactions with their physical and social environments. This
descriptive ecological approach was chosen because we feel that
much research on early development is less productive than it
could be, becuase it tends to focus on narrowly defined
questions before the broad principles and necessary description
of both development itself and its social context have been
established. Research also has suffered, because it often
divides development along traditional disciplinary boundaries
that obscure, if not overwhelm, the whole. The primary aim of
a descriptive ecology is to confront the whole, and combining
many disciplines, and to analyze their interrelations. So we
regard our project as a pilot study, a way of establishing a

---

*
The mother-infant follow-up project is being carried out in
collaboration with Judith Bernal, Frances Barnes, and Paul
Light. We are grateful to all the parents and children for
their patience and cooperation, and to the midwives, general
practitioners, and school authorities for their assistance.
Our research is supported by grants from the Nuffield Foundation
and the Mental Health Research Fund.

starting point from which we can begin work on selected facets
of development in more detail, but still within the same framework.

The use of this approach to the problems of human development arises from the author's background in biology. In recent
years, it has become commonplace to advocate biological
approaches to the study of human behavior, but some confusion
has arisen because many different meanings are encompassed by
this term. For some, it has meant an emphasis of the
physiological level of analysis (so that biological psychiatry
becomes a part of physiological psychology), while for others
it is a continuation of the nature-nurture misunderstanding,
with the main thrust going for the former. Elsewhere, it is
taken as a comparative approach involving consideration of
other species as well as our own. The term *biology* is also
used as a synonym of *ethology*, but even this latter term hides
a wide range of theoretical diversity. Given this wide
diversity of usage, I must take a little space to explain how
I am using the term *biology*.

Our approach has adopted the outlook of animal ecologists
and some ethologists. Ecologists, such as Elton (1960) and
Lack (1947), have attempted to describe and analyze the ways
in which a community of animals lives as part of an ecosystem
in a particular environment. They have been concerned with
the biological adaptations that allow a population to maintain
itself and to live in its particular niche.

Behavior, as well as anatomy and physiology, is modified
by selection pressures, and this has been the particular
concern of the ethologists. Among Tinbergen's classical studies
of Blackheaded Gulls are investigations of the parents' removal
of empty eggshells from the nest, which demonstrates the
ethologists' ecological as well as behavioral concerns.
Tinbergen (Tinbergen, Broekhuysen, Feekes, Houghton, Kruuk,
& Szulc, 1962; Tinbergen, Kruuk, & Paillette, 1962) found that
empty eggshells served as a guide to various predator species,
so that, if they remained in the nest after the young had
hatched, they might lead the predator to the young. Thus egg-
shell removal has a clear selective advantage. For this
analysis, one has to consider several aspects of the gulls'
reproductive biology and behavior as well as the behavior of
predators in the ecosystem. The removal of eggshells could
not be understood without consideration of the predators and
the effects of predation on a population of gulls.

In building a human ecological biology, the system
becomes much more complicated, because we live in a social

structure. We do not simply *react* to our physical and social environment, we *act* as a function of our perception and interpretation of the world around us. These perceptions are part of our culture, and they are acquired during the process of development. For our own species, development *is* socialization. This does not imply any opposition of the biological and the social, merely that we are a social species with a culture. Any consideration of human developmental ecology must rest on the notion of a biological infant, predisposed to social life, who develops as a social being (Richards, 1974a, 1974b).

In applying this approach in our project, we tried to collect a good deal of information about the social world of each family and the social interactions of the children, as well as data related to other aspects of their behavior and physiology. We have described our methodology elsewhere (Richards & Bernal, 1972), so the account here will be both brief and selective.

We set out to collect a sample of about 200 infants and follow them from birth to school age. To reduce variation, we confined our sample to first- and second-born children (both in the same family, where possible), and eliminated cases in which there were any indications of abnormality in the mother's medical records. We wanted a sample of full-term "normal" infants, not complicated by special problems of abnormality. As far as possible, the sample reflected the social class distribution of the population from which it came (defined by administrative area of the City of Cambridge), but we excluded the two extremes of the distribution.

One of our first problems was to choose a suitable sample size. The general approach requires the collection of a great deal of data for each child in the sample. This, together with a reasonable frequency of follow-up visits spaced over a long period of time (birth to five), dictated a small sample size. However, we wanted to have a sample that would be large enough to allow us multivariate statistics and to make comparisons of a whole series of subgroups (social class, sex, feeding method, birth status, maternal attitudes, etc.). Originally we had planned to collect our sample of 200 over a two-year period. However, difficulties in ensuring a regular flow of new cases and other practical problems (e.g., seasonal variations in the birth rate; having only two observers, the author and Judith Bernal) led us to restrict the final sample to just about 100 children. In terms of size, the group is somewhere between the very large samples used in the British National Surveys (e.g., Davie, Butler, & Goldstein, 1972;

Douglas & Blomfield, 1968) and a more individual case study
approach (e.g., Escalona & Corman, 1971; Wolff, 1969). The
hope was to combine some of the advantages of each--the use of
sophisticated statistical analysis, along with a richness of
description. Sometimes this has been possible, but often we
find that we lack the sample size required for some of the
statistical analyses we would like to carry out, and do not
have all the detail needed to interpret some of the correlations
we do find. Perhaps this merely emphasizes the scale of
research required for adequate developmental studies.

The most important problem in studies of this kind is
choosing what to record. Obviously, one has to be highly
selective and can only record a tiny proportion of the possible
data. Description is not possible without theory although the
theory may be implicit rather than being explicitly stated,
and the selection of data must be based on some theoretical
framework. Our work has not been guided by a single theory--
indeed, we wished to get away from the theories which had led
to narrowly selective attention to a few features of development (e.g., the Freudian concern with feeding and elimination).
Instead, we have used a whole series of theoretical considerations
which could only be described by discussion of each item in our
procedures. There are, however, some general principles and some
of the decisions about what data to collect are linked to others
about methodology and sample size.

Studies of mother-infant interaction in captive rhesus
monkeys (e.g., Hinde, Rowell, & Spencer-Booth, 1964) had
convinced us that we would need to have some fine-level
analysis of behavioral sequences. Such data can only be
gathered by direct observation. At the time we were planning
our project, very little systematic observation of mother-infant
interaction in the neonatal period had been attempted (but see
Levy, 1958). Choosing direct observations as a methodology does
not in itself determine the categories of behavior to be
recorded (Cooper, Costello, Douglas, Ingleby, & Turner, 1974),
although it does limit the level of detail and the time span.
We produced our list of categories out of a long series of
pilot observations, using intuitive usefulness and reliability
as the main criteria of selection (Richards & Bernal, 1972).
For observations at later ages, for which much more published
data were available, we relied less heavily on our own pilot
observations and more on methods that had been evolved elsewhere. These, on the whole, have proved less satisfactory.
With hindsight, it is not difficult to understand why, as the
techniques we took over had usually been developed for different
purposes than our own, and this reinforces what I said earlier

about the relationship of theory and description. Methodologies are not always transferable between studies based on differing theoretical assumptions.

In addition to direct observation, we used interviews with mothers, diaries they kept for us on standard forms, and a range of infant assessment techniques. An outline of our time-table for data is given in Table 18-1. From this outline it will be seen that there is a considerable concentration of data collection in the period immediately after birth. This was done for several reasons. We wanted to follow the mother's initial adaptation to her infant. Our pilot studies suggested that this happened very rapidly, and we hoped that closely spaced observations throughout the first ten days would "catch" the critical stages in the process. Also, we were interested in testing ideas about the prediction of later development from neonatal assessments of the infant and the first interaction situations. For the successful application of predictive techniques for pediatric purposes, it is desirable to make assessments during the period in which the mother is in a maternity hospital or under the care of midwives at home (first ten days). More generally, we were struck by the dearth of information about early mother-infant interactions. In spite of widespread beliefs about the long-term importance of the initial formation of the relationship, very little is known about how the process occurs, what variations are related to maternal or infant influences, or the importance of the social setting in which the mother and child form their relationship.

Data collection was also concentrated at sixty weeks, because this is an age frequently selected in studies of attachment (e.g., Ainsworth & Wittig, 1969), and we hoped to use these other results for comparison with our own data.

In the later discussion of some of our results, I hope to illustrate and elaborate some of the points raised in this section. But first I will make some remarks about our method-ology and cross-cultural studies.

CROSS-CULTURAL STUDIES

Our approach to developmental problems has many similarities with some cross-cultural studies. Just as a psychologist or anthropologist may return with a description of child-rearing in the X culture, we set out to provide an account of development

TABLE 18-1. An Outline of Procedures Used in the First Sixty Weeks.

2-6 weeks before delivery	Description of the project to mother, collection of medical social, and attitude information
Delivery	Precoded medical information recorded by midwife. Observation of first mother-infant interaction and infant behavior (when an observer is present)
Days 2, 3, 8, 9, 10	Observation of a feeding session and collection of attitude and interview information
Day 0-10	24-hour mother's diary
Day 8 or 9	Neurological examination of infant, sucking test and test of visual responsiveness
Day 10	Rating of mother on attitude measures
8 weeks (2 visits)	Observation of a feeding session and 2 nonfeeding, baby-awake periods. Infant attention and "rattle" test. 48-hour mother's diary. Interview, including events of previous week and father participation. Assessment of neuromotor development
14 weeks (2 visits) 20 weeks (2 visits) 30 weeks (2 visits)	Same as 8 weeks, but no feeding observations. Tes of responses to novel and familiar objects.
60 weeks (2-3 visits)	2 observations of mother-infant interaction situations with tape recordings. Structured task for mother and infant. Extended interview with mother including events of previous week and significant events since last visit. 24-hour diary. Interview with father. Neuromotor assessment including some neurological items

Further series of visits carried out at 3, 4, and 5 years

in Cambridge, England. But, unlike most anthropologists or
cross-cultural psychologists we are working in our own
community--the community in which we grew up and have spent
most of our adult life.

By definition, *cross-cultural* means moving out from one's
own community to work in another to collect data to compare
with the home culture. But, perhaps surprisingly, descriptive
work is done most commonly outside the researchers own culture.
In fact, until very recently little descriptive material was
available from the home cultures of Western psychologists and
anthropologists. For example, in Bowlby's (1969) study of
attachment, a large proportion of the descriptive material he
relied on came from cultures outside Europe and America or from
animal species. Although some of this selection may reflect
Bowlby's ethological bias, there was surprisingly little data
he could have used from his own country. There are many reasons
why this dearth of detailed descriptive material from "home"
cultures is undesirable. For one thing, it makes clinical
descriptions of problem groups hard to assess. Much of the
detailed descriptive material that is available comes from
clinicians' accounts of their patients. As we have so little
baseline data available, it is often hard to know how far the
behavior described in a problem group is peculiar to that
group. Thus, at one time, it was argued that noncuddliness was
diagnostic of an autistic child. However, descriptive studies
of the relevant populations have shown that a significant
minority of "normal" children may not be cuddly (Schaffer &
Emerson, 1964). An analogous point can be made for many accounts
of the "battered baby syndrome". Here, because so little was
known of the general population, parents' feelings and actions
of anger toward their young children were thought to be rare
outside a small minority. Subsequent work indicates that such
feelings and actions are very widespread (Richards, 1974c).

So, if there are needs for descriptive studies, why do
researchers so often move from their own culture to provide
them? At first sight, it might appear obvious. We do not study
our own communities because we learn about them through our
everyday nonscientific life. Of course, there is truth in this;
as participants in a culture, we will learn a great deal about
it. This knowledge will be unsystematic and probably not very
quantitative, but it may have utility for some scientific
purposes; for others, it will not. We may also need knowledge
that is more detailed and of a quite different kind from that
we assimilate through our daily lives. Or there may be areas
of experience that are systematically denied to most members of
a community (e.g., birth and other aspects of a child's life),

and special efforts are needed to find out what goes on.

But there are more fundamental reasons why we so often choose to go to strange cultures, which stem from the idea of science and objective knowledge. Scientific knowledge is knowledge about the other, a generalized person at a distance, a person with whom we do not have the usual personal and social relationships. Some scientists (e.g., Piaget) have studied their own children, but this is often considered an undesirable practice, especially by psychologists of the more positivistic persuasion. More usual and more generally acceptable is the practice of studying groups who are unlike the researcher by way of gender, status, age, social class, place of residence, etc. This tendency is understandable if one grants that the gaze of the scientist as an observer is antipathetic to many everyday social relationships. An observer in a community that it not his own may be able to adopt a special role that allows him to distance himself from the group and to observe without making his own social position too precarious. Such roles may not often be available or easy to fill in our own communities. Cross-cultural researchers may feel more "at home" observing in a strange culture than they would if they were carrying out an observational study of their family and neighbors at home.

As scientific knowledge is not the same as our everyday knowledge of our own world, and, given that at least in some limited spheres scientific knowledge of human behavior has some practical value, we must recognize both the need to collect it in our own communities and the difficulties in doing so. Some of these difficulties are discussed below.

PROCEDURES

Our first experience of observing mothers and babies was gained in a hospital. Here the situation in many respects is like that for a cross-cultural worker. The observer was introduced to a mother (having previously selected her from a series of medical case histories) by a member of the medical staff. Given that the introduction was rather ambiguous and that the observer was white-coated, most mothers probably assumed that another doctor had come to look at her baby. In describing what the observer wanted to do, interest in the infant was emphasized. As patients in a hospital expect to be asked questions and to be observed, the situation was less odd for the mother than for the staff of the hospital (particularly the nurses). In effect, the observer was using

a preexisting role in the social situation. During this
period we collected most of our pilot data.

For our main sample we wanted to work with home-delivered
infants, because in Cambridge almost half the babies were born
at home, and it simplified matters if mothers and babies did
not move between two very different social situations during
the neonatal observation period. Home deliveries are supervised by midwives, who, together with the general practitioners,
are responsible for the mother's care throughout pregnancy. So
we sought and obtained the midwives' cooperation in recruiting
our sample. The midwives were told of the criteria for
inclusion in the study and were asked to approach any suitable
mother. The mothers were told that we were engaged in a study
of the development of normal children and that we would like to
discuss the project with her if she had no objections. If the
mother agreed, we called on her about two weeks before she was
due to deliver and explained what the study would involve
(again emphasizing our interest in the baby) and asked for her
and her husband's cooperation. Of the mothers approached at
this stage, 95 percent agreed to take part, and over the first
stage of the study (first sixty weeks) no families dropped out
except for unavoidable reasons, such as moving away from
Cambridge. Undoubtedly, using an approach via the midwives,
who are well-known to the mothers and trusted, contributed to
our low refusal rates.

We saw the home-delivered mother frequently over the first
ten days following the baby's birth (see Table 18-1). During
this time, we usually developed a close working relationship
with her. Unlike in the hospital situation, there was no preexisting role that we could use for our purpose as observers.
We were not doctors, midwives, health visitors, or even baby
foods salesmen (as a couple of mothers assumed at our first
meeting), and it was important to us that we were not seen to
be closely related to any of these functions. Previous work
(e.g., Newson & Newson, 1963) had demonstrated that mothers
give different kinds of answers to questions about child-
rearing to people who have "official" functions. Our knowledge
of the community in which we lived undoubtedly helped us to
carve out a special role for ourselves that was understood by
the mothers and allowed them to "place" us. We were members
of a research unit interested in the development of normal
children--or to many families, "the man and the lady who come
to see the baby". Although we wanted to fit the interview
and observation times into our own schedule, we tried as far
as possible to equalize the relationship so that we came at
times suitable for the mother. Similarly, during the actual

observations, we tried to be as flexible as possible within the constraints imposed by the techniques we used, and attempted to avoid a manipulative situation with unequal power for either the observer or the observed.

As our sample approximates to the social class distribution of Cambridge, some families were much closer to our own background than others and a very few were those of colleagues in the university. Clearly, we had to vary our approach and explanations to fit the differing relationships. We did not recruit mothers who were already well-known to either of us, and avoided becoming close friends with any of the members of the sample. We thought that to do so might raise problems in observations and with confidential information about the family that we might be given. We tried to give families as much information as they wanted about the results of the study as they have been published, but to avoid detailed discussion of individual children. Our role was that of observers rather than advice givers, although obviously these cannot always be entirely separate.

The great disadvantage of working within our own culture was that we lacked distance from it. We tend to take for granted what may be problematic. However, we were able to gain some distance through our knowledge of other cultures (both direct and from the writings of anthropologists and others). For example, we only began to appreciate the relative separation of mother and child in our culture and its potential importance after we had read and discussed accounts of child-rearing among hunter-gatherers. Some of the disadvantages of lack of distance are offset by the way in which we could use our knowledge of our own culture to understand and interpret what we saw and heard. As we knew the local institutions for medical care and other social matters related to child-rearing, mothers did not have to explain these things to us. Also, there are very subtle points about the meaning and significance of things that were reported to us, or that we saw, that we probably would have missed in a less familiar culture.

THE PREDICTION OF DEVELOPMENT FROM THE INITIAL STATE OF THE INFANT

As I said earlier, one of the reasons for concentrating our efforts in the immediate postnatal period was that we wanted to see the extent to which later development can be

predicted from measures taken at this time. Some prediction
from neonatal measures has long been possible. Some infants
are clearly abnormal at birth and will develop differently
from normal infants whatever environments they grow up in
(although, of course, this does not mean that their development
is not influenced by their environment). If a whole population
sample is taken that includes some abnormal infants (e.g.,
infants of extremely low birth weight, cases of severe neonatal
asphyxia as well as discrete syndromes such as Down's and
Spina bifida), some correlation is likely between neonatal
assessments and measures taken much later in life. But such
associations may be produced by the obviously abnormal infants.
This is a separate question from the degree of predictability
that may be found in a sample of "normal" infants; in such a
sample, how much of the variance in follow-up assessments can
be accounted for by the neonatal measures?

Very little is known about sources of variability in
normal newborn infants, or, indeed, how such variability may
be assessed. In the following paragraphs, I will discuss
anoxia at birth as one possible source of variation in newborns. It is probable that this is but one factor among many
and that the concept of anoxia itself is much oversimplified.
However, a good deal is known about anoxia because of its
clinical importance, so it is used as an illustration of the
developmental process.

Although anoxia is defined in biochemical terms, it should
be seen within a sociobiological context. Among the many
factors that determine the degree of anoxia suffered by an
infant during delivery will be the mother's attitude toward
the birth, her confidence, and the amount of emotional support
she receives, as well as techniques used in the local culture
by midwife or doctor for the conduct of the delivery. A
"continuum of reproductive casualty" has been postulated to
explain the relationship between birth anoxia and later
intellectual functioning (Pasamanick & Knobloch, 1966). All
infants suffer from, at least, transitory and mild anoxia at
birth. It is well established that severe anoxia can cause
brain damage that leads to later motor and intellectual
handicaps, and it is hypothesized that lesser degrees of
anoxia will contribute to variance in related measures throughout the whole "normal" population. Evidence in support of this
idea is rather mixed (Gottfried, 1973). However, because of
methodological difficulties in the assessment of anoxia at
birth and the failure to take account of infant-environment
interactions in most of the studies, such evidence as there is
does not provide an adequate test of the hypothesis.

In psychological studies of the effects of neonatal anoxia, the degree of anoxia is usually estimated from an Apgar score (Apgar, 1953). This score is based on five parameters: heart rate, respiratory effort, muscle tone, reflex irritability, and skin color, which are noted on 0-2 scales at various intervals after birth. Unfortunately, correlations between Apgar scores and biochemical assessments of anoxia are not impressive, particularly when mothers have received obstetric medication (Saling, 1968; Crawford, 1972). Furthermore, there is not a one-to-one correlation between the degree of biochemical anoxia and the extent or location of changes in the central nervous system (Towbin, 1971). This means that an Apgar score may be a very poor indicator of the important long-term consequences of the neonatal anoxia.

Attempts to find correlations between neonatal assessments and later measures of behavior (most commonly DQ's or IQ's) do not usually take any account of the interactional nature of development. A particular degree of anoxia in particular circumstances may tend to produce placid, noncrying infants. Parents may react to such infants in a variety of ways that could have differential developmental effects. Some parents may regard their placid baby as "good" and leave him alone for long periods, while others may decide that such a baby needs extra attention just because he is placid. To predict outcomes in such a situation, one would need both a neonatal assessment and knowledge of the infant-environment interactions. The importance of effects like this have been demonstrated at the population level. The British National Child Development study (Davie, Butler, & Goldstein, 1972) found that low birth weight infants were not significantly different from the rest of the sample at age 7 if their parents were in Social Classes I, II, and III (Registrar General's Scale), but were different in terms of both school attainment and social adjustment scores if their parents were in Social Classes IV and V.

So we may conclude that, except in extreme cases, prediction of outcome from an infant assessment without taking account of the developmental environment is not likely to be very successful. As our study was designed to investigate the developmental environment, we hoped that we could use it to assess the degree of predictability in a situation where we could take environmental differences into consideration.

We also used the concept of continuum of reproductive casualty to produce criteria for the selection of our "low-risk" normal sample and as one means of deciding what obstetric information to record.

In order to try to restrict our sample to low-risk infants, we made the assumption that factors related to neonatal mortality were also likely to be related to morbidity in survivors. Thanks to the British Perinatal mortality surveys (Butler & Bonham, 1963), the major factors associated with perinatal mortality are well-known, and we used these to set criteria of maternal health and condition during pregnancy and labor for inclusion of a mother and infant in our sample. Information from this same source was used to make decisions on what to record about these events. Our rationale, again, was that a factor known to be related to mortality (e.g., length of labor) was likely to produce significant variance among all infants.

There is, of course, no overall answer to the question of how far neonatal measures can predict later development, because different processes are involved in different aspects of the child's behavior and performance. But to illustrate some of the points I have raised in this discussion, I will now describe some of the results that indicate that a surprisingly high degree of predictability may be found for at least a few measures in a "normal" sample.

Night Waking

One approach to the analysis of our data has been to set up groups within our sample and to compare them on a wide variety of measures drawn from the considerable body of data we have for each child and his parents. Often we have chosen groups that are of interest to parents and/or the medical professions in the hope that we might be able to throw a little light on matters of practical concern.

Throughout the period of data collection we were impressed by the extent of night waking among the infants in the sample, and the anxiety and disruption this sometimes caused for parents. At sixty weeks when we asked mothers about (unspecified) "problems" with their children, difficulties over night waking were most frequently mentioned.

At sixty weeks, twenty-one babies were described by their mothers as waking regularly at night, a further three babies were reported as having had interrupted nights but to have improved in the last few weeks, and five others were said to wake occasionally (this is from a total of seventy-seven babies for whom the relevant data are complete). Mothers completed a diary for us at sixty weeks on a standard form that recorded the child's activities for a 48-hour period. From these we

found that twenty-two babies had woken between 10 p.m. and
5 a.m.   Eighteen were babies described as waking regularly,
two occasionally, and two more as rarely waking.   As there are
difficulties in assessing the mother's meaning of "regularly"
and "occasionally" and because the two nights recorded in the
diaries do not provide an adequate sample of sleep behavior,
the group with sleeping difficulties was defined as twenty-
four infants--the twenty-one described as waking regulary and
three who were reported to have woken regularly but improved
recently.   These I will call the *sleep problem group*, but we
must note that not all of them were considered to be a problem
by their parents.   Using the diary data we found that this
group slept significantly less during the sample nights (see
Figure 18-1).

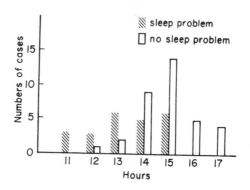

Figure 18-1.   Hours of sleep per 24- hour period at
                14 months (77 cases).   Reproduced from
                Bernal (1973) with permission.

The sleep problem did not differ from the remainder of
the sample in broad biological or sociological terms.   There
was no relationship with   (1) birth order (first or second),
(2) sex, (3) feeding (breast or bottle), (4) social class,
(5) feeding difficulties at 60 weeks, (6) maternal attitudes
to toilet training, or (7) maternal attitudes to feeding
schedules.   But there were many differences between the groups
in early sleep behavior, behavior in the neonatal period, and
in the delivery histories.

Length of labor was significantly longer in the problem

group (13.2 hours against 6.9 hours, $p < 0.02$). Our Apgar-like rating at birth, and times to first cry and regular respiration, all suggested that the sleep problem babies were somewhat depressed. Time to first cry was 36.4 seconds for the problem group against 19 seconds for the rest of the sample ($p < 0.5$). It should be emphasized that the sleep problem group are not "abnormal" by the usual clinical criteria, but are positioned toward one end of the "normal" range.

Over the first ten days, mothers kept a diary for us that recorded time in cot, crying, and feeding. This showed considerable difference between the two groups (Table 18-2), suggesting that the sleep problem babies were wakeful and fussy, and that this was not the result of maternal unresponsiveness. Indeed, as the mothers of sleep problem infants fed them more frequently and allowed them to cry for shorter periods at one time, they might be said to be more responsive. As these diaries are kept by the mothers, it is possible, of course, that the results might reflect a recording bias among mothers rather than a difference in their babies' behavior. Although we cannot totally rule out this possibility, it seems most unlikely that mothers would consistently distort their records of the babies' behavior in the manner required to produce these results. In addition, a partial check of the diaries against our observations when we were in the home provided no evidence of such distortion.

On Day 8 or 9 infants were given a test of nonnutritive sucking, using the technique of Waldrop and Bell (1966), and a neurological examination, by the Groningen method (Prechtl & Beintema, 1964). In the sucking test, the baby is given a teat to suck on for 4 minutes, and then the latency to cry and to a flexion of the knee from the point of removal of the teat are recorded. The test is done after the neurological examination at a time when a feed is due, so all babies were awake and many were crying. Sleep problem babies responded more quickly to the removal of the teat (Table 18-3). Although we have not completed the analysis of the neurological examination results, it is already clear that the sleep problem infants were scored as having significantly increased resistance to passive movement and higher ratings for active power of movements.

At the follow-up visits at 8, 14, 20, and 30 weeks, mothers completed forty-eight-hour diaries of their babies' activities. These have been analyzed in terms of the longest bout of uninterrupted sleep (in cot asleep or peacefully awake) at night (6 p.m. to 6 a.m.). This measure avoids the

TABLE 18-2. Diary Information for the First Ten Days

	Sleep Problem Group	Rest of Sample	N	p
Time in cot--time crying in cot (mean mins./day)	1036	1101	50	< 0.02
Length of uninterrupted bouts in cot (mean mins.)	98	108	58	< 0.01
Interval between feeds (mean mins.)	189	207	61	< 0.01
Total crying (mean mins./day)	110	80	58	< 0.05
Frequency cry bouts/day (mean)	7.5	5.9	58	< 0.004
Length of cry bouts (mean mins.)	12.5	14.3	58	< 0.05

TABLE 18-3. Sucking Test Latencies (70 Cases).

	Sleep Problem Group	Rest of Sample	p
Latency to cry (mean secs.)	12	33	< 0.01
Latency to flex (mean secs.)	5	7	< 0.06

difficulties of defining a baby's "night" when there are wide variations in the time of the last evening feed. The length of the longest bout increases progressively over these ages, but the sleep problem group lags significantly behind the rest of the sample (Figure 18-2 and Table 18-4).

Thus a fairly clear picture begins to emerge. Sleep problem children are born after rather long labors, have an increased degree of respiratory depression at birth, and are fussy, wakeful babies in the neonatal period. Throughout the first year, they sleep (or remain peacefully in their beds) for shorter periods than the other children. This pattern strongly suggests that these babies have differed from the rest of the sample from the time of birth or earlier, and that sleep problems are not the result of any particular style of parental handling, in contradiction to much medical folklore. This latter conclusion is supported by the lack of correlation between the incidence of night waking with social class, or with measures of maternal attitudes, or with feeding schedules, etc. Direct examination of our data on maternal behavior did not produce any consistent differences between the two groups in matters related to sleeping, except that parents of sleep problem children tended to use a wider range of techniques to cope with night waking. This is hardly surprising, as our data suggest that none of the usual remedies are effective, so that parents of these problem children are likely to run through all the available methods. Parents differed greatly in their responses to night waking. In some households, there was a constant battle, in which everybody, except perhaps the baby, seemed to suffer from sleep deprivation. Other families managed to modify their lives around the baby's sleep time. One mother frequently used to spend a couple of hours around 3 a.m. playing with the child.

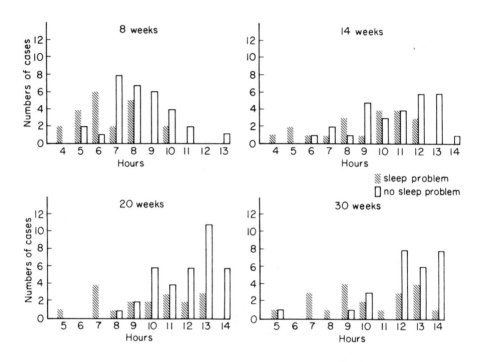

Figure 18-2.   Length of longest sleep bout at night
at 8, 14, 20, and 30 weeks. (77 cases).

Although we have not yet quite completed data collection
at three years, we have enough results to be sure that the
problem group of children still tend to show a different
pattern of sleep behavior. But, at this age, the problem has
changed somewhat, and the children, rather than waking at
night, are often difficult to get to sleep.

Other Developmental Trends

We have been very impressed by the way that in our
"normal" sample, measures taken in the neonatal period show

TABLE 18-4. Mean Length (Hours) of Longest Sleep Bout (Mann-Whitney U Test (2-Tailed)).

Age (Weeks)	Sleep Problem Group	No Sleep Problem	N	p
8	5.6	8.8	52	< 0.0005
14	8.8	11.6	56	< 0.02
20	10.4	12.0	55	< 0.01
30	10.4	12.4	53	< 0.04

such strong relationships with the children's behavior many
years later. Dr. Frances Barnes, who is in charge of the
three-year-old follow-ups, has now begun to search through
the data for other correlations, and several have been found
already. Accidents seem highly correlated with the modified
Apgar scores and latencies to breathing, etc. Children with
the less favorable ratings at birth are much more likely to
have had one or more accidents by the age of three. An
accident is defined as a traumatic incident resulting in
treatment by a general physician or at the casualty department
of a hospital. The majority were cuts or burns severe enough
to need professional help with stitching or dressing, or else
falls leading to X-rays. All X-rays were to the head, as no
child in our sample sustained a fracture or a suspected
fracture of a limb.

Birth events are also associated with the quality of the
relationship with the mother. At three, the picture is of
less favorably rated children as having more distant relationships with their mothers, who frequently see them as difficult
and unpredictable children. These children tend to have a
rather interesting pattern of interaction with the mother.
They are seen as more difficult to leave with other people,
even if they know them, and to be more wary of strangers and
strange places or they will tend to stay near their mothers.
However, at home, they are less likely to be described as
liking to be near their mothers.

While there is much more data analysis to be done, the
trend of the results from our study suggests quite clearly
that behavioral ratings and assessments carried out in the
neonatal period may be much more predictive of later social
and cognitive behavior than is usually realized. Our data on
the later consequences of obstetric medication reinforce this
picture. Clear effects are visible in social interaction
measures at thirty and sixty weeks (the furthest we have gone
with this analysis as yet). For example, at the later age,
"drugged" babies are significantly less likely to be picked
up during a standard observation session in the home.

It is not difficult to see why the long-term effects may
have been underestimated or missed altogether, inasmuch as
studies are usually designed in such a way that these effects
could not be found. This may have produced a systematic
"environmentalist" bias in the literature. In studies of the
development of cognitive and social behavior, it is usual to
search for correlations (or the lack of them) between infant
and parent behavior patterns. When correlations are found,

it is common to see them as evidence for the effects of parental behavior on children. So, as Bell (1968) and others have pointed out, individual differences between children generally are seen as a result of, not a cause of, parental behavior, despite the lack of supporting evidence. Even where the possibility of infant effects on parents is recognized, the individual styles of infant behavior are very seldom traced back to birth. Indeed, the inclusion of any data from the neonatal period is rare in studies of parent-infant interaction. This may have resulted in a systematic playing down of ·the long-term importance of congenital variation. Ecological studies that attempt to look at the whole framework in which development takes place may help to redress the balance and give us a less biased picture of development.

DISCUSSION

There are, of course, many processes that would account for these long-term effects of the initial individual differences between infants. Recent neurophysiological work (Dobbing & Smart, 1973) has drawn attention to periods of high growth velocity in the developing central nervous system. Although the processes are complex and our understanding is far from complete, it seems likely that these periods of high growth rates may represent periods of maximum susceptibility to environmental factors. In our own species, the peak of the velocity curve of brain growth occurs around the time of birth, while in other species it is a prenatal (e.g., guinea pig) or postnatal (e.g., rat) event. Although it might seem prudent to have birth, with its attended dangers of asphyxia and other damaging factors, coincident with the period of maximum vulnerability for the central nervous system, there are presumably many selective costs and benefits involved. This coincidence in our own species could mean that we are uniquely susceptible to brain damage at birth. For our species, variance in later development might be related to events at this time more than in other species.

Even if changes in behavior related to birth events should last only a few days, they could have very long-term effects if they modify the mother-child interaction. We have direct evidence of this. Patterns of feeding interactions in the first ten days are directly related to several obstetric factors. Infants with less favorable records are "difficult" babies and feeds go less smoothly. We think it is likely that particular styles of parental interaction are set up at this

time in response to the infant's behavior. Later differences
seen in the children may well be the outcome both of the
continuing effects of the infant's central nervous system
status and of the cumulative result of the altered parental
interactions. Development is a highly complex interactive
process and it is too simplistic to talk of either infant or
parent effects. One is always dealing with both. I want to
emphasize the contribution of variations between infants to
the process, as these seem to be far more important than one
might guess from reading the psychological literature on early
development.

If this general picture is confirmed in future work, it
could have profound practical consequences. Early intervention
programs are almost exclusively designed to alter mother-child
relationships or the children themselves. This may turn out
to be a very one-sided approach. If birth events do have long-
term effects, there is much that could be done to improve
matters. Our results indicate that we were right in assuming
that the same factors that are related to neonatal mortality
also contribute to individual variations in the later development of children. Comprehensive health care programs are very
effective in reducing perinatal mortality (Baird & Thomson,
1969). Although the techniques are well-known, they are often
not put into practice, as has been demonstrated recently in a
study of perinatal mortality in New York (Chase, 1973). Such
programs not only will reduce mortality, but might also
alleviate many of the developmental problems that are the
targets for the educational early intervention programs. None
of this means that these latter programs are necessarily ineffective or that they should be stopped; simply that they
represent a one-sided approach to a developmental and social
problem. As yet, we hardly know how to design and mount a
postnatal early intervention program, but we do know how to
improve obstetric care, and programs in the field are relatively
cheap.

CONCLUSION

In this paper I have tried to describe a project that was
designed to build up a developmental ecology of a community.
Relationships with comparative psychological and cross-cultural
studies were discussed. It is my belief that any study of
early development must stem from an ecological viewpoint if it
is to avoid the dangers of single-mindedness. Comparative
psychological studies are valuable to those who study a single
community, because they help to define the salient ecology and

draw attention to our ethnocentric attitudes.

REFERENCES

Ainsworth, M. D. S. & Wittig, B. A. Attachment and exploratory behavior of one-year-olds in a strange situation. In B. M. Foss (Ed.), Determinants of Infant Behavior (Vol. 4). London: Methuen, 1969.

Apgar, V. Proposal for a new method for evaluation of the newborn infant. Current Research in Anaesthetics and Analgerics, 1953, 32, 260-267.

Baird, D., & Thomson, A. M. Reduction of perinatal mortality by improving standards of obstetric care. In N. R. Butler & E. D. Alberman (Eds.), Perinatal Problems. Edinburgh: Livingstone, 1969.

Bell, R. Q. A re-interpretation of the direction of effects in studies of socialization. Psychological Review, 1968, 75, 81-95.

Bowlby, J. Attachment and loss. Vol. 1: Attachment. London: Hogarth, 1969.

Butler, N. R., & Bonham, D. G. Perinatal mortality. Edinburgh: Livingstone, 1963.

Chase, H. (Ed.). A study of risks, medical care and infant mortality. American Journal of Public Health, 1973, Supplement No. 63.

Cooper, E. S., Costello, A. J., Douglas, J. W. B., Ingleby, J. D., & Turner, R. K. Direct observations? Bulletin British Psychological Society, 1974, 27, 3-7.

Crawford, J. S. Principles and practice of obstetric anaesthesia (3rd ed.). Oxford: Blackwell Scientific, 1972.

Davie, R., Butler, N. R., & Goldstein, H. From birth to seven. London: Longmans, 1972.

Dobbing, J., & Smart, J. L. Early undernutrition, brain development and behaviour. In S. A. Barnett (Ed.), Ethology and development (Clinics in Developmental

Medicine No. 47). London: Spastics Publications Heinemann, 1973.

Douglas, J. W. B., & Blomfield, J. M. Children under five. London: Allen & Unwin, 1968.

Dunn, J. F. Consistency and change in styles of mothering. In M. O'Connor (Ed.), Parent-infant interaction (CIBA Foundation Symposium 33). Amsterdam: Elsevier, 1975.

Dunn, J. F., & Richards, M. P. M. Observations on the developing relationship between mother and baby in the neonatal period. In H. R. Schaffer (Ed.), Infant interaction. London: Academic Press, 1976.

Elton, C. The ecology of animals. New York: Methuen, 1960.

Escalona, S. K., & Corman, H. H. The impact of mother's presence upon behavior: The first year. Human Development, 1971, 14, 2-15.

Gottfried, A. W. Intellectual consequences of perinatal anoxia. Psychological Bulletin, 1973, 80, 231-242.

Hinde, R. A., Rowell, T. E., & Spencer-Booth, Y. Behaviour of socially living rhesus monkeys in their first six months. Proceedings of the Zoological Society of London, 1964, 143, 609-649.

Lack, D. The natural regulation of animal numbers. London: Oxford University Press, 1947.

Levy, D. M. Behavioral analysis. Springfield: Thomas, 1958.

Newson, J., & Newson, E. Infant care in an urban community. London: Allen & Unwin, 1963.

Pasamanick, B., & Knobloch, H. Retrospective studies on the epidemiology of reproductive casualty: Old and new. Merrill-Palmer Quarterly, 1966, 12, 7-26.

Prechtl, H., & Beintema, D. The neurological examination of the full-term newborn infant. (Clinics in Developmental Medicine No. 12). London: Spastics Publications/Heinemann, 1964.

Richards, M. P. M. The first steps in becoming social. In

M. P. M. Richards (Ed.), The integration of a child into a social world. London: Cambridge University Press, 1974. (a)

Richards, M. P. M. The biological and social. In N. Armistead (Ed.), Reconstructing social psychology. London: Penguin, 1974. (b)

Richards, M. P. M. The "battered baby syndrome" in persepctive. Paper prepared for a conference organized by the Department of Health and Social Security, London, June 1974. (c). Delivered at the Department of Health and Social Security, London, and to be published in the Conference Proceedings, Her Majesty's Stationary Office.

Richards, M. P. M., & Bernal, J. F. An observational study of mother-infant interaction. In N. Blurton Jones (Ed.), Ethological studies of child behaviour. London: Cambridge University Press, 1972.

Saling, R. Foetal and neonatal hypoxia in relation to clinical obstetric practice. London: Arnold, 1968.

Tinbergen, N., Kruuk, H., & Paillette, M. Egg shell removal by the Black-headed Gull, Larus r. ribidundus: II. Bird Study, 1962, 9, 123-131.

Tinbergen, N., Broekhuysen, G. J., Feekes, F., Houghton, J. C. W., Kruuk, H., & Szulc, E. Egg shell removal by the Black-headed Gull, Larus ridibundus, L., a behavioural component of camouflage. Behaviour, 1962, 19, 74-117.

Towbin, A. Organic causes of minimal dysfunction. Journal American Medical Association, 1971, 217, 1207-1214.

Waldrop, M., & Bell, R. Q. Effects of family size and density on newborn characteristics. American Journal Orthopsychiatry, 1966, 36, 544-550.

Wolff, P. H. The natural history of crying and other vocalizations in early infancy. In B. M. Foss (Ed.), Determinants of infant behaviour (Vol. 4). London: Methuen, 1969.

Chapter 19

Social Class Differences in Maternal and Infant Behavior[1]

Steven R. Tulkin

State University of New York at Buffalo

I first became interested in the effects of experience on intellectual functioning in the early 1960s as an undergraduate at the University of Maryland. The civil rights movement was in full swing, and I was hoping to be able to use science to prove that if were truly an egalitarian society, we would not end up with social class and racial differences in intelligence and school achievement. I remember being enraged by the publication of Shuey's (1966) second edition of The Testing of Negro Intelligence and wondering how anyone with any training in research could believe the results of the studies reviewed by Shuey. I was determined to show that environmental

[1] This project was supported by Grant MH 08792 from the National Institute of Mental Health and by a grant to the author from the National Science Foundation. Many people cooperated on the collection and analysis of the data. I would like to thank especially Elizabeth Anderson, Gayle Henkin Brent, Dorothy Largay, Robert Lentz, Cheryl Minton, Doris Simpson, Terry Stagman, Krayna Tulkin, and Julie Vogel. Author's address: Department of Psychology, State University of New York, 4230 Ridge Lea Road, Buffalo, New York 14226.

experiences account for the racial and social class differences found by other researchers (Tulkin, 1968). I might add that presently I find myself much more accepting of the importance of biological influences (including genetics) on development of intellectual skills. We do not know enough to draw any conclusions at the present time, however; and certainly cannot consider any implications.

When I came to Harvard in the mid-1960s I heard Jerome Kagan talking about social class differences in the first year of life and knew that this was the area in which research needed to go in order to explore the nature of environmental influences. I planned to collect data on black and white infants from middle- and working-class homes, but the black community in Boston would have nothing to do with "more research on deprivation". As I now look back, I am glad that I was forced to work only with whites, because I think that racial comparisons are far too complex to be understood by a simple cross-sectional analysis of one aspect of people's life space (Tulkin, 1972; Tulkin & Konner, 1973).

Even working only with whites, I was struck by the naivete of my original assumptions. It is embarrassing for me to admit, but somehow I had assumed that the behavior of middle- and working-class mothers would form nonoverlapping distributions; much to my surprise, I found very "warm", caring (and "stimulating") mothers in my working-class sample, and "cold" mothers in my middle-class sample. I still believe, as I suggested (Tulkin & Kagan, 1972), that the significant class differences were "attributable to a subgroup of middle-class mothers who were highly verbal with their infants--rather than to a 'deprivation' which is uniquely characteristic of working-class families" (p. 38).

I wanted to study these families in greater depth, so I decided to interview mothers who both confirmed and disconfirmed my stereotypes. Two examples of such nonstereotypic cases are presented later in this chapter. I gained a deep appreciation for these families as unique units, each with its own assets and liabilities. The experience was important to me, and I would urge all researchers in this area to spend time getting to know the families they are studying.

Even though we have talked in other sections of the book about the pitfalls of social class as an independent variable, I still believe that investigations of social class differences in maternal and infant behaviors can help to clarify the importance of various experiences for cognitive and emotional development. We need to remember, however, that social class per se is not the critical variable, but is merely a vehicle that allows us to have easy access to populations providing different sets of experiences for their infants. Evaluation of infants' environments and of cognitive and emotional development have become more sophisticated in recent years, and we are well on our way toward answering some of the important questions about early development. We have abandoned our early interest in general terms such as *warmth, control,* and *stimulation* in favor of more specific reporting of behaviors that precede and follow other behaviors (Lewis & Freedle, 1972; Lewis & Wilson, 1971; Rosenfeld, 1973). We are also slowly abandoning our reliance on infant "intelligence tests" in favor of the evaluation of infants' responses to specific sets of stimuli (Kagan, 1971; Lewis & Wilson, 1971; Moss & Robson, 1968; Moss, Robson, & Pedersen, 1969; Tulkin, 1973a, 1973b; Wachs, Uzgiris & Hunt, 1971). Thus we are coming closer to being able to describe infants' experiences and their effects on cognitive development, and social class research has helped us in advancing this objective.

SUBJECTS AND PROCEDURES

The data came from a sample of 60 first-born white ten-month-old girls, half from middle-class families and half from working-class families.[2] They were observed at home for two hours on each of two days, and assessed in several laboratory situations. The specific details of the procedures for each assessment will be presented as the data is reported.

---

[2]Further details of sample selection are as follows:
   Class. The term *middle class* was defined as (1) either one or both parents having graduated from college, *and* (2) the father working in a "professional" job (Occupational Groups One and Two from the Hollingshead [1958] index). The term *working class* was defined as (1) either one or both parents having dropped out of high school but neither having any college, *or* (2) the father working in a semiskilled or unskilled job (Occupational Levels Six or Seven from the Hollingshead [1958] index).
   Prematurity. The original intent was to exclude infants who were either chronologically premature (less than nine months) or premature by weight (less than 5½ pounds). However, because of difficulties in recruiting subjects, the weight criteria was dropped if the pregnancy was full term. The sample includes one middle-class infant and two working-class

DESCRIPTIVE DATA ON HOME AND FAMILY

Demographic Differences

Homes of middle- and working-class infants differed on
several structural dimensions. All of the 30 middle-class
families had both husband and wife present, and rarely did
grandparents or other relatives live in the same house.   In
contrast, fathers were not present in six of the 30 working-
class families (Chi Square = 3.49, p = .062). Two fathers
were in the Armed Services, one couple was recently separated,
and three infants were born out of wedlock.

Working-class homes were more crowded ($p < .001$), and
interaction between the infant and an adult other than the
mother was more common ($p < .03$). The crowdedness was not
necessarily due to smaller living quarters, but to the fact
that a greater number of working-class homes included grandparents and other relatives. Both parents in working-class
families were younger than their middle-class counterparts
($p < .001$) and the mothers themselves came from larger
families ($p < .001$). The number of children in the fathers'
family was not obtained. Religious affiliations also differed
between the classes. Ninety percent of the working-class
mothers were Catholic, while the majority of middle-class
mothers (53 percent) were non-Catholic. Similar differences
were observed for the fathers, and Chi Square analysis for
each parent yielded significant results ($p < .01$). Finally,

infants with birthweights of 4½ to 5½ pounds.

Sample Selection. Names of potential subjects were
obtained from local hospitals, birth records, pediatricians,
and well-baby clinics. It was impossible to contact some
families (moved leaving no address, etc.), some families
were disqualified because they failed to meet the "education-
of-parent" criteria (middle-class occupation but no college;
working-class occupation but some college), and some families
refused to participate. Although the actual rejection rate
was similar in both class groups (32 percent for working
class versus 28 percent for middle class), there were more
unreachable families in the working class than in the middle
class (57 percent versus 33 percent). Further analysis
revealed that the unreachable families tended to have fathers
whose occupational levels were lower than those of the
reachable subjects. Thus the middle-class group is probably
more representative of Hollingshead's occupational levels
one and two than the working-class group is representative
of occupational levels six and seven.

more working-class mothers were employed full-time, while middle-class mothers--if they were employed at all--tended to work part-time (Chi Square = 5.850, p = .054).

Another interesting difference is that no middle-class infant slept in the same room as her parents, while fifteen of the thirty working-class infants did so (Chi Square = 22.059, p = .001). It should be noted that this social class difference reflects an attitude, and is not simply a result of crowded living conditions. Several middle-class families with one-bedroom apartments moved the crib into the living room for the night, while working-class families with two-bedroom apartments often used the second bedroom as a storage area.

Medical Data

Information was also collected concerning pregnancy and delivery. There were no significant class differences in number of previous pregnancies, abnormal course of pregnancy, or abnormal delivery. The only significant difference relating to pregnancy and delivery was that a greater proportion of working-class mothers received gas anesthesia, while more middle-class mothers had injections, mostly spinals (Chi Square = 10.325, p = .006). No class differences were found for infants' birthweight, height or weight at ten months, or illnesses since birth.

Mothers were also asked whether they breast-fed or bottle-fed their infants. Only one of the thirty working-class infants was nursed, and the length of nursing was only one month. Nineteen of the middle-class mothers nursed, and several were still nursing at ten months of age. (This difference was significant beyond the .001 level of confidence by the Fisher Exact Test.)

HOME OBSERVATIONS

Six 20-minute observation periods were conducted on each of two days. The observer carried a small battery-operated timer that, every 5 seconds, emitted a soft tone that the observer heard through an earphone. Code sheets each contained thirty 1 × 2 inch squares and, at the sound of the tone, the observer moved his pencil into the next square. Presence of a particular behavior during a 5 second interval was noted on the code sheet by a number or letter representing that behavior. A particular variable could only be tallied

once per 5 second interval; thus the range for the four hours
of observation was 0 to 2880. Reliabilities based on the
percentage of agreement between two observers were computed
for all variables on ten pretest infants. Median percentages
of agreement ranged from 81 percent to 91 percent for infant
behaviors and 81 percent to 93 percent for maternal behaviors.

In addition to discrete behaviors within 5 second intervals,
variables were obtained by examining sequences of mother and
infant behaviors. These variables were not directly coded in
the homes, but were derived at a later time for the discrete
behaviors of mothers and infants. Sequence variables include
(1) positive responses to infant's nonverbal behaviors (such
as touching mother or giving object to mother); (2) reciprocal
vocalization--the percentage of infant vocalizations followed
within 5 seconds by a maternal vocalization; (3) positive
responses to infant's frets; (4) reciprocal interaction--
defined by both mother and infant acting in response to each
other within 5 seconds of the other's behaviors.

Variables describing particular aspects of the infant's
environment were also recorded during the home visits. These
include the number of toys available, the number of other
environmental objects played with (pots, pans, magazines,
etc.), and the amount of time which the child spent in a
playpen, a high-chair, a crib, etc. Infants who were placed
in walkers or who were free to walk or crawl on the floor
were further described by recording the number of minutes
during which they were free to roam around any part of the
home, rather than being restricted to a particular area.
The free-movement condition was labeled "no barriers". The
number of minutes that the television or radio were played
during each home visit was similarly recorded.

Consistency Between Home Visits

Some authors have suggested that working-class mothers
are less consistent than their middle-class counterparts.
Consistency was investigated by comparing correlations
between visits one and two in the two social class groups.
Correlations were generally higher in the middle-class group,
but the differences in correlations (calculated from r to
z transformations) were significant for five variables only,
and two of those differences showed greater consistency in
the working-class group.[3]   Consistency in the middle-class

---

[3]All correlation matrices not reported in the text are
available from the author.

was higher for amount of time the infant was in a walker
($r = .92$ versus $r = .54$); number of times mother gave the
child an instruction ($r = .78$ versus $r = .29$); and maternal
vocalization within two feet of the child ($r = .78$ versus
$r = .36$). Greater consistency in the working-class was found
for number of people interacting with the child ($r = .69$
versus $r = .27$)--this is probably attributable to the wider
range among working-class families; and amount of time mothers
spent tickling and bouncing the infant ($r = .71$ versus $r = .24$).
These differences are theoretically interesting and consistent
with class differences in frequencies of maternal behavior
(Tulkin & Ragan, 1972), but they do not suggest that the home
environments of middle-class infants are more consistent than
the environments of working-class infants.

The Infants' Experiences

Class differences in the home environments of the present
subjects have been described in detail by Tulkin and Kagan
(1972), and will be presented here in summary only. Homes of
working-class infants evidenced more "extraneous noise" than
homes of middle-class infants, a finding parallel to the data
reported by Wachs, Uzgiris, and Hunt (1971). Working-class
infants lived in more crowded homes, had more interaction with
adults other than their mothers, and spent more time in front
of television sets than their middle-class counterparts.
Second, working-class infants had less opportunity to explore
and manipulate their environments. They had somewhat fewer
toys and fewer environmental objects (pots, pans, magazines,
etc.) with which to play, and spent less time with "no barriers".

With regard to maternal behavior, the total amount of
reciprocal interaction was greater in the middle-class group,
but analysis of specific behaviors revealed that class
differences were significant in some areas and negligible
in others. The majority of differences centered around the
mother's verbal behavior and her attempts to "keep her infant
busy". Other aspects of maternal behavior did not reveal
social class differences. There was no class difference in
the amount of time mothers spent in close proximity to their
infants (within two feet), although the middle-class mothers
more often placed their infants in a face-to-face position.
There were also no significant differences for frequencies
of kissing, holding, or active physical contact (tickling and
bouncing). Contrary to expectations, no class differences
were found in the frequency of maternal prohibitions, even
when ratios were constructed to control for the amount of time
infants were free to crawl around and explore. Finally, when

infants touched their mothers or handed objects to their
mothers, working-class mothers responded positively as often
as middle-class mothers.

Significant differences *were* found on every maternal
verbal behavior recorded (spontaneous vocalization, response
to infant vocalization, and verbal imitation). In addition,
middle-class mothers more often entertained their infants and
more often gave their infants things with which to play. They
also responded to a higher precentage of the infants' spontaneous
frets and responded more quickly.

These results indicate that more middle-class than working-
class mothers were extensively involved in verbal interactions
with their infants and were more likely to provide their infants
with a greater variety of stimulation. Similar findings have
been reported for parents of infants (Levine, Fishman, & Kagan,
1967) and parents of older children (Shipman & Hess, 1966), but
more recent studies have not found social class differences on
these variables. Beckwith (1971; 1972) found no relation
between social class and mothers' behaviors with 8 to 11-month-
old infants, and Lewis and his colleagues (Lewis & Freedle,
1972; Lewis & Wilson, 1971) have reported that lower-class
mothers vocalize as frequently as middle-class mothers to three-
month-old infants and--in fact--there were more "interactive
units" for the lower SES dyads. Lewis and Wilson (1971), however, did report an important class difference that parallels
the present findings. Responses of middle-class mothers were
more likely to be related to behaviors of their infants:
middle-class mothers more frequently responded to an infant
vocalization by vocalizing, even though the overall frequency
of maternal vocalization did not show a class difference. It
is also important to note that Lewis' subjects were only 12
weeks old, whereas the present subjects were ten months old.
Longitudinal data from Lewis' studies may, in fact, be more
comparable to the present findings.

In summary, it seems that working-class mothers care for
their infants as extensively as middle-class mothers, although
there is some evidence that social class differences are found
in areas involving maternal stimulation of cognitive development.

Correlations Among Maternal Behaviors. Correlations were
computed among maternal variables in each class group. Maternal
behaviors were generally positively correlated in both social
classes, but some noteworthy differences emerged. "Tickling-
and-bouncing" was significantly related to only one other

maternal behavior for middle-class mothers, but to several variables in the working-class group. Tickling and bouncing also was more stable among working-class mothers, and may be a type of behavior that is more central to the pattern of mother-infant interaction in working-class families. In addition, two maternal behaviors appeared to be "differentially diagnostic" of the overall amount of mother-infant interaction in the two class groups: the extent to which the infant was held, and the amount of time the infant spent in a playpen. Middle-class mothers who held their infants a great deal interacted with them: holding was correlated with total maternal vocalization ($r = .568$, $p < .01$), percentage of reciprocal vocalization ($r = .500$, $p < .01$), entertaining the infant ($r = .510$, $p < .01$), and the percentage of infant frets to which the mother responded ($r = .502$, $p < .01$). These correlations for working-class subjects were .083, .106, .150, and .278. Similarly, middle-class mothers who put their infants in playpens for extended periods of time tended to be more distant from their infants physically: time in playpen was negatively related to total amount of holding ($r = -.590$, $p < .01$), and positively related to time over two feet away from the infant ($r = .761$, $p < .01$). Both correlations in the working-class group were significantly lower (by r to z transformations): for holding, $r = -.058$; for time over two feet away, $r = .396$.

These class-related differences in correlations suggest that similar behaviors can have different meanings in various groups or individuals. For middle-class mothers, holding the infant was part of a more general cluster of behaviors directed toward the child, and placing the child in a playpen was related to less contact. The absence of these relations in working-class families fits my impression that it was not uncommon for working-class mothers to hold their infants quietly for long periods of time and not engage in any type of interaction. In fact, some working-class mothers seemed to hold their infants on their laps to prohibit them from "getting into everything". Working-class mothers who put their infants in playpens might-- in contrast to middle-class mothers--sit down by the playpen, look at the infant in a face-to-face position, and engage in extensive reciprocal interaction. The point is that research must progress beyond the "counting" stage, in which we look at how much x and how much y various infants are exposed to. The x and y themselves might mean different things in different cultures or in different families.

Infant Behavior at Home

Table 19-1 presents class comparisons of infant behaviors observed in the home. Middle-class infants crawled more ($p = .003$) and played more ($p = .012$) than working-class subjects. Further analysis of play behaviors consisted of an examination of play "episodes". An *episode* was defined as the length of time a child played with one toy before putting it down. Although there were no class differences in the percentages of play episodes of 5 seconds or less, or the percentage over 1 minute, the mean of the three longest play episodes was higher for middle-class subjects. The possible correlation between length of play episodes and number of toys and environmental objects available will be explored below.

Class differences in total infant vocalizations were significant, although not as dramatic as the differences in maternal vocalization. Differences in the subcategories of infant vocalization yielded varied results. Since middle-class mothers also vocalized more, an attempt was made to determine if the class differences in infant vocalizations were attributable to the more frequent vocalizations of the middle-class mothers to their infants. A variable labeled *solitary vocalization* was constructed; this variable was defined by the ratio of infant vocalizations when the mother was over two feet away divided by the total amount of time that the mother was over two feet away. The comparison of the two classes on the solitary vocalization variable was not significant, suggesting that the difference reported for total infant vocalization was at least partially attributable to the fact that middle-class infants were experiencing more interaction with their mothers. Class differences in the infants' propensity to vocalize spontaneously thus appear minimal.

These data are again not consistent with the report of Lewis and Wilson (1971) on three-month-old infants. Lewis and Wilson found that lower-class infants vocalized more frequently than middle-class infants, and also reported that there were no class differences in play behaviors. These inconsistencies emphasize the need for additional research, hopefully longitudinal research that could clarify the ages at which various experiences begin to affect infant behaviors.

Correlations Among Infant Behaviors. Infant behaviors were not as highly correlated as maternal behaviors. Subcategroies of the same general variable were sometimes unrelated (e.g., play, inspect, and relate objects). Only one important class difference emerged: crawling and playing were significantly

TABLE 19-1. Infants' Behaviors at Home.

Variable	Working-Class		Middle-Class		p^a
	Mean	SD	Mean	SD	
Mobility					
Crawl	113.69	110.59	206.40	122.72	.003
Walk	180.00	243.11	121.90	176.98	N.S.
Lift self up	42.50	37.34	55.13	35.39	N.S.
Play					
Relate to objects	12.08	22.35	15.57	23.19	N.S.
Closely inspect object	58.77	27.03	90.73	48.48	.004
All other play	819.27	296.70	985.07	278.48	.036
Total amount of play	890.12	306.32	1091.37	273.74	.012
Percent play episodes under 5 sec.	39.94	5.24	41.54	6.23	N.S.
Percent play episodes over 1 min.	3.62	1.64	3.74	1.98	N.S.
Mean of 3 long play episodes	24.97	7.69	31.76	15.51	.038
Affective Behavior					
Total fret	115.92	75.14	103.37	63.84	N.S.
Cry	7.38	13.52	6.97	16.18	N.S.
Smile	55.19	40.68	71.10	32.18	.108
Vocalization					
Total infant vocalize	666.19	160.60	746.00	140.46	.052
Vocalize while playing	209.77	92.79	258.43	75.72	.035
Vocalize while moving	97.08	77.68	132.60	69.74	.077
Other vocalization	359.35	129.94	354.97	98.18	N.S.
Solitary voc ratio	22.97	7.13	24.81	5.46	N.S.

[a]Independent t-tests; two-tailed.
NOTE: All numbers except for percentages and ratios refer to number of 5 second intervals in which behavior was observed. N.S. stands for not significant.

TABLE 19-2. Comparisons of Catholic and Non-Catholic Middle-Class Mothers.

Variable	Catholic		Non-Catholic		p
	Mean	SD	Mean	SD	
Physical contact:					
Kiss	1.54	1.27	4.29	3.75	.017
Hold	125.15	106.26	234.35	124.93	.017
Tickle and bounce	15.08	12.66	29.47	23.72	.058
Location:					
Time over 2 ft. away	1464.38	574.28	1074.18	337.98	.027
Time within 2 ft.	1344.08	557.51	1664.41	327.70	.057
Time face-to-face	70.69	62.90	141.41	134.75	.092
Prohibitions:					
Verbal	24.62	14.18	13.53	13.68	.039
Physical	15.46	12.48	7.59	5.58	.029
Responses to nonverbal behavior:					
Positive response (percent), child touches mother	52.47	28.26	60.86	20.84	N.S.
Positive respones (percent), child offers object to mother	61.86	30.56	36.22	42.02	N.S.
Reciprocal interaction:					
Reciprocal interaction episodes	52.31	33.55	76.41	35.75	.071
Total reciprocal interaction	192.85	123.10	296.94	146.53	.049
Maternal vocalization:					
Over 2 ft. away	34.62	28.44	24.24	27.48	N.S.
Within 2 ft.	193.69	14.77	251.76	140.06	N.S.
Face-to-face	17.92	16.02	35.06	23.31	.031
Reciprocal vocalization (percent)	19.68	11.51	21.47	9.34	N.S.

Keeping infant busy:					
Entertainment	70.77	62.58	70.18	35.18	N.S.
Give objects	23.62	15.16	28.82	12.99	N.S.
Response to spontaneous frets:					
Frets (percent) to which mother responded	50.62	30.19	64.37	20.10	N.S.
Longest latency to respond (# of 5 sec. intervals)	7.33	6.00	5.76	3.88	N.S.
Other home variables:					
Number of months nursed	0.62	1.04	5.12	3.81	.001
Minutes of television	53.08	84.24	12.41	24.80	.068
Time in playpen	77.23	80.55	21.35	26.15	.016
Time with no barriers	142.15	83.67	188.82	38.39	.051
Interaction with adults other than mother	66.38	79.92	20.59	53.10	.070

NOTE: N.S. stands for not significant.

correlated for working-class infants ($r = .413$, $p < .05$) and not for middle-class infants ($r = -.278$). The difference in correlations was also significant ($p < .05$). Middle-class infants had more toys and environmental objects available to play with, and in addition, had mothers who gave them more things with which to play. Thus, crawling was not necessary in order to play. On the other hand, a working-class infant who wanted interesting things to play with often had to go after them herself--that is, if she was in a "no barriers" situation. This class difference is further illustrated by correlation between time with no barriers and total time playing. The correlation for middle-class infants was .076 (they had plenty of toys and objects to play with wherever they were); the correlation for working-class infants was .396, $p < .05$ (they had to be a position to get the interesting toys themselves).

Demographic Differences and Maternal Behavior

Mother's Age, Birth Order, and Number of Siblings. In the middle-class group, mother's age was correlated with amount of distinct face-to-face vocalization ($p < .05$), but not with vocalization in general. Older middle-class mothers also gave their infants more things to play with ($p < .01$); and were less prohibitive ($p < .01$). These relations were not found for working-class subjects. (The age range of middle-class mothers was 21 to 30 years while the range for working-class mothers was 16 to 34.)

Differences related to mother's birth order were examined in the middle-class group only, since the number of first-born working-class mothers was not sufficient for analysis. First-born middle-class mothers responded more quickly, and responded to a higher percentage of a *subgroup* of infant frets--frets that the mothers themselves had elicited, by leaving the room, prohibiting the child, putting the child down after holding him, etc. Infants of first-born middle-class mothers also spent more time on mothers' laps.

Number of siblings in mother's family was not significantly related to maternal behavior in either class group.

Religious Background of Middle-Class Mothers. The middle-class sample contained 13 Catholic mothers and 17 non-Catholic mothers. Table 19-2 presents the comparisons between these two groups and suggests that the non-Catholic mothers in the present sample were less prohibitive with their infants, spent less time over two feet away from their infants, and spent more time in various types of physical contact. Reciprocal interaction was also more common among non-Catholic dyads, but we can assume that this difference derives largely from physical interactions (such as "mother tickles--baby smiles--mother tickles"), since differences in reciprocal vocalization and "keeping-infant-busy" variables were not significant.

Religious background of the mothers was also related to other aspects of the home environments: Catholic infants spent more time in playpens, less time with no barriers, more time watching television, and more time in interaction with adults other than their mothers. They were also less likely to be nursed.

These data argue that within the middle-class, the experiences of Catholic and non-Catholic infants differed with regard to two clusters of variables: prohibition-restriction, and physical control. It could be argued that the differences reported in Table 19-2 are attributable to factors other than religious background, since Catholic mothers in the present sample tended to be younger ($p = .10$) and to have more siblings ($p < .05$). In addition, the Catholic mothers were less likely to have graduated from college than non-Catholic middle-class mothers (Chi Square = 6.674, $p = .083$). However, mother's age and number of siblings were not significantly correlated with maternal behaviors; and furthermore, comparisons between middle-class mothers with and without bachelor's degrees revealed that none of the maternal behaviors that differed by religious background showed significant difference when analyzed by mother's education. These analyses argue that religious background is an important variable that can influence some specific child-care practices of middle-class mothers.

The behaviors of middle-class infants from Catholic and non-Catholic families were compared to determine if the differences in maternal practices were reflected in theoretically related areas of infant behavior. The non-Catholic infants vocalized more frequently ($p = .005$), but the differences for solitary vocalization was not significant ($p > .25$), which suggests that the difference in overall vocalization may be at least partially attributable to non-Catholic infants' more frequent interaction with their mothers. Religious background of the mother was not related to any infant behavior other than vocalization.

Educational Background of Working-Class Mothers. Only three working-class mothers were non-Catholic, so religious comparisons were not made in the working-class group. Variation was sufficient enough, however, to examine differences beween mothers who graduated from high school ($n = 13$) verus those who did not

(n = 13). No differences were found, except that infants of
working-class mothers who had graduated from high school spent
more time with no barriers (p = .128), and encountered fewer
prohibitions (the difference for the ratio of prohibitions to
time on floor was significant at the .02 level).

Crowdedness. Infants in both classes who lived in more
crowded homes spent more time in playpens and less time with
"no barriers" (p < .05). There were no other significant
correlations between crowdedness and either maternal or child
behavior.

Relations Between Maternal and Infant Behaviors

Separate correlation matrices were generated for each
class group relating the maternal and infant behaviors observed
at home. These matrices revealed interesting similarities as
well as differences in patterns within the two social class
groups. Higher rates of infant fretting were associated in both
groups with delays in maternal response to fretting (for middle-
class subjects, r = .629, p < .01; for working-class subjects,
r = .842, p < .01). Similar results were reported by Beckwith
(1972) and by Ainsworth and her colleagues (Ainsworth, Bell, &
Stayton, 1972; Bell & Ainsworth, 1972). Some authors have
argued that results such as these should not be assumed to
derive from infant's experiences but may, in fact, reflect
individual differences in the infants' behavior that elicit
different maternal responses (R. Q. Bell, 1971; Harper, 1971;
Osofsky & Oldfield, 1971). Ainsworth, Bell, & Stayton (1972),
however, presented longitudinal data (on middle-class infants
only) that emphasized the importance of maternal behavior.
They reported that during the first quarter of the first year
of life there was little relationship between infants' tendency
to cry and mothers' responsiveness. In the third and fourth
quarters, however, babies whose mothers ignore crying or delay
in responding cry more frequently and/or longer than babies
whose mothers were more promptly responsive. Bell & Ainsworth
(1972) further reported that consistency and promptness of
maternal response is associated with a decline in the frequency
and duration of infant crying. The authors stated that "by the
end of the first year, individual differences in crying reflect
the history of maternal responsiveness rather than constitutional
difference in infant irritability" (p. 1171). The present data
argue that similar processes take place in working-class as well
as middle-class families.

Other relations between maternal and infant behavior
indicated that infant smiling was significantly correlated with

various maternal behaviors in both classes, but infant
vocalization showed different patterns in the two classes.
Infant vocalization, as reflected by the solitary vocalization
ratio, tended to be positively correlated with maternal
vocalization variables in the middle-class, and negatively
correlated with these variables in the working class.
Differences in correlations (calculated by r to z transformations) were significant at the .05 level for both total
maternal vocalization and percentage of reciprocal vocalization.
It is possible that infant vocalization had a different meaning
in the two class groups. The author observed that some working-
class infants vocalized continuously, often while examining
their fingers, toes, or clothing. This was not observed in
middle-class subjects. The possibility that infant vocalization
has a different meaning for middle-class and working-class
infants will be important to consider for later discussions of
laboratory assessments.

A final observation from the correlations of maternal and
infant behaviors is that the amount of playing and the mean
length of the three longest play episodes at home appeared to
be relatively independent of maternal behaviors in both groups.
For middle-class infants, the play variables were also
unrelated to the number of toys or environmental objects
available. Among working-class infants (who had fewer toys
and objects with which to play), those who played more had more
toys ($r = .548$, $p < .01$) and more environmental objects
($r = .518$, $p < .01$) available. Thus, the number of toys
available may be unrelated to infant play behavior once a
certain minimum cut-off point is reached, but significantly
correlated below that point.

LABORATORY ASSESSMENTS

Each subject was brought to the university and assessed
in several situations. Some subjects had to be excluded from
various sections of the data analysis because they were
excessively fretful. In some cases, various episodes were not
even run because subjects were crying. Criteria for the
elimination of fretty subjects and the number of subjects
from each group who were eliminated are available from the
author.

In the first series of tasks, subjects were seated in a
high chair and presented various tape-recorded auditory
stimuli. Researchers have commented that investigations of
early cognitive development have paid insufficient attention

to "receptive language" capacities (Friedlander, 1970). The present assessments were designed to explore some potentially useful approaches to tapping the effects of early language experiences.

Variables coded during the auditory passages and reliabilities based on correlations of two observers were: vocalization (.98), fretting (.99), look at mother (.97), look at coder (.91). Mother sat to the infant's right, and the coder sat to the infant's left. In addition to the variables recorded by the coders, two additional measures were taken: heart rate decleration and physical activity.

Meaningful Verus Nonmeaningful Speech

The first set of auditory passages contained tape-recordings of meaningful and nonmeaningful speech, each read with high and low inflection. Two readers were used, and half of the subjects in each class group heard a recording of each voice. Both readers were female and had foreign accents (Chinese and Spanish), which we assumed would control for any dialect differences between mothers of subjects from different groups. (No differences were found between infants who heard each of the two stimulus voices.) Each passage was twenty seconds in length, separated by a ten-second interstimulus interval. The passages were presented twice during the session (separated by other assessments). These two presentations will hereafter be called Series One and Series Two.

No social class differences emerged from analysis of responses to individual stimuli, or means for the entire series of stimuli. Comparisons between "extreme" groups (infants whose parents did not complete high school versus infants whose parents completed college) yielded similar results.

Responses to the high meaning/high inflection passages (Hi Hi) were compared with responses to the immediately preceding passages (low meaning/high inflection in Series One and low meaning/low inflection in Series Two). Changes in responses among infants in each class group were compared by means of second-order t tests (see Table 19-3). It had been predicted that the middle-class infants would (1) babble less and move less during Hi Hi since these activities are incompatible with attending to the stimulus, and (2) show greater vocalization following termination of Hi Hi. The prediction of decreased vocalization of middle-class subjects during the high meaning/high inflection passage was supported

TABLE 19-3. Comparisons of Responses to Hi Hi and the Preceding Stimulus in Each Series.

Variable	Working-Class		Middle-Class		p^a
	Change	SD	Change	SD	
Series One					
Vocalization during	+.296	.791	-.154	.685	.027
Vocalization after	+.121	.858	-.114	.663	N.S.
Move during	+.923	3.322	-.148	2.670	N.S.
Quieting	-.680	3.313	+.333	2.675	N.S.
Look at stranger during	-.011	3.837	-.489	3.527	N.S.
Look at stranger after	-.314	1.987	+.786	2.591	.080
Series Two					
Vocalization during	-.071	.849	-.067	.786	N.S.
Vocalization after	+.092	.668	-.117	.707	N.S.
Move during	+.182	3.096	+.333	2.777	N.S.
Quieting	+.136	3.536	+.565	4.388	N.S.
Look at stranger during	+1.096	3.674	-.158	1.693	N.S.
Look at stranger after	-1.004	1.788	+.583	1.700	.003

[a]Independent t-tests; two-tailed.

NOTE: All numbers refer to number of seconds. N.S. stands for not significant.

for Series One only (p = .027), but no differences were found for physical movement variables or for vocalization following the stimuli. The most consistent class difference was that in both Series One and Series Two, middle-class infants looked longer at the coder following the high/meaning inflection passages than they had following the preceding passages. Thus the middle-class infants appeared to be searching for the source of the meaningful speech, while working-class infants were less likely to engage in this behavior. This finding is consistent with previous work by Kagan (1971) in which meaningful and nonmeaningful speech passages were presented to a group of eight-month old infants, and "upper-middle-class" infants looked longer at the speaker baffle than infants than infants from other social class groups following the high meaning/high inflection stimulus. Since there was no coder visible to the infants in Kagan's experiment, their looking at the speaker baffle paralleled the middle-class infant's looking at the coder in the present study.

Correlations between home experiences and infant's responses to the meaningful speech passages were largely disappointing. None of the maternal behaviors were significantly correlated with increased looking at the coder following the high meaning/high inflection passage. The lack of significant relations between home experiences and laboratory performance is a perplexing problem. Even combining both class groups, no significant correlations emerged.

Mother's Voice and Stranger's Voice

These data have been reported elsewhere (Tulkin, 1971; 1973a) and will be presented here in summary only. Stimuli contained twenty-second excerpts of a standard "fairytale" read by the subject's own mother and by a stranger. Every subject heard the voice of a different stranger from her own social class group. Stimuli were presented alternately four times each with a ten-second interstimulus interval. There was a break between the first four stimuli (Series One) and the last four stimuli (Series Two). The variables coded were identical to the ones observed for the meaningful speech stimuli.

Middle-class infants showed greater differential responding to the two voices, primarily in Series One. They quieted more (i.e., decreased their physical activity) to the passages containing the mother's voice, and vocalized more following the mother's voice passages. Working-class infants did not respond differentially and second-order t-test comparisons for

Series One yielded significane levels of .058 and .090. The
most dramatic differences, however, again involved the infants'
looking behaviors. Middle-class infants looked more at the
mother after hearing the mother's voice and more at the coder
after the stranger's voice (second-order comparisons were
significant at the .055 level for the mother's voice and the
.030 level for the stranger;s voice in Series One). In Series
Two, the only significant difference also involved looking
behavior. Here, the middle-class infants differentially gazed
at mother and stranger *during* the passages.

Correlational analysis argued that middle-class infants'
responses to the stimuli represented a meaningful pattern.
The correlations between looking at the "correct" person
following the passages in Series One and Series Two were .512
($p < .01$) for the middle-class infants, and .029 (not
significant) for the working-class infants. In addition,
middle-class subjects who looked more at their mothers following the mother's voice passages in Series One quieted more
while listening to those passages ($r = .316$, $p < .10$); and
middle-class subjects who looked at their mothers more *while*
listening to the mother's voice passages vocalized more following those passages ($r = .579$, $p < .01$). These relations were
not significant in the working-class group.

Correlations between home experiences and differential
responses to mother's and stranger's voices were again
disappointing. No significant relationships were found
between home variables and differential responding in either
Series One or Series Two. If we look only at differential
responses to the initial mothers' voice stimulus versus the
initial strangers' voice stimulus, we find serveral significant
correlations. In both classes, distinctive face-to-face
vocalization was correlated with greater vocalization following
mothers' voice than following strangers' voice ($p < .05$);
similar relations were found for entertainment and imitations
($p < .05$ for working-class infants, and $p < .10$ for middle-
class infants on both variables). Obviously, these correlations
offer only meager support for the effects of experiences on
infants prelanguage abilities.

Play Behaviors

Mother and infant were taken to a carpeted 9 × 12 ft.
playroom. Subjects were observed through a one-way mirror,
and two coders recorded behaviors on an Esterline Angus Event
Recorder, while the author dictated an audio tape recording
describing other aspects of the play session. The session
consisted of six episodes:

1. A two-minute *adaptation period* designed to give the subject an opportunity to get used to the playroom. The mother was asked (by way of an intercom speaker) to put the infant down on a designated spot on the rug and then to return to her chair at the end of the room. During the adaptation period the following variables were coded: positive vocalization, fretting, looking at mother (defined as looking at mother from the waist up), smiling, exploring the room (defined as intently inspecting any of the fixtures of the room), physical contact with mother (initiated by the infant), amount of time in the 3 × 3 ft. square where the mother was sitting, and number of times the infant crawled from one square to another.

2. Following adaptation, three *single toys* were presented for four minutes each--a block, a ladybug toy, and a chime ball. All of the variables recorded during the adaptation period, with the exception of time spent in the square where mother was sitting, were also recorded for the single toys. In addition, the length of time the infant played with each toy was also recorded. (Each period of noninterrupted play with a toy will henceforth be called *sustained directed activity* or SDA coding, several variables were created: length of time elapsing before the subject touched the toy ("latency"), how long the infant played with the toy the first time she picked it up (first SDA), the longest length of time she played with it before putting it down (long SDA), and the total amount of time she played with it (total SDA).

3. Following the three single toys, two *conflict trials*, of four minutes each, were presented. Each conflict trial consisted of presenting one of the single toys, together with a new toy that the subject had not seen previously. These toys were presented equidistant from the subject and about 2 feet apart. All subjects were presented with the same conflicts (ladybug toy paired with a steam ship, and chime ball paired with a "hanging xylophone").[4] In addition to the variables

[4] Pretesting carried out with subjects who were not included in the present sample demonstrated that preferences between the old and novel toys--if there were any--tended to favor the old toy. Thus choice of novel toys could not be attributed to their intrinsic attractiveness.

coded above, data for the conflict trials included
the toy the infant first chose, the first SDA and
total SDA for each toy, the number of times she
visually shifted from one toy to the other before
making her choice, the number of times she looked at
the other toy while playing, and the number of times
she put down one toy and picked up the other one.
It was predicted (based on results reported by
Rubenstein, 1967) that infants who had experienced
more interaction with their mothers would show
greater interest in the novel toys.

Reliabilities for play session variables were .99 for
vocalization, .91 for fretting, .91 for look at mother, .84
for smile, .99 for explore room, .99 for physical contact and
.99 for total SDA.

Play session data suggest that infants in the two classes
differed only in their responses to the conflict trials.
(These data are available from the author.) Middle-class
infants displayed a pattern of behaviors that could be called
reflective, while the working-class infants displayed behaviors
that might be labeled as *impulsive*. Specifically, middle-class
infants had more visual shifts before touching the toy ($p = .05$),
fewer visual shifts after starting to play ($p = .06$), fewer
play shifts ($p = .124$), and longer periods of play with the
first toy they touched ($p = .151$). Several of the differences
were not significant, but the pattern of class differences
suggests that middle-class subjects resolved the conflict by
looking at the toys before beginning to play, while the working-
class subjects resolved the conflict by switching toys after
they had begun playing.

Middle-class infants also looked at their mothers for
longer periods of time during Conflict One ($p = .01$).
Correlational analysis showed that many of the responses of
middle-class infants during the conflict trials (and the play
session in general) were related to the "look-at-mother"
variable (Table 19-4). Middle-class infants who looked at
their mothers a great deal did less exploration of the playroom, were more hesitant to touch the toys, and looked back
and forth more often before choosing a toy on the conflict
trials. One possible explanation—which is elaborated later—
is that anxiety concerning maternal disapproval led some
middle-class infants to be very cautious in their play
behavior. The absence of these relations in the working-class
group suggests that the maternal disapproval may be a less

TABLE 19-4.   Correlations of "Look-At-Mother" and Other
Play Session Variables.

Variable	Correlations	
	Working-Class	Middle-Class
Vocalization during adaptation and single toys	.152	-.483[a]
Total vocalization	.121	-.029
Explore room, adaptation	-.056	-.459[a]
Total explore room	.181	-.188
Total physical contact	.243	.058
Latency, single toys	.078	.450[a]
Latency, conflicts	-.188	.719[b]
Initial visual shifts	-.113	.447[a]
Later visual shifts	-.016	-.299
Play shifts	.128	-.281
Total SDA, new toys minus old toys	.058	-.039

[a] $p < .05$.

[b] $p < .01$.

salient determinant of behavior in that group.

Relationships between home variables and laboratory assessments were strongest in the area of play behaviors. For middle-class infants (Table 19-5), a cluster of home variables reflecting both positive mother-infant contact (e.g., amount of time mother held the infant and gave things to the infant to play with) and degree of restriction (time in playpen and prohibition ratio)[5] were consistently related to what might be called a *freer* or *less inhibited* style of play. More inter-

[5] The number of prohibitions at home was related to the infants' mobility, so the prohibition ratio is calculated by dividing the total number of maternal prohibitions by the number of five second intervals in which the infant walked or crawled.

TABLE 19-5. Correlations Between Selected Home Variables and Infants' Play Behaviors in the Middle Class.

	Home Variables			
Play Variables	Holding	Give Objects	Time in Playpen	Prohibition Ratio
Mean latency	-.379[b]	-.318[a]	.527[c]	.343[a]
Mean look at mother	-.410[b]	-.008	.403[b]	.371[b]
Initial visual shifts (conflicts)	-.144	-.316	.469[b]	.053
Mean play with new toys	.319	.517[b]	-.524[b]	-.431[b]
Explore room, adaptation	.389[a]	.095	-.363[a]	-.249

[a] $p < .10.$
[b] $p < .05.$
[c] $p < .01.$

action and less prohibition were correlated with shorter latencies to touch toys, less looking at mother, less looking back and forth between the "conflict" toys before choosing one to play with, more play with the new toys on the conflict trials, and more exploration of the playroom during the adaptation period. The correlations in the working-class group were largely nonsignificant.

This data is consistent with reports from other researchers that infants who experience greater interaction with their caretakers have longer latencies to touch toys. Home-reared infants have longer latencies to touch toys than to institutionalized infants (Collard, 1962); middle-class children take longer to respond to a wide variety of tasks than lower-class children (Mumbauer, 1969; Schwebel, 1966; Streissguth, 1969); and first-born infants--who receive more attention from their mothers than later-born infants (Rubenstein, 1967)--also wait longer before touching toys (Collard, 1968). The contribution of the present study lies in the suggestion that at least for some infants, longer latencies derive from *anxiety*, rather than advanced cognitive development. It was my impression, from watching these infants, that subjects with moderate latencies on the conflict trails appeared to be making a choice between the two toys, with no indication that anxiety was playing a role in their behavior. Infants with extremely long latencies appeared to be inhibited or scared to touch the toys. One middle-class infant with an average latency of almost two minutes on the conflict trials was obviously quite anxious: several times, she moved toward one of the toys, glanced back to her mother, and sat back again. Later, she started to put the toy in her mouth, again looked at her mother, and put the toy back on the floor. When she finally did mouth the toy, her mother walked over and took it out of her mouth.

It should be emphasized that these relationships between home experiences and infants' responses to the conflict trials are based on data for middle-class subjects only. These data again point out that variance within social class groups is sufficient to account for large differences in infant behaviors.

DISCUSSION

The major contribution of the present research is the demonstration that social studies can be a useful, but also a limiting, means of exploring the processes of early child development. The usefulness of observing and testing subjects from different classes is that we are provided with groups of subjects with differing experiences; the limitation is that we often do not collect the appropriate data for determining precisely how the experiences are different, and we are left with descriptive results that do not advance our understanding of developmental processes. The present study was able to show that infants in middle- and working-class families differed in some experiences and not in others, and that middle-class infants differed from their working-class counterparts on a number of laboratory assessments. These data, however, do not define the extent to which the class differences observed at home *caused* the differences in the laboratory, and thus the class comparisons do not directly address the question of the effects of experience.

Other aspects of the data analysis--besides social class-- do speak to the issue of relationships between experiences and infant behavior--and these analyses are based on within-class variation. In fact, the most scientifically productive goal for a cross-class study is not a simple comparison of the classes, but rather an analysis of the relationships among a given set of variables in the different groups. The design of the present study provided two groups of mothers who differed in their attitudes toward children (Tulkin & Cohler, 1973), and probably in a variety of other values associated with social status. Examining the same variables in these two groups yielded many of the benefits of a multicultural study. Different patterns of correlations among maternal behaviors in each group, for example, suggested that some behaviors (such as holding an infant), might have different meanings for middle-class and working-class mothers. Recognizing that identical behaviors might have different meanings is a concept that is critical for good multicultural research.

Other examples of class differences in relationships among the variables studied include the finding that the amount of time that working-class infants played in the home was significantly related to the number of toys and environmental objects available; and the finding that a "less inhibited" approach to playing with the toys in the laboratory was related to mother-infant contact and fewer restrictions at home--for middle-class subjects only.

The fact that relationships found in one group did not emerge in the other group is one of the reasons for doing multigroup research. While it is possible to dismiss these findings, because they were not "replicated" in the other social class, it is also possible to examine the particular relationships to determine if they make more sense in one class than in the other. The class difference in correlations between holding and other maternal behaviors has already been discussed in terms of the different purposes that holding an infant appeared to serve in the two classes. With regard to the correlation between playing and number of toys available, the relationship is likely to be nonlinear; once a certain number of toys are available, adding new ones is unrelated to play behavior. Thus the discrepancy in correlations in the two groups makes sense. These data point out how important it is to approach social class studies with the same cultural relativity as one approaches any multicultural research. These precautions have been stressed throughout this book, and need not be repeated again, except to point out that the data reported in this chapter support the argument.

A very striking aspect of the data, which is not readily

apparent from an inspection of the statistics, is the overlap
between the distribution of maternal behaviors in the two
social classes. Even for differences that were highly
significant *statistically,* the distributions are amazingly
similar (see Figure 19-1.). This figure illustrates an
important point: the significant differences are deceiving in
their implication that individual mothers from the two social
classes were grossly different. This quite simply is not true.

To illustrate the large individual differences within
each class, I conducted a series of interviews with some of
the subjects in the present study. I wanted to understand
the child-rearing philosophies of the mothers and to determine
where their attitudes came from. I shall present two summaries
of these interviews to enable the reader to "get a feel" for
what these subjects are like as people.

The specific reasons for interviewing each of the mothers
is given below. The basic philosophies of each of the
mothers will be discussed first, followed by comparisons of
their answers to specific questions.

Mrs. York.

Mrs. York is a 23-year old Catholic middle-class mother.
She was selected for interviewing because she had the least
positive interaction with her daughter, and the second highest
amount of time over two feet away from her daughter in the
middle-class group. During the observations, Mrs. York did
her housework and Baby York played in a playpen. Baby York
experienced only 17 minutes in free exploration (no barriers)
during the four hours of observation, and experienced minimal
interaction of all types with her mother. In a discussion of
how the baby's playing by herself affected her own daily life,
Mrs. York mentioned feeling "strapped down" by her baby.

Finally, Mrs. York was asked to recall various aspects of
her own family life. She characterized her own parents as:

> strict in a loving way; if they said something,
> they meant it. I was disciplined and I'm doing
> all right. I wasn't allowed to run around the
> house. I'm very leary about all the new thinking
> about how you can let you kids do anything they
> want, express themselves 100 percent of the time,
> and all that stuff.

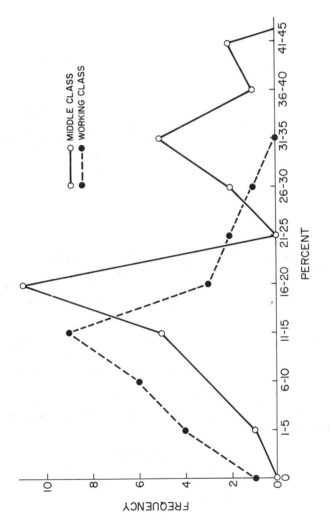

FIGURE 19-1. Percent reciprocal vocalization.

In addition, it is revealing to note that Mrs. York herself
felt that her own mother paid less attention to her than to
her siblings:

> I think I spend more time with her (Baby York)
> than my mother spent with me; on the basis that
> I have more time to spend because I was the
> second one. Like my mother was my father's
> secretary for many years, and my sister after
> me is a Mongoloid--which really strapped my
> mother down... so that she didn't have the
> time.

While minimal data cannot provide definite conclusions,
it appears that a substantial part of Mrs. York's behavior
and attitude toward her daughter are related to her own
personality, and her own family background--and are only
minimally related to experiences associated with social class.

Mrs. Roberts

Mrs. Roberts is a 20-year-old Catholic working-class
mother with a ninth-grade education who accepted her 10-month-
old daughter as a member of the family. This philosophy was
rare among working-class mothers; and Mrs. Roberts, in fact,
commented that she had been criticized by both friends and
relatives because she treated her daughter as if she were
three or four years old. She mentioned, for example, that
people told her that if her daughter walked too early, she
"would get bow-legged because her legs couldn't support her".

The outstanding characteristic of Mrs. Robert's philosophy
was that her daughter was a human being, and deserved to be
treated as one.

> She's just like a person. She has all the feelings
> we do. And anything I tell her, she knows that
> I'm talking about... . She communicates to me
> also. That's why she's just like a person. ...She
> always wants to know something. Anything different
> in the whole house, she noticed it more than I
> would. A simple thing like a little knick-knack
> that I just put out, she walked into the room and
> noticed it right away.

Mrs. Roberts saw this curiosity as resulting partially
from the wide variety of things that she and her husband had

shown Baby Roberts how to do.

> Until they are about 3 or 4 months old, they are
> just interested in themselves--in finding themselves
> out and things like that. After they are through
> with themselves and have looked at their fingers
> a hundred times, they want something else... .
> They should learn to play by themselves, but there
> are certain things that they don't know how to do.
> You should teach them how to play, which doesn't
> take long. And then let them play, and go back
> later and show them something else; because
> naturally they get bored just like we do.

Considerable interview time was devoted to comparing
Mrs. Roberts' philosophies with those of a girl friend who
seemed to be more "typical" of working-class mothers. Mrs.
Roberts said that the girl friend was "more worried about
keeping a beautiful house than keeping a beautiful baby".
She was content not having her infant walking: "Maybe she
wants to keep her a baby" because "she's less trouble that
way. You just sit her in a playpen all day and she doesn't
complain". An attempt was made to determine why Mrs. Roberts
felt differently toward her daughter than her girl friend did
toward her baby. It appeared that Mrs. Roberts' girl friend
grew up receiving very little love, and presently had
considerable difficulty expressing affection. Mrs. Roberts
emphasized, however, that she did not see her girl friend as
a bad mother.

> She's a good mother because she's not neglectful.
> I know she loves her baby, but she's always thinking
> of what to get next. She's always thinking of her
> bills more than her baby.

Mrs. Roberts herself came from a broken home. She said
that she "had a very good life as a baby", although her
parents were divorced when she was in elementary school. She
lived with her father, and remembers that she did not like
her mother anymore. She couldn't recall particular experiences
from her family life except that she was very happy when she
was a young child. What made Mrs. Roberts' life so happy and
contributed to her being the type of mother she is would be
difficult to determine. It is the kind of question to which
social scientists will always be seeking an answer. As to
how she felt about mothers who are like her girl friend, Mrs.
Roberts replied: "I could cry when I think of what they're
missing".

INTERVIEW DATA

The interview was designed to examine the mothers'
philosophies in areas relevant to the behaviors examined in
the present study.

What Are Infants Like?

One of the major concerns of the interviews was the
mother's conception of what infants are like. In particular,
mothers were asked if infants were similar to older human
beings: Do they have emotions? Do they become afraid? Do they
get their own way? Are there particular things they like to
do? etc.

Mrs. York

> Basically, we know that they are human beings, so
> we say that. But, it's just been recently that
> she has actually become an individual in terms of
> learning to express herself the way we express
> ourselves as human beings. For the first six
> months, you can say that they are human, but what
> are they doing? They can't show signs of love!
> They can tell you that they are uncomfortable,
> but a cat out in the street whines because it's
> hungry. Now she shows love. Even on the dressing
> table, if I'm changing her and I go to sit her up,
> she'll snuggle up to me.
>
> [Can kids within the first year of life communicate
> to older people?] They can't say "I'm wet", but a
> baby lets you know. They can't say "I'm hungry",
> but they communicate in the only way they can.

Mrs. Roberts

> I think she's like a person. She does everything
> like a person would do, except that she doesn't
> talk. She has all the feelings that we have.
> When I spank her, she gets mad at me. If she sees
> her father, she's in her glory--just like I am.
>
> [Can you communicate with each other?] Yes. Any-
> thing I tell her she knows just what I'm talking
> about. She communicates to me, too. She can't
> express it, she can't talk about it, but she can

show me what she wants. I can tell when she's
crying because she's mad, or because she wants
something, or because she's hungry, or because
she's scared, or just because she's spoiled.

Summary. There was substantial agreement that by ten
months of age the infants seemed "human" to their mothers,
in terms of having emotions and being able to communicate with
others. Several felt that they were not able to communicate
because the child could not speak.

Effects of Experiences

Mothers were asked a variety of questions concerning the
extent to which they felt that children were influenced by
maternal care practices and other environmental experiences
(i.e., Are intellectual and personality characteristics inborn, or are they shaped by experiences?).

Mrs. York

I think that the mother can be an influence.
Some people just say, "Well, that's the way
she is", but kids have to learn different
things; and your mother is the one to teach
you. For example, I think that it's good
for her to be by herself. Now I keep her
out on the porch for a long period of time,
three hours. She loves it; she's gotten
used to it. I think it's good for her to
learn to amuse herself or play by herself.
A lot of times grown-ups nowadays don't know
what to do with themselves when they are
alone, because they were never let alone to
make use out of time.

Mrs. Roberts

Mothers can become a great influence. I don't
think they can make them smarter or dumber, but
I think they can change their personality. If
we talk to her in stupid sentences, naturally
that's how she's going to talk. If she ever
swears when she's two years old, she'll have
heard it from us. So, she'll get our personality.
As far as smartness, no; I don't think we have
much to do with that... I don't think that

walking her when she was a baby started her to
walk when she was 7 months old. She wanted to
walk; because you can't force a baby to walk.

Summary. It is interesting to note that, in general, the
working-class mothers appeared to see themselves as having less
influence over their children's development than did middle-
class mothers. Another conclusion from the responses to this
question is that Mrs. Roberts, who engaged in extensive
interaction with her infant, was not convinced that her actions
had contributed to daughter's accelerated development. She
felt, instead, that her daughter walked and talked because she
was "active" or becauwe she "wanted to".

Free Exploration Versus Prohibition

One of the clearest differences among mothers was the
extent to which they allowed their infants freedom to move
around the house. A class difference was found on the amount
of time the infants spent with no barriers, but there was a
large degree of overlap. Mothers were questioned regarding
why they permitted or did not permit free exploration and how
they felt these experiences would affect later behavior. Time
with no barriers and the total number of prohibitions at home
is also reported, for each subject interviewed, to illustrate
the relation between the mothers' behaviors and their
philosophies. Finally, since Mrs. York represented the group
of middle-class mothers whose infants appeared to be "anxious"
during the play session, considerable time was spent trying to
understand the attitudes that formed the basis for her behavior.

Mrs. York [17 minutes with no barriers; 46 prohibitions]

A child has to know what he is allowed: what he can
do and what he can't do. Not only on the basis of
what's good for him and what isn't good for him;
but I think children will--because of their nature,
because they are kids--get away with as much as
you allow them. Sometimes letting them get away
with it isn't so bad, but if they were constantly
given in to all the time, or let them do exactly
what they wanted all the time, they wouldn't be
good. A child has to learn to accept limits. We
all live within limits.

I'll let her rip up a newspaper, if everybody has
read it. But when she'll go after a book, that's

all. Or if she aims at the curtains, she doesn't
get away with it. Only so many times you can take
her hands off a curtain or off of something that
you are trying to teach her is a "no no" without
getting mad. I'm human, too, you know, and like
five times you could say "no no" and she could
keep going back to it.

Mrs. York related a recent chain of events that further
illustrates her feelings about the type of infant behavior
that should be prohibited:

> My husband bought her a doll. I let her hold it
> every so often, but it's kind of cute and she'll
> only ruin it, so I put it up. My girl friend came
> over with her three and a half year old girl, and
> I let her play with it because I knew she wouldn't
> wreck it. [Baby York] spotted this other girl
> with her doll and started crying. Then she grabbed
> the arm and it was a real tug of war... I know
> what [Baby York] would have done: ruin the hair or
> the dress. I can't see taking this nice doll and
> ruining it when she really can't play with it the
> way it should be played with. She has other dolls
> just like it that have no clothes, or have raggedy
> clothes. I don't think she's ready for this doll
> yet. Maybe when she's three, she'll really love
> to play with a doll like that; so why have something
> wrecked when I've got things for her level now.

Mrs. Roberts [236 minutes with no barriers; 46 prohibitions]

> She can understand when I say "no". If I say not to
> touch the broom, she knows what I'm talking about.
> And if she touches it, she knows it's against my
> will. So why shouldn't she be slapped for it?
> She's doing it to be spiteful... . She could be
> very destructive if I let her. She's always
> pushing the tables, and the lamps are always
> jiggling... .

> This is a good time for discipline. Right now, when
> they are young. I worry, though. Maybe I'm giving
> her too much discipline. You see all these other
> little kids that have grown up and they are really
> brats. The punks out in the street that smoke when
> they are six and swear in words that I haven't even
> heard. And I just don't want her to be like that.

> I wish I had a book, or somebody to tell how to
> discipline her... .

> Once I counted all the "no no's" I gave her in a
> half-hour; and the poor kid--that's all I said to
> her. I wouldn't stick her in a playpen all day,
> though. How would she learn anything? It's just
> like confining her. Before she'd sit for hours
> with one doll. Now she ·doesn't; she wants
> different things. She's exploring. She gets
> bored easy now.

Summary. Mothers who had occasion to restrict their
infants' behavior believed that verbal and physical prohibitions could be understood by the infants, and, in fact,
were necessary to ensure the development of desirable behavior.
The mothers who believed in early discipline were concerned--
even worried--about the child's turning out to be spoiled, and
suggested that infants try to "get away" with as many things
as they can. Because mothers spoke a great deal about spoiling
their infants, a series of questions was addressed to this
issue.

Spoiling Infants

The interviewer asked how infants can be spoiled and what
types of behavior would result at later ages. One indication
of the mother's concern about "spoiling" their infants was the
extent to which they responded to the child's fretting. Therefore, some of the home observation data on mothers' response
to fretting is given for each subject interviewed.

> Mrs. York   [Responded to 15 percent of the spontaneous
>   frets; mean of two longest times to respond
>   was 45 seconds]

> Definitely, infants can be spoiled. You can spoil
> someone this age the easiest of any because they're
> at a cute age... . I'd hate to see [Baby York]
> spoiled, so I think that to pick her up for no
> reason at all, just because maybe she is fussing
> to be picked up, is wrong... . It's kind of like
> a snowball, you know. You start at one thing and
> then it's two or three; and the older they get,
> the more they try... . I go over to some houses
> where I can't enjoy myself because the baby's
> touching everything. You can't sit down and enjoy

a cup of coffee if they're rocking around the
floor and all.

Mrs Roberts   [Responded to 47 percent of the spontaneous
frets; mean of longest times to respond was
15 seconds]

Yeah, kids can be spoiled. [Baby Roberts] is
spoiled. If she doesn't get her way, she'll wave
her hands at me like she's hitting me. She'll
walk away from me. She'll stomp her feet. She'll
sit on the ground. She'll do anything. But she
usually doesn't get her way with me. I won't give
her anything just because she wants it.

[Is it bad for babies to be spoiled?] There's two
kinds of spoiled. One is when the kid is spoiled
so bad you don't even like him. She's not that
spoiled. That's bratty spoiled--the kind of kid
who takes a tantrum when they don't get something.
She's not bratty spoiled... . But I keep thinking--
I have girl friends who have babies that are four
years old and are really just spoiled sneaks. They
yell back at you and defy their mothers. I keep
thinking that she will be like these kids--these
two and three-year-old devils that know they're
getting everybody mad, but the do it anyway.

Summary. These mothers agreed that infants can be
spoiled, but there was diverse opinion concerning the dangers
of spoiling a child. Mrs. York felt most strongly that spoiling a child was a bad thing, and the data indicated that she
was most hesitant to respond to the child's fretting. Once
when she picked up her daughter, she said that she was
"probably doing the wrong thing". Mrs. Roberts worried that
her daughter might become "bratty spoiled", but was not
concerned about giving the child too much attention. It is
interesting to note that two other mothers who were most
responsive to their infants had similiar theories, i.e., that
there is more than one type of spoiling. Both mothers felt
that it was bad for kids to learn to control adults by crying
(Mrs. Roberts' "bratty spoiled"), but did not feel that
attention per se was bad for the child.

DISCUSSION OF INTERVIEWS

The interview data were gathered originally when it became apparent that large within-class differences were emerging on the home observation variables, and it was anticipated that interviews might help to clarify the source of these differences. The protocols presented-- although admittedly sketchy--do illustrate that variations in maternal behaviors derive from similar differences in maternal attitudes and personality. A mother who needs to be in control and run a "tight ship" is more likely to insist on a great deal of structure in the infant's daily life, and in the mother-infant relationship. On the other hand, a mother who is more flexible is likely to impose only minimal structure. A relativistic philosophy (Tulkin, 1972) would argue that each mother is raising her child according to a "system" that she believes in and the only role for social scientists is to examine the effects of these different experiences so that mothers will better understand the implications of various child-care philosophies.

Social scientists might also help mothers to more accurately interpret contemporary infant behaviors. Parents sometimes misinterpret their infants' behavior, one example being that some mothers see the child's developing initiative between six and nine months of age as intentionally aggressive, and justifying restriction. If mothers better understood developmental patterns during the first year of life, they might be less likely to see their infants as "fresh", "spite-ful", or "destructive" as suggested by some of the mothers in the present study. Mothers also might be less likely to believe "old-wives' tales", such as the warning that teaching a child to walk too early can result in his being bow-legged.

Perhaps the most critical area for parent education involves the importance of early language stimulation. There is no way to determine how many mothers would agree with one mother that it is not important to talk to infants until they themselves begin to talk. Misconceptions like this may be responsible for a substantial proportion of the pre- and early-school-age children who are "retarded" in language development. More research is needed to determine why some mothers do not talk to their infants, while other mothers (like Mrs. Roberts), from similar social class backgrounds, believe that their infants are trying to communicate with them, and that it is important to keep up a conversation.

Large differences in mothers' approaches to early communication with their infants have been noted by other authors, but little data is available on the sources of these differences. Senn and Hartford (1968) observed that some mothers "talked" to their babies from the beginning. Without waiting until words were understood, they conversed with their babies for the purpose of expressing their feelings rather than for achieving specific goals. A second group of mothers used verbal communication from the beginning to direct and control the behavior of their children rather than as a mode of expressing maternal feelings of pleasure in the child. They used language variously to teach, scold, prohibit, and threaten. We conclude that interventionists can play an important function among all social class groups in developing the understanding that families who want their children to develop verbal competence need to emphasize language stimulation in the first year of life.

Finally, our small interview study suggests that a social class difference may exist in mothers' feelings that they can have an influence over their children's development. Minuchin, Montalvo, Guerney, Rosman, and Schumer (1967) also observed that lower-income mothers seemed to see themselves as powerless, helpless, and overwhelmed by their children. These authors found many mothers like one mother in our sample who felt that they were just "not able to do anything" with their children. I have argued previously (Tulkin, 1972; Tulkin & Cohler, 1973) that the feeling among lower-income mothers that they could not influence their children's development probably derives from real life experiences in which these women have been ineffective in producing changes in their environments. Infant intervention and/or parent education programs cannot expect to change these philosophies easily; but by encouraging mothers to feel that they *can* influence their children's development, interventionists might make a start in reducing mothers' feelings of ineffectiveness. However, if we want mothers to really appreciate the influences that they can have over the development of their children, we need to initiate social changes that will increase the effectiveness of these women's efforts to influence their environment in other ways. As the above protocols have suggested, a mother's feelings and behaviors toward her child derive from her own experiences; and the need to change the experience of powerlessness.

REFERENCES

Ainsworth, M. D. S., Bell, S. M., & Stayton, D. J.
    Individual differences in the development of some
    attachment behaviors. Merrill-Palmer Quarterly,
    1972, 18, 123-143.

Beckwith, L. Relationships between attributes of mothers and
    their infants' IQ scores. Child Development, 1971,
    42, 1083-1097.

Beckwith, L. Relationships between infants' social behavior
    and their mothers' behavior. Child Development,
    1972, 43, 397-411.

Bell, R. Q. Stimulus control of parent or caretaker behavior
    by offspring. Developmental Psychology, 1971, 4,
    63-72.

Bell, S. M., & Ainsworth, M. D. S. Infant crying and maternal
    responsiveness. Child Development, 1972, 43, 1171-
    1190.

Collard, R. A study of curiosity in infants. Unpublished
    doctoral dissertation, University of Chicago, 1962.

Collard, R. Social and play responses of first-born and later-
    born infants in an unfamiliar situation. Child
    Development, 1968, 39, 325-334.

Friedlander, B. Z. Receptive language developments in infancy:
    Issues and problems. Merrill-Palmer Quarterly, 1970,
    16, 7-51.

Harper, L. V. The young as a source of stimuli controlling
    caretaker behavior. Developmental Psychology, 1971,
    4, 73-88.

Hollingshead, A. H., & Redlich, R. C., Social class and mental
    illness: A community study. New York: Wiley, 1958.

Kagan, J. Change and continuity in infancy. New York: Wiley,
    1971.

Levine, J., Fishman, C., & Kagan, J. Sex of child and social
    class as determinants of maternal behavior. Paper
    presented at the meeting of the Society for Research
    in Child Development, New York, March 1967.

Lewis, M., & Freedle, R. Mother-infant dyad: The cradle of meaning. Paper presented at Symposium on Language and Thought: Communication and Affect, Erindale College, University of Toronto, March 1972.

Lewis, M., & Wilson, C. D. Infant development in lower-class American families. Paper presented at the meeting of the Society for Research in Child Development, Minneapolis, April 1971.

Minuchin, S., Montalvo, B., Guerney, B., Rosman, B., & Schumer, F. Families of the slums: An exploration of their structure and treatment. New York: Basic Books, 1967.

Moss, H. A., & Robson, K. S. Maternal influences in early social visual behavior. Child Development, 1968, 39, 401-408.

Moss, H. A., Robson, K. S., & Pedersen, F. Determinants of maternal stimulation of infants and consequences of treatment for later reactions to strangers. Developmental Psychology, 1969, 1, 239-246.

Mumbauer, C. C. Socioeconomic background and cognitive functioning in preschool children. George Peabody College DARCEE Papers, 1969, 3 (5).

Osofsky, J. D., & Oldfield, S. Children's effects on parental behavior: Mothers' and fathers' responses to dependent and independent child behavior. Paper presented at the meeting of the American Psychological Association, Washington, D.C., September 1971.

Rosenfeld, H. M. Time-series analysis of mother-infant inter-action. Paper presented at the meeting of the Society for Research in Child Development, Philadelphia, April 1973.

Rubenstein, J. Maternal attentiveness and subsequent exploratory behavior in the infant. Child Development, 1967, 38, 1089-1100.

Schwebel, A. I. Effects of impulsivity on performance of verbal tasks in middle- and lower-class children. American Journal of Orthopsychiatry, 1966, 36, 13-21.

Senn, M. J. E., & Hartford, C. (Eds.) The first born: Experiences

of eight American families. Cambridge, Mass.:
Harvard University Press, 1968.

Shipman, V. C., & Hess, R. D. Early experience in the
socialization of cognitive modes in children: A
study of urban Negro families. Paper presented at
Conference on Family and Society, Merrill-Palmer
Institute, April 1966.

Shuey, A. M. The testing of Negro intelligence (2nd ed.).
New York: Social Science Press, 1966.

Streissguth, A. P. Social class differences in children's
cognitive functioning. Paper presented at the
meeting of the Society for Research in Child
Development, Santa Monica, California, March 1969.

Tulkin, S. R. Race, class, family, and school achievement.
Journal of Personality and Social Psychology, 1968,
9, 31-37.

Tulkin, S. R. Infants' reactions to mother's voice and
stranger's voice: Social class differences in the
first year of life. Paper presented at the meeting
of the Society for Research in Child Development,
Minneapolis, April 1971.

Tulkin, S. R. An analysis of the concept of cultural
deprivation. Developmental Psychology, 1972, 6,

Tulkin, S. R. Social class differences in infants' reactions
to mother's and stranger's voices. Developmental
Psychology, 1973, 8, 137. (a)

Tulkin, S. R. Social class differences in attachment behaviors
of ten-month-old infants. Child Development, 1973,
44, 171-174. (b)

Tulkin, S. R., & Cohler, B. J. Child-rearing attitudes and
mother-child interaction in the first year of life.
Merrill-Palmer Quarterly, 1973, 19, 95-106.

Tulkin, S. R., & Kagan, J. Mother-child interaction in the
first year of life. Child Development, 1972, 43,
31-41.

Tulkin, S. R., & Konner, M. J. Alternative conceptions of
intellectual functioning. Human Development, 1973,

16, 33-52.

Wachs, T. D., Uzgiris, I. C., & Hunt, J. M. Cognitive
    Development in infants of different age levels and
    from different environmental backgrounds: An
    explanatory investigation. Merrill-Palmer Quarterly,
    1971, 17, 283-317.

Chapter 20
Mother–Infant Interaction
and Development in Infancy

Leon J. Yarrow, Frank A. Pedersen, and Judith Rubenstein

National Institute of Child Health and Human Development
National Institutes of Health

Our thinking about the significant dimensions of early
experience has undergone vast changes during the past twenty-
five years. For a long time, psychoanalytic theory was the
main inspiration of research on early development. Sometimes
explicitly, often implicitly, it provided the framework within which research problems were formulated; but more importantly
it specified the variables. Much of the research on early

[1] This paper is a condensation of data and discussion presented
in more detail in the book, Infant and Environment: Early
Cognitive and Motivational Development. Halsted, 1975.

[2] We are indebted to Dr. Joseph Jankowski, Mrs. Myrna Fivel
and Miss Joan Durfee for their assistance in the development
of the observation scale and in the collection of data; and
to Mr. Richard Cain for his contribution to the data analyses.

**Social and Behavioral Sciences Branch, National Institute of
Child Health and Human Development.

***Tufts University School of Medicine

experience stimulated by psychoanalysis was concerned with the effects of severe trauma or of severe sensory or social deprivation, or it dealt with a fairly limited domain of experience--early feeding, weaning, and toilet training. In a review of the literature more than 25 years ago Orlansky (1949) pointed out the essentially negative conclusions from this research. The data from the many studies did not add up to any clear and consistent findings. In a comprehensive review of the effects of infant care, Caldwell in 1964 again emphasized the lack of consistent unequivocal findings regarding the effects of oral gratification, breast- or bottle-feeding, sudden or gradual weaning, severe or easy toilet training. The early studies, on the whole, were overly literal in their attempts to test psychoanalytic theory. Obviously much more goes on in mother-infant interaction than feeding or training in sphincter control.

Gradually the psychoanalytic orientation to early experience has given way to new theoretical framework. Among these theoretical formulations are adaptation level theory, information theory, operant learning theory, Piagetian developmental theory, and Hunt's synthesis of several theoretical positions around the concept of intrinsic motivation. Such theoretical systems are, on the whole, more modest and more circumscribed than psychoanalytic theory. Their concepts (from these theoretical formulations) are more easily translated into observable variables, and the basic propositions generated by the theories can more readily be tested in experimental or natural situations. These theories have had a significant impact on our conceptualization of the early environment. They have conceptualized the environment in different ways; they have emphasized different dimensions of the environment and have come to a different view of the organism.

Common to many of these theories is an emphasis on stimulus seeking. The infants' activities are not simply directed toward reducing tension, they are concerned with maintaining an optimal state of arousal. Paralleling this conceptual shift has been a change from the simple model of stimuli acting on a passive organism to the conception of the infant or child who reaches out to elicit stimulation. and who mediates the effects of stimuli through his or her specific sensitivities and vulnerabilities.

Our own interest in a differential analysis of the early environment has evolved gradually. It began with the involvement of one investigator, Leon Yarrow, in a longitudinal

study from a psychoanalytic perspective, and continued during
another longitudinal study of the impact of infants of separation
from the mother during the first year of life. This research
experience and a thorough immersion in the literature on early
influences led to the conviction that we needed more precise
specification of the variables of the environment in order to
study the full range of an infant's experiences in the natural
environment. This conviction crystallized after a critical
review of the literature on maternal deprivation (Yarrow, 1961).
In this review, Yarrow pointed out the many different conditions
subsumed under the term maternal deprivation: insufficient
sensory stimulation. inadequate emotional involvement, and the
many trauma associated with loss of the mother and subsequent
instability of caretaking. The conclusion was that uncritical
acceptance of this blanket concept as an explanatory model
clouded out dynamic understanding and was detrimental to
research.

While there seems to be some general agreement on the
inadequacies of older theoretical perspectives and on the
importance of differentiating the infant's experiences, there
is still no consensus regarding the extent of differentiation,
the level of variables, or the specific types of variables
that are most useful for the analysis of early experience.
Sharply polarized views have emerged on the important
dimensions of the early environment. Some have emphasized
intangible qualities of mothering, such as warmth, responsiveness,
acceptance; others have emphasized objectively defined variables
of sensory stimulation. The present investigators came to feel
that both types of variables were necessary. We arrived at the
view that many important qualitative dimensions of maternal
care could be given careful definition and indexed by quantitative
measures: others could only be captives by global ratings
after a long period of observation.

Our interest in these methodological and theoretical
issues was heightened when the federal government began to take
responsibility for the development of compensatory educational
programs in an attempt to undo the effects of the severe
deprivations that many underprivileged children had suffered.
Many programs for disadvantaged children have been developed,
for the most part, without detailed knowledge of the
characteristics of their environments. When we were faced
directly with the tasks of specifying the conditions that
would promote healthy intellectual and personality development,
we could only make very general recommendations. Social action
and theoretical considerations converged in strengthening our
conviction that we needed to look at the early environment in

more differentiated ways, to analyze the components of early
experience, and to investigate their differential effects on
the developing organism.

In summary, the major aims of this investigation were to
differentiate the early environment in conceptually meaningful
terms, to coordinate these concepts with observational
categories for studying the natural environment, and to analyze
the relationships between these differentiated dimensions of
the environment and infant functioning. A more detailed
presentation of the procedure and findings is given elsewhere
(Yarrow, Rubenstein, & Pedersen, 1975).

SAMPLE OF METHOD

The subjects were 41 five- to six-month-old black infants,
21 boys and 20 girls, who were cared for by a stable primary
caretaker. The mother was the primary caretaker in 33 cases,
a relative in five cases, and an unrelated babysitter in three
cases. Throughout this report we will use the term *mother* or
primary caretaker interchangeably. Although the majority of
the subjects were from lower socioeconomic levels, the sample
encompassed a broad socioeconomic spectrum. The fathers'
education ranged from six years to graduate school, with a
mean of 11.5 years; their occupations ranged from unskilled
worker to professional. The mothers' education level ranged
from 7 to 17 years, with a mean of 11.6. The age range of
the fathers was from 18 to 40 years, with a mean of 26.5; the
mothers' age range was 16 to 41, with a mean of 24.2. Such
demographic data are useful in characterizing the sample, but
we believe that social class membership per se does no affect
the infant's development; rather it is the proximal variables,
the kinds of stimulation and the patterns of caretaking, that
are significant.

There were great variations in the living conditions,
life-styles, and value orientations of the families in this
study. Their residences ranged from modest detached homes in
suburban developments and well-maintained high-rise apartments
to deteriorated inner-city housing. Most of the families lived
in old urban apartments or in attached homes in older neighborhoods in the inner city. The interiors of the homes showed
equal diversity--from spacious, amply furnished rooms to dimly
lit, crowded rooms with dilapidated furniture.

These households were similarly diverse in family

composition. Many conformed to the nuclear family model of
mother, father and siblings (44 percent); others represented
some variation of extended families (51 percent); with
various combinations of relatives; a few were lone mother-
infant pairs (5 percent). There were many father-absent
families (39 percent). Some mothers were not married, some
were divorced; others were separated because the fathers were
employed in another city or were in military service.

All infants were of normal birth weight and free from
gross complications of pregnancy and delivery. In addition
to being screened through the pediatric records, they were
all examined by our staff pediatrician to eliminate cases in
which there were any indications of neurological damage.

The mothers and infants were observed in their homes when
the infants were 5½ months old. The infants were also given
the Bayley Test (1969) at this age. A test of exploratory
behavior and preference for novelty was given at 6 months.
The two home observations were made about a week apart. Each
involved three hours of time-sampling when the baby was awake.
The time-sample cycle consisted of a 30-second observation
period and a 60-second recording period. There were 45
categories of caretaker behavior recorded and 15 categories
of infant behavior. To analyze the characteristics of the
inanimate environment, we recorded all objects within reach
of the infant, and later rated these objects in terms of their
complexity, their feedback potential (i.e., responsiveness),
and their variety.

The variables used in the analyses were on several
different levels, and reflected the several theoretical
orientations from which the central questions and hypotheses
of the study were derived. Some were at the concrete
behavioral level, e.g., touching, holding, rocking, looking at,
and talking to the infant. Other variables were concerned
with process, i.e., responses contingent on the child's
behavior; at still another level, we rated the mother's
demonstrativeness in expressing affect. From the composite
scores of several behavior categories, we derived other high-
order variables, such as Variety of Social Stimulation. As
noted above, three variables were concerned with the properties
of inanimate objects: Complexity, Responsiveness, and Variety.
These variables will be defined in more detail.

ENVIRONMENTAL VARIABLES

Modalities of Stimulation

Our interest in the modalities of stimulation comes from a variety of sources. For many years, there has been a continuing controversy between proponents of "mother love" and the advocates of sensory stimulation. On the other hand, psychoanalytic theory has maintained that a warm, affectionate relationship with the mother is essential for healthy development. Others have argued that the infant will thrive if he is simply given adequate sensory stimulation. In a sense, this is a pseudocontroversy. The mother's basic feelings toward the infant are transmitted largely through her behavior-- through talking to the infant, touching and holding him. Although mother love may not be completely reducible to sensory stimulation, it is possible to analyze the sensory components of maternal affection and investigate their contribution to development. If we find significant relations between stimulation in given sensory modalities and the infant's development, from a practical standpoint it is essentially irrelevant whether these relations can be attributed to love or to the character of the mother's social stimulation.

There have been a few theoretical papers and a small number of experimental studies on the role of specific modalities of sensory stimulation. Some theorists have emphasized the importance of tactile and kinesthetic stimulation in infancy for maintaining the young infant's internal equilibrium (Frank, 1957; Prescott, 1971); others have elaborated on the role of distance receptor stimulation in the development of social responsiveness (Walters & Parke, 1965).

The animal studies of Harlow and Mason were most dramatic in drawing attention to the importance of tactile and kinesthetic modalities. Harlow's (1965) studies indicated that "contact comfort" is more important than oral gratification as an antecedent of attachment. Mason (1968) found that "swinging" mother surrogates (moving inanimate objects) that provided kinesthetic stimulation were more effective in preventing the usual effects of deprivation than the stationary surrogates, which provided only tactile stimulation. Anthropological studies have commented on the precocious development of infants who were given a lot of tactile and kinesthetic stimulation by being carried around strapped to the mother's body (Geber, 1958).[3]

In our study, there were five variables dealing with the modalities in which stimulation was given: three measures of near receptor stimulation and two of distance receptor stimulation. The near receptor stimulation measures were Passive Tactile, Active Tactile, and Kinesthetic. Passive Tactile was the amount of time the caretaker spent holding or touching the baby; Active Tactile consisted of more vigorous stimulation--patting or caressing the baby. Kinesthetic stimulation involved movement of the baby's whole body, and included rocking, jiggling, carrying it around the house. The two distance receptor measures were Visual stimulation, the amount of mutual visual regard between infant and care-giver; and Auditory stimulation, the amount of talking the caregiver directed toward the baby. Scores were frequency counts summed for the two days of observation.

Table 20-1 presents the intercorrelation among the modality measures. There were moderate intercorrelations among the near modalities--Passive Tactile, Active Tactile, and Kinesthetic stimulation. The correlations were within a narrow range, from .53 to .57. Similarly, Visual and Auditory stimulation correlated .60. The most interesting findings were the low level of relationships between distal and proximal stimulation; the range was from .10 to .43, with a median of .27. These data suggest that mothers in the population we studied cannot be characterized simply as depriving or stimulating; it is more meaningful to characterize them according to their preferred patterns of stimulation. Some give stimulation predominantly through vision or audition, others prefer the tactile and kinesthetic modalities. The mother who rocks the baby and pats him a lot may not necessarily talk to him or engage in much eye-to-eye contact.

Contingency Measures

Although clinicians have emphasized for a long time the importance of a responsive environment and have documented the harmful effects on the child of the mother's failure to respond sensitively to the child's cues, it is only recently that these clinical convictions have been documented by findings in the laboratory. Operant learning theory and the controlled studies (Brackbill, 1958; Gewirtz, 1969) that have been carried out from this theoretical orientation have begun

---

[3]Warren (1972) has recently pointed to the methodological shortcomings of some of these studies and has questioned whether African precocity has been demonstrated.

to specify the temporal conditions under which responsiveness to the child's signals effectively reinforces desired behavior.

Studies of institutional environments (Provence & Lipton, 1961; Yarrow, 1961) and of depriving home environments (Wortis, 1963) have emphasized the lack of contingent interaction in caretaking. In institutional settings, children are often fed, diapered, and even played with by schedule rather than in response to their signals. The developing apathy and progressive withdrawal of these children have been attributed to the lack of contingent responsiveness.

In this study, we did not attempt to measure all varieties of contingent response to the child, but limited ourselves to two measures. The first, Contingent Vocal Response to the Infant's Positive Vocalizations, was a count of the frequency with which the mother or caretaker vocalized immediately following an infant vocalization. The second variable, Contingent Response to Distress, was based on a five-point rating scale defining the *immediacy* of the mother's response to crying or other signs of distress. The low point on the scale signified long delay before the caretaker responded. A score of five indicated that the mother typically responded immediately to minimal signs of distress such as increased motor activity or mouthing movements.

We had anticipated that maternal responsiveness might be a generalized characteristic, and that therefore these two measures of contingency would be highly correlated. We found, however, a moderately low relationship between Contingent Response to Distress and Contingent Vocal Response to Positive Vocalization, $r = .31$. This finding suggests that mothers who are responsive to positive behavior on the part of the infant may not be equally responsive to the baby's indications of unhappiness or tension, or vice versa.

Expression of Positive Affect

The dimension Expression of Positive Affect was based on ratings made by the observers at the end of the time-sampling observations. This measure of the caretaker's characteristic level of demonstrativeness was rated on a five-point scale, ranging from quiet, subdued, or low-keyed positive affect to highly demonstrative, intense expressions of positive affect. Although we recognize that there is not a one-to-one relationship between demonstrativeness and depth of feeling, we thought this measure might have some meaning in regard to the affectional

TABLE 20-1. Interrelations Among Environmental Measures.

	Active Tactile	Kines-thetic	Visual	Audi-tory	Contingent Response Positive Vocaliza-tion	Contingent Response Distress	Contingent Pos-itive Affect	Variety Social Stim-ulation	Variety of Inanimate Objects	Respon-siveness of Inanimate Objects	Complexity of Inanimate Objects
Passive Tactile	57	54	24	--	--	45	--	38	--	--	--
Active Tactile		53	43	27	35	41	52	57	--	27	--
Kinesthetic			29	39	32	37	38	60	--	--	--
Visual				60	47	25	55	56	--	--	--
Auditory					70	26	59	58	--	--	--
Contingent Response to Positive Vocalization						31	51	45	--	--	--
Contingent Response to Distress							23	48	31	--	--
Positive Affect								64	20	23	--
Variety of Social Stimulation									29	33	--
Variety of Inanimate Objects										--	--
Responsiveness of Inanimate Objects											70

NOTE: Correlations marked -- < .20.

relationship between mother and infant. We found this variable was moderately related to most dimensions of the social environment but insignificantly related to the characteristics of the inanimate environment. The highest correlations were .59 with Auditory Stimulation, .55 with Visual Stimulation, and .52 with Active Tactile Stimulation. With Contingent Vocal Response to Positive Vocalization the correlation was .51, whereas with Contingent Response to Distress the correlation was only .23, again emphasizing the very different meaning of these two contingency measures.

These data indicate that there is a moderate relationship between the demonstrativeness of expression of positive affect and the amount of sensory stimulation a mother gives her infant. Although positive affect is communicated through the sensory modalities, the sheer amount of visual, auditory, or kinesthetic stimulation is not a simple, direct index of the mother's positive emotions toward the infant. Surprisingly, the mother who is demonstrative in expression of positive affect does not necessarily respond with dispatch to the infant's distress.

Variety of Social Stimulation

Several theoretical positions, especially information theory, have emphasized the importance of variety. Varied stimulation, it is hypothesized, serves to arouse the infant and to elicit his attention, whereas repetitive, unchanging stimulation is quickly adapted to and loses evocative power. We combined several discrete categories of maternal behavior to obtain the measure Variety of Stimulation. This measure of the richness of experience consisted of four components of maternal behavior, three of which measured manifestly different activities that go beyond routine caretaking: (1) encouraging emergent motor skills, such as postural control or locomotion. (2) directing the child's attention to inanimate objects by presenting or highlighting toys (social mediation of play materials), and (3) engaging in interactive play, which characteristically elicits smiles, vocalizations, and positive affect. The fourth component was the number of changes in physical contexts, measured by noting how often there was a change in the baby's "container", e.g., an infant seat, playpen, the caretaker's lap, etc. Each component score was converted to a standard score and summed.

The Inanimate Environment

The analysis of the inanimate environment along three

dimensions--Variety, Responsiveness, and Complexity--was also based on theoretical considerations.

At a conceptual level, Variety of inanimate stimulation is analogous to Variety of social stimulation. It reflects the richness and nonrepetitive character of the inanimate environment. An environment high in inanimate variety provides greater opportunities for assimilation of and accommodation to various properties of objects, thereby differentiating perceptual, cognitive, and motor skills. Adaptation to high levels of variety is also hypothesized to result in motivation to maintain high levels of variation in stimulation. Our measure of Variety was a count of the number of different play objects which were observed to be within reach of the infant at any time during the home visit.

The second dimension of the inanimate environment, Responsiveness, was a measure of the feedback potential of objects. The theoretical significance of responsiveness comes from operant learning theory, and from Hunt's (1965) ideas concerning intrinsic motivation. Objects were rated on four scales describing the extent to which they change or provide stimulation when the infant does something to them. An example of a responsive object is a rubber toy that changes shape when the infant squeezes it; if it also squeaks, it is even more responsive.

The importance of Complexity as a dimension of the inanimate environment also comes from information theory, especially from Berlyne's (1960) work. Essentially, Berlyne holds that an optimal degree of complexity, based on the organism's capacity to assimilate the information provided, is most facilitative of cognitive growth. To obtain a complexity score, we rated the objects within reach of the infants during the home observations using such criteria as: the number of colors, the amount of visual and tactile pattern, the extent of variation in the contours of the object, and the degree of responsiveness of the object.

Looking at the interrelations of the variables of the inanimate environment, we found Variety essentially unrelated to Complexity or Responsiveness. Since Responsiveness was one of the components of Complexity, these two variables were more highly correlated, r being .70. The most striking findings were the consistently low relationships between the inanimate environment and the social environment. Most of the correlations were around zero. Homes that provide highly stimulating play materials to infants are not necessarily rich in social

stimulation. These findings again emphasize the inappropriate-
ness of global characterizations of environments as depriving
or stimulating.

THE INFANT VARIABLES

There were sixteen variables indexing infant development,
eleven of which we shall discuss in this report. They were
derived from several sources: the Bayley Scales of Infant
Development, some supplementary items given immediately after
the Bayley Test, and a structured situation designed to measure
exploratory behavior and response to novel objects (Rubenstein,
1967).

Exploratory behavior was measured when the infants were
6½ months of age. The first step in the procedure involved
presenting the infant with an attractive toy--a bell--for ten
minutes. We recorded the amount of time the baby spent looking
at and manipulating the bell and the amount of time vocalization accompanied the exploration. Then a series of ten new
toys were presented, each one paired with the now familiar
bell for one-minute intervals. Two measures of preference for
novelty were obtained, the amount of time the infant spent
looking at the novel object and the time spent manipulating
it.

From the Bayley Test eight distinct clusters of infant
behavior were derived: (1) Social Responsiveness, (2) Language,
(3) Fine Motor, (4) Gross Motor, (5) Goal Directedness,
(6) Reaching and Grasping, (7) Secondary Circular Reactions,
and (8) Object Permanence. From the supplementary items,
another cluster, Problem Solving, was developed.

The procedure for grouping the Bayley items involved
several steps. We first eliminated items that all infants
in our sample either passed or failed. We then sorted the
remaining items on the basis of conceptual considerations.
For each cluster, Spearman-Brown split-half reliabilities were
computed; for one cluster with only two items, tetrachoric
correlations were obtained. After reassigning some items, the
final clusters had split-half reliabilities (or tetrachoric
correlations) ranging from .74 to .92. These variables are
described in detail in Yarrow, Rubenstein & Pedersen, (1975)
and in Yarrow & Pedersen (1976).

RESULTS

Modalities of Stimulation

Both near and distance receptor stimulation were significantly related to infant development at 6 months (Table 20-2). However, near receptor stimulation had many more significant relationships with the dependent variables than did distance modality stimulation. Visual and auditory stimulation were related significantly only to Social Responsiveness ($r = .31$ with visual, and $.37$ with auditory).

Of the near receptor modalities, kinesthetic stimulation seems to be the most important in terms of the magnitude and number of significant relationships with the dependent variables. Kinesthetic stimulation was highly related to Goal Directedness ($r = .57$) and moderately related to Object Permanence ($r = .44$); it showed lower but significant relationships with Social Responsiveness ($r = .36$), Fine Motor development ($r = .31$), and Secondary Circular Reactions ($r = .28$). Kinesthetic stimulation was also significantly related to both Bayley developmental indices, the Mental Development Index ($r = .41$) and the Psychomotor Developmental Index ($r = .36$).

Why does kinesthetic stimulation seem to have such pervasive effects? The kinds of activities involved in kinesthetic stimulation--rocking, jiggling, moving the whole body--can be either soothing or arousing, depending on the state of the infant when it is initiated. Our speculation is that appropriate kinesthetic stimulation serves to maintain an optimal state of arousal. This means that the infant is in an optimal condition for attending to and responding to people and objects in his environment. A number of studies support this interpretation. For instance, Korner and Thoman (1970) found that neonates who received special vestibular stimulation showed more visual alertness than infants not receiving such stimulation. White and Castle (1964) found that institutionalized infants who receive extra handling from their caretakers showed significantly more visual exploration than infants who were given ordinary institutional handling. These results are also supported by data from several multicultural studies reported in this volume (Brazelton, Konner, Goldberg, and Leiderman). In cultures that provide high levels of kinesthetic stimulation, infants are characteristically advanced in cognitive and motor development.

TABLE 20-2. Relationships Between Measures of the Social Environment and Infant Measures

Environmental Variables	Bayley M.D.I.	Bayley P.D.I.	Social Responsiveness	Goal Directedness	Secondary Circular Reactions	Object Permanence	Reaching and Grasping	Gross Motor	Fine Motor During	Vocalizing During Exploration	Manipulation of Objects
Passive Tactile	--	--	.25	.30[a]	.31[a]	--	--	--	--	--	-.35
Active Tactile	.41[b]	--	.21	.33[a]	.33[a]	--	.24	--	--	--	--
Kinesthetic	.36[a]	.36[a]	.36[a]	.57[b]	.28[a]	.44[b]	.25	.25	.31[a]	.09	--
Visual	--	--	.31[a]	--	--	--	--	--	--	--	--
Auditory	.23	--	.37[a]	.21	--	--	--	--	--	--	--
Contingent Response to Positive Vocalization	--	--	.22	--	--	--	--	--	--	.30[a]	.31[a]
Contingent Response to Distress	.32[a]	.37[a]	--	.38[a]	.30[a]	--	.29[a]	.28[a]	.33[a]	--	.24
Expression of Positive Affect	.23	--	.26[a]	.31[a]	.30[a]	--	--	--	--	.24	.28[a]
Social Variety	.34[a]	.23	.34[a]	.48[b]	.35[a]	.47[b]	.28[a]	--	.26[a]	.31[a]	--

NOTE: Correlations marked -- < .20.

[a] $p < .05$, one-tailed test.

[b] $p < .01$, one-tailed test.

In the present study, the strong association between kinesthetic stimulation and the two infant variables Goal Directedness and Object Permanence seem to be especially meaningful theoretically. If kinesthetic stimulation increases the general level of alertness and enhances outer-directedness, as indicated by the studies above, then it might be expected to relate to Goal Directedness, a measure of the infant's focused attention and persistence in attempting to secure objects out of reach. The relationship with Object Permanence cannot be explained so simply. At this developmental level, Object Permanence is present in only a very rudimentary form. The terms in this cluster are concerned with the infant's tendency to look for an object that is partially hidden or going out of view. Our speculation is that kinesthetic stimulation may help the infant in defining the boundaries of his own body, thus enhancing his awareness of an external environment that exists independently of himself.

On the whole, these findings do not offer simple support for either Frank's (1957) speculations regarding the primacy of tactile stimulation or Walter and Parke's (1965) emphasis on stimulation through the distance modalities. They seem to indicate that both near and distance modalities of stimulation have a significant impact on development in early infancy; more importantly, they indicate that their impact is selective. Auditory and Visual stimulation are more highly related to the development of Social Responsiveness and the beginnings of language. Near receptor stimulation has stronger relationships to early cognitive functions and cognitive-motivational characteristics, but kinesthetic stimulation is significantly related to social responsiveness as well. These findings probably cannot be interpreted as simple one-way relationships. Infants who involve their mothers in mutual regard, who vocalize and smile at them, are likely to elicit more auditory and visual stimulation from their caretakers. Infants who adapt comfortably to being held and rocked probably elicit more tactile and kinesthetic stimulation from their mothers.

Contingency Measures

We find that response to the infant's positive vocalizations and response to his distress signals have very different implications for infant development. Contingent Vocal Response to Positive Vocalization showed only one significant relationship having conceptual meaning, a correlation with the amount of infant vocalization during the exploratory behavior test ($r = .30$). Even though its magnitude is low, the specificity of this relationship offers

support for an operant learning interpretation. Our results
in the natural situation extend findings obtained under more
controlled laboratory conditions (Rheingold, Gewirtz, & Ross,
1959; Weisberg, 1963; Todd & Palmer, 1968). Since our measure
of vocalization was obtained in a different situation from the
one in which maternal reinforcement generalize beyond the
immediate learning situation.

Contingent Response to Distress had many significant
relations with the infant variables (Table 20-2). Its relations
with the cognitive=motivational variables, Goal Directedness,
Reaching and Grasping, and Secondary Circular Reactions, support
the thesis that rapid response to crying frees the infant to
attend to the environment (Ainsworth, 1967). To the extent that
these measures are indices of the infant's attempts to reach out
and master the environment. The data also support the hypothesis
(Lewis & Goldberg, 1969) that contingent response to the infant's
signals strengthens his awareness that he can have an impact on
the environment. The relationships with motor development
suggest one possible explanation for the accelerated development
of young infants in several African cultures. In some of these
societies, the infant and mother are in close proximity much of
the time, and she responds rapidly to even minimal signs of
distress. (See Korner and Leiderman, this volume.)

Expression of Positive Affect

Psychodynamic theories have emphasized the importance for
the healthy development of the infant of a warm, nurturant
relationship with his mother. Unfortunately, we had no
adequate measures of the depth of the affectional relationship.
Our variable, Expression of Positive Affect, was simply a
global rating of the caretaker's demonstrativeness in expressing
positive affect. There were a number of low but significant
relationships to infant development. More demonstrative
expressions of positive affect were associated with higher
levels of Social Responsiveness, Goal Directedness, Secondary
Circular Reactions. and more Manipulation of Novel Objects.
The fact that even so crude a measure of affect shows
significant relationships emphasizes the need to come to grips
with the elusive problem of operationalizing warmth, and to
define its behavioral components.

Variety of Social Stimulation

In addition to the discrete behavioral measures of the
social environment, we derived a composite measure that
represented a more global and abstract level of description

of the environment. The findings on this measure, Variety
of Social Stimulation, have methodological as well as theoretical
significance. Although we have emphasized the importance of
differentiating the environment, we see that global variables
can be meaningful if the constituent behaviors are carefully
defined. This measure included many different types of social
stimulation, e.g., playing, providing toys, and encouraging
motor responses; it also included changes in the physical
contexts in which these interactions occurred. Variety had
significant relationships with many of the infant variables.
Its pattern of relationships was similar to Kinesthetic
Stimulation, and most of the correlations were of comparable
magnitude. Two relationships stand out as being of special
theoretical significance: tne correlation of Variety to Object
Permanence was .47 and to Goal Directedness, .48. Its relationship with Goal Directedness, a measure of the infant's persistence in trying to secure objects out of his immediate reach,
suggests that varied social stimulation enhances early motivational development. The relationship with object permanence also
has special theoretical significance. Our interpretation of this
finding is that the development of the object concept is facilitated by the richness and diversity of the infant's experience.

The Inanimate Environment: Responsiveness, Complexity, and
Variety of Objects

     The findings regarding the inanimate environment are
especially noteworthy, because there have been so few studies
of the role of inanimate stimulation in natural settings. We
found several theoretically meaningful relationships. None of
the variables of the inanimate environment was related
significantly to social responsiveness or language; however,
they were related to Goal Directedness, Reaching and Grasping,
Secondary Circular Reactions, and both Fine and Gross Motor
Development (Table 20-3).

     Responsiveness, a measure of the feedback potential of the
objects available to the infant, also had conceptually meaningful relationships to two variables: Secondary Circular Reactions
($r = .51$) and Reaching and Grasping ($r = .46$). The developmental
implications of secondary circular behavior are far-reaching.
According to Piaget, its acquisition is necessary before the
child can use more complex means-ends relationships in problem
solving. The significant relationships found in this study
suggest that the intrinsic reinforcement associated with
responsive objects seems to foster behavior directed toward
eliciting feedback from the environment, and also affects the
development of manipulative skills and the motivation to

TABLE 20-3. Relationships Between Characteristics of the Inanimate Environment and Selected Infant Measures

Environmental Variables	Bayley M.D.I.	Bayley P.D.I.	Social Responsiveness	Goal Directedness	Secondary Circular Reactions	Object Permanence	Reaching and Grasping	Gross Motor	Fine Motor	Vocalizing During Exploration	Manipulation Of Novel Objects
Responsiveness of Inanimate Objects	.28[a]	.27[a]	.21	.30[a]	.51[b]	--	.46[b]	.27[a]	.33[a]	--	--
Complexity of Inanimate Objects	--	--	--	--	.46[b]	--	.32[a]	.22	--	--	.34[a]
Variety of Inanimate Objects	.36[a]	.51[a]	--	.41[b]	.33[a]	.30[a]	.38[b]	.42[b]	.37[a]	--	.48[b]

NOTE: Correlations marked -- < .20.

[a] $p < .05$, one-tailed test.
[b] $p < .01$, one-tailed test.

secure objects.

The variable Complexity of Inanimate Objects showed fewer significant relationships than did Responsiveness, but the infant variables with which it was significantly related are ones that reflect receptivity to stimulation: Reaching and Grasping, Secondary Circular Reactions, and Manipulation of Novel Objects. Although theories of the importance of complexity emphasizes an "optimal" level, we found no evidence of curvilinear relationships with the infant variables. In future investigations, we would hope to sharpen our differentiation of Complexity from Responsiveness; in this study they were intercorrelated .70. We would also want to study further the relation of complexity to the infant variables by choosing the variables so that they have a tighter conceptual link to this dimension of the environment. For example, we might measure preference for complexity.

Variety of Inanimate Objects was a measure of the number of *different* materials and objects the young child had available to look at and manipulate. This variable was correlated significantly with every infant variable except Social Responsiveness and Vocalization. There were strong relationships with exploratory behavior (Manipulation of Novel Objects, $r = .48$) and goal-directed behavior (Goal Directedness, $r = .41$). The pervasive relationships of Variety of Inanimate Objects with early development suggest that this aspect of the early environment may influence the infant in several different ways. It may affect the arousal level, keeping the infant alert and ready to "tune in" to the environment; it may establish a high adaptation level to variation in stimulation, making the infant more receptive to novel and varied experience; and it may provide opportunities for the infant to develop more differentiated schema through encounters with different properties of objects.

We have shown that variation in dimensions of the inanimate environment, particularly Responsiveness and Variety, have significant associations with early cognitive and motivational development. In this way, we have extended (to the home environment) the findings of experimental intervention studies in institutional and other settings. The absence of relationships between the inanimate environment and social responsiveness and vocalization, moreover, shows that these effects are selective.

SUMMARY AND DISCUSSION

Many studies of early environmental influences have limited

themselves to rather global variables. Anthropological studies
of other cultures, although richly descriptive and communicating
a feeling for the experiences of the young child in those settings, have often portrayed the normative child and the modal
mother. Rarely do they give a differentiated analysis of the
environment or a picture of the range of variation within a
given culture. In this study, we have differentiated the
environments of infants on many dimensions, some of which are
moderately related to each other, while others are essentailly
independent. A mother's profile may show highs and lows in
different aspects of her behavior.

This study extends our understanding of early environmental
influences beyond the simple associations of gross deprivation
with gross developmental retardation. The fact that these
diverse dimensions of stimulation show differential relationships with such aspects of infant functioning as goal directedness, secondary circular reactions, problem solving, and fine
and gross motor development emphasizes the importance of
analyzing the components of the environment. Some environmental
variables are more highly related to certain infant characteristics than are other dimensions of the environment. Some
striking examples are the different relationships with near and
distance receptor stimulation. Visual and auditory stimulation
in social contexts are related only to social responsiveness,
while kinesthetic stimulation is related significantly to many
cognitive and cognitive-motivational characteristics as well.

Although both Kinesthetic stimulation and Variety of
Inanimate Objects seem to have a pervasive influence on infant
development, the magnitude of their relationships tends to be
quite different with given variables. For example, Kinesthetic
stimulation is most highly related to Goal Directedness and
Object Permanence, whereas Variety of Inanimate Objects is
related to the infant's interest in manipulating novel objects
and his motor development. These findings show that specific
environmental variables are especially important for certain
infant functions. They also indicate that there are differing
degrees of relationship between given dimensions of the
environment and certain cognitive and cognitive-motivational
functions. They show a selective impact of different kinds
of stimulation.

Of special interest are the several significant relationships between the environment and motor development. The amount
of kinesthetic stimulation the infant received, the degree of
the mother's responsiveness to the infant's distress signals,
and the variety of play objects and materials available to the

infant were all significantly correlated with the Bayley
Psychomotor Index. These findings lead one to question the
prevailing view that motor development is primarily a
maturational process, relatively uninfluenced by environmental
factors.

We are aware that in this study we have concentrated on
only a few pieces of the total mosaic of early experience.
One important issue with which we did not deal is the problem
of environmental continuity and discontinuity. Our methodology
and, to some extent, our conceptual model assume that there is
a single primary caregiver, usually the mother, who has
maintained a stable relationship with the infant. Early in the
study, we planned our observations of the infant and caregiver
on the assumption that they would provide us with a reasonable
approximation of the infant's early experience. There were
subjects, however, whom we decided could not be included in
the analyses, inasmuch as there had been such major changes in
caregiving arrangements that we could not be confident that our
observations were representative of the infant's past experiences.
In some cases, there were several changes in caregivers during
the first few months; in others, there were shared or multiple
caregiving arrangements such that no single person assumed a
major share of the infant's care. While these families did not
fit our model for assessing early experience, they do represent
important patterns of discontinuity in caretaking that may be
significant for development.

Much of developmental research on early influences has
assumed environmental continuity. Multicultural research on
the other hand has pointed up discontinuities in caretaking.
In some cultures, young infants may be treated very permissively
and granted immediate gratification of most of their needs,
but when a new sibling is born or after a certain age is reached
there may be an abrupt change in care characterized by longer
periods of delay and more frequent experiences of frustration.
A new caregiver may also assume major responsibility, while
the mother devotes her full attention to the new infant.

The fact that longitudinal studies generally show only
moderate relationships between early characteristics and later
functioning may in part be due to a failure to distinguish
degrees of discontinutiy in the environment. Rather than
eliminate cases with gross discontinuity, as we have done in
this investigation, perhaps we should attempt to study discontinuity longitudinally by detailed analyses of patterns
of similarities and differences at successive time periods.

In this study we have obtained a highly differentiated picture of variations between primary caregivers, but we have an incomplete picture because we have ignored the larger cultural context. We need to examine how the environmental variables we have studied are modified by this context. Multicultural studies have sensitized us to the importance of looking at the values of the society as a background for child rearing. This is an area in which the concepts of social anthropology and developmental psychology might be meaningfully integrated. It is clear that such basic variables as amount of kinesthetic stimulation or encouragement of gross motor activity will be influenced by the society's and the caretaker's modal values and idealized images of the young child. Similarly, the patterns of contingent responsiveness are likely to be affected; the culture that values stoicism may not sanction rapid responsiveness to the infant's distress.

Cross-cultural research, on the other hand, in its emphasis on describing differences between societies has often not paid sufficient attention to differentiating the proximal environment or to the range of variation within a given culture. We believe that cross-cultural studies can make a more effective contribution to understanding early experiences by more differentiated analyses of the environment and by more differentiated assessment of the infant.

In this discussion, we have pointed out some ways in which anthropology and developmental psychology can benefit each other. We should not be too glib, however, about the ease of interdisciplinary collaboration. We must recognize that there are important differences between the two disciplines. The central problems of each discipline differ, and their theoretical constructs are on different levels. The distinctive contributions of each are undoubtedly a function of these differences.

When we differentiate the environment, we are impressed with how important it is to avoid drawing any simple conclusions about the effects of stimulation or deprivation. We are aware of the possibility that the patterns of interrelationships of the environmental variables, and their relations to infant functioning, may hold only for the particular sociocultural group we studied.

We must also be cautious about drawing too simple conclusions about the effects of single, isolated variables. We cannot conclude that mother-infant interaction consists of separate, isolated packets of stimuli between which there are no meaningful relationships. Our isolation of variables in the natural environment is an artificial one; in reality many variables are acting simultaneously. Although we have found significant correlations between specific dimensions of the environment and infant characteristics, associations that exceed chance expectations and that are consistent with theoretical assumptions, we cannot conclude that any single variable alone is decisive for any particular function. For example, despite the pervasive and consistent relationships of kinesthetic stimulation to infant characteristics, it is unlikely that any infant would develop optimally if he were given only kinesthetic stimulation mechanically.

In developmental research, we are still asking very complex questions in oversimplified form, and are using overly simplistic models and statistical analyses in trying to deal with terribly complicated problems. We need to ask questions that recognize the complexities of real environments; e.g., whether certain environmental variables may be interchangeable, whether certain combinations of variables are additive in their effects, and to what extent certain variables interact to strengthen or diminish each other's impact. Our view of the infant and his relationship to the environment has changed dramatically in the last ten years. From the view of the infant as a passive recipient of stimuli, we now see him as a competent and constantly changing organism in a dynamic system of interaction with the environment. To this perspective, we have added further complexity by underscoring the multifaceted character of the environment.

REFERENCES

Ainsworth, M. D. S. _Infancy in Uganda: Infant care and the growth of love._ Baltimore, MD.: Johns Hopkins University Press, 1967.

Bayley, N. _Bayley scales of infant development._ New York: Psychological Corporation, 1969.

Berlyne, D. E. _Conflict, arousal and curiosity._ New York: McGraw-Hill, 1960.

Brackbill, Y. Extinction of the smiling response in infants as a function of reinforcement schedule. _Child Development_, 1958, _29_, 113-124.

Caldwell, B. M. The effects of infant care. In M. Hoffman
    and L. Hoffman (Eds.), Review of child development
    research, Vol. 1. New York: Russell Sage Foundation,
    1964.

Frank, L. K. Tactile communication. Genetic Psychology
    Monographs, 1957, 56, 209-225.

Geber, M. The psycho-motor development of African children
    in the first year and the influence of maternal
    behavior. Journal of Social Psychology, 1958, 47,
    185-195.

Gewirtz, J. Mechanisms of social learning: Some roles of
    stimulation and behavior in early human development.
    In D. Goslin (Ed.), Handboodk of socialization
    theory and research. Chicago: Rand-McNally, 1969.

Harlow, H. The affectional systems. In A. M. Schrier,
    H. F. Harlow, & F. Stolnitz (Eds.), Behavior of non-
    human primates (Vol.2). New York: Academic Press,
    1965.

Hunt, J. M. Intrinsic motivation and its role in psychological
    development. In D. Levine (Ed.), Nebraska symposium
    on motivation. Lincoln: Univeristy of Nebraska
    Press, 1965.

Korner, A. F., & Thoman, E. B. Visual alertness in neonates
    as evoked by maternal care. Journal of Experimental
    Child Psychology, 1970, 10, 67-68.

Lewis, M., & Goldberg, S. Perceptual-cognitive development
    in infancy: A generalized expectancy model as a
    function of the mother-infant relationship.
    Merrill-Palmer Quarterly, 1969, 15, 81-100.

Mason, W. A. Early social deprivation in the nonhuman primate:
    Implications for human behavior. In D. C. Glass
    (Ed.), Environmental influences. New York:
    Rockefeller University Press, 1968.

Orlansky, H. Infant care and personality. Psychological
    Bulletin, 1949, 46, 1-48.

Prescott, J. W. Early somatosensory deprivation as an
    ontogenetic process in the abnormal development
    of the brain and behavior. In I. E. Goldsmith

and J. Moor-Jankowski (Eds.), Medical primatology.
New York: Karger, 1971.

Provence, S., & Lipton, R.   Infants in institutions.   New York:
International Universities Press, 1961.

Rheingold, H., Gewirtz, J., & Ross, H.   Social conditioning
of vocalizations in the infant.   Journal of
Comparative and Physiological Psychology. 1959, 52,
68-73.

Rubenstein, J.   Maternal attentiveness and subsequent
exploratory behavior.   Child Development, 1967, 38,
1089-1100.

Todd, G. A., & Palmer, B.   Social reinforcement of infant
babbling.   Child Development, 1968, 39, 591-596.

Walters, R., & Parke, R.   The role of the distance receptors
in the development of social responsiveness.   In
L. Lipsitt and C' Spiker (Eds.), Advances in child
development and behavior.   New York: Academic Press,
1965.

Warren, N.   African infant precocity.   Psychological Bulletin,
1972, 78, 353-367.

Weisberg, P.   Social and nonsocial conditioning of infant
vocalizations.   Child Development, 1963, 34, 377-
388.

White, B., & Castle, P. W.   Visual exploratory behavior
following postnatal handling of human infants.
Perceptual Motor Skills, 1964, 18, 497-502.

Wortis, H.   Child-rearing practices in a low socioeconomic
group.   Pediatrics, 1963, 32, 298-307.

Yarrow, L. J.   Maternal deprivation: Toward an empirical and
conceptual re-evaluation.   Psychological Bulletin,
1961, 58, 459-490.

Yarrow, L. J., & Pedersen, F. A.   The interplay between
cognition and motivation in infancy.   In M. Lewis
(Ed.), Origins of intelligence.   New York: Plenum
Press, 1976.

Yarrow, L. J., Rubenstein, J. L., & Pedersen, F. A. Infant and environment: Early cognitive and motivational development. New York: Halsted, 1975.

PART IV

CONCLUSIONS

Chapter 21

Dimensions of Multicultural Research in Infancy and Early Childhood

Steven R. Tulkin

State University of New York at Buffalo

In this chapter, assisted by P. H. Leiderman and A. Rosenfeld, we will focus on the potential contributions of multicultural research to our understanding of early development. We would like to emphasize both the "pros" and "cons" of multicultural studies and to suggest some ways to think about research in this area.

The first question we need to ask before packing our bags to go off and do multicultural research is whether, in fact, a multicultural design is the most appropriate way of addressing the questions we want to answer. Observing and interpreting the interplay of biological and environmental factors on child development is hard work in our own culture; in a foreign culture, it is infinitely harder, both practically and theoretically. We have stated, in Chapter 1, that a multicultural approach can add considerable variability to the independent variables one is investigating. A first question, therefore, would be whether the variability that is needed in order to answer our questions can be observed in our own culture, either through natural variation or through an experimental intervention program. If we can find enough variability at home, we may not need to pack our bags. There are some questions, however, that can only be answered by comparative research. If we want to study the effects of polygyny on mother-infant relationships, for example, we have to go to another culture. There are subcultures in the United States (like the Mormons) who practiced polygyny, but this practice was not accepted by the majority culture, making it, in effect, a different experience.

In discussing the selection of groups for cultural comparative research, LeVine (at the conference) mentioned that he had previously (1970) criticized the idea of selecting groups on the basis that certain environmental conditions would provide a natural experiment--because "some researchers had incorrect notions of the specific conditions that existed in a particular group." Now, however, he feels differently, because now we are beginning to know enough about different groups so that we can design studies that will give us appropriate information. LeVine noted, for example, that there is tremendous variation in severity of weaning. Yoruba women wean their children first in the daytime and then at night; and, if the child makes a big fuss, they relent and let him go back to breast for awhile. Among the Hausa, weaning is done in one day (always on a Friday, among the Muslims), and from then on the child is forbidden the breast. If we can control for other differences between the Yoruba and Hausa, we have an excellent opportunity to study the effects of extreme variations in weaning that would be more difficult to find in our own culture.

Too often, however, multicultural research is simply the study of individual differences in a nice place. We need to be careful to use multicultural designs only when we are sure that there is no other way to jeopardize our hypotheses. The reason for such caution is that although going to another culture may add considerable variability along the dimensions we are investigating, it also adds variability along a number of other dimensions, some of which may not be immediately obvious to us. If we decide that the variability gained by traveling to another culture is necessary, we need to ask a second question: Do we know enough, or can we learn enough, about the culture we are visiting to enable us to attribute the differences we observe to the specific set of independent variables we are studying? There are two ways in which we would like to approach an answer to this question: (1) do we know enough about the culture to appreciate how it works--its values, goals, etc., and (2) do we know enough about factors that affect infant behavior to collect adequate data. We will consider first the question of understanding our own biases and how they can influence our research. In the next chapter, we will discuss what kinds of data are needed for a comprehensive investigation of culture and infancy.

WESTERN BIASES AND IMPLICATIONS FOR DATA GATHERING

One of the most pervasive themes of the conference was the Western bias of researchers. It was pointed out that the very study of development (focusing on childhood and future outcomes) can be seen as a Western phenomenon. Certainly the comparison of groups or individuals to determine who is better or faster is a concept that would not be familiar to many of the people we study in other cultures. The questions we have asked and the ways we have viewed the child in his social context have again the subtle biases and concerns of our own culture. Thus, for example, our pragmatic, environmentalist, and behavioristic orientation has led to far more stress on the influence of mother and child than the converse. Somewhat related to this bias is the emphasis on the mother as the major figure for the child, to the neglect of other caretakers. Similarly, we tend to emphasize the effects of environmental stimuli (both social and physical) on development rather than the unfolding of the child's own biology and maturation.

Looking more closely at individual studies, it is possible to find that our own cultural expectations and norms color our choice of measures when dealing with other cultures. By now, most sophisticated social scientists are aware that infant tests are not culture-free. Yet other intrustions of cultural bias may be less familiar. For example, we tend to see social interaction as including behaviors such as face-to-face looking and talking, whereas the more passive physical presence and availability of a parent or caretaker who holds a child or lets a young child climb over him might not be scored as social interaction.

One of the most insidious aspects of our cultural bias (often denied, but nonetheless present, even among ostensibly sophisticated social scientists) is the notion that what is "normal" in our culture is what is "right", and that cultures that are different are likely to be "wrong" or "inferior". The researcher who recognizes the social and cultural roots of his own inquiry improves his own chances of perceiving another culture freshly, in its own terms. This recognition is an essential first step in preparing to do meaningful research across cultures.

One example of the need for cultural relativism came from the conference discussion itself. LeVine noted that, in the Hausa culture, mothers have minimal interaction with their first-born children. They have a custom that involves the extreme avoidance by mothers of their first-born children, starting at birth. Although the mother nurses the child, she does not play with him, call him by name, or look him in the eye. LeVine found that all the mothers abided by this norm, although not with uniform intensity; and it did have an impact on attachment. There were systematic differences between the attachments of first- and later-born children. Later in the conference, as we were discussing the value of multicultural research, it was suggested that research among the Hausa could help us to understand the effects of rejection. It was pointed out that what to a Western observer is rejection has a different meaning in the Hausa culture. LeVine noted that the cultural norms compensate for the mother's low level of involvement by customs that involve other caretakers with first-born children. Therefore, a comparison of first- and later-born Hausa would probably tell us little about rejection; and certainly tell us nothing about the effects of rejection in our own culture.

This does not imply that we should not do cultural comparative research, but it does suggest that we need to be aware of the ways that our assumptions, derived from our own experiences, can blind us from understanding the phenomena we observe in other cultures.

The major implications of this discussion is that we need to understand the culture we study, before we study it. This necessitates a two-phase approach to cultural comparative studies: first, we need to discover how the experiences we want to study vary in the culture, and how these variations fit into an overall cultural matrix of values, economics, politics, and belief systems. The researcher at this level is a kind of "participant observer" and the research is carried out within the "context of discovery". Only after these understandings have been reached in the second phase can a researcher attempt to prove or disprove a hypothesis with sufficient rigor that the results will be defensible. There is reason to question whether our state of knowledge about child care in various cultural contexts is sufficient for us to be engaging in hypothesis-testing research; perhaps for now we must be satisfied with simply discovering cultural diversity in infant care, and *generating* hypotheses that are suggested by our observations.

Anthropologists appear more willing to accept the idea of hypothesis-generating research as legitimate and valuable, but psychology seems less willing to do so. Participant observation research is rarely done in psychology, and, in fact, great efforts are made to keep the researcher as a person, as well as his impressions, out of the research report. Psychologists have few tools with which to engage in research within the context of discovery, which puts them at a disadvantage for determining what are the important questions to be asked in a particular culture. We would encourage the development of methodologies appropriate to this task, and encourage our colleagues to accept the legitimacy of this approach to scientific discovery.

What is important to remember is that the outcome of a study done within this framework does not provide answers; it provides questions. Attempting to use this method to answer questions is inappropriate. However, it makes sense to know the right questions before we try to answer them, and this type of exploration can be used as a way of identifying variables to be examined more systematically later.

Researchers attempting to test hypotheses via multicultural research have a much more difficult road to travel. These investigators are usually interested in very important questions, such as the universality of ontogenetic principles, or the effects of early experiences; work in these areas needs to be well controlled in order to yield valid conclusions. A researcher is not justified in electing to do multicultural hypothesis-testing research, and then in apologizing for methological sloppiness because "things are harder to control in a field study". We are much better off--as one conferee suggested--if we "stop fooling ourselves and pretending that we are going to do definitive studies", and instead recognize that, in most aspects of infant development, we are still at a stage of *generating* hypotheses.

For those who want to engage in hypothesis-testing research, several precautions are important. First is a problem that some might see as only semantic, but in fact it is relevant to the type of conclusions we draw. As we discussed in Chapter 1, the work that most of us are doing is not really "cross-cultural", in that the culture itself is not under study. In the following discussion, therefore, we focus on research in comparative child development, and emphasize the type of understandings that we feel are necessary for researchers using this approach.

The Importance of Context[1]

The critical concept we wish to emphasize is the need to

---

[1] Many of the ideas discussed below were developed by Dr. Robert LeVine.

study behavior in its context. Most researchers in mother-infant interaction are aware of the need to describe the immediate environment and to specify behavioral contingencies; this can be called the "situational-behavioral" context. Psychologists, however, are less likely to consider two other meanings of the word *context*: the cultural or ideological context and the sociohistorical context. It is these larger contexts, together with the more limited situational-behavioral context, that give meaning to the behaviors we study: and we must recognize all three.

Situational-Behavioral Context. Most researchers observing mother-child interaction are aware of the need to carefully specify the environmental context in which the observed behaviors occur. It is clear that, within a single culture, a given item of behavior such as a child's crying or touching his mother may have different meanings at different times, and for different children. If a behavioral scientist uses a purely statistical approach and counts instances of crying, he may lose sight of the behavioral context within which that crying occurs, and may obscure or misinterpret the behavior. If a mother does not respond to a child's behavior, for example, the meaning of that nonresponsiveness depends on the adult's prior pattern of response. If she had been saying "good" and is then silent, the silence may mean "bad"; if she had been saying "bad" and then is silent, it may be interpreted to mean "good". Giving no response, therefore, can have two different meanings, good and bad.

The problem for the behavioral scientist is to describe the structural contingencies that shape the meaning of behavior. Lewis (at the conference) noted that one way of approaching the problem is to give greater attention to the "structural relationships of behavior". He argued that we can no longer look only at behavior in isolation, such as the number of times a mother touches her infant. We must look at the context in which it occurs. We may find, as we do in social class comparisons, that mothers differ not in how many times they touch the child, but how many times they touch when the child cries. One major problem facing researchers in this area is that there is at present no satisfactory descriptive language or model for describing such contingent relations. Some steps in that direction might come from a "game theory" orientation or from Piaget's "logical operational model" of cognitive development, which, although nonstatistical, allows one to "mathematize" the description of behavior that is not necessarily quantitative.

As a practical matter, there is also the problem of

developing a common terminology for describing and specifying
the situational and interpersonal environment. There is a
certain similarity among the variables reported in many studies,
but it is really not clear that they represent common
definitions and mean the same things. It is particularly
important, in talking about divergent findings, to be clear
and specific about what we mean by *tactile contact*, or
kinesthetic stimulation, or even more simple terms like
contingent vocalization. Researchers seem to be working on
these problems with considerable energy, as is clear from the
papers in the present volume. Similar enthusiasm is not
evident, however, for attempts to clarify the importance of
the larger contexts.

    Ideological Context. If one observes mothers "sitting
around doing nothing" in two different societies (e.g., Bushman mothers and Gikuyu mothers from Kenya) their behavior
would probably be quite different in the two societies.
Whiting has indicated:

> The Bushman woman has relatively little to do
> and therefore has a lot of time for her child.
> In a horticultural society such as the Gikuyu,
> she's out there digging and getting wood and
> water from morning to night. Then somebody
> comes along and invents the plow and harnesses
> an ox to it. In the first place, because the
> woman is an economic asset, you get polygyny
> highly correlated with horticulture and no
> plow. You invent the plow and you have monogamy
> (ox is cheaper than a woman). ...When you've
> got a plow or a tractor, you've got a woman
> having a chance to have more time with her
> children, but curiously enough, she spends this
> time in a different way than the Bushman mother
> does, because along with this plow you get social
> stratification. You've got to get up that ladder.
> So the mother takes to spending her time seeing
> that her kid's going to get up that ladder.
> That's quite a different ballgame from the Bushman.

    If one is to understand how behavior fits into a cultural
pattern, and comprehend how that behavior is viewed by the
people being studied, it is essential to study the attitudes,
values, expectations, and ideologies of that culture. To an
anthropologist, this is self-evident; to a psychologist,
particularly a behaviorally oriented one, the ideological

context may be of minimal interest, although it offers important clues to ongoing behavior that may not be observed directly. The problem is that child-rearing studies in our own society have led to skepticism about the relationships between maternal attitudes and maternal behaviors. Recent studies have begun to make progress toward understanding this question (Tulkin & Cohler, 1973; Moss & Jones, Chapter 17, this volume); but, regardless of findings in our own culture, it is extremely important at the cultural comparative level to know what mothers and other caretakers think they are doing, what their goals are for their children, and what some of the overall values are for the society. If we just go out and look at what mothers do in a context completely different from our own, we put too much burden on the small samples of maternal behavior that we collect.

Gathering this data has several purposes. First, of course, it may help us to understand how caretakers interpret what they are doing. There are several examples of the utility of this understanding throughout this book. Tulkin (Chapter 19) reports class differences in the correlation between mothers' holding their infants and other interaction variables: Middle-class mothers who hold their infants a lot also interact with them a great deal in both verbal and nonverbal modalities; in the working-class group, correlations are not significant. The difference is interpreted as supporting the notion that working-class mothers were more likely to hold their infants in order to restrict them from "getting into things", while middle-class mothers held their infants in order to have them more accessible for interacting.

A second purpose in collecting attitudinal data is that it provides a link with the institutional structures of a society. Beliefs and values of caretakers are likely to come from the larger ideology of that group, or from the institutions in which they participate. In an earlier chapter LeVine suggested that parental goals are related to different phases in sociocultural evolution and also emphasized the importance of social class in the formation of attitudes related to child-rearing. He emphasized that "attitudes and values are really the mediator between the macrosocial environment that anthropologists tend to be interested in. and the microsocial environment in which infants are being raised". It is clear that psychologists need to rely on techniques developed by other disciplines in order to adequately gather data on the ideological context of child-rearing. This suggests the need for cross-disciplinary training and/or cross-disciplinary research teams. Cooperative of this type seems imperative, if advances are to be made.

   Historical Context. Taking an even broader perspective,
one can look beyond the ideological context to the historical
context, recognizing that child-rearing serves a critical
function for all societies. According to LeVine, child-
rearing practices are guided by principles and attitudes that
seek (consciously or unconsciously) to encourage behaviors in
children that will lead to their adaptation to the demands of
their society. This is congruent with Caudill's perspective,
which urged that we look at differences between infants of
different cultures, not in pathological terms as one group
being defective or deficient, but rather as attempts to sow
the seeds of future adaptive behaviors. By adopting an
historical perspective we can see how child-rearing patterns
are related to cultural evolution and natural selection.

   Biologists reconstruct the history of life by comparing
different species, organizing them in a certain way, looking
at their similarities and differences, and reconstructing
what must have happened during evolution to produce the range
that is observed. Similarly, when we look at cultures, the
differences are for our understanding of cultural evolution.
If we go about it carefully, we might be able to find out
what has happened in the history of human infancy and infant
care by ordering cultures historically as hunting-gathering,
herding, gardening, or industrial societies, and so on. This
perspective is not purely academic, however. It can offer us
some important suggestions about our current attempts to
influence mother-infant interaction and child development.
If we find various patterns that seem to have persisted
throughout our evolution, it seems unwise to attempt to alter
them, even though we may be able to do so through technology
or through political and social changes. Just as ecologists
talk of "natural balances" in the environment, we may also
find natural patterns in child development as we examine the
history of our species.

   We do not want to imply that this type of analysis needs
to be a part of every cultural comparative study. Researchers
using comparative designs, however, should be aware that they
are studying much more than behavior itself. When we pack our
bags to do a multicultural study, we must bring along some
books on anthropology, sociology, and maybe even evolution.

Social Stratification

   One way to tie together and concretize this discussion is

to focus on one specific type of multicultural study that has been used by many researchers investigating the processes of child development: social class. Social class has been used as an explanation for observed differences on a variety of cognitive and affective tasks assessed in children and adults, and, in many ways, the multicultural research design parallels social class studies done in a single culture. By applying the strategies discussed above to research on social class, we hope to provide a model that will be relevant for all researchers conducting multicultural research.

The first problem facing researchers is to define criteria for social class membership. Immediately we must abandon our "Western biases". It is obvious that when making assessments of socioeconomic status or social class membership in non-industrial non-Western societies, one cannot use conventional Western criteria; instead, one must study the society's own bases for establishing stratification and wealth, and assess how these variables might affect child-rearing. One of the many problems in studying what we call *social class* in other cultures is that--in addition to specific problems of measurement--the conceptions of social class are likely to differ. In the United States, for example, *status*, as defined by prestige within the community, is likely to be related to incomes and amount of material possessions. Leiderman (at the conference) pointed out that among the Gikuyu, economic criteria were not as closely related to *status*. As economic indicators, easy access to water and amount of land (over two acres versus under two acres) seemed to be critical variables; however, one might not be able to predict "the power relationships in the village" from these indicators: The important persons in the village may have cash income, but they may not have water piped to their households. "Educated" people in the village may have more of the modern amenities, but are still less important than the elders and the chief of the village.

From culture to culture, even comparing relatively unwesternized societies, socioeconomic and stratification criteria will differ. Thus, while acreage was a significant criterion for Leiderman working among the Gikuyu, in Klein's Guatemalan study in this volume the number of rooms in the house seems to be the most useful economic measure. If we are to understand how economic stratification affects child development, we need to know (1) the characteristics that differentiate economic levels in a particular group, and (2) how these differences affect the experiences of the infants. These are questions that are difficult to answer, and clearly they are not answerable by relying on assessments derived from Western populations. We need to understand the phenomenology of social stratification and to do this we need to know what it is like to be a Gikuyu or a Bushman.

Once having defined the criteria for social class, we are faced with assessing its impact. Social class as a crucial variable in developmental research engenders heated debate, largely because it is often used as an explanatory concept, rather than as a means to understand how experiences produce the effects on development which we observe. As we stated previously, we feel that in order to really understand these processes, we need to look at ideological and historical contexts of behavior as well as environmental and biological influences.

The theoretical foundations of the concept of social class and SES are essentially sociological, arising from the observation that all complex societies are stratified to some extent, with unequal access to goods, services, and presumably, power. While stratification is widespread, the factors on which it is based--economic, historical, educational, occupational, and sometimes familial-hereditary--may vary from one society to another, making it difficult, if not impossible to use uniform criteria for class membership in the comparison of different cultures. While sociological theories of social class provide a useful framework for study-ing social structure, its origins, and its perpetuation, and allow one to make some predictions about behavioral differences among large populations, they do not provide an adequate explanation at the psychological-interpersonal level of how these differences come about. Social scientists have long investigated the gross relation between social class or SES and aspects of child development, often finding significant relations, but usually have neither an adequate theoretical framework nor sufficient empirical data to understand how these relationships arise. As Kagan said (at the conference), we should stop the practice of using social class as an explanation, but that is hard to do, because class comparisons always yield significant results, and there is no single set of behaviors that produce the same effects. Whenever we begin to look at what seem to be its significant components, the predictability is greatly reduced. Even given this history, we would like to push for continued dissection and study of social class, and would suggest that future explorations focus on the following components:

1.   Medical-biological: e.g., maternal health and
     nutrition, pre- and postnatally; birth procedure
     and conditions; child health and nutritional status
     at birth and later; physical growth patterns; and
     familial genetic and health background.

2.   Behavioral-situational context: the familial life-
     style and rhythms, particularly those that directly
     affect the child, such as patterns of verbal and non-
     verbal interaction; feeding, holding, etc.; and
     household characteristics, e.g., density, house size
     and spatial logistics, play areas, toys and other
     stimuli, lighting, heat, etc.

3.   Ideological context: the values, attitudes and
     expectations of parents, caretakers, and other
     relevant household members toward themselves, their
     society, and the children under study; also, the
     attitudes and behaviors of members of other groups
     toward the children and families of the group being
     studied.

In addressing ourselves to questions of research strategy
in the study of social class influences on child development,
it is important to distinguish between research addressed to
the sources and meaning of social class membership as it
affects children, and research in which social class variables
are merely used as a means of obtaining variation in the
populations under study. This distinction is in some respects
similar to the differences between cross-cultural studies and
comparative studies of child development (Chapter 1). Broad-
gauge studies of social class, like cross-cultural studies,
are addressed to the *total context* within which infant development occurs, and to the totality of variables that derive from
one's position in the social hierarchy. However, when studies
are addressed to more limited aspects of social class (such as
differences in child-rearing practices), many class-related
variables such as parental attitudes, health, and environmental
factors become merely background variables to be understood
and controlled for, but not the focus of the study. Warren
(at the conference) noted that in studies of this latter type,
investigators often feel that if they use social class as an
independent variable, it is in order to get rid of it as fast
as possible, and replace it with more detailed variables that
it represents.

We would argue that, at this stage of the field's develop-

ment, with insufficient theoretical and empirical knowledge of
the effects of class-related variables on infant development,
the wise investigator, regardless of his research interests,
will cast the widest possible data-gathering net before set-
tling on a more limited set of variables. It is only by understanding the total configuration of variables that make up
social class that we can come to understand which are most
salient for child development, and how these can be separated
out by those who wish to focus on them.

   Biological and Medical Variables. Some behavioral
differences that are reported as social class differences can
probably be traced to biological factors that covary with
social class. It is essential, therefore, that both cross-
class and cultural comparisons of child-rearing include an
assessment of maternal and child health and nutrition.

   Whatever one's definition of social class or socioeconomic
status, it is clear that within many societies, there are
relatively widespread differences in diet, eating patterns,
family size and spacing, breast- versus bottle-feeding practices,
use and access to health care, and physical demands on parental
time and energy that can vary from one class to another.
Furthermore, certain populations in many societies do not
usually intermarry with one another, and traditionally have not
intermarried, giving rise to the possibility, particularly at
the extremes of the stratification system, that the biological
states of mothers and children due to genetic factors differ
appreciably in ways that ultimately may affect the cognitive
and even the social-affective development of children. In
England and America, for example, significant differences in
infant mortality and morbidity across social classes have been
demonstrated, usually with lower rates in the upper classes.
Lower-class infants generally stand a greater risk of low birth
weight, congenital malformations, pulmonary disease, or poor
pre- and postnatal nutrition or protein deprivation, and many
other health problems that might interfere with normal development and optimal performance. It is therefore important that
health inventories for both child and mother include such data
as: familial health background and congenital malformations;
maternal health and nutrition, pre- and postnatally (including
prior fertility, miscarriages, and infectious disease); birth
procedure, use of anesthesia, complications; newborn birth
size and competence (i.e., Apgar score or Brazelton score);
postnatal child nutrition, disease history, and physical growth
patterns. For scientists interested primarily in social
influences in normal child development, a health inventory can
help to eliminate unwanted sources of variation by screening

out subjects likely to have developmental handicaps. For those
who wish to account for behavioral differences in children
across social classes, whatever their cause, such an inventory
can provide a clue to one of several sources of variability.

Studies of this latter type, focused on the interaction
of biological and social variables in accounting for class-
related differences in development are extremely difficult,
but sorely needed, as the recent literature on social and
physical deprivation attests. One finding might be cited to
illustrate this point. Drillien (1972) has found in Great
Britain that low-birth-weight infants (who are usually considered to be developmentally at risk, both physically and cognitively)
follow different developmental courses, depending on their social
class background. At age seven, those in the first three social
classes were not significantly different from the rest of the
sample, while those in the lowest two social classes differed
both in school attainment and social adjustment. It is not
clear to what extent this difference arises from variations in
the *causes* of low birth weight (prenatal malnutrition, with
subsequent minimal brain damage may be more likely in the
lower classes, while other causes of short gestation or low
body weight that are less damaging developmentally may be more
common among the upper classes); differences in postnatal care
and long-term nutrition; attitudinal differences in the way
parents and caretakers in the two classes raise their children;
differences in the quality of schooling and responsiveness of
teachers; or some combination of these and/or other factors.

There are a number of problems such as these that require
the long-term combined efforts of medical and social science
researchers if solutions are to be forthcoming. In some
instances, multicultural studies may provide natural
experiments in which social and biological variables normally
inseparably correlated within our own social classes may be
found in isolation. Questions such as the effects of pre- and
postnatal protein deprivation or malnourishment on cognitive
development (or for that matter, on maternal energy and the
quality of child care); or those concerning developmental
plasticity after early deprivation or illness; or those
concerning the interplay of genetic and social factors in
development across social classes are going to require a long
partnership between the medical and behavioral sciences.

Behavioral-Situational Context. The thrust of most recent
research concerning the impact of social class on infant
behavior has been to specify the environmental variables to
which infants are exposed. Studies such as these, often based
on direct observation in the home, have provided a significant

link in the causal chain from caretaker to child behavior, but in the absence of attitudinal and environmental data, as well as health data, they probably tell us more about variations in parenting and their effects on children than about the effects of social class membership on child development. It is important to keep these two areas of inquiry distinct.

For investigators primarily interested in the relation between parenting behavior and child development, for whom the use of SES is merely a way of obtaining needed variation in parenting behavior, alternative strategies might be preferable. Researchers can pool the behavioral data, obtained from members of various social classes, to see whether there are natural groupings of parental and child behavioral patterns other than those defined by SES. Another approach would be to choose families randomly in a community, observe parental and child behavior, analyze the data for natural groupings, and then test their correlation with SES (Leiderman & Leiderman, Chapter 16 of this volume). Such approaches might suggest more specific behaviorally relevant variables than SES.

Considering now the selection of behavioral variables, most of the behavioral data obtained to date have focused on interaction of mothers and their children. Key variables have been touching, holding, verbalizing, eye-contact, playing with an object, feeding, changing and so on. While these are un- doubtedly central to infant care and socialization, we suggest that, for a thorough understanding of the behavioral correlates of social class, further study should also be given to patterns of infant interaction with others in the household (e.g., fathers, sibs, baby-sitters, extended family members, friends, etc.), to differences in the quantity and quality of these contacts, and to different behavioral-situational contexts in which these contacts occur. Another aspect of the behavioral environment of the child that may well be related to social class concerns the differences in styles of child-rearing when an infant has multiple caretakers (Leiderman & Leiderman, this volume). When the caretaking responsibilities are shared by a variety of relatives, baby-sitters, and day-care center staff members, discontinuities in the physical as well as the social environment are introduced, and the effects of these dis- continuities are likely to be different depending on the attitudes of the caretakers. Simple observations of behaviors are likely to yield very limited results.

Another aspect of the behavioral-situational context is the physical environment itself. Only minimal attention has been given to dimensions of the physical environment. While

most investigators recognize that physical environments can
vary significantly with social class, it is difficult to
characterize and conceptualize these influences in any
systematic way. Again, we find ourselves without a theory
by which to understand our data. Many investigators,
particularly those interested in cognitive development, assess
the variety and responsiveness of inanimate objects with which
children interact (Yarrow, Pedersen, & Robenstein, this volume),
or the numbers of toys and other objects for play, the use of
playpens, walkers, highchairs, etc. (Leiderman & Leiderman,
and Tulkin, earlier in this volume). Rarely, however, is an
attempt made to describe systematically the physical environment of the home, or other environments to which the infant
may be exposed, and the ways in which families use their living
space. For example, Whiting (at the conference) mentioned that
house size, a variable often overlooked, can be used as a
predictor of both behavioral and health variables, since
infants in a large house may more often be separated from their
mothers than those in smaller quarters, and may undergo more
stress, which itself can affect physical growth patterns.
The amount and quality of light is another factor, known to
affect animal development, which might be relevant in infant
studies as well.

Perhaps greater definition of the social environments,
utilizing methods developed by Moos and associates applied to
family units (1974) might be the best approach. Given the fact
that a considerable amount of the variance for predication of
behavior resides in the "situation", it would seem that
systematic evaluation of the individual-situation interaction
is necessary. Such qualification of environments could then
be adapted for comparisons between classes and cultures along
common dimensions.

Ideological Context. Some investigators of infant
behavior would argue that whatever is in the "hearts" of
caretakers is irrelevant, since, to preverbal infants, social
class variables are experienced only through the direct behavior of those who interact with them. Their studies reflect
this perspective, focusing almost entirely on caretaking
behavior across social classes, with little or no attention
to other types of variables. However justified this position
may be on practical grounds (it undoubtedly allows one to
focus one's efforts on a clearly deliminated problem), it is
unduly limiting heuristically. As LeVine (Chapter 2) has
observed, when attitudinal data are omitted, one not only
precludes the possibility of explaining why parental behavior
varies across social classes (thus minimizing opportunities

for social structural explanation), but one also loses
potentially valuable sources of corroborative evidence
concerning ongoing *behavioral* practices. For example,
Richards (1973) points out that we often presume that social
class has the same meaning across an entire country, and
presume a similarity in life-style between a laborer living
in a village and an unskilled worker in a densely populated
industrial city. Not only do physical environments vary
across situations like this, but so do social environments--
the degree of community solidarity and organization, the
importance of kin networks, the availability of social, medical
and educational institutions, the values of the subculture,
etc. Clearly, further work is needed to clarify the extent
to which presumably uniform class subcultures are indeed
uniform. By obtaining attitudinal and ideological data,
students of child development can shed light on this question,
while illuminating the sources of class-related behavioral
differences.

One attitudinal variable that appears to derive directly
from social structural position, and has behavioral correlates
in child-rearing practice, is the parent's sense of his or her
own power and ability to control fate, both personal and
familial. Tulkin (this volume) reports that he had informally
interviewed some of the mothers in his study and found that
working-class mothers did not believe they could interact
with and affect the intellectual development of their infants
while middle-class mothers did believe possibility of
effective interaction. Behavioral observation supported these
attitudinal differences, with greater amounts of interaction
between middle-class mother-infant dyads than between working-
class dyads. Further, attitudes of middle-class mothers, as
assessed by Cohler's Maternal Attitude Scale (Cohler, Weiss,
& Grunebaum, 1967), were significantly correlated with their
behaviors toward their infants (Tulkin & Cohler, 1973). Some
working-class mothers may have held similar attitudes, but
were less likely to translate their attitudes into behavior,
possibly because of their feelings that whatever they did
would make no difference. Thus, the assessment of a specific
attitude is insufficient to explain the presence or absence
of a behavior; more comprehensive belief systems must be
studied.

Analysis of the feeling of personal (or internal) control
provides a plausible conceptual handle for theory development
and research concerning one source of behavioral differentiation
across social classes. A recent study that supports the importance of the parents' sense of control over their own fate was

reported by Falender and Heber (1974). Working with lower-class, low-IQ mothers, half of whom were randomly selected to participate in an intervention program, Falender administered the Cohler scales, did behavioral observations, and also administered Rotter's (1974) I-E Scale, which assesses the degree of internal versus external "locus of control". Mothers who had participated in the intervention program had scores reflecting a significantly greater sense of internal locus of control than the control group. Furthermore, correlations between the Cohler Scales and maternal behaviors were higher in the intervention group than in the control group parallel-ing the findings for social class reported by Moss and Jones (this volume), and by Tulkin and Cohler (1973). Thus one of the process variables we need to look at in our efforts to understand social class is likely to be related to the way in which lower-class status carries with it a sense of power-lessness and fatalism. Clearly, however, far more work is needed to document the demography of attitudinal and behavioral differences across social classes before it can be assumed that this is indeed a significant and widespread indicator of class characteristics and differentiation within our own as well as socially stratified non-Western cultures.

Finally, we would like to suggest that researchers interested in understanding the ideological context of behavior behavior begin to explore the "meaning" of class membership for the family being studied in relationship to the membership of other social classes. Here, we are talking about variables such as the degree of stratification within a society, "class consciousness". The attitudes and behaviors of other groups may impinge directly on the infant where the infant is in contact with these groups, and the attitudes can influence parents' personalities as well as their specific child-rearing goals and behaviors. While in most instances the infant is relatively isolated from direct contact with members of other classes, certainly the parents and other family members may not be so isolated. Where the infant has direct contact with other social groups, such as through the practice of hiring nurses to care for upper-class infants, this multiplication of cross-class caretaking patterns will surely have some effect on the development of the child (see Hardy, 1972). The variations in behaviors of the adults and older children, based on class differences that directly affect the family and infant, should be part of the total assessment of the effects of social class.

SUMMARY

We recommend that in studying the impact of social class variables on infant development:

1. The characteristics that differentiate socioeconomic status in a particular culture need to be defined.

2. Naturalistic observational studies should be used to explore social class environments before more detailed and focused studies are begun. In the aggregate, these studies should span all social classes within a given culture.

3. Data collection should include attitudinal, behavioral medical, and environmental aspects of the setting.

4. The correlations between SES categories and class-specific attitudinal, behavioral, and environmental characteristics should not be assumed, but be put to empirical test.

5. Investigators not inherently interested in the origins, meaning, and impact of social class differences on child development should attempt to find behavioral and attitudinal bases for caretaking variability that are not necessarily linked to SES demarcations.

6. An attempt should be made to explicate the theoretical assumptions and purposes behind studies of social class influences on infant development. This can aid in theory and hypothesis development: and, in the absence of formal theory to guide research strategy, can aid in developing research strategies appropriate to research goals.

REFERENCES

Cohler, B. J., Weiss, J., & Gruenbaum, H. Child-care attitudes and emotional disturbance among mothers of young children. Genetic Psychology Monographs, 1970, 82, 3-47.

Drillien, C. M. Later development and follow-up of low birth weight babies. Pediatric Annals, 44, 1972.

Falender, C., & Heber, R. Attitudes and behaviors of mothers
        participating in the Milwaukee Project. Unpublished
        manuscript, University of California at Los Angeles,
        Department of Education, 1974.

Richards, M. P. M. Social class and the early development of
        children in Britain. Paper presented at the Wenner-
        Gren Conference on Cultural and Social Influences
        in Infancy and Early Childhood, Burg Wartenstein,
        Austria, June 1973.

Tulkin, S. R., & Cohler, B. J. Child-rearing attitudes and
        mother-child interaction in the first year of life.
        Merrill Palmer Quarterly, 1973, 19, 95-106.

Chapter 22
Ethics, Politics, and Multicultural Research

Susan Goldberg
Brandeis University

Social science has traditionally been a Western enterprise
shaped by Western ideologies. Those of us who do research
carry these ideologies into our work, often unwittingly. If
we work in other cultures, what we do, what we see, and what
we can learn is determined by ideology. In the United States
and in Britain, the prevailing ideology is a competitive one
(Reigel, 1972; Buck-Morss, 1975): the individual succeeds only
in comparison with others, and our approach to child development reflects this attitude. One is rewarded for individual
achievement and the hallmark of achievement is beating out
everyone else. Indeed, the words *competence* and *complete*
share a common Latin root. Our concern is for individual
accomplishment, regardless of the consequences to the group.
In many non-Western cultures, the shared concerns of the group
are primary (Hsu, 1973). Our approach to infant development
is a reflection of this attitude and the thrust of much
research is to see whether development can be accelerated
(e.g., White, 1969). It is accepted by many that more rapid
development is better development!

It is not surprising then, that many studies of African
infants focus on comparisons with European infants to see
which group is more precocious. (Warren, 1972). Everything
we believe leads us to expect that African infants, without
the benefits of modern medicine and our notion of a balanced

diet, should lag behind more privileged Europeans. If the reverse is found to be the case, we do not decide that European infants are retarded. We conclude that European infants are normal and African infants who are more advanced are extraordinary.

Often we take Western experience to be "normal", and label other patterns *pathological*. The concept of intelligence, for example, has come to mean possession of those skills that ensure success in Western school systems. We judge the intelligence of others by these standards, rather than by the skills that are valued in their own cultures (Tulkin & Konner, 1973). Even where attempts are made to adapt our approach to local experience, the premises remain Western. When I was testing infants in Zambia, I tried to use familiar materials wherever possible. I continued to use inanimate objects, although I felt the social domain was more salient for these infants. Only later, after Dasen (1973) made the same observation in his work with Ivorian infants, did I realize that I could have used this knowledge in my testing.

Several recent papers have commented that, in many cultures, both children and adults are more responsive to the social domain than to the physical, where we have assessed skills that only relate to the physical world (Cole, 1973; Hsu, 1973; Lewis & Ban, this volume). By and large, we have failed to study the area of development acknowledged to be a major failure in industrialized cultures: personal relationships. Often, where we do study personal realtionships in infancy, it is to assess their influences on cognitive development (e.g., Ainsworth & Bell, 1974; Bell, 1970; Goldberg, Chapter 9, this volume; Lewis & Goldberg, 1969).

Some observers find that Western emphasis on independence and achievment may be destructive of personal relationships. Brazelton (this volume), for example, notes that, in comparison with Zinacanteco infant care, American practices set the stage for independence and individual striving in a way that does not encourage trust in human relationships.

ETHICS IN THE FIELD

Thus, Western assumptions bias the questions we ask and the interpretations we make of the answers. But even more important, our ideologies structure the evaluations we make of others, and therefore the kind of respect we can accord

to them. If we were on the other side of the relationship,
we might see this more clearly. Suppose a Kpelle psychologist
came to test Westerners on a task that most Kpelle can do
easily: the classification of leaves according to the type of
plant they grow on (bushes, trees, or vines). Even if the
task were administered in English, with leaves chosen from
local plants, most of us would perform poorly. Yet we would
resent the conclusion that our classification skills were
inadequate. We would reject the conclusion that we were
lacking in intelligence.

In the past few years, social scientists have become more
concerned about the ethics of the researcher-"researchee"
relationships. Various documents have been published with
recommendations on the major issues. These include such
matters as the confidentiality of information gathered by a
researcher, the kind of information an investigator should
provide to the participants, and the appropriate compensation
for participants. These issues should be of specific concern
to those of us who work in other cultures. If nothing else,
the unwitting assumptions we make about normality and
pathology, about success and failure, may easily lead us to
exploit those we do not consider equals.

Ordinarily, participation in research is a voluntary
activity. An individual decides to participate on the basis
of information provided by the investigator. However, it is
often the case that participants have little knowledge of
what has actually been taken from them. It is not that social
scientists are all deliberate deceivers. Our sins are more
often the sins of omission rather than those of commission.
Usually we are concerned that we may make people unnecessarily
self-conscious, or assume that people are not sophisticated
enough to understand the details, so we leave out some
information that we might provide. In nonindustrialized
countries, we are even more likely to omit information. We
may assume that even the elite have little basis for understanding our research. For example, Ainsworth (at the
conference) stated that she could not use data from her research
in the United States to publish case studies without violating
the confidentiality of her informants. Yet some years ago she
published studies from her work in Uganda (Ainsworth, 1967),
because it seemed safe to assume that none of the informants
would ever see them. In many of the studies described in this
volume, infants were observed in their homes. We also observed
and recorded information about mothers. However, we rarely told
mothers that they were being watched. This was deception, and
many of us felt uncomfortable about it. At the time, we assumed

that this was essential to the conduct of research. Part of
our ideology says that you cannot trust what you see when
people know you are watching.

Often researchers are permitted to observe events that
would ordinarily be private. Some of us were present, for
example, at births, where even the infant's father and siblings
are usually excluded. At the very least, we had to believe
we were doing no harm, for we were intervening in the lives of
others. We were there, when normally we would not be. Most of
us believed that whatever disruptions attended our observations,
they were minimal and relatively unimportant. If we were
psychologists, we did our best to be distant and objective and
to avoid involvement. While anthropologists and sociologists
are often allowed to be participant observers, the ideology of
psychology tells us to remain apart from what we observe.
Ainsworth suggested that if a study involves repeated observations at home, it may be unethical to be uninvolved. It is
very threatening for someone to sit and take notes without
ever reacting to what happens. Indeed, in the name of research,
we often behave in ways that would ordinarily be considered
very peculiar, if not inhuman. This can be very disturbing to
a family. Paradoxically, Ainsworth also suggested that the
effects of potential disruptions may be minimized by longer
and more frequent visits. As the observer becomes more
familiar, the threat value of being observed may diminish.
However, more natural behavior and involvement on the part of
the observer can also minimize such threats.

In a relatively unfamiliar culture, it is even more
difficult to sense what is an invasion of privacy, what is
offensive, and what is appropriate. In most of the homes I
visited in Zambia, a male may not visit a woman's house when
her husband is absent without violating the family's sense of
propriety. We should not think that being a doctor, a
psychologist, or an anthropologist overrides such customs.

Another issue involves compensation. Usually, we exchange
money, services, or even academic credits for the time and
information that participants contribute. In some cultures,
our usual compensation may be inappropriate. Often the people
who are approached can make clear what they wish in exchange.
Ainsworth found that the Ganda mothers in her study were so
eager for information about feeding and nutrition that the plan
of the study had to be changed so that this could be provided.
To refuse this information was unethical. It would also have
been impossible to maintain their cooperation in a research
project without meeting this need. Sometimes the exchange

expected by participants may present some difficulties.
Leiderman (at the conference) told us, for example, that he
was disturbed to find that his wife was expected to provide
transportation to the hospital for residents of the village
where he was working. Eventually, a satisfactory agreement
was reached so that transportation was available specifically
for families in the research project.

Compensation to individual participants is, of course,
important. Even more important is the return to the community
and the host country. In industrialized countries where a
great deal of research is carried out, it is generally assumed
that, in the long run, society as a whole benefits from the
findings of research projects. When Westerners do research
in less wealthy nations and take the data home to analyze, the
benefits generally accrue to Western science and Western life-
styles. The host country may have little access to the
information gathered. Even in Western countries, the findings
of research studies are not readily available to participants.
When they are, they are often of little immediate use or
applicability. When a country has permitted outsiders to do
research without any return of information, there may be
increasing resentment at the diversion of local resources and
talent to foreign interests.

Recently, for example, the New York Times (September 1,
1974) printed a small item about the result of exploitation
by social scientists in Canada's Northwest Territories. It
seems that the Eskimos and Indians get tired of being helpful
to anthropologists ("Who's your anthropologist"? was a common
joke), and of answering the same questions over and over without ever seeing the findings. Hereafter, social scientists
wishing to do research in this area must apply for a license
from local authorities. A detailed proposal must be submitted
and the local board may reject projects that are judged to
threaten daily life. Furthermore, the researcher who is
licensed is required to submit progress reports to the
licensing board. Similar application procedures exist for
research projects on kibbutz life in Israel.

Less formal, but similar procedures may be required by
minority communities in the United States. In the summer of
1974, I helped to initiate a research project in the black
community of an urban center in Massachusetts. Most of the
summer was devoted to public relations work, meeting with
community organizations and agencies. A committee representing
the community read our proposal and approved the project, with
the understanding that we were responsible to the committee

for the submission of regular progress reports. Many times
we were asked, Who would control the data?   Were we going
to be comparing blacks and whites?   Would our findings be
subject to negative interpretations about the black community?

Sigel (1973) described his experiences in establishing a
program for preschoolers in a black community. He had to
explain to parents what the project was about, what it meant
for an outsider to establish such a program, how parents'
expectations for their children related to his goals, and so
on. Constant communication on a two-way basis was essential
throughout the duration of the project.

These examples suggest that many groups of people who
have been studied repeatedly are now wary of being exploited.
They are insisting on some input and control of projects that
concern them. This is a welcome sign.

DOING GOOD

As social scientists, few of us have any intention of
changing the people we study. Yet, as the foregoing examples
show, those who have been studied repeatedly often feel that
their way of life is threatened by the process.

> Into each life, it is said, some rain must
> fall. Some people have bad horoscopes,
> others take tips on the stock market... .
> But Indians have been cursed above all
> other people in history. Indians have
> anthropologists.
>   [DeLoria, 1969, p. 83]

At the conference, someone said "I have never heard of any
society that was destroyed by social science". Apparently
this view is not shared by American Indians. It is not shared
by Canadian Eskimos, and it is not shared by many black
communities in the United States. What social scientists
consider harmless, may in fact, be damaging in the eyes of
others.

Similarly, what social scientists see as good, may be
rejected by others. Many of us believe that in exchange for
the time and information people give us, we should try to

"do good" to "uplift" the people we study. (Of course, only
those who are inferior can be uplifted. We never speak of
"uplifting" our equals.) The greatest harm, Whiting said (at
the conference), is done by those who think they are doing
good. During my stay in Zambia, I occasionally hosted other
researchers in my field. On one occasion, when I escorted
some American colleagues to a Zambian farmer's home, they were
offered a basket of eggs. They began to refuse, feeling that
they could do good by saving a few more eggs for the family.
The insult of refusing a gift, however, would have been far
more important to that family than the few extra eggs.
Ainsworth was advised not to bring milk powder to the babies
she visited. The mothers would use it while it was free, but
could not afford to buy it on their own when she left. A child
might become dependent on this gift and suffer serious
nutritional problems when it was no longer available.

We disagreed among ourselves about what we could contribute
to the people we study without doing harm by doing good.
Whiting felt that the most important thing he could give away
with a clear conscience was knowledge of scientific method.
This involved the training and development of local scholars
and making research findings broadly available to local people.
Many of us were less sanguine about this. For example,
training scholars requires some input in local school systems,
which might be viewed as meddling. But even more serious, is
not spreading behavioral scientists around the world tantamount
to spreading Western ideology? This is not an easy question to
answer.

RESEARCH AND POLITICS

It is impossible to do research without politics. Scientific research was once the exclusive province of wealthy gentle-
men who could afford to support themselves. Today, science is
supported by governments, and by public and private foundations;
wealth and power continue to determine what is done. In recent
years, Western research literature has been filled with studies
of minority-group children. Why? Because there is money
available for intervention research. Often this means research
aimed at shaping minority-group children in the image of the
white middle class. Social scientists are still ready to assume
the model in which deviation from white middle-class behavior is
considered pathological. The rationale for such research is
that ostensibly it will increase these children's chances to
succeed in the system. Most of the scientists who engage in

this kind of research believe they are doing good. But if
they succeed, perhaps they will also succeed in alienating
poor children from their parents and their ethnic origins.
It rarely occurs to us that the system may be changed, that
the fault may be in the system, not in the children. That
is part of the ideology: the belief that the system is good
and right and such interventions are in the interest of
progress. Again, we must ask if we are doing harm by doing
good.

It is rich and powerful nations that can afford to send
researchers to other countries. Thus, Americans can do
research in Third World countries, but rarely does an African
or Asian come to study Americans. The British and French send
researchers to their former colonies, but when does someone
from the colonies come to study the British or the French?
Even with the most careful efforts at cooperation between
scholars of different nations, the economic and political
reality is that it is the richer country that has the resources
to do research and it is the poorer country that has the
information. Cooperative efforts in this climate are doomed
to be "helping" on one side, and "giving" on the other
(Tajfel, 1968), at best, a benevolent academic imperialism.
Even within the rich nations, where power and resources are
increasingly available to social scientists so that they will
solve our social problems, the poor get the short end of the
stick. The result is an increasing concentration of power in
the hands of the "helpers" at the expense of those who are
"helped" (Richards, 1973).

Both Whiting and LeVine stressed repeatedly the
importance of developing collegial relations with local
scholars when possible. But political reality interferes
with the equality of the participants in such relationships.
Nonwhite social scientists have felt that, while they are
encouraged to study their own culture, it is primarily in the
role of providing information to the "real" (white male)
social scientists (Hsu, 1973; Jones, 1970). It is a sobering
thought that a conference on "cultural and social influences
in infancy and early childhood" could consist only of white
Westerners and with few exceptions, exclusively from the
United States. Few of us thought to suggest our local
colleagues as participants, myself included. This sheds a
harsh light on the nature of collegial relations between
researchers from wealthy nations and those from the poor.

A Western scientist need have no desires to intervene in
the interests of social change or political causes. But the

very fact that Westerners can invite themselves to poor
countries to do research is political reality (Frank & Smith,
1976). Anthropology, remarked LeVine, would not exist now
if we had waited for people to invite research in their
communities. Social science may represent a threat to the
status quo. There is always the possibility that careful
scrutiny by an outsider will reveal what governments would
prefer to hide. Invited or not, social scientists who have
financial support from governments or foundations can go.
Once there, a social scientist may actually lend validity to
repressive governments. Social scientists have worked in
countries with oppressive minority governments and allowed
their presence, their money spent, and their subsequent
silence to lend tacit support and approval to such governments.
While anthropology gave us "cultural relativism", it had its
origins in colonial history. Often anthropologists were sent
to their country's colonies to discover information that would
help control local populations. Reverence for traditional
cultures can still serve to support and maintain existing
colonial and neocolonial conditions (Gjessing, 1968; Jones,
1970). It is not surprising that social scientists are
sometimes suspected of being intelligence agents of their
governments.

CONCLUSIONS

     What does all this have to do with the goals of research?
It may seem that we have been speaking of matters that are
peripheral, if not extraneous, to the research enterprise.
However, political realities have theoretical implications.
If Westerners are allowed to study both their own cultures
and those of others, while scientists from poorer nations can
only work at home, an important perspective is missing. Many
theoretical views can be overlooked in this way. For example,
I have often thought that if psychology had originated in
Zambia, our concerns would be quite different today. We would
have assumed from the start that contact comfort was essential
for the development of infant-mother relationships. The role
of feeding, if considered at all, would have been discovered
only recently. The ideologies of different cultures should
lead to different approaches to human behavior, different
problems for study, and different styles of research. We
have, at present, few clues as to what these might be, because
many possibilities are now closed. As long as social science
is dominated by Westerners, we will discover only what Western
ideologies unveil. When we are willing to lay ourselves open

to the scrutiny before which others lay themselves bare for
us, we will understand ourselves differently.

Until that time, I do not think I can do multicultural
research with a clear conscience. The years in Zambia were
very productive for me. I would like to return, but I will
not invite myself as I did before. I would like to think that
some day a Zambian scholar might invite me as a collaborator,
and that I could extend a similar invitation. I hope that
time is not too far away. Perhaps then, such chapters as this
one will no longer be necessary.

REFERENCES

Ainsworth, M. D. S. Infancy in Uganda: Infant care and the
        growth of love. Baltimore, Md.: The Johns Hopkins
        University Press, 1967.

Ainsworth, M. D. S., & Bell, S. M. Mother-infant interaction
        and the development of competence. R. J. Connelly
        and J. S. Bruner (Eds.) The Growth of Competence.
        New York: Academic Press, 1974.

Bell, S. M. The development of object as related to infant-
        mother attachment. Child Development, 1970, 41,
        291-312.

Buck-Morss, S. Socio-economic bias in Piaget's theory and
        its implications for cross-cultural studies. Human
        Development, 1975, 18, 35-39.

Cole, M. An ethnographic psychology of cognition. Paper
        presented at Conference on the Interface Between
        Culture and Learning, Honolulu, February, 1973.

Dasen, P. R. Preliminary study of cognitive development
        among Ivorian children (Baole and Ebrie): Sensori-
        motor intelligences and concrete operations. Early
        Child Development and Care, 1973, 2, 345-354.

DeLoria, V. Custer died for your sins. New York: Avon, 1969.

Frank, J. E., & Smith, R. A. Social scientists in the policy
        process. Journal of Applied Behavioral Science,
        1976, 12, 104-117.

Gjessing, G.   The social responsibility of the social scientist.
        Current Anthropology, 1968, 9, 397-402.

Hsu, F. L. K.   Prejudice and its intellectual effect in
        anthropology. American Anthropologist, 1973, 75,
        1-19.

Jones, D. J.   Towards a native anthropology. Human Organization,
        1970, 29, 251-259.

Lewis, M., & Goldberg, S.   Perceptual-cognitive development in
        infancy: A generalized expectancy model as a function
        of mother-infant interaction. Merrill-Palmer
        Quarterly, 1969, 15, 81-100.

Reigel, K. F.   Influence of economic and political ideologies
        on the development of developmental psychology.
        Psychological Bulletin, 1972, 78, 129-141.

Richards, M.   Social class and early development of children
        in Britain. Unpublished paper, Unit for the Medical
        Application of Psychology, Cambridge, England: 1973,
        Cambridge University.

Sigel, I. E.   Contributions of psychoeducational intervention
        programs in understanding of preschool children.
        Paper presented at Biog. Wartenstein Symposium No. 87,
        Cultural and Social Influences in Infancy and Early
        Childhood. Cloggnitz, Austria, June, 1973.

Tajfel, H.   Cross-cultural research and international relations.
        International Journal of Psychology, 1968, 3, 213-
        219.

Tulkin, S. R., & Konner, M. J.   Alternative conceptions of
        intellectual functioning. Human Development.
        1973, 16, 33-52.

Warren, N.   African infant precocity. Psychological Bulletin,
        1972, 78, 353-367.

White, B. L.   The initial coordination of sensorimotor schemas
        in human infants: Piaget's ideas and the role of
        experience. In D. Elkind & J. Flavell (Eds.),
        Studies in cognitive development: Essays in honor of
        Jean Piaget. New York: Oxford University Press,
        1969.

RECOMMENDED READING

Baratz, S. S., & Baratz, J. C. Early childhood intervention:
     The social science base of institutional racism.
     Harvard Educational Review, 1970, 40, 29-50.

Berrien, F. K. Methodological and related programs in cross-
     cultural research. International Journal of
     Psychology, 1967, 2, 33-43.

Berrien, F. K. A superego for cross-cultural research.
     International Journal of Psychology, 1970, 5, 33-39.

Kelman, H. C. A time to speak. San Francisco: Jossey-Bass,
     1968.

Sroufe, L. A. A methodological and philosophical critique of
     intervention-oriented research. Developmental
     Psychology, 1970, 2, 140-145.

Tulkin, S. R. An analysis of the concept of cultural
     deprivation. Developmental Psychology, 1972, 6,
     326-339.

Chapter 23
Looking Toward the Future

P. Herbert Leiderman
Stanford University School of Medicine

Steven R. Tulkin*
, State University of New York at Buffalo

Anne Rosenfeld
State University of New York at Buffalo

Up to this point we have attempted to present a sample of the state of the art of multicultural research on infancy. It should be obvious from the chapters in this volume that the theoretical underpinnings for this research area, the number, variety, and rigor of empirical studies, permits, if not requires, considerable expansion of research endeavors in the future. In this chapter we shall present our views of some of the possible pitfalls to avoid before embarking on this most challenging and rewarding approach to understanding the ontogenesis of human behavior.

HOW WE LOOK: METHODOLOGICAL ISSUES

Assuming that one has made a decision to do mulitcultural study, the question arises as to the specification of methods to be employed. It is now apparent that one cannot readily export techniques of psychological observation, measurement, and analysis developed in white, Western, middle-class populations and apply them blindly to studies in other cultural groups. Great caution, sensitivity, and often modification are needed if these techniques are to be used at all. Even observational techniques cannot be used without knowledge of the culture being observed. "Evil eye" beliefs, mentioned by

*Present address: University of Cape Coast, Cape Coast, GHANA.

Brazelton (Chapter 7, this volume) serve as one example of the way in which cultural norms affect observed behavior. Another example involves the differences between maternal behaviors toward first-born and later-born infants among the Hausa, mentioned by LeVine (this volume). Typical Western methodology of controlling for birth order by observation only first-borns would result in a very biased picture of Hausa child-rearing.

An even more troublesome example is a recent study by Randall (1975), which argues that the effects of observation are different in middle-class and working-class U.S. families. Randall found that working-class mothers of ten-month-old infants vocalized significantly less when the observer was present than when he was absent, but that for middle-class mothers the differences were negligible. Thus, even in our own culture, we need to be aware of how our methods can affect different populations differently (Tulkin, 1972; see also Zegiab, Arnold, & Forehand, 1975).

The necessity of using assessment tasks whose meaning is relevant to the subjects being tested has been fully described by Cole, Gay, Glick, and Sharp (1971), and will not be discussed here at length. An example of the need to be aware of this issue comes from a study by Fjellman (1971), who compared schooled and unschooled Akamba (Kenyan) adolescents and found that when classifying geometric shapes the schooled subjects used more abstract, and the unschooled used more concrete, principles of classification. This supports previous research demonstrating that schooling is related to the development of abstract thinking skills. However, Fjellman also had subjects classify animals--a task that is more closely tied to "adaptive behavior" in Akamba life. On this task, she found that the unschooled children used more abstract (e.g., domestic versus wild) and the schooled more concrete (e.g., color) classifying principles. Thus, their respective positions in a developmental sequence were reversed, depending not even on the nature of the task, but merely on the objects to be operated on.

Despite the necessary diversity of methodologies, there is emerging an overreaching approach to comparative child development that promises, in the future, to permit a greater degree of comparability and reliability across cultures than we now have (see Munroe & Munroe, 1975). To some extent, this approach is based more on recognition of common problems than on common methodological solutions, but the realization that problems exist represents at least a first step toward their solution. In the following paragraphs, we will focus on methodolgocial issues relating specifically to the study of infancy.   Readers interested in a broader review of cross-cultural methodological issues, especially as they apply to survey and questionnaire techniques, are referred to Brislin. Lonner, and Thorndike (1973).

Use of Multiple Measures and Approaches.

As we have gained greater appreciation of the complexity of infant behavior and the state of our own theoretical and empirical ignorance, we have come to realize that we must design studies that take into account the widest possible search for sources of variance in the populations under study. This means careful, explicit description of the cultural and physical context (and this applies to studies in our own cultures as well), the medical, biological, and genetic factors affecting mother and child, and the attitudinal and behavioral milieu surrounding the child.   It means, as well, that studies of infant development must utilize multiple measures of infant response and activity.

The necessity for interdisciplinary cooperation in accomplishing the design and implementation of such studies is obvious.   There is ample room for studies more limited in breadth and scale, so long as the limits of conclusions drawn from them are understood at the outset.

During this exploratory phase of comparative child development research, it is important to "hedge one's bets", both theoretically and methodologically, allowing for a variety of approaches to the same subject matter, e.g., time-sampling observation, interviews, participant observation, use of naturally occurring structures and experiments, testing, etc., to gain a firm grasp on slippery variables.   While one runs the risk of spreading one's research efforts too thinly, there are few multicultural research studies to date that would not have benefited from a broader initial investigation.

Statistical Analysis

Although there are few, if any, explicit, experimentally oriented models of the nature of developmental interaction between the infant as a biological and psychological organism and his social and physical environment, there is an implicit dynamic model developing in the field that is nonlinear, non-stimulus-response and only fragmentarily described by current correlational techniques.   However, while many researchers are aware that even the current popular techniques do not provide

the best statistical answers, there are as yet few better tools
available. It is tempting to believe that there are nonlinear
mathematical models developed for other fields, but none have
been adapted or developed to suit the needs of current developmental research.

Until such techniques are developed, it is important that
scientists in this field design studies that can yield the
clearest data, while appreciating the limits of this statistical
approach. This is still a time in the field's development when
careful, naturalistic observation can yield as many or more
clues to fundamental relationships among causal factors as
utilizing rigorously, but naively formulated correlational
analyses. A wise strategy would combine both approaches, with
a preliminary exploratory study, designed to discover key
variables, followed by more careful investigation of those
variables under more carefully specified conditions.

While we do not have a satisfactory mathematical description
of the bidirectional effects we know to be characteristic of
mother-child interaction, it is still possible to describe
behavior with greater rigor and attention to the behavioral
context in which other behavior appears; so, for example, in
analyzing when a child cries, one describes his prior and
immediate state, the responses of other people that preceded
his crying, and other people's current responses to the child's
cry. By such painstaking analysis and observation, it is
possible to build a more dynamic model of the give-and-take
of social interaction than we have had to date. Longitudinal
studies are also essential to our understanding of these
"bidirectional" influences. Moss and Jones' data (Chapter 17,
this volume), based on maternal interviews before the birth
of the child, demonstrate the importance of the mother's
contributions, as does the longitudinal data on crying by
Ainsworth and her colleagues. Thus, although we lack statistical sophistication, we can improve the designs of our
research so as to yield more meaningful results. The short-
term longitudinal study may be the best available approach,
combining rigor and creative exploration.

Measures and Infant Behavior

A central problem for scientists studying infant
development across cultures or social classes is to find a
common basis for comparison. Until we know which aspects of
infant development are universal, and to what degree these are
the result of common biological programing, it is difficult,
if not impossible, to measure infants and children across

cultures with the same metric, and to assume that valid
comparisons can be made. However, the problem of metrics
remains with us, and it may well be necessary as an intermediate step to establish metrices based on norms for a
particular society or cultural group, leaving comparisons to
be made at a later time.

Certainly, an age-graded metric is unsatisfactory in most
instances, since there is wide and as yet inadequately explained
variation in the chronological achievements of children the
world over. A more promising approach (unless one is specifically interested in the causes of *chronological* differences)
is to use a stage-related metric, assuming, as we do, that there
is probably a universal sequence of general stages in motor,
cognitive, and affective-social development through which all
children must pass to become fully functioning adults in any
human society. Known universal developmental milestones and
events, such as the first social smile, early preverbalization,
walking, weaning, separation from mother, etc., can form the
basis for meaningful comparisons to be explored in their social
meaning, the response of various cultural group members to
them, and the ways in which infants themselves respond to them.

Recognizing that cultural needs and expectancies, as well
as genetic, medical, and biological considerations can all
affect the timing and quality of developmental progress and
style, we have yet to devise criteria of infant adequacy that
are appropriate to this perspective. While we sense that there
are certain minimal physical and psychological needs and
conditions at birth that, if unmet or uncorrected, place any
infant in developmental jeopardy, we do not yet know the limiting conditions, worldwide, nor de we know the extent to which
infants "at risk" by standards developed in our society can
survive, adapt, and develop normally as viewed by members of
their *own* societies. We tend, for example, to view flaccid,
passive infants and children as abnormal, retarded, or possibly
diseased, but greater study of worldwide patterns of development reveals passivity frequently to be nonpathological and in
fact modal in many societies in which children nonetheless grow
up to be fully functioning members. Kagan and Klein's
observations in Guatemala (Chapter 12) provide a good example.

In our choice of subjects, of tests, and our interpretation
of results, greater caution is warranted in the future. Within
culture comparisons, with acute attention to the choice of
samples for study and the state of their pre- and postnatal
health and nutrition can provide one important check on hasty
generalizations and comparisons across cultures about infant
adequacy and adaptive capacity.

WHAT TO LOOK FOR: GOALS AND CAUTIONS

One becomes immediately aware, when discussing cross-cultural and comparative research, of the tension between those whose goals are to look for similarities between cultures and those who search out the differences. Many Western researchers (especially psychologists) seem to use comparative developmental studies to search for differences among groups of children: If experience X seems to relate to skill Y then a culture high in X should be higher than other groups in Y. This approach can be characterized as a psychological expression of our consumer culture, continually looking for the small differences that will make one product "better than another". Lewis and Ban (Chapter 16) have discussed our cultural emphases on differences, and on "the psychology of more, better, and faster". They have pointed out that even though cultures vary widely in their child-rearing patterns there is convincing evidence of similarity across groups.

On the other hand, those who seek out differences argue that, in the best scientific tradition, they are attempting to tease out the critical elements that link related phenomena, and the only approach to the establishment of "casual" change is to examine differences. Multicultural studies, they assert, are one way to magnify the small differences, especially when the cultural components have an important place in this causal chain.

Neither the homogenizers of the heterogenizers should be confused with those researchers interested in individual differences. It should be obvious that comparative and cross-cultural approaches cannot contribute to research on individual differences--and, in fact, can introduce considerable uncontrolled variance into any experimental study concerned mainly with individual differences.

These ideas push us to spell out more explicitly why we choose to do comparative developmental studies. Can our scientific objectives be met through the study of individual differences within our own culture? If so, this would obviate some of the need for doing comparative research. In an attempt to answer this question, we have outlined a set of goals for comparative studies and a set of questions that we believe researchers should ask before they elect to engage in comparative research.

Going from the general to the specific, a list of goals for research and comparative child development would include the following objectives:

1. To delineate the social, psychological, and biological invariances that determine the course of development in our species.

2. To gain an appreciation of the adaptive significance of child-rearing practices through studies of cultures living under conditions vastly different from industrialized Western societies, thus providing an evolutionary perspective to developmental research.

3. Establish the relationships of child-rearing practices to other aspects of societies, e.g., economic, political, and social systems.

4. To elucidate the interrelationship between processes as they shape the early development of this child.

5. To expand our understanding of developmental processes by investigating the effect of certain child-rearing practices on cognitive and social development, e.g., relationship of an infant being carried in a sling to the kinesthetic stimulation received by the child.

Given these general goals, there are several questions that might be asked before embarking at any type of comparative study. While this is not the place to provide a general checklist before beginning research, it seems to us there are several issues peculiarly germane to comparative studies that might be raised.

1. Specifically what do I wish to study? What is the theoretical or practical importance of the comparisons I wish to make?

2. Who are the people I propose to study? What is known about them, and how feasible is it for me to establish rapport with them in the time allotted for the study?

3. Is this the proper group in which to examine the issues or answer the questions I am interested in? Can the same information be obtained from other

groups within my own culture? Can the questions I
want to ask be explored by looking at other variations among individuals or by introducing an
experimental intervention in a group of subjects
from my own culture?

4.   Will my research lead to the possibility of
     invidious comparisons and possibly potentially
     harm subjects and/or detract from further work
     with them?

5.   Do the known physical and cultural features of the
     societies possibly have a significant effect on
     their relationships and/or the behavioral processes
     I propose to examine?

6.   Can the study itself be performed adequately with
     the skills at my command or will I need assistance
     and/or collaborative efforts to obtain information
     with satisfactory precision?

7.   Are the methods I hope to employ taking into account
     differential experiences and/or value systems of
     the people under study?

8.   Can I determine whether my racial, ethnic, or
     cultural heritage influence the observations I
     may make? If so, is the magnitude of this effect
     greater than the effects that I am studying?

9.   Brislin. Lonner, & Thorndike (1973) list fifteen
     factors suggested by Campbell and Stanley (1966)
     that can jeopardize the validity of a cultural
     comparative study. They suggest that the designer
     of a carefully planned study should be able to rule
     out these fifteen threats so as to support his
     preferred interpretation of cultural differences.
     Researchers should consult this list when planning
     multicultural research.

It is obvious that we have chosen a highly complex set of
phenomena to investigate. By recognizing the complexities, we
can begin to make progress toward untangling them. It is
important to recognize that we must move slowly and carefully,
and our moves need to involve interdisciplinary collaboration.
If we have succeeded in communicating this message, the
endeavor is a success.

REFERENCES

Brislin, R. W., Lonner, W. J., & Thorndike, R. M. Cross-
     cultural research method. New York: Wiley Inter-
     sciences, 1973.

Campbell, D. T., & Stanley, J. Experimental and quasi-
     experimental design for research. Chicago: Rand
     McNally, 1966.

Cole, M., Gay, J., Glick, J. A., & Sharp, D. W. The cultural
     context of learning and thinking. New York: Basic
     Books, 1971.

Fjellman, J. Myth of primitive mentality: A study of semantic
     acquisition and modes of characterization in Kamba
     children in South Central Kenya. Unpublished doctoral
     dissertation, Stanford University, 1971.

Munroe, R. L., & Munroe, R. H. Cross-cultural human development.
     Monterey, Calif.: Brooks-Cole, 1975.

Randall, T. M. An analysis of observer influence on sex and
     social class differences in mother-infant interaction.
     Paper presented at the meeting of the Society for
     Research in Child Development, Denver, Colorado,
     April 1975.

Tulkin, S. R. An analysis of the concept of cultural depriva-
     tion. Developmental Psychology, 1972, 6, 326-339.

Zegiob, L. E., Arnold, S., & Forehand, R. An examination of
     observer effects in parent-child interactions. Child
     Development, 1975, 46, 509-512.

Index

A
B 7
C 8
D 9
E 0
F 1
G 2
H 3
I 4
J 5